12 ⁹⁵

MUSIC IN A NEW FOUND LAND

MUSIC IN A
NEW FOUND LAND

*Themes and Developments
in the History of American Music*

WILFRID MELLERS

New York
OXFORD UNIVERSITY PRESS
1987

Copyright © Wilfrid Mellers 1964, 1987

Copyright © Wilfrid Mellers 1964, 1987

First published in the United States in 1965 by Alfred A. Knopf, Inc.

This revised paperback edition first published in 1987 in Great Britain by
Faber and Faber Limited, London, and in the United States by Oxford University
Press, Inc., 200 Madison Avenue, New York, New York 10016

Oxford is a registered trademark of Oxford University Press

Library of Congress Cataloging-in-Publication Data

Mellers, Wilfrid Howard, 1914–
    Music in a new found land.
    Originally published: London : Barrie and Rockliff,
1964.
    Bibliography: p.
    Includes index.
    1. Music—United States—History and criticism.
I. Title.
ML200.M44   1987   781.773′09   87-1566
ISBN 0-19-520526-x (pbk.)

2 4 6 8 10 9 7 5 3 1

Printed in the United States of America

TO AARON COPLAND
AND TO THE
MEMORY OF
MARC BLITZSTEIN

Contents

Foreword to the 1987 Edition

This book, first published in 1964, has been out of print in both the English and American editions for some years. When my present publisher suggested that it ought to be in print, and that I might consider bringing it up to date, I at first concurred. Having, however, surveyed the musical landscape on a visit to the States, I decided that since several hundred American composers unknown to me seemed to have made some mark in the years after 1964, I was too old to sort out which among them I thought worth writing about. Publisher and author therefore mutually agreed that the book should be republished in its original form, and that I should add this new foreword, roughly charting subsequent developments and looking back on the past with older, if not necessarily wiser, ears and eyes.

I have not changed or emended the text of the original book, since its imperfections are part of the "documentary" point. This includes the list of Recommended Books (p. 450), which was never intended to be a comprehensive bibliography but simply an acknowledgement to publications which I'd found helpful, and the Discography (p. 452), to which there is frequent specific forward reference in the main text. It would ideally now require a book all on its own in order to do justice to the plethora of recorded material that has come out in the past twenty years. Obviously, I would do some things differently now, and the thud of the years has brought changes of emphasis. The crucial chapter on Ives I would now present in more widely consequential terms. The account of Elliott Carter would have to take account of his consistent evolution through the last twenty years, while the career of Harry Partch is rounded off by his last and most substantial work, *Delusion of the Fury*—a title of significant general application. I could write more adequately, today, about Varèse. Lou Harrison, since the death of Partch, has become a more considerable figure, taking on the mantle of guru composer of the East-West. Morton Feldman has embarked on his phase of "extended composition" without fundamentally modifying the Feldman experience. The chapter headed "Today and Tomorrow" has naturally proved most vulnerable. Most of the composers discussed are still around though some have faded. The brilliant Lukas

Foss has hardly fulfilled his promise, though he is no less a "documentary" figure in the pluralism of his interests and abilities. The Grand Old Man of the avant-garde, as John Cage has become, is still copiously inventive, and still "puts down" the modern world at the same time as he invents it.

More surprisingly, I also hold by most of my valuations in the jazz section. In a world where the reputations of performing rather than composing musicians are volatile, there are, of course, a few players and singers who have gone the way of all flesh, and there are a few I wish I'd included. But there have been no significant developments in jazz over the last twenty years, since its creative energies were subsumed into pop. "Free" jazz and the jazz-rock fusion have thrown up some interesting music, without substantially changing the story.

About ten years ago I had come to admit that, as a panorama of American musics, the book suffered from one major and several minor omissions. Although it offered an inevitably selective account of American "art" musics from the beginnings to the 1960s, and a representative if no less selective survey of the Black American demotic musics we call jazz, it almost totally ignored white demotic music, whether under the categories of folk, jazz, country or pop. Whatever one thinks of these musics—about some of them I had been, when working on the book, distressingly ignorant—one cannot deny that they are part of the rich, or at least multifarious, pattern of American (and everyone else's) life. Largely to repair that omission I wrote my book *A Darker Shade of Pale: A Backdrop to Bob Dylan*, which sets the greatest American folk-rock artist in the context of American folk and country music generally. This year (1986) I've published another book, *Angels of the Night: Popular Female Singers of Our Time*, which concerns white as well as black performers and singing poet-composers, considering Joni Mitchell, for instance, as Dylan's female counterpart. These two books have gone some way towards rounding out the partial picture I'd given of the American scene.

Two further themes remain to be explored in this Foreword. One is topics within the scope of the original book which through ignorance or inadvertence had been evaded or distorted; the other is developments which postdate 1964. In the early reaches of the book I wrote somewhat scampingly of nineteenth-century American concert music because most, not all, of it seems to me interesting historically and sociologically rather than in intrinsic musical terms. Deeper knowledge of the music of nineteenth-century America would lead me (or anyone) to deeper understanding, but I doubt if it would lead me to a radical reassessment of the account originally given.

These supplementary comments will therefore start where indigenous American music comes to flower: with the generation of Ives, Ruggles and Varèse. At least five composers of this generation don't appear in the original book for the basic reason that I did not know their music well enough, if at all, to appreciate its significance. The first, Charles Seeger (1879–1982), is not so much a creator as a mover and shaker, born a decade later than Ives and surviving him—he lived to the age of ninety-three—by five years. Between Ives and Seeger there are direct parallels. Both came from a comfortable, in Seeger's case affluent, background; Ives was a Yale, Seeger a Harvard, man. Both were activators and explorers, though whereas Ives's musical adventures were in his own creative interest, Seeger aimed rather to shake up a stuffy musical Establishment by injecting into New England university circles the then avant-garde musics of Europe, from Debussy and Scriabin to Stravinsky and Satie: composers about whom Ives, during his years of creative ferment, knew and cared little. That Ives's experimentalism was self-help whereas Seeger's was a shot in the arm for a moribund society points to the basic distinction between them: Ives was a genius, Seeger a man of talent. Ives's songs are a scrapbook of "moments of truth" which, in their democratic eclecticism, are grist to the mill of his creation; Seeger's songs, often superficially comparable, stay within the European (Teutonic) tradition of the nineteenth-century American parlor song, from which they escape only when Seeger discards piano and relies on solo voice, unconsciously forecasting his later career as folk song collector and scholar. His setting of John Wheelock's "The Letter" is deeply affecting; whereas even the best of his piano-accompanied songs offer no Ivesian startlements and do not—despite or because of their graceful writing for voice and keyboard—attain to intrinsic rather than to sociological identity.

There's a similar parallel between Seeger's and Ives's chamber music. The layout of Seeger's big violin and piano sonata (1908–13) resembles that of Ives's three violin sonatas of about the same date. The post-Brahmsian piano writing is spacious in an American pioneering vein; the violin sings sweetly as it approaches folky pentatonics; neither piano nor violin is, however, new made for a New World. Ives's transcendentalism grows spontaneously out of his American experience; Seeger's takes the form of an explicit quotation from Scriabin inserted into the first movement's climax. Only in the slow movement, dedicated to the composer's first, violin-playing, wife, does Seeger make music that hints at an Ivesian awareness of democratic contrariety, for it is a dialogue between "man and wife" that does not flinch from disparities that disturb, even alarm, as well as enliven.

There may be an autobiographical undertow to this, for Seeger voluntarily relinquished composition in 1919, two years before Ives's "retirement" in 1921. Ives's abdication was prompted partly by ill health, which may—since he had come to admit that his radical democratic identity was not to win acceptance in genteel musical circles— have been psychosomatic. Seeger, one suspects, retired because, although he had fought to change the established musical order, he found that he hadn't himself creative energy adequate to the task. Ives supported radical causes, musical and social, while remaining independent of them as a self-sufficient artist; Seeger, realizing that change in the musical establishment wouldn't occur without change in the structure of American society, threw in his lot with radical politics. Collaterally, he directed his attention to "people's music" in the forms of folk song and dance: in which fields he toiled for the last fifty years of a long life, and in the process founded a dynasty of performing folk musicians and scholars still active today. That made and makes sense, in the context of his life: though it is regrettable that in eschewing Art for Life he took his second wife, Ruth Crawford, with him.

For she, born in 1901 and therefore more than twenty years his junior, was a composer of genius who, though a woman, might have stood craggily with the grand American eccentrics who were really central—Ives, Ruggles and Varèse. If she wrote little music, so did Ruggles and Varèse; everything she produced makes a resounding impact, being (in Ezra Pound's phrase) "news that STAYS news". Especially is this true of her String Quartet which, composed in 1931, packs into four movements lasting *in toto* less than ten minutes maximum content, electrical melodic impetus, rhythmic energy and harmonic charge. The strenuous linear counterpoint of the first movement and the eel-like whirligig of the scherzo have nothing in common with Hindemithian busy-ness or Schonbergian serial tenuity. There is some affinity with the denser polyphonic writing of Ives, and perhaps with Wallingford Riegger; more startlingly, the textures anticipate the quartet writing of Elliott Carter twenty years later. The slow movement works by an infinitesimally slow expansion and contraction of tone clusters around nodal points, in a manner that was to become a cliché of the 1960s; while in the extraordinary finale, scored in counterpoint for solo violin and the other strings muted in unison, the two voices function in fantastically complex inverse metrical proportion. These techniques too were to bear strange fruit thirty or forty years later, though this is not to praise Crawford merely for historical prescience. Her quartet is a stunning masterpiece in its own right, and it is pitiful that it was both a climax to and a virtual end of her creative evolution. For Ruth Seeger abandoned composition to devote herself to her husband's related causes, those of American folk music and radical politics; and whereas Charles was probably right to decide that *his* music wasn't "relevant" in the social situation, Ruth Seeger's quartet was and is. Its tensity and angry wit voice protest not merely or mainly against inequable and iniquitous social systems but also against the frustrations inherent in living, especially as a woman in a man-made industrial technocracy. We cannot know whether Ruth Crawford felt creatively victimized; if she did, any personal exacerbation is only one instance of the general truths her music promulgates. The last twist of the knife is that she died at the age of fifty-three, of cancer.

Charles Seeger not only introduced avant-garde European music into Harvard, New York and Los Angeles; he also fostered local iconoclasts, especially Henry Cowell, discussed in the original book as an American Boy of the Woods who experimented with a battered piano until, grown respectable, he introduced ethnomusicological pursuits into university circles. It was Seeger too who launched on the New York scene a still wilder man of the *Russian* woods: Leo Ornstein who, born in southwest Russia in 1892, had been fêted as a child prodigy at the Petrograd Conservatory. With the encroaching threat of the Revolution he escaped with his family to New York in 1907. In youth Ornstein seems to have been a phenomenal pianist in the Russian virtuoso tradition, from which his own music at first stems. His gigantic Piano Quintet of 1927 outdoes Rachmaninov in profligate fecundity of notes if not invention, and emulates his "big" tunes without attaining their memorability. Ultra-romantic afflatus is toughened by Russian and Central European barbarism in passages built on fourths and fifths and on incremental ostinati and drones. The big American city gives a more febrile edge to the overburdened heart; it is not an accident that Tchaikowsky and Rachmaninov, both White Russians and both neurotics, obsessively appeal to industrialized common men.

Ornstein's most characteristic music is more directly molded by his American environment. Much of it is for solo piano, written for himself to play on his concert tours, and often not rotated for many years after its formulation at the keyboard. Although not improvised, this is *ad hoc* empiricism in the American grain; and this is true even of ostensibly formal pieces like the four piano sonatas, the (recorded) last of which is a soberer yet more characterful piece than the Quintet. A big romantic sonata, as are the two great sonatas of Ives, it is rooted in Rachmaninov rather than in Beethoven, while its intermittent "transcendental" elements spring not from Concord but (again) from Scriabin. The sonata is impressive, though its pioneering virility does not attain Ives's indigenous veracity.

It is significant that Ornstein owed his contemporary notoriety to his short piano pieces which, like Ives's "studies" and "sketches", start as a young virtuoso's party-pranks. Seated at a piano, he allows his jaunty mind and fiery fingers to toss off genre pieces for a global village; the famous "A la Chinoise" of 1918 dizzily plays with pentatonic ostinati, whirling glissandi and jangling clusters, with neither harmonic development nor formal evolution. Only in its static nature is it oriental; in spirit, the music is as New Yorkan as it is un-Chinese. Global village music crops up too in the miniscule *Arabesques* of 1918–20. These genre pieces flash by in a minute or less (the most violently "radical" lasts twenty-six seconds); multi-ethnically ear-tingling in sonority, they are musically insubstantial in much the same way as the multi-racial stores in Greenwich Village market used to be enlivening, but unreal or surreal, excrescences on everyday life. Sometimes the pieces may (perhaps?) be jokes—for instance the "Raging and Wailing Wind" that briefly shatters the set.

These American "moments", Ornstein's most distinctive contribution, resemble Cowell's juvenile piano pieces in being of their nature ephemeral. We noted that in later years Cowell, without Ives's genius for Making It New, had to leave behind childish things to become either academically conservative or ethnically orientated. Ornstein, with an elaborate European technical equipment behind him, lacked either Ives's genius or the boy Cowell's pristine innocence; perhaps for this reason his fame or notoriety spluttered out like spent fireworks. With his wife he founded his own Ornstein School of Music at which, in relative obscurity, he taught for many years. Yet without seeking to promote his music, he continued to compose intermittently, way into his and the century's eighties; he has enjoyed something like a comeback at Yale, to which he has bequeathed his copious manuscripts. He remains a peripheral figure in a culture which, of its nature, has no one center, as does another exotic of the same generation, Dane Rudhyar, who was born in Paris in 1895 but emigrated to New York of his own volition, in the same year (1916) as Varèse.

Rudhyar is, or has become, a figure typically American in his very exoticism. At one time an actor, he played Christ in a 1924 movie; he is poet and painter as well as composer; he is an internationally celebrated authority on astrology; and he is a student of oriental philosophies and of various brands of mysticism. Not surprisingly, he has found a home from home in California, where he has lived and worked for half a century. Most of his music is now written for piano, which he regards as a "resonant mass of wood and metal, a sort of condensed orchestra of gongs, bells and the like". It reverberates in "the one Harmony": Nature's overtone series which is independent of man-made harmonic systems and implies no pre-ordained forms. Notation and printed scores are for him only a necessary evil: perhaps not even really necessary, if we recall that Ornstein didn't bother to write out even his more artfully sophisticated piano works for years after their creation.

Rudhyar's pieces are not as formless as his philosophy might suggest; astrological pentagrams and the like make for patterns and recurrencies, while eschewing forward momentum. Nonetheless, the pieces are self-generated from bell-like sonorities massive or tinkling, and from tones and intervals (Rudhyar calls them "words", implying an intrinsic expressivity) which move in free rhythms untrammeled by time, without extended melodic span or harmonic direction. "Stars", a pentagram of 1925, exquisitely auralizes stellar space; "Paeans" (1927) and "Granites" (1929) have a monolithic grandeur evoking some magical stone-circle. The complete set of *Pentagrams* consists of four five-sectioned pieces headed the Coming Forth, the Enfolding, the Release and the Human Way. Such theosophical concepts reach consummation in a late work written in 1976, in the composer's early eighties. *Transmutations* lives up to its title, for in its nearly half-hour duration it slowly *alchemizes* its initial sonorities and gestures ("words") in an attempt to "communicate inner experiences of human growth, of crisis, of fulfilment". This late Rudhyar music is at an opposite pole to Ornstein's, being unostentatious and totally humorless; if there is a parallel to its indrawn meditation it must be in the late music of Scriabin, though Rudhyar is at this stage far more exiguous. So introspective a music puts a heavy burden on "inspiration". Calling for total commitment, it occasionally deserves it.

Dane Rudhyar is a real, if slightly mad, composer who belatedly found acceptance on the West Coast where his theosophies chimed with the post-Beat generation that sought alternatives to Western technocracy. He has a place in my original chapter, "From Noise to Silence", though he remains a marginal figure rather than a renovative force like Partch or Cage, while he lacks, and did not seek, Lou Harrison's contacts with a wider, more humane society. The remaining Outsider who found no place in my book seems, at this date, the most significant: perhaps because, although in a sense another exotic, he is also a composer of the big city. Conlon Nancarrow, born in the same year (1912) as John Cage, belongs to a generation later than Ornstein, Rudhyar and Crawford. He shares with the woman composer an electrical energy born of the social ferment and political protest of the 1930s. Unlike her, he creatively survived to make a music positively affirmative, even ebullient. His music and biography are interlaced.

Born in an outpost of Arkansas, he came to New York as a music student, working with those different but related props of American academicism, Walter Piston and Roger Sessions. Early works of the 1930s—a piano sonatina, a string quartet, a toccata for violin and piano—transmute, indeed begin to demolish, conventional techniques mainly through the prestidigitous speed (reflective of New York's urban frenzy?) of their articulation; recently the violin work has been dazzlingly performed with the piano part taped and speeded up to the vertiginous tempo the composer wanted but could not expect from merely human performers. There is an affinity between this early Nancarrow music and the music Ruth Crawford was making in the same years—not only her String Quartet, but also the hair-raising "Piano Study in Unequal Rhythms", almost exclusively in octave unisons. In the 1930s, however, Nancarrow's composing career was disrupted for reasons different from but related to those that terminated Crawford's: he went to fight in the Spanish Civil War. After his return to the U.S. in 1939 he was subjected to political harassment, as a consequence of which he settled in Mexico City. In this pullulating if exotic conurbation Nancarrow has lived for the past forty-five years.

These biographical facts bear on the composer's status as an outsider; and this in turn is related to his abandoning conventional instruments in favor of the player-piano, for which all his music since 1948 has been composed. In his youth Nancarrow had been a jazz trumpeter, and the earlier of his pianola "studies" relate to the "alternative culture" of jazz, as do Ives's studies for (ostensibly) normal piano. In particular, Nancarrow's music recalls the crudest and rudest types of big city jazz, for both the polymeters and the clattery metallic sonorities sound like piano boogie in the barrelhouse, somewhat exoticised with touches of voice and trumpet blues, flamenco guitar and Mexican marimba band. By means of his perforated rolls Nancarrow creates miracles of polymetrical intricacy that would be beyond the control of human fingers, however agile the mind behind them. So the music's corporeality merges into its intellectuality.

Later studies explore extremities of metrical proportion and disproportion, one tempo being related to another in (say) the ratio of 2 to the square root of 3; or two "metrical canons" continuously accelerate and decelerate on overlapping planes—a mechanical fulfillment of the experimental finale of Ruth Crawford's quartet and an anticipation of some aspects of the music of European Ligeti, who acknowledges a debt. If the concept is mathematically abstract, its musical consequence is of tremendous physical excitation. Body and head, for too long separate in our Western world, are reunited; and although comparable complexities are now easily negotiable by electronic means, no electrophonic music has created such presence out of "distinguished and divided worlds", to use the phrase in which seventeenth-century Sir Thomas Browne, himself both artist-theologian and putative scientist, referred to body and spirit. This is the deeper meaning of today's mating of men and machines and explains why this self-exiled loner now occupies so crucial a position in world music.

Of course there are ranges of experience—for instance tragedy and pathos in the Greek senses—that Nancarrow's music of its nature bypasses; he cannot claim to be a "great" humanist composer of Ives's ilk. But that is the measure of his historical import; if he embraces black jazz within white intellect, he also anticipates those "process" composers who effect a deliberate return to quasi-tribal "necessity". This takes us into areas developed since the publication of my book, for "minimal" or "process" musics have become the most influential, if not necessarily significant, forces during the last twenty years. An ultimate extreme was adumbrated, back in the 1960s, by La Monte Young, for whom the "I" loses identity in surrendering to the aural cosmos of a single tone or interval sustained (as though) *in eternitatum*. Terry Riley's aural meditation less radically denies in an oriental abnegation of works: in the 1960s through identification with a single sound-source, as in "In C"; in the 1970s through improvisation, mostly pentatonic, on electric keyboards; in the 1980s through an incantatory use of traditional resources such as the string quartet. The objection to such negation is that although to reject European humanism may be understandable and even excusable, we do not, even if we're West Coast Americans, belong to an ancient oriental culture but irremediably to Western traditions which, as European composers like Debussy and Messiaen have demonstrated, may be modified but not denied. Young's and Riley's willessness amounts to a prodigious exercise of will.

If a similar objection may be urged against Steve Reich's Africanism it is less damaging since the "process" the live performers undergo on their live instruments is indeed enlivening, calling for a high degree of skill, in which the audience participates vicariously. The body, expunged by Young and Riley, proves for Reich a launching-pad for "transcendence", as may happen in real tribal magic and in African-based jazz. In a substantial Reich work like *Drumming* the slow exfoliation of metrical and linear patterns in the tingling orchestration of percussion instruments pitched and unpitched tends to enhance rather than engulf "consciousness". As with Chopi xylophone bands, Mexican marimba bands and Balinese gamelan—with all of which Reich has lived and worked—mind, nerves and senses are activated as one becomes momentarily part of a ritual performance, living in the noise while it lasts. The danger is that since we, unlike the Africans or whomever, have no defined notion as to what the ritual signifies in relation to our lives, act may degenerate into habit. Perhaps with this in mind Reich has in recent works, such as *Desert Music* and *Tehillim*, relaxed the abstraction of his pattern-making to the point of calling on melody instruments, incantatory voices and even verbal content. Minimalist fanatics tend to sniff at these pieces on the grounds that they betray the integrity of the abstraction which is apposite to, even as it counteracts, a mechanistic civilization. On the other hand a vast new public has discovered in a piece like *Tehillim* a substitute tribal pop music. Momentarily and near-infantilely we live in the noise's process *as though* we were real near-Eastern folk dancing as we chant a Hebrew version of a Psalm. An ancient "way of life" is rendered immediate—legitimately enough, at least for a (even if non-practicing) Jew in New York's urban community.

The transition between Process and Pop has been effected still more successfully—in economic if not musical terms—by Philip Glass, who in his early days wrote middle-of-the-road Copland-affiliated music but has arrived at a minimalism relatable to the "libidinal" philosophy of Jacques Derrida and J.-F. Lyotard. Freud's distinctions between ego, id and libido may have been too restrictive, encouraging division into "higher" and "lower" moral categories that are at best over-simple, at worst misleading. Nonetheless such categories are not meaningless, and being human inevitably involves a balance between conscious and unconscious forces. Totally to surrender to libidinal impulses is to deny part of our birthright; although we have learned much from "savages" about aspects of human nature that we had, to our cost, forgotten, we cannot *be* savages because we cannot extrapolate ourselves from history. The attempt to abolish history becomes ultimate slavery to it, for Freud was on the mark when he equated submission to the libido with the death instinct. This correlation has been overtly admitted by many pop groups, whose names (and functions) have shifted over the last twenty years from cheerfully animistic Beatles, Byrds and Animals into Boom Town Rats, the Stranglers, the Enemy, the Clash, the Sex Pistols and even (ultimate irony) the Police. It is difficult to avoid seeing Glass's prodigious success in the 1980s—records of some of his works have sold over a hundred thousand copies, and he has had four or more operas or theatre pieces running concurrently in capitals of the world— in relation to this most fundamental negation. His music, if in some (not many) ways more complex than that of pop groups, functions in the same way, both in its incremental remorselessness and in the fact that although—unlike most of the music of Riley and Reich—it admits to the existence of Western harmony, it employs it without reference to antecedence or consequence. Through electric keyboards very loudly and unremittingly playing reiteratively phased patterns, Glass creates an aural womb that becomes a tomb. Seeking an identity of time and space, he offers an anti-teleological interpretation of Einstein, the subject of one of his operas. His later opera, *Akhnaten*, set in ancient Egypt and with a transvestite Hero, carries phased repetition to the point of mummification. Despite the splendor of the visual images achieved through dance, mime, lighting and cinematic devices, one comes away reflecting, after four hours' submission to Glass's music, that although one is not against commercial success and popular appeal, one prefers it to be on behalf of life—as it is with Reich—rather than on behalf of death.

There is an ultimate paradox in the position of the minimalist composer in our consumer-orientated world. Pecuniarily, we value art in terms of dimension if it is visual, of duration if it is aural. On this basis a minimal work of Glass lasting three hours (a modest span for him) is in performance rights worth sixty times as much as a maximal piece of Webern lasting three minutes. This gives us pause for thought: from which comes the further reflection that humanity today surely needs more, not less, thought—and art and craft and care—if it is to survive, or even to deserve to survive, the criminal imbecilities of our world. One cannot discount a force as potent as Glass's music; one may, however, find its implications alarming.

If Nancarrow's pianola works more richly anticipate process music, they also strikingly forecast developments in electronic music, which can likewise negotiate metrical complexities beyond mere human resource, as well as theoretically embrace any conceivable sonority. Like process music, electronic music has bifurcated into two streams, one populist and concrete, the other elitist and abstract. The fathers of electrophonic music—just emerging when I was writing the book— tended to be sound engineers rather than composers, specializing either in electronic means of redisposing the sounds of the natural world (*musique concrète*), or in the making of mathematically ordered structures of "pure" electronic sounds. In those days only the great Varèse used electrophonics to musical ends, though his inspired electrophonics in *Deserts* are, by later standards, technically simple-minded.

The leader of the "intellectual" camp was Otto Luening, not a highly creative talent but one who earns respect as a disciple of Busoni, whose notions of a New Music wedding Art and Science he hopefully promulgated. More influential in "abstract" electrophonics was Milton Babbitt, perhaps because he already had—as recounted in the original book—a dedicated following in his attempt totally to serialize "live" music. Electronics made possible the fulfillment of this ideal: not only pitch relationships but every aspect of composition could be preordained to create the most intellectually intricate music yet invented. At the heart of American democracy Babbitt and his disciples, functioning within universities which financed their gadgetry, made a music intentionally *anti*-democratic. Babbitt himself even maintained that his music's "value" lay in its mathematically demonstrable *truth*, which could only be sullied by communication with any, certainly with *the*, public. That there is psychological and semantic confusion in this ivory-towerism is suggested by the fact that Babbitt is passionately devoted to American musical comedy and in particular to "escapist" Jerome Kern, the composer he, at least in waggish moments, would most like to have been. Yet the pure abstraction of electrophonics is itself an escape from the toil and moil of living: which is probably why it sometimes seems that pure electronic composers are or ought to be a dying breed, if breed they ever did.

Such a judgment is obviously too hasty because it is too early to assess the potential of what has become, with the aid of computer science, a new approach to music's nature and function. Whether the experimental work of a Charles Dodge or John Chowning in American universities will amount to discovery as well as exploration is in a very real sense bound up with the question of the future or non-future of our electronic civilization; the same applies to the investigations at Pierre Boulez's IRCAM, on the European side of the Atlantic. In the interim, "impure" electronic composers have naturally been more prolific and more communicative than pure ones. For them, electronics are an enrichment of live music and theatre: as we may hear, among the older generation, in the work of the lively Robert Erikson, whose imagination, however attuned to new resources, always maintains a recognizably "humanist" basis. One may say as much of some composers born in the 1930s, such as Roger Reynolds, Erikson's successor and colleague at San Diego, and Donald Erb, whose powerfully emotive music for electronics with live orchestras has had a measure of popular success. A similarly accessible aural imagination is manifest in the music of Morton Subotnick, whose purely electrophonic *The Silver Apples of the Moon* creates an aural universe of delicate precision, while his *Electric Christmas* of 1967 combines synthesized electrophonics with film and light projection to make multi-media theatre, invoking both medieval cantillation and twentieth-century rock music. *Return*, an impressive recent piece devised to celebrate Halley's Comet, also calls on medieval techniques, perhaps to evoke the eternity of interstellar space. In creating a continuum of sound from an immensely magnified harpsichord, it resembles process music, both in the sound and in the fact that the aural events are visually mirrored. *Return* was intended for performance in a planetarium, with full-scale sky show.

It seems not improbable that the future evolution of electronic music will steer this product of highly sophisticated technology towards a manifestation of precisely those "mystical" and numinous ranges of experience which science was supposed to have obliterated. The often deeply moving (part electronic) mystical music of Britain's Jonathan Harvey demonstrates this more potently than any American example: though Robert Eaton's *Mass* for microtonal Japanese soprano, clarinet and synthesizers is touchingly American in offering a grotesque but not intentionally comic parody of twentieth-century religious experience. The piece, if with more (slightly scary) sociological than musical import, is weirdly fascinating; a male speaking voice declaims the

Creed in American, in the portentous tones of a March of Time news-caster, while the microtonal soprano squeaks and squawks and the elec-trophonics emit their habitual bleeps, burps, gibbers and gobbles.

It is odd that the repertory of electrophonic sounds, theoretically of infinite variety, has so soon become so rigidly stereotyped; and it is interesting that a partial exception to this is provided by *Akwan* (1972), for piano, another piano and strings electrically transmuted, and sym-phony orchestra, by Olly Woodrow Wilson—one of the new genera-tion of black "art", as distinct from jazz, composers. Based on African mythology and to a degree on African musical techniques, the piece recreates both in the spirit of our machine age: an evolution (again) hinted at in Nancarrow's pianola music.

If, over half a century, electronic music has produced little of humanely musical substance, it may be because music, a performing art, battens on human agency. This may be why electronic music has proved more successful—artistically as well as in audience appeal—the more it has veered towards pop. In this context a minor, exclusively electronic composer, Jon Appleton, merits more attention than many who are both more ambitious and more esteemed. Appleton's early work, dating from the late 1960s, is mostly an extension of the primi-tive techniques of *musique concrète*, juxtaposing and collating natural and unnatural noises of the external world to create hilarious, sometimes bizarre, science-fictional dreams and nightmares. The pieces— "soundscapes" rather than music as we have known it—are usually amusing, often stimulating, sometimes imaginative. Appleton's later work is more conventionally musical, being composed for a digital sys-tem called the Synclavier, devised by Appleton in collaboration with engineers Sydney Alonso and Cameron Jones. The pieces are usually played straight at the keyboard, though the instrument stores comput-erized material. The synthetic sounds, even when microtonal, are clearly defined, often ripely sonorous and euphonious, and the struc-tures are not radically distinct from those of orthodox music. If the glinting sonorities remind us (as does some process music) of Balinese gamelan it is never in the spirit of "the old exoticism trip", to call on Steve Reich's phrase. The music merely takes over such sonorities as part of our global village birthright. The sounds are so clean, light and airy that they prompt visual analogies: a tapestry of bell sounds is a mixed metaphor that goes some way towards defining the spatial and temporal effect of a piece such as "Syntropia" (1977).

Although influences are not in question, there is a tie-up between the

"Appleton experience" and the music of children of all times and places; that of the simpler exotic cultures, notably the Balinese; that of Satie both early and late; and that of early Cage and, in the clean lines, open textures and non-Western modalities, of Lou Harrison. Harry Partch, pioneer of a simultaneously old-new global village, believing that the Western world had lost its bearings in surrendering just intonation and the contact between word, body and tone, spent a lifetime trying to recover tonal and human truth, evolving new-old notational systems and instruments in the process. Appleton's electric instruments are more practical because more portable than Partch's "live" ones fashioned from the natural materials of the environment; here technology, though anathema to Partch, would seem to be vindicated in that it allows the newborn global village to function in total audibility. No one, certainly not Appleton, would claim that his is great music; but in that it is innocently concerned with new worlds, always sounds beautiful, and never loses its sense of humor, it does offer qualities which our beleaguered race (not merely avant-garde music) is in dire need of. Jon Appleton, like Erik Satie, may be an important, little composer. By way of a modern machine, his music says something about birth and human potential; at the same time it offers a dispassionately comic assessment of our no less human limitations.

Throughout the twentieth century the barriers between the genres have been slowly eroded. In Appleton's music electrophonics, a bastion of hyper-intellectuality, join hands with a form of popular entertainment that is enlivening rather than amnesiac. Inversely, the dream factory of the American Musical has shown signs of coming-of-age, catching up with that great theatre piece, Gershwin's *Porgy and Bess* (really a fully-fledged opera) and, at a somewhat lower level, with Bernstein's *West Side Story*, a Broadway musical distinguished alike by its seriously contemporary theme and its brilliantly professional musicianship. That the generality of musicals has remained escapist pap is counterbalanced by the emergence of Stephen Sondheim, who has proved—especially in *Sweeney Todd*—that the musical may still be used to adult ends. For this powerful, subtle, funny, frightening and paradoxically *enlivening* piece deals with that very *death*-wish which underlies and undermines our culture, as manifest alike in (some) tribal pop and process music. At the same time "pop" has itself burst the banks. It is difficult to know in what category to place a Laurie Anderson, androgynous priestess of a tragi-comic sci-fi world in which, through sounds, mime and visual images, we alarmingly recognize the lineaments of the present, and are induced to laugh even if and as we are scared. Complementarily, basically traditional jazzmen like Ornette Coleman and Keith Jarrett have entered the realms of notated composition, and may present their music theatrically. Media-men such as David Behrmann and Max Neuhaus are effacing distinction between the artist and the technician.

And what of the "straight" composers, who are still the central tradition if one may be said to exist? A few, notably Elliott Carter, now approaching his eighties, have continued to advance as well as evolve, creating his difficult music for ideal listeners. The concept of such a listener at least implies a *potential* public; the dichotomy of music as mathematical truth (Babbitt) as against music as evasion (Kern) is meaningless to Carter, who wants to communicate with human beings willing to accept him on his own terms, but has little interest in music outside accredited artistic traditions, and no interest at all in music of which the motivation is overtly commercial. Assured of critical acclaim, even regarded by some as "the greatest living composer", Carter's relationship to a public remains equivocal; and this applies too to more recent composers, such as Jacob Druckman, who in intellectual and imaginative probity may count as his successors. Not surprisingly, composers of less formidable assurance have proved less austere. Especially fascinating is the case of George Rochberg, a severe post-Schonbergian serialist who returned to tonality on the grounds that the music of the Viennese classics and their romantic successors is still our musical bread and wine, as well as bread and butter. Though his recent quasi-Beethovenian and Mahlerian music often has power as well as dignity, pastiche and near-quotation can be no substitute for creation. If ever there is a "new tonality" it must discover its own *modus vivendi*.

In any case Rochberg's music, though admired in some quarters, can hardly be called popular. For that kind of success we must look to the "new romanticism" of a David del Tredici, who in the 1960s had an elitist reputation as a composer of hyper-refined, texturally complex serial music, but re-embraced tonality in a sequence of works based on Alice in Wonderland. *Final Alice*—evocative of childhood's wonder in expressive immediacy yet glossily sophisticated in orchestral expertise—deserves the phenomenal success it has achieved with a wide middlebrow public. Yet a fixation on Alice cannot promise a future; indeed Sondheim's *Sweeney Todd*, originally spawned on Broadway, is a far more "adult" piece than Tredici's *Alice*, which Disneyizes the semi-artistic, semi-industrial medium of the mammoth symphony orchestra. Del Tredici's cult of illusion is overt; no less illusory, if more covert, is the political fixation of Frederic Rzewski, a one-time experimentalist who now makes romantic piano music in the nineteenth-century idiom, calculated to appeal to the broad masses. Only it does not. One may admire its ideological probity and technical skill while doubting whether a self-designated music of the future can be rooted in conscious regression—even when the past revoked is a brilliant excursus around 1920s barrelhouse boogie.

Rzewski's jazz-orientated pieces veer towards the ethnic tributary which now runs parallel to the mainstream: notably in the music of the acute-eared George Crumb, wondrously responsive to non-Western and "primitive" vocal and instrumental techniques. Though the sonorous seductiveness of Crumb's music doesn't, perhaps, wear well, he is a composer to be grateful for in that he has reminded us—as have Appleton's electrophonics—that music may still afford sensuous delight. In this context one might mention too the lucidly eclectic William Balcom; Donald Argento, exquisitely sensitive to words and the human voice, and with an almost Brittenesque vernality; Daniel Lentz, Lorin Rush and Paul Chihara, Californians whose music variously invokes magic; perhaps even Harold Budd, who has gravitated from Californian New Romanticism into Zen-affiliated pop, as did minimal Terry Riley in his *A Rainbow in Curved Air*.

But a roll call can only mislead. Our inconclusion must be that American music, like American society, is even more "open" than it was twenty years back. In the light of that the magnitude of the mind and music of Charles Ives seems the more formidable. At the beginning of the century he voiced the cultural and psychological quandary of modern democracy. From one point of view he was an Artist reared in the nineteenth century, an American Beethoven courageously concerned with an affirmation of the human spirit against whatever odds. From another point of view he was a seismograph to a pluralistic global culture, potentially involving "everyman" in music as game-playing, improvisation, contest, chance operation and demotic high-jinks, functioning in an eternal Present as does an African tribesman, though in a world transitional between Art and Science, wherein signs and signifiers have no clearly defined meanings. It is not extravagant to say that *all* the "themes and developments" uncovered in this book were at least latent in the music of Ives; whatever survives of his work—it should be a lot, if our world survives at all—we can only wonder at his courage in creating such life-affirming music out of the muddlement of his and our world. He seems an even more commanding figure than I had thought him twenty years ago. In a world context, he is the first *great* composer of democratic principle.

Highbury Fields, London   W.M.
September 1986

Preface

The nature of this book is accurately defined by its sub-title—themes and developments in American music. It is not an attempt at a comprehensive history of American music, and in no sense competes with Gilbert Chase's admirable *America's Music*, which takes some 400 pages to discuss the "pre-history" that I cover in a shortish chapter. Even when I reach what seems to me authentic American music, I make no attempt at a roll-call or catalogue. I deal, in some detail, with comparatively few composers, most of whom have well-established reputations. Of course, while I have discussed no composer who does not seem to me worth writing about, usually for a positive reason, it does not follow that composers whom I have omitted are *ipso facto* not worth consideration: I may not know their work, or may know too little of it to form a judgment, or I may simply be impervious to its virtues. But I have written of what I know, not of what I might have known, and have tried to understand rather than to evaluate. From this effort comes, I hope, a sense of direction, or at least of possible directions; and if one knows a little more clearly where things are going one has some enhanced awareness of their value and significance. It may be that at no period of history has it been more difficult to forecast the shape of things to come from our knowledge of things past; but at least we may feel greater confidence if we have decided, merely to our own satisfaction, which elements in the present and the immediate past are genuine and meaningful, which are not. This I have tried to do; and I hope my many friends among American composers and musicians will forgive me if they think I have misunderstood either their country or themselves.

Since my interest in American music has always been inseparable from its immediate relevance to the twentieth century, my theme inevitably involves discussion of the relationship between "art" music, jazz and pop music. The segregation of the genres is both illogical and artificial; each is a form of organized sound, or music, and qualitatively as in other ways their contributions overlap. If the pop music of Tin Pan Alley *may* be anti-art, it has also produced Gershwin, who is certainly among the three or four finest composers ever produced by the United States; if jazz is a limited art, it has produced composers such as Ellington and composing-improvisers such as Louis Armstrong, Charlie Parker and Miles Davis, whose work is certainly of greater creative significance than that of (literally) hundreds of art-composers whose music is performed, intermittently if infrequently, in the concert hall. So in writing Part II of this book I have used the same musical criteria as in writing Part I. I have tried to write of the musical experience that jazz is, keeping to a minimum the sociological and anthropological aspects which have been discussed in a number of books, such as Marshall Stearn's *The Story of Jazz*. In writing of jazz I have not kept strictly to my intention to deal only in positives; a certain amount of negative, deflatory criticism seemed to me unavoidable, because in jazz history so much has happened in so short a time, and very few attempts have been made to distinguish the truly creative from the up-to-the-minute gimmick. As a "straight" musician, I didn't find it difficult to decide what, in the world of jazz, seemed to me musically genuine, and I found this fact somehow comforting. I hope the professional jazzman, should he see this book, won't say I'm talking through my hat; for if jazz is not music I don't know what it is, and if it is music it ought to be intelligible to a musician.

Apart from this, the only difference in approach in Part II, as compared with Part I of the book, is that I have based my musical commentary on specific recordings, giving detailed references, and have not used examples in written notation. These are inadequate even with published "art" music (the musical examples in Part I are intended merely to whet the appetite, not to serve as a substitute for perusal of the scores); and since jazz is basically an improvised art which cannot be accurately notated, the citation of written examples may even be misleading rather than helpful. Where possible, I have chosen recordings that are readily available, and the jazz section of the book is meant to be read in close association with the sound of the recordings. In writing of Gershwin and other pop composers I have reverted to music-type illustration, with full awareness of its inadequacy. Again, as in Part I, reading of the book is supposed to be supplemented by reference to scores and by the *sound* of the relevant works. The discography lists extant recordings of the principal works referred to in the text.

The study of American music—no less than of American literature and painting—is deeply relevant to any enquiry into the nature of the world we live in, and this is true for Europeans, as well as for Americans.

This book contains a large number of quotations from American writers, because it seemed to me self-evident that the word-creation of Americans of sensibility should parallel, reinforce, and comment on American sound-creation. The quotations thus provide a link between the original sound-experience and my critical exposition, which has no choice but to be, like the quotations, in words. For this reason the literary quotations are not chi-chi, but part of the book's substance; they should not be skipped! In general, my approach, in this more restricted field, is similar to the approach to European music which I adopted in my share of *Man and his Music*; and while I may, as an outsider, miss many qualities, musical, psychological and social, that a native American would be aware of intuitively, there is also a chance that, as an outsider, I may see and hear things that cannot be experienced from within the American context. Certainly I must acknowledge a debt to those American composers, friends and acquaintances, with whom I have talked about their work and (more dangerously) about that of their colleagues. I should also express gratitude to the Mellon Trust and the University of Pittsburgh which, in enabling me to live for two academic years in the States, made it possible for me to become familiar with much music I would otherwise have missed. My final debt is to an Englishman, Mr Kenneth Dommett, who not only prepared the discography but also awakened my dormant interest in jazz, and stimulated it by discussion, admonition and disagreement.

W.M.

Department of Music
University of Pittsburgh
December, 1962

The living fact commemorates itself. Why look in the dark for light? Critical acumen is exerted in vain to uncover the past; the *past* cannot be *presented*; we cannot know what we are not. But one veil hangs over past, present, and future, and it is the province of the historian to find out, not what was, but what is. Where a battle has been fought, you will find nothing but the bones of men and beasts; where a battle is being fought, there are hearts beating.

I too would fain set something down beside facts. Facts should only be as the frame to my pictures; they should be material to the mythology I am writing . . . My facts should be falsehoods to the common sense. I would so state facts that they shall be significant, shall be myths or mythological. Facts which the mind perceived, thoughts which the body thought—with these I deal.

Thoreau: *A Writer's Journal*

PART ONE

The Pioneer and the Wilderness

If there was a road, I could not make it out in the faint star-
light. There was nothing but land: not a country at all, but
the material out of which countries were made. . . . I had
the feeling that the world was left behind, that we had got
over the edge of it, and were outside man's jurisdiction. . . .

Between that earth and sky I felt erased, blotted out. I did
not say my prayers that night: here, I felt, what would be
would be.

On some upland farm, a plough had been left standing in the
field. The sun was sinking just behind it. Magnified across
the distance by the horizontal light, it stood against the sun,
was exactly contained within the molten red. There it was,
heroic in size, a picture writing on the sun. Even while we
whispered about it, our vision disappeared; the ball dropped
and dropped until the red tip went beneath the earth. The
fields below us were dark, the sky was growing pale, and
that forgotten plough had sunk back to its own littleness
somewhere on the prairie.

She was a battered woman now, not a lovely girl; but she
still had that something which fires the imagination. . . .
She had only to stand in the orchard, to put her hand on a
little crab tree and look up at the apples, to make you feel the
goodness of planting and tending and harvesting at last. All
the strong things of her heart came out in her body, that had
been so tireless in serving generous emotions. It is no wonder
that her sons stood tall and straight. She was a rich mine of
life, like the founders of early races.

In that singular light every little tree and shock of wheat, every
sunflower stalk and clump of snow-on-the-mountain, drew
itself up high and pointed; the very clods and furrows in the
fields seemed to stand up sharply. I felt the old pull of the
earth, the solemn magic that comes out of those fields at

nightfall. I wished I could be a little boy again, and that my way could end there.

WILLA CATHER: *My Antonia*

We Americans are the peculiar, chosen people—the Israel of our time; we bear the ark of the liberties of the world . . . We are the pioneers of the world; the advance guard, sent on through the wilderness of untried things, to break a path in the New World that is ours.

HERMAN MELVILLE: *White Jacket*

She had wandered, without rule or guidance, in a moral wilderness and regarded whatever priest or legislators had established with hardly more reverence than an Indian would feel.

NATHANIEL HAWTHORNE, of Hester,
in *The Scarlet Letter*

It was about this time I conceiv'd the bold and arduous project of arriving at moral perfection. I wish'd to live without committing any fault at any time; I would conquer all that natural inclinations, custom, or company might lead me into. As I knew, or thought I knew, what was right and wrong, I did not see why I might not always do the one and avoid the other.

BENJAMIN FRANKLIN

The founders of a new colony, whatever Utopia of human virtue and happiness they might originally project, have invariably recognized it among their earliest practical necessities to allot a portion of the virgin soil as a cemetery, and another as the site of a prison.

NATHANIEL HAWTHORNE

into the American wilderness, "descended into smallness, condemned to be unflowering". In the words of William Carlos Williams—a poet who has experienced the "making of Americans" by an act of imaginative empathy—"they stressed the spirit, for what else could they do? They had nothing else. But the spirit is really an earthly pride which they, prideless, referred to heaven and the next world. They had a tough littleness to carry them through the cold; their religious zeal was not a thrust upwards towards the sun, but a stroke in: the confinement of the tomb. In fear and without guidance, really lost in the world, it is they alone who would later, at Salem, have strayed so far, morbidly seeking the flame—that terrifying unknown image to which, like savages, they too offered sacrifices of human flesh. It is just such emptiness, revulsion, terror in all ages, which in fire finds that which lost and desperate men have worshipped."[1] Only with reference to this horror can we understand the forms that the transplanted European traditions were to take.

Roger Williams was reviled by the settlers for suggesting that they ought to buy their land from the Indians; to take the land from the "savage" was, they maintained, an act on behalf of their God, who, indeed, placed the Indians (offspring of the devil) in positions convenient for "divine slaughter at the hands of the English". So, as the Puritan who fought for the liberty of his conscience struck off from the community into the vastness that is America, he left his "spiritual" justification behind. He never forgot the Savage he had had to destroy; and his simultaneous hatred and fear were only intensified when the exterminated Indian was replaced by the enslaved African. The Red-Black Man became the pioneer's consciousness of guilt; and the guilt was inherent in the very attempt to conquer and subdue a strange land. The lonely pioneer, fighting for his spirit's freedom, became the hunter, the killer, fighting for his life, and for the plot of land on which to live it. Because he was alone, each man for himself in the wilderness, he dreaded, yet thrived on, competition. Hunter was killer and trapper; trapper was trader; trader became boom-town manufacturer; manufacturer became cut-throat gangster. Counting heads turned into counting money—"for the glory of God and the advancement of the beaver trade".

In the fusion of the Puritan and the Tracker we find, as the wilderness was opened up, the first great American mythological figure, immortalized by Fenimore Cooper in the Leatherstocking saga. The

[1] William Carlos Williams: *In the American Grain.*

A pre-history of American music: the primitives, the retreat to Europe and the conservative tradition

Though born on the cheating banks of Thames,
Though his waters bathed my infant limbs,
The Ohio shall wash his stains from me:
I was born a slave, but I go to be free.

WILLIAM BLAKE: *Thames and Ohio*

Every composer should be his own Carver.

WILLIAM BILLINGS

America is a polyglot culture, different from any other in that it is non-indigenous. For the native American culture, which was that of the Indian, was exterminated by the settlers, or withered away of inanition; and the settlers brought with them a rag-bag of European traditions, out of which America grew. In this sense America is an extreme evolution from the European consciousness; we see in America what happened to "the mind of Europe" when, separated from the traditions of a civilized past, it was faced with "nothing but land—not a country at all, but the material out of which countries are made".

One might almost say that America begins with the disintegration of the Middle Ages and the triumph of humanism. In Europe's High Renaissance flesh and spirit were one; but belief in man's individual will in the long run led to spiritual impoverishment. Man, proud of his god-like potentialities, sought to conquer Time and Space; having conquered them, he no longer knew what to do with them. Puritanism became the Plain Man's attempt to be responsible for his own destiny. The Puritan left Europe because he fought for his individual soul against entrenched privilege and moribund convention. But in fighting he lost the sense of religious ecstasy; his soul, indeed, became *his* privilege, of its nature littler, meaner, than those of Church and State which he had relinquished. So the souls of the Pilgrims, transplanted

Pioneer Hero had both a positive and a negative aspect. His positive virtues are described in Cooper's initial account of Deerslayer as a young man:

> In stature he stood about six feet in his moccasins, but his frame was comparatively light and slender, showing muscles, however, that promised unusual agility, if not unusual strength. His face would have had little to recommend it except youth, were it not for an expression that seldom failed to win upon those who had leisure to examine it, and to yield to the feeling of confidence it created. This expression was simply that of guileless truth, sustained by an earnestness of purpose, and a sincerity of feeling, that rendered it remarkable. At times this air of integrity seemed to be so simple as to awaken a suspicion of the want of the usual means to discriminate between artifice and truth; but few came in serious contact with the man, without losing this distrust in respect for his opinions and motives.

Deerslayer's "guileless truth" is American man's innocence, his power to be born anew because, indeed, he is in a world that he has yet to make; and his ideal, platonic, a-sexual friendship with the Noble Savage is a wish-fulfilment, an expiation of guilt. At the same time Deerslayer is, and must be, a slayer if he is to conquer the wilderness; and the negative aspect of the pioneer myth is revealed in the complementary figure of Hurry, the giant of a man who looks half bear, and will obey no law but that of the jungle. When Deerslayer reprimands him for threatening any possible suitor to Judith Hutter, whom he desires, Hurry replies:

> If an inimy crosses my path, will I not beat him out of it! Look at me! Am I a man like to let any sneaking, crawling skin trader get the better of me in a matter that touches me as nearly as the kindness of Judith Hutter? Besides, when we live beyond the law, we must be our own judges and executioners. And if a man *should* be found dead in the woods, who is there to say who slew him?

Hurry's position is logical and there is no answer to it in terms that he would understand. Deerslayer's innocence is the American search for a rebirth of belief, not in the Puritan's God (which had been degraded in Man-alone, or Hurry), but in a power greater than his Will. "You are wrong", says Deerslayer at a later stage of his career,

> to distrust the power of God in anything. Them that live in the settlements and towns get to have confined and unjust opinions consarning the might of His hand; but we who pass our time in His very presence, as it might be, see things differently. I mean such of us as have white natur's. A redskin has his notions, and it is right that it should be so, and

if they are not exactly the same as a Christian white man's, there is no harm in it. Still, there are matters that belong altogether to the ordering of God's providence, and these salt and fresh water lakes are some of them. I do not pretend to account for these things, but I think it is the duty of all to believe in them.

Now the first art-music to be created by Americans manifests—as one might expect—both the virtues and the vices of the Puritan inheritance and of the pioneer's innocence and savagery. The settlers that came over, especially from Britain, Germany and Holland, brought with them their folk-songs and the religious music which expressed the faith for which they were self-exiled. The folk-songs survived, were handed down in remote rural areas from generation to generation, were changed, and became—as we shall see in Part II of this book—one of the sources from which an indigenously American folk-art was derived. But the only music the Puritan settlers could officially tolerate was religious music, which could help them in their hard struggle with Nature; and although at first they did no more than sing the music they had sung at home, they increasingly came to sing it in ways that were changed by the wilderness. Thus the early seventeenth-century settlers in New England brought with them the psalm-singing traditions of the Reformation. In 1640 the pastors published the *Bay Psalm Book*, which consisted of metrical versions of the psalms made by members of the Massachusetts Bay Colony: these were to be sung to "very neere fourty common tunes, as they are collected out of our chief musicians by Thos. Ravenscroft". For worship in church the psalms were sung at rather fast tempi and in unison—so that God would have no difficulty in understanding the words. At home, for recreation, they were often sung in parts, as harmonized by British seventeenth-century composers such as Ravenscroft himself, Tomkins, Allison, East and the elder Milton. Both tunes and harmonizations were thus imported from the old country and—as in the archaic *cantus firmus* technique—the main melody was usually sung by the tenors. This comparatively sophisticated style could not, however, for long weather the conditions of pioneer life; as traditional skills were forgotten in the urgent necessity of keeping alive, the music began to acquire some of the barbarity of the land. In the eighteenth century, when the New England communities had acquired a measure of order, if not of the graces of civilization, the pastors made a conscious effort to revive religious music. Itinerant choral directors travelled around establishing singing schools, and published their own music in "tune-books". As musical literacy increased, so did the number of mainly amateur composers. In the later half of the eighteenth century enthusiastic New England amateurs produced in abundance hymns, metrical psalms, anthems and "fuguing tunes" for use both in church and at home. This music was based on recollections of the old English and German Reformation music, only the memory had become a little fuddled, so the technique was clumsy and inexact. The half-intuitive composers, thinking modally, like folk-singers, did not know how to achieve the highly civilized equilibrium between horizontal polyphony and vertical homophony that characterized their European forebears. Yet their rawness was also their authenticity. Their "mistakes" in harmony and part-writing could be at times inspired; indeed, they were not mistakes at all, since they were a creative manifestation of their identities. For the first time we thus hear, in their music, the accent of a New World; their "guileless truth", like that of Natty Bumppo, is inseparable from their barbarism.

Some part of the crudity of the New England hymnodists was, of course, an invention of their first critics who, nurtured on the strictest nineteenth-century principles, would undoubtedly have made similar objections to Machaut or Stravinsky. They objected strongly, for instance, to the New Englanders' prosody, which followed sixteenth- and seventeenth-century tradition in disregarding the bar-accents, leaving changes of time to be inferred from the verbal stresses: so that it was precisely the independence of the melodic thinking that produced some of their most characteristic harmonic effects; it is also possible that some of the modal survivals in their music were modified in performance by the introduction of accidentals that they were chary of notating. As texts, the New England hymnodists favoured the Tate and Brady metrical versions of the Psalms, the hymns of Isaac Watts, and various biblical paraphrases. The metrical psalms and hymns were set in simple homophony, or as "fuguing tunes" usually in two sections— the first being in the customary triadic homophony with occasional passing notes, the second being in fugato of a rudimentary type derived directly from English and Scottish psalter style of the seventeenth century. Often the homophonic hymn is in triple time, the fugato in duple. The anthems were longer pieces usually on biblical texts in prose; they tended to be sectional (a series of linked hymns and fuguing tunes), or in repetitive forms such as the rondo and variation, since the composers had little skill in, or even interest in, the modulatory techniques of European eighteenth-century music.

The primitivism of the New Englanders' music consists not so much in their "incorrect" harmony as in their avoidance of true polyphony. The dissonant suspension—the core of sixteenth-century style—is unknown to them: so consequently is the concept of music as a gradation of harmonic tensions. When they wrote in fuguing style (sometimes spelt fuging or fudging, and perhaps so pronounced, the unconscious pun being appropriate), they did not really depart from homophonic principles. The fudging was exciting, and lent an animation to the sturdy triadic harmony; but it did not create that harmony, and if a few "wrong notes" resulted from the very free imitation, they added to the stimulation. Even in the metrical psalms and hymns the odd dissonance tended to be fortuitous—a consequence of the composers' desire to give each part a good singing line. These lines were modal because modal melodies are the most "natural" to sing; and the modalism sometimes came into conflict with a fumbling attempt to accommodate it to the principles of eighteenth-century tonality. To us, perhaps, the composers who succeed least in this compromise, and therefore appear the most archaic, seem the most imaginative and truthful; and in view of the subsequent history of American music there is a sense in which they may, in fact, be so.

Timothy Swan, for instance, was born in Worcester, Massachusetts, in 1758, and began to compose when, at the age of seventeen, he became a fifer in the Revolutionary Army. His *Leghorn*[2] published, in 1800, opens with soprano solo, in unaccompanied monody; intuitively, the music is modal (aeolian), though a naïve form of post-baroque illustration introduces some F sharps, and an implied modulation, when the billows roll in a lilting dotted rhythm; and this makes the more disturbing the return to F natural in the modal cadential phrase for "his holy soul":

EXAMPLE I

Deep in our hearts ——— let us re - cord the deep-er sor - row of our Lord. ——— Be -

hold the ri - sing billows roll. ——————— To o - - ver - whelm his ho - - ly soul.

Note how in this example the bar-lines have no accentual significance.
The hymn begins in 3 : 2, as indicated by the square brackets.

---

2 Some of the examples referred to in this section are republished in *Landmarks in Early American Music,* edited by Goldman and Smith (Schirmer).

If this is "primitive", it is also strangely moving, with a kind of awkward truth comparable with that which we find in the monodic writing of our twentieth-century English composer, Holst. Swan then repeats this line, harmonized in four parts. He does not attempt to accommodate the wandering modulation to his part-writing; banishing the F sharps, he sets the tune in consistent modality, without a single chromatic alteration. The empty fifths and flat seventh give the music a grave dignity, like that of folk-song; and the occasional dissonant passing notes, which are without harmonic implication, impart a rough strength to the simplicity (consider what happens to the tune's cadential F natural at the end):

EXAMPLE 2

In *Rainbow*—for which Swan used words by Isaac Watts—we find a quiet, unambiguously triadic homophony for the hymn section, with a rhythm that preserves something of sixteenth-century flexibility; the fuguing section has a gracefully lilting dotted rhythm for the calming sea, and is harmonically almost all tonic and dominant:

EXAMPLE 3

Reprinted from *Choral Music of the American Folk Tradition*, edited by Jeanne Behrend, by permission of Elkan-Vogel Co., Inc., Philadelphia, copyright owners.

The beauty of the music—in performance—lies in the spare, "open" texture: a characteristic we shall meet with again in the work of composers such as Copland and Harris, who are establishing a twentieth-century American tradition.

The "folk" flavour of New England hymnody is nowhere more evident than in the work of Swan. In the music of Justin Morgan—who lived from 1747 to 1798, and was teacher, innkeeper and horsebreeder as well as musician—the folk element is combined with other more sophisticated elements that still tend towards the archaic. *Amanda*, published in 1792, has a very crude form of sixteenth-century false relation to express death's nastiness:

EXAMPLE 4

our awareness of life's dreaminess and emptiness, however, flows into a purely modal tune, with bare fifths and flat seventh cadences that are, like folk-song, melancholy yet resigned. That this folk-modalism was Morgan's natural musical idiom is suggested by comparison of *Amanda* with *Huntingdon*, from his *Philadelphia Harmony*. Here the hymn section gains a rugged boldness from the parallel fourths and octaves, while the fuguing section makes an unsuccessful attempt at the European harmonist's sense of progression, for there is a long dominant pedal that "prepares" nothing. The fortuitous clashes of the passing notes and the driving energy of the descending scale phrase have, on the other hand, considerable power, making us aware of the slipperiness of the rocks and of the determination necessary to avoid their perils:

EXAMPLE 5

Reprinted from *Choral Music of the American Folk Tradition*, edited by Jeanne Behrend, by permission of Elkan-Vogel Co., Inc., Philadelphia, copyright owners.

In some of the composers the folk flavour seems to be accommodated to the more "civilized" contours of European melody by instinctive assimilation. Simeon Jocelin, who lived from 1746 to 1823, has a beautiful setting of a metrical version of the 89th Psalm that might pass as a traditional Lutheran chorale—of a rather old-fashioned nature, however, for there are still empty fifths and implied false relations. From his setting of the 146th Psalm, the modalisms have gone. The relationship to the chorale tradition is still evident in the long-sustained initial notes, to get the congregation together; but the part-writing, though consistently diatonic, is oddly fortuitous. Sometimes the bumps have a naïvely illustrative intent, as in the Lombard rhythm, that makes his voice shout against death; more often they are an accidental consequence of the simple voice progressions:

EXAMPLE 6

I'll praise my Ma - ker with my breath

The final cadence, after the fuguing, sounds a little like unconscious parody of the noble eighteenth-century peroration.

Those primitives who lack the deep imaginative instincts of Timothy Swan or Justin Morgan are apt, inevitably, to produce music that sounds to us quaint rather than affecting. Samuel Holyoke's *Andover*, published in 1791, is a case in point. When "this feeble body" fails, it "faints" in a comic dissonant appoggiatura and dies in a cadence separated by rests. The disembodied saints are represented by fluttery quavers in scalewise motion, while our "long-sought rest" becomes a procession of bare fifths (even this "literalism" is to find an echo, however, in the music of Ives):

EXAMPLE 7

Shall join the dis - em - bod - ied saints and find its long sought rest

Join and find its long sought rest

Jacob Kimball, who lived from 1761 to 1826, shows a comparable naïvety in employing—in his *Leicester* and *Marblehead*, both published in 1793—a stern homophony for the world's cares and sorrows, and a somewhat jittery fugato for the "destructive way" of "youthful sinners". We can find this music amusing, even touching in its primitivism; but we cannot find it beautiful as the best of Swan's music is beautiful: which proves that true musical inventiveness has nothing to do with the presence or absence of "technique". Among the American hymnodists the more technically proficient tend, as one would expect, to adopt an idiom closer to what was then contemporary style; but those who employ, with least ambiguity, an eighteenth-century manner are not necessarily the latest in chronological sequence. Josiah Flagg (1738–94) published an *Hallelujah* in 1764; to us it sounds ludicrous because its jaunty trumpet arpeggio tune is fugued in such perfunctory brevity, and rounded off by an extended plagal cadence that is almost as long as the fugato. In reminding us of Handel, it reminds us of the world Handel celebrated; and this doesn't seem apposite to Flagg's world in the way that Timothy Swan's new oldness is apposite to his. The *Jubilee* of Supply Belcher, published in 1794, has also a Handelian trumpet theme, and a final grandiose peroration. Here, however, the style seems acceptable. Though the ripe Handelian sonority has holes in it and the parts behave "incorrectly", the music does make "a gladly solemn sound"; this is how Handel might sound, with a wilderness behind him instead of Augustan England.

By far the most celebrated of the New England hymnodists—in his own day and in ours—is William Billings, who was born in Boston in 1746 and died there in 1800. His fame may be partly due to the fact that he was a most colourful character and an excellent self-advertiser; and had physical peculiarities—a withered arm, lame leg, blind eye and rasping voice—that seem to correspond to the "crudeness" of his music. More important, however, is the fact that, starting as a tanner, he was the first New England hymnodist to turn fully professional. He thus had time in which to learn his new trade; and although or because his empiricism was the essence of his creativity, there is evidence in his published work that he did learn it, the hard way. In his first singing-book, *The New England Psalm-Singer*, published in 1770, he said, with characteristic boastfulness, that since Nature is the only true dictator every man must be "his own Carver"; he would acknowledge no rules coming from precedent or authority that seemed irrelevant to an aboriginal New Englander. In his last collection, however, *The Continental Harmony*, published in 1794, he uses a title that possibly implies a reference to Europe, and acknowledges that he has been "fool enough to commence author before I really understood either tune, time, or concord". Yet his argument makes clear that he did not mean that he had had to go to someone else's school in order to learn a technique: only that he had needed time and experience to understand the nature of his own technique adequately. Thus he leaves us in no doubt that he knows of the rule about parallel fifths, while continuing to write them with enthusiasm because he likes the noise. (Somewhat oddly, to our ears, he finds them "luscious and fulsome", not austere.) Similarly, he advocates the use of the modern major and minor scales ("the only two scales are C and A") for theoretical reasons; but repeatedly insists that the demands of a good singing line must take precedence over harmonic considerations. Always he appeals empirically to the ear: so that if he uses fewer false relations than many of his colleagues, he displays a fondness for some modal archaisms (such as the so-called Machaut cadence and the Landini cadence) which they do not share. He maintains his Yankee innocence until the end; and for all the respect for Science that he shows in his last collection, we find him blandly admitting that expediency counts for more than academic law: "The first part (the tenor) is nothing more than a flight of fancy, and the other parts are forced to comply and conform to that, by partaking of the same air, or, at least, as much of it as they can get: But by reason of this restraint, the last parts are seldom as good as the first; for the second part is subservient to the first, the third part must conform to the first and second, and the fourth part must conform to the other three." But if Billings is saying in this passage that no man can do more than try his best, negligence of rule can have a more positive aspect, too. One may flout rules not because one is not clever enough to obey them but because Fancy, when she "gets upon the wing, seems to despise all form, and scorns to be confined or limited by any formal prescriptions whatever". Thus Billings composes an anthem based on Psalm 60[3] in which he expresses God's displeasure by violent ungrammatical transitions, rather than modulations, and by rapid metrical changes. The happy ending is in F major, after the G minor lamentation. Billings subtitles the anthem "Variety without Method", but the imputation is that method is not always desirable: an opinion in which Charles Ives would have concurred. Experience must make music anew, just as texts—even sacred ones—must be rewritten to accord with topical and local needs: "by the rivers of Waterton", sings Billings in an early anthem, "we sat down and wept, yea we wept as we remembered Boston".

One may suspect that Billings's music appealed to his contemporaries because it was melodically fertile, and grateful to sing: and also because it reflected so spontaneously all the musical potentialities that were in the air. There are innumerable tunes by Billings that might be folk-tunes; there are also others that incorporate vestiges of eighteenth-century melismatic elegance, and many that combine a folk-like

---

[3] This and other Billings examples are taken from the facsimile re-issue of *The Continental Harmony*, edited by Hans Nathan for the John Harvard Library.

modal lyricism with eighteenth-century illustrative arabesques, like this delightful tune from *I charge you* (which anthem boasts not one accidental or modulation):

EXAMPLE 8

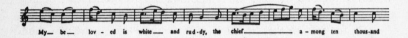

Others again make an unusually direct use of eighteenth-century dance rhythms—gavotte, bourrée and jig—such as were fashionable in the towns: but do so with a folklike uncouthness and vivacity, and with an occasional piquant asymmetry prompted by the words. (Consider the Christmas carols *Judea* and *Emmanuel* and the many tunes that contain reminiscences of *Greensleeves*, such as *Clarimont*.) Billings's superiority over his colleagues, if it exists, would seem to lie in the spontaneity with which, in his unartful art, these various elements cohere. We do not feel with him that the contributory elements are pulling in different directions, and it was probably this wholeness of personality that made him so effective as teacher and educator, as well as composer. Even his larger anthems, though rudimentary in structure, make formal sense, and exploit alternations of solo and duet passages with chorus in a manner that is varied and charming, if seldom dramatic. The short anthems (such as *I charge you* and *The Rose of Sharon*) are the best, because Billings's music always convinces most when it seems most unpremeditated. This applies equally well to his more learned compositions, as we can see from his comments on fuguing in *The Continental Harmony*: "while the tones and words do most sweetly coincide and agree", he says,

> the words are seemingly engaged in a musical warfare; and excuse the paradox if I further add that each part seems determined by dint of Harmony, and strength of Accent, to Drown his Competitor in an Ocean of Harmony, and while each part is thus mutually striving for Mastery, and sweetly contending for victory, the Audience are most luxuriously entertained and most sweetly delighted. Now the solemn Bass demands their attention, now the manly tenor, now the lofty counter, now the volatile Treble, now here, now there, now here again. O enchanting! O ecstatic! Push on, push on, ye Sons of Harmony.

If we consider these words alongside a passage such as this from *Creation*, probably the most vigorously stimulating of all fuguing tunes:

EXAMPLE 9

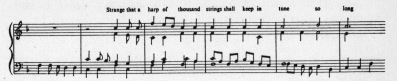

we shall understand how Billings was indeed a man living and breathing new music in a new world. He is the true American naïf in that his "art" is an overflow of wonder, of energy, of released delight. It is as though he—and we—were experiencing music for the first time; and the sensation is strange and enlivening, especially for those who belong to a world grown old. There is a similar sense of shock, of child-like excitement, in the fuguing descent of the "angel of the Lord" in Daniel Read's *Sherburne*—a New England version of "While shepherds watch their flocks by night". Such moments seem to justify the interminable stretches of common triads in root positions, the five- or six-minute anthems that have lost modal fluidity without being able to rise to a single modulation! Such music reflects the positive aspects of the American "new man" who, as Crèvecoeur put it, had passed from "servile dependence, penury and useless labour" to "toils of a very different nature, rewarded by ample subsistence".

Billings habitually kept the tune in the tenor, as in the old three-part Reformation psalm-singing; and expected his pieces to be sung by a preponderance of male voices. The heavily weighted bass was a part of the rugged, manly effect: as was the fact that the tenor tune would be sung by some of the women an octave higher, creating an organum part in and around the treble part proper, and incidentally correcting some of the incorrect harmony. The quality of pristine wonder that Billings's music represents could not, however, be long preserved; or at least, the more "civilization" encroached on New England, bringing with it professional teachers of polite music from Europe, the more the primitive American hymnody moved back into the wilderness. Now it was disseminated not only along the eastern seaboard, but also south and west, written in a curious notation called "shape-note", which was a compromise between normal staff notation and the empirical method of tonic solfa. Many of the tunes of Billings and the other New Englanders were thus transported by the travelling singing teachers, who themselves wrote similar tunes; as they were carried through thinly populated regions of the vast rural continent, their primitive features were naturally encouraged. The melodies tended to revert to the original three-part setting; their modal character was reinforced by direct contact with surviving folk-songs, as in the beautiful tune *Wondrous Love*:

EXAMPLE 10

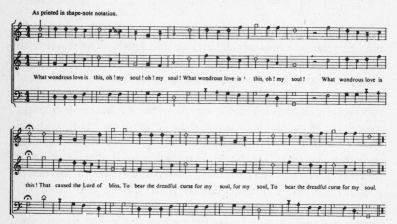

and the New Englander's attempt at eighteenth-century harmonization was abandoned in favour of an instinctive folk-organum, as in this strange version of *Holy Manna* from "Southern Harmony", where Rousseau's original tune has become almost purely pentatonic and the harmony almost consistently parallel fourths and fifths:

EXAMPLE 11

If, on paper, the music looks crude and gauche, we must remember that it is not paper-music. It came empirically from the sound made by massed voices: as, indeed, the technique of medieval organum had originally done. The sonority the music produces in performance is extraordinarily impressive and resonant, the more so because the New Englanders' habit of allowing men or women to sing any part—"up" or "down" according to sex—was, in the remoter rural areas, adopted with complete spontaneity. The consequent octave doublings give the sound its awe-inspiring reverberation: nor is it ever certain which part will receive the main emphasis, since that depends on the proportionate number of people who decide to sing each part. The shape-note tunes proliferated with remarkable rapidity, and the revivalist sects that flourished in every state took them up the more readily because they could appeal immediately to the illiterate. Shape note method encouraged the singers to make up their own versions of the tunes on the spur of the moment, so that a wild heterophony must often have resulted. This would have accorded, musically, with the physical excesses of revivalist fervour; and contemporary descriptions make clear that this was not far removed from the ritual exercise of voodoo-worship. In the South the shape-note tunes were the main "white" source for the Negro's spirituals; together, white and black Christian sought a refuge from Calvanistic fire and brimstone.

By this time the shape-note tunes had ceased to be a part of American "art" music and had become part of the origins of the American folk-art that is jazz: not until the twentieth century did they play a part in the evolution of art music, as we can see in the setting of the 67th Psalm by Charles Ives. It says much for the vitality of this indigenous American music that—preserved in many teaching books such as *Kentucky Harmony, Sacred Harp, Harp of Columbia* and *Southern Harmony* (at first in the traditional three parts, but later with an alto added) —it should be still be performed, in much the same manner, in the remoter regions of the Southern states. Meanwhile, however, the development of art-music in the American cities was associated with the assimilation, and then perhaps with the imposition, of European models. Indeed, there had been a precedent for this way back in the eighteenth century, contemporary with the New England hymnodists: for the Moravian Brethren in Pennsylvania had attempted to transport their European culture, along with their way of life, to their new home. The musical activity of the community at Bethlehem was especially rich both ecclesiastically and domestically, and their technical skill did not noticeably decline in the relatively harsh conditions in which they were forced to live. How deeply their music was rooted in European tradition is indicated by a beautiful piece such as the choral and instrumental arrangement, possibly by Johannes Herbst, of "O Sacred Head now wounded". Hassler's noble chorale tune had been treated as an organ prelude by J. S. Bach's pupil, Peter Kellner; and this organ version was used by Herbst as the basis of an arrangement suitable for performance by the Moravian Brethren. There is nothing specifically

American about it, unless the freely moving inner parts, the wandering modulations and the somewhat wild climax may be said to hint at the pioneer's uncertainty. Normally, however, the Moravians cultivated a civilized fluency, rather than a deep passion: an aria of John Frederick Peter such as "The Lord in his Holy Temple" (written in 1786) exemplifies rococo charm with an undercurrent of Bohemian energy, while John Antes's "Loveliest Emmanuel" manifests an almost Mozartian lyricism, with soaring leaps and a flexible, moving bass beneath a vamping accompaniment that is operatic in origin, though it could become both American and "popular". This John Antes, who was born in Pennsylvania in 1740, went to Europe as a Moravian missionary, met Haydn, returned to Bethlehem and wrote music copiously for the delectation of the Brethren, and then spent the last years of his life in England as a watchmaker. He composed not merely church music but also chamber music, most of it modelled directly on Haydn's European style. His trios for two violins and cello (prompted perhaps by Haydn's works for this unusual combination) were published in London, ascribed to a "Dilettante Americano". The music has a simple grace and rather frail pathos; the frailty is perhaps the only evidence that the competently written, ingratiating idiom does not really belong to the old world, though it shows little positive evidence of the new. The Moravians tried to preserve, musically as in every other way, a home from home. Unlike Billings, they had no desire to create a new musical world, though increased familiarity with their work may reveal that their piety achieved, in their strange environment, a wide-eyed simplicity such as Europe had long lost.[4]

The new arbiters of taste were not, however, the Moravians; they were rather the more sophisticated Europophiles who lived in the big cities, especially Boston and Philadelphia. We can see the change—and decline—with clarity in the development of the secular patriotic songs. Andrew Law (1748–1821) wrote some noble Billings-like hymn tunes such as *Blendon* (which is eighteenth-century in manner, despite the occasional parallels and false octaves); he also composed *Bunker Hill*, which is one of the finest patriotic songs ever written. The stern modal tune, the harsh passing notes, the empty fifths, make us aware that the reality it speaks of does indeed involve "Blood and Carnage and Death Groans", while at the same time the simple grandeur of the period tells us that the horror was necessary, even justifiable. This is

---

[4] Vocal and instrumental music of the Moravians has been edited in modern editions by Hans T. David (Peters).

why *Bunker Hill* is accurately subtitled "The American Hero". One has only to compare this truly heroic piece with Alexander Reinagle's *Federal March*[5] of 1788 or with George Jackson's *Funeral Dirge for General Washington*[5] of 1799 to see how heroism may turn to platitude. If Jackson's sanctimonious drooping cadences are evidence mainly of a deficient talent, there is a general principle involved, too. The polite symmetries of the eighteenth-century echo-effects deprive the experience of authenticity: maybe an old European civilization could make such elegance a means of objectifying profound feeling, but a new American civilization cannot. So the piece becomes a gesture towards a dead hero by a gentleman who knows little of either heroism or death. We can relate it to the genteel tradition of Francis Hopkinson, who had written a toast to the (living) General Washington which, in the comic *politesse* of its cadence-phrase, unconsciously deflates the glory, pride and virtue it is supposed to celebrate:

EXAMPLE 12

This Francis Hopkinson (1737–91) was a writer, painter and politician as well as musician. For him, as for his friends and colleagues, whether musically educated or not, music was a social rather than professional activity; the point of his psalms and parlour songs in the English manner of Arne, Storace and Dibdin was that they were, in his own words, "easy and familiar". Their "rational" simplicity would have appealed to another amateur musician, Benjamin Franklin, while their European grace would have pleased Thomas Jefferson, who wrote comparable songs himself, hoping that such music could be aristocratically civilized and democratically easy at one and the same time. The hope was vain: as is testified by Hopkinson's prettified, faintly false songs, dedicated to Washington, who never told a lie. In "Beneath a Weeping Willow's Shade" the mocking echo of the mocking bird is hardly necessary, for the banality of tonic-dominant habit has already ironically deflated the plaintiveness of the maiden's "moan". Even when the polite composers, such as Alexander Reinagle (1756–1809), had acquired a more proficient technique than Hopkinson could

[5] These are republished in *Landmarks of Early American Music*.

boast of, their music remained unreal in its elegance, pretentious (in the strict sense) in its aristocratic charm, as we can see from the sprightly yet excessively long first movement of Reinagle's D major Sonata. This unreality becomes comic in the many programmatic "battle" sonatas to which Washington was partial. James Hewitt's seemingly interminable "Military Sonata" describing the Battle at Trenton is a case in point: one wonders what the infantrymen who went through the crossing of the Delaware would have had to say about the footling tootle that represents their exploit; while even the grief of the Americans for their lost comrades is expressed through Lombard sobs that are rendered platitudinous by the placid conventionality of the harmonic progressions. It would seem that the dream of Jeffersonian democracy is over, musically as in other ways: and that by the turn into the nineteenth century the only art-music that maintained a brash vitality was—as we shall see in Part II of this book—that which was intended for commercial entertainment: the banjo music and minstrel songs that, beginning as an American complement to the popular style of English ballad opera, led to the work of Stephen Foster and Louis Moreau Gottschalk.

The genteel musical tradition was a direct complement to the apparent taming of Calvinistic fervour when the wilderness seemed to have been civilized. Practical rationality succeeded religious conviction, as God Almighty was accepted (in Franklin's phrase) as "Himself a mechanic, the greatest in the universe, respected and admired more for the variety, ingenuity and utility of his handiwork than for the antiquity of his family". Thus, for the genteel, music was moralistic and educational rather than religious. We can see this in the urban development of the hymn tune itself, which was emasculated in becoming polite. Timothy Dwight, a President of Yale—for so many years to be the pillar of American musical respectability—composed hymns himself, as well as enormously ponderous epic poems about Washington and the Revolution, and pastoral poems such as *Greenfield Hill,* which attempted to regard the American scene in the mellow light of the English eighteenth century. Dwight's four-part settings ushered in—rather than heralded—the conventional hymn style of the nineteenth century, with correct leading notes and passing dominant sevenths after the English-Teutonic model. The educational, rather than mystical, bias is evident when Lowell Mason introduced his immensely popular singing-books for children with the admonition that everyone "ought" to be able to read music because it "improved the mind and added to the refinement of the heart". That, perhaps, was no mean ambition, and many of Lowell's hymns have deservedly become a part of American popular culture. None the less, it was an ambition that made music a pleasing smoothing of the surface of life rather than an attempt to express the energy of a new world. Unlike the Primitives, the Genteel used art as a refuge from experience; and Walt Whitman fulminated against the polite musicians, the "piano songs in rooms stifling with fashionable scent", the trifling ballads and lacrymose hymns, no less than he did against the "male odalisques" and "dandies and ennuyees" who had come to represent Poetry in his generation. Maybe it was inevitable that music, a social art, should for the time being shut up house. But prosperity and plenty, which brought the American buoyancy and optimism, had not really destroyed the negative aspects of the pioneer myth: which is why in the nineteenth century the American spirit had to seek its ultimate salvation in a solitary personal destiny. Gentility would not or could not follow the great literary figures on the path they had to take. The polite blurred the white and the black aspects of the Pioneer's innocence, while the almost mythological solitaries of American literature saw the dark as complementary to the light: as both inevitable and terrifying.

Thus even in Fenimore Cooper there is not only the relationship between Natty and Hurry; there is also that between Natty and Chingaghook—between the white man and the redskin who is at once the Noble Savage and the unknown terrors and violence within us. In Poe—significantly a Southern writer—the white innocent becomes a puppet, the baby-doll or child-wife, poised against the Ape, the blackness of sadism, masochism and necrophilia; while his most representative stories are vampire-parables about the disintegration of the self-consuming ego. In Hawthorne the Calvinistic sense of Innate Depravity seems the more appalling because the Fall has happened a second time, in the New Eden which was America; the "blackness" of guilt becomes a fear of the flesh that must burn and destroy, even as it creates the white, blond, directionless licence of Hester's child. Much grander is Melville's parable of Ishmael, the American alien and outcast, the man of heart who is redeemed by his dark brother-spouse Queequeg, whose coffin becomes a womb: and of Ahab, the Puritan Pioneer who is self-exiled from his kind and, driven by his dark brother, Fedalla, strives to conquer the mystery, the unknowable Nature—god or devil —that lurks in the sea's depths. Exalting Will at the expense of spirit, heroic in courage yet doomed to destroy his humanity in the act of asserting it, Ahab becomes a prototype of Modern Man, hopelessly challenging a sublimely purposeless universe. The whale is white because eternal and unanswerable; and the truth of the whiteness becomes Ahab's black death.

This same dichotomy is apparent in the ostensibly optimistic figure of Whitman, whose "free" verse sings a "song of Myself". The single ego is to become all things, achieving the unity of multiplicity; society must put itself to his test, not the other way round, for "I resist anything better than my own diversity". As James said, the poem has "a look of being committed to nothing in particular, of standing in an attitude of general hospitality to the chances of life". Society is to be redeemed by Adamic man, who is unique and alone, yet at the same time a cosmos, a "knit of identity". Having become the universe, however, Whitman has nothing to long for but nirvana; so his surging, buoyant rhythms lead into the great paeans to Death. Out of the cradle of the unknown sea he sails to the ultimate oblivion; and the elegy on Lincoln—wherein the blackness of the coffin creeps through the vast, lilac-springing land—becomes an elegy on Whitman himself, and on the ideal of the American pioneer:

> Over the breast of the spring, amid cities,
> Amid lanes and through old woods, where lately the violets
>   peeped from the ground, spotting the gray debris,
> Amid the grass in the fields each side of the lanes, passing the end-
>   less grass,
> Passing the yellow-spear'd wheat, every grain from its shroud in
>   the dark-brown fields uprisen,
> Passing the apple-tree blows of white and pink in the orchards,
> Carrying a corpse to where it should rest in the grave,
> Night and day journeys a coffin.

Most terrifying of all, perhaps, is the figure of Emily Dickinson, who made herself a Lady in White: who said in a letter to Thomas Higginson: "I had a terror since September I could tell to none; and so I sing, as the boy does of the burying ground, because I am afraid." Her family, she says, are "religious, except me, and address an eclipse, every morning, whom they call their Father". But she is alone, without God or Man: "You ask of my companions. Hills, sir, and the sundown, and a dog large as myself, that my father bought me. They are better than beings, because they know, but do not tell; and the noise in the pool at noon excels my piano."

No wonder that Emerson, reacting against the "blackness upon blackness" of Calvinist inheritance, sought to "transcend tragedy": to render Ahab comfortably positive, without the sense of evil, immersing the soul pantheistically in the world of appearances. No wonder Thoreau, that other recluse at Walden, also listened for "the noise in the pool at noon", the only respite for the terror of the solitary heart, for there he had "a little world all to myself", with his "own moon, and sea, and stars". No wonder Thoreau said that, in his private Eden, he could "walk and recover the lost child that I am"; no wonder the aboriginal American was always trying to recapture the pristine innocence of the Boy in the Forest, before the predatory instinct has destroyed him, as he had destroyed other living creatures. We see this supremely in the boyhood myths of Mark Twain. Tom Sawyer is the boy Twain was: the teller of tall stories, dreamer of the dreams of *bourgeois* pretence. Huck Finn is the boy Twain would have liked to be: preserving before puberty his "guileless truth", accepting Light and Dark on equal terms, so long as he is on the raft, on the river, with Jim. ("Other places do feel so cramped and smothery, but a raft don't. You feel mighty free and easy and comfortable on a raft.") Riding the raft, Huck can face the terror and violence of the wilderness, even the ghastly spectacle of his dead father in the broken, drifting boat. When, however, he goes ashore he meets the sharks and sharpers, the murdering partisans of Southern chivalry who are the reality of Tom Sawyer's dream; and when Tom comes into the story Huck seems to capitulate to his values. The farce of the mock-escape, though very funny, is very savage, and a sacrifice of the humanity Huck has discovered. It is not final, however, for Huck's equation of alienation (he calls it lonesomeness) with the death-wish is more profound than Tom's flesh-creeping boyhood horror of the cave wherein lurks Injun Joe; and Huck's admission of alienation leads to his second rejection of society, when he lights off into the woods. But he is a boy no longer, and Twain does not tell us what happens to him: whether he ends up like his father or miraculously manages to live as outcast, preserving his humanity. Later American writers have tried to continue his story: in Salinger's Caulfield he suffers a nervous breakdown; in Faulkner's Ike he attains a kind of metaphysical, if not religious, absolution; in Hemingway's Nick Adams (whose name makes him both First Man and Devil!) he exchanges the woods for war, sudden death, the pointless wound and the lost generation. In a sense, Hemingway's own death by shot-gun completes the parable; and the conclusion was already implicit in Huck Finn, since the true morality and heroism of the raft was doomed to fail. In fact, it carried Huck and Jim not to escape, but deeper into the dark heart of the hostile South.

For Mark Twain, as for Whitman, the Civil War—in which American agrarianism was finally routed by industrialism—was the historical expression of the failure of the Pioneer Ideal. The Puritan virtues of the men of the pre-War world had been real, if restricted, and Cobbett cannot have been altogether wide of the mark when he said, after his American travels, "there are very few really ignorant men in America of native growth. Every farmer is more or less of a reader . . . well-informed, modest without shyness". After the War, however, the salt of the earth was no longer the farming class; the new bosses were men like Jim Flask (a pedlar), Daniel Drew (a cattle dealer), Jay Gould (a promoter), and for them "the dog that snaps the quickest gets the bone". Inevitably, perhaps, the frontiersman had become a mixed-up character; the training and beliefs of his earlier days had been "overlaid by successions of unrelated and violent experiences, like geological deposits". The experience of Nature in the raw, of the violence of war, of the impact of "scrofulous wealth" (in Whitman's phrase), all conflicted with his inherited traditions and his memories of the past. As a result there was a "total lack of fusion and mutuality" in the texture of his life; he had lost his European standards, and he had acquired no others apart from a brash assertion of his equality. Mark Twain himself became a victim of the spirit he intuitively deplored. It was necessary that democratic man should become a "berserker", debunking the past, asserting the validity of his materialistic convictions. But to pillory the past, as Twain did in *Innocents Abroad*, was only an inverse form of reliance on it. Twain had to "know" the old world so that he could pretend to be superior to it; at bottom there was not much difference between his hysterically asserted hate and the all-consuming love with which "sensitive" Americans, in reaction to the post-War American world, sought to pillage Europe. Unable to face the solitariness, as Melville and Hawthorne and Emily Dickinson had faced it, these artists pretended that they could still have a tradition of solidarity; and because this was no longer spiritually possible—as it had been, in their raw fashion, for the American primitives—their art became more false in proportion to its increasing technical proficiency. It was not merely, or mainly, that they studied abroad and employed European techniques, for American techniques inevitably came, with Americans, from Europe. But whereas the American Primitives had transplanted their European conventions in American soil, and had allowed them to grow as they would, the nineteenth-century "art" writers—and composers—preferred to stick artificial (European) flowers into American earth. "Europe" became an abrogation of responsibility for one's destiny: a theme which Henry James profoundly explored in his studies of the love-hate relationship between American Innocence and European Experience. James wrote of this theme with conscious understanding; lesser men, however, became the playthings of the past, childish in a sense that was diametrically opposed to the boyhood-integrity of Mark Twain. We can see this as early as Washington Irving's *Bracebridge Hall*; a dream-revocation of the Old World as it never was or could have been. This is not far removed from the *second*-childishness of Irving's Rip van Winkle myth, which is not a re-creation of the child's "guileless truth", but a pretence that the adult can and should behave with non-adult responsibility. This again is a wish-fulfilment. Though we can't all be Robber Barons, democracy's Little Man, like Charlie Chaplin, may sometimes come out on top— through luck, not judgment. It is interesting that the white man is here equated with the black: who had, in Brer Rabbit, his own weak but lucky charm against misfortune.

Most nineteenth-century American music is "Bracebridge Hall music". Like that of Edwardian England, it manifested a passive veneration for the Teutonic, which represented Art; and was usually well written, cheerful and agreeable: a pretence that the wilderness did not exist, that the heart was not a "lonely hunter". We have seen that Lowell Mason (1792–1872) tamed the fuguing hymnody of the primitives into technically more sophisticated, Europeanized forms, closer in harmony, cosier in texture. John Paine, George Chadwick and Arthur Foote inflated the cosiness to oratorio-like or symphonic proportions (Paine considered Wagner subversive, and recommended "the present *and future* adherence to the historical forms as developed by Bach, Handel, Mozart and Beethoven".) Perhaps only one of the "Bracebridge Hall" composers, Horatio Parker (1863–1919), managed to discover, beneath the "massive oak beams" and old-worlde charm, a truth that preserves a modest vitality. This was partly because his passion for England was a positive if mild virtue which, in his social life at Yale as well as in his music, he attempted to re-create; and was partly because he was, within limits, a man of genuine religious conviction. His most celebrated, and perhaps best, work—the oratorio *Hora Novissima*—may turn its back on the wilderness and on the terrors of the solitary heart; but something more comes across than pietistic aspiration. The fugal movements, with their two-bar periods and chromatic sequences, tend to be tepidly conventional; but the soft sweetness of the arias has a genuine poignancy that derives direct from the literary theme: which is that of the New Eden which has now become a dream. "Spe modo", for instance, combines a lilting momentum with Macdowell-like chromatic harmony in a manner that touchingly expresses the longing for freedom: while "O bona patria" is a lovely evocation of a dream-Eden, with passive mediant modulations and fluctuating enharmony that make a fairy-tale from the conventions of German oratorio and Italian opera. In the chorus "Urbs Syon Unica", and still more in the final chorus, Parker succeeds in creating from Parry-like conventions a manner that is his own and, at least incipiently, American. The pure diatonicism of the fugal entries preserves some of the freshness of the old Puritan hymnody, while the slowly accumulating chromatic inner parts induce a hazy nostalgia. The final chorus, with its wandering modulations over which soars the soprano solo, becomes a lament for the New Eden that had been betrayed; one can see the piece as a swan-song on the dream of Jeffersonian democracy. The hope that Europe might be reborn in the New World, that "the Ohio will wash my sins away", as Blake put it, had been undermined by the Civil War and by the triumph of industrial commercialism—which exploded in the European War of 1914–18. For Parker, this war meant the end of all he believed in. It broke him, and he died because he had nothing more to live for. Parts, at least, of *Hora Novissima* survive as evidence of what might have been; and in the final chorus of *The Legend of St. Christopher*, Parker attains a truly epic or "pioneer" grandeur in the broad periods and the deeply resonant sonority, to which the rapidly shifting modulations give a hint of instability, if not of fear:

EXAMPLE 13

Here the largeness of conception overrides the polite symmetries of the sequences, in a manner that is remote from the kid-gloved piety of Parker's English master, Parry. Parker's opera *Mona*, indeed, occasionally touches on passional depths which could hardly be accommodated in Bracebridge Hall at all. One suspects that Parker, looking back at *Mona* in the latter part of his life, must have turned over some pages rather furtively and have talked, firmly, of something else: just as he did when the young Charles Ives showed him the more—or even the less—adventurous of his student exercises.

Parker's best music is a vision of an American future that was to be Europe reborn. It did not turn out like that at all; and when commercial values had come to dominate the New World, the more conservative artists tended to look back not merely to Europe, but also to America's innocent past. Rip van Winkle art comes to complement that of Bracebridge Hall; and Parker's friend and colleague, Edward Macdowell, is an admirable example of a Rip van Winkle composer whose work, perhaps significantly, is the only music by a nineteenth-century "art" composer that is still modestly current. Like Parker, Macdowell was trained in Europe, being deeply influenced not by the oratorio tradition but by Edward Grieg—a minor romantic who imbued simple, folk-like melodies with a plaintive nostalgia by harmonizing them with seductive chromatics and enharmonic sequences. Macdowell's music is more honest than that of the Bracebridge Hall composers precisely because it admits to its nostalgia. All Macdowell's best pieces are short, and are a boy's view of the American past, looked back to from a premature middle age; and they are most successful when most unequivocally boyish. This is why the sea always brings out the best in Macdowell. The first three of the *Sea Pieces* are probably his finest achievement. *To the Sea* has in its open spaciousness a quality that is unteutonic, a pioneering nobility that (like that of Parker's homophonic choruses) is inseparable from the music's fundamental simplicity; the initial theme is pentatonic, and there is comparatively little harmonic movement, despite the sonorous power of the "added note" chords and the deeply ringing piano sonority. In the piece about the *Mayflower*—A.D. 1620—the resonantly singing bass line is combined with a swinging $\frac{6}{8}$ modal-tending theme that acquires great breadth through the intrusion of duple cross rhythms: the Puritan hymnic spirit is here musically equated with the American heroism. In *To a Wandering Iceberg* the chromatic harmony acquires, despite the modest proportions, an almost Delius-like flow:

EXAMPLE 14

The slow-swinging rhythm carries us forwards, the melodies make us feel simple and good, the booming bass sonorities imbue the simplicity with grandeur, while at the same time the chromatic harmonies and fluctuating passing notes induce a "personal" sensuousness and wistfulness.

The *Sea Pieces* attain a beautiful freshness in recognizing that they are a Dream of Long Ago. Most of Macdowell's nostalgic pieces admit, however, that their dream, although lovely and good, is, compared with Billings's sturdy modalism and crude harmony, neither entirely guileless nor true. The *New England Sketches* and the *Woodland Sketches*, for instance, express Hawthorne's sentiment without the blackness that is its heart's core. The best pieces are the simplest—such as the once popular *To a Wild Rose* and *To a Water Lily*: in which the rudimentary two-bar sequences and the trance-inducing pedal notes preserve an innocence that is not belied by the tenderly stabbing, bitter-sweet appoggiaturas, or by the nostalgic haze of "added notes". In some pieces (*An Old Love Song, By Smouldering Embers*) irregular, overlapping phrases touchingly suggest a tremor of uncertainty: the pathos, rather than the sentimentality, of regression. In some of the more pretentious nature pieces, however, the anchoring of the chromatics by pedal notes and sequences seems to make the "epic" intention no more than a rhetorical gesture. (Macdowell is prone to inflation in his verbal directives; you do not make a piece impressive by labelling it "largo impressivo", as we can see from *To an Old White Pine*.) At the worst, this becomes a synthetic self-indulgence, which is most embarrassingly evident in Macdowell's songs, such as *The Robin Sings in the Apple Tree*. The words (Macdowell's own, one regrets to say) turn on the familiar Stephen Foster cliché about Bygone Days, when "I" was happy, in love and at peace. The chromatics that tell us that his heart is "now forlorn"—$\frac{6}{4}$, augmented triad, dominant ninth—are a classic instance of emotion self-induced, each chord delivering an additional stab of "pathos":

EXAMPLE 15

so we are not surprised when, at the reference to "days gone by", the music oozes out in ninths and chromatic passing notes that link the Victorian ballad directly with the twentieth-century pop number:

EXAMPLE 16

This manner is quite uncharacteristic of Foster, though similar to that of his more sophisticated and Europeanized colleague, Ethelbert Nevin. The augmentation of the rhythm at the end ("when she was at my side") is a more arty device, but no less contrived; nothing could better reveal how the clichés of nineteenth-century pop music and art music represented the same kind of corruption.

It is significant that although Macdowell's most artistically pretentious pieces seldom sink as low as this, they have not—unlike the best of the mood pieces—survived. His sundry Viking and Norse sonatas attempt, somewhat self-consciously, to invoke the heroic Pioneers of Yore; yet the invocation happens only within the mind of a sensitive, somewhat timid academic who had dreamed hard dreams, maybe, but lived soft. The dreams retain life only when, in a moment of memory, Macdowell re-creates his youth. In his sonatas he tends to expatiate on his short-lived themes in order to encourage them to live up to the ideal of sonata. In this sense, rather than in the nature of his melodic and harmonic material itself, he is victimized by Europe. Perhaps only in one of his large-scale works, the Second Piano Concerto, does Macdowell make a virtue even of his vices. It opens with an exquisite string prelude, all elegiac chromatics, like the dream-pieces for piano. Then the piano enters with a grand romantic gesture, sweeping the memory away; and a barn-storming allegro follows, full of pianistic bravura—an episodic, adolescent "tragedy" wherein the soloist fronts a hostile destiny with Tchaikowskian fervour. The melodrama is extraordinarily naïve: yet the naïviety is its strength; and the episodic technique justifies itself in the tender coda, where the piano at last plays the strings' nostalgic melody. The freedom to dream, to regress, turns out to be the ultimate reality, which we can heart-easingly admit to after the grandiose peroration of the cadenza. The other two movements of the concerto are, experientially, hardly necessary. They no longer attempt the heroic gesture, the second being a brilliant Scherzo, a boyhood joke in Macdowell's Uncle Remus mood, while the Finale—after a solemn introduction, hymnic but brief—becomes a brashly energetic expression of a New World's vitality. The second subject again introduces a nostalgic reference to the American past, but it isn't sustained. The ebullient mood is soon reinstated, and the coda brings the house down.

Macdowell was one of America's Boys in the Wood, and his pitiful personal destiny has the quality of a moral fable: suffering a brain-lesion, he became, in his early forties, as a little child, responding only to fairy-tales until, in the last years, he could respond to nothing at all. Most of his music relies on the American Past; when, in the second and third movements of this concerto, it invokes the American Present it can do so only by pretending that the American experience is a joke— by a denial of artistic (as well as moral) responsibility that carries it into the world of entertainment. Both aspects of his work have had innumerable progeny. His pupil, Henry Franklin Gilbert (1862–1928) is particularly interesting because he was the first American composer to receive a completely American training; and that fact is related to his desire to create a crude, brightly coloured art related to American popular music. Deliberately he discarded the Griegian chromatics he had learned from Macdowell, and produced—in his *Negro Dances* for piano solo, *American Dances* for piano duet, *Comedy Overture on Negro Themes* and *Humoresque on Negro Minstrel Themes* for orchestra—a vivacious, extravert, diatonic music that uses the nigger minstrel as a musical equation for Rip van Winkelism. Though an "academic" musician, educated at Harvard, Gilbert was the child-adult who tried musically to live in irresponsible hedonism; and is probably unique—

and uniquely American—in being a composer who, unlike the true American primitives, consciously attempted to write amateurish music—on the model of the empirical Russian nationalists whom he admired. He is not in the least interested in the exoticism of his pseudo-Negro material, only in its irresponsible naïvety. It is significant that his latest, most extended, and most academically "worked over" essay in this manner—the *Dance in Place Congo*, a fantasy on Creole themes for orchestra—has lost some of the spontaneity of his earlier work. It is colourful, and formally more satisfying than the earlier pieces, as a concert work. But Gilbert was not by nature a concert composer; he was a popular entertainer who stands somewhere between Gottschalk and Bernstein. His talents failed to come to fruition, perhaps, because there was no one to help him discover where he truly belonged. With pathos and irony Gilbert said that in his *Dance in Place Congo* he hoped to treat Creole melodies "in the manner of Grieg and Tchaikowsky". When, in 1927, the piece was performed at the International Festival of Contemporary Music at Frankfurt, as an example of Americana, Gilbert, who suffered from a rare disease, made his first trip to Europe to hear it. Appropriately enough, the trip killed him.

Gilbert's vivid if superficial response to the American scene has remained one strand in the academic tradition that harks back to Horatio Parker. As Parker's dream of an American Eden which was to be Europe remade has been overshadowed by the reality of an industrial and commercial world, the dream of the innocent American Past has taken its place: so the composers of the conservative tradition combine something of Parker's academic sobriety with Macdowell's elegiac nostalgia and with Gilbert's naïve delight in American superfices. There is a consistent pattern in the careers of the senior American conservatives. Most of them were Parker's pupils at Yale, all of them went to study in Europe. Paris took the place of Leipzig; but their Parisian master was Vincent d'Indy, who came closer than any other Frenchman to fusing the French tradition with the German. The affiliation with German tradition preserved a Parker-like earnestness; while at the same time contact with France encouraged a more hedonistic approach. The music of Douglas Moore, who was born in 1893, is an example of this American conservatism. His technique, like his master's, is basically nineteenth-century and Teutonic; yet in writing a symphony he aims at recovering the form's original entertainment value, and the mood of his Symphony in A (1946) alternates between Macdowell-like elegy and Gilbert-like eupepticism. When he turns to the theatre—

which is his main interest—he uses a basically nineteenth-century European idiom to deal with such American subjects as *Daniel Webster* and *The Ballad of Baby Doe*. Puritan hymnody, hill-billy songs, military music, primitive ragtime are embraced within the "regressive" style: so the pieces tend to sound like tasteful, superior film music, being a dream of the American Past to complement Parker's dream of an American Future that did not come true. But the myth in Moore's ballad operas is genuinely felt and awakens an immediate response in the hearts of Americans: which is why Moore's operas have preserved their audience-appeal more consistently than any other American operas except Gershwin's *Porgy and Bess*. His biggest and most recent opera, based on Henry James's *The Wings of a Dove*, explores the American-European theme at a deeper level. Though the spiritual implications of the novel are beyond Moore's range, he has here found the subject that, of its nature, called for the American-European, nineteenth-century idiom in which he spontaneously expressed himself. Only one younger composer, Carlyle Floyd, has achieved any success in attempting this kind of compromise between regional Americana and the box-office appeal of a conservative musical style capable, in the theatre, of Puccinian immediacy. His *Susanna*—which transplants the biblical story to small-town America—makes considerable dramatic impact, probably because its theme of repression, guilt and expiation acquired a deeply American significance both for the composer and for his public. Such a success could not, it seems, be repeated; in Floyd's later and larger operas the validity of an American myth is replaced by the grandiose intention, and the Puccinian rhetoric becomes the Hollywood gimmick.

The mythic quality in Floyd's *Susanna*, no less than in Moore's operas, is its strength, and the myth is normally elegiac. Quincy Porter —another pupil of Horatio Parker who went to Paris to study with Vincent d'Indy and, in 1946, took over Parker's chair at Yale—employs a basically nineteenth-century idiom with French elegance and grace. He excels in the classical medium of the string quartet and, for all his sophistication, comes closest to attaining distinctive character when his long singing lines and spacious textures remind us remotely of the "man and mountains" mood of American mystics like Ives and Harris. The slow movement of his Eighth Quartet is mildly beautiful; yet even here we have to admit that the total impression his music makes seems curiously irrelevant to our lives. To some degree this is true of two other senior conservatives—Howard Hanson and Walter Piston—

whose virtues are opposed but complementary. Hanson was born in Nebraska, of Swedish descent, in 1896. His Nordic ancestry is a part of America's roots; and he has thus been able to accept the nineteenth century heritage unselfconsciously, giving to Teutonic romanticism a spacious sweep that differentiates it from its European origins, just as the Nebraskan Swedes and Germans became, inevitably, a new people. That Hanson is aware of the nostalgic element in his music is evident in the fact that he subtitled his Second Symphony (1930) "the Romantic"; but there is more than regression in his music because, like Parker, he is genuinely a man of religious sensibility. Being a dramatic symphonist in the nineteenth-century tradition, he is concerned with struggle and conflict: the assertion of the Will that is necessary to create a new world. But his affiliations are not so much with Beethoven as with Sibelius, from whom he learned his technique of motivic evolution: and still more with Vaughan Williams, whose lifelong struggle was to achieve reconciliation between the "conflict" symphony and the "religious" principles of vocal monody. Hanson's Fourth Symphony is a requiem dedicated to the memory of his father. It is both an elegy on the past and a search for a God who has some of the qualities of Bunyan's Puritan Father and also of the deity of Nature that Fenimore Cooper referred to in the passage quoted earlier in this chapter. The first movement, Kyrie, is a fight between a turbulently rhythmic motive and a modally lyrical theme that suggests both Swedish folk-song and liturgical chant. The lyricism is segregated in the slow movement, the rhythmic racket in the Dies Irae scherzo; and the opposing forces are reconciled in the last movement, when a harmonically fierce climax resolves into peaceful modal cantilena, very close in mood and technique to Vaughan Williams's Fifth Symphony. An affiliation between Vaughan Williams's *Pilgrim's Progress* and that of the Pilgrim's American descendants is natural enough, especially when the liturgical manner becomes fused with Sibelian nature-mysticism. This happens in the coda, wherein scalewise movement flows over a deeply humming pedal, and comes to rest in an eternal tolling of bells. Such music —and the closely related Fifth Symphony (Sinfonia Sacra) and the choral and orchestral *Cherubic Hymn*—in being so closely reminiscent of Vaughan Williams and Sibelius, serves to demonstrate the difference between the minor talent and the great Original. It will make no difference to history, and it may be too retrospective to survive; but at least it conserves qualities that Hanson believes in—and does so without emotional bombast.

There is a similar sobriety in the less patently retrospective music of Walter Piston, a New Englander who was born in 1894. He is a conservative in that, almost exclusively an instrumental composer, he has adhered scrupulously to the classical conventions of Europe. The Teutonic origins of this academicism are, however, modified by prolonged residence in Paris, where he was not—like Moore and Porter—a pupil of d'Indy, but of Nadia Boulanger. This gives his music affinities with composers of a slightly later generation: he rides a middle path between two other Boulanger pupils who were to become leaders of the indigenous American tradition. The long, sinewy, asymmetrical nature of his themes and the polyphonic nature of his textures suggest Roy Harris; while the precision of the contours and the transparency of the sonority remind us of Copland. Piston's relationship to these composers is, however, no more than superficial. He has not Harris's "religious" pioneering vein, whereby structure is equated with lyrical evolution: nor, on the other hand, do we find Copland's "geometric" integrity, which extracts human strength and tenderness from the hardness of the machine and the emptiness of space. Experientially, Piston is a much less radical composer: which is why he can employ what have become orthodox academic forms: the European sonata, aria, scherzo and rondo. In the Sixth Symphony, for instance, the first movement is a normal classical sonata structure. Though the chromaticized diatonicism is flexible, like that of Hindemith, the tonal basis is as clear as is the opposition of the two subjects—the first built from a nagging minor third and second around a tonic C, the second a lyrical, "feminine" cantilena in the mediant (not dominant), in stepwise movement interspersed with vocal thirds and fifths:

EXAMPLE 17

In the development, the clean polyphonic texture and the luminous scoring deprive the prancing melodies of any American aggressiveness: while the austerely Italianate cantilena—perhaps remotely derived from Piston's Italian ancestry—preserves a distant relation with New England hymnody. The spring and the open-air resilience of the music are

American; the structural conformity is not. This conformity has, indeed, the same effect as Parker's "correctness', for it renders the American experience harmless. It is significant, too, that the textural resemblance to Stravinsky is only skin-deep, whereas the relationship to Hindemith's traditionalism is basic.

In the Scherzo and the Adagio the elements that in the first movement were complementary—American bounce and American hymnody—are separated. The exquisitely scored Scherzo disembodies the American rhythmic exuberance, so that qualities that had originally been of the earth, earthy, become glinting fairy-music of almost Mendelssohnian elegance; the large percussion battery employed in this movement seldom plays louder than *mp*. The Adagio Sereno is an aria that polyphonically extends a swaying, stepwise-moving melody against a background of hymnic string chords. Though the serenity is genuine, and draws on springs buried deep in American tradition, the quiet content in the hymnic movements of composers such as Moore or Hanson has here become less communal, more personal in feeling—and highly sophisticated in texture. The short rondo-finale reinstates the American zest, with bouncing, fourth-founded themes and a reiterated rhythmic pattern. The lucidity of the texture carries this graciously rowdy dance out of the barn into the concert-hall, and a Bostonian concert-hall at that. Indeed, the total effect of the symphony, which was written for the Boston Symphony, is in every sense Bostonian; and while both the polish and the reticence are admirable, they are somewhat negative virtues. As a Bostonian, Piston takes something from both worlds, the old and the new, while getting the best of neither; something valuable is lost, along with primitive crudity, and even in the lovely Adagio the strength of the melodies is less remarkable than the radiant gravity of the sonority. Piston is a composer to be grateful for, since his beautifully written music is always delightful to play and agreeable to listen to, and his professionalism marks the beginning of a truly American—as opposed to the old-fashioned Teutonicized—academic tradition. When one has said that, however, one has to admit that his somewhat clinical music is "civilized" only because it is in part ignorant of what America is and might be.

The American academics, from Parker and Macdowell to Porter and Piston, are all in some sense composers of the Might Have Been. The great writers of the nineteenth century knew that though "there are always dreamers on the frontier", the dreams were both light and dark. Courage and optimism drove the pioneers on, and the eyes of the settlers shone at the new prospect. At first, moreover, when the initial hardships had been weathered, the settlers' efforts were rewarded; in colonial America land was so plentiful and so fertile that any man who failed adequately to support himself and his family could lay the blame only at his own door: he had not sufficiently exhibited the American virtues of industry, sobriety and practicality. On the basis of this agrarian economy, wherein every man could live more or less "free" because there was enough for all, was founded the "general happy mediocrity" to which Benjamin Franklin paid tribute—and which is reflected in the Primitives' music. Then the great trek west revealed the darker impulses—the malignancy, violence and greed—behind the American virtues; and Francis Parkman, greatest of American historians, saw the democratic procession of the Covered Wagons as a second Decline and Fall. Franklin may have been justified in remarking, after a tour of Britain, that "the effect of this kind of civil society seems to be only the depressing multitudes below the savage state that a few may be raised above it"; Jefferson may even have spoken with passionate conviction, if not accuracy, in stating that "of twenty millions of people supposed to be in France, I am of opinion that nineteen millions are more wretched, more accursed in every circumstance of human existence than the most conspicuously wretched individual of the whole United States". None the less, the light of the American vision went out, and as that happened the new prospects began to seem an inadequate return for the traditions that had been left behind. Virginian agrarian society (Jefferson said he knew "no human condition happier than that of a Virginian farmer might be") declined into a foolish and oppressive archaism, and the destructive aspects of pioneer life grew stronger as agrarianism weakened. The fight against Nature and the legacy of Calvinistic Puritanism led to a denial or perversion of the most fundamental creative instinct, that of heterosexual love; and the lust for power and the dedication to death became the more efficient when allied to material wealth and to the machine. The superman of Jack London has become a subman. Henry James wrote of the "black and merciless things that lie behind great possessions", and of death as an epitaph on the failed human—especially sexual—relationship.

It was these facts that the conservatives wished to deny, though this does not mean that the myths inherent in Moore's American Past, in Hanson's Puritanic nature-mysticism, or in Piston's Bostonian gentility, have not their own partial truth. But more was asked of an American composer if he was to face up to the central American themes: to something comparable with Whitman's "multiplicity in unity", with Melville's transcendental terror, with Hawthorne's conscience, Thoreau's and Dickinson's search for the music in the pool at noon, Twain's vision of the boy-child's integrity. Not until the birth of Charles Ives in 1874 did America produce such a composer; only then do we see that, in one sense at least, the American artist has some advantages that are denied to the European. We have lived through a period of slow cultural disintegration that has inevitably affected our approach to creation; we have worked from a consciousness of loss, from an awareness that the stable values that were acceptable to our forebears can no longer be acceptable to us. The American artist may, as we have seen, do the same, though he has lost much less; but the very fact that he has little sense of history, that he is *living through* his loss offers him a supreme opportunity. When the artist is alone, with no religious or social orthodoxies to guide him, his moral responsibility becomes the greater. Potentially he becomes an "unacknowledged legislator of the world". Charles Ives was the first American composer since the Primitives to accept the loss of the wisdom that respect for tradition brings; to become, unafraid, his "own Carver", who would make what he could of the chaotic world he lived in. For that reason he became the first authentic American composer—and is still the closest America has come to a great composer, parallel to her nineteenth-century literary giants. He showed us, creatively, what the pioneer world was really like, not what it might have been: so through his reality shines—still alive, not embalmed—the heroic light of a New World's struggle.

II

Realism and transcendentalism: Charles Ives as American hero

Earth's the right place for love:
I don't know where it's likely to go better.
I'd like to go by climbing a birch tree
And climb black branches up a snow-white trunk
Toward Heaven, till the tree could bear no more,
But dipped its top and set me down again.
That would be good both going and coming back.

ROBERT FROST

Here is the hospitality which for ever indicates heroes. Here the performance, disdaining the trivial, unapproached in the tremendous audacity of its crowds and groupings, and the push of its perspective, spreads with crampless and flowing breath, and showers its prolific and splendid extravagance.

WALT WHITMAN: Preface to *Leaves of Grass*

We see steadily pressing ahead and strengthening itself, even in the midst of immense tendencies towards aggregation, this image of completeness in separatism, of individual personal dignity, of a single person . . . in pride of himself or herself alone. . . . This idea of perfect individualism it is, indeed, that deepest tinges and gives character to the idea of the aggregate.

WALT WHITMAN: *Democratic Vistas*

When the music of Charles Ives was first belatedly disseminated one was conscious mainly of its apparent freakishness. With familiarity, however, the sense of oddity has worn off: or rather we have come to see that his integrity is synonymous with his experimental audacity—which springs from two related characteristics that are the core of his Americanism. One is the pioneer's courage: his desire to hack a way through the forest since he has, indeed, no alternative. The other is that radical innocence of spirit without which—as we have seen in the literary figures—the pioneer could hardly embark on so perilous an adventure. Ives was a complex personality; yet his innocence shines through his literalism, his acceptance of the texture of life in provincial Danbury, Connecticut, where, in 1874, he was born.

For having so strong a sense of moral responsibility Ives could not be content to write second-hand music in the German academic tradition. If he was to be an honest creator, he had to take his materials from the world around him: which was the provincial community of the hard-bitten farmer, the small business-man and tradesman. Here was a certain measure of pioneering vitality, mixed with a somewhat blighted religious ethic; of refinement or "culture" there was no trace. In musical terms, this life meant the town band (which Ives's father directed), ragtime, the corny theatre tune, the chapel hymn. All these were crude but full of conviction, since they were aspects of a way of life. Moreover, the remoteness of this music from academic convention stimulated the aural imagination. The music was not what it would seem to be, rudimentarily notated on paper; it was unpredictable sound-stuff which was also human experience. Ives's father had given him a training in conventional harmony and counterpoint and a respect for the "manly" classical composers, Handel, Beethoven and Brahms, while at Yale Ives was to acquire a thorough, if somewhat grudging, academic technique.[1] Yet for him this was insignificant compared with the stimulus offered by the sounds of life as it was being lived; and in the category of (potential) artistic material he included noise as well as the sundry types of "music" that were made in his local community.

What excited Ives's imagination was the vast body of singers yelling or croaking slightly different versions of the same hymn, thereby creating something like folk-heterophony: or the horn-player who

[1] In their fascinating biography of Ives, Henry and Sidney Cowell relate many anecdotes that indicate how much Ives owed to his remarkable father. Significantly, Ives himself identifies the *musical* stimulation his father gave him with his "understanding of the ways of a boy's heart and mind". When father invented contraptions to play quarter-tones or encouraged polytonal performances of "Swanee River" it was not as a technical exercise, but to develop open-mindedness, to "stretch the ears" and the imagination. In a most moving passage Ives compares what he learned from his father with what he learned, at Yale, from Horatio Parker. While Ives respected Parker (whose music was "seldom trivial"), he knew that Parker would hand back his score after glancing at a measure or so, would make a little joke about hogging all the keys at one meal—and then talk about something else. Parker, having at bottom only the academic's fear of life to offer, "made me feel more and more what a remarkable background and start father had given me in music. Parker was a composer and Father was not; but from every other standpoint I should say that Father was by far the greater man".

got left behind his fellows in the town band, producing weird effects of harmonic and rhythmic dislocation. Similarly, the several bands that, at celebration time, played different music simultaneously in the four corners of the town square suggested to Ives a fresh aural experience:[2] as did chapel singing heard over water, mixed up with the sounds of wind and rustling leaves. All this is at once music and life; the only criterion of "correctness" is the music's truth to experience. On a wider and deeper scale we have here an extension of the phenomenon we referred to in the American primitives such as Billings: the "mistakes" may be, musically and experientially, more interesting than the art-creation. Ives would have agreed with his father, who, when asked how he could stand hearing old John (the local stonemason) bellowing off-key at camp meetings replied: "Old John is a supreme musician. Look into his face and hear the music of the ages. Don't pay too much attention to the sounds. If you do, you may miss the music."

The nature of the (often very) raw material of Ives's art can be most conveniently examined in his numerous songs, which he produced intermittently throughout his working life from around 1890 to the early 1920s; and which served in part as sketches—or annotations of experience—to be further explored in large-scale works. In their immediacy and their realism they express the pioneer instinct to "make it new"; and it is significant that so many of them imaginatively notate the "moments of truth" that we experience in, and remember from, childhood. Consider four little songs that appear to range, technically, from the tritest banality to the most complex sophistication. *Two Little Flowers* looks like a sentimental parlour song such as the more respectable inhabitants of Danbury would have entertained themselves with on a Saturday night, if not Sunday afternoon. Ives's own words, about two little girls, are arch, the tune metrical and smilingly diatonic, the accompaniment simply arpeggiated. What makes the song truly touching—not a sentimental platitude but an apprehension of tenderness—is the unexpected dislocations of rhythm on the words "in green" and "passing fair":

> [2] "I remember hearing, when a boy, the music of a band in which the players were arranged in two or three groups around the town square. The main group in the bandstand at the centre usually played the main themes, while the others, from the neighbouring roofs and verandahs, played the variations, refrains, and so forth. . . . The bandmaster told of a man who, living nearer the variations, insisted that they were the real music and that it was more beautiful to hear the tune come sifting through them than the other way round. Others, walking round the square, were surprised at the different and interesting effects they got as they changed positions." (Ives.)

EXAMPLE I

One dressed,at times, in   brightest pink and one   in   green.___   The ma-ri-gold is   rad-i-ant,   the_ rose___   passing fair.___

It is not merely that the effect has a tinge of irony that counteracts the coyness; it is also that it gives a little quiver of first-hand realization, so that we see the girls in their bright, frail dresses, and know, in wonder, that they *are* passing fair.

Alongside this, consider *The Circus Band*, a reminiscence of childhood which this time is comic, though quite without condescension. The tune, if blatant, is splendid for marching to ("Ain't it a glorious noise"); and what gives it its authentic vitality is again its literalness— the rhythmic oddities that emulate the hiccuping effect of the band, the syncopations that make the music prance. In the swinging trio-tune the cross-accents are really mistakes, as the players are carried away by their enthusiasm, by the exuberant chromatic swirls of the brass. *The Side Show* is another circus piece which involves literal imitation, in its hiccuping rhythm, of the merry-go-round that gets stuck; yet again the realism is emotional as well as physical, for the creaking jerks of the machine become synonymous with a kind of crippled grotesquerie in the sound-portrait of "Mister Riley" himself. The imitation becomes, in Arnold's sense, a criticism of life; and this is still more so in the evocation of the pacing beast in *In the Cage*. This again is a reminiscence of childhood: Ives's recollection of a small boy, watching the leopard in his cage, and wondering whether life was "anything at all like that". The beast's pacing is conveyed through a vocal line so unstably chromatic as to be non-tonal: while the cage's prison is suggested by Schoenbergian fourth-founded chords and a complex metrical "series" that, in 1904, anticipates the metrical series of post-Webern music. But there is no difference in approach between this song and *Two Little Flowers*, which is, in fact, chronologically the later of the two. Both songs are moments of truth; both utilize the techniques that are to hand and appropriate. All that matters is the empirical reality of the experience.

Another group of Ives's songs deals with childhood experience viewed not immediately, but retrospectively. *Tom Sails Away* is a beautiful example, in which the vocal line moves mainly by step, without metrical accent, as though the singer were ruminating to himself; the words, which are Ives's own, may well be autobiographical. The piano texture is amorphous, floating, dissolving into free polyrhythm and polyharmony. Gradually, through the haze of memory, the scene is recreated, and comes to a climax when Tom, as a boy, meets Dad coming over the hill. Then, as the song recalls how Tom sailed away "over there", the music returns, with nostalgic quotation, to the ruminating present; and fades away into nothing, metreless, in ambiguously telescoped tonality:

EXAMPLE 2

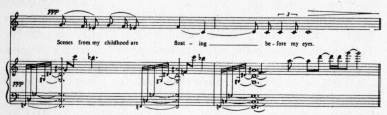

Scenes from my childhood are   float - ing _____ be - fore my eyes.

This is a true musical impressionism, extending Debussy's liberation of the harmonic moment.

Ives's finest songs, however, are those which discover the richest allegory in personal recollection. *The Greatest Man*, for instance, is another song about a little boy: but this time the perkiness of his boogie-rhythm, his circus-band pride in his father's exploits as horseman, the pathos of the father's tenderness and the mother's death, the comedy of the throw-away conclusion, are not merely a naturalistic sound-picture of a specific boy in a specific locality; they are also an evocation of the American small-town "way of life". In a more general sense they are also a revelation of fundamental aspects of the American character, for Ives's indication that these words from the *Saturday Evening Post* should be sung in a manner "half wistful and half boastful" is touchingly realized in the music. At a deeper level we find a similar allegorical generality in three songs about the American innocence. *Serenity* sets Whittier's hymn—"take from our souls the strain and stress And let our ordered lives confess The beauty of Thy peace"—against the background of America in 1919. The gentle undulation of the vocal line around A and B, in a flexible rhythm unobtrusively following the speech-movement, should be a unison chant: massed voices whispering together in the unity of prayer. Against this, the soft swinging pendulum of the bitonal accompaniment goes on for ever, reminding us simultaneously of the ticking of Time's clock and, in its regularity and remoteness, of Time's end—or eternity. The final unresolved tritonal chord epitomizes this simultaneous awareness of mobility and immobility, of stress and resolution. In microcosm we have here the "kind of furious calm" which Ives sought for in his large-scale works.

Evening is another lovely song about the peace of innocence—this time Milton's Paradise that was lost. Evening becomes synonymous with innocence forgotten, as whole-tone progressions in the vocal line and whole-tone swayings in the piano figuration create an impressionistically hazy sonority. Against this, the pentatonic phrase for "silence" and the repeated notes, rising fifths and melismatic undulations that represent the nightingale's "amorous descant" stand for life—for Paradise Regained. This is why "silence was pleased". Once more we see how Ives's literalism is never merely that; the imitation of the nightingale, emerging from the mist, is musically the point of the song, as well as the essence of the allegory. *The Indians* presents the theme of Innocence Lost in a specifically American environment, for Ives's words deal with the American who is, in William Carlos Williams's phrase, "an Indian without a home". The winding, wandering vocal line is basically primitive and pentatonic; yet it achieves an extraordinary poignancy as it floats aimlessly across the bar-lines, contradicted rather than supported by the oscillating chromatic harmonies, which are themselves consistently dislocated. These harmonies, indeed, act the "pale man's axe and plough", which deprive the Indians of their birthright—and in so doing perturb their pentatonic ululations (consider the setting of the words "bounds" and "axe"). The final vocal phrase (note the meaningful stress on the word "their", the movement upwards through a major third to the word "go", then the suspiring breath to a minor third on the word "die") is irremediably desolate: a profoundly musical expression of inanition, of the tragic decay of a race:

EXAMPLE 3

And the tragedy is not confined to the Indians.

All these lyrical-reflective songs are crystallized drama; and perhaps the most impressive of all Ives's songs are those that are both dramatic and narrative. In *General William Booth enters Heaven*—a setting of part of Vachel Lindsey's poem—the moments of reality which he re-creates in songs like *In the Cage* or *Soliloquy*[3] are used cumulatively to evoke a scene, a man, a human situation. The song is an imitation of the hot gospeller's march-tune, wherein the savage percussive dissonances in the piano part add the *noises* incidental to the experience felt, the scene described: the yawp of the out-of-tune instruments, the bump of the drum (often in the wrong place), the yells of the throng. Even the nontonal meanderings and rhythmic displacements of the vocal line are realistic: the singer, transported by enthusiasm, bellows off-key and distorts words in jazzy syncopation, as a means of making a rhetorical point. Yet the chaos is part of the music: which builds up to a superb climax of religious frenzy, as syncopations become savager, dissonances more wildly percussive, until the appearance of Jesus. Then the din is hushed, and the vocal line vacillates in a triplet cross-rhythm between C flat, B flat and A flat over simple tonic and subdominant chords. When the march starts again—yanked back from the A flattish tonality to a cross between D, G and C (simultaneous tonic, dominant and subdominant)—it is with a difference, for the miracle has happened. "Are you washed in the blood of the Lamb" sounds remotely, wonderingly, not, as at first, with the gospeller's belligerent rhetoric. The art of this marvellous song is thus inseparable from its literalism. It renders incarnate the heart of the gospeller's experience, without destroying its grotesque comedy, its macabre horror. It does not praise or blame, it presents. With a vividness that takes the breath away, we become the gospeller, share in his vision.

This song contains two qualities that lead us to the core of Ives's work as a whole. The first is its acceptance of life-as-it-is, in all its apparent chaos and contradiction; and it is this that encouraged him to employ any and every technique that seemed empirically appropriate, whether drawn from conventional European music, from folk improvisation, from chapel or bar-parlour, or from the sounds of the natural world. In his larger works all these and many more elements may be

[3] Ives describes this extraordinary song—which, written in 1907, makes free-atonal Schoenberg look as straightforward as early Brahms—as "a study in sevenths and other things", and also as "a parody of the Yankee drawl". It is a technical exercise, that is, which is also an imitation of reality; and in so describing it he is admitting that it is not art but—like many of his shorter works—material out of which art might be made.

used as experience dictates, and often simultaneously, since all experience is related and indivisible. In *General Putnam's Camp*, from the orchestral *Three Places in New England*, several military and ragtime tunes are played together in different rhythms and tempi, and often in different keys, mixed with the huzzaing of the crowd and various a-rhythmic, non-tonal sounds of nature. The music evokes, with astonishing immediacy, the physical and nervous sensation of being present at such a vast outdoor celebration: yet the flux of life becomes one through the organizing power of the imagination. Ives tells us that the piece derives from a recollection of his childhood, when he heard two bands pass one another on the march. It is difficult to think of any art that conveys more precisely the experience—common in childhood, rarer in later years—of being at once identified with the flux of appearances and detached from it, as watching eye and listening ear. In this sense Ives's art is discovery: a new found land.

This brings us to the second quality of Ives's music inherent in *General Booth*: which is that the attempt to discover unity within chaos is in essence a transcendental act. The beautiful *Housatonic at Stockbridge*, the third of the *Three Places in New England*, starts from another transient personal reminiscence—from (as Ives puts it) "A Sunday morning walk that Mrs Ives and I took near Stockbridge the summer after we were married. We walked in the meadows along the River and heard the distant singing from the Church across the River. The mist had not entirely left the river bed, and the colours, the running water, the banks and the trees were something that one would always remember." This personal reminiscence becomes, in the music, a visionary moment. The lovely horn melody, with its almost Mahlerian orchestration, suggests both the chapel singing that Ives heard floating over the water, through the mist, and also the tranquil security of the love between himself and his wife (charmingly called Harmony Twichell). This melody is absorbed in a haze of strings that play, as from a distance, more or less independently of the rest of the orchestra. Gradually these sounds of Nature—of river, mist, and rustling leaves—grow wilder and stronger until they engulf the love-song: at which point the tumult abruptly ceases, and the song is left suspended, unresolved on a sigh. With great poignancy the piece reveals both the centrality of human love and also its impermanence in the non-human context of the natural world. Some years later Ives (surprisingly and characteristically) made a version of this piece for voice and piano. The solo melody, slightly adapted, becomes vocal, with Ives's own words, which oppose the serenity of the melody to the tumult that threatens to drown it, and imply that facing up to the turmoil is more important than submitting to the quietude. This does not, of course, invalidate the positive beauty of the melody itself, nor the sigh of regret with which the music ends. Something more is involved here than the pioneer's wide-eyed vitality; there is also the power of love to make a world anew.

Sometimes—perhaps more frequently—the dichotomy between Man and Nature takes the opposite form in that Nature, if indeterminate, is peaceful, whereas Man is turbulent and unresolved. That strange and lovely piece *Central Park in the Dark*, from *Three Outdoor Scenes* (1898–1907), is a case in point. The vaguely oscillating strands of the orchestral texture, without harmonic root or rhythmic definition, evoke the natural sounds of night in the park: which being natural are directionless yet without tension. They remain ultimately impervious to the sounds of the man-made world—car hooters, subway roars, yelling newsvendors, jazz bands and theatre hubbub—that burst spasmodically into them. The effect is emotionally ambiguous, and the richer for its ambiguity: one is not sure whether the man-made noises, against the eternal hum and simmer of nature, are courageous or pathetically desperate. Ives offers a still more extreme expression of this ambiguity in the justly celebrated short orchestral piece, *The Unanswered Question*. Here muted strings, distantly playing immensely slow diatonic concords with virtually no temporal pulse, represent eternity and the unknowable mysteries. A solo trumpet becomes Man asking the "Perennial Question" in an angular, jagged, upward thrusting phrase: to which what Ives calls the "Fighting Answerers" (flutes and other people) heroically attempt to give answers. The string concords proceed implacably on their way, however; so the Fighting Answerers get increasingly distraught, bumping into one another in polytonal, polyrhythmic chaos until they end in despairful mockery of the trumpet's phrase. But it is typical of Ives that he does not leave us with a *dusty* answer. Though the unknown seers will not reply and the silence of eternity remains unruffled, Man's trumpet is undismayed. At the end it calls in its original form—not in the agitated permutations into which the Answerers had whipped it. Ives, though a "modern" questioner, is essentially a positive artist; this is why he can, on occasion, create an exquisite miniature like *The Pond*, the second of the *Three Outdoor Scenes*, in which man's hymn-creating solidarity and the indeterminacy of the natural world are momentarily in perfect equipoise.

The prophetically revolutionary technique of pieces such as *The Unanswered Question*—the conception for independent orchestral groups, one of which involves, as the Answerers grow more frantic, a degree of improvisation—is not basically a technical experiment. It is a human exploration; and this is why the piece remains as stimulating today as it was when it was written, well over fifty years ago. While Ives did not believe that the Real and the Transcendental—the two realms represented in this piece by his two orchestras—could be reconciled in the conditions of temporal mortality, he believed that it was the duty of every man to attempt such reconciliation. He resembles Whitman in his appetite for experience; yet the obverse side of the American myth is present in his work, too, for the Ego that would swallow all experience becomes progressively more aware of its isolation. The more immediate his response to the external world, the more he had to seek a transcendental reality beyond the flux. One can see this in his life as well as in his music. He regarded his art and the insurance business in which he made his fortune as complementary activities:

> My business experience [he said] revealed life to me in many aspects that I might otherwise have missed. In it one sees nobility, tragedy, meanness, high aims, low aims, brave hopes, faint hopes, great ideals, no ideals, and one is able to watch these work inevitable destiny. . . . It is my impression that there is more open-mindedness and willingness to examine carefully the premises underlying a new or unfamiliar thing in the world of business than in the world of music. It is not even uncommon in business intercourse to sense a reflection of a philosophy, a depth of something fine, akin to a sense of beauty in art. To assume that business is a material process, and only that, is to undervalue the average mind and heart. To an insurance man there *is* an average man and he is humanity. I have experienced a great fullness of life in business. The fabric of existence weaves itself whole. . . . There can be nothing exclusive about a substantial art. It comes directly out of the experience of life and thinking about life and living life. My work in music helped my business and my work in business helped my music.

In other words, he who would create a New World must first put his own house in order; to renew the individual spirit is to re-create society, for in the last resort the material and the spiritual are inseparable.

This attitude Ives inherited from his father who

> Felt that a man could keep his music interest keener, stronger, bigger and freer if he didn't try to make a living out of it. Assuming that a man lives by himself and with no dependants, no one to feed but himself, and is willing to live as simply as Thoreau, he might write music

that no one would play prettily, listen to, or buy. But—if he has a wife and some nice children, how can he let his children starve on his dissonances? So he has to weaken (and if he is a man *should* weaken for his children); but his music . . . more than weakens—it goes ta-ta for money! Bad for him, bad for music!

This is why Ives, who did not approve of formal absolutes, was fascinated by the sonata as a principle of composition. Like Beethoven, whom he revered above all creators, he saw the sonata as an attempt to impose the unity of the Will on the chaos of experience; and his awareness of contradiction (like Beethoven's) was so violent that it had ultimately to seek resolution in a transcendental act. He differs from Beethoven, of course, in that he had behind him the American wilderness, not Viennese civilization and a long musical tradition; so that he cannot accept Beethoven's positives—especially that of eighteenth-century tonality, on which the classical idea of sonata depended. He differs from Beethoven, too, in that he glimpses, but does not enter, his paradise, for there is nothing in his music comparable with the lyrical efflorescence of the Arietta that ends Beethoven's opus 111. Yet there is a truly heroic quality in his search for a reality beyond the flux. He is a New World's stumbling approach to a figure of Beethovenian power: which is enough to ensure his place in history.

If one had to choose one work which most effectively embodied Ives's lifelong search it would probably be the tremendous piano sonata—written, on and off, between 1908 and 1915—which he explicitly dedicated to the Transcendentalists, those New England Heroes who lived in Concord between 1840 and 1860. Emerson is the hero of American Strife, Hawthorne of Conscience, Thoreau of Contemplation; and before the Thoreau movement Ives inserts a picture of the Alcott family, representing the cosy domestic pieties that form a background to the Heroes' lives. Each one of the heroes is also, of course, an aspect of Ives's own character.

The first movement of the "Concord" Sonata was originally conceived as a concerto for piano and large orchestra. It is both the longest movement and the most difficult: for it deals with Emerson, who preached "the infinitude of the private man", who "unsettled all things", who "simply experimented" with no past at his back. These words are Emerson's own; Ives described him as "an invader of the unknown", "the soul of humanity knocking at the door of the Divine Mysteries, even in the common heart of Concord: radiant in the hope that it will be opened—and the human will become the divine". The work begins with an enormous, almost bar-less period which asserts the multifariousness of experience—the "fierce complexity of reality", as Ives put it:

EXAMPLE 4

A "lyric" motive, moving mainly by step, descends in the bass in powerful minims, and ascends in the treble in crochets. It proliferates in flowing semiquavers, in a polyphony of chords; and a violently contrasted "epic" motive (the motto from Beethoven's Fifth) intrudes, syncopated off the beat. This motive begins on C, descends to G sharp, then to E, then to C sharp; and then from D sharp to C natural. It thus plunges through the widest possible tonal range, while being surrounded by a web of grindingly dissonant counterpoints, in free cross-rhythms. These come to momentary rest on a unison only when the bass returns to C natural: so that this surging clause is a preludial statement of the progression from diversity to unity which is the impulse behind the whole work.

The unison C is marked by one of the rare bar-lines; but it does not stop the music's momentum. The piece is perpetual evolution; and while Ives seldom employed strict contrapuntal procedures, which to him suggested a preordained organization of experience and therefore a denial of life, most of his music is polyphonic, and usually poly-rhythmic and polyharmonic as well. The artist's creation, he believed, should resemble the creativity of Nature; and "Nature loves analogy and abhors repetition and explanation. Unity is too generally conceived of, or too readily accepted as, analogous to form, and form as analogous to custom, and custom to habit". So his themes are always growing, and change their identities as they are related in wildly opposed rhythms or on separate (polytonal) planes of harmony. On the printed page the music looks as though it falls into a number of sections that Ives himself referred to as "prose" and "verse": the prose sections being unbarred, complex and expansive, the verse sections barred, and comparatively simple. But both motives appear in the prose and verse sections equally, and the texture is continuous and evolutionary. The closest approach to a second subject grows into a singing melody in a kind of mixolydian C. The song tune does not, however, preserve its identity; it is absorbed into the kaleidoscope of experience. In the second verse section it approximates to the opposing "epic" forces in being subjected to octave displacements similar to those in Schoenberg's serial technique: the pitch relationships remain more or less constant through several restatements of the theme, though the notes are frantically scattered through progressively widening octaves of the keyboard:

EXAMPLE 5

The ultimate climax comes at the end of the next prose section when the epic motive is enunciated fortissimo, and fast, at Beethoven's original pitch. After that, the music gradually disintegrates over a slowly oscillating chromatic bass that finally swings between the notes of the tritone D sharp to A. It is significant that the manifold permutations of the motives do not, at the end, coalesce into a sustained melody. The movement ends with overtone echoes of the third, E to C sharp, sounding remotely, unresolved, while the bass plays the motive descending from A to F natural.

This disintegrative conclusion—or inconclusion—suggests how radically Ives's technique differs from Beethoven's, despite their consanguinity. Both start from dualism and contradiction. Beethoven's transformations of his themes are, however, positively controlled by the will and by the shaping force of the imagination; so that the form of the Fifth Symphony is the gradual revelation of the theme's destiny, its triumphant major apotheosis in the last movement. The unity Ives achieves is more ambiguous, and for that reason less satisfying, because the transformations of his themes are more protean, like life itself. He has immense courage; but he has not—perhaps no one, living in a rootless world, could have—Beethoven's positive assurance. It is as though he felt it was his moral and artistic duty, in a world in which the assertive Will of the pioneer had been degraded into a lust for material power, to insist that experience is not only indivisible but also incomplete, and never to be completed except by death, and maybe not even then. He is the polar opposite to an American artist like Poe, with whom the chiselled perfection of verse-forms and the obsession with cross-word ingenuities of plot are the technical equivalents to his neurotic power-complex, existing in a void. Ives, on the contrary, would have said that all his music, including the "Concord" Sonata, was only a "sketch", as was the song *Soliloquy*; all he would have claimed is that some sketches were less incomplete than others. Such unity as he could attain must be sought within, not imposed upon, the context of a given work; and while a fully-fledged, *a priori* serialism would have been regarded by Ives as musically and philosophically monstrous, the impulse *towards* it might be good and necessary, in so far as it might be a search for order within the psyche, without reference to pre-ordained law. So serial processes exist in the "Concord" Sonata, but are intuitive rather than systematized. In a sense the "Concord" Sonata—which Ives continued to rewrite and revise over a period of thirty years, so that it is hardly possible to establish a "definitive" version—remained unfinished at Ives's death, as did the gigantic Universe Symphony which he left in fragments that might, he hoped, be seeds to be nurtured and tended by future generations. In so far as the "Concord" Sonata attains, in its last movement, an extremely equivocal resolution of conflict, it does so in almost hermetic quietude. Beethovenian forcefulness is most evident in the first movement, where tension remains unresolved.

In the Emerson movement the conflict between lyric and epic forces has been largely subjective. The fight goes on within the consciousness, and the Will attempts, with only partial success, to control destiny. This is the heroism of the American Pioneer in spiritual terms, and in conception—though not, as we have seen, in realization—this is Beethovenian music. The second movement, however, is quite un-Beethovenian, for it deals with the subconscious life of dreams, nightmare, and the sensory impressions of childhood. Ives says that he has not stressed the most significant aspect of Hawthorne—his calvinistic sense of guilt. Instead, he has written an "extended fragment" (the term suggests the inconclusive nature of the experience) dealing with Hawthorne's excursions into "half child-like, half fairy-like phantasmal realms. . . . It's something about the ghost of a man who never lived, or about something that will never happen, or something that is not." That final negation is interesting, and suggests that the childhood reminiscences ("frosty Berkshire morning, and the frost imagery on the enchanted hall window . . . the old hymn tune that haunts the church and sings only to those in the churchyard to protect them from secular noises, as when the circus parade comes down Main Street") touch off disturbing, even sinister, undercurrents of feeling. The American obsession with childhood complements, after all, the Puritan sense of guilt, which probably entered Ives's music by the back door: for in our dreams and phantasms, not to mention our nightmares, our sense of guilt is most manifest.

The very fast, whirling opening is like the chaos of the subconscious mind. There is virtually no tonal feeling, no metre and, one might almost say, no rhythm, since almost every crochet and quaver is violently syncopated off a beat that is merely implicit. The texture is dominated by hard, glittering fourths—the interval that, in European music, played so important a part in the breakdown of classical tonality:

EXAMPLE 6

Into this amorphous hurly-burly are hurled fragments of both the lyric and the epic motives. But they have no controlling force; they are flotsam, thrown up on the waters of the unconscious. They do, however, provoke dream-recollections of daytime experience. A circus tune (the *Slave's Shuffle*?) emerges out of the mist; and a horn-like theme, related to the lyric idea, sounds as though it might be a love-song, which dissolves in a pianissimo haze of note-clusters, pressed down with a strip of board. The song emerges out of sleep, only to subside again.

Similarly, the crazy syncopations of the dream-life turn into a direct recollection of ragtime heard in the bar, before sleep; in dream, the syncopations attain a complexity to end all ragtime. Then the haunted churchyard hymn flows into the dream, singing permutations of the epic theme in bare diatonic triads: the spacing of the chords here reminds us of late Beethoven's "personal" re-creation of the divine music. This hymn is surrealistically juxtaposed with the circus-band episode we heard earlier; but its holy metaphysics do not seem to be very powerful, for the music soon reverts to drunken ragtime, from which moment the unconscious takes over, without inhibition. The music gets faster and faster, the tonality becomes vaguer, the rhythms still more wildly distraught; the player is encouraged to make it up, if he cannot get round the written notes with sufficiently tipsy abandon. At the very end there is a distant, bitonal echo of the hymnic version of the epic motive, reminding us of man's potential divinity even when —or especially when—he is "beside himself", possibly drunk, certainly half-conscious, between sleeping and waking. The echo is, however, swept brusquely away by an arpeggiated note-cluster.

Emerson was the life of the mind and soul, Hawthorne the life of the subconscious. With the third movement, Ives turns to everyday reality: to the "commonplace beauty" of Orchard House, home of Bronson Alcott, amateur philosopher, pedagogue, teacher, talker and family man, whose life with his wife and daughter was a "witness of Concord's common virtue". Here the daughter Louisa wrote *Little Women*, supporting the family and at the same time enriching "the lives of a large part of young America, starting off many little minds with wholesome thoughts and many little hearts with wholesome emotions. She leaves memory-word-pictures of healthy New England childhood days—pictures which are turned to with affection by middle-aged children—pictures that bear a sentiment, a leaven, that middle-aged America needs nowadays more than we care to admit". So "The Alcotts" deals with another aspect of the American innocence: with "the richness of not having: with the memory of that home under the elms, the Scotch songs and family hymns that were sung at the end of each day". Here, both lyric and epic motives appear in simple form, naturalistically: for Beethoven's Fifth is being "played at" on the Alcott's parlour piano. The opening hymnlike version of the epic motive is a tune now unambiguously in B flat; but it is harmonized with tonic, dominant and subdominant chords of A flat: which may have begun as a realistic imitation of the out-of-tune instrument, but becomes a wonderfully touching symbol of stability and immobility, as compared with the turbulence of the two previous movements:

EXAMPLE 7

None the less, as Ives says, "common sentiment may contain a strength of hope, a conviction of the power of the common soul as typical as any theme of Concord and its Transcendentalists". It is thus not surprising that the lyric motive should flow into bitonal polyphony recalling the first movement; nor that the climax should be a heroic presentation of the epic theme in diatonic triads. The heroic outburst is not however, consummatory; we return to Concord simplicities as the music subsides in a brief version of the lyric motive. Again the first movement is recalled in a kind of mixolydian cadence that telescopes the B flat of the tune with C major.

If resolution is achieved in the sonata, it is in the last movement, which deals not with the fight of the ego with destiny (Emerson), nor with dreams (Hawthorne), nor with simple domesticities (the Alcotts), but with the individual spirit alone with Nature. Surprisingly, yet on reflection not inappositely, Ives relates Thoreau to Beethoven, who in his last years also heard the music in the pool at noon, and could do so *because* he was deaf, cut off from the normal means of communication, from social institutions, from *a priori* beliefs. Both men were "deeply conscious of the enthusiasm of Nature, the emotion of her rhythms, and the harmony of her solitude. In this consciousness [they] sang of the submission to Nature, the religion of contemplation, and the freedom of simplicity—a philosophy distinguishing between the complexity of Nature, which teaches freedom, and the complexity of materialism, which teaches slavery . . . . In their greatest moments the inspiration of both Beethoven and Thoreau expresses profound truths and deep sentiment. But the intimate passion of it, the storm and stress of it, affected Beethoven in such a way that he could not but be for ever showing it, and Thoreau, that he could not easily expose it. . . . The message of Thoreau, though his fervency may be inconstant and his human appeal not always direct, is, both in thought and spirit, as universal as that of any man who ever wrote or sang—as universal as it is contemporaneous—as universal as it is free from the measure of history, as solitude is free from the measure of the miles of space that intervene between man and his fellows". So, far from being parochial (as Henry James called him), Thoreau explores precisely that sublime and elemental simplicity that Beethoven entered in the Arietta of Opus 111 or the celestial folk-song that concludes the last of his quartets. The kind and range of experience are the same, though Thoreau merely seeks, where Beethoven finds. This, again, is what makes Thoreau a part of Ives; and it is legitimate to say that the

Thoreau movement of the "Concord" Sonata bears a similar relationship to late Beethoven as does the Emerson movement to Beethoven's middle period music.

At the beginning of the movement Thoreau sits in his sunny doorway at Walden, "rapt in revery, amidst goldenrod, sandcherry and sumach". "He grew in those seasons like corn in the night." Though "he realized what the Orientals meant by Contemplation and forsaking of works", he does not, as Ives points out, contemplate in the same way. "Thus it is not the whole tone scale of the Orient but the scale of the Walden morning which inspired many of the polyphonies and harmonies that come to us through his poetry." The music is at first barless, almost rhythmless, like a fluttering of leaves and wind: which involves, too, the fluttering of human nerves in response. Gradually the human element—the song melody which had begun to define itself through the rustlings—grows stronger; and the quivering harmony comes to rest on a swaying ostinato A, C, G. This is an inverted form of the epic motive, now rising instead of falling, but implying both an A and a C root to the harmony. Little by little these fragments of song grow into a long, winding melody that fuses the lyric idea with the epic. Ives directs that this melody should be played on a flute if you happen to have one handy. This is not merely quixotic, nor merely programmatic, since Thoreau played the flute in his rural solitude.[4] The musical point is that the sostenuto character of the flute line and other-worldly colour of the instrument emphasize the effect of the melody as the goal of the whole sonata. The spirit is liberated from inner strife, from nightmare, even from everyday reality. The lyric and epic contrarieties become one, in a mystical communion; and if the melody seems tentative, misty, groping as compared with the serene lyrical fulfilment of Beethoven's Arietta, that is as much as one has a right to hope for, in a divided and distracted world.

---

[4] Cf. Thoreau's Journal: "Our minds should echo at least as many times as a Mammoth Cave to every musical sound. It should awaken reflections in us. . . . Now the day's work is done, the laborer plays his flute—only possible at this hour. Contrasted with his work, what an accomplishment! Some drink and gamble. He plays some well-known march. But the music is not in the tune; it is in the sound. It does not proceed from the trading nor political world. He practises his ancient art. There are light, vaporous clouds overhead; dark, fuscous ones in the north. The trees are turned black. As candles are lit on earth, stars are lit in heaven. I hear the bullfrog's trump from afar." Compare Ives's warning—in his comments on the singing of old John the stonemason—that one shouldn't pay too much attention to the sound, or one might miss the music.

The "flute" melody is in or around B flat (is it an accident that this was the Alcotts' key, representatives of the "common heart" of Concord?). One developing version of the ostinato involves the major and minor third above A, the fifth C to G, and the third G to B. All the forms of the epic motive's thirds and fifths now rise instead of fall, and are telescoped in a timeless moment. The end of the work is, however, characteristic. The ostinato continues, emulating the "faint sound of the Concord bell—'tis prayer-meeting night in the village—a melody . . . imported into the wilderness"; but it fades away in "a certain vibratory hum" that may be the voice of the woods or the transcendental tune of Concord, wherein the "whole body is one sense" and, in final submission, one possesses "the Freedom of the Night". The epic motive sounds high up on the bare fifth, D to A. This time it neither rises nor falls; it remains suspended at the same pitch. This sounds like a resolution of the A–C sharp relationship into D. But the C natural-G complex is still audible, reminding us of the point from which we started; and into the last measure softly intrudes C sharp, the leading note of D, seeming to suggest how for Ives each resolution into Being is only a stage in the eternal flux of Becoming:

EXAMPLE 8

So although serenity is achieved, at the end of the work the cyclical process starts again. This, too, emphasizes both the resemblance to, and the difference from, Beethoven. The "Concord" Sonata, though of course a much less significant piece, is the same *kind* of music as the "Hammerklavier" Sonata, which also ends at the point where it began. But Beethoven's opus 111, the last sonata of the supreme composer of "Becoming", has reached its heavenly destination. It is, as Thomas Mann pointed out, not only the last of Beethoven's sonatas but, in a sense, the end of the sonata principle; its end is an end eternally, for what could come "after" Paradise?

While the "Concord" Sonata is Ives's most developed exploration of the relationship between the Real and the Transcendental, the same theme dominates, at varying levels, most of his works in sonata style.

In the First Piano Sonata (1902–8), which is scarcely less impressive than the second, the astonishing ragtime movements are "moments of truth" like *General Booth*. They bring to immediate reality a time and place: the bar-pianist's exuberance, the jangle of broken strings, the clusters of wrong notes, the tipsy croaking of hymns, floating on the smoke through the half-opened door:

EXAMPLE 9

But in the first and third movements the composer leaves his social environment and walks into the hills; and the sonata's generating motive of minor second and major third develops not through tonal conflict to resolution, but with an evolutionary, polymodal, poly-harmonic, polyrhythmic freedom that suggests improvisation. A New World is liberated, and in the last movement sweeps to a climax of purposeful grandeur. Man-alone, communing with Nature, has achieved this assurance: which is not destroyed by the fact that in the last bar we hear, remote above the resonant E major triad, a broken statement of the original "tension" motive:

EXAMPLE 10

Like the "Concord" Sonata, this work thus returns to its initial impulse.

In media other than piano music Ives developed still further the contradictions inherent in the sonata principle. The Second String Quartet, for instance, written between 1907 and 1913, being for four melody instruments, explores the possibilities of linear and rhythmic independence between the parts in two movements called Discussions and Agreements. A character called Rollo—derived from a contemporary newspaper column but given by Ives a mythic quality as representative of the academically and emotionally "safe", the "lilly-pads and ladybirds"—is reluctant to allow his viola to follow the creative enterprise of the other players. The independent polyphony that results anticipates more developed experiments in this direction in the quartets of Elliott Carter. In the last movement of Ives's quartet human dissension is characteristically stilled by a walk into the hills.

In some passages of his Fourth Symphony, the most "advanced" of all his works, Ives attempts to explore this free polyphony in the texture of a symphony orchestra. The first movement is turbulent and atonal (the strife of the personal life). The second movement is diatonic, hymnlike, straightforward in rhythm (the simple, communal life). The third movement is tipsily syncopated in its attempt to notate the improvisatory rhythms of the bar-parlour. The fourth movement seeks a "transcendental" synthesis in combining all these elements simultaneously, attaining a linear and rhythmic complexity so great that it would seem to require three or four conductors—at once separate and co-ordinated!—if it were to be adequately realized in performance. Henry Cowell relates how, when Nicholas Slonimsky conducted "Washington's Birthday" from Ives's "Holidays" Symphony "he gave seven beats with the baton (in itself not a thing every conductor finds simple), three with his left hand, and lead two beats by nodding his head"; and this piece is ludicity itself, compared with parts of the Fourth Symphony.

While Ives put his most complicated "pioneering" music into his large-scale works, his American innocence is manifest in them also. Thus the Third Symphony, as compared with the Fourth, is a hymnic, diatonic piece that specifically looks back to the simple pieties of the small-town life of Ives's youth. His free polyphony re-creates the hymn tunes he quotes, while accepting their virtues as a positive. If the music sounds primitive, even commonplace at times, this is not because Ives was himself a primitive, like Billings, but because, typically, he accepted the primitive community on its own terms. Though much less interesting, at least to a non-American audience, than his experimental pieces, this music has, even in its quiet commonness, the distinction of its integrity, for it is a part of Ives's and America's roots. The violin sonatas, as compared with the piano sonatas, occupy a similar

position in the total pattern of Ives's work. He had a particular affection
for his four violin sonatas; and if he sometimes described them as
"harmless little works", he knew that their qualities came in part from
the nature of the medium. For Ives, and the same is true of Beethoven,
a sonata for violin and piano was apt to be "easier" than a piano sonata,
because lyric song or "verse" could be readily associated with the
violin, as against the amorphous, evolutionary "prose" of the piano.
Thus the first movement ("Autumn") of his Second Violin Sonata
(1903–10) is the same kind of music as the Nature movements of the
piano sonatas, only shorter, less complex. The two themes—a noble
adagio phrase growing from a falling fifth, and an allegro moderato
hymn tune—interact in shifting modal and rhythmic identities until
the violin plays the "fifth" theme inverted and syncopated, while the
piano plays a triplet extension of the allegro tune with descending
chromatic bass. The music sweeps to a series of impetuous climaxes,
each of which breaks off abruptly, unresolved.

The second movement, "In the Barn", is Saturday-night-hop
music, in which both instruments imitate the raucous off-beat ragging,
the off-key squawking, the false starts and non-coordinations of the
primitive music-makers. The excitement generated by the cross-
rhythms and tonal contrasts is not primitive at all, however: except
in so far as it reveals the violence beneath the pioneer's apparently
insouciant need to "make it new". The third movement has a slow
introduction recalling the material and the nature-mysticism of the first
movement. This leads into a hymn tune—the movement is called "The
Revival"—first presented in close canon at the tritone, and followed
by four variations wherein the hymn is fused with the hymn-tune of
the first movement. The variations grow increasingly ecstatic until the
piano accompanies the violin hymn with a clangorous stomp of telescoped tonic, dominant and subdominant chords: an effect at once
thrilling and weird:

EXAMPLE II

The Fourth Violin Sonata, sub-titled "Children's Day at the Camp Meeting", makes explicit the interdependence between Ives's complexity and his simplicity. From his awareness of contradiction comes his search for a transcendental unity; but this can be attained only by one who can preserve, or rather resurrect, the direct honesty of the child's heart. Thus the first movement harks back, like the Third Symphony, to the roots of New England music in eighteenth-century English polyphony, which it remakes in open-air exuberance: the organ is being played in chapel while the boys march outside, singing a different tune (Lowell Mason's "Work, for the night is coming"), often in a different key; and those who sing the loudest sing the most wrong notes. The beautiful largo makes afresh the hymn "Yes, Jesus loves me", dissolving hymnic innocence in polytonal, polyrhythmic nature-noises. The middle section ("allegro slugarocko!"), wherein the boys, gone beserk, indulge in stone-throwing, is rhythmically destructive and harmonically savage; but the naughtiness, being childish, serves only to deepen the heart-easing quietude of the enriched recapitulation, when the pulse of the day runs down and the chapel bells float mistily through the hymns' murmur. That the child's simplicity is a quality the adult must repeatedly recapture is revealed in the last movement: an erratic oom-pah of ninth chords, over which the violin sings a hymn. At the end, the violin-song stops with the first clause, "Shall we gather at the river?" leaving the players to *think* the remaining words, "that flows by the throne of God". The child would know. We, grown up, are left with a question and with (musically) a disturbing hiatus.

That we return to the affinity between Ives's experimentalism and his innocence is significant, for this is what defines his stature as an *embryonically* major composer. It is interesting that he anticipated by several decades the more advanced techniques of Hindemith, Bartók, Stravinsky and Schoenberg: that in *Tone-Road no. 3* he produced a complete twelve-note row, with angular leaps, as early as 1915: that his exploitation of noise, his polyphony of harmonies, tonalities and rhythms (as well as of lines), and his attempts to combine composition with improvisation should have pointed a way to the most advanced developments in the music of the mid-century. But to initiate an experimental technique is one thing; to possess the genius and the aural imagination that can give the technique substance is another: and that Ives had such genius, even if but fitfully, is the measure of his importance in the history of music. Thus, in listening to such a piece as the second of the *Three Harvest Home Chorales* (1912) for chorus, brass, string bass and organ we will be astonished at the extraordinary technical experiment when the tenor enters with a melody in slow triple rhythm, while a pizzicato bass plays nine equal notes stretched across *two* bars: this contradiction being taken up by the voices against an organ accompaniment of starkly dissonant triads in duple rhythm:

EXAMPLE 12

But we are also deeply moved by the passage, because the technical experiment is at the same time an experiment in human understanding. The "ugliness" of the sound helps aurally to create the scene: the chapel wherein choir, congregation, organist and instrumentalists combine to praise the Lord to John Hampton Gurney's text—and if their yells and blowings are not entirely coordinated in rhythm, and if some of the singers land, in their enthusiasm, on a ninth instead of an octave, that only makes the sound more exciting, the praise the grander. As Ives puts it:

> If a Yankee can reflect the fervency with which his gospels were sung— the fervency of Aunt Sarah, who scrubbed her life away for her brother's ten orphans, the fervency with which this woman, after a fourteen-hour work day on the farm, would hitch up and drive five miles through the mud and rain to prayer-meeting—her one articulate outlet for the fullness of her unselfish soul—if he can reflect the fervency of such a spirit, he may find there a local colour which will do all the world good. If his music can but catch that spirit by being a part with itself, it will come somewhere near this idea—and it will be American too. In other words, if local colour, national colour, any colour is a true pigment of the universal colour, it is a divine quality. And it is a part of substance in art, not of manner.

So, in this *Harvest Home Chorale*, the ugliness turns out to be beauty, the real to be transcendental, as all the contradictions become one in an act of worship. The last of the three Chorales ends, after the lines have become progressively more wide-flung and ruggedly ecstatic, with the telescoped tonic, dominant and sub-dominant of C major.

The vindication of what might appear to be the empirical amateurism of such a score is found where it should be found—in performance. Of recent years it has been proved that, given patience and understanding, even Ives's most complex scores are playable[5] and, listening to *The Housatonic at Stockbridge*, we can no longer doubt that Ives possessed an aural imagination of acute sensitivity, the more remarkable in that he heard none of his major works performed until years after he had ceased composing. Moreover, in performance Ives's amorphous American eclecticism reveals an unexpected consistency of style. This is partly because, although remote in his raw vitality from the autumnal ripeness of Mahler and early Schoenberg, he none the less belonged to their generation, and shares something of their sensuous richness. Still more, however, it is because of the integrity of his vision, which remained unafraid of the almost complete isolation in which he had to work. This is not to say that isolation had no effect on him. We can hardly complain that he attained complete artistic realization only occasionally and fortuitously (in, say, *The Housatonic at Stockbridge* and *The Unanswered Question*), since we have remarked that the idea of completion seemed to him illusory. It remains true, however, that a proportion of his large-scale works, including the fascinating Fourth Symphony, remains in part incommunicable as well as experimental. There are passages that seem to give up the struggle: to be confused simply because they accept life's confusion in passivity; just as there are times when Ives seems to rely on hymn tunes for his positives when creative melodic invention might have served him better. No man was more capable of strenuous effort nor more powerfully humane in his response to the world; yet the things he stood for seemed so antipodal to the things the world—especially the musical world—valued that we cannot be surprised that he occasionally lapsed into rage or cynicism. One finds this not only intermittently in some of his large-scale works, but also in a number of small pieces that would seem to be private jokes directed against authority. While we must beware of reading our own sophistication into Ives's empiricism and must remember that for him the banal and the trivial were no less a part of the Real, and as capable of revealing the Transcendental, as the tragic or sublime, we cannot but find these works disturbing, because we can never be sure how far,

[5] See Appendix I.

and in what way, they are seriously intended. It is as though the pressure of realizing his experience in isolation becomes, at times, too great to be borne: so Ives sticks out his tongue at "Rollo" and momentarily tries to kid himself and us that music does not matter.

Since music was for Ives the heart of reality and therefore in the last resort the *only* thing that mattered, we can see that Schoenberg was not entirely accurate when he said that Ives "responded to negligence by contempt". Quite certainly, Ives was affected by the fact that people considered him a crank, if not a madman; and it is probable that the illness which was the ostensible reason why Ives relinquished composition in the early 1920s was in part psychosomatic. Though he lived for another thirty years and saw his music become a seminal influence upon the young, he never forgot his early experiences, nor entirely grew out of the feeling that if he wished to write music that he considered worth-while he must "keep away from musicians". Ives's account of his encounter with a celebrated professional violinist—as quoted by the Cowells in their biography—is at once comic and tragic:

> Well, the "professor" came, and after a lot of big talk he started to play the first movement of the First Sonata. He didn't even get through the first page. He was all bothered with the rhythms and the notes and got mad. He kept saying "This cannot be played. . . . This is awful. . . . It is not music, it makes no sense." Even after I had played it over for him several times, he could not get it even then. I remember he came out of the little back music room with his hands over his ears and said: "When you get awfully indigestible food in your stomach that distresses you, you can get rid of it. But I cannot get those horrible sounds out of my ears with a dose of castor oil."
>
> After he had left, I had a kind of feeling which I have had, on and off, when other celebrated musicians have seen, or played, or tried to play my music. It was only temporary, but I did for a time feel that there must be something wrong with me. Said I to myself: I am the only one, with the exception of Mrs Ives and Ralph D. Griggs, who likes any of my music—except perhaps some of the older, more conventional things. Why do I like to work in this way and get all set up over what just upsets other people. No one else seems to hear it the same way. ARE MY EARS ON WRONG?

They were not: as the livelier professional musicians came ultimately to discover. But by that time it was too late to encourage Ives to resume composition; or if he responded to encouragement, he was too ill for hard work.

Though we must deplore the wastage of thirty potentially creative years, we can hardly deplore Ives's isolation, since it was the condition of his achievement. He had to be alone to reveal the heart of a new world that had no traditions; one might even say that to reveal that heart as it authentically was he had to cut himself off from most of the opportunities for performance that his society offered. As a young man he resigned from the New York church where he was organist because he felt that his duties to his congregation conflicted with his duties to himself as artist. Bach's musically devoted and knowledgeable public had been disturbed by the complexity of his improvisation; how much more would not Ives's fashionable, business-world congregation be upset by the occasional dissonances, overtone series and polytonal embroideries which, try as he would, he could not entirely banish from his hymn accompaniments? While his friend Dr Griggs assured him that "God must get awfully tired of hearing the same thing over and over again, and in His all-embracing wisdom could certainly embrace a dissonance—might even positively enjoy one now and again", Ives thought that his public, as well as God, deserved some consideration. "When a body of people comes together to worship, how far has a man a right to do what he wants, if he knows by so doing he is interfering with the state of mind of the listeners, who have to listen regardless and are helpless not to? I seem to have worked (in composition) with more natural freedom when I knew that the music was not going to be played, at least publicly—or rather, before people who could not get out from under, as is the case with a church congregation. . . . One has a different feeling in playing his music before an audience or public that cannot help itself. In other words, a public audience, or a congregation, has some rights."

So, working alone, without public or performance, Ives embraced within his embryonic art America's musical past, present, and potential future. The Emersonian strife in his music was a still more violent development from the European sonata principle; and its very violence led him to a new—in part monistic—search for order, and to a polyphony of independent ensembles that may have more to suggest to the future of music than any of the European masters who are, in intrinsic achievement, greater. Isolated in a vast, rapidly industrialized society, he found that a New World, materially considered, could grow only from a new world of the spirit, which each man must seek from his own inner resources. If his music has something of the rawness of a new world it has also, at times, the authentic note of grandeur. It is a note that is becoming rare. We should be grateful for it.

III

Men and mountains: Carl Ruggles as American mystic; Roy Harris as religious primitive

> This old man died last winter, having lived eighty-one years
> under open sky,
> Concerned with cattle, horses and hunting, no thought nor
> emotion that all his ancestors since the ice-age
> Could not have comprehended. I call that a good life;
> narrow, but vastly better than most
> Men's lives, and beyond comparison more beautiful, the
> wind-struck music man's bones were moulded to be the
> harp for.
>
> ROBINSON JEFFERS: *The Wind-struck Music*

We have observed in the music of Ives two poles of the American experience. On the one hand he manifests a Whitmanesque energy and comprehensiveness, an ubiquitous love of humanity and of every facet of the visible and tactile world; on the other hand he is a solitary, alone with Nature, seeking a transcendental order within the flux of reality. Carl Ruggles, a composer of the same generation, born in 1876, is in no sense the gregarious democrat, but is unequivocally an isolated spirit. Also a New Englander, descendant of a Cape Cod whaling family, he has not, like Ives, entered the big world of commerce and industrialism. He studied at Harvard, held a few university appointments; but has remained in his Vermont home for many decades and, in his old age, has become almost literally a hermit. The walls of his study, indeed, are papered with the exquisite calligraphy of his own manuscripts. Shut within the world of his own creation he has, it would seem, allowed the chaos of the American scene to pass him by. Yet although his music—unlike Ives's—contains no direct reflection of the external world, he is still concerned with the New. It is not for nothing that he is a solitary in New England, where so much that went to make America is rooted.

The eclecticism of Ives's technique—his simultaneous use of modal, diatonic, and chromatic materials from multifarious aspects of the past and present—is part of his immediacy, his awareness of environment. Ruggles, on the other hand, is neither eclectic nor profuse. In a long life he has written—and rewritten, again and again—only a handful of works; and they are in style as consistent as Ives's music is protean and inconsistent. This style is comparable with, and related to, one aspect only of Ives's music: the freely evolving, non-tonal polyphony in which he expressed both his freedom from the past and his desire for identity with Nature. From Ruggles's music all those tune-filled, rhythm-dominated, harmonically-ordered conventions which approximate to the values of Society are rigorously banished. His is a dedicated art; and it is dedicated to the integrity of his own spirit.

Ruggles started composing at about the same time as Schoenberg, in Europe, had arrived at his free atonal phase: which was in essence a rejection of the "public" conventions of the past, a desire or a need to concentrate exclusively on personal response, on an "expressionistic" immediacy, even if this meant confining oneself to works of small dimensions. It is improbable that Ruggles knew Schoenberg's music well, though, discounting their opposed backgrounds, there is much in common between the two men. Both were amateur painters who, in their visual work, sought the expressionistic moment of vision. Both, in their music still more than in their painting, found that the disintegrated fragments of the psyche could be reintegrated only by a mystical act. Schoenberg, as Viennese Jew, had an ancient religion and the spirit of Beethoven to help him; Ruggles had only the American wilderness and the austerities of Puritan New England. For this reason he sought freedom—from tonal bondage, from the harmonic straitjacket, from conventionalized repetitions, from anything that sullied the immediacy and purity of experience—even more remorselessly than Schoenberg. His chromaticism, like Schoenberg's, began with the Wagnerian identification of the "world" with the Self; then the burden of consciousness proved too great to be borne, so the harmonic chromaticism sought a linear release. The sequences of *Tristan* both yearningly impel the music forwards and express frustration, since each sequence must return to the point it started from. In Schoenberg's "free" atonal music and in Ruggles's chromatic polyphony there is a minimum of repetition, for each piece is a new birth. Self-consciousness is lost as the polyphony sings and wings.

The implications of this are already evident in the earliest work which Ruggles admits to the canon—*Angels*, originally written for six trumpets in 1921, but revised for four trumpets and three trombones (or four violins and three celli) in 1938. This is the only work of Ruggles that has any affinities with classical tonality and form: within an A:B:A: and an A-flat key-flavour it uses vocal form intervals and a close harmonic texture to create a "neo-baroque" brass sonority. That this does not, however, remind us of the ceremonial or public aspects of baroque music is due in part to the muted tone colour, in part to the way in which the rhythms of the individual voices tend to flow in triplets, tied syncopations and other irregularities across the duple pulse. The harmony is also complicated because each line oscillates chromatically around its nodal point:

EXAMPLE I

So both tonally and rhythmically the lines aspire to freedom, towards absolute expressionism, and it is in this freedom that their "angelic"— their superhuman—quality consists.

Despite the vocal and tonal bases, the harmonic texture created by the chromatic oscillations and elliptical rhythms of *Angels* is sharply and uncompromisingly dissonant. By the time of *Men and Mountains* (1924) for chamber orchestra Ruggles's characteristic manner, which has remained unchanged since, is defined. The hardness of the harmonic texture—with a preponderance of minor seconds, major sevenths and minor ninths—is similar to Schoenberg's; but in place of Schoenberg's density, Ruggles cultivates a clear, open resonance, a winging polyphony that overrides the harmonic passion. There may be a peculiarly American quality in both the harshness of the harmony and the sweep of the lyricism, in which the reiteration of notes is discouraged, though not prohibited. The violence of the harmony reminds us of the American axe in the wilderness, and of the savagery within the mind that it came to represent. But the violence does not stay rooted in (sadistic) sensuality. The surge of the lines, their rhythmic independence, carries them away from the earthward tug of harmony, as the dissonant pain becomes itself an agent of liberation. One can sense this especially in

"Lilacs", the beautiful second movement of *Men and Mountains*. It is
not merely the spring flower that the lyricism evokes; the vast hidden
energy of the lilac's tentacular roots, spreading all over New England
or even the American continent, is contained in the web of dissonant
counterpoint. The surging spring of the lines, the persistent tension of
the dissonance, is like the pain of birth; nothing is preordained, all is a
growing. It is revealing to compare Ruggles's *Men and Mountains* with
Delius's *Song of the High Hills*. Delius starts from the burden of his own
passionate heart—the Wagnerian appoggiatura-laden harmony that
tries to drag down the singing lines. Ruggles's chromaticism is not,
historically speaking, so far from Delius's; but the prancing energy of
the lines, the hardness of the harmonic texture, transform a personal
melancholy into an epic celebration of the organic processes of Nature.
Delius is a belated and weary humanist; Ruggles is a mystic in a non-
religious society. Paradoxically, his mysticism is his Americanism: for
it is also his "newness", his search for personal integrity. His "inhumanism", springing from his humanism, parallels that of the poet Robinson
Jeffers; perhaps only against the background of the American wilderness could an artist possess this sense of man's identity with the immensity, the beauty, the terror and cruelty of the natural world.[1]

The title *Men and Mountains* refers to Blake's "Great things are done
when men and mountains meet". The nature of these "great things" is
suggested by another work for string orchestra, *Portals* (1926), which
bears an inscription from Whitman: "What are those of the known
but to ascend and enter into the unknown." Here there are two themes,
one strenuously human, with energetic tritones, leaping sevenths and
double dots, the other remotely floating, in a flexible triplet rhythm.
Texturally, the piece is all melody, in twelve real parts. The two
themes (the known and the unknown?), coming into collision, grow
towards climax, then break off, unresolved, to start again. At the
second climax the lines whirl wildly, in grinding dissonance, until a
brief, distant coda telescopes the themes vertically in an immense
spread chord that fades into silence. Again, the process of growth is
both natural and painful; and the pain is freed, but not resolved, in
silence and space.

Ruggles's *Evocations* for solo piano, written between 1937 and 1945,

---

[1] Certainly there is no European artist strictly comparable with Ruggles or
Jeffers. The term "inhumanism" is Jeffers's own. It does not, of course,
mean anti-humanism: only an awareness of man's littleness against the
background of animate and inanimate Nature.

are his most recent work and his only work for a solo instrument. Habitually, he has been an orchestral composer, and the restriction of the medium here would seem to coincide with his (un-Ivesian) desire to achieve ever greater clarification and concision. Each of these "chants for piano" is short, though not as short as the pieces of Schoenberg's opus 19; each is growth to and from a single climax; each involves a minimum of repetition; each creates an impression of unexpected breadth. The first piece reveals most clearly its genesis in Wagnerian chromaticism, for it is built on a rising, upsurging phrase—a fifth striving up to a semitonic dissonance—which occurs three times. Each attempt at the rise thrusts higher, in freer and more complex rhythms and in increasingly dissonant polyphony. At the ultimate climax perfect fifths appear in rapid sequence (E to B, A flat to E flat, E to B, F to C, D to A): from which high point the lines descend in thundering fourths, which are fifths inverted. As coda, there is a reference to the opening, but not a return: for the fifths are now obscure, augmented into whole-tonal ambiguity:

EXAMPLE 2

The second Evocation has a twelve-note theme in extremely flexible rhythm. Alternating perfect and imperfect fourths imbue it with a quality at once wistful, yet strong and resilient. The theme is not treated serially; and such contrapuntal (in particular canonic) devices as occur do not impede the lines' movement. Indeed, the canons, which begin strict, become canons in variable rhythm:

EXAMPLE 3

and the flow grows the more free as the hard sonorities of sevenths and ninths serve to boost the soaring polyphony. After the explosive climax, there is again a quiet reference to the original version of the theme, but with rhythms and sonorities now more tenuous and amorphous. Subtle use is made here of the Ivesian piano technique of "afternotes": a haze of subsidiary tones which appear and disappear as overtone-shadows of the harmony notes. The final deep resonance of the E flat seems to hark back to the opening statement of the theme, to which it now gives a tonal, or at least nodal, fundament.

The third piece returns to the perfect fifths of the first piece, only now they descend. The fifths, both falling and rising, then grow in triplets, in semiquavers and in quintuplets, striding across the bars in free stretto, building up a series of climaxes each more vibrant than the last. The final climax covers the entire range of the keyboard. Once more there is a "da capo" coda, beginning strict but very quiet, fading away in semitonic dissonances through which, however, the fifth E flat to B flat shines clear:

EXAMPLE 4

Whereas Ives "accepts the universe"—the tawdry and the trivial along with the sublime—Ruggles concentrates exclusively on strife towards an identification of his own consciousness with the processes of Nature. His achievement has a heroic quality, though the heroism is limited by its exclusiveness: throughout his career the compositions get shorter and fewer. His dedication to the sublime also means that he has to be inspired to carry it off; and whereas *Lilacs* and *Portals* are certainly inspired, alive in every phrase and rhythm as the lines come to birth, the later *Organum* (1945) for full orchestra is not. The title of this piece is significant, referring not merely to the fact that it is in essence linear, but also, perhaps, to the *organic* nature of the compositional process. Here, however, the "evolutionary" polyphony seems dammed up by the viscidity of the orchestral sonority; and if the lines cannot take wing the explosive violence seems pointless. What Ruggles had to say was valid and, within limits, important; but the relative failure of *Organum* —and perhaps the aphoristic restriction of the *Evocations* also—suggests that his experience of "inhumanism" was in more senses than one self-destructive.

With Ruggles we may compare and contrast a composer of the next generation, Roy Harris. His parents were pioneers of Scotch-Irish descent, who had built their own log cabin in the Cimarron frontier rush; one of his grandfathers had been a Kansas circuit rider, the other a rider of the Pony Express from Chicago to the western ports. Harris himself, born in 1898, became a farmer in his teens, and took up music full time only on the cessation of the First World War. Though he went to study in Paris, as a pupil of Nadia Boulanger, he did not absorb Parisian sophistication; the strength of his musical character is indicated by the fact that even his first (Parisian) works, such as the Concerto for piano, clarinet and string quartet (1927), preserve something of the rugged, Whitmanesque character of Ives in his folk-hymnodic vein. The link with Ruggles lies in the fact that Harris's music, too, relies on continuous melodic and polyphonic flow: in which respect it is fundamentally a religious affirmation. But whereas Ruggles, single-minded and simple-hearted though he is, is an artist whose introspection relates him to such highly sophisticated composers as Schoenberg and Berg, Harris is essentially a primitive and naïf. This is why he could accept, as Ruggles could not, the modal and diatonic materials of America's past; it is also why he could treat these materials in direct, affirmative lyricism, without the complexities and ambiguities—the recognition of "other modes of experience that are possible"—to which Ives submitted them. At first, indeed, Harris's primitivism seemed almost gauche. In a work such as the early Piano Sonata the composer's obsession with organum-like parallel fifths and fourths and with freely sweeping non-metrical rhythms creates a sense of crude, pioneering vitality; but the momentum remains undisciplined and is—like the original westward migration itself—directed to no clearly foreseeable end.

By the time of the Piano Trio of 1934 Harris has discovered the direction which is natural to him, though he has not yet achieved his talent's fulfilment. His compositional principle is unequivocally that of linear growth; starting not so much with a theme as with an interval (the major and minor third), the texture of the two stringed instruments and the piano (treated preponderantly in octave unisons or in two parts) grows gradually more sustained and more song-like. Thus the initial assertive phrase:

EXAMPLE 5

evolves into sundry permutations:

EXAMPLE 6

while the harmony grows not thicker but more sonorously spaced in its triadic formations. The movement builds up to a tremendous climax in which all three instruments play in unisonal monody; but the music's raw vitality is not, in this movement, lyrically consummated. Its rhythmic vigour has to be succeeded by the hymnic song of the slow movement, in which the rising and falling thirds are absorbed into a melodic line that is basically stepwise. Again the texture is thin, though sonorous, and the piano, scored monodically two octaves apart, is consistently a melody instrument. Here the rhythms are vocal, with the flexibility of song: not with the jaunty, rather aggressive irregularities of the first movement, which may reflect the inflections of American speech. Again there is a starkly resonant, mainly unisonal climax over a pedal G; and a coda which, beginning as a cadenza for the two strings, reminds us of the affinity between the Andante's song-theme and the first movement's more aggressively metrical, melodically frustrated material. The resolution of these two opposed impulses is achieved, in the finale, through the monistic unity of fugue. Both the falling thirds and the agitated repeated notes of the first movement are now subservient to the "heroic" rising fourths with which the theme opens:

EXAMPLE 7

Organum-like parallel fourths and fifths give resonance to the piano texture without complicating the harmony, and the exposition ends with stretto and augmentation. Then the $\frac{10}{8}$ rumba-rhythmed theme of the first movement returns as a counter-subject, to be combined in double fugue with the first theme. The climax is immensely powerful and affirmative, though the last notes we hear are the falling minor third, in triplet rhythm.

Harris's Trio is linear in essence and contrapuntal or polyphonic in development; but it is still, perhaps, lyrical in intention rather than in effect. The spontaneous-seeming growth of the phrases is to some extent impeded by the nagging reiteration of intervals and rhythms; the contrapuntal unity may still be more the imposition than the revelation of order. The full emergence of Harris as a musical personality coincides with his realization that his kind of "religious" affirmation must be lyrical of its essence, as well as polyphonic. The greater maturity of the *Soliloquy and Dance* for viola and piano (1939), as compared with the Trio, lies in the much more sustained quality of the line which, beginning with pentatonic fundamentals, grows into long, surging cantilena, like plainsong, a hymn of praise. The evolution of song from silence is, as it were, the basic relationship between man and God, even in the wilderness; and once created, the song can lead to the dance, a social act wherein the clipped, fourth-founded phrases and bouncing rhythms are a blithe acceptance of a new world's solidarity.

Though this progression from song to dance is in a sense a synonym for the evolution of the—or a—New World, Harris's music demonstrates that it cannot, against the background of the American wastes, be achieved easily or unambiguously; indeed the Dance, though exuberant, is much less positive, more disrupted, than the climax of the Soliloquy. The implications of this, as it were, anti-development are revealed in a larger—in this case orchestral—work which Harris produced in the same vintage year. His Third Symphony is his best-known work and certainly one of his best; and the "pioneer" myth that is latent in the viola piece seems, in the symphony, to be given explicit formulation. Beginning in religious primitivism, it resembles Bruckner if one could imagine a Bruckner with no past: with no Schubert, Beethoven, Mozart, Haydn, baroque counterpoint, Renaissance polyphony or medieval monody behind him—with nothing, indeed, but the American wilderness. Like a Bruckner symphony, it starts with the emergence of life from the void: not with Ruggles's chromatic disintegration and rebirth, but with an enormously long cello melody based on stepwise movement, with undulating pentatonic thirds and "open" arpeggiated leaps that sound the more spacious because the ends of the phrases are "resonated" by unison violas:

EXAMPLE 8

The vision of empty distances the music thus evokes, the sense of growth and endeavour in the length of the melody, powerfully suggest man alone in the prairies: the music is "religious" in that the continuously evolving monody sounds like a rudimentary, open-air plainchant, a spontaneous God-given creativity; while it is modern, and perhaps specifically American, in the speech-inflected plasticity of its phrasing and in its harmonic fluidity. And as the unbroken texture flows on, the music enacts the growth of a civilization. Monody leads to organum (fourths and fifths in parallel motion); organum leads to contrary motion; contrary motion to harmonic tension; harmonic tension into Wagnerian enharmony. But there is no disintegration into chromatic introspection. The music's primitivism is comparable with Bruckner's faith in that the Wagnerian awareness of harmonic personality—of the sensual self—is absorbed into the flow of the lines. The lyrical continuity implies, at first, an identity between man and nature which can be accepted, not (as in Ives and Ruggles) arrived at by a transcendental act. The acceptance is part of the naïvety, which can substitute for Bruckner's heaven the empty prairie.

Yet the innocence of this affirmation cannot be sustained; and in this respect Harris is Ruggles's complement and also his polar opposite. Ruggles's chromaticism starts from the isolated consciousness, from which he seeks lyrical release in the "inhumanism" of the natural world. Harris starts from the primitive identity between man and nature and imaginatively re-enacts man's apparent conquest of nature and his achievement of civilization: in which process the religious lyricism is lost. Thus, though the texture of his Third Symphony remains unbroken, it evolves into four sections that grow progressively less "vocal" in melodic contour. First, the undulating lines cease to be song and, grown faster, become figuration—an impressionistic rustle like a Sibelian moto perpetuo. As in Sibelius, the moto perpetuo is like the hum of Nature herself. Woodwind and brass begin to pick out brief, comparatively fragmentary *tunes* which are derived from the long, plainsong-like melodies, but which become progressively more rhythmic, perky and assertive, less lyrical and "religious". Ultimately they turn into American hill-billy and shanty-tune: the crude music the pioneer makes to assert his humanity *against* Nature. The Ivesian acceptance is replaced by a bouncy aggression; and this becomes overt in the third section when the undulation of nature is banished and the eternally-flowing polyphony turns into a brusquely American fugued dance in alternating $\frac{3}{2}$ and $\frac{6}{4}$:

EXAMPLE 9

This sounds like a fusion of a late medieval hocket or hiccup (which had disrupted the continuity of plainsong line and rhythm) with the fuguing hymn, and with the music of Middle West dance-hall and honky-tonk. The cruelty within the American wilderness comes to the surface as the creative spontaneity of religious lyricism is defeated. The broken rhythms are savage, the scoring harsh, the tunes, with their open fourths and sevenths, resilient and bouncy, but unflowing, non-lyrical. It is significant (as we shall see) that this is the only part of Harris's score which reminds us of the urban idiom of Copland.

The fugued dance grows increasingly vehement until melody—or even tune—disappears completely, and the savagery blows up in venomous reiterated brass notes, separated by silence:

EXAMPLE 10

At this point, however, the innate heroism of the pioneer re-establishes itself in an extended coda that combines the aggressive metrical hammering of the honky-tonk episode with the arpeggiated flow of the work's opening. A level timpani pedal on D suggests the courage a new world needs if it is to reconcile its brash vitality with the spirit's aspiration. At the end the pulse breaks again; but though the raucously scored, modally and enharmonically related minor triads sound grim, and the silences that separate them are apprehensive, we feel, at least, that the future is before us. Though we may have lost our religious innocence, we know what is at stake.

A chamber work that followed immediately after the Third Symphony deals with the same kind of experience with perhaps even greater power. This is the Quintet for piano and strings which although ostensibly in three movements—Passacaglia, Cadenza and Fugue—is again a completely monistic and evolutionary work. The passacaglia convention is, indeed, a classical parallel to Harris's normal technique of growth by permutation: once more the work opens with a unison statement of the theme with "resonated" overtones, and then throughout the passacaglia-repetitions the initial oscillating semitone and descending third proliferate in "divisions" that grow gradually more vocally lyrical, more flexible in rhythm. Here is the theme and some of the permutations:

EXAMPLE II

Again the piano writing includes vast stretches of octave unison, interspersed with occasional modally or enharmonically related diatonic triads.

The Passacaglia's unity is a "religious" affirmation: a continuous, unbroken evolution from the initial "seed". In a sense, indeed, it forms one vast climax, at the ultimate point of which the monodic unity explodes into separateness. For each instrument, beginning with first violin, then enters playing its own rhapsodic, quasi-improvisatory cadenza growing from the passacaglia. Out of the pentatonic rhapsody, fragments of theme begin to emerge: until the strings become a wild whirling of trills and the piano enters with the most extended and abandoned of all the cadenzas. It is as though the piano becomes, here, the *individual* consciousness: the soloist leaping out of, even rebelling against, the "monism" of the passacaglia. And this personal freedom, this rhapsodic liberation, would seem to be a necessary stage towards fulfilment: for it leads directly into the final fugue, wherein the original passacaglia theme has become an extended, free-rhythmed song:

EXAMPLE 12

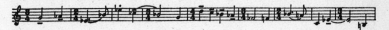

The texture, like that of the Passacaglia and still more of the Third Symphony, is evolutionary rather than strictly fugal: like an immensely expanded version of seventeenth-century ricercar or canzona style, rather than like a Handelian fugue. Again the note-values grow progressively faster, as in seventeenth-century divisions, and the temper of the music not only more animated but also more agitated. Ultimately the figuration has become savage repeated notes in semiquavers on the strings, with stark parallel fifths in jerky six-eight rhythm on the piano. As in the Symphony, the religious lyricism has been metamorphosed into the American violence: perhaps even more disturbingly, since the process happens within a single fugal movement. As in the Symphony, the coda reasserts a kind of stoic heroism, so that the total effect of the work is, if grim, positive rather than negative.

Harris's Third Symphony and his Piano Quintet made a tremendous impact on their first performance, and the symphony has probably been more widely played abroad than any other major American work by a "serious" composer. The impact of these works must have been in part attributable to their significance as an American parable; and it may also be that what Harris achieved with such power and conviction in this climacteric year of his career could not be repeated. Certainly, though Harris's later works sacrifice nothing of his music's rugged authenticity, they do not attain again the driving momentum of the works of 1939–40, while at times they descend to passive self-imitation. The Third Symphony and the Piano Quintet are, in their vigorous originality, beyond the vagaries of fashion, whereas the primitivism of later works seems anachronistic in the sophistications of the Big City: as does also, perhaps, the home-spun, free-rhythmed verse of the later Carl Sandburg, whose background is comparable with that of Harris. Only the Seventh Symphony among Harris's later works suggests a possible line of development, and that development is of a negative nature. Again, the symphony is all lyrical-polyphonic evolution—a passacaglia with five divisions, followed by a series of asymmetrical variations that grow gradually more metrical until they turn into a coda that brings back the passacaglia theme in augmentation. What is new in this music is the manner in which the proliferating variations now *conflict* so violently with the noble spaciousness of the passacaglia theme that Harris's rural music acquires an undercurrent of neurotic fury, incarnated not so much in harmonic tensions as in the piercing and most original orchestration. The symphony is impressive, though it is difficult to imagine where Harris can go from this point.

If Harris's music seems to have reached an impasse, it preserves its integrity: whereas that of his one-time pupil, William Schuman, has sacrificed the validity of the pioneer tradition. The essence of Schuman's music—as of Harris's and Ruggles's—lies in melody, quasi-vocal in contour and modality, long and flexible in rhythm. For this reason its structures tend to be polyphonic rather than harmonic; and Schuman's symphonic works are seldom symphonic in the same sense as are those of the Viennese classics. He attempts to create "evolutionary" forms like those of Harris: and in so far as he has employed pre-ordained criteria of order he, too, has favoured the monistic forms of the baroque era—chaconne, fugue and toccata—rather than the dualistic forms of the sonata.

To write music that grows inevitably from sustained melody calls for emotional stamina and also, one suspects, for a visionary, if not dogmatically religious temperament. Roy Harris, in his finest works, has both stamina and vision. William Schuman has stamina in plenty, but—even in his best pieces—seldom attains vision. The strength of his music is attested by the heroic opening of his *Symphony for Strings* or by a long sustained line such as this from the choreographic poem *Judith*:

EXAMPLE 13

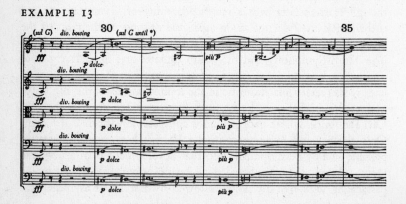

Here the widely arpeggiated, resiliently rhythmed phrases and open textures are even bigger, more confidently epic, than those of Harris: while the interrelation between modal contours and a sonorous triadic harmony (involving multiple false relations) is immensely assured. Both the athletic exuberance and the elegiac lyricism are Whitman-esque; both seem to develop to higher potential qualities found in Harris. Yet in total effect Schuman seems a smaller composer than Harris—or than Ruggles, whose concept of the Sublime would seem to be also applicable to him; and paradoxically the limitations of his music are directly associated with what appears to be its greater assurance. Significantly, Schuman's works tend to be more impressive in their opening clauses than in development, when the grand gestures are apt to become inflated. Harris's music at its best owes its power, we have seen, to his spiritual innocence: which would seem to be inseparable from his primitivism and even from his technical gaucherie. In being technically more expert, emotionally more sophisticated, Schuman sacrifices the raw authenticity that makes Harris's best music memor-able. If the long asymmetrical lines, the fourth-founded buoyancy, the stark triadic harmony, cannot be sustained by lyricism there is a temptation to inject into them a dose of harmonic punch and orchestral bravura. The more streamlined the technique, the more the concept of the American Sublime approximates to the "colossal" epic of Holly-wood. Schuman's later symphonic works indicate how myth may become cliché; there is something about the Seventh Symphony and (still more) the United Nations piece *Credendum* which is not so much grand as monstrous. The sheer professional efficiency of the music turns it into an emotional bulldozer; we are left physically shattered and deflated by the rumbustiousness of the gestures.

There is a similar tendency in the symphonies of Peter Mennin (born 1923). The long-spanned lines and rhythmic gusto of his Third Symphony, for instance, relate it to the pioneer tradition: but as with Schuman, though less damagingly, the professional competence seems to make the music less, not more, authentic. It becomes mannered music, where manners are least appropriate, and the manners are to some degree parasitic on the later work of Vaughan Williams. The appeal of the English Puritan tradition, as exemplified by Vaughan Williams, is under-standable enough; so is the fact that the tradition, in becoming Ameri-canized, should become also streamlined. Perhaps there is only one composer of a later generation whom we may consider a true heir to Roy Harris, and he is Robert Palmer, who was born at Syracuse in 1915.

Though his music has been described as Stravinskian, it has little in common with Stravinsky except a partiality for clean lines and driving rhythms. The continuity of texture in a work such as the Piano Quartet (1949)—its slow, almost nagging evolution from small motives—is as untypical of Stravinsky as it is typical of Harris. Equally Harris-like are Palmer's fondness for complex cross-rhythms, for bare, widely spaced textures and organum effects, and for obsessive ostinati and pedal notes. Palmer himself has said that—admiring Ives, Harris, and American transcendentalists such as Thoreau, Whitman and Hart Crane—he aims at a kind of religious expression: and admits that musically he has been influenced by polyphonists such as Taverner and Byrd. He does not achieve the religious ecstasy of Byrd, and his music never takes wing as Harris's sometimes does. This may be because his basic material is not sufficiently interesting, so that the patterns tend to get the better of the lyricism: in which respect it is instructive to compare the slow movement of Palmer's Piano Quartet with that of Harris's Piano Quintet. But if Palmer is a composer of religious intention rather than achievement, he is to be honoured for preferring his constricted harmonic range, his unfulfilled melody and polyphony, to technical and emotional inflation. In his most recent music—such as the *Memorial Music* for orchestra—there is a hint that he is finding his way out of his emotional impasse, not, perhaps, by way of the development of a richer melodic sense, but by way of a bolder exploration of Ivesian heterophony and rhythmic multiplicity, combined with a formal discipline more suggestive of Copland than of Harris. The music creates a sharp, exciting resonance which preserves pioneering vitality, but is harsh and acrid, as befits our post-war world, rather than heroic. The American Sublime, it would seem, is no longer possible; or at least, with the growth of urban civilization, the American Sublime has to be balanced by another tradition that, insisting on absolute precision of personal statement, would seem to be the sublime's antithesis. Only gradually do we realize—especially in the music of Aaron Copland—that such minimal integrity may carry its own sublimity.

IV

Skyscraper and Prairie:
Aaron Copland and the American isolation

> It is easier to sail many thousand miles through cold and
> storms and cannibals than it is to explore the private sea, the
> Atlantic and Pacific Ocean of one's being alone: herein are
> demanded the eye and the nerve.
>
> THOREAU
>
> I wish to see the earth through the medium of much air or
> heaven, for there is no paint like the air.
>
> THOREAU
>
> And I and silence, some strange race
> Wrecked solitary here.
>
> EMILY DICKINSON

In considering the music and personality of Charles Ives we have come
into contact with the essential American themes. In so far as the Pioneer
is an ego alone in a vast, savage land he must, like Whitman, attempt to
subjugate the physical universe; but precisely because he is alone, it is
only by way of a mystical act that he, like Thoreau, can find reality
beneath the flux. Response to the physical must involve a rebirth of the
spirit; the New World, materially considered, must grow from within
the psyche. So Ives was always a seeker, as—in their less comprehensive
way—were Ruggles and Harris; his art had to remain in part unrealized
because it was, of its nature, embryonic—a world coming to birth.
When in a later generation an American composer appeared who
sought, and achieved, complete artistic realization, and thereby began
to establish an American tradition, he could do so only by a severe
limitation of range. That composer was Aaron Copland. To refer to
his limitation of range is not a pejorative remark; both Copland's
limitation and Ives's incompleteness were inevitable: a part of the
integrity that makes them key figures in American music.

Ives was born in small-town America; Copland was born, in 1900,
in a "drab street" (his own phrase) in Brooklyn. His parents, Russian

Jews whose name was originally Kaplan, had migrated to New York in early youth. They ran a Brooklyn department store, were reasonably successful: and totally impervious to music.[1] That Copland was a big-city boy, whereas Ives was a small-town boy, has more than biographical interest. Copland grew up in the polyglot industrial society that was no more than implicit in Ives's world. Ives unselfconsciously accepted the materials his world offered him, stayed at home, and expressed his rebellion only by making anew the world he loved. Copland absorbed the temper of big-city life at a level below conscious understanding; being aware that he was alone, however, he felt that to acquire a technique he had to separate himself from the world in which he lived. So, as self-reliant Brooklyn youth, born and bred in American democracy, he saved enough money to enable him to go abroad to study; and "abroad", for an American of his generation, meant Paris. Copland's prentice works, written in France while he was a pupil of Nadia Boulanger,[2] have a somewhat clinical flavour. Their lean, spare texture, their preoccupation with rigid formal discipline (consider the piano *Passacaglia* of 1922), were a purgation of what then seemed the bad blood of romanticism. The purging process was advisable for a European—as Nadia Boulanger's idol Stravinsky proved; for an American it was essential, since he had no choice but to start *ab ovo*. Copland's Big City—which had sprung out of Ives's America—did not even offer him the tangled, inchoate awareness of inherited human values, if not of musical traditions, that Ives so vigorously embraced.

While Copland's first works were in this sense clinical, they were not entirely negative. Their bareness was a positive quality also; and

[1] "I was born on November 14, 1900 on a street in Brooklyn that can only be described as drab. It had none of the garish color of the ghetto, none of the charm of an old New England thoroughfare, or even a pioneer street . . . I mention it because it was there I spent the first twenty years of my life. It fills me with mild wonder every time I realize a musician was born on that street. Music was the last thing anyone would have connected with that street. In fact, no one had ever connected music with my family or with my street. *The idea was entirely original with me.*"

[2] Copland did not know of Nadia Boulanger's existence when he went to Paris; he accidentally heard her giving a class and knew at once she was his teacher. Later, the pilgrimage to the "Boulangerie" became almost obligatory for advanced American composers; Paris and Nadia Boulanger became their protest against Horatio Parker—and the German academic tradition which was still taught in their own country. Copland may have realized subconsciously that Stravinsky—being in many ways non-European—was one of the few composers from whom he and other Americans could learn.

in a piece such as the charming setting of Richard Barnefield's "As it
fell upon a day" for voice, flute and clarinet (1923), the "open"
texture—with a prevalence of fourths, fifths, minor sevenths, major
seconds and major ninths—creates a tingling freshness which is more
than an evasion of romantic lushness. By the late twenties Copland's
music already betrays all the representative features of his highly
personal manner. Consider, for instance, the *Two Pieces* (1928) for the
most respectable of all classical media—the string quartet. The first has
a superficial affinity with Stravinsky in the spare, luminous spacing of
the parts and in its slow, quiet, almost ritualistic movement. The
oscillating diatonic concords of the opening bars, with the second
violin's falling ninth that creates a "blue" false relation, are, however,
quintessential Copland, evoking both a hymnic sobriety and a wistful
urban loneliness such as we shall meet repeatedly in his work:

EXAMPLE I

Equally characteristic—and unlike any European music with the partial
exception of Stravinsky—is the immensely slow harmonic movement
of the piece as a whole. The "blue" opening figure is repeated, almost
obsessively, in varying permutations, but it does not grow; and the
climax is harmonically static, being built over an ostinato, or revolving
"cam", in the bass.

The second piece, *Rondino*, brings the thin texture of Copland's
Parisian works into direct contact with his New York home, for it
adopts the agile, nervous rhythmic contradictions of jazz to a linear
style. It is not jazz, since there is no compulsive earth-beat for the
melodies to swing against; but it uses the tension of rhythmic contra-
diction—mainly a conflict between $\frac{2}{2}$ and $\frac{3}{8}$ plus $\frac{5}{8}$—to suggest an urban
gaiety that is at the same time a little jittery. The piece has more har-
monic movement, as well as surface animation, than the *Lento Molto*;
its rondo form means, however, that it does not develop climacterically. Repeatedly it returns to its starting-point; and in so far as it moves,
it is by linear permutation rather than by harmonic progression. Here
are three permutations of the opening phrases:

EXAMPLE 2a

EXAMPLE 2b

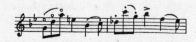

EXAMPLE 2C

Although this piece is delightful and successful, it initiated a phase which deflected Copland from his true path. The works of this period which borrow directly from jazz—notably the Piano Concerto—have not worn well, because they were a too conscious attempt to use techniques that must, of their nature, be spontaneous. They preserve the nervous twitch without the earthy vitality. Copland's music, as the creation of an urban American, had a real and profound affinity with some aspects of jazz: which affinity did not, however, involve imitation of the superfices. This we can see in his first masterpiece, the Piano Variations of 1930, which is still a key-work in his career and in the history of American music.

While one might say that Bartók's percussive use of the piano and Stravinsky's "geometric" organization of rhythmic patterns and of telescoped diatonic chords had some effect on Copland's Variations, one might also say that there has never been a work more decisive in its originality. The ragbag of the past is no longer relevant. The American Jew, expatriated and alienated, accepts the life of the big city and of a machine-made civilization. From it, he must draw what succour he can; unlike Ives, he must sacrifice the multifarious variety of life to achieve economy: which may or may not be a start towards a new order.

The Piano Variations is thus in texture so bare and hard as to be almost skeletal: because it is in essence a skeletal experience. Its most obvious difference from European music—or from most of the music of Ives, Ruggles or Harris—is its lack of lyrical growth. It is as though Copland—an a-religious, non-sentimental artist in an arid machine civilization—felt that he had no choice but to sacrifice the "natural" principles of musical growth, and to see whether anything of human worth could still be salvaged. So he starts, in the Variations, from the broken bones of a disrupted culture: in particular from the ambiguous thirds, sixths and sevenths of the Negro blues, and from the declamatory leaps of Jewish synagogue music. It is significant that both Negro and Jew are dispossessed peoples who have become, in a cosmopolitan urban society, representatives of modern man's uprootedness. Since the dislocated fragments cannot grow spontaneously, they must be reintegrated in a personal vision: much in the same way as the cubist painters attempted a personal reintegration of the broken facets of the visible world. So the technique of the Variations is rigidly—not (like Ives's music) amorphously—serial, being based on a five-note figure. The theme begins with the "blue" ambiguous third, continues with a redistribution of the same notes, and concludes with a further statement of them with the E natural extended to a declamatory E major triad:

EXAMPLE 3

Everything that happens in the variations is strictly derived from the theme which is also a "row". Sometimes the procedures are canonic, though in modified rhythms (variation 1); frequently the notes are transposed to widely separated octaves; all the figurations are thematic and the infrequent chords are derived from the theme, so that there is no accompanying material. Here is an example of the thematic figuration:

EXAMPLE 4

and here is one of thematic chords:

EXAMPLE 5

It will be observed that apart from octave displacements the thematic notes are not transposed, and there is no modulation. The brief, broken phrases may vary greatly in mood—may be tender, naïve, warm, protesting, angry, fierce: yet they cannot grow, either lyrically or in harmonic implication; and the inverted climax of the work, before the Coda, is a rhythmic disintegration wherein the "row", in its original, inverted and retrograde forms, gradually splinters in jazzy syncopation until it flickers into silence.

The Piano Variations thus explore, with uncompromising honesty, the experience implicit in the first of the *Two Pieces* for string quartet. Whereas that piece was short, slow and quiet, however, its tension being beneath the surface, the Variations embrace all the physical and nervous energy of city life. Yet although the sharp, hard, metallic piano texture has the precision of a machine, and the lyrical heart, the harmonic blood, and the rhythmic pulse would all seem to be disrupted, there is an impressive nobility in the way in which the serial permutations shore up the fragments against our ruin. It is *because* line, harmony and rhythm are so disintegrated that every facet must be serially related with such rigid fanaticism. This is what one can do, the music seems to be saying, with the minimal material our world offers' us. The energy may be broken and distraught; but in the "disintegrative" climax it is liberated into stillness. Then the coda, stating most of the theme's permutations simultaneously, can attain a grandeur that is steely and monumental, yet at the same time a profoundly human expression of courage. As a whole, the work is immensely invigorating. If it has the hardness of the New York skyline, it has also the sense of new vistas. It asks a question: Shall these bones live?

The hard inevitability of the Piano Variations was scarcely imitable, though in the early thirties Copland produced a number of works which have a similar aphoristic quality. The *Statements* for orchestra is perhaps the most powerful example; and the work's laconic title is appropriate. The brief, uncompromising pieces seem to tell us that this is the rock-bottom nature of our experience, here and now in this

American city. If the hardness may become at times almost savage, it is at least stringently controlled; if the tenderness cannot grow or sing, it is at least admitted to. Copland must have felt, however, that it would have been exhausting to confine himself to such severely economical, such boldly lonely music, even though it was at bottom an affirmation of the human spirit. He must have felt the need for relaxation and—complementarily—the need for wider communication.[2] So, in the mid-thirties, he deliberately turned from the creation of these fiercely personal works to the creation of music for radio, cinema and ballet. Living in an industrial city, he admitted that he ought to make use of industrial techniques. Perhaps he also realized intuitively that the typical "cubist" technique which he had evolved lent itself admirably to functional use. A pattern of short phrases, possibly serially related, was a natural means of giving order to the discontinuous images of the screen; and Stravinsky—the composer Copland most admired—had repeatedly demonstrated the relationship between such patterns and the stylized gestures of ballet.

The commonly expressed view that Copland's "popular" works of the thirties are in some way a denial, even a betrayal, of his earlier integrity would thus seem to be illusory. The simpler style of the ballets and film music does not belie the techniques of Copland's previous "abstract" pieces, though the music's deliberate lack of progression or development may be less disturbing when allied to immediately recognizable, folk-like tunes and to physical action or visual drama. Certainly the folky vein of Copland's ballets is not an evasion of the steel girders—within which he so miraculously discovers a human warmth—of the Piano Variations: for he sees the prairie as symbol of the irremediable loneliness of big cities, the hymn as symbol of the religious and domestic security that urban man has lost. The difference between the ballets and the abstract works consists, that is, rather in the nature of the material than in the treatment of it. The melodies, deriving from and often directly quoting hill-billy tunes or American

[2] "During these years I began to feel an increasing dissatisfaction with the relations of the music-loving public and the living composer. The old 'special' public of the modern music concerts had fallen away, and the conventional concert public continued apathetic or indifferent to anything but the established classics. It seemed to me that composers were in danger of working in a vacuum. Moreover, an entirely new public for music had grown up around the radio and phonograph. It made no sense to ignore them and to continue writing as though they did not exist. I felt it was worth the effort to see if I couldn't say what I had to say in the simplest possible terms."—Copland's autobiographical sketch.

Puritan hymnody, are more diatonically stable than the bony or sinewy fragments of the Variations; but the phrases still tend to be short and repetitive, capable of treatment in Copland's "geometric" manner. The rhythms, influenced by bar-parlour stomps—by a primitive rural environment rather than by the sophistications of urban jazz— again lend themselves to Copland's development by "dissection" and reintegration rather than by cumulative growth. The harmonies appropriate to the diatonic and modal tunes are naturally less tense and elliptical than those of the Variations, and have more of the conventional sense of progression. The harmonic movement is again, however, immensely slow compared with the melodic and rhythmic animation; and Copland's fondness for ellisions of tonic, dominant and subdominant chords isolates simultaneously, in a moment of time, the basic norms of progression in European music. This harmonic feature is also typical of Stravinsky, of course: though Copland associates it particularly with the triadic formation of cowboy songs and Puritan hymns—and with the empty spaciousness of the prairie.

It is significant that the first of Copland's "Wild West" ballets, *Billy the Kid* (1938), has for theme the conflict between Society and the Outlaw. Billy was a historical figure who, at the age of eleven, stabbed a man who shot his mother in a brawl. Later he shoots a man who accuses him of cheating at cards; there is a gun battle between Billy's gang and the Sheriff's representatives in the course of which Billy is captured and gaoled. He escapes from prison, however, and joins his Mexican sweetheart in the solitude of the desert. He is betrayed to the Sheriff by an Indian guide; the Law closes in on him in the silence of the night, and he is shot by the Sheriff as he lights a cigarette. The ballet concludes as it began with a march of the pioneers, moving westward with the Sheriff at their head.

While this myth seems like a moral tale, the music complicates our response to it, for it reveals the Outlaw as at least in part the Hero. Billy is against the world because the world's hubbub destroyed the basic human relationship, that of son to mother; and his second murder was a protest against dishonesty. By far the nastiest music is given to Society —in the settler's savagely rhythmed, bitonal dance of triumph after Billy's capture; by far the most beautiful music is given to Billy as Outsider, when he is alone with his love in the desert, while the dark (and the Law) closes in. In this twilit music, full of telescoped tonics, dominants, and subdominants, the music's pulse almost comes to a stop. The bare, open texture becomes the emptiness of the desert and an emptiness in the human heart, the forces that destroy love; while Billy's humanity is represented by a slow waltz version of the cowboy tune "Come wrangle yer bronco", rendered forlornly tender by unexpected suspensions and hiatuses in the phrasing, because the life of simple fellowship which the tune stands for is torn and broken:

EXAMPLE 6

There is not, however, a straightforward opposition between Billy and the World. At the beginning the settler's music is dignified and noble, the social-hop music sturdily vigorous. Only in the middle do we see how the "public" values may conflict with the fulfilment of the private life; only at the death-scene, when the music so remarkably deepens in effect, do we see Billy as a tragic figure. At the very end the World comes into its own again; the final march returns to the dignity of the opening, though we cannot hear it with the same ears, now that we know what is at stake.

The second ballet *Rodeo* offers a comic version of the Outsider theme, this time with a happy ending for the cowgirl heroine. *Appalachian Spring* (1944), the third of the ballets and the most beautiful, is entirely positive and a ritualistic rather than a dramatic piece. A note on the score says that it "depicts a pioneer celebration in spring around a newly-built farm house in the Pennsylvania hills in the early part of the last century. The bride-to-be and the young farmer-husband enact the emotions, joyful and apprehensive, aroused by their new domestic partnership. From time to time an older neighbour represents the rocky confidence of experience. A revivalist and his followers remind the new householders of the strange and terrible aspects of human fate. At the end the couple are left quiet and strong in their new house". The prelude's marvellous evocation of spring in the world and in the heart is achieved through an open texture, a luminous scoring, and a harmony of telescoped concords exactly comparable with the techniques of Copland's earlier abstract pieces; and the "quiet and strength" of the noble conclusion occur as variations on the Shaker tune "'Tis the gift to be simple" gradually slow the music down to immobility. As at the conclusion of *Billy the Kid*, we hear the folk-tune against the background of silence and space; but whereas in *Billy* the tune seemed wan and lost in the emptiness, the Shaker tune remains strong in its simplicity, and we accept its dissolution into time and space as naturally as we accept the cycle of the seasons. *Billy the Kid* stresses the heart's loneliness; *Appalachian Spring* stresses the love—the togetherness—that can make emptiness meaningful, or transform it from threat to comfort.

Similar musical images may be found in Copland's film music. In the threshing scene from *Our Town*, for instance, telescoped triads suggest vast space and also the quietude of evening light; both of which become a serenity within the heart. In the score for the dog-shooting scene in *Of Mice and Men*, on the other hand, the forlornly repeated flute tune, poised over telescoped diatonics, suggests loneliness and the cutting off of communion between creature and creature; and the music points the "universal" significance of the incident since it returns, in expanded form, at the play's climax, when poor Lennie has to be shot, as the dog had been. Coplandesque techniques express irremediable isolation in cinematic terms in the scene wherein Curley's wife sits at a table, playing with ice-cubes in a glass. The sound suggests a subdued waltz tune, a banal murmuring monotonously repeated by cello and piano in low register, accompanied by the clink of glass, spoon and ice. In the next sequence, when the girl tries to seduce George, the waltz tune flits aimlessly through a number of keys until it finally skims fragilely over the guitar. The girl's wantonness and vacuousness, her boredom and exasperation with her jealous and bestial husband, her tawdriness and pitifulness, the pointlessness of her action are thus exquisitely suggested. Copland's characteristic techniques lend themselves equally well to moments of violence, as when Lennie, the giant simpleton, attacked with a whip by the viciously sadistic Curley, finally comes to his senses and crushes Curley's hand. The cracking of Curley's whip generates a snapping rhythm and bright, harshly instrumented concords peppered over the orchestra. These unrelated concords meet in an inverted resolution—an immense grinding discord when Lennie grips Curley's hand. The music collapses with Curley's prostrate figure.

The basic identity between Copland's "functional" and his "absolute" music—and between his rural and his urban manners—is indicated if one compares the final elegy over Lennie, or still more the elegy over Billy the Kid, with *Quiet City*, a short piece for trumpet, cor anglais and strings which he composed in 1939 from incidental music originally written for a play. Now the image derived from the play was that of the big city in the quiet of the night, through which a young Jewish boy, lonely among multitudes, sang of his sorrow on his jazz trumpet. In Copland's score the nervously agitated, highly declamatory trumpet solo is both Negroid in its blue notes and Jewish in its incantatory repetitions:

EXAMPLE 7

As it merges into cor anglais solo the (speech inflected) manner is not changed, but sounds, in the modified tone-colour, still more plangent. The solo voices of trumpet and cor anglais pierce through a dragging, limping string figure which evokes emptiness and isolation by precisely the same open intervals and telescoped concords as we have referred to in the "rural" pieces. It is worth noting, too, that Copland's earlier *Music for Radio*, composed in the heart of New York, as urban music for an industrial society, was given the subtitle *Saga of the Prairie* as the result of a competition for a descriptive title.

During the 1940s Copland's talent came to full maturity in a fusion of the uncompromising honesty of the Piano Variations with the more relaxed manner of his popular works. The key-piece is again a piano work, this time a Sonata (1939–41). The first movement uses the technique of the Variations in a harmonically less austere form. Again we have the brief figures, the "blue" false relations:

EXAMPLE 8

Again the phrases are split up into their component parts, producing a kind of inverted development-by-dissection, in which the texture gets thinner and thinner. Thus although the material here is directly comparable with the "American vernacular" of Harris's quicker movements, the treatment of it could hardly be more opposed to Harris's evolutionary growth. In Copland the buoyant upward lift of fourths, fifths and minor sevenths is pinned down by the immense slowness of the rhythmic and harmonic design: so that the energetic phrases seem curiously wistful, suggesting both man's ant-like energy and his ineluctable loneliness. When the original phrase comes back triple forte as recapitulation, it has somewhat the same effect as the Coda to the Variations: the music seems the grander, the more noble, because of the development's near-disintegration.

The Scherzo is built from a nagging, wedge-shaped figure which continually tries to "take off", but is always frustrated:

EXAMPLE 9

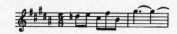

The more it fails to break away from its anchor—to reach the empty distance which is hinted at in its rising sixth—the angrier and the more hysterical it becomes. The sickening $\frac{5}{8}$ rocking sounds obsessive; and there is virtually no modulation until the music explodes with its frustrated fury. The trio is wavering, wandering, tentative, and diaphanous in texture; little fragments of song try to emerge out of the oscillating sixths, but peter out in inanition. Then very softly, "with suppressed excitement", the wedge figure comes back and there is a modified "da capo", ending with a distant promise of B major radiance and an augmented statement of the wedge in canon. The tension seems to be in part released by the final luminous chord of the added sixth, in second inversion.

It is not an accident that these two movements of frustrated energy should lead—by way of a strange reminiscence of the first movement, all telescoped tonics and dominants, like a sublimated hill-billy stomp—into an Andante which is a quintessential expression of immobility. The tender, cool melody, with its widely spaced fourths and fifths, floats out of the embryonic song of the Scherzo's trio. Its delayed, tentatively dotted rhythm is a Copland "fingerprint" that sounds like an infinitely remote echo of the world's bustle—a frail, disembodied boogie-woogie. But the melody does not become a self-contained song; its life is suspended above empty harmonies that pulse as unobtrusively as a heart-beat. Though the pendulum swings wider at the climax, the regularity of the beat is never broken—not even when the machine-clangour of the first movement's false relations returns at the pendulum's apex. Then gradually the music runs down like a clock, sinking in tonality to A flat with flat seventh (a tone below the original modal B flat minor). There is no more modulation and virtually no more movement, as the texture gets still sparer and more widely spaced, dissolving away into space and eternity. Echoes of the first movement's grinding false relations sound from a remote distance, absorbed into the emptiness:

EXAMPLE 10

The music that here stills the heart's agitation is closely related to the film score to Wilder's *Our Town*, which is also associated with images of vast space. Its serenity is the more impressive and (to most of us) moving because Copland is not a mystic like Ruggles, or a primitive like Harris.

The Violin Sonata of 1943, though apparently a slighter work, carries on at the point where the crucial Piano Sonata ceases; for its quiet happiness—a quality rare in twentieth-century music—seems a positive flowering from the stillness of the piano work's conclusion. It opens with a rarefied version of Copland's New England hymnody, the telescoped tonics, dominants and subdominants supporting the "freely singing" thirds and fifths of the violin with radiant confidence. But the phrases, though lyrical, are characteristically brief; and the "form" of the movement is an attempt to build up, from the fragments, a more extended line. An allegro motive—a rising sixth, two falling thirds and two rising fourths—emerges out of the hymn; and the development consists of an investigation of all the permutations of this figure. The music alternates between passages wherein the violin lyricism sings in the brief passivity, accompanied by the simplest diatonic concords: and passages wherein a mainly two-part texture, vernal yet tinglingly dissonant, tries to build up rhythmic animation and tonal movement (the music modulates rapidly, but in an architectural cycle of fifths, not dramatically). The movement concludes with a restatement of the introduction: so between the moments of hymnic tranquillity the nervous bustle of the permutations of the reiterative, upward-tending phrase is enclosed with an effect that is oddly timeless. Here, the inner tension involves a kind of blithe buoyancy rather than violence. As in the Piano Sonata's first two movements there is still, however, a contrast between the energetic desire of the phrase to prance upwards, and the tortoise-like slowness of the harmonic and metrical pattern that will not allow it to.

The slow movement, similar in mood and texture to the Piano Sonata's finale, with a slowly swinging pendulum and telescoped triads, is short and interludial. The air's off-beat entries—accompanied by a static form of the first movement's sixths and fourths—sound hurt and lonely as well as tender; the warm, stepwise-moving melody seems to float, disembodied, over the distant pedal. Because this slow movement is not a consummation, it can be followed by a movement which, in its jaunty rhythmic obliquities, strident, cleanly patterned tunes and episodic, rondo-like organization, is directly related to the shanty-town music of "popular" works like *El Salón México*. But the precision of the texture now gives the popular style a kind of sublimatory quality: so that the elided tonics, dominants and subdominants of the allargando passage can lead into a most beautiful coda referring back to the first movement's hymnic introduction. The violin sings its fifths and thirds "freely", while the piano makes ghostly references to the last movement's dance-hall stomp, and the work fades out on widely spaced twelfths and tenths in G major.

It is interesting that this phase of Copland's career should have concluded with two large-scale vocal works: *In the Beginning* for mixed chorus "a cappella" (1947), and *Twelve Poems of Emily Dickinson* for solo voice and piano (1949–50). Up to this point Copland had written very little for the human voice; and since he started—as we have seen—from a denial of the "natural" principle of lyrical growth, this is hardly surprising. While these two works are far from being traditional in their handling of vocal resources, they manifest a remarkable development of Copland's speech-inflected declamation towards lyricism, and in this sense represent a deepening maturity. The text of *In the Beginning* is from the book of Genesis. A mezzo-soprano solo serves as narrator, and the story of the Creation is told in antiphonal dialogue between the narrator and the people, as represented by the chorus. The form is a vast rondo, each section being introduced by the narrator, extended by the chorus (sometimes in dialogue with the narrator), and rounded off by a refrain for each of the seven days of creation. The declamatory part ("in a gentle, narrative manner, like reading a familiar and oft-told story") suggests both the Negro preacher and the Jewish cantor; the repetitions of falling major thirds, balanced by rising minor thirds, have an almost hypnotic effect as they reappear, between the days of creation, throughout the work. The material of the choral parts is usually derived from the declamatory phrases. The lines are not sustained, but move in brief periods, following speech rhythm in a kind of declamatory counterpoint, but building into ever more complex patterns as the days of creation unfold. The familiar open intervals and telescoped chords are all diatonic; but though each section tends to be tonally non-developing, the transitions between the sections are extremely rapid and often enharmonic. This modulatory freedom—unusual in Copland's music—subtly suggests the burgeoning of life from the void.

After the third day the speech-movement of the solo line becomes jazzily syncopated at the reference to "lights", while the chorus blaze into long sforzando notes. This increasing animation sweeps us through the fourth and fifth days and leads to a big unisonal climax—a vast-leaping expansion of the original declamatory phrase—at God's decision to make man in his own image. The "multiplying" of created nature is expressed by way of level homophonic movement and of a long solo, built from a tonally oscillating melodic version of the descending thirds, over an F sharp pedal. At the seventh day the "refrain" music becomes the main theme, for God's contemplation is now the universe. The coda, beginning with a "breathless" unaccompanied monody, builds up first in primitive organum, then in solidly sonorous homophony, with swiftly shifting modulations, as God breathes into the dust and man becomes "a living soul". Telescoped triads in eight parts culminate in a tremendous chord of E flat—a semitone up from the declamatory opening.

In the Beginning is a remarkably impressive work, though it is not, in its deliberate primitivism, in the main stream of Copland's development. The Emily Dickinson songs, on the other hand, are among the most central of his achievements; and we can understand how the isolation, the innocence and (in Blake's sense) the terrifying honesty of this strange hermit-poet would be likely to release the deepest aspects of Copland's experience. In nineteenth-century New England, Emily Dickinson wrote of the isolated heart and the contagion of the world: of the necessity for, and the impossibility of, human love: of love's complement, death: of man alone, against the background of Nature and eternity. In the mid–twentieth century, Aaron Copland, at Sneden's Landing, New York, set some of these poems to music which is a lyrical distillation of both his rural and his urban loneliness.

The first song, "Nature, the gentlest mother", deals with the two poles of experience: Nature and human love on the one hand, Eternity and death on the other. The "crystalline" piano texture of the beginning, with its twittering bird and animal noises, has Copland's familiar luminosity; but the sonority is no longer sharp and metallic. The spacing of the fourths and sevenths produces a warm radiance as well as a pristine freshness; and when the voice enters, its phrases, though still short and declamatory, are shaped as tenderly—in their falling thirds and fourths—as a caress. The piano texture glitters as the words refer to Nature's variety, until at the word "flower" the pentatonic chitterings blossom into multiple trills. Then, over a double B flat pedal very high and very low on the keyboard, we return to humanity, as Nature gives her benediction to the sleeping children. The song concludes—like the Piano Sonata—with a gradual slowing down of life's momentum, as Nature "wills silence everywhere". The expansion of the vocal line—both in time values and in pitch relationships—again equates emptiness with peace:

EXAMPLE II

The fourth song, "The World feels dusty", concerns the vindication of death by human love. It is another of Copland's "pendulum" pieces: though this time the swing of eternity, built on dissonantly telescoped concords, becomes a compassionate sigh. The elided chords grow fierce when the poem reflects that "Flags vex a dying face"; but return to an infinite tenderness to tell us how a friend's hand "cools like the rain". The "lost" wistfulness of the added sixth effect is soon intensified by acute false relations. The song fades out unresolved, but with the drooping thirds now rising. The tonality, modally ambiguous throughout, ends in equivocation, the voice's low, B minorish A sharp changing enharmonically to B flat, accompanied by a swaying pendulum chord that seems to contain implications of E flat, C, G minor and possibly D.

The twelfth and final song, "The Chariot", looks back to the tremendous declamatory song that forms the cycle's climax. This seventh song, "Sleep is supposed to be", had concerned the relationship between sleep and eternity; and Copland's "suspended" boogie-rhythm, widely arpeggiated vocal line, and metallic bell-clanging climax indicate how the song's vision of the "break of day" parallels the deepest, most revelatory moments of Copland's mature instrumental music, especially the Piano Sonata. The grandeur of this song is a kind of rhetoric that complements the American innocence; in the last song, however, the same theme and the same sublimated boogie rhythm acquire a tragic dignity and—as Copland puts it—a "quiet grace". Here the boogie rhythm, which is in origin the world's bustle, becomes the gentle ambling of Death's carriage. The composer, like the poet, accepts Death on terms of courteous familiarity; sees the gambolling schoolchildren alongside the "swelling of the ground" that is both a tomb and a pregnant womb. For the first time in the cycle, rhythm attains a gently regular pulse which flowers into sustained melody: in which the occasional big leaps suggest not strain, but freedom. The final *tierce de picardie* is an ultimate consummation of the Dorian B minor.

During the last decade Copland has to some extent returned to the dichotomy between "serious" and "popular" works which characterized his early years. The Piano Quartet, written immediately after the Emily Dickinson songs, takes up again the highly personal type of serialism that Copland had explored in the Variations; and this trend reaches apotheosis in the tremendous Piano Fantasy (1955–7) which Copland must have intended as a companion piece to the Variations. It is a piano work in one movement lasting half an hour: in which all the material is derived from the opening phrase, which Copland himself describes as "declamatory". The technique is again one of variation or rather dissection and reintegration; and again the harmonic and rhythmic movement is vastly slow as compared with the variety—now fierce, now brisk, now tender, now desolate—of the contributory phrases. While the piece is identical in principle with the Variations, it is not a mere inflation of that work. At least its gargantuan proportions, its superb exploitation of the piano's sonorous resources, are justified by the emotional pressure behind them. To create so long a work out of such brief and apparently fragmentary material is a heroic achievement. While the music has not the comprehensive humanity of Ives's two sonatas, it has a comparable grandeur that comes, in this case, from its acceptance of the spirit's isolation. The grandeur remains when the music fades into the emptiness of the stellar spaces and, after a long silence, the bells of the opening fourths sound in eternity. The Fantasy—the third of Copland's major piano works—is also the greatest: for it fuses the stark energy of the Variations with the still serenity of the Sonata's last movement.

Also in the mid-fifties Copland attempted—in his first full-scale opera *The Tender Land*—a comparable ripening of his "popular" vein. He wanted to create a folk opera in the sense that it concerns ordinary American folk and a common psychological situation. The story, set in the Mid-West of the thirties, at the spring harvest and at graduation time, tells of a lower-middle-class, mother-dominated teenage girl who wants to "graduate", in every sense, into life. She does so, painfully, with the help of two strangers from the outer world; and in the process is simultaneously hurt and absolved. The fable is simple and also—as presented by Horace Everitt—true and touching, if in the expository first act somewhat unnecessarily protracted. If the opera appears less convincing as a whole than a minor masterpiece like *Appalachian Spring*—which also deals with the year's renewal and the tension between private love and communal tradition—that is only because it attempts more. In the ballet, the stylization of common life can be done in mime, so the tricky elements involved in a verbal-lyrical presentation of everyday experience do not arise; moreover, because of the subservience to lyrical movement Copland can—as we have seen—readily create an equilibrium of brief lyrical phrases, rhythmic ostinati and triadic harmonies, breaking into sustained lyricism only when he quotes or refers to traditional material. In a sung opera, however, the lines must expand in vocal lyricism; must seek the lyrical-harmonic climax which has never been typical of Copland's music—not even of the Emily Dickinson songs. When he seeks such expatiation and climax in the love duets and other ensemble numbers of the opera, the music, though theatrically effective and well placed, does not quite ring true.

To put it another way, one could say that while he marvellously conveys the yearning within adolescence, he is less convincing in dealing with the pain of growing to maturity. The fulfilment, in terms of personal relationships, has not the absolute rightness of the more detached, epic, and ritualistic manner of *Appalachian Spring*; the lyricism of *The Tender Land* ever so slightly adulterates the integrity which *Appalachian Spring* shares with the "absolute" works, perhaps by unconscious compromise with some conventional image of what a popular work ought to be. Yet Copland genuinely has "the gift to be simple", which is a gift as rare today as it is valuable; and his desire to fulfil this simplicity in lyrical and vocal terms sprang from a desire to go further than he had gone in his earlier "popular" works. In particular, we may see *The Tender Land* as an extension into adolescent experience of Copland's school opera *The Second Hurricane*. Despite a slightly false-naïve, preachy libretto this piece is wonderfully successful at expressing by way of sharply scored, bouncing phrases in clipped, simplified jazz rhythms the American child's innocent assurance: while it also conveys, through the rocking, static ostinati and modal flat sevenths of a number such as Gyp's song, the child's complementary lonesomeness. Because they are childlike, the melodic phrases, whether vivacious or wistful, cannot develop; *The Tender Land* makes similar phrases *grow*—and it can do so because its dramatic theme is a more human extension of the somewhat jejune morality of the earlier piece. In carrying us over the threshold of childhood, *The Tender Land* becomes a "popular" equivalent to the intimate lyricism of the Emily Dickinson songs. Though the opera may not be a success in the same way as is the chamber work, it is a more important piece in Copland's career and in modern music than its unpretentious nature might suggest.

It is, however, interesting that the most expansively lyrical and balladlike of the Emily Dickinson songs—the one that approximates most closely to the lyricism of the opera—is the least characteristic and one of the least convincing. (Though it is a personal love song the words—"Heart, we will forget him"—turn out to be an admission of love's impossibility.) Perhaps this suggests that Copland is unlikely to explore further in this direction: that, having become a kind of father-figure to American music, he will in his "late" phase devote himself to works concerned, like the Piano Fantasy, with the uncompromising integrity of his personal vision. We come back to the contrast between him and Ives. The elder composer, though, in fact, he had no public, accepted the world in which he lived, and made out of it the music that seemed to him to be inherent in it. Creatively he behaved, that is, as though he were at one with his society: though he knew, and demonstrated in his music, that in the last resort the unity beneath the chaos can be perceived only by a transcendental act. In this sense he was a religious humanist. Copland, on the other hand, started from—and has perhaps returned to—the individual sensibility alone in a mechanized world: from an awareness of disintegration and of the necessity for a personal ("cubist") reintegration. His attempt to come to terms with the world, in his ballets and film scores, was consciously separate from his "personal" works, though, as we have seen, it was deeply related to them. Out of the denial of lyricism and of spontaneous growth which was the essence of his honesty, he won through to a kind of serenity: but that serenity is in no sense—like the polymorphous texture of Ives's music or the lyrically evolutionary texture of Harris's —religious. It is not so much a dissolution as a suspension of move- ment: a running down of Time's clock as the pulse beats slower, the simple harmonies become more statically interlocked, the melodies become the quiet reiteration of one or two (usually falling) intervals. Verbally, this peculiarly American experience—which is not un- connected with America's geographic immensity—has been described by Scott Fitzgerald in a famous passage from *The Last Tycoon*:

> I looked back as we crossed the crest of the foothills—with the air so clear you could see the leaves on Sunset Mountains two miles away. It's startling to you sometimes—just air, unobstructed, uncomplicated air.

This is an accurate description of the conclusion of Copland's Piano Sonata and Piano Fantasy; and, in contrast with the screwed-up ner- vous and physical energy of the big city, the emptiness is a positive experience, not merely a negation.

It is not, perhaps, an accident that there should be precise parallels between Copland's musical achievement and the visual arts, and here again he may be compared and contrasted with Ives. The sprawling, amorphous texture of Ives's music is like the early American scene itself, with both the chaos and the dynamic movement that came from pioneer migration. In accepting his environment, chaotic though it was, as a basis for the creation of order, Ives resembles another heroic figure, Frank Lloyd Wright, who insisted on the organic relationship between Man and Nature precisely because, in a new world, man seemed to have asserted his whim, rather than his will, with promiscu- ous blatancy. Copland, on the other hand, started from an admission that the only order that now seemed valid was that imposed from within the personal sensibility: so that the "geometric" pattern-making of the Variations is related to the geometry of abstract painting in the same way as his elongations or foreshortenings of phrase or figure may be related to the distortions of cubism. The order implies the imprisonment of dynamic movement: as does the configuration of the American city. In each case it is a geometric or mathematical order, crystalline rather than cellular: a static construction rather than a living organism. It is significant that the New York skyline is said to have had considerable influence upon the visual abstraction of Mondrian.

But the apparent "constriction" of this personal order becomes a kind of liberation, releasing us into the free air and the white light: and reminding us that, though the experience reaches its apotheosis in big city life, it has its roots in the American past, no less than does Ives's—or Whitman's or Melville's—all-inclusiveness. In the rectangularity of early American architecture we can see the influence of the hard, sharp American light, with deep shadows and clean angles, and can trace the relationship between the flat elevation and the open plan on the one hand, the razor-blade edge of sawn wood on the other. Although Copland is essentially an "original"—and it is part of his representatively American significance that he should be such—the texture of his music has points in common with the painting of a nineteenth-century master such as J. S. Copley, who gave so sharply linear a reinterpretation to baroque or rococo flamboyance, even when he was painting portraits.

Copland is not a "great" composer—perhaps not even a great composer *in potentia*, like Ives. But he is a very important composer in twentieth-century history, for he is the first artist to define precisely, in sound, an aspect of our urban experience. There is a beautiful Appalachian folk-song called *Nottamin Town* which is now a children's song, though it did not begin life as such. In it the singer tells how "in Nottamin Town not a soul would look up, not a soul would look down" to show him the way, so that—in almost Blakean imagery—he set himself down

> on a hard, hot, cold-frozen stone,
> Ten thousand around me, yet I was alone;
> Took my hat in my hands for to keep my head warm,
> Ten thousand got drownded that never were born.

There is no music which conveys this big-city experience more honestly than Copland's: which is more compassionately human in its acceptance of spiritual isolation: or which attains, through tension, a deeper calm. In his music we can see the neat, bland-eyed, rugged-souled Americans of a Copley portrait—when they have lived through the nervous and physical stresses to which a machine-age has submitted them.

V

The Pioneer's energy and the Artist's order: Elliott Carter

> Out of what one sees and hears and out
> Of what one feels, who could have thought to make
> So many selves, so many sensuous worlds,
> As if the air, the midday air, was swarming
> With the metaphysical changes that occur
> Merely in living as and where we live.

WALLACE STEVENS: *L'Esthetique du Mal*

There are, we have seen, two main "positives" in the evolution of American music in the twentieth century. One we may define as pioneer heroism: Ives's desire to make anew the toughness, power, copiousness, triviality and grandeur of the American scene and the American spirit. The other we may define as the search for order from authenticity: Copland's attempt to reintegrate, in a kind of musical cubism, the disintegrated fragments of the present. The two complementary modes have their essential techniques. Thus Ives's music, in accepting the chaos of the external world, accepts, too, the eclectic variety of the traditional and untraditional materials of music: but in so far as it re-creates them, it tends to liberate them into a polymorphous, polymodal, polyrhythmic, polyharmonic flux, wherein the "outer" life and the "inner" life become one. Copland, on the other hand, makes what he can of the broken fragments of the present; there is no "transcendental" re-creation flowing into non-tonal polyphony, no continuous lyricism, no mystical element in the loneliness that becomes a kind of peace. Copland's experience is the more limited, and also the "later"; it belongs, we have suggested, to the Big City which emerged out of Ives's America.

A third stage in the American musical evolution is approached in the work of Elliott Carter, wherein the values represented by Ives and Copland begin to come to terms. Born in 1908, and also a New Englander, he shares with Ives a multifarious energy, an awareness of contradictory realms of experience, of life's protean mutability. Unlike Ives, however, he is not content to accept life's incompleteness, but would impose upon it something like Copland's disciplined order—without Copland's limitation of emotional range. On the face of it, it would seem that one can have Ives's virtues or Copland's, but not both at once. Of its very nature, such a compromise is an undertaking of extreme difficulty, and Carter admits that his music is difficult, both to perform and to listen to. None the less, in the evolution of American music, the attempt at compromise had to be made; and Carter's historical importance is undeniable, whatever conclusions one may come to as to the ultimate value of his compositions.

Carter was a comparatively slow starter and probably only by hindsight can one discover, in his earlier work, hints of the remarkable developments to come. His early vocal music, for instance, is Copland-esque, with declamatory rather than lyrical phrases, built on fourths and minor sevenths, and with open, resonantly spaced textures; it differs from Copland mainly in having a more normal, traditional sense of harmonic and tonal progression. In the *Pastoral* for viola and piano (1940) one can first sense the germ of his later music: for though the texture still owes much to Copland and is still fourth-founded both melodically and harmonically, the extreme rhythmic fluidity and the continuous linear evolution suggest Ives. One would not say that the music betrays Ives's influence, for it remains somewhat bare and austere, without Ives's copious variety. None the less, it is Ives's kind of music rather than Copland's; and it is significant that the flowing texture attains, as climax, to a quasi-improvisatory cadenza.

Carter emerges as a major composer with the Piano Sonata of 1945–6: a large-scale work which demonstrably combines elements from the piano sonatas of both Ives and Copland, while achieving a powerful individuality. The nature of the material reminds us of Copland,[1] both in the declamatory opening phrase, exploiting wide-ranging piano sonorities, and also in the tingling, luminously spaced part-writing of the fourth-dominated "scorrevole" sections. But the methods whereby these contrasted materials are developed are unlike Copland and much closer to Ives: for as in an Ives sonata the motives interact "polymorphously" and are transmuted in the process. So the static, steely, monumental sound of Copland-like piano declamation:

[1] Most of Carter's earlier music suggests, too, that he admires Stravinsky: though the Russian's influence on him is probably not direct, but—by way of Copland—second-hand.

EXAMPLE I

flows into a "liquid" texture related to Ives's transcendental polyphony; becoming in the process increasingly free in tonality:

EXAMPLE 2

The personal element in this Ivesian evolution is perhaps centred in
Carter's sense of rhythm. The work is written—like the comparable
passages in Ives—without regular bar-lines, and achieves its characteristic flow because, though Carter gives crochet equals 132 as a unit, he
seems to think in terms of the semiquaver (which equals 548). This
tendency to think of rhythm in its smallest rather than largest units is a
salient feature of American music which was commented on, many
years ago, by Roy Harris. The passage[2] has been much quoted, and too
much, perhaps, has been made of it. None the less, it is true that there
is a distinction between the use of small metrical units in irregular
combinations such as we find in European composers like Stravinsky

---

[2] "Our rhythmic sense is less symmetrical than the European rhythmic
sense. European musicians are trained to think of rhythm in its largest
common denominator, while we are born with a feeling for its smallest
units. That is why the jazz boys, chained to an unimaginative commercial
routine which serves only crystallized symmetrical dance rhythms, are
continually breaking out into superimposed rhythmic variations which
were not written in the music. This asymmetrical balancing of rhythmic
phrases is in our blood; it is not in the European blood. . . . Children skip
and walk that way—our conversation would be strained and monotonous
without such rhythmic nuances."

and Bartók, and the irregular rhythms of Ives, Copland, Harris, and
jazz; and the implications of this difference are consciously explored in
Carter's music, beginning with the Piano Sonata. In the "scorrevole"
sections of the first movement one might say that the irregularities
suggest the displacements of jazz improvisation *with the metrical beat left
out*—and not even implied. It is this which gives the music its vigour:
and also its quality of springing elation. There is nothing in European
music to which one can compare it, except possibly the combination of
madrigalian polyphonic rhythm with jazz syncopation in the later
music of Michael Tippett.

As in Ives's sonatas, the contradictions in Carter's sonata remain
unresolved at the first movement's conclusion; and after an ecstatic,
toccata-like cadenza the tonality sinks abruptly from the basic B to
B flat. The second (and last) movement separates the declamatory and
tocca features of the first movement into two sections ("andante" and
"allegro giusto") which are independently developed, yet telescoped.
The andante transforms the declamatory motive into a Coplandesque
hymn, though it contains more harmonic movement than is common
in Copland. The allegro starts from rather fragmentary phrases thinly
scored: again a Copland-like sonority. In evolution it acquires, however, some of the characteristics of Ives's nature-polyphony; and the
two modes finally become one in the impressive coda, where the
metallic clangour of Copland's Piano Sonata (especially the first movement) has accumulated also something of the hymnic grandeur of the
conclusion to Ives's First Sonata:

EXAMPLE 3

Though this thrilling coda is still dependent on other composers, it
is certainly not parasitic; and its fusion of the "urban" with the "religious" indicates the direction in which Carter's talent was to develop. A
large-scale work which he produced in the following year (1947) was
a further aid towards self-realization, for being a theatre piece, with an

explicit programme, the ballet *The Minotaur* called for a relatively direct approach. Carter had long been preoccupied with classical mythology and, as a young man, had written extensive incidental music for Sophocles' *Philoctetes* (1933) and Plautus' *Mostellaria* (1936). It probably was not fortuitous that Carter chose the Minotaur story, for the violence, the sense of bewilderment in the episode of the maze, and the expiatory theme are in tune with American as well as Greek mythology. Because the music must become manifest in terms of physical movement on a stage, the rhythms cannot be as complex as those of the Piano Sonata; but the tension of opposing rhythms can and does remain, and is rendered the more potent because it is reinforced by (Stravinskian) harmonic tensions far more acute than anything in the piano sonorities of the sonata. Along with this goes a development in melodic approach. The Piano Sonata, though continuously evolutionary, is not remarkable for purely melodic invention. The themes of *The Minotaur*, on the other hand, are strong, long, and deeply expressive: consider the undulating flute cantilena over Pasiphae's "heartbeat" rhythm, or the noble expansion of the Coplandesque lyrical phrases in the final chaconne. Indeed, all the energetic, Copland-like motives tend, in this work, towards a sustained harmonic impetus which also extends into lyricism. Perhaps projection in theatrical terms was necessary before the violence within Carter's experience could be released. Certainly there is a comparably "dramatic" release in the most recent of his vocal works, *Emblems* (1947), for chorus and piano, to poems of Allen Tate. In this remarkable piece the music's extreme difficulty is justified by its dynamic power; and most significantly, it is the closest Carter had yet approached to the uncompromising immediacy of Ives. It is also Carter's most "American" piece—especially in its Ivesian use of rhythmic displacement; the poem deals with the American pioneers.

But if dramatic projection was a necessary stage in Carter's development, this was not because he is naturally a vocal, let alone a theatrical, composer. Though (like Beethoven) an intensely dramatic artist, he is (again like Beethoven) concerned with the drama of the inner life; and experience with ostensibly theatrical techniques was merely a step towards treating an "abstract" musical argument in dramatic terms. We can see this in the Sonata for cello and piano of 1948: a work which marks the beginning of Carter's mature phase. Here the drama is inherent in the nature of the instruments themselves; they are the protagonists—one a stringed instrument of lyrical character, the other a (basically harmonic and percussive) piano. The instruments' incompatibility becomes a virtue, for they are "personified" as independent identities which have to seek a relationship. Although this approach is Ivesian, the idiom is now authentically Carter's. Consider, for instance, this tremendous paragraph:

EXAMPLE 4

Here there are three sharply disparate elements: the thudding bass, separated by silences; the regular yet surging quintuplets of the piano's right hand; and the cello's lyrical-declamatory line which, compared with the piano part's regularity, seems rhapsodic, especially since it usually comes in just before or just after the beat. Two other features should be noticed, one tonal, one rhythmic. The music is in incessant linear movement and the tonality is as free as the evolution of the lines. Like much of Ives's music, it is not a-tonal but polymodal, and the freedom of tonal movement complements the flexibility of line; for Carter, as for Ives, life is movement, and in this sense his mature work is at the opposite pole to Copland's. (In this passage the basic tonality is B major, which is, however, telescoped with D major and G sharp minor, which becomes enharmonically A flat.)

Although Carter has employed key signatures in none of his works subsequent to the Cello Sonata, his sense of tonal direction remains strong even when his polymodal complexity and harmonic tension increase. This attempt to discipline creative exuberance has a rhythmic counterpart, too: as we can see from the use in the above example of the device that has come to be known as "metrical modulation". "Device" is a crude term, for the technique arose spontaneously out of Carter's creative practice. He wished to preserve the sense of almost improvisatory freedom that the polyrhythms and continually transmuted metrical groupings gave to his music, while establishing a relationship between the parts and the whole. He therefore began to think of groups of (say) three or five notes against a duple metre not as cross-rhythms, but as new units in their own right, which can, by process of transition, become a new basic rhythm. Thus, in the above passage, the five-pulse of the first two bars changes into quintuplets in $\frac{4}{4}$ time; and it is easy to see that by such means the most subtle and flexible changes of tempo may be notated, wherein the evolutionary freedom becomes not opposed to, but a means towards, structural control.[3]

The Cello Sonata was the first work in which Carter explored these possibilities; and the exploration is still, perhaps, a little tentative, powerful though the work is. The fulfilment of Carter's originality—of his fusion of the apparently contradictory modes we have associated with Ives and Copland—occurs in the immense String Quartet which he completed in 1951. Although in a number of sections, this forty-five minute work is really in one vast movement evolved by linear and rhythmic permutations or "modulation". The first section is headed Fantasia, which we are probably meant to interpret both in the technical sense as a polyphonic discourse of four instruments (as in the seventeenth-century fantasia), and also in a philosophical-psychological sense as a seemingly spontaneous overflow of the fancy or creative imagination. We begin with an exposition wherein each instrument enters in turn, each with its distinctive material, appropriate to its own genius, separate from, indeed opposed to, that of the others. Metrical modulations lead us from the cello's solo at crochet equals 72 (tonally

[3] A very simple instance would be this: music in $\frac{2}{4}$ time, four quavers to the bar; the quavers become quintuplets; the time signature changes to $\frac{5}{8}$ at the quintuplet speed. When it returns to $\frac{2}{4}$—and perhaps to the original or related material—the speed will be proportionally faster. Arithmetical gradations of speed, that is, are dependent on the linear behaviour of the music; the proportions are part of the expression. In his later work, notably the string quartets, Carter employs different metrical modulations in independent parts, simultaneously, producing effects of extreme freedom by means of feats of prodigious organizational skill.

oscillating between E major and C minor) to crochet equals 120, when all four voices are proceeding in their independently contradictory directions:

EXAMPLE 5

Like Ives's "Concord" Sonata, the quartet thus opens at the point of maximum complexity—at the most extreme expression of life's multiplicity and diversity. The parts evolve, unbroken, by continuous melodic and rhythmic mutation. Though the music is all polyphony, there is virtually no *literal* repetition but, as in Ives, all growth and continuity, like the life-process itself.

As the lines grow more lyrical, impelled by a long, swaying cantilena in ¾ on the viola, they seem increasingly to seek to live together—to achieve, in Beethovenian as well as Ivesian terms, unity out of multiplicity. So, while still preserving their independence, the lines increasingly interact the one on the other until, at bar 290 *et seq.*, they attain an almost unisonal climax in triplet figuration, through which the viola sings the still, off-beat oscillating theme which, in the exposition of contrarieties (bar 22 *et seq.*), had been associated with the first violin. After this there is a coda in which all four instruments play a kind of developing recapitulation of all the themes, each now keeping *consis-*

tently to its given pattern of fives, threes or sixes, over a rhythmically
level bass. The acute tension of the harmony is the direct consequence
of the linear and rhythmic independence; it is as though the attempt to
create unity out of contrariety leads to a frenzy of desperation, as in the
fugue of Beethoven's "Hammerklavier" Sonata.

The texture blows up with its inner tension: splinters, with another
metrical modulation, into semiquaver figuration, "allegro scorrevole",
to initiate what approximates to the Scherzo. The texture is now fragmentary and chromatic, disintegrative rather than reintegrative, so
there are no metrical modulations, no lyrical evolutions, in this section.
The part writing is, however, highly imitative, even—in Ives's manner
—quasi-serial, as though the splintering atoms must be held together,
saved from chaos, come what may.[4] And against this whirling atomi-
zation sounds, as trio to the Scherzo, an icy stillness: an immensely
slow, non-metrical succession of telescoped dissonances that remind us
both of Ives's music of the stellar spaces in *The Unanswered Question*
and also of Copland's music of the empty air, especially at the conclusion of the Piano Fantasy. The emptiness, being sharply dissonant, is
hostile, and brings no hint of peace, as it does in Copland. The Scherzo
returns and flickers whimperingly to nothingness:

EXAMPLE 6

It is at this point that Carter indicates a pause, and writes II above
the next passage of music. But this passage turns out to continue the
re-created recapitulation of the Scherzo at the point where it broke off,
and it is clear that there is really no break in the evolving structure of

---

[4] This passage, extraordinary as it is, is not entirely without precedent; we
may think of it as a most audacious development from the famous scamper-
ing-mice movement of Berg's *Lyric Suite*.

the quartet: a pause is indicated simply because players and audience need some respite in a work physically, intellectually and spiritually so strenuous. It seems probable, moreover, that Carter introduces the break at this point precisely because it is so unlikely: one can have no doubt, when the music starts again, that it is a continuation, not a beginning. This time the Scherzo peters out into the music of still dissonance; and with a metrical modulation to crochet equals 36 we reach an Adagio which is the emotional climax of the quartet.

As a result of the Scherzo's disintegration, its glimpse of the stellar spaces, we at least see more clearly. The multiple contrarieties—the *four* instruments that seem to be four poles of experience—are reduced to a dualism, viola and cello forming one unit, the two violins the other. Although the pulse is so slow as to be almost inapprehensible, the viola-cello unit is divided into rapid, irregular and agitated note-values, returning to something like the strenuous human activity of the cello's rhapsodic opening. The two violins, on the other hand, continue the glassy, cold, spatial music in a glintingly dissonant texture deprived of all sense of metrical accent by continual elisions and suspensions. Here is the transition from the viola-cello motive to the violins:

EXAMPLE 7

This duality has a close affinity with the real-transcendental opposition in Ives's *The Unanswered Question*, and also with the human energy-empty space opposition in Copland's Piano Sonata and Piano Fantasy. The difference is that for Ives, in that piece though not in all his work, the question *is* unanswered and in the Copland the only answer is silence: whereas Carter attempts to resolve the opposition. The agitated questions of viola and cello are heard against the stillness, and grow increasingly distraught as the violins descend lower in tessitura until the music becomes completely immobile: at which point the life-cycle starts again.

The four instruments regain their identities in music which recalls the quartet's opening, though it is not the same. This time the disparities flow into continuous triplet movement, forming a transitional passage that parallels the transition, after the break, from Scherzo to Adagio. There is then another (very brief) pause before the last movement, which is headed "Variations". The whole work has been variation—at least in Ives's sense of evolutionary mutation; the use of the term here would seem to indicate that a point of definition has been reached, in that—by way of the explicit dualism of the Adagio—the themes emerge in a less amorphous form. Certainly the long, winding $\frac{5}{4}$ theme introduced on the second violin reappears in recognizable shape intermittently: contains a hint of tonal stability against the music's perpetual flux: and leads to a passage in which the four parts move in shorter, more balanced periods and even homophonically (bar 52 *et seq.*). But the approach towards homophonic union does not bring rest; instead, it leads to a strange, numb sequence of non-metrical dissonances marked "non vibrato", wherein the tension seems to be locked in stasis, rather than resolved. In a sense the texture of the variations, as they proceed, becomes simpler because polyphonic-harmonic movement slowly gives way to a kind of heterophony of twos against threes against fours against fives:

EXAMPLE 8

through which shimmers a composite thread of melody. As in the first movement, there is a unisonal climax at bar 432; but the unison no more brings peace than the numb homophony, and the work ends in fragmentation, as the cello's original rhapsodic phrase and minor thirds, transferred to first violin, dissolve into their elements, fading into the music of the stellar spaces.

Carter's First Quartet is a work of tremendous power and originality and stands among the handful of American masterpieces. Its difficult integrity is achieved, perhaps, at a price. Though it attempts much more than even Copland's finest works, it cannot emulate Copland's remarkable achievement in creating a human strength and serenity from the apprehension of emptiness; and though it attains a greater degree of organization of its quasi-improvisatory[5] complexities than does the music of Ives, it loses, in the process, some of the human immediacy, the sense of life's physical as well as nervous texture that makes Ives's best music so memorable. The American heroism and grandeur glow through the rich, sharp sonorities of Carter's quartet, as they do in Ives's two piano sonatas; but Carter calls for heroic listeners, too, for unlike Ives he makes no allowance for the more commonplace realities, let alone the fun, of our everyday lives. The comparison with late Beethoven is pertinent here. Carter's quartet is the same *kind* of music as the late Beethoven quartets and sonatas: only—as Carter would be the first to admit—it does not reach Beethoven's *Paradise Regained*—the lyrical efflorescence of the Arietta of opus 111 or the variations of opus 131. Beethoven demands the same kind of effort from us as does Carter; and rewards us with as luminous a glimpse of heaven as we are likely to see in the conditions of this life. Carter's quartet leaves us spiritually as well as physically exhausted: in the same way, but to a much greater degree, as do the quartets of Bartók and Schoenberg, which bear a similar relation to the late Beethoven quartets as Carter's. There is a direct parallel between the glassy, still sonorities in some of Bartók's slow movements and Carter's stellar-space music; and the shimmering, quasi-heterophonic string textures in both composers' quartets are also comparable. The texture of Carter's

---

[5] Carter wants his music to *sound* like improvisation, as Ives's often does, but to be composition—a placing together. He distrusts the fashion for introducing improvised passages into composed music, as a denial of the composer's responsibility. The frequently cited analogy with the baroque period he believes to be illusory: because the composer was then so often his own performer and the division between the creative and the interpretative artist scarcely existed.

quartet is, however, immeasurably more complicated, the sense of strain more painful, the lack of resolution more disturbing; and this is not, in the last resort, merely a personal matter but also a difference of environment. Bartók, as a European, could have a more direct relationship to Beethoven than could Carter, as an American. Carter's relationship to Beethoven is like that of Ives: except that he turns the struggle unequivocally inwards, accepting nothing of the external world. The difficulty of his music is thus inherent in its nature; though we may find Ives more humanly rewarding, we cannot flinch from the wild integrity of Carter's courage.

Carter's moral courage may be technically equated with his desire to make his music as free and as rich in evolution as Ives's, yet paradoxically to achieve an ever-increasing degree of control. But this discipline must come from within. If on the one hand he distrusts (as we have seen) the resort to improvisation, he is on the other hand still more suspicious of preordained systems of organization, including serialism.

> The tendency to fad [he writes] has been greatly encouraged by the promulgation of systems, particularly harmonic systems. Many recent composers, following Schoenberg, Hindemith and Messiaen, have gained renown by circulating descriptions of their systems even in places where their music was not known. This kind of intellectual publicity can lead to a dead end even more quickly than the older fads derived from the actual sound of music in styles the composer did not even bother to explain. . . .
>
> Obviously the only way to withstand the disturbing prospect of being swept away by a change in fad is to plunge into the even more disturbing situation of trying to be an individual and finding one's own way, not bothering too much about what is or will be sanctioned at any given moment by the profession and the public.

Thus, far from being serially preordained, Carter's metrical modulations are no more than a means of notating the rhythmic evolutions that grow "organically" from the lines; just as the kind of "composite" melody he seeks in the last movement of the First Quartet grows from the interaction of a number of different, polyrhythmic strands. There is a harmonic parallel also: for although Carter's later music is non-tonal, we find that in the Quartet, for instance, he makes use of a "key" four-note chord that seems to be itself generative both of melodic material and of harmonic tensions. The chord, built of secundal intervals within a diminished fifth, appears in intervallic inversions and in total inversion. While in later stages of the quartet Carter undoubtedly introduced permutations of this chord intentionally, as an element of control within the rhapsody, it was neither conceived nor used systematically; it was a point for growth, and a point for return.

Carter's investigation of the "organic" processes in composition is continued in his next large-scale work, the Variations for Orchestra of 1954–5. Being scored for a full orchestra, the work does not explore further the extreme linear independence of the quartet, but it follows the same compositional principle in that Carter conceives of variation as a method of transformation—which he himself, in a programme note, compared to the transformation from one life-stage to another of some marine animals:

> As in all my works [he has said], I conceived this one as a large, unified musical action or gesture. In it, definition and contrast of character decrease during the first variations, arriving at a point of neutrality in the central variation, then increase again to the finale, which contains many different speeds and characters. This work was thought of as a series of character studies in various states of interaction with each other both within each variation and between one and the next. Activity, development, type of emphasis, clearness or vagueness of definition, I hoped would also contribute to characterization. Form, rhythmic and development processes as well as texture and thematic material differ in each one for this reason.

Of course, some such "organic" description of the process of composition would apply to most good composers, at least since the epoch of the sonata, and especially—as Carter himself points out—to Beethoven. The difference lies in the fact that the premises Beethoven started from —his basic assumptions—were fairly clearly defined both to himself and to his public: whereas in Carter, even more than in Ives, the process of definition is part of the composition. This is true even of a relatively accessible work like the orchestral Variations, which is a more inward and intense version of the Carter of *The Minotaur*: freer in tonality and rhythm, more flexibly evolutionary in structure, but no less strong and pliant in melodic contours. Still more is it true of the most recent phase of his work which, beginning with the Second String Quartet, takes up even more uncompromisingly the First Quartet's attempt to "be an individual", unequivocally self-reliant.

What makes Carter's First Quartet and his Orchestral Variations so impressive is that he has accepted the challenge of some of the most significant developments in twentieth-century music—the Bartók of the quartets, the Berg of the Lyric Suite, the Schoenberg of the Variations for orchestra—and has used them as a spring-board for new discoveries. In his recent works he has drawn further away from the European masters and has explored, ever more exhaustively, the more radical newness suggested by his American forebear, Ives; indeed, it is difficult to see how the concept of linear independence could be carried further than Carter carries it in his Second String Quartet (1959). Here each of the four instruments has its own character and its own style of playing, its typical intervals and rhythmic figures; the composer's original idea was that the players should be segregated at the four corners of the platform, but this had to be abandoned as impracticable. Thus the first violin's temperament is bravura; its characteristic intervals are minor thirds, perfect fifths, and major ninths, its characteristic rhythms involve extravagant alternations of longs and shorts. The second violin is anti-lyrical in temperament, characterized by more regular rhythms, by major thirds, minor sixths, and major sevenths: and by the employment of all kinds of pizzicato. The viola is the "expressive" temperament, making much use of glissandi and portamenti; its characteristic intervals are augmented fourths and minor sevenths. The cello's temperament is lyrically rhapsodic, characterized by gruppetti of accelerating and retarding notes which function independently of the other tempi; its intervals are the perfect fourth and the major sixth. Each of these instrumental "personalities" is given its head, and tries intermittently to impose itself on the others—a very Ivesian concept. Apart from the fact that each instrument gravitates around its characteristic intervals and "techniques", there is no literal repetition of material, no recapitulation, no fugal device, no *a priori* schematization. The quartet, Carter has said, is a "series of events in time"; what happens happens because the characters are what they are. The order is that which is inherent in their properties: nor are we *consciously* aware that there are two "cells" that recur, epitomizing the interaction of linear, harmonic and rhythmic characters.

The quartet opens with an introduction wherein we meet the four instruments as individual personalities, each playing its own kind of music regardless of the others: the cello its rubato phrase, dominated by fourths; the first violin its dramatic rhythms dominated by thirds and fifths; the second violin its pizzicati and anti-linear, double-stopped sixths and sevenths; the viola its lyrically expressive tritones and portamenti. After the characters have been thus introduced, an "allegro fantastico" is initiated and dominated by the first violin, whose bravura nature is manifest in its spurting cantilena and spasmodic rhythms, rendered powerfully affirmative by the frequent thirds and fifths:

EXAMPLE 9

The other instruments enter severally, at first very tentatively. The cello begins "sul tasto" with single notes that grow into fourths, "senza vibrato"; the viola with single notes "molto vibrato"; the second violin with isolated notes and chords in its various kinds of pizzicato. Gradually, the other three instruments attain parity with the first violin; their lines grow more sustained, while the first violin incorporates into its rhapsodic sweep ever wider, more elastically bouncing leaps through which, however, the perfect fifths still ring strongly sonorous. When all the instruments have reached equality—though not conformity—the viola takes over in an accompanied cadenza, through which the other instruments grow gradually more fragmentary. This leads without break into a "Presto scherzando", which is lead by the second violin's pizzicati. The first violin's "assertive" intervals are wide-flung and tenuous, while the lyrical viola and cello begin disjointedly. The cello grows more sustained and songful as the first violin is reduced to a broken muttering and whinneying of its thirds and fifths, and the second violin's double-stopped sixths and sevenths grow savager. The cello's dominance leads to its own cadenza, in its typical rubato manner: against which first violin mutters thirds and fifths with grim persistence, now unheroic, while the viola has broken sighs and the second violin broken pizzicati in triplets.

Again without a break follows the "Andante espressivo". This is lead by the lyrical viola, supported by the cello, with the two violins reduced to long-held, ostinato-like notes, rhythmically displaced one against the other. The lower instruments are gradually affected by the upper instruments' paralysis, so that the music grows ever more immobile. As all the parts acquire displaced rhythms, the sense of a pulse almost disappears. A return to life is initiated, characteristically, by the first violin, who has the only unaccompanied cadenza and the only music that is (very freely) recapitulatory. The first violin becomes long sustained and "molto cantando" as the cello establishes more regular, stepwise movement: which leads into the final Allegro where-in, for the first time, there is some interchange of "characteristics" between the instruments. (The cello's use of the second violin's sixths and major sevenths and of the first violin's minor thirds and perfect fifths is particularly obtrusive.) It is in this movement that the instru-ments between them form the two "cells" which are, as it were, a crystallization of the work's basic tensions:

EXAMPLE 10

But while this is an admission of mutuality between the characters, it is not a resolution; the polyrhythmic structure reaches its climax, indeed, in an extraordinary passage wherein the four instruments play, very rapidly and all out of "character", in fours against sevens against threes against fives:

EXAMPLE 11

This explosion—which is arrived at by a long series of metrical modulations—is the end of any attempt at synthesis, and the end of the work; the Conclusion is in a sense an anti-conclusion, dissolving the music away into the elements first presented in the Introduction, only isolating the characteristic intervals and "techniques" in time and space. The heroic first violin now plays its fifths off-beat, pianissimo and non vibrato, so that they become numb, empty. Finally the first violin is reduced to single notes, non vibrato, rhythmically displaced; the viola teeters out in its tritonal sigh, making a false relation with the cello's perdendosi B naturals; and the second violin's pizzicati fade out on a dry G harmonic.

Despite its conceptual resemblance to Ives, and an occasional suggestion of the sonority of the Schoenberg of the String Trio, Carter's Second Quartet is a new development in string quartet writing. It is superbly "heard" as well as felt: exciting aurally because its technical exploration is an exploration of experience. One's only doubt is that the tension generated out of its very nature is so great as to seem incapable of relaxation. Though the work is—and must be—short compared with the First Quartet, it is still more exhausting to listen to; and it offers scarcely any hint of the (glassily forbidding) calm explored in the First Quartet's slow sections. So uncompromising a response to contrariety is magnificent, and perhaps one should not, in present circumstances, ask for more. It is, however, a little disquieting that Carter's most recent work seems to offer even less hope of any resolution than the Second Quartet. His Double Concerto (1961) adapts the principle of independence to two antiphonal instrumental groups, one led by a harpsichord soloist, the other by a piano soloist. The harpsichord is associated with an ensemble of flute, horn, trumpet, trombone, viola and double bass with a percussion group made up of metallophones and lignophones; the piano is associated with an ensemble of oboe, clarinet, bassoon, horn, violin, cello with a percussion group consisting of membranophones. Each ensemble is isolated from the other; each—like the instruments in the Second Quartet—has its characteristic intervals and rhythms. The harpsichord ensemble is dominated by minor seconds, minor thirds, perfect and imperfect fourths, minor sixths, minor sevenths and minor ninths. The piano ensemble exploits major seconds, major thirds, perfect fifths, major sixths, major sevenths and major ninths. Each of these intervals is associated with a certain metronomic speed; rhythmically the two groups have "fields of specialization", the harpsichord ensemble specializing in derivations of polyrhythms of 4 against 7, while the piano ensemble uses 5 against 3. "The motion of the work", Carter has said, "is from comparative unity with slight character differences to greater and greater diversity of material and character and a return to unity. The form is that of confrontations of diversified action-patterns and a presentation of their mutual interreactions, conflicts and resolutions, their growth and decay over various stretches of time."

In intention, therefore, the work is a development from the "organic life" metaphor that Carter employed with reference to his Variations for Orchestra. The difficulty would seem to be that, whereas the characters and destinies of the four parts of the Second String Quartet can still be aurally apprehensible, the multiplicity and complexity of characters and destinies in the Double Concerto are so extreme that they cannot be adequately performed or heard. The whirlwind-like corruscations of sound may be more "organic" than the polyrhythmic textures of Ives; but the virtual disappearance of lyricism means that the "life-process" of the musical characters seems decidedly less human. The very important and complex percussion parts emphasize this tendency to dehumanization: or at least if they are human they are often cruel. The strength of Carter's middle-period music was essentially the strength of his humanity. That he should feel the nervous strain involved in the attempt to "be an individual" is understandable; one may question, however, whether the way out could, for him, involve any approximation to Varèse's pseudo-scientific view of his art. One wishes he would write more lighter, if not light, works. Though this seems an odd thing to say of a composer who has established himself as one of the most stimulating and original creators in (not merely American) modern music, the beautiful and comparatively relaxed Sonata for flute, oboe, cello and harpsichord of 1952 points to a path that Carter might explore further.

In this work the first movement begins antiphonally, with widely contrasted material for the various instruments: but achieves resolution as the harpsichord evolves a slow melody out of an extraordinary sustained resonance, while the melodic instruments interject phrases in a texture that grows gradually airier and more spacious. The Lento develops from the changing coloration of a single note, G; both the tempo and the momentum increase by metrical modulations until the movement returns to its initial Gs, which are now affirmative. The last movement carries a clear suggestion not merely of song, but of dance, for the lilt of the forlane is implicit beneath the surface, always dissolving into Carter's typical rhythmic fluidity. Again the piece is all evolution, gaining momentum incrementally; again there is no schematization or recapitulation, apart from a very brief, retrospective coda, when fragments of earlier motives bubble up to the mind's surface. This metaphor suggests the analogy between Carter's musical processes and the "stream of consciousness"; and this may be linked with Carter's own "marine organisms" analogy in that our subconscious minds inherit the legacy of the remotest and most rudimentary forms of the life-process. In the Sonata—as in the quartets—one is aware that the processes, whatever their origin, have become quintessentially human. The danger—which may be evident in the Double Concerto—is that conscious awareness of the unconscious may lead to an almost complete isolation of our own life-processes from the world around us. The twitchings and twitterings may seem amoebal: sub- rather than super-human. There may be something to be said for the old-fashioned view that the lyrical instinct—so strongly if uncompromisingly manifest in the Carter of the First Quartet and the Orchestral Variations, and in a slighter way in the Sonata—affirms man's humanity, and is his first offering to God. Perhaps the denial of this could occur only in a civilization in which art has ceased to have a social and religious context.

VI

The American frenzy and the unity of serialism: Wallingford Riegger and Roger Sessions

> O caught like pennies beneath soot and steam,
> Kiss of our agony thou gatherest:
> Condensed, thou takest all—shrill ganglia
> Impassioned with some song we fail to keep
> The sod and billow breaking—lifting ground—
> A sound of waters bending aside the sky
> Unceasing with some Word that will not die.
>
> HART CRANE: *The Bridge*

> The nearest approach to discovering what we are is in dreams. It is as hard to see oneself as to look backward without turning round. And foolish are they that look in glasses with that intent.
>
> THOREAU'S JOURNAL

In Europe, Schoenbergian atonality started from Wagner's disintegration of harmonic stability, dissolving chromatic passion into independent polyphonic lines. The "freedom" which the music sought was at bottom an attempt to achieve a mystical liberation of the Self; and Schoenberg, an Austrian Jew, was a fundamentally religious composer without a faith—as is manifest in the central work in his career, the opera *Moses und Aron*. Perhaps there is an allegorical quality in the fact that Schoenberg should have ended his life in the United States; certainly we have observed that some American composers—Ruggles consistently, Ives in his transcendental moments, Carter in his later work—have employed "free" atonality as part of their attempt to express a peculiarly American, anti-traditional mystical experience. While these composers have, however, affinities with Schoenberg in that they associated atonality with linear and rhythmic freedom, they did not follow him into a consistent use of serial technique as a new principle of order, superseding the harmonic and tonal order of the pre-Wagnerian past.

For Schoenberg, the twelve-note row became analogous to the search for a faith; it was the Law, comparable with the medieval *cantus firmus* or the Hindoo *raga*—the Word from which all the permutations of human experience derive sustenance and, indeed, life itself. This would seem to apply still more to Schoenberg's more uncompromisingly serial successor, Webern: who habitually set religious and mystical texts and who might well have said, with the Scandinavian serialist Valen, that for the twelve-note composer the row was God's will. It is hardly surprising that the American composer, fanatically democratic, was reluctant to accept such an *a priori* conception of order; for him—as we have seen—his "mysticism" became synonymous with his freedom. So the first American composer to make consistent use of serial technique employed it in a manner radically different from, even diametrically opposed to, that of Schoenberg. That he did so is the measure of his integrity: which makes his best music, crude though it may seem compared with Schoenberg, still powerfully disturbing.

Wallingford Riegger was born in Albany, Georgia, in 1885, though his family moved to New York in 1899, and Riegger's music is related more to the big city than to the South. Presumably of German descent, he studied in Berlin; and his early works stemmed from the traditions of German romanticism, especially from Brahms and Reger. It is interesting that these early pieces, notably the Piano Trio of 1919–20, show nothing of the lyrical-visionary quality of the early works of Schoenberg. Riegger had not yet discovered what, as an American composer, he had to do with his Teutonic materials: so that these pieces, though often powerful and always professional, are somewhat characterless. When, in the late twenties, Riegger finally settled in New York, two things happened which helped him to discover his true direction. One was that he met the pioneers of the "modern movement" in America—Ives, Ruggles, Varèse and Henry Cowell. Recognizing a spiritual kinship with them, he threw in his lot with theirs and devoted an immense amount of time and energy to the Pan-American Association of Composers. The other event was his introduction to the art of Martha Graham, "through whom I was drawn into a new sphere of creative activity: writing for the modern dance. I had not been impressed with the prettiness of the ballet, so alien to the American scene, but so generously patronized. The modern dance, being vital and expressive—and an American product—fascinated me".

These two impulses worked together to free Riegger's music from its retrospective German romanticism. The wilder music of Ives, Ruggles and Varèse revealed to Riegger that his romanticism, if it were to spring from the whole man, heart and nerves and sinews, must acquire a fiercely febrile intensity rather than an elegiac poignancy: while the influence of dance rhythm revealed that this intensity involved the release of kinetic energy. This is why Riegger's first "advanced" compositions are so different in effect from those of Ruggles or Ives. There is no "religious" continuity, no winging abundance; instead, the chromaticism splinters the lines into fragments, and only the dynamism of the driving rhythm thrusts the music forwards. In the famous or infamous *Study in Sonority* for ten violins (or any multiple thereof), which, appearing in 1929, was the first work of Riegger to create a sensation both of approval and of disapproval, the most traditionally lyrical of all instruments is driven to frenzy by its inability to sing, while it is simultaneously sustained and assaulted by the metrical pulse of Time. Despite their Germanic rather than Franco-Russian roots, the technique and the experience have affinities with those of the early experimental works of Copland, another composer of the big city. But whereas Copland, as we have seen, accepts frustration and wrests from it a kind of strength, even peace, Riegger finds that frustration generates fury: a secundal tension that becomes at the climax almost insupportable. The lid blows off the savagery within the American wilderness; and this is true whether the music affects us as horrid or as grotesque.

Something similar happens in one of the earliest of Riegger's works to employ serial technique—*Dichotomy* (1932), originally for chamber orchestra but later rescored for full orchestra. Whereas Schoenberg's rows are not usually apprehensible as themes, but exist to give an inner unity to the apparently amorphous texture, Riegger's rows have recognizable identity and their various permutations are labelled as such in the score. Since the melodic rows are combined with metrical rhythms of extreme violence, it almost seems as though the rows are present to prevent the music from going mad. Unstably chromatic though they may be, nervously jittery and angular in line, they must be heard as themes, intermittently recurrent, because if they cannot impose order on the chaos of chromatic dissonance and the ferocious assault of metrical Time, nothing can; they are the human will's desperately stammered assertiveness—certainly not, in Riegger's universe, the will of God. In *Dichotomy* the row theme is stated at the outset, but is then immediately battered into insensibility by savage, jagged syncopated metre:

EXAMPLE I

The "dichotomy" of the title is, indeed, between the row's attempt to establish thematic identity and the savagery of the syncopation; the frequent growth of the serial element into explicit fugato imitation (again labelled as such) is indicative of this search for a recognizably thematic unity. In the "meno mosso" section it seems that there is to be an expansion into lyricism; the widely leaping lines acquire an almost Ruggles-like ecstasy, while the piano's percussive dissonances change into shimmering, hallucinatory bitonality. The lyricism is not, however, sustained; a frenzied climax is built up over chromatically oscillating double basses and piano; and the concluding "quasi passa-caglia", though based on the unity of the row's perpetual repetition, proves an ultimate climax of fury. The obsessional repeated notes of the first section return and are transformed into chromatic scurryings, until the work ends with a scream. The savagery the music reveals is an urban complement—more chromatically strained and metrically jagged—to the rural barbarism revealed in Harris's music; and it is significant that both composers are obsessed with "monistic" forms such as the passacaglia and fugue. In Harris's case the monism is both a religious affirmation and a protest against the threat of chaos; in Riegger it has become almost entirely a protest.

In *Dichotomy* it is the metrical beat of Time that annihilates both fugal unity and lyricism. The relationship between song and dance in Riegger's music is usually more complex than this, however; and in the music he composed specifically for dance movement, kinetic energy tends to become a positive. The power of the full orchestral version of the *New Dance* (1934) derives from the release of inner tension into physical action, and although Riegger intermittently employs serial processes in the texture, we do not here feel that the serialism is neces-sary to safeguard the music from hysteria: the lines, serial or otherwise, ride on the rhythmic momentum. Though Riegger's modern dance music is not in itself particularly valuable, it would seem that this relatively extrovert projection of nervous into physical tension was essential if Riegger was to continue composing; certainly the maturing of his talent in the three symphonies which he composed in rapid sequence between 1945 and 1947 could hardly have occurred without the release offered by the dance music. The symphonies do not resolve the tension; but they now face up to it with formidable fortitude.

We may take the Third Symphony, opus 42, as representative; in it all the fingerprints we traced in *Dichotomy* reappear in extended and more powerful form. After a brief declamatory gesture (a descending chromatic undulation) the oboe sings the row, which is also a theme:

EXAMPLE 2a

Beginning moderato, the music makes repeated attempts to whip itself into an allegro and to establish a continuous fugato texture. But the patterned semiquaver figuration is threatened by snarls from the brass, which soon turn into an angular, metrically obsessed version of the row theme that banishes all hint of tenderness. When the clamour dies down, fragmentary wisps of the lyrical version of the row sound frail and forlorn through floating chord blocks on the violins. During the development the chromatic undulation of the introductory figure creeps in with insidious and sinister effect, being extended in Riegger's characteristic chromatic parallel seconds. The climax is a percussive explosion, generated by the wriggling seconds: which leads back to the introductory figure and to a telescoped recapitulation in which the remote lyricism of the second subject motive significantly does not reappear. Instead there is another attempt at fugal unity, based on the first seven notes of the series. This turns, however, into reiterated jumping sevenths, like a cat on hot bricks:

EXAMPLE 3

and then into the secundal undulations and the hammered repeated notes, forming an immense grinding dissonance, an apex of tension.

Even the slow movement, though it is marked "andante affetuoso", has the introduction's chromatic undulation and the wriggling seconds as its core:

EXAMPLE 4

and since Riegger tells us that the first sixteen bars of this movement are taken unaltered from a modern-dance piece he composed for Doris Humphrey in 1936, it would seem that this motive was rooted deep in Riegger's consciousness and was the germ of the whole symphony. Although the violins sing a much more expansive and lyrical permutation of this theme, they cannot escape from the nagging, self-tormenting undulation; and soon the phrases become broken, the parallel seconds threatening, as they were in the first movement. Again, out of the whirring seconds an attempt is made to establish fugal order: which leads only to increasing frenzy and an explosion of percussion. The "undulation", having failed as a fugue subject, returns to the serpentine seconds, now thickly scored for woodwind, brass and strings in unison. Then the movement whimpers out in fragments of theme and an unresolved dissonance.

The fragmentary texture is preserved in the introduction to the Scherzo. The allegro proper begins with a more or less unisonal texture and with an easily recognizable row theme, which is the slow movement's theme inverted and with octave displacements. Wriggling chromatic triplets like those of the first movement intrude to break up the dance momentum; once more there is an explosion of side-drum hammering, followed by an attempt to impose fugal unity. The domination of metrical rhythm is fanatical, screwed up—at the opposite pole to the freedom of Ives, Ruggles or Carter. The battering reaches a climax; then, as trio, the texture splinters into chips of the row over sizzling viola trills. The chromatic parallel seconds return on bassoons, in remorselessly regular minims; and drive the music into a much curtailed da capo. A stretto coda vanishes in double-bass grunts and a brief ejaculation on full orchestra. The effect—like that of the movement as a whole—is grotesque, though hardly comic.

The last movement, like the conclusion of *Dichotomy*, is a passacaglia and fugue, but is no more resolutory than the earlier piece. Indeed, the passacaglia theme, consisting merely of seven chromatic semitones with some octave displacements, is the most acutely painful of all the work's attempts to impose order on chaos, and the rigidity with which it obtrudes becomes cumulatively frightening. The classical passacaglia convention, in Bach or Couperin, had been an affirmation that disciplined the harmonic awareness of pain. Here it becomes more like an obsession, and as it is sickeningly repeated the melodic phrases above and around it grow shorter, more jagged, more twittery. Gradually the nervous jitter affects the bass itself, which changes from

EXAMPLE 5

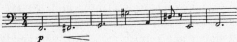

to

EXAMPLE 6

The fugue subject, into which the passacaglia theme is metamorphosed, is—with its sevenths, tritones, and reiterated notes—the most "feroce" of all the permutations:

EXAMPLE 7

and there is no further point of repose. The violence increases as the sliding chromatics in parallel motion return; a fury of percussion alternates with full-orchestral hammerings from which all element of fugal line has vanished: until the music blows up, as does *Dichotomy*, in a screech. This was the original end of the work—the form in which it was first played. In the published score Riegger has added a brief, soft coda which retrospectively reveals the derivation of the fugue theme and the undulating seconds from the oboe row theme of the first movement. The music fades out on an unresolved string dissonance. The coda increases, rather than alleviates, the horror.

Although the Third Symphony is a more extended and more powerful piece than *Dichotomy*, and to that degree a still more courageous one, it is not experientially an advance. It is music virtually without a moment's rest, offering no hint of spiritual assuagement (as does Ives) or of lyrical fulfilment (as does Ruggles), while in its metrical obsessiveness it lacks the sense of grandeur that Carter achieves from tension. Because Riegger's music attempts much less it is, for all its ferocity, easier to listen to than the music of Ives, Ruggles or Carter, and there is some truth in the waggish description of it as "the common man's Schoenberg". But this description should not be interpreted pejoratively: for the Common Man cannot but be aware, however inarticulately, of the frenzy within his heart and within the Big City, and it would be salutary if he could face the frenzy as fearlessly as Riegger. From this point of view Riegger's lifelong devotion to communism is interesting. Though the People certainly would not listen to his music by choice, or accept it with pleasure if they heard it by chance, Riegger knew that he had no alternative but to fight, as revolutionary, for an honest expression of the reality of urban man's experience: not what it ought to be, nor even what it might be, but what it was. And if it is true that serialism is a kind of faith, that it was Schoenberg's search for the Law of Moses, might not one say something similar of Riegger's serialism? The Law he sought was not God-given but man-made; and his works' perpetual search for fugal unity is the will to a faith without the spiritual sanction. In this sense the non-resolution of his art was the consequence of its honesty: and will remain its essential value.

In the last phase of his work it did indeed seem that there was some promise of reward for Riegger's anger. The *Variations* for piano and orchestra of 1954 abandon the grinding, cumulative tension of his symphonies; and although the serial motives are still fragmentary, the textures sharp, the dynamic contrasts explosive, the music is in total effect more relaxed—even comic and tender, and often both at once. The use of "monistic" variation form, culminating in fugue, instead of "dualistic" sonata that haltingly attempts fugato, is indicative; and the music of Riegger, in his seventieth year, has come to sound wonderfully youthful, with both the fearfulness and the promise, rather than the cruelty, of the new, big city life. The fearfulness is present in the glinting, dancing arabesques which the thinly scored piano interjects into the somewhat limping lyricism of the (infrequent) slow sections: or in the broken boogie-woogie variation, which has an almost Chaplinesque pathos. The promise is present in the sheer resilience of the textures, in the suppleness and "cheek" of the lines, unsustained though they may be. The Riegger of the pieces for the Modern Dance movement seems born anew—in something as close to grace as the big city can hope for.

That Riegger's art depends in part on shock tactics is an aspect of the Americanism that grows from his Germanic roots; and there is an element of shock in the mere fact that he found it necessary to jump direct from a valedictory post-Wagnerian and Debussian romanticism to a "modern" aggressiveness. The career of Roger Sessions, whose compositional roots are also Germanic, has no such hint of the sensational. This is partly because he belongs to the next decade, by which time protest did not seem so urgently necessary: and partly because of a difference in environment. Riegger was born in the South, but, very early, became and remained a New Yorker. Sessions, though in fact born in New York, soon returned to Massachusetts, where for generations his family had been New England clergy. The ethos of Bostonian gentility and of respect for the past conditioned his outlook, and he has remained—in so far as the term can be applicable to an American—an aristocratic artist. He belongs to a cultural *élite*, is highly intelligent, sophisticated, cosmopolitan. Respect for tradition has made it possible for him to accept the European techniques on which most American composers had been reared; vitality of response to the world around him has made it possible for him to develop those techniques progressively, not retrospectively. The nature of his music has changed slowly (whereas Riegger's changed very quickly) over the years; but the change has been both steady and logical.

Despite his respect for New England tradition, Sessions seems at first to have no affinity with the religious aspects of American Puritanism. In a sense one could say that he has carried his ingrained Protestantism to its ultimate end; the religious element that is present in Ives, Ruggles, Harris, and even Carter, is replaced by a more radical Protestantism, a basic assertion of human rights and civic liberties. Because he is representative of the flower of American "consciousness", he and his art must stand for the human spirit, anti-denominational, and not even deliberately pro-American. A citizen of the world, he has studied and lived for long periods in France, Italy and Germany—and has a linguistic gift hardly less precocious than his musical talent. His first and most influential teacher was Ernest Bloch—a Swiss Jew and ex-patriate; and it was through Bloch's example that Sessions learned how to absorb so many elements of Europe's past without being absorbed by them. Since America is a polyglot civilization an American must, in Sessions's opinion, have the strength to take what it offers. This may mean, to some, hymn tunes, popular songs, primitive textures and jazzy syncopations; but it may also mean, to a highly cultivated, cosmopolitan New Englander, something very different. As Sessions has said:

> I reject any kind of platform or dogma. I am not trying to write "modern", "American" or "neo-classic" music. I am seeking always and only the coherent and living expression of my musical ideas. . . . The Flemish and Italian composers of the sixteenth, seventeenth and and eighteenth centuries, Bach, the Mozart of *Die Zauberflöte* and the *Requiem* represent to my mind the highest perfection that music has yet reached. . . . I have no sympathy with consciously sought originality. I accept my musical ideas without theorizing as to their source or their other than musical meaning.

Sessions's enthusiasms, among the music of Europe's past, are interesting in the light of his own creative development; what concerns us, however, is how the things he took from the past became his own, and in the process became imperceptibly but inevitably American.

To begin with, Sessions was—as a traditionalist—unequivocally a tonal composer, though the European composers to whom he owed most were those who came to be associated with the dissolution of tonality. The astonishingly expert juvenile work *The Black Maskers* (written as theatre music at the age of sixteen, but cast into its present orchestral form in Session's early twenties) may show no trace of Wagner; its orchestral virtuosity and rhythmic zest may, however, be related to Strauss, while its linear independence is Mahlerian, its sensuous harmonic colour Debussian. While not a piece of pronounced character—one would hardly expect it to be—it demonstrates more than technical acumen. Both the nature of the style and the somewhat *fin de siècle* nature of the dramatic subject (based on a Russian play) may seem a far cry from New England Puritanism; they are not, however, extraneous to Session's later development.

We can see this even in a work such as the First Piano Sonata of 1930, a comparatively austere piece which makes no attempt pianistically to emulate the sensuous richness of an orchestral texture. For though the sonata is tonal, in chromatically extended diatonicism, and the keyboard layout traditional, the essence of the music is long, sinuous cantilena which, though basically diatonic, proliferates in chromatic arabesques. The Jewish cantillation of Sessions's teacher Bloch may have had some effect on his exploration of this kind of melody; but it becomes Sessions's most distinctive characteristic and one which is to relate him, later on, to more ostensibly American composers such as Ives, Ruggles and Carter. Development by melodic evolution implies, too, the second feature of Sessions's sonata—its prevailingly polyphonic texture. While it is a true sonata, seeking dramatic climax through harmonic and tonal means, the harmonic tensions are the consequence of polyphonic movement, and are the more nervously wrought because the independent rhythms are so complex. The telescoping of lines involves the telescoping of harmonies, so the climaxes are often polytonal—as is the ultimate climax in the Piano Sonata, which needs four staves for adequate notation.

All the typical features of Sessions's Sonata—its chromatic arabesques flowing from diatonic melodies, its sinuous rhythms, its sensuous response to sonorities—tended to lead him, as similar qualities had led Mahler, away from tonality; and as this happens Sessions becomes an original composer and, for that reason, inescapably American. Sessions himself said that the key-work in his career was the Second Symphony of 1946; and certainly this is a different kind of music from anything that he—or anyone else—had written previously. It is scored, with extreme virtuosity, for a very large orchestra. Though it still employs key-signatures, the texture is almost as consistently chromatic as that of Berg, and its sensuous richness and complexity are no less great. The nature of this complexity is, however, peculiar: as is the first movement's handling of the traditional dualism of sonata form. The first subject group, "molto agitato", consists of a fiercely biting secundal chord combined with a chromatic string arabesque: a fragmentary declamatory motive on the brass: a figure in lurching brass chords, with delayed accents: and a skipping motive built out of sixths, first heard on the oboe. All this material is presented more or less simultaneously in a whirring, whirling kaleidoscope of sound. The texture is more sophisticated than anything in Ives and more elegantly sensuous than anything in Carter, but it has more in common with those composers than with anything in the European tradition.

Though it seems hyper-civilized compared with the raw intensity of Riegger's music, Sessions's Symphony evokes a comparable bustling nervosity. But in Sessions's Symphony the tension of the world—and particularly of the city—has an opposite pole: for the directionless momentum of the first subject group is sharply contrasted with the second subject group, marked "tranquillo e misterioso". This retreats into the inner life: perhaps into the life of dream, since a long, undulating chromatic cantilena on solo violin floats high and metreless, mysteriously veiled by melismata on cellos and clarinets. It is interesting that the arabesques produce a somewhat Oriental impression, as do the melismata in the last movement of Mahler's *Das Lied von der Erde*; but the dreamy, introverted wandering of Sessions's music sounds more amorphous, more lost, because Mahler was singing an elegy on a great civilization, whereas Sessions is opposing the heart's loneliness to a raucous world. Perhaps the "mystery" in this most poetic passage involves a reference to spiritual sanctions also; the long, winding lines would be airborne:

EXAMPLE 8

If so, the spirit remains unfulfilled. There is no resolution of the dualism; and the development is rather an anti-development wherein the two poles of experience—the frenzy of the present and the "lost" tranquillity within the mind—are hurled against one another, unreconciled. Reality and dream even seem to change places: trumpets blare fortissimi a distorted, rapid malformation of the oboe's dream-motive to form the ultimate climax; which leads to a complete breakdown of the music's momentum and a hallucinatory extension of the second subject themes, with the woodwind melismata becoming more complex, more flexible, more chromatic, over a haze of divided viola chords and violin trills. The recapitulation brings us back with a bump to the world-as-it-is. But though we do not hear the second-subject dream motives again, the first subject group itself fades out in a puff of smoke. We are left asking which is the more illusory.

This first movement, the most remarkable and original part of the Symphony, is followed by a tiny Scherzo, only sixty-five bars long and built on a single tune. Basically diatonic, with chromatic side-slippings, this perky tune reminds us of Prokoviev or perhaps of Shostakovitch and, through him, of Mahler. The tonal displacements and rhythmic distortions make the comedy wry, even rather pathetic:

EXAMPLE 9

Even the movement's brevity is part of the effect: for it suggests that if this is a simple, foolish happiness, we cannot expect it to last long; it is likely to be swept away by the first movement's kaleidoscopic twitter. What, in fact, follows it is a funeral elegy—dedicated to the memory of Franklin D. Roosevelt, who, more than any man, symbolized the values of Protestant democracy and a New Deal. The chamber-music orchestral texture of this movement has obvious affinities with the Mahler of the Ninth Symphony, which was an elegy on another and much older civilization. The texture interweaves three related themes in free chromatic polyphony; the melodies are broken by a heavily dragging chordal climax on woodwind and brass, and peter out in equal quavers high on the violins, with so many chromatic appogia-turas that there is nothing left of the basic B flat minor tonality:

EXAMPLE 10

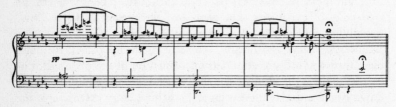

The concluding Allegramente looks as though it is going to repre-sent the world's triumph, and perhaps even the triumph of the big city: for it begins in a brashly assertive metrical rhythm and in a clear D major with polytonal overtones. Two fragmentary trumpery-trumpety tunes are blared together with many subsidiary motives, so that the hubbub sounds almost like one of Ives's march-conglomera-tions, though with a parodistic feeling that Ives would not have allowed himself. This brass-band episode gives way to a weird passage wherein muted trumpet and cor anglais indulge in stuttering repeated notes, trying to break away, but getting no further than a minor third. This leads into a mysterious climax over complex percussion: from which point the vigorous motives begin to disintegrate. The texture becomes kaleidoscopic, as in the first movement: an Orientally melismatic wriggling over sustained ostinati. The brusque vigour reasserts itself for a final, full-orchestral statement, but after a terrific rumpus over a D pedal, the end is ironically bathetic. The woodwind's tootling D major arpeggio sounds more like a giggle than an affirmation.

It will be observed that although this Symphony starts from traditional values and a European idiom, it in effect inverts those values. Tonality becomes a negative, associated with the most virulently assertive, even cruel music; a-tonality becomes a positive, in that it is associated with a search for tenderness and compassion, if not serenity, within the inner life. It was therefore natural that, after the Second Symphony, Sessions should tend to leave tonality behind and to make a (partial not systematic) use of serial techniques. Nor is it surprising that in his first atonal works his Berg-like European sensuousness should become subservient to a kind of "religious" austerity associated with his New England heritage. His later music—of which we may take the Second String Quartet as representative—sounds more like the "religious" Schoenberg than Berg; and it is not an accident that it should have, too, something of the lyrical continuity of Ruggles's Man and Mountain's mood, and something of Carter's attempt to achieve organic growth from the disparities of experience. The cosmopolitan Sessions has become a New England composer, just as, in the whirlwind of the Second Symphony's first movement, he had become at a deep level American.

Like Riegger, Sessions often uses fugal techniques in employing themes serially, so that the thematic significance is immediately apprehensible. The first movement of the Second Quartet opens with this beautiful, chorale-like theme:

EXAMPLE 11

The evolution of the movement depends on tension between the note B (which is the work's tonal centre) and its leading note A sharp which, becoming enharmonically identical with B flat, leads to a subsidiary tonality of E flat. The theme's hymnic quality suggests the communal Puritan heritage; but the tonal tension gradually conquers the song-fulness as the sonorous fugal polyphony grows increasingly complex, if transparent. The evolving chromaticism suggests an increasing intro-version, as against the communal nobility; and although the fugal order is reinstated, it now appears in a remote, rarefied sonority, as though such tranquillity cannot be grasped in the conditions of temporality:

EXAMPLE 12

And then the turmoil of a scherzo bursts upon us, the lines wide-flung, bounding, full of physical energy but far distant from song. The rhythms of each part are fiercely independent: not in the kaleidoscopic whirlwind of the first movement of the Second Symphony, but with a contrarious multiplicity such as is explored in Ives's Second Quartet and—to a more extreme degree—in the quartets of Carter:

EXAMPLE 13

Whereas the symphony seems to be swept along on the flux of experience, the quartet attempts to wrestle with it: while the almost static trio hints at a metaphysical reality outside Time's contradictions.

This scherzo thus states explicitly what would seem to be inherent in the first movement; and we hear this with new ears in the slow movement, which balances the fugal oneness of the hymn with the oneness of lyrical song or aria that flows into variations. Though this is the same kind of music as Beethoven's last quartets, here the humanly expressive chromaticism—the awareness of pain and contradiction—makes the texture grow more and more complex, self-destroying: until the song is swept away by another kinetic scherzo, simpler but for that reason more savagely aggressive than the previous scherzo. And this time facing up to the savagery seems to bring its own relief: for the violence is followed by an epilogic adagio in which the theme at last sings in untrammelled lyricism:

EXAMPLE 14

But the lyricism grows increasingly remote, tenuous, until nothing is left but the undulating thirds:

EXAMPLE 15

As the $^6_4$ chord on B gently glides into a $^6_3$ E flat chord we return to the tonal ambiguity which had generated the opening fugue. This time the tension is left suspended in time and space. This is truly a moment of vision: perhaps the most beautiful music Sessions has created. But the glimpse over the horizon vanishes almost before we have become aware of it. Though radiant, the music is, in its wide spacing, also forlorn; and the songful quality of the first movement—which, being hymnic, at least potentially involved a public—does not return.

When Sessions employs serial rows he often—as we have seen—does so thematically. In any case he does not believe that the twelve-tone "system" provides "an answer to the question of how the ear perceives, co-ordinates, and synthesizes the relationships involved". The series may be a practical aid to the composer; but his job will still be to define the "tonal areas" which must be implicit in the row, if the music is to make sense. "What is needed is a new and far more inclusive description of the various relationships between tones, and of the means by which the 'musical ear' discriminates, selects, and arranges these relationships." In the last analysis, Sessions believes, the acoustical effect derives not from the manipulation of the series as such, but "from the relationships between notes, as the composer has by these means set them up. . . . Two tones a fifth apart still produce the effect of a fifth, and, in whatever degree the context permits, will convey a sensation similar to that of a root and its fifth, or of a tonic and its dominant". The traditional basis to Sessions's serialism is perhaps a little modified in his most recent phase, which opens with a series of works that oppose a single melodic voice to a massed polyphony. The Violin Concerto of 1959, the *Idyll of Theocritus* for soprano and orchestra, and the odd and somewhat frightening Mass for unison voices with organ indicate that New England transcendentalism is not the only element in Sessions's work that is opposed to his sophisticated cosmopolitanism; or rather they indicate that his cosmopolitanism has a deeper significance, in that the melismatic writing explored in parts of the Second Symphony and still more in the pieces involving solo instruments or voices hints at a retreat from the West. We have already seen that the curling melodic tendrils and bell-tolling ostinati of the Thoreau movement of Ives's "Concord" Sonata reveal an affinity between New England transcendentalism and an "Oriental contemplation and forsaking of works". In the later music of Sessions this process is no less spontaneous but more developed, being encouraged, perhaps, by his response to some of the European composers—the Mahler of *Das Lied von der Erde*, Debussy, Berg, Bartók and Stravinsky—who have most interested him. It is as though, in the "kaleidoscopic" parts of the Second Symphony, the physical and nervous energy of modern industrial America is fragmented, atomized with its own excess; and the atomized world seeks, but does not for long attain, an immense, remote calm. In Sessions's Third Symphony he develops the kaleidoscopic aspects of the Second to a more extreme degree; in his Fourth and most recent Symphony, written in 1958, he patently reveals the relationship between his sophisticated, allusive, European-derived style and the American experience of Ives.

For the three movements of his Fourth Symphony (which Sessions, characteristically using Greek terminology, calls Burlesque, Elegy and Pastorale) correspond to three complementary aspects of the human consciousness. The first movement is aware of life's contradictions and tensions and has, despite its free chromaticism, many of the features of a sonata movement. Though the themes are row-derived, and developments are as much contrapuntal as harmonic, there are two clearly defined thematic groups with "male" and "female" characteristics, there is a recognizable recapitulation, and a brief coda that resolves the rhythms of both themes. Since the movement is the spirit of Comedy, however, the conflict is not long sustained; we can accept the angularities and sinuosities of the themes, and also the disparities between them, and can deal with them in an economical, classical structure. In this sense the movement suggests how Tradition may, even in the distraught world in which we live, help us to behave like civilized beings. In the second movement, however, we face the spirit of tragedy, and the pretence is dropped. Despite the European, Berg-like sensuousness of texture, the awareness of contradiction is here of Ivesian vehemence; only in Carter's later music does one find such wild juxtapositions of long elegiac cantilena on the strings, mostly in slow tempo, with furiously whirling allegro sections scored for full orchestra. As in Ives and Carter, the music seems to well up from depths below consciousness, with a minimum of logical connection, but with permutatory evolution which becomes an extremely free serialism. These savage oppositions we experience against the background of an almost motionless passage for woodwind, with delicate and mysterious percussion noises. This appears as prelude, reappears in modified scoring between the various episodes, and as postlude dissolves away—rather than resolves—the contrarieties. How close this is to Ives's and Carter's half-fearful, half-hopeful awareness of the eternal silence that surrounds the hurly-burly of our lives becomes evident in the last movement, which is a Pastorale not merely because it opens with classical siciliano rhythms on rustic oboe and cor-anglais, but also because it is a piece of nature-mysticism comparable with Ives's "Thoreau". As in Ives's movement, the texture of the cantilena now flows continuously. This "religious" note is similar to that of the finale of the Second Quartet, though the melismatic nature of the lines suggests "Oriental contemplation" rather than the New England flavour of the quartet. It is pertinent to note that the row is here, as in the quartet's finale, unambiguously a theme, which reappears as coda, in augmentation. So we feel that the discovery of the row theme is the goal of the Symphony, just as the discovery of Thoreau's flute melody is the goal of Ives's "Concord" Sonata. Both discoveries are, if non-doctrinal, a religious act.

That Sessions's music is sophisticated, European, and at the same time responsive to a central American theme may explain why it has made so potent an appeal to young musicians, despite Sessions's lack of interest in dogma. They welcome the music because it is meaningful to them as Americans; and they do so the more readily because it no longer needs to insist on its Americanism, but can take its place in the community of musical nations, old and young. The music of Andrew Imbrie shows the advantage of this civilized European-Americanism: for while Imbrie has taken from his teacher Sessions something of his austere New England polyphony and something of his sensuous melismatic texture, he has none the less arrived with apparent spontaneity at a manner of his own—partly because his melismatic melodic writing has led him to explore the tonal ambiguities of augmented and diminished intervals. Imbrie's quartets may be related to the New England intensities of the quartets of Sessions; and the rich and complex texture of the orchestral *Legend* has affinities with Sessions's symphonic style. Yet there remains room for Imbrie's own identity; and the same is true of Ben Weber, whose Symphony on poems of William Blake for baritone and chamber orchestra disturbingly combines a neurotically acute, Berg-like and Sessions-like chromatic polyphony with a direct, almost melodramatically theatrical projection of experience. This odd mixture of tortured sophistication with naïvety may well be the kind of art that Blake might create, had he indeed been born on the banks of the Ohio, and were alive today. There are similar qualities in the explicitly theatrical music of Hugo Weisgall; it is not an accident that his one-act, one-character opera *The Stronger* should "adapt" Strindberg from nineteenth-century Sweden to a ·twentieth-century American cocktail lounge.

One of the central traditions in American music today would seem to derive from an interaction of the influence of Sessions and Riegger: as is indicated in the career of a senior composer, Ross Lee Finney. In his early years Finney produced prolifically chamber music that was extremely well made, but somewhat characterless, deriving from German conservatism by way of Hindemith, with a spicing of Prokoviev, and perhaps, Stravinsky: more interestingly he also attempted to combine this relatively academic proficiency with something of the raw vigour of the New England primitives, using psalm tunes, in more or less their original harmonization, as a basis for extended choral and orchestral works. After the Second World War, however, Finney found that his own idiom, growing increasingly chromatic, could no longer be accommodated to the modalism of American folk-tune and hymn. On the other hand, it seemed to him that even a music which was like his, reluctant to sever completely the roots of tonality might profit, in cogency of argument and richness of reference, from the use of serial devices. This led him to take up creatively the serialism which he had rejected when, as a young man, he had been a pupil of Alban Berg; it seems clear that, in adopting serialism, he has found his talents' fulfilment.

In his Second Symphony of 1959 the chromatic sensuousness which he shares with Berg and also with Sessions (who was also his teacher) comes to terms with a Riegger-like rhythmic athleticism. The work employs serial processes in the sequence of its note-durations as well as in pitch; and it may be that in its impeccable lucidity of texture and structure it loses something of Riegger's raw power and of Sessions's introspective intensity. In a sense, however, this is part of a necessary historical process: the American vehemence cannot be denied, but must acquire some element of civilized propriety; similarly, the American introspection must turn outward, if the new man is to live adequately in the world he has made. Thus Finney's Second Symphony has considerable nervous and physical tension, as has the urban society in which he now lives; at the same time its extreme clarity, its complete aural realization, give it a quality of buoyancy and exuberance. If Berg is, in one sense, a composer of Europe's twilight, Finney, using comparable techniques, becomes a composer of an American dawn. The serial processes may be there to hold back chaos, but they are also a liberating agent; and in the rowdy coda to the last movement their presence is least felt, because it is least necessary. Civilized, even meticulous, though the music may be, it re-creates in urban form something of the open vigour of the Mid-West, where, in 1906, Finney had been born.

That Finney is becoming a "successful" composer, both in terms of commissions and of audience-response, is significant: for it is salutary that a composer so honest in feeling and so expert in technique should be accepted, in the mid-twentieth century, as a representative of the new age's conservatism. Even "advanced" techniques may become part of a tradition; in his big choral and orchestral work *Still are New Worlds*, for instance, Finney employs a row involving several fourths proceeding to thirds in the traditional manner of the choral suspension;

and when he introduces electronic tape to reinforce the hubbub and horror of the climax, he is using a modern technique in the same manner and spirit as the nineteenth-century oratorio composer called on the 32-foot stops of the organ. Nor is it an accident that Finney should have devoted more attention than any other American composer except Quincy Porter to the classical medium of the string quartet. He has composed eight quartets, the last three of which are serial, though no. 6 is also described as being in E. The Eighth Quartet, in particular, is a remarkably convincing one-movement, "permutatory" structure, moving in circular form from slow, intimate, rhapsodic lyricism to the point of maximum ferocity (wherein glissandi represent the breakdown of song), and then back to lyricism. One might say that the quartet is directly concerned with the relationship between introvert contemplation and extrovert energy; and the piece remains positive in effect even though lyrical intimacy does not, after all, win the day. The completion of the circle—the return to the initial rhapsodic version of the row theme—is succeeded by a vigorous allegro coda, and the concluding music consists of stabbed syncopations and the disintegrative glissandi:

EXAMPLE 16

If, however, the introspective lyricism and the assertive energy would seem to be opposed, the effect is no longer—as in Riegger—one of frenzy. As at the end of the Second Symphony, we can now find compromise acceptable, even life-enhancing.

A composer of a younger generation, Leon Kirchner, has a dual relationship to Sessions and Riegger, comparable with that of Finney. In his impressive Concerto for violin and cello with wind orchestra and percussion (1960) the lyrically expressive cantilena of the string soloists is affiliated, by way of Sessions, with Schoenberg and Berg: while the clarity of the melodic contours and the luminosity of the textures give to the music a new-world freshness remote from the introverted romanticism of the Viennese. The treatment of the wind ensemble, on the other hand, reminds us of the Schoenberg of opus 29, refelt in Riegger's more aggressive spirit; and this relatively extrovert buoyancy is reinforced by the complex and vivacious percussion parts. As with Finney, the technical mastery—the precision of the aural realization, the always "telling" sonority—is part of the emotional effect. Kirchner is a more complex personality than Finney; yet his music, too, suggests that it is the creation of a sensitive and passionate man who is also on top of the world—as a twentieth-century American would like to be. The romantic cantilena is so shapely and clear that it is entirely without self-pity: while the zest is neither thoughtless nor complacent. In some works—for instance, the Piano Concerto of 1952–3—Kirchner's romanticism is more explicit. The intricate texture of the first movement suggests the Berg of the Chamber Concerto: within which sensuous subjectivity an andantino middle section tries to establish a cooler, more detached lyricism. Then the slow movement becomes a dialogue between piano and orchestra, on the analogy of the slow movement of Beethoven's Fourth Concerto; here lyrical lucidity and dynamic frenzy are separated in the two contrasted forces, and attempt integration. The romanticism of the music—as compared with Finney's —lies in the fact that the integration is not successful. The rondo finale returns to the structural principle of the first movement: a mood of extreme tension and complexity is opposed to a mood of cool remoteness, exploiting a thin, widely spaced piano texture, and the work reaches a climax by inversion in a long piano cadenza which is the quietest, stillest music in the score. So the final effect is neither one of Riegger-like fury nor of Finney-like optimism; it is, indeed, oddly wistful, as though the music were seeking, from its state of nervously wrought energy, the primitive American innocence that is lost for ever. The sharpness and thinness of the sonority mean that this wistfulness cannot be mistaken for nostalgia. Kirchner's music accepts the modern urban world as it is, with strength and sensitivity; a man of his generation, however, finds that world somewhat more difficult to assimilate than does Finney.

It is perhaps significant that no post-Schoenbergian composer of a later generation than Finney has continued in his vein of chromatic conservativism. The highly sensitive Irving Fine might have done so: for having started as a Stravinskian neo-classicist whose work was distinguished by meticulous clarity, if not by passionate intensity, he found himself when, in his String Quartet of 1952 and in his posthumously published Second Symphony and Fantasy-Trio, he adopted serialism without surrendering consciousness of tonal roots. The tender, fine-spun lyricism of his slow movements suggests a Berg reborn in the clear New England air; if some of the Viennese "morbidity" has gone, so has some of the strength. For this reason, perhaps, Fine's lyricism, though sustained compared with the fragmentary lyricism of Riegger, does not coalesce with his furious motor-rhythms to create an art both muscular and optimistic, like Ross Lee Finney's. He affects us as being, *in toto*, an elegiac composer; and there is an allegorical quality in the fact that he should have written very little music, created at once exquisitely and painfully; and that he should have died, prematurely and unexpectedly, in his forties.

There is, indeed, evidence to suggest that most of the young men who started in the Riegger-Sessions tradition are now turning in a different direction. Kirchner's Piano Concerto initiates what will probably be a far-reaching change in his music; while the talented George Rochburg—whose powerful Second Symphony is related to Riegger in its relentless exploitation of row *themes*, of aggressively metrical rhythms and of harsh tone-colours—seems to be moving towards a Webernesque serialism in his *Time-Space* for orchestra. Composers like Kirchner and Rochburg prove that though in part disillusioned they still live in a new world, rather than in a world grown hoary. They preserve much of the rhythmic energy and textural richness of their first masters, Riegger and Sessions; and in becoming aware of atomic disintegration, their music none the less rejects the elegiac. This concern with the New finds explicit formulation in the music of those composers who have made a more radical departure from Western tradition than have the chromatic serialists. In them we shall find an end to the adventure in American democracy which composers such as Ives, Ruggles, Carter, Riegger and Sessions represent. In their work Ahab's odyssey is over and—in Charles Olsen's words—"the Atlantic crossed, the new land America known, the dream's death lay around the Horn, where West returned to East. The Pacific is the end of the UNKNOWN which Homer's and Dante's Ulysses opened men's eyes to. END of individual responsible only to himself. Ahab is full stop."

VII

The retreat from the west: science and magic: Charles Griffes, Henry Cowell and Edgard Varèse

> everything
> and nothing
> are synonymous
> when
>
> energy in vacuo
> has the power of confusion
>
> which only to
> have done nothing
> can make
> perfect.
>
> WILLIAM CARLOS WILLIAMS

In so far as Sessions is a composer within the Schoenbergian tradition, he derives from the German—the Beethovenian and Wagnerian—view of the artist as a moral force. Though he ends, like Ives, with a desire to relinquish the personal will in the transcendental, the will is none the less the point from which he starts. Now, there was in Europe a composer more directly and profoundly revolutionary than Schoenberg. That composer was Debussy, who inherited Wagner's awareness of the senses' burden: but differs from Wagner in that for him dedication to the sensory moment became a release from the weight of time-obsessed passion and an abnegation of the will. In *Pelléas et Mélisande* Debussy, a sensual and passionate man, created an operatic myth about what happens to human passion when the will is extinct. Technically, the consequence of this is, negatively, the destruction of the sense of harmonic progression (which is still evident, in however frustrated a form, in the Wagnerian sequence); and positively, the exploration of melismatic and ostinato techniques having affinities with medieval, and still more with Oriental music. The passivity that Debussy's music seeks is certainly more Oriental than Occidental; and it is valid to describe his techniques as impressionistic in that they go some way

toward rendering music a spatial rather than temporal art. For Debussy the chord—including the higher chromatic discord—may exist
in its own right, as a moment of sensation, with no before or after.

Debussy once said that there was more to be gained by seeing the
sun rise than by listening to the "Pastoral" Symphony. His desire to
lose the personality in submission to the world of appearances found a
response in the heart of the American composer: who had little consciousness of tradition: whose will was weary with its attempt to
conquer the wilderness. At first, perhaps, the implications of Debussy's
revolution were not evident to the Americans. Sensory passivity could
be no more than a refusal to face the wilderness, rather than a release
from the experience of it: so that much American music composed in
Debussian idiom between 1900 and 1930 (by men such as Edward
Burlinghame Hill) now seems, if genuinely sensitive, also precious and
parasitic. There was one composer, however, who—starting from
Debussian premises—created music characteristically personal and
American. He was Charles Griffes; and he died young, when he had
just discovered what he had in him to do.

In view of the "spatial" tendencies of Debussy's music, it is interesting that Griffes should have been a talented visual artist as well as a
musician. He was born in New York in 1884 and died there in 1920
after a career both physically and nervously distraught. His earlier
compositions are remarkable mainly for their technical competence;
the piano works are beautifully laid out for the instrument, the orchestral pieces expertly scored. The piano piece *The White Peacock* (1915)
could be by any post-Debussian, post-Ravelian composer, European
or American. Only a certain wildness at the climaxes sounds personal,
and American rather than French; and our response to these climaxes
may be effected, retrospectively, by our knowledge of Griffes's last
work. In *Clouds*, however—the last piece, written in 1916, of the set to
which *The White Peacock* belongs—a quality enters the music which
we cannot find in Debussy. In the Frenchman's *Nuages* the cor anglais
phrase that wanders in and out of the clouds' organum-like procession
of concords may suggest the desolation of man's littleness, but the
exquisite lucidity of the piece is none the less tranquil and assuaging.
In Griffes's *Clouds* the bitonal floating of the ostinato chords and the
unresolved appoggiaturas over a swaying drone induce a sense of
separation, as well as of emptiness. Despite the refinement of the
writing, there is a chill in the music remote from Debussy's sensuous
elegance; and the implications of this disturbing quality become mani-

fest in Griffes's last work, the Piano Sonata of 1917–18, which reveals him as an American composer of potentially major talent.

Whereas in the orchestral *Kubla Khan* the Orientalism is superficial, the Piano Sonata proves that Griffes is no longer out of his depth in tackling a Coleridgian, hallucinatory theme. The technique of the work is perhaps closer to late Scriabin than to Debussy, in that it is based on a kind of harmonic serialism. All the material is derived from an Oriental scale or raga: only the raga is now a moment of harmonic sensation, within the psyche, as well as a Law of pitch relationships, existing "absolutely". Although the "raga" forms tritonal and augmented chords which, like Debussy's whole-tone harmonies, tend to be tonally neutral, it is introduced with the opposite of Debussian passivity, seething upward in spasmodic gusts, marked "feroce". Even when the first theme proper ("allegretto con moto") appears, its sinuous cantilena repeatedly threatens to boil over in cascades of fioriture in cross-rhythms of $\frac{3}{4}$ against $\frac{6}{8}$, with frequent quadruplet and quintuplet groupings:

EXAMPLE I

And the music, in its violently alternating moods, seems the more frenzied because the harmony created out of the whirling monothematic texture is almost static: we are reminded of a bird frantically beating its wings against the cage of the harmonic obsession. When a "molto tranquillo" section succeeds the first movement's whirlwind, its tranquillity is that of exhaustion. The quasi-pentatonic melody, in level crotchets over a drone, is incantatory: Oriental with a Russian (Moussorgskian) flavour:

EXAMPLE 2

The trance is, however, hypnotic—a drugged stasis rather than a
mystical vision; and it leads only to further frenzy, a whirring moto
perpetuo in tarantella rhythm, wherein the raga chord-obsession
becomes even more obtrusive than in the first movement. After a wild
climax the trance passage is heard again, from a distance; but the
ostinato chord-complex and the furious $\frac{3}{4}$ $\frac{6}{8}$ opposition return and lead
into a delirious presto coda exploiting the entire range of the keyboard.
Despite the sensuousness of the tritonal chords, the sonority is at once
savage and metallic—the music of an asphalt jungle:

EXAMPLE 3

Indeed, this disturbingly powerful sonata is an American parable in
musical terms, telling us what happens to the ego alone in the industrial
wilderness, if it cannot attain Ives's capacity to embrace all aspects of
experience, or Copland's strong acceptance of emptiness, or the pan-
theistic religious sense of Ruggles, Harris or (perhaps) Sessions. In this
sense it is a young man's music, comparable with the art of the poet
Hart Crane, or the novelist Thomas Wolfe: men of extreme nervous
sensitivity who also wore themselves out in youth: who uttered a yell
of desperation because, opposed to the industrial society they lived in,
they were imprisoned within their own senses, as Griffes is imprisoned
within his raga-chord. Despite the sensuous pliancy of the themes, with
their chromatics and augmented intervals, Griffes's Sonata is an astonishing and frightening work. Its Orientalism is not an escape into dream
but a consequence of desperation such as could have occurred only in a
spiritually barbarous world. Debussy's revolution was balanced by his
artistic conscience and by centuries of French civilization; certainly he
was not aware of the sense in which his art's amorality was a return to
the primitive. Griffes's Sonata shows us how an American composer,
given strong enough nerves, could experience Debussy's revolution
"raw".

Griffes was a sophisticated composer who was trained in Europe.
The American vehemence that spurts up in his Piano Sonata took him

unawares, perhaps even killed him, for so much nervous stress may well have had physical consequences. Such frenzy was not, however, the only possible manifestation of the American violence and the retreat from the West: both could be an indigenous product, part of the American naïvety, as we can see in the personality and career of Henry Cowell. Strength, with Cowell, becomes a blithe insouciance; and although he is an important figure in American music, he is so as an explorer rather than as a composer. Born in 1897 of eccentric Anglo-Irish parents who believed that children, like plants, should be left to grow, he spent his childhood in San Francisco (where he visited the Chinese Theatre and listened to and watched the street games of Chinese children), and on farms in California, Kansas, Iowa and Oklahoma (where he became familiar with Anglo-Irish folk songs and fiddle tunes). Brought up in contact with these spontaneous manifestations of both Oriental and Occidental music, he played the fiddle (by ear) at the age of five, and was composing empirically by the time he was eight. Apart from violin lessons, he received no formal education in childhood; from the age of twelve he supported himself and his mother, largely by collecting and selling rare wild plants. He even saved enough money to furnish a shack with a ramshackle upright piano, on which he produced music as prolifically as Nature produced the plants he lived by. Although Cowell was later sent by admiring friends and acquaintances to Seeger University, where he acquired intellectual know-how and a conventional training in harmony and counterpoint, he remained emotionally a naïf, a "natural"—as the highly complex Ives was not.

Perhaps we may relate Cowell to Ives's father, rather than to the composer himself. Just as Ives senior indulged in acoustical experiments to "stretch the ears", so Cowell, in his shack with the upright piano, investigated the instrument's aural properties as only an American boy, self-educated, with no contact with civilized traditions, could have done. Ives took over hints from his father and turned them into musical experience, introducing note-clusters (for instance) to mark a climax or for a special effect in relation to the whole. But for Cowell, as for Ives senior, the experiment was itself the experience. Cowell's early piano pieces are the doodlings of an American aboriginal; each one starts, not from a human experience, but from an aural gimmick, so that they are "moments of Sensation" with a capital S, using the term in the modern American, rather than in Debussy's, sense. As material out of which art might be made, they are often immensely invigorating.

The earliest of Cowell's piano pieces to be published dates from 1911, when he was fourteen. Called *The Tides of Manaunaun* it is, like many of these works, a bit of Celtic Irishry which is, as composition, banal enough. The folksy tunes are pentatonic, but are rhythmically square, with hymn-book harmonies. The experiment consists in the tone-clusters, played with fist or forearm on the low registers of the keyboard, surrounding the tune with a mysterious reverberation like Oriental gongs. Other Celtic pieces—such as *Lilt of the Reel*—use tone-clusters as an overflow of animal high spirits; they do not disguise, and are not meant to disguise, the fact that this is a jolly, conventional Irish reel with no harmonic or rhythmic surprises. *Jig* uses the same technique with more interesting, jerkily displaced, rhythms. This may be a naturalistic piece, like Ives's barn dances; the wrong notes and wobbly rhythms are a consequence of tipsiness: which quality links the piece with the more obviously "audacious" numbers, wherein the interest is proportionate to the stimulating power of the gimmick. *The Snows of Fujiyama* is explicitly Debussian, if one can imagine Debussy as unembarrassed barbarian! The tune is pentatonically Oriental; the static impressionist harmonies are reinforced by overtone resonances. *Fabric* literally weaves three voices in independent rhythms; it sounds like a Chopin nocturne gone askew. *Fairy Answers* literally answers a hymn-book phrase with mysterious plucked-string resonances; *Sinister Resonance* and *Dynamic Motion* use plucked and stopped strings with more telling effect as "moments of sensation". *The Aeolian Harp* creates some beautiful portamento effects from plucked piano strings; while *The Banshee* produces weird and exciting noises from crossed string glissandi. These sounds have a prophetic relationship to some of the sounds produced by electronic means, though they are, on the whole, more haunting and evocative. In the notorious *Tiger* ferocious tone-clusters, played with fist and forearm, chittering sevenths and ninths and reverberating overtones emulate the creature's growls, pounces, snatchings, grunts and even purrs. Although the piece is a barbarous din it is not in the least frightening, except as a physical assault on the nerves. Indeed, like *The Banshee*, it is a comic piece: the extrovert complement to the finale of Griffes's Sonata, which reveals the banshee and the tiger within the heart.

These piano pieces were written between 1911 and the early twenties, independently of the percussive works of Stravinsky and Bartók, and probably independently of the contemporary works of Ives. Most of the theories to be explored twenty or thirty years later by *avant-garde* composers were touched on by Cowell during these years. As early as 1914 he employed rhythmic serialization; and he investigated indeterminacy in his *Mosaic Quartet* (in which the performers create their own continuity from composed "blocks") and in his *Elastic Music* (from which parts may be omitted at random). When Cowell began to produce, in cornucopia-like profusion, more conventionally "composed" music, he significantly attempted a fusion of the modality and the rhythmic and tonal simplicity of the American primitives with the melismatic and percussive styles of Eastern music. *Set of Five* (1952) for violin, piano and percussion is one among the hundreds of examples that Cowell's eupeptic temperament has created. The violin sings a home-spun modal line, lyrically mellifluous; the piano adds melismatic arabesques and percussive sonorities that are reinforced by gongs, tom-toms, porcelain bowls and other specifically Oriental instruments. There are moments of relaxed beauty, especially in the central andante: and an exciting use of plucked string resonances in the finale. The music is, however, destitute of the strangeness and wildness that characterizes Griffes's Orientalism. Even the charming *Toccanta*[1]—an almost completely monophonic or at least heterophonic work for soprano vocalize with flute, cello and piano—is so suavely prettified as to seem slightly factitious. It is not Western; but it is not really Eastern either. It would make a delightful accompaniment to the visual gyrations of a Hollywood-Polynesian maid, for its sensuality has just about as much, or as little, relationship to reality.

In his most recent phase Cowell still "exposes himself"—to use the American phrase—to non-Western music, Indian, Asiatic, Chinese and Japanese, while at the same time asserting his roots in the modal and diatonic hymns and fuguing tunes of the American primitives. He feels this is valid because an American is essentially a polyglot, open to all things, in democratic gregariousness. His Fourth Symphony, based on the styles of American hymn, ballad and fuguing tune, has a certain guileless charm, and is impeccably scored. It sounds like a home-spun American Vaughan Williams, without the religious conviction; and the qualification is important since without this conviction an American primitivism is likely to sound no less cinematic than an amiable Orientalism. The emotional naïvety in Cowell's "early American" pieces complements the naïve response to the aural gimmick that we

[1] The title—an ellipsis of toccata and cantata—means that the voice is an instrument along with the other instruments, but that all play-sing in vocal style.

commented on in his experimental works: and makes them seem in every sense facile as compared with Vaughan Williams or with Ives's works in hymnic vein. Cowell's Eleventh Symphony (*Seven Rituals of Music*) exhibits both his strength and his limitation. Beginning with a touching lullaby for a child, it covers the cycle of man's experience: but is in every phase childlike. The work-music is percussive factory noises, the love-music Hollywooden solo violin, the play-music country jigs mixed up with barrel-organ, fairground and cinema-organ noises, the magic-music weird sonorities extracted from glissandi on strings and bells: while the final, death-confronting lament is no more tragic than the growl of Cowell's piano Tiger is scarifying. Whereas Ives's multiplicity is an aural realization of the multiplicity of experience, Cowell's multiplicity is a simple acceptance of the variety of aural gimmicks that a new world offers the composer; and this is equally true of Cowell's mildest works and of his most ferocious—such as the middle-period Piano Concerto, which is the closest Cowell approaches to Ives's grandeur, yet becomes, in its reliance on percussive violence unrelated to line and structure, grotesque rather than sublime. Even the grotesquerie has a kind of innocent charm. At least Cowell is a phenomenon that only America could have produced.

If not a great composer himself, Cowell has been a seminal influence on other composers: neither his experimental nor his relaxed manner has been a dead end in American music. A composer of a younger generation, Henry Brant, who was born in Montreal in 1913 and came to New York as a boy, may be compared with the "experimental" Cowell, not only because he was a child prodigy, but also because he is as composer inspired by the gimmick rather than by human experience. Characteristically American, he has been a collector of odd sounds; and has written works, like *Galaxies*, designed to explore unexpected possibilities of instruments, more or less without reference to harmony or structure. He is particularly fascinated by Ives's concern with "multiplicity", and has composed works for independent orchestras requiring several conductors, each group having its own tempo and metre. *Antiphony No. 1* is scored for normal symphony orchestra instruments in four groups with four conductors, with a fifth conductor to cue in the ensembles. *Ceremony* has only one conductor, but vocalizing groups associated with bizarre instrumental combinations are placed in front of him, in different parts of the hall. *Millenium no. 2* is scored for ten trumpets, ten trombones, eight horns with two tubas, segregated in various parts of the auditorium; there is also a percussion group (timpani, chimes, bells, vibraphone) and a soprano vocalize. The groups are brought in by conductors, but then play freely, without precise co-ordination; at the climax there are six conducted parts and eighteen independent melodic strands going simultaneously. The musical material itself is usually—as with Cowell —quite simple, even rudimentary: which is probably why the least pretentious pieces, such as *Angels and Devils* for solo flute accompanied by an orchestra of flutes (including piccolos and bass flutes), tend to be musically the most satisfying. This work combines orthodox harmonic materials with Ivesian tone-clusters, dissonant heterophony in ten or more parts, bird-sounds, jazz and circus-tootles, in delightful limpidity. Perhaps it is pertinent to note that this is a 'young' piece, written at the age of eighteen, when the aural gimmick can still be a genuine stimulus to experience. In the later, more complex works the sounds that result from the heterophony are still often fascinating; but like Cowell's sounds they tend to be aural excitation rather than composition. This would seem to be Brant's own attitude; composing, for him, is having fun, investigating gimmicks. Certainly this relatively non-creative audacity has place in a mechanized society; it is good that a man who, like Brant, makes his living as an extremely ingenious commercial arranger, should thus preserve the liveliness of his senses and faculties.

Cowell's "relaxed" manner has had somewhat more rewarding progeny. Alan Hovhaness, a composer no less fecund than Cowell himself, has attempted to create an American-Oriental music that may be justified by more than a preoccupation with the empirical moment, since Hovhaness is an American of mixed Armenian and Scotch descent. Born in Massachusetts in 1911, he composed vast quantities of Nordic, Sibelius-dominated symphonic music which he has destroyed or renounced. The music of his second creative life dates from his investigations into Armenian folk and church music: which induced him to create a music no longer based on the Western conception of harmonic tension, but rather on monody and heterophony both medieval and Oriental. The first movement of the piano concerto *Lousadzak* (1944) has no chordal harmonies; the strings flow in continuous stepwise or pentatonic organum over long-sustained drone notes, while the piano imitates the percussive qualities of certain Armenian instruments. There is no climax, only a spiral mounting of the melodic lines until stillness is reached: at which point the lovely slow movement unfolds, liquid piano melismata being twined around the drone of eternity, as in classical Indian music. In the third movement the timeless cantilena soars into a dance, but there is still no harmonic development. The work ends with a "chime and symphony of Nature", a glowing ecstasy that fulfils the title, which means "the Coming of Light". Nothing could be further removed from the end of Griffes's Sonata, which is also orgiastic.

Not all Hovhaness's music is as consistently Oriental in approach as *Lousadzak*; when he employs European techniques, however, they are usually those of the Middle Ages or early Renaissance, and are therefore unconcerned with harmonic tension. The Hymn that concludes the Second Violin Concerto (1951) combines Oriental melismata in the solo line with a modal homophony comparable with Vaughan Williams's re-creation of archaic styles. *Arevekal* also has medieval hymnic movements and a delightful estampie, alternating with Armenian monody and heterophony. Hovhaness's best music achieves—perhaps because of his ancestry—a relaxed calm that goes deeper than Cowell's facility; and since a serenity that is at once easy and honest is unusual in contemporary music, it is not surprising that Hovhaness should have become a much-performed, much-commissioned composer. While there is a positive side to this—implicit in the fact that Hovhaness's music makes an immediate appeal to children—one wonders how far his art can be relevant to urban, industrial America, except in an evasive sense. There is nothing in his work comparable with Vaughan Williams's attempt, in the Pastoral Symphony and subsequently, to reconcile the technical and philosophical opposites of vocal monody and the sonata principle; and although fluency is a joy in a creatively constipated society, one cannot help suspecting that Hovhaness's music is too easy to write and too easy to listen to. To pretend one is an Ancient Armenian may be part of the American Dream: which cannot be identified with the *avant-garde's* attempt to enter the emptiness that surrounds the music of so representative an American composer as Copland.

A composer whose music is related to that of Hovhaness—though he is less prolific, more individually sensitive, and perhaps in closer touch with the urban world—is Lou Harrison, who was born in 1917 and brought up on the West Coast, facing east. In so far as his work borrows elements from European tradition it returns—beyond the sonata principle and even the harmonic universe of the baroque—to the vocal modality of the Middle Ages and the Renaissance. The chorale-like adagios and the fugal movements of his suites for strings, and the vocal and brass writing of his *Mass*, demonstrate how Harrison handles these materials in a less spontaneous, more hieratic manner than Hovhaness. While this aspect of his work is strongly reminiscent of Stravinsky, Harrison carries to a further point the "non-progressive" use of European harmony; and frequently dissolves it into a quasi-medieval or Oriental music in which line is as important as harmony is insignificant. Thus in the Suite for Symphonic Strings (completed in 1960, though it includes material going back as far as 1936) the most personal, and also the most beautiful, movements are those which have least sense of harmonic progression: such as the epilogic *Nocturne*, in which modal song-lines flow around a drone, or the *Chorale* "Et in Arcadia ego", in which telescoped diatonic triads, in the manner of Stravinsky's *Apollon Musagète*, float into a tender lyricism reminiscent of Vaughan Williams in his folk-hymnodic vein. Yet more successful are the pieces that have no harmony at all, since they are purely monodic: the exhilarating *Estampie*, for instance, depends on a spirally evolving, resiliently rhythmed line that flowers into pentatonic arabesques, accompanied by cellos and basses, used in a variety of original ways as percussion instruments. Similarly the *Ductia in honour of Eros* manages to suggest, through a subtle rhythmic lilt combined with a sinuous, reiterated lydian phrase over a drone, both the eagerness and the innocence of adolescent sexuality:

EXAMPLE 4

with drone

Something similar happens in the lovely Suite for cello and harp, for the (Stravinskian) Chorale leads into a singing-dancing Pastorale in three melodic parts, in which there is no modulation and virtually no harmony, the interest centring in the glinting lyrical arabesques and the glancing contrarieties of rhythm. One of Harrison's most convincing works—the Concerto for violin and percussion orchestra—is literally all melismatic line, rhythm and colour, and he has often scored for instrumental combinations that have patently Oriental associations. His *Canticles* for percussion (the quasi vocal and lyrical title is pertinent) are among the most poetically evocative percussion works ever created by a Western composer: and can probably be so because Harrison has never attempted to make Orientalism a *substitute* for the Western tradition that is still manifest in his suites for strings. It is relevant to note that he has frequently used the Viennese-derived idiom of chromatic serialism, creating from melodic arabesque a sensitive, attenuated texture of almost Japanese delicacy. His post-Renaissance passion can thus come to terms with his medieval innocence: so that in a long work like the Suite for Symphonic Strings he can, without incongruity, group highly chromatic movements like the Lament and the two Fugues alongside pentatonic and modal pieces like the Estampie and the Canonic Variations.

Though a composer of true distinction, Harrison is a marginal figure: as are, more obviously, some younger composers who may count as his disciples. The music of Daniel Pinkham, who was born in 1923, lacks the passionate sensitivity that makes Harrison's best work so moving; yet it distils from its prettified medievalism a genuine tenderness and radiance. The tinkling bells and melismatic patterns of the Concerto for celeste and harpsichord, or the elegantly pure vocal writing of the *Easter Cantata* (in which the voices are haloed by more bells and by muted brass) are delightful to listen to, and unassuming in their acceptance of their emotional limitations. They are true to their composer's talent, though to most of us they cannot but seem anachronistic. Even less than the music of Hovhaness, and much less than that of Harrison, can we consider Pinkham's music a sequel to Griffes's sonata. The man who ultimately followed through the implications of that extraordinary work was Edgard Varèse: who fought to get Griffes's later music performed and who in the years following Griffes's death, himself produced a series of works that radically reinterpret the Debussian revolution. Ignored for many years, these works have, in the mid-twentieth century, become a seminal influence upon *avant-garde* composition.

Varèse was born in Paris in 1885—the year after the birth of Griffes. He did not finally settle in the States and become an American citizen until 1916; yet we can see him as a predestined composer of a New World, both because he understood—more completely, perhaps, than anyone—the implications of Debussy's music, and also because his early training was in mathematics and engineering. As a young man, however, he decided on a musical career and entered the Schola Cantorum and the Paris Conservatoire, where he was a pupil of Roussel—but also of Vincent d'Indy (who had taught so many of the conservative pupils of Horatio Parker) and of Charles Widor! He knew Debussy personally and later, in Berlin, became an unofficial pupil of Busoni. As conductor and as practical musician he vigorously associated himself with progressive developments in Europe; whether or not his early attempts at composition conform to European traditions is obscure, for he has disowned, and has been successful in suppressing, any music that deviates from his chosen path. All the works he admits to the "canon" were written after he settled in the States; all contribute to a conception of music that is opposed not only to European tradition, but also to the post-Renaissance view of music as expression and communication. Significantly, however, the earliest pieces reveal the affinity between Varèse's notion of music and the Debussian revolution.

It was perhaps as a symbolic gesture that Varèse called the first work he still recognizes *Amérique*: it was intended to be, and is, a New World of orchestral sound. How this new world was hinted at by Debussy is better indicated by the second work that Varèse admits to: the *Offrandes* of 1921-2, which are settings of surrealist poems for soprano and chamber orchestra. Debussy, in treating each chord as a moment-in-itself, sought to liberate us from the Will: to make the listener an aural seismograph who would be fulfilled in becoming one with the natural world. The musical materials he employed were still, however, those sanctioned by tradition and by French civilization. Varèse saw that logically the Debussian aesthetic involved the rejection of conventional musical stylizations and of clearly defined distinctions between musical sound and noise. For Varèse, as for Debussy, the post-Beethovenian conception of music as psychological drama rooted in the Self was irrelevant; but he went further than Debussy in that he discarded, too, the conventionalized materials of diatonic and chromatic melody, of harmony, and of rhythmic pattern related to harmonic tension. In *Offrandes* there are many passages in which he uses these traditional elements in Debussy's anti-traditional way, divorced from the sense of temporal progression: indeed, there are passages for trumpet and harp that sound almost like quotations from Debussy. There are also passages, however, where the barrier between sound and noise is crossed, and the organized sounds of music and the sounds of the natural world—not only semi-musical sounds such as bird-song, but also car hooters, barge sirens, clattering milk cans, etc.—are identified, far more radically than they are, intermittently, in the music of Ives. The fact that the words in *Offrandes* are surrealist is pertinent. Looking within the mind and the senses, they encourage us to respond to music "concretely". Music should be created, like the dance, as an act of the body itself: not as communication of feeling, but as a magical performance.

So Varèse starts from the sound-characteristics of each instrument—what he calls its density: its timbre and quality independent of pitch relationships. The instrument is a sound, like any other, relatively accidental, noise; and Varèse's music becomes a polyphony of timbres, each instrument having its own typical figure or rhythmic pattern, which remains constant or changes, if at all, only very slowly, as some "fact of Nature" suffers permutations beyond its conscious volition. Varèse has likened this process to crystal-formation; indeed, "form is the result of process. I have never tried to make my compositions fit into a known container. . . . Musical form, considered as the result of a process, suggests an analogy with the phenomenon of crystallization. The clearest answer I can give to people who ask how I compose is to say: 'By crystallization'. . . . The crystal is characterized by a definite external form and a definite internal structure. The internal structure is built on the unit of crystal, the smallest grouping having the order and composition of the substance. The extension of the unit into space forms the whole crystal. In spite of the limited variety of internal structures, the external forms of crystals are almost limitless. I believe that this suggests, better than any explanation I can give, the way my works are formed. One has an idea, the basis of internal structure; it is expanded or split into different shapes or groups of sounds that constantly change in shape, direction and speed, attracted or repulsed by various forces. The form is the consequence of this inter-action. Possible musical forms are as limitless as the exterior forms of crystals." So construction, for Varèse even more than for Debussy, is spatial rather than temporal; and while harmonically conceived music achieves purposeful order through the development of themes in time, and the movement to and away from a central key, Varèse achieves his "opening of space" through the addition and contrast of rhythms and timbres which, in so far as they behave like crystals, *seem* to be as impervious to the dictates of the human will as is Nature herself. Such a conception has something deeper in common with the magical properties of primitive music, or the ritualistic properties of Eastern music, than has the Orientalism of Cowell or Hovhaness; and Varèse believes that to encourage forgetfulness of self is a musical necessity of our time, because the hyper-self-consciousness of modern man is the basic reason for twentieth-century chaos. At the same time he insists that his ritualistic music is modern as well as primitive, because (unlike the music of Cowell and Hovhaness) it is directly related to scientific process and therefore to a machine-dominated civilization. Certainly the percussive noises and patterns in his music have affinities with the sounds of city life, which have become part of our everyday consciousness. The artist's task is to help us perceive the (mathematical?) patterns of order and beauty that lie beneath Man's and Nature's chaos, if we have eyes to see and ears to hear. When we can all see and hear—Varèse would say, along with some painters of visual abstraction, such as Jackson Pollock—the artist will no longer be necessary.

Since Varèse's music is anti-harmonic, we can examine its essence in *Ionisation* (1931), which is purely percussive, and in *Density 21.5* (1936), which is purely linear. *Ionisation* is scored for thirteen players on a very large variety of hissing, banging and scraping instruments. Its effect is, at one level, primitive and orgiastically exciting, and its reliance on cumulative repetition relates it to the scarifying metallic fury of the last section of Griffes's sonata. The imprisoned melodies and harmonies of Griffes's sonata are abandoned; noise, especially the noise of the modern city, comes into its own: which we must respond to, and become one with, as Debussy invited us to be identified with the rising sun. Though the noise is savage, often even vicious, it becomes both an assertion of controlled power and also a release from horror. For if *Ionisation* does not have a sense of temporal progression in the post-Renaissance sense, it has an architectural or spatial awareness of periodic Time: and even an awareness of climax in that pitched instruments (piano, chimes, glockenspiel) appear at the end, as the hissings, bangings and scrapings gradually slow down Time's pulse into one eternal-seeming reverberation. Here pitch becomes equated with an ultimate stillness, for as pitched instruments gain ascendency we are progressively less exacerabated by wailing sirens (which remind us of air-raids and police-cars, but are probably meant to symbolize the infinite gamut of pitches that Varèse later explored through electronics). This conclusion[2] is both Oriental and also a consequence of the

[2] The final pages of Stravinsky's *The Wedding* are directly comparable with the end of *Ionisation*, though the relationship of Stravinsky's deliberately primitive work to modern life is less direct, if not less real. Shortly after *The Wedding*, the American George Antheil produced, in Paris, his *Ballet Mécanique* for a similar battery of pianos and percussion. The noises of modern life (aeroplane propellers, etc.) are introduced alongside Stravinskian geometric pattern-making, and Antheil claims that the piece is built mathematically on the Time-Space concept, like musical engineering, or modern architecture in sound. He admits that Varèse preceded him in this concept. In any case, compared with the works of Stravinsky and Varèse, *Ballet Mécanique* has only historical, not musical interest.

evolution—and maybe of the decline—of the West. The modern composer, Varèse would maintain, is an artist in that he must *discover*, through an activity of the mind, nerves, body and senses, the aural order which is inherent in Nature; but he will be a scientist in that his discovery can emerge only from knowledge of the way sound behaves. Only if he can use his humanity to *reveal* Nature will he escape the yell of desperation with which Griffes's sonata ends. One can see this more easily in *Density 21.5* which, being purely melodic may be more readily compared or contrasted with "conventional" music. The piece was written for George Barrère, as an inauguration work for his platinum flute. 21.5 is the density of platinum; and the title presumably means that this music is the "aural reality" of the metal: the sound-experience that can be revealed through it. The work is short enough to quote complete.

In this piece the use of melismatic arabesques oscillating around nodal points, and of incantatory repetitions that change very slowly, suggests affinities both with Oriental music and also with the European re-creation of non-Western melody inherent in Debussy's magically beautiful *Syrinx*. At the same time, however, the piece's investigation of pitch relationships and dynamic levels is "scientifically" planned. Thus the first clause—which covers seventeen bars up to the high fortissimo G—is built around the "node" (or internal crystal) of the sequence F sharp, C sharp and G. In the first eight bars the chromatic wriggle around E expands into a perfect fourth and then into a tenser imperfect fifth. It then stretches up, through oscillating pentatonic thirds, to C natural. The second half of the clause repeats the pattern, with the C sharp changed enharmonically to D flat, the G natural transmuted into G sharp, and with sundry octave displacements and rhythmic complications, especially in the use of the minor thirds. The next clause begins with the chromatic wriggle on B natural—a tone we have not heard up to this point. The minor thirds are now on E and C sharp, low in register, almost percussive in attack. The appearance of E flat—the only tone not yet sounded—leads to an increase of intensity in the wriggling semitones, now in octave displacements around F sharp. The "new note" E flat also promotes release on to undulating pentatonic thirds on D and B, very loud and high in register. The abrupt descent to a low A flat re-establishes the tritonal relationship; the final cadential clause (bars 50–60) returns to the original C sharp–E–G complex (or crystal) which now merges into the B flat–D–F sharp polarities in a phrase covering all the registers of the instrument. The tensions of the polarities

EXAMPLE 5

* Always strictly in time - follow metronomic indications.
** Notes marked + to be played softly, hitting the keys at the same time to produce a percussive effect.

and densities are thus neutralized: as are the rhythmic tensions at the conclusion of *Ionization*, when the interlocked planes of rhythm and timbre are relaxed by a gradual enlarging of the silences between the sounds.

In most of his works Varèse combines the melodic techniques of the flute piece with the polyphony of rhythms and timbres characteristic of *Ionization*. *Intégrales*, the longest of the early pieces, is representative.

Though played on normal wind and percussion instruments, it sounds like a *collage* of the noises of city life, with sirens, hooters, automatic drills and the din of traffic. At the same time it does not sound, because it is not, disorganized; and it achieves an almost majestic grandeur out of the impersonality of its violence. This impersonality is manifest in the clearly defined three-sectional form. In the first section there are two vertical chord-structures (rather than harmonies) which never change except in sonority and dynamics: and a variable melodic pattern oscillating around a single note. Each of these elements is a noise which (even more than Debussy's chords) is incapable of "development", though it may suffer crystal-permutation. The section ends with an enormous shimmering cadence-chord in which the two vertical structures and the one linear pattern are stated simultaneously:

EXAMPLE 6

In the second section there are two "polarities" derived from the original pattern: a woodwind chord D, E, B flat, F, and a brass tritone F sharp to C. Only duration and rhythm fluctuate in this section, the reiterations of pattern being dominated by repeated tones on trombone. The rhythmic fluctuations slow down until they, too, become static, and a cadence-phrase again dissolves the two elements into one. In the third section the oboe has a more extended version of the basic pattern:

EXAMPLE 7

This, too, revolves around itself, proliferating horizontally through the chord-clusters of the brass. The opposition between the vertical and horizontal elements here creates an effect comparable with those passages in Ives's music that bring together the aural disparities of the natural world. But whereas Ives is content to be humanly amorphous,

Varèse attempts the scientist's precision. The attempt must fail because an artist, being human, is humanly fallible. None the less there is grandeur, as well as excitement, in Varèse's attempt to emulate, through human means, the processes of Nature. Perhaps only God can make a tree, but Man may at least make sounds behave like crystals.

The *Octandre*, written in 1924, offers a further exploration of Varèse's crystal-forming analogy. The texture is here more consistently polyphonic—even fugal, if one can imagine a fugue without thematic contours or harmonic implications, but with a crystal-figure that is mutated, not developed, and with "entries" that establish increasing and diminishing planes of tension. The heterophonic second movement, indeed, achieves formal resolution mainly through oscillating dynamics: gradations of tension may become independent not only of line and harmony, but even of rhythm:

EXAMPLE 8

A more extended form of this principle is evident in *Arcana* (1927), which is scored for an enormous orchestra, including forty percussion instruments and numerous exotica such as sarrusophone, heckelphone, contrabass clarinet and contrabass trombone. The title comes from the *Hermetic Astronomy* of Paracelsus, and while it refers to the "science" of alchemy, it also implies that the generator of change—the transmuter of base metal into gold—is the human imagination. Varèse has described the piece as a kind of passacaglia on the eleven-note figure that opens the work, but the structure is neither thematic nor harmonic. Such recollections of "normal" music as bubble up to the surface (there are fragments of street songs, of military tunes, as well as recollections of

Debussy and of the Stravinsky of *Firebird, Petrouchka* and *The Rite of Spring*) are sub- or at least semi-conscious; the true form of the work is the arch of tensions it creates from permutations of the "passacaglia" crystal, and from the noises of the external world.

In so far as Varèse's conception of structure is related to the impact of "pure" sounds ("I was the first to explore, so to speak, musical outer space, the first to be moved by living sounds and to make music with them"), it is clear that his art-science could be fully realized only through electronic means. Way back in the twenties he recommended the electronic development of acoustical resources in order to make possible an infinite variety of pitch relations and timbres (or overtone complexes). Few took him seriously, which may be why he gave up composing between the late thirties and the early fifties. The development of magnetic tape has encouraged Varèse to compose again: and has led to a revival of his early works, which are valued as much for their prophetic insights as for their intrinsic merits. In writing electronically, however, he insists that "a machine can only give back what is put into it. It does not create. . . . No matter how obedient a machine is, it will encounter situations for which it is not prepared. A bad musician with instruments will be a bad musician with electronics. An electronic instrument is an additive, not a destructive factor in the art and science of music. . . . Electronic instruments do not mean that old instruments will be abandoned. Just because there other ways of getting there, you do not kill the horse. . . . The composer should, in building his sonorous constructions, have a thorough knowledge of the laws governing the vibratory system, of the possibilities that science has abundantly placed, and continues to place, at the service of his imagination. The last word is: Imagination."

In 1953 Varèse reappeared as composer with a work called *Deserts*, for orchestra and pre-recorded tape. He has commented on the nature of the piece as follows:

> *Deserts* was conceived for two different media: instrumental sounds and real sounds (recorded and processed) that musical instruments are unable to produce. After planning the work as a whole, I wrote the instrumental score, always keeping in mind its relation to the organized sound sequences on tape to be interpolated at three different points into the score. I have always looked upon the industrial world as a rich source of beautiful sounds, an unexplored mine of music in the matrix. I went to various factories in search of certain sounds I needed for *Deserts* and recorded them. These noises were the raw material out of which, after being

processed by electronic means, the interpolations of organized sound
were composed.

The score of *Deserts* is made of two distinct elements: (1) an instrumental ensemble composed of fourteen wind instruments, a variety of
percussion instruments played by five musicians, and a piano as an
element of resonance; (2) magnetic tapes of organized sound transmitted
on two channels by means of a stereophonic system to provide a sensation of spatial distribution of sound sources to the listener. There are
four instrumental sections of different lengths, and three stereophonically
interpolated sections of organized sound introduced between the first
and second, the second and third, and the third and fourth instrumental
sections.

The live instrumental ensemble (which includes all varieties of flutes,
clarinets, horns, trumpets, trombones, tuba, piano and percussion)
evolves in opposing planes and volumes, which are decided by "the
exigencies of this particular work, not by any fixed system of intervals
such as a scale, a series, or any existing principle of musical measure-
ment". They thus produce a sense of "movement in space" and are
associated with the element within which the human operates—for
which Varèse's term is "presence". The taped interpolations, on the
other hand, are associated with "distance", with the non-human
aspects of the physical universe, symbolized in "the industrial sounds
(of hissing, friction, grinding, puffing) filtered, transposed, transmuted,
mixed, by electronic devices", which appear in the first interpolation.
The second taped interpolation, played by an ensemble of percussion,
perhaps provides a link between the non-human and the human world;
and the third interpolation mixes industrial noises with fragments of
humanly operated percussion. The interplay of the human and the
non-human produces increased intensity, and the higher the intensity
the briefer the section. The music rises to its climax in the third interpolation and fourth instrumental section: after which it fades away in a
long pianissimo.

Varèse has said explicitly that the word "Desert" is to be understood
as suggesting not merely "all physical deserts (of sand, sea, snow, of
empty space, of empty city streets), but also the deserts in the mind
of man; not only those stripped aspects of Nature that suggest bareness,
aloofness, timelessness, but also that remote *inner* space no telescope
can reach, where man is alone, a world of mystery and essential
loneliness". The remorseless honesty with which Varèse explores
this basic modern theme explains why *Deserts* is one of the most
impressive, and certainly the most frightening, of his works. The

extreme rhythmic dislocation, the use of piercingly high and growl-ingly low sonorities create an entity wherein factory, subway and aeroplane noises merge into the cries of birds and beasts. Although so new, the searingly dissonant heterophony, the microtonally wailing portamenti and the immensely slow rhythmic organization remind us of something immensely old—of Japanese gagaku, the imperial court music that flourished from the eighth century onward. The lyrical continuity of classical Indian music or the mellifluous suavity of Balinese gamelan is utterly remote from this music, which, though highly sophisticated, is also cruelly barbaric (the flute and oboe set the teeth on edge, being deliberately tuned to the maximum degree of distonation), yet emotionally deflated (the voice sings of the most passionate or gruesome occurrences in a dead-pan moan). Though Varèse knows a great deal about Oriental music, it is almost certain that the affinity between his work and gagaku is unconscious. The American twentieth-century, and the Japanese ninth-century, violence have deeply entwined tentacular roots—as is perhaps evident in the relation-ship between some American films and some much-lauded Japanese films about medieval Japan. Maybe the violence cannot be evaded: though it would seem to represent an ultimate "desert" in the heart and senses.

At least Varèse never forgets that man *has* a heart and senses. His first completely electronic work, the *Poème électronique* composed for the Brussels Festival in 1957, to be performed in a pavilion specially designed by Le Corbusier, introduces the human voice into taped sounds that include both processed natural noises (i.e. *musique concrète*) and also vibrations produced by "pure" electronics. Varèse again describes the work as "ordered sound" rather than music: by which definition he indicates that while all music is ordered sound, not all ordered sound is, in the orthodox sense, music. But although he has extended the boundaries of sound by admitting an infinite variety of pitches and timbres instead of the few conventionally accepted ones, and although these sounds are, in this piece, mathematically ordered by graphs, creating a sound-universe that is half scientific, half magical, none the less the ordering agency is still human. It is a *human* voice that cries from the vast prison of space and the physical universe; and objec-tions that have been made to this work on the grounds that the human instrument is not miscible with the electronics surely miss the point. The piece is uncannily disturbing—as most electronic music, as yet, is not—because it is thus aware of the human predicament. Like Reg

Butler's sculptured Unknown Political Prisoner, it is a parable of our time; and the "prisoner" theme takes us back to the Sonata of Griffes, who was an exact contemporary of Varèse and, had he lived to work along with him, would surely have produced electronic music also. In any case, *Poème électronique*, being the creation of a real composer, has a force that goes far beyond acoustical experiment. Whether it marks the triumph of the desert or the beginning of our passage through it remains to be seen.

VIII

From noise to silence: Harry Partch, John Cage and Morton Feldman

> As the truest society approaches always nearer to solitude, so the most excellent speech finally falls into Silence. Silence is audible to all men, at all times, and in all places. She is when we hear inwardly, sound when we hear outwardly. Creation has not displaced her, but is her visible framework and foil. All sounds are her servants and purveyors, proclaiming not only that their mistress is, but is a rare mistress, and earnestly to be sought after. They are so far akin to Silence that they are but bubbles on her surface, which straightway burst, an evidence of the strength and prolificness of the under-current; a faint utterance of Silence, and then only agreeable to our auditory nerves when they contrast themselves with and relieve the former. In proportion as they do this, and are heighteners and intensifiers of the Silence, they are harmony and purest melody.
>
> **THOREAU**

> The movement with the wind of the Orient and the move-ment against the wind of the Occident meet in America and produce a movement upwards into the air—the space, the silence, the nothing that supports us.
>
> **JOHN CAGE**

> The poem supreme, addressed to
> emptiness—this is the courage
> necessary. This is something
> quite different.
>
> **ROBERT CREELEY**

Varèse's music is new, in sound and technique, because it implies a new philosophy: and also a rejection of the immediate past and the re-creation of a very old philosophy. As a French American, however, Varèse had roots in Europe: whereas another composer of a somewhat younger generation is both as radical as Varèse and as empirically American as Cowell. Harry Partch—whose very name has allegorical overtones—was born in Oakland, California, in 1901, and spent much of his early life in remote areas of the Arizona and New Mexico deserts. Here, not surprisingly, he received no formal education in music, although—like Henry Cowell, whose background in youth was comparable—he used his freedom from tradition as an impetus to experiment in sound. At the same time, living where he lived, he came to believe that the future of music—and, indeed, of civilization—lay in a rebirth of the instinctual springs of life that had animated ancient cultures; and this rebirth called, inevitably, for a re-creation of the media through which the spirit was to be made manifest.

So he did not, like Cowell, make do with such conventional instruments (however unconventionally used) as came to hand; he designed and built his own instruments, derived from the sounds of primitive, especially Polynesian, percussion and plectrum instruments, but including some bowed strings, pipes, and keyboard-operated reed organs. All these were adapted to a forty-three-tone-to-the-octave system of tonality that could give coherence to a monophonically conceived music based, like primitive chant and any single-line music, on Just Intonation. In a key passage from his book, *Genesis of a Music* (University of Wisconsin Press), Partch has described the difference between his "monophony" and the harmonized music of Western tradition:

> The major contribution of Monophony as an intonational system is its realization of a subtle and acoustically precise interrelation of tonalities, all stemming from unity 1/1. This interrelation is not capable of manifold modulations to "dominants" or any other common scale degree; it is not capable of parallel transpositions of intricate musical structures; it does not present any tone as any specific tonal identity. Conversely, it is capable of both ordinary and hitherto unheard of modulations to the natural limits imposed by just intonation, and the arbitrary limit of 11 ... it is capable of an expanded sense of tonality . . . and of great variety in that expanded sense. Few composers will regard the total virtues of Equal Temperament and those of Monophony as equal in value. Whichever of the two sets is accepted as superior, it can be stated unequivocally that they cannot co-exist in the same musical system, given the present ideas behind musical instruments and the present conception of musical values, and that—short of a mechanical revolution in the construction of instruments and a psychic evolution in musical conceptions—they will not co-exist in the same system in the future.

It will be observed from Partch's book that while his attempt at a scientific understanding of "monophonic" Just Intonation is modern, the philosophical and psychological ends which the theory serves are not. Partch's views on the religious-social effects of his Intervals of Power, of Suspense, of Love, of Approach and so on have obvious analogies with Greek theory and with Oriental theory and practice; he has composed "studies" in justly intoned Greek modes and nowhere in his music is there any rapprochement with modern Europe, or any harmony, except for parodistic purposes. Even those who, like the present writer, are unqualified to assess the validity of Partch's mathematics, may feel sympathy with his intentions, both because we have no reason for complacency about our civilization as it is, and also because the "system" has enabled Partch to create monophonic works on a fairly extended scale which can be formally satisfying.

This form is not, however, an end in itself; for Partch, even more than for Varèse, all music is magic and also ritual. The *active* incarnation in ritual explains why Partch's music, unlike Varèse's, has no scientific-mathematical relationship to our industrial society, but is always "corporeal", not "abstract" (to use his terms): and is thus always associated with the word, or with dance movement, or with both. His closest European counterpart is Carl Orff, who likewise seeks the salvation of a moribund society in orgiastic ritual, embodied simultaneously in music, dance and mime. But whereas Orff adheres—at least until his most recent works—to the more rudimentary forms of the modal and diatonic materials of tradition, Partch, as an offspring of the American deserts, returns to a more radical equation between musical sound, noise, human speech, and physical movement. His music *has* to be monophonic and in Just Intonation *because* it is a corporeal, theatre ritual as were classical Greek drama and the Japanese Noh play: and as the "popular" tradition of Japanese Kabuki theatre still is. His works, like Aristophanes and Japanese Kabuki, use monophonic chant, dance, mime, slapstick and juggling for social-religious ends. It is not his fault that the religion he celebrates is that of the outsider, the bum. For a period of eight years he, in fact, lived by "riding the rails", identified with the outcast and the Beat Generation; and the first of his large-scale works—*U.S. Highball*, written in 1943—was a musical commentary on that phase of his career. Here Partchian instruments represent both railway noises and also the "bums" as characters, and the text, intoned or chanted by a hobo called Mac, consists of the names of railway stations culled during a journey east from San Francisco, mixed up with fragments of hobo dialogue, Mac's random thoughts, snippets of advertisements and wayside graffitti. Little bits of pop songs, hill-billies, and bar-tunes float in and out of the hobo's railroad journey-to-no-end; naïve pentatonic cries sound wistful against the corny seventh and ninth chords of the vamping "guitar-bass", disembodied yet mysteriously magnified on Partchian percussion.

U.S. Highball is directly "about" the disintegration of urban civilization and the pathos of the outcast's search for the springs of life. In Partch's later works the positive and the negative aspects of this situation are more sharply differentiated, the rebirth of (pre-Christian) vitality being opposed to the mechanization and bureaucracy-ridden sterility of the modern world. Partch epitomizes this duality by calling some of his works "satyrs"; they are satires in the modern sense on the present, but they also reinvoke the satyrs who were the source of man's potency. So although Partch does not accept a scientific-mathematical universe as Varèse does, he does not present a simple case of white against black. He offers not a churlish lament against our industrial civilization, but a passionate desire that industry's power should serve the ends of life, not death. This is evident even in those few works of Partch that have no explicit theatrical connotations. Thus he describes *Even Wild Horses* (1953) as Dance Music for an Absent Drama, adding that "music and dance enter the consciousness through the gate to illusion, lost recollections, and dimly seen prophetic projections. This music might be considered as autobiographical by almost anyone, in darkly humorous moments." "One's beginning is a decent and honourable mistake, and long before life has run its course one is obliged to contemplate—both dazed and undazed—the endless reaches of one's innocence." While this music is often surrealistically funny (the score includes an Afro-Cuban Minuet on "Happy Birthday to You!") the innocence of the dadaism releases energy. Significantly, the music starts from those elements of primitive (especially Latin-American) music that have found a place in our commercial world; and the point is not to guy the clichés of samba, conga or rumba but to reveal again—as the commercial or jazzy stereotypes revert to the wilder wails and grislier grunts from which they sprang—the mysterious power that makes for life. Even *Rings Around the Moon*, which seems to be a negative parody of the affectations of sophisticated "culture", creates a positive quality of strange abandon from its microtonal distortions of parlour platitude and tea-shop tinkle. If the negative here becomes positive, in *Castor and Pollux,* a danced allegory of rebirth, a certain farouche hilarity imparts satyrical overtones to the grand theme of the mating of Leda and the Swan: the inseminated eggs that produce Castor and Pollux, who become Partch instruments, require precisely 234 beats each for the cracking. The Polynesian sound of Partch's gigantically magnified plectrum and percussion instruments, wailing microtonally without reference to tempered scale, charms away contemporary contrariety: with the mating of pairs of Kitharas and Cloud Bowls, Giant Marimbas and Harmonic Canons one can indeed believe that, in Partch's words, "misfortune is impossible". It is interesting that Partch says that watching his instruments being played is part of the experience. In this sense his music would be ritual and theatre even if there were no stage action; and this is true whether the pieces employ words and dance or not. The first work to which he still owns—the settings of poems by Li Po for intoning voice and adapted viola (1931) is a series of charms or incantations; the voice speaks, chants, or vocalizes in the simplest pentatonic phrases, while the forty-three-tone viola microtonally moans in the background, or is on occasion strummed or plucked; *Bless this House*, composed nearly thirty years later for intoning voice with adapted viola, oboe and three Partchian percussion instruments, is precisely what its name implies—an oddly touching, pentatonically naïve, even infantile "blessing" over a lulling percussive accompaniment; and there is no difference in kind between these pieces and, say, the *Cloud Chamber Music* of 1950, which sounds like Balinese gamelan music, and quotes a ritual tune of the Zuni Indians of New Mexico.

But Partch's most representative works are all actively theatrical, a cross between masque and drama. In 1952 he set Yeats's marvellous translation of Sophocles' *Oedipus Rex* for voices speaking, wailing and chanting, with a monophonic women's chorus, and dance movement supported by some normal instruments and many of his invented instruments. For the recorded version he was obliged to make a new translation, and therefore to modify the music, since permission to use the Yeats translation in a recording was refused. Even though Partch's text falls a long way short of Yeats's, enough comes over in the recording to suggest that the version might be extremely effective in the theatre. Certainly it must be closer in spirit and technique to the original character of Greek drama than any previous revival, not excepting Orff's musically more impressive *Antigone*—the only attempt strictly comparable with that of Partch. More commonly, however, Partch finds his model in the conventions of Japanese Kabuki theatre, which, unlike Greek drama, is still a living tradition, and a "popular" art—like the American musical comedy. In *The Bewitched* (1956) a group of Lost Musicians represent the instinctual life; "they are primitives in their unspoken acceptance of magic as real, unconsciously reclaiming an all-but-lost value for the exploitation of their perception". The piece deals satirically with these Clown Musicians' dadaistic, unmalicious destruction of sundry fake products of twentieth-century mechanization and intellectuality: "A Soul Tormented by Contemporary Music finds a Humanizing Alchemy", "The Cognoscenti are plunged into a Demonic Descent while at Cocktails", "Visions fill the Eyes of a Defeated Basketball Team in the Shower-Room", "Two Detectives on the Trail of a Tricky Culprit Turn In their Badges", and so on. At first the Lost Musicians think they are unhappy to be lost, so they appeal to an Ancient Witch to help them. But she—a "prehistoric Seer untouched by popular malevolence and with that uncanny power to make others see"—leads them to understanding. At the end, they know that they already know the only truth that is humanly apprehensible; in their clownish innocence, they are true to the moment. The moment of insight gone, they wander away, because "perception is a sand-flea. It can light only for a moment. Another moment must provide its own flea". So the twentieth-century musical parody dissolves into what Partch calls slapstick; and again it is this dadaism that leads to the moment of truth, and links contemporary non-values to values so old that they seem eternal. Humans who microtonally yell, moan, shout and grunt in jazzy abandon or hysteria may become indistinguishable from hooting owls, barking foxes, and the wild cats of the woods; and in returning, below consciousness, to Nature they may rediscover their true selves. The long, wailing pentatonic chant that occurs at the end of the prologue and again in scenes 8 and 10 evokes, with magically therapeutic effect, an age-old quietude that is none the less full of longing. Significantly, it is based on a chant of the Cahuilla Indians—aboriginal Americans who still live in the emptiness of the southern Californian deserts, where Partch grew up. We remember again William Carlos Williams's remark that "every American is an Indian without a home". This weird chant—sounding the more disturbing against the wavering ostinati of Partch's forty-three-tone reed organs—sings simultaneously of what home means, and of how it feels to be homeless.

In his next theatre piece, *Revelation in Courthouse Park* (1960), Partch adapts classical mythology to his own use. The work draws a contemporary psychological parallel to the *Bacchae* of Euripides, shifting in time and place between ancient Thebes and the courthouse of a modern park. The twentieth-century Dionysius is Dion, Hollywood King of Ishbu Kubu; and the ritual of Hollywood substitute-living ("The Happy Way, Right or Wrong, Dead or Alive") is celebrated with Hollywood music—that of TV entertainment, revealed as fatuously inane, partly through imbecilic reiteration, partly through the distortions occasioned by Partch's forty-three-tone system which, being melodically conceived, can only distort harmonically derived music. Yet again the distortion is not merely parody; it also gives an Ives-like veracity to the off-key blowing of the park bands, played on Partchian instruments and on conventional instruments simultaneously; and when the party really gets going to Latin-American rhythms, the synthetic Hollywood product is once more metamorphosed into a revelation of the wildness—and the longing—within the heart. Compared with Ives (whom it resembles in its realistic exploitation of "popular" performing techniques), or with Varèse (whom it resembles in its use of the noises of the external world, sometimes electronically reproduced), Partch's score to *Revelation* has very little musical substance. But this criticism is hardly relevant, since his scores are not meant to be musically self-subsistent. Their ritual is viable only in the theatre, where too much musical substance, in the wrong place, may be a liability; their theatrical impact may well be proportionate to their intuitional naïvety.

This would certainly seem to be true of *Water! Water!* (1961), his most recent theatre piece, which consists of eleven prologues and nine epilogues, separated by an intermission. Here the Partchian duality is presented in its simplest form, for the stage is divided into two. On the audience's left is a largish American city, Santa Mystiana, humanly represented by such characters as a disc jockey, an alderman, a Lady Mayor and a radio baseball commentator. On the audience's right the stage presents the open countryside, with a dark, mountainous horizon. The control over Nature which Society and Civilization have achieved is symbolized in the city's possession of a huge dam. None the less, the city is suffering severely from drought, and Lady Mayor, alderman and disc jockey are driven to the desperate expedient of calling for help on a Negro jazz band, who are said to be able to invoke rain through voodooism and an appeal to the Dark Gods. Not surprisingly, agreement between the parties is difficult; the Lady Mayor thinks the jazzmen's music isn't Nice, and the jazzmen think the city dwellers are not sufficiently respectful of the Water Witch. After sundry disputations between the beats and the squares, jazz incantations produce rain, which becomes so heavy that a baseball game has to be abandoned, and civilization falls in ruins. After the Intermission we find that chaos dominates the city as the result of a Second Flood. Both Arthur, the jazzman and God of Rain, and Wanda the Witch are put on trial and sued for a million dollars, but this is of no consequence, since, as climax to the floods, the dam bursts—and with it man's attempt to control the waters of the unconscious. To the strains of the "Santa Mystiana the Beautiful" hymn—the Nice Tune the Lady Mayor asked for—both beats and squares resign themselves to the deluge. When the disc jockey has been whisked into nothingness, the mobile instruments are finally driven down into the orchestral pit by the producer: for the "highest goodness is like water. It seeks the low place, that all men dislike" (after Lao-tze). Partch calls this American Kabuki play a "tragic farce", and also a musical. In the conventional sense there is virtually no "music" left in it, though some of the parodies (especially the Santa Mystiana anthem and the Beats and Squares attempted reconciliation, "We really love each other In 43 Whines to the Octave") are very funny. It is interesting that the more Partch deals with the human, the more anti-musical he becomes, though that does not mean that his work may not still be good theatre. Perhaps the most *musically* beautiful and significant moments in his work occur in his score to *Windsong* (1958), a film version of the Apollo and Daphne story, wherein the human is metamorphosed into animate Nature. Partchian instruments here create a *collage* of sounds, aural cuts complementary to the visual cuts of the film: musical images suggested by "dead trees, driftwood, falling sand, blowing tumbleweed, flying gulls, wriggling snakes, waving grasses"—the non-human elements of Nature. In this aspect of his work Partch carries to an extreme that element in Varèse's music which was concerned with the desert, both within the mind and without.

Perhaps the film is Partch's most congenial medium. Certainly, since he is at heart a composer of the desert, it is hardly surprising that there should be a paradox inherent in his theatre work: which is that although he is a ritual composer for the theatre—with a simple "message" comparable with that of the novelist Henry Miller and the poet Kenneth Patchen, who are his contemporaries—his ritual is likely to be experienced only by a few "cognoscenti" of the type he despises. Part of his creative career has been spent in departments of American universities, which have given him grants to pursue his researches and to build his instruments and have generously financed the performance of his theatrical pieces. One can hardly imagine his works being taken up by other than university theatres, both because the theme of his pieces is a denial of the values the commercial theatre lives by and, complementarily, because the general public, to whom Partch's message is addressed, is naturally conservative and chary of experiment. In any case, the practical difficulties involved in transporting his unique instrumental resources would probably be insurmountable. This paradox may explain why Partch has had comparatively little influence on other artists. If his position seems a bit unreal, that is not a denial of his integrity; and we can see clearly enough where he stands if we think of him as the connecting link between Varèse and John Cage.

While Cage holds views about modern civilization which are in many ways comparable with Partch's, he has had, through his music, a considerable influence on other artists, perhaps because he was at first content to carry Varèse's process of magical-mathematical abstraction a stage further, rather than seek for a public manifestation of ritual in the theatre. Debussy had accepted the chord as a moment in itself, without before or after; Varèse accepted as a moment in itself the single tone, or an aggregate of tones and timbres. Cage—born in 1912, and a West Coast man like Partch—acknowledges a debt to both Debussy and Varèse, and carries this conception to its ultimate conclusion. He takes each single sound or noise—each sand-flea, to use Partch's term— as an audible event which is complete in itself, and is therefore incapable of development. So there is, in the traditional sense, no melody and no harmony in his music: and not even rhythm as European composers have conceived it—in relation to melody and harmony. Cage merely places his sound-events one after another, and they are related only because they co-exist in space. Since he wishes his compositions to be "free of individual taste and memory in their order of events", they have no logical sequence and are planned only chronometrically; the only element that is pre-ordained is the points-in-time at which their "space" erupts into the silence of eternity. Henry Cowell has likened a Cage work to a "shower of meteors of sound" in that each event is "an aggregate of materials of sound that cohere, much as physical elements find themselves joined together in a meteorite". We may compare this meteor analogy with the metaphor of crystal-mutation that Varèse used about his own music; and that we may compare with the analogy from marine life that Carter employed and the metaphor of organic plant life (the tentacular roots of the lilac) that we applied to Ruggles. The four metaphors represent a process of dehumanization which becomes—from Ruggles to Carter, to Varèse, to Cage—progressively less living, more abstract.

Though Cage did not arrive at this extreme point immediately, his earliest music is extraneous to Western tradition. His first works—such as the Sonata for clarinet solo, the Sonata for two voices, and the *Three Pieces* for flute duet, which were all written in 1933—tend towards the Orient in that they are purely linear, non-harmonic; and these linear works were followed by a phase in which Cage wrote exclusively for percussion instruments. The Trio and Quartet of 1935 and 1936 use, in addition to bass drum, specifically Oriental instruments such as Chinese wood blocks, tom-toms, tam-tams, and bamboo sticks. Structurally the pieces employ talas—pre-ordained rhythmic series, often of great complexity, their order being based "not on durations of notes but on spaces of time". Cage's fully characteristic music emerges with the series of works for prepared piano, stretching from the *Amores* of 1943 to the *Sonatas and Interludes* of 1947. The prepared piano, which was Cage's invention (prompted, perhaps, by some of the experiments of Cowell), is an ordinary grand piano with some of the strings muted by the insertion at specified points of bits of wood, glass, rubber or metal. The resultant sound should not resemble a piano so much as a Balinese gamelan orchestra; indeed, the prepared piano is a highly ingenious means of producing a one-man percussion band of most varied and sensitive sonority. *Amores* consists of two pieces for prepared piano and two for ordinary percussion instruments (tom-toms, pod rattle and wood blocks). Piano and percussion pieces are similar in character, for the percussion instruments use different pitches in a linear if not melodic way, while the piano is restricted to very few pitches in mainly pentatonic patterns, hypnotically repeated; many of the "prepared" tones of the piano are also of indeterminate pitch, like the tom-toms. Since there is no melodic *line* and no modulation the sound-event is, again, spatial rather than temporal. The delicate, tranquilizing pieces have no beginning, middle and end, though the chronometric proportions of sound to silence are calculated.

The *Sonatas and Interludes* specifically employ ragas and talas. Each Sonata has a two-part structure with both parts repeated, consisting of x times x bars of $\frac{2}{2}$, divided into different arithmetical proportions for each piece. The Interludes do not have this pre-ordained pattern, though each lasts four minutes, as against the Sonatas' two or two and a half minutes. Cage says that he intended to express the "permanent emotions" of Indian tradition. The magic or ritual they celebrate can hardly, however, be identical with that celebrated by the Indian musician. They seek, like the *Amores*, a haven of quiet within the mind, and their sensory passivity betrays an obvious relationship to the pentatonic-Oriental moments in Debussy's piano pieces and in the early works of Satie, despite the more radical nature of the technique:

EXAMPLE I

Sometimes—as in the exquisite first Interlude—there is a distant, disembodied reference to the contemporary world, because the rhythmic patterns (like some of Partch's) here suggest the Latin-American rumba, reminding us not only of ancient Polynesian music but also of twentieth-century jazz. The hurly burly of the world is, however, purged, sublimated into a timeless grace. This is strictly true, for one must relinquish the Time sense in order to listen to these pieces. As a whole, the work lasts well over an hour and is, in sonority and dynamics, of extremely restricted range. To complain that it is "monotonous", or that it goes on too long, is as irrelevant as it would be to make this objection to the improvization of a classical Indian vina player or—to take a less exalted example—to that of a first-class jazz combo, playing through the small hours of the night.

The Oriental and abstract elements in Cage's music tend to be equated, as they are in the music of Varèse; and the equation is at once magical and mathematical. The abstract-mathematical aspect was

directly manifested in two works, composed in 1940, to which Cage
gave a title that implies an analogy with the visual arts. His *Constructions
in metal* are scored for bells, thundersheets, muted piano, gong, various
sizes of cowbell and of Japanese temple gong, automobile brake drums,
anvils, Turkish and Chinese cymbals, water gong, tam-tam, sleigh
bells, rattle, wind bell and snare drum; and again we are invited to
listen to the sound-events in space, at chronometrically predestined
periods. The magical—as compared with the abstract—aspect of Cage's
work was explored in pieces written during the 1940s, wherein he
introduced the human voice, singing-speaking-chanting in its lowest
register, in a mixture of determinate and indeterminate pitch. *The
Wonderful Widow of Eighteen Springs* (text from Joyce's *Finnegan's
Wake*) was the first of these pieces, scored for voice and closed piano,
used as a percussive and resonating instrument; it was followed in 1945
by *She is Asleep*, a work in two parts, the first purely percussive for
twelve tom toms, the second for wordless voice and prepared piano.
The quartet of tom-toms play in a cyclical tala, continuing in an eternal
circle, so that they induce hypnosis; the vocalize ululates in an extremely restricted vocal range, sung in folk-like incantation:

EXAMPLE 2

Like some of Partch's chants, this invokes a primordial American-
Indian music; it is an American's night-music whispered, in a profound
hush, from a state below consciousness. The submission to sleep, and
therefore to the subconscious, suggests how Cage is already turning
away from pre-ordained serialism. The raga and tala may be a Law
which can liberate one from the will; but how far can they be valid
for an aboriginal American? In the last resort, he must find his will-
lessness in submission to the waters of the unconscious, which float in a
primeval void.

It is interesting that when Cage temporarily returned to conventional instruments he was able to use even the medium of the string quartet in a manner that has no connection with European tradition. His strange Quartet was begun in 1949 in Paris and finished the following year in New York. Intended as a tribute to the Parisian Erik Satie, whom Cage reveres for his abnegation of the will, it is almost unique in Cage's work in that it employs chords vertically. These harmonies are, however—like Satie's and unlike Debussy's—the simplest diatonic concords; and they are virtually without movement, let alone modulation. They revolve around themselves, occasionally bumping into one another, thereby creating dissonances which are, however, arbitrary, without sense of progression or climax. Perhaps these clashings in space may be related to the meteor analogy; certainly in the slow movement, which is the heart of the work, we reach a condition of near-paralysis. Indeed, the heart almost stops; the pendulum of the ostinato figures swings so slow as to be, in Cage's directive, "almost stationary". Again the music induces trance: is a *reductio ad absurdum* of the slowing-down pendulums in Copland's music. After this "spatial" stasis, the tiny last movement, called "Quodlibet", introduces fragments of Satiean street tunes in ostinato patterns, still played 'non vibrato', as is the whole work. The effect is most odd, for it makes the streets, whether of Paris or New York, seem infinitely forlorn, childishly pathetic, as compared with the eternal silence. It would seem that human life is a *quodlibet* because we have no choice in the matter: or rather should have no need of choices.

So Cage's concern with will-lessness, with the levels below consciousness, led him to a doctrine of irrationality, if the term is not self-contradictory. He gave explicit formulation to this in the *Music of Changes* for piano solo, written the year after the Quartet, in 1951. Although the piano is not "prepared" for this work, it is used entirely as a timbre or dynamics instrument, without melody and harmony. The spatters of sound-noise are precisely notated; the frequency and duration of their occurrence, however, are dictated by I-Ching, an ancient Chinese method of throwing coins, or sometimes marked sticks, for chance numbers. The *composition* of the sounds, in the strict sense, is Cage's creation; their succession in time is governed by a game of chance, and the laws of the game are so complex that continual variation is inevitable. The creating mind is still not negligible, because the beauty and interest of the kaleidoscopic patterns that chance makes depend on the potentialities of the original materials. But Cage has here gone a long way towards releasing music from "memory and desire", as well as from "individual taste"; and he goes still further in work such as the notorious *Imaginary Landscape* for twelve radio sets playing twelve different programmes simultaneously, with their tuning, dynamics and durations (whether of sound or silence) all determined by chance. Since the material provided by the radios is independent of Cage there is no longer even an initial inventor; the "ideas" are the radio station's, while the durations and proportions are produced by the toss of a coin.

Presumably Cage is making a philosophical gesture rather than composing; he is saying that all sounds have their values, not merely the extremely refined and indeed personal sounds that he himself invents. "A sound", he has written, "does not view itself as thought, as ought, as needing another sound for its elucidation, as etc.: it has no time for any consideration—it is occupied with the performance of its characteristics. . . . It does not exist as a series of discreet steps, but as transmission in all directions from the field's centre. It is inextricably synchronous with all other sounds and non-sounds, which latter, received by other sets than the ear, operate in the same manner." Thus sounds have their value as sound—rather than as psychological "meaning"—only in relation to the silence that surrounds them; and from the *Music of Changes* onwards the silences between Cage's chronometrically disposed sounds tend to become longer and longer.[1] Cage has compared the silences in a passage such as this from *Music of Changes*:

EXAMPLE 3

---

[1] Antheil, in his *Ballet Mécanique*, used arithmetical durations of silence as early as 1924, partly as a result of studying Oriental music. As we have seen, however, the work's motor rhythms relate it to Western music, and it does not get far with the space-time concept.

to the space between the objects in Japanese stone gardens. Just as the stones are there so that we may be aware of the space between them, so the sounds are there in the music so that we may be aware of the silence that separates them. We have seen that other American composers— for instance, Ruggles and Harris—have been concerned with man's will and ego as they are affected by solitude and space: and that such representatively American composers as Copland and Varèse—and in some aspects of their work, Ives, Sessions and Carter, too—have seen twentieth-century man's struggle towards spiritual equilibrium as an attempt to accept, even to derive strength from, his loneliness. To all these men, however, the emptiness of space is to some degree inimical; the ends of Copland's *Piano Fantasy*, of Session's Second Quartet, of both of Carter's quartets, of Varèse's *Deserts* and *Poème électronique* tell us that empty space is opposed to man's humanity, even though man must, if he is to survive, come to terms with it. Cage, on the other hand, invites us to lose consciousness of our selves in entering, in embracing, space itself. Much though he has in common with Varèse, he has come to deplore what he considers the philosophical and psychological implications of Varèse's music. We have reached the ultimate oblivion that Wagner's Isolde yearned for as she sang (maybe) the death-song of the European obsession with personal will and passion.

In the most recent phase of his work Cage has made considerable use of graphs and of electronics as a means of producing "abstract" sound. The opening page of his *Music for Carillon*, 1958, looks, in score, as shown on pages 184 and 185:

The transcription Ex. 4a and 4b is a graphed version of the more normally notated version. The position of the point, horizontally and vertically, determines a tone's place in time and pitch. "An inch, horizontally, represents a second"; and in performance the player uses a chronometer. "Since it had been decided", Cage says, "that the piece would last four minutes, 240 inches of graph paper were required. Eleven rectangular pieces of paper were folded (some symmetrically, some asymmetrically) and cut. When unfolded, they were placed one at a time at structural points in the total area, points being inscribed on the graph through the cuts in the paper patterns. Chance operations determined what patterns were to be used, in what frequency, and in what relation to the structural points. No record was made of the nature of the structure nor of the chance operations; and no history was kept of the processes involved. The neglect to do this is of little consequence, since the objective was not to make a composition, but rather to bring about a situation in which the sounds themselves would be autonomous."

In this case the result (in the recorded performance) is strangely beautiful: like a tolling of Japanese temple gongs dedicated not to a god, but to Nothingness. Cage's works for electronic tape, which use similar principles, are more difficult to relate to any notion of "music", since, despite the acute sensitivity of his ear, Cage seems deliberately to have selected and processed the most grotesque noises available. In *Williams Mix* the sounds consist of city sounds, country sounds, pure

EXAMPLE 4a

1 System = 7 Seconds

electronic sounds, manually produced sounds (including the literature of music), wind-produced sounds (including songs) and small sounds requiring amplification. The frequency, loudness, pitch and duration of the sounds that make up the "mixture" are controlled by chance operations. In some of his later works Cage has extended the notion of chance in that he allows succession and duration, in humanly operated instruments, to be controlled surrealistically by caprice. He says, for instance, that in the *Concert* for piano and orchestra (1957–8) his "intention is to hold together disparities much as one finds them held together in the natural world—in a forest or a city street". So there is a sixty-three-page piano part containing eighty-four different sound aggregates to be played in whole or part, and in any sequence. There

EXAMPLE 4b

are also a number of solo parts, of a similar nature, for wind and string instruments; this is what a page of the trombone part looks like:

EXAMPLE 5

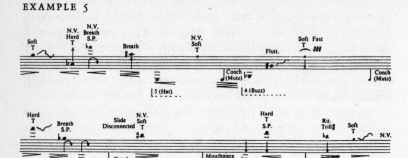

An "aria" for voice also exists, which may or may not be sung simultaneously: and there is a part for a conductor who may or may not indicate temporal durations for the various entries. His function is not, of course, to beat time, for there is no temporal pulse. Cage no longer notates the basic material (as he does in *Music of Changes*); he merely offers hints for improvisation, and the succession and duration of the parts are dependent partly on chance operations (the throwing of coins, the noting of imperfections in the paper), and partly on the sub- or semiconscious reactions of the participants. Each performance is, inevitably, different, the texture of the sound being in some ways comparable with Varèse, since both strings and wind instruments play microtonally in an infinite gamut of pitches. The chance- or subconscious-derived "structure" means, however, that the music has a chaotic, even relaxed, amorphousness in place of Varèse's impersonal order. The forest, or the city street, here takes over from man; and we cannot help feeling that the loss of Cage's own aural sensitivity is regrettable. Cage would consider our regret in the strict sense impertinent, for he is no longer concerned with "so-called music". Indeed, since each player in the *Concert* is instructed to play all, any, *or none* of the notes allotted to him, it is theoretically possible, if improbable, that a performance could result in complete silence.

Perhaps, indeed, this is music's ultimate goal; and in view of Cage's conception of his art as an agent of his own brand of Zen Buddhism the remark need not be merely facetious. The beauty and delicacy of Cage's earlier music for prepared piano is as undeniable as its however unobtrusive individuality. If, in opposing individuality and in cultivating mathematical determinacy along with human indeterminacy he seems to have thrown out the baby with the bath water, and to have created some tediously ugly taped noises into the bargain, we cannot dismiss his motives as merely frivolous. That they are irrational is part of the point, since music, in itself, is "inclusively and intentionally purposeless", and any relevant *action* must be theatrical, as Cage has demonstrated in his *Theatre Piece* of 1960. This provides a set of eight parts for from one to eight musicians, dancers, and mimers, "to be used in whole or part, in any combination". Time-brackets are given within which an action may be made. These actions are from a gamut of twenty nouns and/or verbs chosen by the performer. This gamut changes at given points, so that each part involves a performer in a maximum of fifty to a hundred different actions. Means are supplied for the answering of four questions with regard to the activities within any one time-bracket. The composing means are the materials of *Fontana Mix*. (One of Cage's processed tape works.)

In considering musical abstraction and theatrical "corporeality" as complementary, Cage has begun to approach Partch's philosophical position and, in works such as this uproarious *Theatre Piece*, has cultivated a still more uncompromising Dadaism. This release from "consciousness" is prompted by motives similar to those that gave rise to Dadaism after the First World War; but Cage's search after the Fool's will-less state differs from Tristan Tzara's, and resembles Partch's, in that it exists in emptiness, independent of any tradition and almost without reference to a past. With far greater validity than Europe's Paul Klee, Cage could say: "I want to be as though new-born, knowing nothing about Europe, nothing, knowing no pictures (or music), entirely without impulses, almost in an original state." Stravinsky has acutely pointed out, in conversation with Robert Craft, that the Cage "phenomenon" is related to the Henry James theme of American innocence and European experience. "Is it only that Mr Cage does things that Europeans do not dare do and that he does them naturally and innocently, not as self-conscious stunts? Whatever the answers, no sleight of hand, no trap-doors, are ever discovered in his performances; in other words, no 'tradition' at all, and not only no Bach and no Beethoven, but also no Schoenberg and no Webern either. This *is* impressive, and no wonder the man on your left keeps saying *sehr interessant*." So completely *blank* an innocence can be compared only with that of another American of the earlier Dadaist movement: for Gertrude Stein abstracted the word—in the same way as Cage abstracts the individual sound—from antecedence and consequence. There is also a (less significant) parallel between Cage's "landscapes" for radios and the visual "ready-mades" that Marcel Duchamp produced in the American phase of his strange career. They invite us to look at objects or to listen to sounds as they are "in themselves", without the intrusion of taste, memory or desire. Both are anti-art in that they destroy the barriers between objects existing in the visible and audible world and those few objects which are artificially segregated in museums, art-galleries and concert-halls. For Cage, the accidental sounds that may occur (in the street, in the apartment above, or in the basement) during the performance of *his* sounds and silences are part of the experience.

We may think, we probably do think, that the human will has unexpected resilience and that the pain of consciousness—the spiritual and nervous energy that went to make a Beethoven—can be, must be, borne. At the same time we cannot merely laugh away Cage's belief that we have reached a point of no return. He states, after all, a truth which we have seen to be latent, in less fanatical terms, in composers as diverse as Ives, Ruggles, Harris, Carter, Copland and Sessions, as well as in his direct predecessors, Griffes, Cowell, Varèse and Partch; and there is evidence of a comparable evolution in European music also, as we can see from aspects of the work of Debussy, Satie, Stravinsky, Webern, Messiaen, Orff, not to mention Boulez, Stockhausen and Nono. Indeed, if Western man does not to some degree go his way, we may literally blow ourselves up: so perhaps it is not surprising that so apparently eccentric a figure as Cage should have become, not an isolated figure, but a beatnik saint whose disciples proliferate. Composers such as Christian Wolfe, Earle Brown and Morton Feldman are a new phenomenon in that they did not even start from our post-Renaissance concepts—from what they dismiss as "so-called music". Earle Brown has specifically stated that the impulse towards his kind of composition came from the visual arts of Alexander Calder and Jackson Pollock; he has tried to create a musical "mobile" in which control and non-control work together, "finding" aspects of a work within the process of "making" it. His first representative works combine strict Webernian serialism with passages in what he calls time-notation—a highly ambiguous graphic scoring that indicates not metrical proportions, but approximate spatial relationships relative to the performer's time-sense. The *Music* for violin, cello and piano of 1952 uses a strict twelve-note row in a way that has recognizable kinship with Webern; but the *Music* for cello and piano of the following year sounds like a cross between Webern and Varèse. The cello wails, howls, grunts and shrieks in a way that is as uncannily evocative as Varèse's hooters and sirens; because the serialism is tempered by ambiguous "time-notation", the music is in total effect quite unlike Webern, being strangely relaxed, despite its explosiveness. *Hodographs* (1959) carry further the attempt to make a virtue of the discontinuous and disembodied. In No. 1, for flute, bells, vibraphone, marimba, piano and celeste, Brown uses two systems of notation. One, which he calls explicit, is similar to that which he employs in the cello and piano work, in that it gives frequency, intensity, timbre, mode of attack and *relative* duration; the other, which he calls implicit, indicates by means of line drawings the amount and character of activity the players should indulge in. The piece is "mobile" in that it achieves an equivocation between the performers' spontaneous doodling and the varying degrees of ambiguity and explicitness in the notation. The result—at least in the recorded version—is exhilarating: and not too protracted.

If Earle Brown effects a compromise between Webern and Varèse, Morton Feldman suggests, more directly, a liaison between Webern and Cage. The Webernian element in his work probably came by way of Stefan Wolpe, whose pupil he was, for Wolpe—a German composer now resident in America—began by writing somewhat aggressive Schoenbergian music, but then joined the post-Webern *avant-garde*. In Feldman's earlier pieces, such as the *Extensions* for violin and piano of 1951, the complete serialization of pitch, rhythm, dynamics and even of the succession of metronomic tempi, relates the music to Webern, though the fragmented (Viennese) lyricism has all but evaporated. The extraordinary stillness which the isolated tones evoke, however, already reminds us of the inner world of Cage's *Sonatas and Interludes*; and like Cage, Feldman soon retreated from the "academic" determinacy of serialism. The *Four Structures* for string quartet, composed in the same year, are non-serial and without any of the formalization of a classical sonata. Single notes, chords, figures, rhythmic patterns

are played mostly 'non vibrato,' in various kinds of harmonic and pizzicato, often repeated many times hypnotically: so that the effect is, in
Feldman's words, "as if you're not listening, but looking at something
in nature". Here Feldman follows Cage in carrying to its ultimate point
the "liberation of the note" that Webern initiated—as a sequel to
Debussy's liberation of the chord.

This naturally led Feldman, as it had led Cage and Brown, to a
degree of indeterminacy, which he explored in his graph pieces. In
Projection 4 for violin and piano a graph indicates whether the performers are to play a high, middle or low register tone, but does so
without definition of pitch. Other signs indicate the approximate
duration of the notes (long or short), and the relative length of the space
between them: the violinist is also told when to use special effects such
as pizzicato. The choice of pitches is determined by the players, so no
two performances will be exactly alike. Again, the hermetic tranquillity
of the music comes from the tones' isolation. In later works Feldman
has employed predictability and unpredictability in about equal proportions. The *3 Pieces* for string quartet of 1954–6 are notated music
which carries the immobility of Cage's *Quartet* of 1950 over the
border into nirvana. The separate notes are much longer sustained than
in the earlier *Structures*, and all three movements are equally motionless; there is no hint of Cage's ghostly reference to the external world.
If we might think that musical abstraction could be carried no further,
the most recent phase of Feldman's music proves us wrong. In the *Piece*
for four pianos of 1957 all the players read from the same score and
start by playing simultaneously a sensuous, and to that degree "world-
ly", sonority which is gently, even tenderly concordant. After the
simultaneous start, however, each pianist repeats the same sequence of
notated tones at intervals dictated by individual choice. "The repeated
notes", says Feldman, "are not musical pointillism, as in Webern, but
they are where the mind rests on an image—the beginning of the piece
is like a recognition—not a motive—and by virtue of the repetitions it
conditions the mind to listen." As we listen, the time-responses gradually co-ordinate, or seem to co-ordinate, until the mind can rest, and
this is the piece's end. The players must enter a state of trance in order
to be able to play the music slowly and quietly enough; and the performers' trance induces in the audience something very like hypnosis.
Feldman has continued in this vein in all his recent music; one of the
appropriately titled *Last Pieces* for piano solo is short enough to quote
complete:

EXAMPLE 6

The *Durations* of 1960–1 apply this technique to a number of wind and string instruments as well as piano, though these instruments are deprived of any melodic potentiality. The various instruments—alto flute, tuba, piano, vibraphone, violin and cello—again all play from the same part—the ultimate monism—always sounding single, precisely designated pitches. They begin simultaneously, but remain free to choose their own durations within a given general tempo. So the instruments, in changing combinations, set up a "reverberation" from a single sound-source; the tones are always isolated, immensely slow, and delicately soft, and when instruments play together, because the durations overlap, the simultaneous sounds are often unisonal or concordant. An infinitely slow drone on muted tuba, a major third on muted string harmonics, sound as though the players are creating the tones out of the eternal silence, and we are being born afresh in learning to listen to them. Music seems to have vanished almost to the point of extinction; yet the little that is left is, like all of Feldman's work, of exquisite musicality; and it certainly presents the American obsession with emptiness completely absolved from fear. The music's passive, rarefied tenderness seems to have the therapeutic property of making us saner, rather than more mad. Since the question of sanity or madness can hardly be decided, however, without some human criterion as reference, it may be that the cycle of "consciousness" has, willy-nilly, started again.

This would seem to be the crucial point: for if there is no past in the music of Cage and Feldman, there is no future either. Paradoxically, the "purer" music or any other art becomes, it also becomes the simpler and the less "artistic". The purest music is the random sound in the air, the purest painting the accidental splash of colour on a fence, the purest poetry the prattling of an infant. As soon as choice comes in, the human will, with memory and desire in its wake, is not far away, and it is from the tension between the activity of the human and the passivity of the material that the thing made—the artefact—results. In this sense Stravinsky is right in saying that the "Cage phenomenon" is "not a purely musical development, or even a musical development at all". If it is "metamusical", however, there may be some validity in saying that it is an anti-experience which we have to go through before music can be born again, out of the silence; certainly the phenomenon is already influencing many composers, both American and European, who are more recognizably "musical". Cage himself has put the matter beautifully in saying that although the *collage*-like actions and the underlying philosophy in his music are like Dada, yet "what makes this action unlike Dada is the space in it, for it is the space and emptiness that is finally urgently necessary at this point in history (not the sounds that happen in it—or their relationship)". This purgation is not merely a negative act, "for nothing is, in the end, denied. It is simply that personal expression, drama, psychology and the like are not part of the composer's initial calculations: they are at best gratuitous. . . . For what is the purpose of writing music? One is, of course, not dealing with purposes but with sounds. Or the answer must take the form of paradox: a purposeful purposelessness or a purposeless play. This play, however, is an affirmation of life—not an attempt to bring order out of chaos nor to suggest improvements in creation, but simply a way of waking up to the very life we're living, which is so excellent once one gets one's mind and one's desires out of its way and lets it act of its own accord." There is a truth in this, whether the music of Cage and Feldman, or the art of Calder and Pollock, is a prelude to the disappearance of the artist as communicator and professional, or whether it is merely —as seems more probable—a transitional stage, necessary before the new "communicators" can emerge. At the very least we must be grateful to Feldman for some sounds that are a more healthful tranquillizer for our nervous distresses than the common drugs of the market: and to Cage for the tenuous beauty of his prepared-piano music and the charm of his personality. As Stravinsky has put it: "I have enjoyed many things Mr Cage has done, and always when he is performed side by side with the young earnests, his personality engages and his wit triumphs—he may bore and frustrate, but he never puts me in a dudgeon as they do."

IX

Innocence and nostalgia:
Samuel Barber and Virgil Thomson

There was a child went forth every day,
And the first object he looked upon, that object he became.

WALT WHITMAN

A world of made
is not a world of born.

E. E. CUMMINGS

I think that no experience which I have today comes up to,
or is comparable with, the experience of my boyhood. . . .
My life was ecstasy. In youth, before I lost any of my senses,
I can remember that I was all alive, and inhabited my body
with inexpressible satisfaction; both its weariness and its
refreshment were sweet to me. This earth was the most
glorious musical instrument, and I was audience to its strains
. . . For years I marched as to a music in comparison with
which the military music of the streets is noise and discord
. . . With all your science can you tell how it is, and whence
it is, that light comes into the soul?

Through our recovered innocence we can discern the innocence of our neighbours.

THOREAU'S JOURNAL

So far we have traced the deepest lines in the evolution of American
music from Ives to Cage. While what is deepest is most revelatory and
is therefore, ultimately, most representative, it is not what first meets
the eye and ear. With the exception of Copland, the composers we
have discussed in detail are not those most frequently played in the
States. There is a tiny audience of initiates for the music of the *avant-
garde*; there is a slightly larger "minority" audience for tough modern
music that is not afraid of the nervous tensions of our urban lives; but
there is a much larger middlebrow audience for a softer modern music
that will offer us opportunities for nostalgia or self-dramatization.
Though we are told that Tchaikowsky and Rachmaninov are slipping
a little in the popularity-poll, it would still probably be true to say that

the middlebrow concert-going public finds its most direct satisfaction in the music of these neurotic misfits. They were composers of talent—in Tchaikowsky's case a composer of genius: but also composers of adolescence, of arrested development. A large public's dedication to adolescence cannot be a sign of emotional health, though one understands the motives that prompt it, and knows that one has not the right to be priggish oneself.

To be born anew, in innocence, as Cage invites us to be, is likely to be upsetting; nothing, on the other hand, could be cosier than to regress to our memories of lost childhood and youth, and we saw in Chapter I that such regression was a dominant theme both in American literature and in the music of the American conservatives. There are, however, other composers who explore the theme of adolescence more immediately and more deeply; and it is probably not an accident that they include some of the most inventive talents nurtured on American soil. Samuel Barber—a New Englander who was born near Philadelphia in 1910—is probably the most frequently performed of "serious" American composers; and it is not extravagant to say that his music is meaningful to comparatively large numbers of people precisely because it is not experientially "mature". His appeal depends on qualities that his music shares with Tchaikowsky and Puccini. It matters because it is heart-felt, never second-hand: and its awareness of adolescence strikes deep into the American experience. It may involve regression to childhood and the womb; but it is a specific child, "realized" in sound, not an idealized abstraction of an American Past.

It is typical that the piece that first called attention to Barber's talent should have been a setting for voice and string quartet of Matthew Arnold's *Dover Beach*—that cry of the young heart, lonely in a hostile world in which Faith is extinct:

> Ah, love, let us be true
> To one another! for the world which seems
> To lie before us like a land of dreams,
> So various, so beautiful, so new,
> Hath really neither joy, nor love, nor light,
> Nor certitude, nor peace, nor help for pain;
> And we are here as on a darkling plain
> Swept with confused alarms of struggle and flight,
> Where ignorant armies clash by night.

Barber was a boy of twenty when he set these words (and sang them himself, in a most touching recorded version). Living in a great industrial civilization, he clearly felt them as personally as did the British

Victorian in the darker years of the Industrial Revolution. The lyrical contours of the voice part, the flowing sea-figuration of the strings, the unabashed sobbing of dominant ninths at the climax, have nothing in common with the antiseptic textures of the music characteristic of the early thirties. This music, unlike that of Walter Piston, for instance, wears its heart on its sleeve, and the sleeve is cut in a nineteenth-century European fashion familiar in Philadelphia. The heart, however visible, is none the less true: so the music is still meaningful.

When Barber turned from such small and intimate pieces to attempt the large romantic gesture he was less successful. His First Symphony opus 9, written in 1936, has another of the qualities of adolescence in that it inflates passion with rhetoric. Although in one movement, it is not, like Harris's Third Symphony, a pioneering "religious" piece. Its texture is not continuous and evolutionary, but falls into three clearly defined, though related, sections: an exuberant Allegro, a Scherzo, and a consummatory Epilogue, beginning andante but growing quicker. In the first movement the harmony and scoring, and even the rhetorically prancing themes, suggest Tchaikowsky with a dash of Mahlerian sophistication, rather than Ives or Copland. Only the metamorphosis of the theme (with "blue" false relations) in the third section has something of the open, declamatory quality of Harris and Copland, and this may be unconscious imitation rather than instinctive affinity. The symphony is a young man's piece, expertly theatrical and melodramatic. But for the brashness of its rhetoric, one might not know that it represented the birth-pangs of a new world, rather than the swan-song of an old one; and there is a sense in which even its buoyancy is stale, being close to the synthetic emotion of Hollywood. The big gesture does not come naturally to Barber, as it did to Harris; nor is he entirely happy when, in a later work such as the "Capricorn" Concerto for flute, oboe, trumpet and strings (1944), he deliberately tries to write music of Coplandesque incisiveness, more in tune with "contemporary" thought. This was not, for Barber, an adequate answer to the lure of romantic inflation: he needed not to evade his romanticism, but to preserve its intimate integrity. The true Barber of *Dover Beach* is present in the exquisite *Adagio* for strings (1936), with which Toscanini scored so remarkable a success both in America and in Europe. The piece's international celebrity was attributable in part to the fact that its elegiac nostalgia found a ready response during the war years; it became a dirge for the young dead, combining in American naïvety the lyrical appeal of Tchaikowsky with a touch of Mahler's world-weariness:

EXAMPLE I

None the less, the potency of the *Adagio*'s appeal comes from its musical merits. Its tender emotionalism goes to the heart because it springs from the heart; if a tear-jerker, it is not a Hollywood tear-jerker. The wide-arched, finely spun cantilena gives to the harmonic opulence a frail pathos, so that one is involved, but never emotionally bullied.

Among Barber's later instrumental works the finest is probably the Piano Sonata opus 26 (1949); and this owes its success to the fact that it is unashamedly lyrical and romantic. While being subtler than the *Adagio*, its passion has a comparably intimate quality; the "American" fourths and Coplandesque dotted rhythms create a sensuous harmonic texture through multiple false relations, and a continuously surging flow by way of triplet and quintuplet rhythms against regular quaver movement. The work is conservative compared with the sonatas of Copland: the first movement is an orthodox sonata movement, the finale a real fugue, the slow movement an aria with Bach-like baroque decoration, the Scherzo a bitonal Mendelssohnic fairy-music. The piano sound is, however, original and beautiful; and the work convinces because any tendency to rhetoric dissolves in the romantically fluid texture. The attempts at modernity—such as the slow movement's twelve-note ostinato—support rather than hinder the music's sensuous intimacy; and in so far as the piece departs from tradition it reminds us most tellingly of the Piano Sonata of Griffes. The richly glinting texture is similar; and while Barber's Sonata does not approach Griffes's ferocity or his revolutionary, eastward-tending conception of form it makes—in the slow movement and the coda to the first movement—a comparable use of ostinati.

Whether in a simple piece like the *Adagio* or a relatively complex piece like the Piano Sonata, Barber's instrumental music depends on the continuity of its lyrical flow. This reminds us that the core of his music lies in his understanding of the human voice. His first meaningful piece, *Dover Beach*, was vocal; and throughout his career he has excelled as a writer of songs—an unusual bent for a twentieth-century composer.

Though his emotional range is limited, he seldom writes vocal music that is factitious in the manner of his First Symphony. One reason for this is that the intimate song form was appropriate to the themes that meant most to him. Born under a lucky star, with a fluent talent, a generous home-background and a ready entry into musical circles, he has found regression to youth more congenial than an attempt to confront those "ignorant armies" of the wide world; and it may not be fanciful to hear in the rocking semiquaver accompaniment to *Dover Beach* not only the sound of the sea that nurses us all, but also the lulling of the cradle. All his best and most typical songs set poems dealing with adolescence—consider the many songs from Joyce's *Chamber Music*. In all of them the conservativism of the technique, its polish and inti-mate charm, suggest a regressive dedication; in all of them the con-servativism is not merely academic, because it is part of Barber's desire to conserve, not merely a musical tradition, but also the emotional aura of his youth. This "personal" implication comes through in the extreme sensitivity of the vocal line, both to verbal inflection and to the vagaries of mood and feeling: and also in the occasional piquancy of harmony or rhythm.

It is typical, even symptomatic, that Barber's most recent song-cycle, and also his best, should be the *Hermit Songs* opus 29 (1953). These are settings of translations of medieval Irish poems by monks and scholars; and the last of them is specifically called "The Desire for Hermitage". It evokes the soft security within the monastery's walls, the tolling bell of the reiterated Gs being the point of rest. Similarly the vocal line, meditating to itself in plainsong-like speech rhythm, un-dulates around the note G, revelling in being "alone, with nobody near me, Singing the passing hours to cloudy Heaven, feeding upon dry bread and water from the cold spring; That will be an end of evil, when I am alone in a lovely little corner among tombs, far from the houses of the great":

EXAMPLE 2

The warmly lapping texture of the piano part, beneath the sensitive vocal line, makes this anti-experience seem subjectively self-involved, almost narcissistic, so that the dry bread and cold water become an exquisite repast, and the graveyard a place to hug oneself in. It is essentially irreligious, and also a bit unreal in the context of the contemporary world; but the feeling is re-created by Barber with authenticity, because it is, indeed, the heart of his work. Sometimes it crops up, more acceptably, in comic form, as in the delightful song about the monk and his cat Pangur. Here the voice's cross-rhythm over the lilting rumba movement:

EXAMPLE 3

Pan - gur, white   Pan - gur

the piano's mewings, and the sinuosity of the middle section (when the monk stretches in his chair and the puss weaves in and out of his legs?) give an edge of self-mockery to the self-regarding cosiness.

It is significant that the two most beautiful "serious" songs from the cycle deal directly with the mother-child relationship. "Ita's Vision" opens with dramatic arioso, wherein the vision occurs. The modal, pentatonic-tending vocal line wonderingly shifts its tonal centre, the piano chords reinforcing the pentatonic simplicity with corruscations of added seconds. The aria itself is a lullaby sung by Mary to the infant Jesus. The line is smilingly lyrical, but slightly insecure, owing to metrical fluctuations between $\frac{6}{8}$, $\frac{9}{8}$ and $\frac{3}{4}$; the piano envelops the voice's melody in a haze of shimmering semiquavers in fourths. At the end the rocking slows to rest as the tune's time-values are augmented from quavers to crotchets to dotted crotchets. The self-involved brooding has here a heart-felt tenderness; and in the fifth song, *The Crucifixion*, Barber's innocence admits to the fact of pain. Most of the song is derived from the bird-cry at dawn—a perfect and an imperfect fourth —with which it opens. At the climax the lyricism is supported by tritonal chords with added seconds; but as the desolation of Calvary becomes equated with the desolation of the mother who must lose her son to a hostile world, the rising fourth theme returns. The immediate reality of the pathos is manifest in the addition of a single quaver before the line resolves in a fourth that, instead of rising, slowly descends:

EXAMPLE 4

In the last bar the bird cries again, its suspended B echoing into silence.

This little song is probably the most deeply affecting music Barber had written up to this point: and may be so because, although rooted in the mother-child relationship, it sings from the mother's point of view, and from the agony, as well as the comfort, of their mutuality. In this sense, this song from Barber's opus 29 may well have been the seed from which sprang his opus 30, the *Prayers of Kierkegaard* for mixed chorus, soprano solo and orchestra. This work, which is in every sense Barber's biggest piece, is not mystical nor even specifically religious. Indeed, it takes us back to the Barber of *Dover Beach*, for the prayers are addressed to a God who is unchanging, as compared with the restlessness of Man's longing. As in the *Hermit Songs*, here God is both father-figure and mother-image: only Barber is now more aware of the nature of his own feelings.

The work opens with unaccompanied, plainsong-like declamation for tenors and basses: man's prayer, which alternates with homophonic outbursts for full chorus, to represent God's unchanging power. Growing from the initial prayer, the chorus appeals for rest in a fugato phrase that is an almost exact quotation, in the same key, of a phrase from *The Crucifixion*. Fourths, both perfect and tritonal, increasingly dominate the texture and are, indeed, one of the few fingerprints that Barber's music shares with more recognizably American composers such as Harris, Copland and Piston. The fugato fourths lead to a soprano solo addressed to Christ: in which sustained orchestral pedal notes suggest the divine Home, while the soloist's flexible rhythm and wide leaps reflect Man's going astray. The chorus joins with the soloist, singing diatonic triads, modally juxtaposed in false relation: the music thus combines, once more, naïve humility with insecurity, especially since the modulations are rapid. When the prayer refers to longing that "lays hold on us" the vocal lines become more chromatic, with Mahlerian major sevenths in false relation, though the flowing fourths continue unbroken in the orchestral figuration. Contrast between the yearning, chromatic soloistic lines and the speaking homophony of the choric prayers grows more acute: until it leads to a climax for divided choirs, both stressing the word "longing" in their chordal declamation, while the orchestra develops the anguished lyricism. The appeal to "hold fast God's highest good" explodes in the first quick, purely orchestral passage, in strong fifths and fourths, but with a hint of desperation in the barking rhythms. The turmoil dies down until nothing is left except an ostinato oscillating between D and E: out of which the original prayer emerges, still for divided choirs singing antiphonally. The "regressive" effect of this passage is, in the context, extraordinary: it is as though, after the orchestral hurly-burly, we retreat into childhood, lisping "Father in Heaven" in a rudimentary pentatonic incantation, without tonal movement, to a distant accompaniment of bells on the note E. But at least our prayer is, in some sense, answered. The music does not fade out on the incantation, but rises to a noble chorale in modally related concords. The work acquires a simple strength from its humility.

Perhaps it is true to say that Barber's music becomes more moving—even, paradoxically, more "mature"—when it is content to admit to its adolescent, childish quality. In the *Prayers of Kierkegaard* Barber treats the Man-God relationship as synonymous with the child-parent relationship; the music has always a gentle distinction and is free from either the inflated bombast of his earlier symphonic works or from the embarrassing archness that disfigures some of the *Hermit Songs*. The failure of Barber's art to grow up becomes a liability only when he seeks to give it more weight than it can bear. This doesn't happen in the *Prayers of Kierkegaard* because the level at which Barber treats the religious theme is unambiguous. It does happen, disastrously, in his opera *Vanessa*, to a libretto by Gian-Carlo Menotti, because here Barber attempts to deal with his hermit theme in an adult way, making a tragic heroine out of a girl who is forced through circumstances to deny life. Regressive innocence is replaced by a most unpleasant gloating over the woman's self-imprisonment, both physical and mental;

the vocal tessitura and the orchestral fabric have Puccini's febrile intensity and neurotic self-involvement without the lyrical panache and the harmonic punch that may justify them. It would seem that Barber needs God, in a negative sense, in order to preserve his innocence: to make it possible for him to retreat to the security of "home" without self-embarrassment.

In this respect it is interesting that his most completely representative work—and one of his most beautiful—is in fact supposed to be sung by a child: or rather by a man re-living his childhood so intensely that the child's voice speaks through him. "We are talking now of summer evenings in Knoxville, Tennessee, in the time that I lived there so successfully disguised to myself as a child", says James Agee in the autobiographical prose-poem that serves as prologue to his novel, *A Death in the Family*. The little boy meditates to himself with Joycean immediacy; and Barber begins his setting of *Knoxville: Summer of 1915* for soprano and orchestra (1952) with a soft-flowing, diatonic-modal texture of Coplandesque luminosity, but with more lyrical continuity. It is like the river of memory: which turns—as the child-voice sings in a pentatonic simplicity of how at evening "people go by, things go by, a horse, a buggy, a loud auto, a quiet auto"—into the rhythm of a rocking cradle. A delicately jazzy section re-creates the bustle of life remembered from the past; this fades into stillness, to evoke the night that is "one blue dew". And out of the quietude comes the memory of Home: father and mother, uncle, aunt and I, lying there, talking of nothing in particular, of nothing at all. The equation between God's love and Home, implicit in the *Prayers of Kierkegaard*, is here explicit in a simple modal line which is similar to the homely-liturgical manner of the *Prayers*:

EXAMPLE 5

May God ⎯⎯ bless⎯ my peo-ple, my uncle, my aunt, my mother,⎯ my good fath - er

and the climax comes with the recognition of the disparity between this tranquil security and the unknown terrors of the "ignorant armies" of the world. The momentary outburst of orchestral dissonance subsides, however, into the original rocking cradle motive in A major. The boy sings of being put to bed, to sleep, "familiar and well-loved in that home", by those who, loving him, yet will not, "not now, not ever, will not ever tell me *who I am*". The voice's final cry, agonized then wistful, is that of the child who cannot break away, cannot grow to independent self-awareness. We are left with an ineffably tender version of the rocking. In James Agee's powerfully evocative text—which the vocal line follows with almost "pre-conscious" spontaneity Barber would seem to have found his quintessential theme.

We have seen that the subject of childhood is crucial and recurrent in American art. A great deal of Ives's music, for instance, starts from recollections of childhood, for being concerned with the New in a new world, Ives saw that "the child is father to the man". But whereas for Ives the child was the beginning of growth, for Barber the child is symbol of the desire to go back, to evade "the fury and the mire of human veins". He is in every sense a much easier, more comfortable composer than Ives: which is why he is, relatively, a box-office success. The commercial appeal of adolescence explains the precariousness of Barber's position—his ability to create a work as honestly touching as *Knoxville: 1915* and also one as perversely nasty as *Vanessa*. Both facets are present simultaneously in a minor piece like *Dei Natali* for orchestra (1960). That Barber should be able to produce at this date this pot-pourri of Christmas carols is evidence of his innocence, which re-creates in pliant polyphony and bright, sharp orchestral colours a medievalism both blithe and tender. But while the most "medieval" sections (the quick, estampie-like movements) preserve the boy's sense of Christmas wonder, they are essentially a reversion to what Christmas "felt like" when one was a child; and this becomes clear in the context, since the slow carols are harmonized and orchestrated with a saccharinity comparable with that of the commercial Christmas card and the TV show. Though Barber is always a more musical composer than Menotti, there is not much to choose between the slower parts of *Dei Natali* and *Amahl and the Night Visitors*, which has become a TV perennial. In both, the Hollywood gloss is a prostitution of the Christmas mystery. It seems sacrilegious, whether one believes in that mystery or not.

Another composer preoccupied with the theme of childhood has avoided this kind of exploitation by making no attempt to court popular favour. Barber excels in songs, but has become a relatively popular composer because he has expressed himself readily in the large-scale conventions of the concert-hall and symphony orchestra: whereas Theodore Chanler—a small talent but a true one—has said everything he has to say in terms of a voice and a piano. His style has affinities with

Barber's in that it is lyrical (diatonic with modal tendencies), conservative, and related to French tradition both in its approach to prosody and in its use of the piano as an atmospheric harmony-instrument. Chanler's melody is, however, more reticent, his harmony more chaste—as one might expect of a self-confessed disciple of Fauré. Both the lyrical intimacy and the purity of harmony help Chanler to achieve his child-like, rather than childish, simplicity: so that it is not surprising that the key-work in his career should be a cycle of settings of that supreme poet of childhood, Walter de la Mare. That the *Eight Epitaphs* should be epitaphs is also part of the point. The verses are supposed to be inscriptions on gravestones, memorials to the forgotten dead, to child, simpleton, spinster, to the odd bit of human flotsam or jetsam, rather than to the great who make a nation's destiny. So the cycle expresses in miniature the American obsession with innocence: and with death as its complement. This may be why it is, for so apparently slight a work, unexpectedly disturbing, as well as charming.

In the first song, "Alice Rodd", the vocal line exquisitely follows the speaking inflections of the words, and in so doing makes the dead child breathe again: consider the transition from the pentatonic parlando of the opening phrase to the flattened E on the words "She were so small":

EXAMPLE 6

The piano adds a delicately twining modal polyphony, like tendrils growing over the grave. "Susannah Fry" has an almost motionless piano figure: softly undulating false relations and flat sevenths over a telescoped tonic and sub-dominant. The pentatonic vocal line dreams in the haze of an eternal summer afternoon. Susannah was "weak in the head, maybe", but the stabbing G natural in the cadential phrase makes us aware of the pathos of all humankind, ourselves included, as the piano's drowsy rocking fades to silence. There is a similarly wistful quality beneath the sprightliness of "Three Sisters". The softly whirring moto perpetuo of scales suggests the sisters' busy domesticity and gaiety of heart, while the cross-rhythms of the vocal line convey their old-maidishness, their hate-fear of Man. The moto perpetuo is in a mixolydian G; when this subsides to the subdominant at the end we feel that the sisters have found, in that high, luminous C major triad, their quietus, for if there is no more scurrying, there is no more fear either. "Thomas Logge" is another scherzo, in which perpetual changes of metre in a unisonal piano texture create the "rascally dog's" peevish malcontent. Yet although Thomas was clearly a prickly customer, and his epitaph is comic, it is not ill-temper that we're left with. There is compassion in the apparently petulant concluding phrase; he should be left in peace, as we hope to be. "A Midget", hero of the fifth epitaph, seems to have known this peace in his life, as in his death. The vocal line, in a dorian B flat, sings a stepwise-moving threnody over a ground-bass-like figure on the piano; a texture of soft, detached scales suggests the little man's minuscule movements—with a hint of the tender gravity of the Stravinsky of *Persephone*.

The remaining three songs run to one small page each. "No Voice to Scold" is explicitly a lullaby for a dead child, with gently stabbing semitonic clashes in a rocking dotted rhythm. "Ann Poverty" becomes a little lament for the weak and pitiful, whether young or old, living or dead; it is built on the simplest texture of falling fifths, with an occasional quavering enharmonic. Then, as epilogue, the cycle has an epitaph on childhood in general, "Be very quiet now". The F sharp major harmonies—like the B major harmonies of "Susannah Fry"— are almost static, and remind us of the telescoped tonics, dominants and subdominants of Copland, though the intimate lyricism is not at all Coplandesque. The song evaporates on an added sixth, leaving us suspended between death and life: for the child's grave has become a cradle wherein life is nurtured, so that the cycle starts again. The beauty and purity of these tiny songs seem impervious to fashion. One cannot imagine they will ever sound dated. They are a part of history—as many big, well-intentioned symphonic works are not—because they have realized, to perfection, their modest truth.

The childhood theme becomes explicit, too, in the work of another

"middle path" composer of a somewhat earlier generation. Virgil
Thomson does not (like Ives) grow up from childhood, nor (like
Barber) look back to it; he rather preserves the inconsequential spontaneity of a child into adult life. Born in 1896, he was a bright boy from
Kansas whose musical legacy consisted of the kind of American bric-à-
brac—hymns, parlour songs, ragtime—that was also the background to
Ives's experience. Intellectually precocious, he won his way to Harvard
and then to Paris, where, as an American cosmopolitan but not ex-
patriate, he became a poor student—who "might as well starve where
the food is good". He also became a member of the Gertrude Stein
circle; and wrote wildly experimental, often satirically debunking
works as a protest against a (post-war) world that had had its day. The
protest was itself that of a child; and in returning to diatonic fundamentals and in deliberately disrupting musical grammar and the logic
of connection, Thomson achieved an American equivalent to the
music of the Parisian Erik Satie, who deflated Europe's post-Wagnerian
pretence and egomania. There is a direct relationship between Thomson's bringing together of emotionally disparate elements—plainsong
and café-tune, Bachian fugue and Middle-West hymn—and Satie's
surrealistically childlike unsentimentality; and both composers discover a personal logic in unexpected collocations of triadic harmonies.
There is an American insouciance and cheek in Thomson's bizarre
juxtapositions which we do not find in Satie's fundamentally grave,
chaste art. Given the difference between an old world and a new, however, both the technical methods and the cultivated naïvety are the same.

This irresponsible spontaneity has two complementary, though
apparently opposed, manifestations in Thomson's first Parisian works.
One is associated with the Church—organ pieces on plainsong themes,
"a capella" settings of Roman liturgy. Thomson wrote these works
not because he was a member of any Church, but because he loved
ritual—and hated too obsessive a concentration on the self. Unexpected
modal and enharmonic relationships between the simplest diatonic
triads give to these pieces a curious quality of *serene instability*; in
technique and mood they are close to the Satie of the early Rose Croix
works, such as the *Messe des Pauvres*. Indeed, Thomson's pseudo-liturgi-
cal works are "poor men's masses" in much the same spirit as Satie's:
ritual music without a faith, but with a Pierrot-like, clown-eyed
gravity. The complementary manifestation is a clown's Black Mass, to
balance the White Mass of the Catholic pieces. The *Sonata da Chiesa* of
1926, for clarinet in E flat, trumpet in C or D, viola, horn and trom-

bone is a key-work, in which irresponsibility does not so much evade formality as deliberately misuse it. The first movement, called Chorale, is based on a primitive pentatonic undulation on solo violin and later clarinet, against starkly dissonant parallel fifths and ninths on the other instruments. The effect is disturbing, much more prankishly perverse than Satie's harmonic dislocations, though it has an affinity with them. Its raucousness is its Americanism: for Thomson tells us that the solo undulation was suggested by a negro preacher he heard in a Kansas church. The chorale proper occurs when, at the end, all the instruments join in hymnic homophony; they are the congregation, inspired by the preacher to the enthusiasm of misplaced accents and wrong notes. The effect is here affectionately parodistic, and thus quite unlike the comparable passages in Ives. The second movement is a tango in alternating $\frac{4}{4}$ and $\frac{5}{5}$, with a slippery theme announced by viola, with triplets and quintuplets sliding across the already irregular tango rhythm:

EXAMPLE 7

The viola tune sounds more appropriate to trombone; and the perversity is increased by the fact that the wind instruments emulate plucked strings, the horn playing grotesquely low in the bass register. This clown-devil's dance is an odd piece to find its way into a "chiesa"; and the inversion of values is completed in the final fugue, which is almost a parody of Bach's "Wedge" fugue, growing cumulatively more sharply dissonant and more contradictory in rhythm. The piercing, "unnatural" sonorities of the E flat clarinet and D trumpet (in place of the customary B flat instruments) are wickedly exploited.

But the naughtiness, being clownish, is as innocent as the goodness of the "a capella" pieces. The music is "beyond good and evil" in no high-falutin sense, but simply because it is unconcerned with moral choices. The *Variations and Fugues on Sunday School Tunes*, for organ, written in the late twenties, must have shocked congregations if they were ever played in American Protestant churches; but they are not irreligious (like Barber's *Hermit Songs*), merely a-religious and non-sentimental (like Satie). The frivolous figurations, the polytonal embroideries and "wrong" notes are to be accepted for their own sake; their "wrong" is as good a "right" as any other. Thomson's gospel of childlike spontaneity thus led him to the series of works he produced with Gertrude Stein. The first of them, *Capital, capitals*, for four male voices and piano, appeared in the following year, 1927. Together, Stein and Thomson make their protest against entrenched propriety, and against the European obsession with Time, for the point of the text is that it is pointless. The four capital cities converse endlessly, but no one answers anyone, and nothing ever happens. Thomson's music "acts" this by using C major clichés traditionally associated with progression and finality in a manner that is continuous but static. Triads, tootling scales, arpeggios, bells, fragments of European folk-clichés and Protestant hymn-tunes pass by kaleidoscopically, without modulation except for some polytonal addenda in the "Mediterranean" passage. Though consistently busy, the music has no climax and no excitement. Perhaps it is significant that the only faintly emotive moment occurs when the Protestant hymn tune—redolent of Thomson's own Kansas community—accompanies the words "as they say in the way they can express in this way tenderness".

While this piece has historical rather than musical interest, Thomson used its technique to greater artistic purpose in his first Gertrude Stein opera, *Four Saints in Three Acts*, which followed in 1928.[1] Here he

[1] Cf. Gertrude Stein's *Autobiography of Alice B. Toklas*: (See page 209)

attempted to give literal expression to the child's spontaneity, for after living with the text a while, he improvised each act at the piano, using only the simplest triadic material. He then revised the improvised version with knowing sophistication: but retained its quality of seeming at once irrational and ordinary. This naïvety goes far beyond Satie and could have been created only by an American; beneath its *enfant terrible* elegance it reaches a homespun humour that gives an odd poignancy to the apparently endless succession of tonic, dominant and subdominant triads. The opera reveals the poetry in the tedium of everyday triviality. Fragments of children's tunes, street songs and hymns appear and disappear; but nothing could be more remote from the amorphous polyphony of Ives than this homophonic sequence of rudimentary concords. In Ives, the quotations are part of the external world: which the artist's consciousness absorbs and translates. In Thomson, the quotations are the ephemera of everyday life: in which the Will would be lost. In this sense *Four Saints*, despite its Parisian chic, portrays in rock-bottom terms "the making of Americans" which is the theme of Gertrude Stein's interminable novel. That it should seem equally interminable is the point: for the high point of the libretto (which of course has no climax, in the accepted sense) is St. Ignatius's vision of Pure Being. In the famous "Pigeons on the grass alas" episode Thomson finds a musical image for this condition of passive will-lessness that is touchingly memorable; the Holy Ghost pigeons (not doves) flutter in a graceful boogie rhythm over an ostinato of a "Salvation Army band" bass that remains constant throughout:

In the meantime as I have said George Antheil had brought Virgil Thomson to the house and Virgil Thomson and Gertrude Stein became friends and saw each other a great deal. Virgil Thomson had put a number of Gertrude Stein's things to music, *Susie Asado*, *Preciosilla* and *Capital Capitals*. He had understood Satie undoubtedly, and he had a comprehension of prosody quite his own. He understood a great deal of Gertrude Stein's work, he used to dream at night there was something he did not understand, but on the whole he was very well content with what he did understand. . . . She delighted in listening to her words framed by his music. . . . Virgil Thomson asked Gertrude Stein to write an opera for him. Among the saints there were two saints whom she always liked better than the others, Saint Theresa of Avila and Ignatius Loyala, and she said she would write him an opera about these two saints. She began this and worked very hard at it all that spring and finally finished *Four Saints* and gave it to Virgil Thomson to set to music. He did. And it is a completely interesting opera both as to words and music.

EXAMPLE 8

If a mag-pie in the sky in the sky can-not cry if the pigeon on the grass a - las.

In its quasi-religious denial of the Will, *Four Saints* has obvious affinities with some of the eastward-tending composers discussed in the previous chapter. Gertrude Stein had conceived the book as one of her "landscape" plays in which people, things and (implicitly) stories are present, but not progressive in the given moment:

> All the saints I made and I made a number of them because after all a great many pieces of things are in a landscape all these saints together made my landscape. These attendant saints were the landscape and it the play really is a landscape. A landscape does not move nothing really moves in a landscape but things are there, and I put into the play the things that were there. . . . All these things might have been a story but as a landscape they were just there and a play is just there. That is at least the way I feel about it.
>
> Anyway I did write Four Saints an Opera to be Sung and I think it did almost what I wanted, it made a landscape and the movement in it was like a movement in and out with which anybody looking on can keep in time. I also wanted it to have the movement of nuns very busy and in continuous movement but placid as a landscape has to be because after all the life in a convent is the life of a landscape, it may look excited a landscape sometimes does look excited but its quality is that of a landscape if it ever did go away it would have to go away to stay.
>
> Anyway the play as I see it is exciting and it moves but it also stays and that is as I said in the beginning might be what a play should do.

As a credo, this has much in common with the beliefs or assumptions of John Cage, who uses the term "landscape" in precisely this sense to describe some of his compositions (of sounds in time, equated with things in space). Indeed, Gertrude Stein's Parisian-American saints bear a distinct resemblance to Cage, and it is pertinent to note that both Thomson and Cage revere Satie. Although Thomson has never practised Cage's ultimate liberation of the *individual sound*, as distinguished from the basic rudiments of tradition, he has always, as author and critic, been sympathetic towards Cage's more radically Steinian abstraction: while Cage in his turn has written a generous and perceptive study of Thomson's work, which he now finds almost the only normal music—apart from Satie and Debussy—that he can listen to. The *Four Saints* were thus never really European, let alone archaic. On the stage they were personified by "childlike" Negroes against a décor of black and white abstraction. The traditions of the past were worn out; in becoming part of a landscape, process without progress, we were born again, reiteratively stammering our childish little phrases. What Gertrude Stein said of her *The Making of Americans* would apply also to *Four Saints*: "It is singularly a sense of combination within a conception of the existence of a given space of time that makes the American thing the American thing, and the sense of this space of time must be within the whole thing as well as in the completed whole thing. . . . Think of anything, of cowboys, of movies or detective stories, of anybody who goes anywhere or stays at home and is an American and you will realize that it is something strictly American to conceive a space that is filled with moving."

Certainly, when Thomson returned to the States he gave a specifically American interpretation to Steinian naïvety. Twenty years later, in 1947, he produced his second Gertrude Stein opera, *The Mother of us All*, which directly concerns "the making of Americans", since the characters are figures from American history, mingled with real and imaginary representatives of the present moment. Again there is no chronological sequence, and no apparent succession in harmony or tonality. But although "there is there and where is where", the texture of everyday life is now immediately recognizable as such. The banalities that float to the surface of the music—reminding us of the Salvation Army Band at the street corner, Aunt Emily on the parlour piano, the band at Billy's graduation time, Uncle Joe playing the chapel organ at his wife's funeral—these are real and true: seemingly unalterable because they are accepted, as Satie would have accepted them, in their own right. In fact, only one quotation ("London Bridge is falling down") appears in the opera, as compared with the innumerable quotations in *Four Saints*. Yet there seems to be no tune that we have not known since we were born. A piece such as the tender Wedding Hymn or the Funeral Hymn in *The Mother of us All* attains a truly Steinian sublimation of the commonplace; and the diatonic simplicities are scarcely modified throughout the opera, apart from some (Satiean) triadic polytonality to suggest the frigidity of snow or the heat of temper. In so far as the tunes appear and reappear throughout the opera, without development but in different permutations, the effect (John Cage has suggested) is rather like that of a chaconne or passacaglia. Since these were originally ceremonial dances, the comparison emphasizes the ritualistic quality of the work, as compared with the "Becoming" of a sonata. What is being celebrated is the sanctity of the commonplace. Like Satie, Thomson achieves his extraordinary originality from a deliberate denial of personal identity.

Only in his settings of Stein texts does Thomson carry the cult of banality so far. Her child-vision is, however, the impulse behind most of his music; nor is it fortuitous that one of his most successful works should be the *Five Songs from William Blake* for baritone and orchestra, which are concerned with the Blakean Innocence rather than Experience. In these most touching songs Blake is, as it were, new-born in the American small town. Thus "The Divine Image" transforms the metre of eighteenth-century English hymnody into an American parlour song, with subtle rhythmic modifications suggested by the words, in a manner comparable with that of Ives in "Two Little Flowers":

EXAMPLE 9

The tune itself is extremely affecting, because it is based on affection for its models; and the Christian implications of the "terrifying honesty" of Blake's words are not belied by the music's apparent triviality: which reveals "the heart of the common lot" no less than the Alcott movement from Ives's "Concord" Sonata. "Tiger, Tiger", though no less simple in means, is very different in mood. The creature's savagery is created by way of broken phrases in Thomson's bugle-call manner, over bare fifths and a regular, sinister march-beat. The slow percussive rhythm, with intermittent silences, manages to hint at an Asiatic quality beneath the here-and-now of Kansas City. The middle section of the ternary form sings of the Lamb in exquisitely tender, diatonic lyricism. "The Land of Dreams" is technically more complicated. Thomsonian bugle-calls serve to wake up the little boy, but the dream-vision introduces chromatically wandering major triads, major-minor bitonality, parallel scales in chromatics, twelve-note transitions and abstruse modulations, ending up in B major, the furthest extreme from the original C. This is one of the pieces that reveal the relationship between the child's vision and a preconscious state. "The Little Black Boy" returns to the small-town parlour. Its model is Stephen Foster; again the tune is extremely touching and quite unparodistic. The mother's words, in the middle section, are through-composed, the vision of the New Eden provoking Ivesian polytonality, telling contractions and elisions of rhythm (consider the setting of the words "pointing to the east" and "bear the beams of his love"), and a radiant use of obbligato violin. This suggests a celestial folk-fiddle music, while the harp becomes a seraphic cowboy's guitar. "And did those feet" is the most remarkable of all these American rebirths. The violin and harp melismata over a drone sound, at first, exotic and Oriental; but the violin turns into the Kentucky folk-fiddle, the drone into the chapel harmonium and the village-hall squeeze-box, while the voice sings a swinging, buoyant bugle-call that seems likely at any moment to become a gospel shout. Yet there is no debunking of Blake's experience. The meticulous prosody (which originally came from Thomson's Stein-like dedication to the word-in-itself, divorced from sentimental associations) gives to the music a delicate immediacy and truthfulness, so that if the song is comic it is also strangely moving. The exquisitely scored conclusion, when the "reality" of the American small-town dissolves into pentatonic arabesque, proves that the child mind may perceive the New Jerusalem.

Thomson must have been aware, however, that such a vision is difficult to preserve in the conditions of the modern world. This may be why some of his finest music is elegiac; and is certainly why the death of Gertrude Stein in 1949 prompted him to a work of unexpected emotional depth. *A Solemn Music* for wind band is a ceremonial piece which effectively marries all the constituents of his art, except his satirical wit. The Satiean liturgical manner of his youth, the polytonal sophistications and the simple gravity of American hymnody meet in a structure that is serial in that it is based on themes that are also a row, involving every note of the chromatic scale. Since the harmony consists almost exclusively of diatonic concords the effect is utterly remote from that of Viennese serialism; indeed, the serialization reinforces the sense of "serene insecurity" which we commented on in the liturgical pieces, and gives a kind of resigned grandeur to the music's awareness

of innocence lost. The Thomsonian bugle-calls reach apotheosis in a
brass sonority that sounds as though Bruckner had been reborn in
Kansas City! We may recall that Bruckner had himself a noble simplicity, if not naïvety, and that the chromaticism and enharmony of his
music may point to a certain insecurity beneath his faith. *A Solemn Music*
is not a religious work, but it is more than a requiem for Gertrude
Stein; it is an elegy on her and Thomson's vision of a world new-made.

In this context it is interesting that Thomson's biggest work should
be a *Missa Pro Defunctis* (1960) for chorus and orchestra: the profoundly
equivocal effect of which depends on the fact that, though based on the
interval of the major third, it employs that stable interval with no
sense of tonal centrality. Thomson has commented on his intentions
in an unusually informative programme-note:

> Harmonically the work is dominated by the major third, which is used
> in parallel lines, in canons, in stacked-up position as augmented triads,
> in chromatic chords (combined with the major second), and in major
> chords that often run parallel and at other times are arpeggiated into
> bugle-calls and vocalizes. The constant presence of the major third
> produces constant tonal shifts in the melody and, through its frequent
> appearance in stacked-up form as the augmented triad, generates whole-
> tone harmonies as well as constant modulation. This non-stable tonality
> aspect—of evanescence with iridescence—resulted from the wish to
> express the idea, constantly present in the text, of "eternal light". Also to
> suggest a region neither heaven nor earth but in some outer space between
> the two where it may be imagined music is freed from both the frictions
> of twelve-tone chromaticism and the gravitational "pulls" of classical
> harmony.

Such a neutral limbo—a genuinely American extension from the
a-religious ritual of Satie—is evoked in triadic and whole-tone passages
such as the following:

EXAMPLE 10

It is disturbing in the same way as is Satie's music; and the comedy of the military percussion and bugle-call motives in the *Dies Irae*, or the seraphic New Orleans band to which the Saints dance in the Sanctus are no more a deflation of the sublime than are the comparable effects in Satie. The military motives remind us of the martial and materialistic horrors of the world we live in, while making it possible for us to regard them dispassionately, since they are trivial compared with eternal matters. The delicately jazzy Sanctus, on the other hand, tells us that heaven may be where we find it; and we can find it anywhere if we have not lost our innocence. The humour is part of the music's discretion, its spiritual modesty. For this reason the piece, though a Fool's Requiem, is an affirmation of human dignity: moving because it is aware of human limitations.

Despite the large forces involved—a normal full orchestra and separate men's and women's choruses at opposite ends of the platform —Thomson has designed his *Missa Pro Defunctis* for liturgical use; and this subservience to function is in tune with the music's nature. Liturgical function is not, however, that most typical of the modern world, so perhaps it is not surprising that Thomson should have epitomized his experience as American *naif* in a very different kind of functional music. As far back as 1927 he had explored—in his *Symphony on a Hymn Tune*—the possibilities of an instrumental version of his Steinian technique of musical *collage*. Not only the main hymn "How firm a Foundation", but also sundry other hymns and one secular song ("For he's a Jolly Good Fellow") are interwoven without temporal sequence but with Steinian cross-references between modes and moods. One tune will be harmonized in severely Roman organum, another in the parallel thirds of Puritan hymnody; bits of European bric-à-brac will jostle alongside shanty tunes, toy waltzes and lobster quadrilles, in structural relationships that, being architectural, are spatial rather than temporal, even visual rather than aural. On returning to the States, Thomson realized that this musical-visual technique had cinematic potentialities. His film music derives, indeed, from the prophetic *Entr'acte cinématographique* in Satie's *Relâche*. It may not be an accident that his American simplicity, which complements the American complexity of men such as Carter and Sessions, should be so completely realized in submission to a function that involves a highly mechanized technique.[2]

[2] Thomson's most characteristic music, like Copland's, lends itself readily to the film, because it depends on very short phrases in reiterated and per-

Thomson's earliest film scores were for documentaries—*The Plow that Broke the Plains* (1936) and *The River* (1937): both of them dealing with the making of modern America. Thomson used real cowboy tunes, blues and hymns in a thin, diaphanously scored, almost Satiean texture; and employed his musical materials without progressive sequence, to underpin the visual images. How close this cinematic method is to the *collage* technique he had evolved spontaneously is indicated by the fact that *The River* includes much music from the *Symphony on a Hymn Tune*, with a minimum of reworking. Ten years later Thomson was asked to write a score for Robert Flaherty's *Louisiana Story*. What he produced is not only a landmark in the history of film music, but also one of Thomson's most satisfying works in purely musical terms. The semidocumentary film, significantly, saw the clash between man and Nature through the eyes of a child, opposing the Acadian existence of the boy's family life to the impact of the oil prospectors. The contrast, rather than conflict, is not, however, an excuse for moral comment; the meeting of disparate ways of life is accepted by the boy's imagination as a fact, and this quality of wide-eyed acceptance comes over in the music. In the Chorale that accompanies the arrival of the derrick the boy's simplicity is musically equated with an Acadian folk-tune, which expresses both his own nature and also the traditional, rural values he has been nurtured on. The derrick's slow drifting is evoked by Satiean unrelated diatonic triads, harmonizing a twelve-note theme:

EXAMPLE II

and this passage is in part visually descriptive (following the derrick's almost directionless movement), and in part psychological (reflecting

---

mutating patterns which can thereby simultaneously follow and disguise the fluctuations of cinematic "cutting". More detailed discussion of the film-music techniques of Satie, Copland and Thomson can be found in the present writer's article on film music in the current edition of *Grove's Dictionary of Music and Musicians*. The reader is also referred to the section on film music in Virgil Thomson's *The State of Music*.

the wonder and fear which the weird mechanical river-beast creates in the boy's mind). To be physical and psychological simultaneously is an ideal which film music cannot often live up to. Here Thomson has achieved it marvellously, perhaps because the experience the film is concerned with is so close to the "serene insecurity" we have referred to in Thomson's early liturgical works, in *A Solemn Music*, and in his *Missa Pro Defunctis*. The composer's description of the piece as a Chorale is appropriate; it evokes, by similar means, precisely the combination of humility and awe (with a slight undercurrent of fear) which we find in the Kyrie of the Mass.

There is a similar fusion of visual-physical description with psychological revelation in the music that accompanies the boy's fight with the alligator. This is a fugue in which the subject, or rather subjects, are derived from the animal's wriggling and snapping. The structure is not, however, thematically and tonally planned as it would be in a traditional fugue. Instead, disparate subjects are introduced in a series of expositions which are put together architecturally, on the *collage* principle, the sections being in increasingly remote keys, returning to the point of departure with a major *tierce de picardie* at the point when the boy is rescued by his father. Again, the music's physical description is inseparable from the agitation within his mind. Something similar is true even of the various Acadian songs and dances, most of which are based on folk tunes, treated naturalistically. Thus the squeeze-box is actually being played in the film, but the imitation becomes also a revelation of character and motive. In "Papa's tune" the contrast between the F major oompah vamp and the G major tune suggests bewilderment; in "Sadness" and "Super-sadness" the wistfulness is inherent in the whole-tone and bitonal movement and in the un-related keys of the threefold repetition of the gentle melody, always in two-part counterpoint. We can see in this simple and tender music how the cinema—or at least a reflective film like Flaherty's—offered Thomson what he needed. He could surrender the sense of personal identity—of "desire and loathing"—in submission to the visual image; yet in doing the job it had to do the music reveals Thomson's character through the character of the film's participants. He becomes the film-boy's clear eye, honest heart—and sensitive ear.

The relationship between the boy and Nature in *Louisiana Story* is instinctive, not mystical; and it may be that Thomson was able so completely to reconcile his American innocence with his Parisian sophistication because the people of this part of Louisiana are still in part French in culture and language. In any case the music to *Louisiana Story* is idyllic, Arcadian as well as, strictly speaking, Acadian; and one finds a similar quality in a few purely orchestral works, such as *Wheat Field at Noon* or *Sea Piece with Birds*. The former uses *collage*-like blocks, placed sectionally like the layout of wheatfields. Serially related diatonic concords similar to those of the derrick Chorale produce, within the geometric proportions, a shimmering, vibratory effect—a precise aural equivalent for the visual effect of a hot day. The sea-piece uses whole-tone scales and bitonality to imitate sea-sounds and bird-calls; here personal identity is so dispersed in the observation of natural phenomena that the piece has virtually no structure and no thematic repetition. The birds' cries are in double or triple chromatics, simply stopping at the height of the hubbub, when there are no more instruments left to play augmented triads or whole-tone swirls. The piece, though fascinating, is a *ne plus ultra* of the American naïvety, and the closest Thomson comes to the more radical American composers who stem from Debussy. The literalism is itself child-like, however. Such music, the creation of a sophisticated Parisian New Yorker, preserves the innocent eye of the Louisiana boy who wonderingly, even apprehensively, watched the great derrick floating on the river. We can still see this boy, this aboriginal American, in Thomson's blandly cherubic face, as he approaches his seventieth year. We are reminded again of Thoreau's words: "Not by constraint and severity shall you have access to true wisdom but by abandonment and child-like mirthfulness. If you would know aught, be gay before it."

Another veteran composer whose best work may be associated with the theme of American innocence is Bernard Rogers, who was born in New York in 1893, had an international training in that he studied with the American Arthur Farwell, the Swiss Jew Ernest Bloch, and the Parisian Nadia Boulanger: but has lived for most of his life unambitiously in Rochester, where he teaches at the Eastman School of Music. Since he is a prolific composer who has written many works in many styles, and is one of the few Americans to tackle the big religious theme, it may seem odd to group him with the innocents. Yet in a sense his ability to write a Passion, with spontaneity and conviction, in 1944, is an aspect of his innocence; and the music of this and other large-scale works has the same radiance and simplicity—in the lucidity of its orchestral and choral texture—as has the considerable number of his works that deal with the world of the fairy-tale, of Once upon a Time. Sometimes these pieces are addressed directly to children, as are the

Leaves from the Tale of Pinocchio: but the most recent development of his work suggests that they go to the heart of his experience. This is evident in the beautiful *Variations on a Song of Moussorgsky* for orchestra (1960). The theme, significantly, is Moussorgsky's *Child Song*, which combines the child's direct response with Moussorgsky's own empirical integrity: the qualities Rogers probably admires above all others. The briefly rocking modal theme, with its incantatory pentatonic phrases, contains no possibility of symphonic development; and Rogers makes his variations a *revelation* of the theme's innocence that carries us outside Time. In earlier works his interest in Oriental (especially Japanese) music and culture had been combined somewhat uneasily with a traditionally European harmonic sense; here, the harmonic texture is as bare as Moussorgsky's own, while the extreme clarity of the instrumentation makes the spare score glow with light. Thus in the first variation the tune is almost disembodied; fragments of it are heard over sustained ostinati and pedal points. The second variation is mostly unisonal, metamorphosing the tune into rhythmic subtleties, while in the third variation the theme becomes bird-twitters on woodwind, again over long ostinati. The fourth variation opens monophonically, the line scored with "liturgical" resonance, which then turns into medieval-sounding brass polyphony. Ostinato drones continue during the fifth variation, when plucked strings become a balalaika orchestra; then the sequence of sixth, seventh and eighth variations build up a cumulative grandeur that is hardly dependent on harmonic momentum. The lines become melismatic fanfares over an F sharp pedal; and a brief fugato leads into a restatement of the song, this time for full orchestra. A sequence of two codas starts with the non-harmonic concept of tolling bells, which become canonic chorale-like phrases, without harmonic progression. Thus the piece demonstrates, like some of Thomson's music, the relationship between the American innocence and the retreat from the West; and it is interesting that this phenomenon should occur too in the by no means esoteric work of a middle-path composer such as Rogers. The freshness, the sense of re-creation, in these Variations implies, perhaps, some kind of renewal for him as artist; it could certainly have a "therapeutic" value for some thousands of listeners for whom the liberation of Cage or Feldman, or even Partch, would be too far out to be apprehensible.

X

Today and Tomorrow: Lukas Foss
and the younger generation

> It is easier to discover another such a new world as Columbus
> did, than to go within one fold of this which we appear to
> know so well; the land is lost sight of, the compass varies
> and mankind mutiny; and still history accumulates like
> rubbish before the portals of nature.
>
> THOREAU

Barber and Thomson are probably the two most creative of America's
"middle path" eclectics, and one is a composer of adolescence, the
other a composer of adult childhood. Thomson's vision, like that of a
real child, is too direct, and therefore disturbing, to make him a widely
popular composer; Barber comes closer to popular appeal in offering
a milder, more topical and local, version of the regressive neuroses
(which we all in part share) of his European forebear, Tchaikowsky.
Even if Barber were, instead of a minor talent, a composer of a genius
to match Tchaikowsky's, he could hardly be adequately representative
of "the American experience". The composers of a later generation
seem to feel that it is now too late for innocence: so that knowingly,
even self-consciously, they take what they can from the bewildering
range of styles and conventions their world offers them.

The example of Harold Shapero—the most talented of the group
that, stemming from Stravinsky and Copland, attempt a "geometric"
reordering of the fragments of a disintegrated world—suggests that the
withdrawal from innocence is not necessarily an asset. He made his
name with a triptyque of piano sonatas exquisitely written in a twentieth-century modification of rococo style. The model was earlyish
Haydn, re-created with Stravinskian harmonic ellipses and rhythmic
displacements, and with Prokoviev-like lyricism and tonal wit. A
distinctively personal, and perhaps American, quality finds its way
into the texture, for the gaiety has a translucent limpidity, and the slow
movements (which are never really slow) combine lyrical tenderness

with an austere elegance and prim precision that reminds us of the chiselled poetic forms of Emily Dickinson:

EXAMPLE I

In music, the closest parallel is with the work of Theodore Chanler; but a man of Shapero's generous inventiveness could not be content with Chanler's deliberate limitation of range. Shapero wanted to "grow up"; yet could not or would not tear himself from the past. So, for the model of Haydn and rococo music, he discovered a more challenging—and more dangerous—substitute. The *Symphony in Classical Style* and the big *Piano Variations* are impressive pieces, remarkable for their very attempt to use Beethoven as (in Stravinsky's sense) a mask. One may still think, however, that the attempt was misguided: for Beethoven's essence is a revelation of identity rather than a manifestation of tradition. Identity can never be emulated, only superseded. This is why the sheer (Bostonian) musicality and facility of Shapero's invention becomes, in these works, almost a liability. Where is Beethoven without the sense of struggle? If Beethoven has won his victory, why fight the fight again? Shapero's refusal to stand on his own feet was an abdication; and it is hardly surprising that, since assuming the mask of Beethoven, he has written less and less. That he feels that fashion is against him may be a partial, but cannot be the whole, explanation. Creativity will never be stifled by fashion—so long as it is convinced of its creativeness.

Another composer of the same group—Alexei Haieff—has "grown up" into individuality, but only at a cost. A Siberian who was brought up in China, he came to America at the age of seventeen. Less richly endowed by nature than Shapero—in particular less melodically fertile —he has developed a voice which, if small, is his own. Like his masters, Stravinsky and Copland, he likes to "build" his pieces geometrically from tiny figures, so that the mosaic metaphor is frequently applicable to his forms. The Piano Concerto of 1952, for instance, starts with a descent E flat, D flat, C, accompanied by a first inversion A minor chord. This brief motive generates the mosaic-patterns of the whole work. The Stravinskian vitality has gone, so has the austere heroism of Copland; as a consequence, the music's lack of sustained melodic interest produces an oddly dehydrated effect. The music's fascination lies almost exclusively in its texture—in the melismatic decorations, in the rhythmic nervosities that suggest a desiccated jazz, in the tingling bitonality of the prevailingly two-part polyphony. The music's brittleness, though not uncommunicative, is curiously non-committal: the alternating-hand octaves at the end even remind us of Saint-Saëns, with the saccharine turned to acid! The later Piano Sonata (1956)—in which the generating motive is a falling minor third and rising fifth— is not lyrically more sustained, but is less acerbative because harmonic-ally more fulfilled. Though the wide-spaced piano texture looks superficially like Copland, the sound is quite different, because the implied chords are so often tritonal or augmented. Indeed, when Haieff writes for strings, in a work such as his charming and poetic String Quartet, we realize that both his melodic and harmonic dialect are, by nature, much more romantic than those of his master Stravin-sky: which may be why the fragmentation of texture and the disloca-tion of rhythm produce an effect of half-comic, clownish pathos. Haieff seldom writes a real slow movement; this quartet concludes with a slow, exquisitely lyrical coda—which is, however, almost apolo-getically brief.

Most post-Stravinskian American composers of the middle genera-tion tend to be, like Haieff, light-weights. Their position is somewhat ambiguous, for they would seem to be creating "entertainment" music, yet no one knows precisely what public they entertain. Haieff, it is true, frequently writes for the ballet, where his music finds a natural home; yet there is something faintly forlorn about the "ab-stract" chamber and orchestral music of most of these American light-weights, since it is neither "functionally" justified, nor a "new experience". The tastefully eclectic music of a "modern" academic like Vincent Persichetti, for instance, implies the existence of a cultural élite which is not, in fact, available; it is neither advanced nor commercial, yet too subtle and refined for a middlebrow public. This is probably why such American composers who still follow the path of middle-period Stravinsky are increasingly tending to emphasize Stravinsky's incipient Orientalism. The powerful Piano Sonata of Robert Moevs is a case in point, for here Stravinskian ostinati, melismatic embroideries and bitonal filigree go towards the creation of a bold, hard, spacious piano style that reconciles the Orientalism of tolling gongs with something comparable with the American grandeur of Copland's large-scale piano works.

Neo-classic Stravinskianism can thus enter the swim, and a composer such as Moevs need not feel an outsider; he can share a private-public consisting of other composers, artists and their hangers-on, even if he cannot contact the public at large. Post-Schoenbergian serialism—as we saw in discussing Finney, Kirchner and Imbrie—has become more fashionable with American composers, probably because it offers some ready-made answers to compositional problems that perplex an artist living in a world of shifting (if not shifty) values. Post-Webernian serialism has still additional attractions in that its pointillism may provide direct contact with the quasi-oriental techniques of the *avant-garde*. The composer may thus feel that he belongs to an evolving Western tradition, while sharing something of the philosophical re-orientation (the term is exact) that provides the *avant-garde* with a more than musical *raison-d'être*. Given this religious-social justification, the presence or absence of a public, in the accepted sense, becomes of minor account. The senior composer in this group, Milton Babbitt, began by writing sensitive, if rather anonymous music in the manner of Webern: consider his song-cycle *Du*, to German texts. He then turned to complete serialization, of pitch, rhythm, timbres and dynamics, in his abstract "compositions" for various instrumental groups; and from there he took the logical step to electronic means which could effect mathematically accurate serialization at speeds and intensities of which normally operated instruments were incapable. Babbitt's abstraction is so extreme that he favours pure electronic sounds, not the processed natural noises that Varèse and Cage commonly employ. The result does not seem very meaningful in terms of human experience, though it is too early to tell whether this is due to Babbitt's deficiencies as a composer, or to his inexperience in handling a new medium. That electronic sounds may have significance as a *background* to human experience seems, at least, to be demonstrated by Babbitt's *Vision and Prayer*: a setting of Dylan Thomas's poem for voice speaking, chanting, and singing, to the accompaniment of electronic tape. Thomas's poem, declaimed, would make its effect anyway. Whether the effect is enhanced by the poppings and bubblings and squeakings may be debatable, but to hear the poem and the tape together is certainly not a negligible experience.

A younger composer, Mel Powell, started from a compromise

between Hindemith's chromaticized tonality and Schoenberg's serialism, as we may see from his *Divertimento* for wind instruments which consists of serial studies that are given tonal centres. He then turned to a post-Webern idiom related both to Babbitt and to the Orientalism of Cage. His *Haiku* settings for soprano and piano (1961) are poetic and evocative, using vocal wails, howls, whispers and hisses in the manner of the musical "theatre" of Partch or Cage—and demonstrating thereby a return from extreme sophistication to an almost preconscious immediacy, with the lisping, wide-eyed wonder of a child. Thus Powell's post-Webernian qualities become directly related to the musical-philosophical preoccupations of Cage; and this is no less evident in the Filigree Setting for string quartet,(1961), wherein Powell uses the medium in the same fragmented, disembodied way as he employs the human voice. The process seems to be complete in his purely electronic works, for the gurgles and jibbers of the sounds, however mathematically organized, return us to the most primitive, de-humanized utterance—in default of the ability to sing. The rebirth of the monkey—and a mechanical one at that—may be a stage we have to go through; since Powell is a composer of musicality we may hope that he may find humanity again as, and if, he discovers his own identity. Certainly there is a positive aspect to his electronic music, for if one considers it alongside the orientalism of his *Haiku* settings one can see how pure electronic sound might provide a valid—"modern" because mathematical and scientific—link between western vocal and instrumental resources and the microtonal intervals and complex rhythmic patterns of the East.

Most of the younger composers manifest a retreat from the West in one way or another. Seymour Shifrin, for instance, has employed serial techniques with extreme aural sensitivity in a manner that has led him not specifically to Orientalism, but towards the sonority and texture, though not the rhythmic impulse, of jazz. Nor is this surprising, since—as we shall see in Part II—the jazz phenomenon also involves a partial retreat from the West. Serialism, Orientalism, and jazz, in fact meet in the work of Gunther Schuller, a sophisticated art-composer who has worked, both as horn player and as composer-arranger, in the jazz world. It is significant that his *Seven Studies after Paul Klee* for orchestra should be *visually* inspired. Many of the pieces have a minimum of movement in time: the first study, for instance, is all colour in space, suggesting both medieval organum and Oriental gongs; the specifically jazzy piece is jazz disembodied, its momentum broken; the twittering-machine piece simply twitters, without necessary be-

ginning, middle or end; the explicitly "Eastern" piece (no. 5) is beautifully evocative as sonority, but might be background music to a film,
which would imply the action which the music intentionally lacks.
Still more, the "Eerie Moment" implies an accompaniment of theatrical
action (in Cage's sense), as complement to its exciting, Varèse-like
noises. In such works—however acute an ear they manifest—music
has abrogated responsibility: not, as in Cage's case, for the purpose of
ritual that may also be a game, but for a kind of showmanship, if not
salesmanship. Schuller here renders Varèse commercial, making his
kind of music subservient to a cinema that is not even visible; and he
does something similar for jazz in his sundry works for John Lewis and
even in the big Symphony for brass and percussion, since the expertise
of the writing, the "stunning" command of sonorities, sometimes seems
to control the invention, rather than the other way round. In a sense
this happens, too, in a work of much greater musical substance, the
String Quartet of 1957. Here Schuller takes over the techniques of the
avant-garde—serialism of pitch and rhythm, alleviated by passages of
improvisatory freedom—and renders them dazzlingly "effective".
Some degree of authenticity, of intensity, is relinquished, but one cannot
say that the process is all loss. Maybe, in a commercialized world, something like this has to happen; certainly the world of art and the world
of commerce are, in Schuller's music, willy-nilly coming to terms.

Faced with so vast a range of creative or imitative possibilities, the
American composer in the mid-twentieth century is apt to feel unsure
of his identity; nor can we find it surprising that the most naturally
gifted American composer born later than 1920 should be an eclectic
whose career comprises a pocket-history of American music during the
twentieth century. Lukas Foss was not, in fact, born in the States, but in
Berlin, in 1922. He was composing by the age of seven, wrote two
operas in his early teens, and by the time he came to America at the age
of fifteen had a virtuoso command of classical European techniques.
By this time Hindemith was already settled in the States; his lucid
counterpoint and chromatically expanded diatonicism were a natural
point of departure for a German composer who had become part of an
international, polyglot culture. Foss's virtuosity, moreover, gave him a
chameleon-like adaptability; in his new home he achieved his first big
success with a work, to Carl Sandburg's quintessentially American
words, on a quintessentially American theme. *The Prairie* (1943) for
soli, chorus and orchestra, offers us buoyant, fourth-dominated themes,
speech-founded rhythms, jazzy syncopations, a spacious, open texture

and a luminous orchestral sonority that are almost unadulterated Copland. The technical mastery of the piece is, however, astonishing from a boy of twenty, and the music is truly moving, not merely clever. If it speaks another man's language, it does so from the strength of admiration, not from the weakness of imitation. This is why, in the space of a few years, Foss could learn to combine his Coplandesque Americanism with the more traditional skills he had acquired in Europe. In the String Quartet of 1947 the sonorities (with telescoped tonic, dominant and subdominant chords) still derive from Copland, as do the rhythmic agility and the metrical displacements. The music's drive, however, its incessant tonal momentum, suggest a gayer, more elastic Hindemithian counterpoint; and create perhaps the only quartet-texture that is comparable with that of Michael Tippett.

The catalyst that fused the American and the German elements in Foss's music proved to be the Old Testament and—as musical synonym for it—Jewish cantillation. In the first movement of *The Song of Songs* for soprano and orchestra the clean, glinting, Copland-like texture flows into curling tendrils of Jewish-Oriental lyricism: while the characteristic Coplandesque ostinati become related to the incantatory repetitions of Eastern chant. The pastoral $^6_8$ aria similarly enriches tingling Hindemithian counterpoint with melismatic decoration; and in the third movement exciting use is made of heterophonic arabesque against a passionate vocal arioso. The short, consummatory fourth song attains unexpected depth in thus relating the American Present to the Jewish Past; and the later *Psalms* for chorus and two pianos (1957) develop this mode in more powerfully personal terms. The basically pentatonic cantillation has a sumptuous vigour; and the pianos are brilliantly used as percussion instruments, sometimes in harp-like arpeggiated pentatonics, sometimes in wildly clashing heterophony:

EXAMPLE 2

The dance-song of rejoicing that forms the centre-piece has a paradoxical quality of ingenuous brilliance that reminds one of Britten; and the soprano's oscillations between D and D sharp, in the resolutory setting of Psalm 23, also effect, through the simplest means, a Britten-like moment of illumination:

EXAMPLE 3

That the elided harmonies still derive from Copland no longer matters; the virtuosity sweeps us off our feet because it is, emotionally as well as technically, a revelation.

There are similar revelatory moments in most of Foss's later works —in the dazzlingly extrovert Second Piano Concerto (which Foss plays so magnificently himself), no less than in the introversion of *A Parable of Death*, set for speaker, tenor solo, chorus and orchestra to a text of Rilke. In the Prologue to this piece Copland and Hindemith are present on equal terms; but in the first tenor solo with chorus the sinuous Jewish cantilena fuses these contributory elements into a music at once intimately expressive and theatrically projected. The second tenor solo becomes the work's emotional climax, beginning with weeping quavers, in pairs, over an Oriental drone:

EXAMPLE 4

and gradually expanding in sonorous choral polyphony. The narrating voice—usually a dangerous device in a large-scale work—is handled with uncannily theatrical flair: in which respect Foss is again comparable with Britten. Both men are remarkable for sheer musical ability combined with dramatic instinct; both are fine conductors and pianists of acute sensitivity. Both use their theatrical instinct to objectify their twentieth-century awareness of neurosis. It is not an accident that *A Parable of Death* should be what its title says it is: in this centre-piece in his career the German-born Foss uses his new-world expertise as a release from a death-obsession that is both German and American.

A Parable of Death thus led Foss inevitably to the *Time-Cycle* for soprano and orchestra with improvising chamber ensemble: a work which he regards as the beginning of a new phase in his music. Having "dealt with" Death, and therefore implicitly with the Western Time-sense, Foss can join the anti-traditionalists of the *avant-garde*, setting two poems by Auden and Housman in English (his adopted language) and two prose passages from Kafka's Diaries and from Nietsche's *Thus Spake Zarathustra* in German (his native language). The first song, a setting of Auden's "We're late", expresses with uncanny precision the breakdown, in the West, of the sense of organic Time; words and tones are splintered, fragmented, sung-spoken with a kind of childish or perhaps idiotic bewilderment, like a puppet incapable of self-direction, while the clocks of chronological Time toll and tick imperviously. This experience naturally lends itself to techniques borrowed from post-Webern serialism; but the music itself remains dramatic, not abstract—the "theatre" is implicit in the music (as in Britten), not extraneous to it (as in Cage). In the second song the jangling bells of both orchestra and voice evoke the neurasthenia of Housman's quatrain; the music has a typically American literalism, for the bells become an equation for the frenzy of chaos—and only negatively a desire to escape from chaos. In the two German songs the dramatic and theatrical affiliations of Foss's new style become overt. The Kafka passage relates mental breakdown to the dislocation of Time: the clocks do not synchronize, "one chases another in an inhuman manner", so that again the text provides a musical image for a dramatic event occurring within the mind. In the final song the striking of the midnight clock offers a serial organization in both pitch and metre, but as this happens we become most acutely aware of the human identity that Time would obliterate. Thus the music of the two German songs, and of the second in particular, is much closer to Foss's roots in European humanism—more lyrically sustained, more harmonic in implication, more Mahlerian in scoring. *Time-Cycle* is a middle-path work in a very real, and deeply moving, sense: for it starts as anti-Time music, in reaction to the Western obsession with "the pain of consciousness", but ends with a somewhat desperate and elegiac assertion of man's humanity. We can see this, too, in the remarkable improvisations for chamber ensemble that Foss inserts between the composed songs. In the recorded performance the composer on piano, Richard Dufallo on clarinet, Howard Colf on cello and Charles DeLancey on percussion improvise on material suggested by Foss: in the spirit of jazz improvisation, though without the help of a compulsive beat. While these improvisations are not directly connected with the songs (which may be performed without them), they have an experiential relationship, for they affirm the gift of spontaneous creativity. Foss significantly says that for him improvisation is "chance—*corrected by the will*": so the improvisations, which are perhaps more beautiful than the composed songs, tell us that even when organic Time seems broken, man's humanity may precariously survive.

Foss's eclecticism is thus far from being a denial of authenticity. Even his instinct for fashion—which makes it possible for him to write a *Time-Cycle* one week and a brilliantly gimmicky "nine-minute opera" like *Introductions and Goodbyes* the next—is part of his Americanism. If his virtuosity seems to lack a core compared with that of Britten, we cannot attribute that merely to the fact that Britten's genius is the deeper rooted in human experience; there is also the fact that Britten had an English tradition, and in particular Purcell, to give direction to his eclecticism. Whether a central American tradition, beneath and beyond the variety of fashions old and new, is slowly establishing itself is difficult to tell. If it is, it seems probable that it has nothing to do with Harris-like regionalism, and little direct relationship to chromatic serialism or *avant-garde* Orientalism: but that it rather stems from Ives by way of Carter. This would seem to be the affiliation of the young composers who have most strikingly attained personal identity. The two big sonatas of Hall Overton—for viola and piano and for cello and piano, published and recorded in 1960—are cases in point. These are highly complex pieces, written for their medium with a superbly sonorous assurance that recalls early Kirchner. The Cello Sonata in particular is distinguished by some extremely imaginative writing—consider the fantastic pizzicato variation, with Busonian bitonal piano filigree; and the expertise of the technique has little discernible relation to fashion. Overton borrows certain poetic overtone and note-cluster effects from the piano writing of Ives; but what most deeply relates him to the pioneer master, as well as to middle-period Carter, is the largeness of conception, the richness of texture, the idea of form as evolutionary variation or metamorphosis. One may think that Overton has bitten off rather more than he can chew, and one would not expect the quality of "felt life" in the sonatas to be as convincing as it is in the best works of Ives and Carter, for Overton is still a comparatively young man. But there is enough here to suggest that this line, stemming from Ives and Carter, may be both the central and the truly progressive tradition in American music; and this is reinforced if one considers the Overton sonatas alongside the music of Billy Jim Layton, possibly the most impressive talent to appear in American music since the meteoric rise of Lukas Foss.

If Foss's eclecticism is part of his Americanism, Layton has no need of it. Born in 1924, in the depths of Texas, he studied at Yale, Harvard, and widely in Europe. He learned what he had to learn; but the technical skill he acquired was directed towards the revelation of personal identity. Despite a generic relationship to the quartet-writing of Carter, it is not often that the opening bars of the work of a young composer seize one by the throat as unmistakably as does the opening of Layton's *String Quartet in Two Movements*. This arresting opening states, or rather hurls at one, three seminal motives: a scream in trills, an ostinato stamping bass, and a sustained, almost motionless chord-motive in cross-rhythm:

EXAMPLE 5

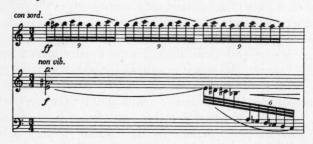

The concept is Ivesian and Carterian in its concern with multiplicity and contrariety, with heterogeneous ideas yoked together by violence. The contrasts of mood—metrical ferocity alternating with a glassy quietude—are extreme; yet the first movement has a cumulative growth, or rather an attempt at growth, for the ostinato bass tries to establish a stability sufficient to support a flowing line. The attempt at song is defeated, as it is in Carter's quartets; the ostinato gets stuck on one obsessively reiterated note which slowly and frighteningly rises, until the trills take over and the movement ends with a prolonged scream. Yet the effect of this movement is not negative and destructive; the magnificent richness of the string sonority (which bears a similar relationship to Bartók as does Carter's string writing) gives us a sense of abiding vitality and courage. This is why the mainly rhythmic energy of this first movement can lead into the complementary second movement, where the impulse is in part lyrical. The form is that of evolutionary variation, or rather permutation, which "seeks" the basic theme; and freely melismatic lyricism grows over static harmony, in a manner that recalls Ives's *The Unanswered Question*, as well as the slow movement of Carter's First Quartet. For Layton, too, the question remains unanswered: the more passionate and jagged the melismatic interjections become, the more remote and impervious the motionless chords seem, until—as though man cannot stand a moment longer the heavens' indifference—there is an explosion in multiple rhythms, like a Carter scherzo, a stuttering and jibbering of monkeys:

EXAMPLE 6

But Layton does not end with this return to the jungle, this descent below consciousness. The alternation of moving lyricism and moveless chords returns, immensely distant; and though the melodic texture thins out and dissolves irresolutely into space, the lyricism survives as the theme, in comparative simplicity, emerges. The music's honesty, and no doubt its topicality, lies in the fact that the answer to the question, when (and if) it appears, should sound so frail and so forlorn.

It is worth noting that some of the very young composers are attempting to incorporate the radicalism of the *avant-garde* into something approaching the "central tradition" of Ives and Carter. The highly musical talent of William Sydeman—a Sessions pupil who has also the by now customary affiliations with Webern and Boulez—is increasingly betraying signs, too, of his admiration for the later music of Carter; while it is probably Carter's influence that gives a sense of direction to the eclecticism of the lively and brilliant Charles Wuorinen. His Third Symphony of 1957, written when he was in his early twenties, is a shatteringly sensational, brash, technicolored piece that brings Copland, Harris and Riegger up to date with superb irreverence. Two years later we find him writing a *Sinfonia Sacra* for solo voices and chamber orchestra in a style that is chromatically serial, neo-medieval, and at the same time highly, if somewhat luridly, imaginative. In the *Evolutio Transcriptio* of 1961 he is using a Carter-like evolutionary polyphony and polyrhythm, with aggressive Ivesian note-clusters. In the *Duiensela* for cello and piano, written in the following year, he has added Earle Brown's time-notation and other semi-improvised techniques to the manner of the *Evolutio*. Another lively, perhaps less pretentious young composer, Yehudi Wyner, has employed post-Webern-like textures not with the strict rigour of serialism but with something resembling the permutatory and evolutionary techniques of Carter; his music contains a minimum of repetition or of pre-ordained organization. Even Ralph Shapey, a relatively senior composer who as conductor has strenuously and brilliantly devoted himself to the *avant-garde*, reconciles in his own music a Carterian approach with the radical differentiation from "Western" techniques that may have been sparked off by his teacher, Stefan Wolpe. Though Shapey's music is far more fragmented than Carter's: though his compositional processes are closely related to the crystal-formation analogy of Varèse: though he views his explosive linear-rhythmic images against the background of the eternal silence, as does Cage: none the less the *nature* of his melodic and rhythmic and even harmonic materials is closer to Carter than to any other composer. One may think that, given so much human energy, Carter's methods of dealing with it are the only relevant ones. Whether or not one finds Shapey's music convincing, however, one cannot deny that it has a powerful documentary interest in that, in a work such as the recorded *Evocation* for violin with piano and percussion (1959), it fuses elements belonging to both Carter and Cage—the most painfully involved, and the most uncompromisingly non-committed, of contemporary American composers.

All this ferment is probably a healthy sign, at least with composers as creatively vigorous as Wuorinen and Shapey. The ferment reminds us, however, as we look at the American scene in the mid-twentieth century, that it would seem that it is best, now as at any other time, for a composer to have creative invention, with or without the support of an indigenous and flourishing tradition. If he has no creative invention, then a deeply rooted is better than a shallowly rooted tradition; and if he does not have *that*, today's fashion is probably more helpful than yesterday's. The problems of the American composer centre around the fact that although in one sense a raw, new world, America seems in another sense a very old world, since a high degree of mechanization has brought phenomenal developments in every kind of skill. The level of technical accomplishment among the later generation of American composers is no less remarkable than their numbers; yet with the growth of this professionalism something is in danger of being lost. If Ives's multifarious complexity was often chaotic, it was generously responsive to the texture of American life; if Copland's technical perfection involved a severe limitation of emotional range, it was a means of attaining personal authenticity. An evolving American tradition has to have more formal control than Ives's empiricism allowed for, and a wider experiential range than Copland could completely realize. Yet the only growth that matters is that wherein technical and emotional assurance are collateral; and that this has not always or often happened in American music is not basically a musical matter. As Thoreau pointed out well over a hundred years ago, it is easier to discover a new world than to penetrate "one fold" *within* it; and, in default of such imaginative penetration, one is apt to substitute for the experience of living a mental canniness—a desire to "know how", to see what makes the works go round. This modern psychological disease—so trenchantly castigated by D. H. Lawrence—has economic consequences also, in that for the advantages of an Affluent Society one may have to pay a price. The Pioneer Spirit and the Efficiency Chart are not readily miscible, and an artistic tradition is one thing that cannot be computed or machine-made.

This is not to advocate despair: only to remind us that the problems inherent in a vast mechanized society have as yet hardly been tackled, let alone solved. To be an artist in such a society is not going to get any easier, except possibly in a material sense; but the importance of the true artist's function must increase rather than diminish. There are still composers who can, in Elliott Carter's phrase, "be an individual"; and this applies not only to a man such as Billy Jim Layton, but also—in a slightly different sense—to the eclectic Foss, and maybe to young

Wuorinen, and even to Feldman, in so far as his anti-individualism exists, individualistically, within the context of an increasingly mechanized society. One can hardly be alive at all without being aware that one lives in a world that has such and such characteristics, rather than others. Layton's or Kichner's art may seem to protest against their world, Foss's to be unsure of it, Feldman's to renounce it; yet the protest, the dubiety, the renunciation, help to make their—and our——world what it is. All that matters, in the long run, is the artist's faithfulness to the "reality" he has to experience, for there are many different truths, in many fields of activity. The only betrayal of art is spiritual dishonesty; and although this, in the nature of things, occurs most frequently in commercial art, the commercial world holds no monopoly in this quality. When we listen to such an expertly concocted bon-bon as Walter Mourant's *Valley of the Moon*, whether we hear it in the cocktail lounge, or in our own armchairs, or in the Carnegie Hall, we are so debilitated by the chronic chromatics and syrupy strings that we grow panicky, fearing we may be glued to our cinema seats for bad and all. We can in this case easily recognize what is being done to us; and it is perhaps not very difficult to see that a massively Hindemithian, chromatic-plated piece like Gerald Trythall's Symphony of 1960 is doing much the same thing, even though we would not be likely to hear it in the cocktail lounge. As successor to the nineteenth-century self-dramatizing symphony it was meant to be tragic and deep; beginning and ending as a rhetorical gesture, grossly overscored, busy-textured, and emotionally inflated, it turns out to sound like a noise going on as background to some other, more important activity—probably a TV programme.

But if there may be death in commercial music, and in "straight" music and in jazz no less, there may also be life in all three. We have merely to recognize the creative spirit whenever and wherever we may meet it; and this is why the segregation of the genres, in our much divided and departmentalized society, is meaningful no longer, if ever it was meaningful. Foss's eclecticism has embraced most aspects of twentieth-century music from native folk material and jazz to chromatic serialism and *avant-garde* Orientalism; Gunther Schuller and Hall Overton—a dedicated composer if ever there was one—have worked in the jazz world; there are similarities between what happens in the work of the far-out jazzmen such as Ornette Coleman and what happens in the music of Varèse, Cage, and Feldman; Tin Pan Alley has produced a Gershwin; academically trained composers such as

Bernstein and Blitzstein have entered the musical theatre on Broadway. All this is a matter of historical necessity, for a composer's "individualized" music cannot be separate from the music that his society produces, however commercialized the latter may be—and this remains true, whether the relationship be one of attraction or of repulsion. There is some evidence, we have seen, to suggest that attraction may be becoming more potent than repulsion: which may be a development of some significance in the checkered history of our civilization. This is the theme we shall be considering in the second part of this book. To approach it, it will be necessary to make some preliminary enquiry as to how the phenomenon now known as entertainment music grew up. We must take a momentary excursion to Europe, and to the period when democracy was established.

PART TWO

The world of art and the world of commerce: the folk-song of the asphalt jungle

This land which man has deswamped and denuded and de-rivered in two generations so that white men can own plan-tations and commute every night to Memphis and black men own plantations and ride in jim crow cars to Chicago to live in millionaires' mansions on Lakeshore Drive, where white men rent farms and live like niggers and niggers crop on shares and live like animals, where cotton is planted and grows man-tall in the very cracks of the sidewalks, and usury and mortgage and bankruptcy and measureless wealth, Chinese and African and Aryan and Jew, all breed and spawn together until no man has time to say which one is which nor cares. . . . No wonder the ruined woods I used to know don't cry for retribution!

The people who have destroyed it will accomplish its revenge.

WILLIAM FAULKNER: *Delta Autumn*

If one examines the myths which have proliferated in this country concerning the Negro, one discovers beneath these myths a kind of sleeping terror of some condition which we refuse to imagine. In a way, if the Negro were not here, we might be forced to deal within our selves with all those vices, all those conundrums, and all those mysteries with which we have invested the Negro race. Uncle Tom is, for example, if he is called Uncle, a kind of saint. He is there, he endures, he will forgive us, and this is a key to that image. But if he is not Uncle, if he is merely Tom, he is a danger to everybody. He will wreak havoc on the countryside. When he is Uncle Tom, he has no sex—when he is Tom, he does—and this obviously says much more about the people who in-vented this myth than it does about the people who are the object of it. The Negro is penalized for the guilty imagina-tion of the white people who invest him with their hates and longings.

JAMES BALDWIN

I

Introductory: Music and entertainment in nineteenth-century America: Stephen Foster, Louis-Moreau Gottschalk and John Philip Sousa

> That you should ever think, may god forbid
> and (in his mercy) your true lover spare.
>
> E. E. CUMMINGS

> and you say goodbye
> just as George did, good-bye poetry
> the black sand's got me, the old
> days are over, there's no place
> any more for me to go now
> except home—
>
> WILLIAM CARLOS WILLIAMS

Wyndham Lewis once said that America was merely the first country—because of her comparative youth—to become Americanized. While the American Way of Life is not necessarily implicit in the triumph of the machine, it seems possible that the physical impact of industrialism has been, in its spiritual effects, both more violent and more widespread than any of the great religious movements of history. Machine-dominated, we think, feel, act differently from our predecessors; and part of the evidence of this radical change in human consciousness lies in the art we produce and consume.

It is a truism that in a machine-made world we must expect to find two contradictory types of art which do their best to cancel one another out. One kind gallantly (and precariously) keeps flying the flag of the human spirit; the other exploits mechanistic techniques to prostitute the spirit for material gain. By and large, the distinction is valid; but it is a tall order thus to convict an entire culture of schizophrenia. Different groups of people accept (say) Carter or the Beatles as the Music of the Twentieth Century. In the deepest sense, both may be wrong. On the other hand, there is a sense in which both are certainly right, for these (and many other) kinds of music are made and played in our time. One may preserve the integrity of the human spirit, the other may debase it. But the human mind has never shown much reluctance to being debased; the only difference is that today machine-techniques make the process easier and more efficient. Moreover, the nature of the debasement is not fortuitous. Hollywood prostitutes our feelings in the way that seems likely to yield the biggest financial return; even commercial techniques assume, however, the existence of proclivities that await exploitation. Though the Hollywood Dream may be shoddy compared with the myths in the light of which great civilizations have lived, we do not preserve our precious integrity by pretending that it has nothing to do with *us*. In a sense, we make our own myths, which imply codes of behaviour relevant to our society. Though we may not like them, and may suspect that the techniques of TV and radio have given them greater power than we bargained for, yet we cannot deny their existence, nor the part we ourselves have played in shaping them. For this reason we should be suspicious of the too glib distinction between Art and Commerce.

Moreover, although the differentiation between "minority" art and "mass" entertainment is new, it is not as new as all that: for its origins are inseparable from the origins of democracy. Mozart, at once an aristocrat and a democrat, wrote music that is simultaneously art and entertainment; his successor Rossini, however, hints that art-as-entertainment implies a slightly different scale of values. Consider how—in *The Barber of Seville* as compared with Mozart's *Figaro*—Rossini tends to substitute for Mozart's psychologically dramatic sonata-aria the non-developing Cavatina or the Rondo with stretto and coda to work up the applause. In the Serenade at the opening of Rossini's opera the comedy depends on the contrast between the simplicity of the tune (a street song) and the extremely stylized elaboration of the ornamentation, which "exhibits" the Count's passion. The chromatic twiddles are his sensual excitement: and also his showing off to impress the girl. They *are* sensual, even gallant; but they are not love-music. The exhibitionism introduces an ironic, almost deflatory element; we do not need to take his passion seriously, since he does not do so himself, and for Rossini as Entertainer this is an asset, since love can be, usually is, disturbing as well as, or even rather than, amusing. Something similar happens in Rossini's substitution of the Crowd Scene for Mozart's dramatic ensembles, with their interplay of character and motive. The comedy of the musicians' chorus that follows the Serenade depends on the simple opposition between the wheedling musicians—their physical gestures being vividly evoked in the cringing appoggiaturas—and the Count's irritation and impatience. The crowd is a crowd, not an aggregate of human creatures. There is no interaction between the private and the public life. The two planes never cross, and the comedy lies in the impossibility of human communication; probably this is why it seems so "modern".

When Rossini does write an ensemble number it is almost always an "ensemble of perplexity". Instead of Mozart's sonata-resolution of conflicting impulses, we have a deliberate exploitation of non-understanding for risible effect. When in Act II, the soldier is revealed first as an impostor, then as the Count, the hurly-burly of the arrest is followed by a moment of utter stillness and stupefaction. They say, pathetically, they "can't breathe", and try limply to keep up the social pretences, as manifest in the elegant vocal decoration. But then, gradually, mass hysteria takes over, sweeping everyone into a wild rhythmic gallop. They cannot deal with experience except at the most superficially hedonistic level; so when they are up against Perplexity, it turns to frenzy. Perhaps this is inherent in farce, as opposed to Mozart's tragi-comedy. The slip on the banana skin reveals us as we are when our social masks fall off. The element of cruelty in Rossini's humour is a retreat from love and tenderness, because such emotions are difficult to compass. This is why his young girls are so often Cinderellas who try to preserve a bucolic innocence in a cynical urban society. Their intermittent folk-like tunes, hauntingly nostalgic as they are, tell us that their pertness is in part a defence. In a sense this is true of all the young and loving, irrespective of sex, as the terzetto at the end of *The Barber* beautifully proves. After the multiple misunderstandings that Society involves them in, the lovers are reconciled and sing together in twining thirds a tune exquisitely, *extravagantly* ornamented. Their lyricism is "sincere"; but it is also (the extravagance reveals) both comic and pathetic in the situation in which they are placed, for if they do not run away immediately all their hopes will come to nothing. So while they coo together in dippy rapture, Figaro tells them, in rapid patter-music, to hurry up, there is no time for that kind of behaviour. In his world, the remark applies to life in general, not merely to this particular situation; and it is significant that Rossini's Figaro, unlike Mozart's, is not himself involved in the action, but is a detached observer, even a manipulator, of other people's lives.

Exactly comparable characteristics may be found in the work of the great artist-entertainer who was Rossini's successor—Offenbach. Both lived in hedonistic societies that hovered on the brink of chaos; both celebrate the passing moment in music of surpassing rhythmic zest and melodic *allure*. In both, these positive qualities are balanced by negative qualities of deflatory irony, and an awareness of innocence lost: in both, the intoxication may at any moment be metamorphosed into fear and frenzy. *Orpheus in the Underworld* is almost a punning title, for the shifty behaviour of the gods is pointed with contemporary parallels. This is the best we can do, nowadays, at the classical humanist's concept of man as god. Social conventions exist to serve sensual appetite; public opinion can be manufactured so that no public truth is possible; everything is sacrificed to money. The glamour that surrounds the apparatus of material power is mocked out of existence; and against the mockery stands the melancholy of John Styx, who once had a True Love in Arcady. "But that was in another country; and besides, the wench is dead": so he is alone, and a back-number, while the gods are bored stiff with their indulgences. The climax comes when the old-style aristocratic Minuet is changed into a Galop Infernale: no innocent Arcadian revel, but a dionysiac orgy that, resuscitating the post-Revolutionary can-can, ends in self-destruction. The "commercial" motive has become explicit in Offenbach, for he wrote for the new, bourgeois aristocracy whose power derived from high finance, not from titular right. His basic theme is prostitution, in one form or another; in Offenbach we are all merry because we are rich, melancholy because our earnings are immoral. With breath-taking zest *La Belle Hélène* celebrates the Legendary Prostitute epitomized in the glamour of Cora Pearl. The aristocracy of money attempts to buy up Paradise in what is literally a vulgarization—a making common—of the heroic ideal; there is a gradual descent from the radiant, never-never-land beauties of Watteau, who live in a dream within the heart, to the saucily fleshy nymphs of Boucher, who are painted on the bedroom wall, to the tinsel crowns and paste pearls of the Second Empire queens, who become the more meretricious the more they are marketable. The climax comes in the justification of adultery for reasons of State: "*il faut bien que l'on s'amuse*" or one will go mad with tedium and so bring Civilization to ruin. The effrontery is as superb as the abandon of the music; but the audacity sprang from an awareness of the abyss. It is significant that Offenbach ended his career with a "serious" opera—*Les Contes d'Hoffman*—which centres around a romantic necromancer who can simulate life.

We may, indeed, observe in Offenbach even more than in Rossini a curious paradox typical of all attempts to create popular entertainment, as distinct from art: which is that although the play and music seem to be "up to the minute", immediately in touch with the texture of life, they depend on a denial of reality. The zest can be indulged in only by obliterating the natural impulses of the heart: which is why the brittle shell of frivolity hides emotion that is both gloomy and cruel. The strength of Rossini and Offenbach is that, although they may have been afraid in their lives—Offenbach had a pathological fear of solitude, while Rossini relapsed into neurotic silence at the height of his fame— they were not afraid in their art-entertainment. Offenbach's music admits that life is not really an eternal can-can, though we may have to pretend it is, if we are to survive; the Rossini crescendo tells us that the Mannheim orchestra's "steam-roller", which had expressed the confidence of the Common Man, may be grotesque and frightening as well as powerful. This core of bitter honesty within the pretence is not maintained by lesser, and especially later, composers of "light" music. In Gilbert and Sullivan the zest is milder, the dream cosier—the cruelty blunter, but still present. In the operettas of Johann Strauss the dream becomes not—as in Tchaikowsky's fairy-tale ballets—an ideal fulfilment of our lives' imperfections, but an escape, a substitute for living. In *Die Fledermaus* the centre of the action is a ball; a waltz, Vienna's expression of life in the physical moment, becomes the focal point of the drama. Moreover, it is a *masked* ball, which hints at the contrast between appearance and reality. The story deals with petty deceptions and adulteries, the masquerade of human passions; yet the point is that none the less everyone loves everyone else: except for the Bat who, in a fit of petty spite, wants to reveal the truth about themselves to these charming people. Because he invokes Reality, the Bat is the villain; but it turns out that he invokes reality only in order to defeat it. The Grand Finale looks as though it has achieved a degree of honesty, for along with the dominant hedonistic motive it shows us the military theme, the prison theme, even the death-fear—all of which permeated Viennese life, as we can see from the music of Schubert and Mahler. The Bat admits that everyone deceives everyone else, that the military shadow darkens the charms of Lilac Time, that one may end up not in a palace but in a prison; he even admits that we may ultimately die. Having done so, however, he would then persuade us that all this is exquisitely funny. While there is true grace, vivacity and ebullience in Strauss the Waltz-King, celebrating physically the passing moment, we can understand why it was his soft evasion, rather than Rossini's or Offenbach's effervescent cynicism, that degenerated into the tabloid feeling of Lehar, Oscar Strauss and Leo Fall. Tin Pan Alley was spawned in the gutters of Vienna.

In our remarks on the genesis of entertainment music in Europe, we have referred to several basic themes: dedication to the passing moment; a strain of cruelty that comes from denying the complexity of human passion; an awareness of lost innocence and a complementary desire to recover the immediacy of a child; an adolescent instinct to evade reality in a dream. Now all these themes have appeared, at varying levels of subtlety, in our discussion of American composers who belong to the world of art, not that of commerce: which fact should remind us how closely the strands are twined. The problems of art composers in America cannot be separated from the forces that have created their civilization. Since this civilization has developed by way of the rapid impact of industrialism upon a wilderness, we would expect to find a rapid development of industrialized entertainment music, within the context of this civilization. It is also consistent that many of the impulses behind this music should re-appear, no doubt in more complex forms, in the work of "art" composers; and it is interesting that it took the art composers longer to realize what these impulses were. In nineteenth-century America there was, as we have seen, no dearth of deadly serious composers bent on revealing as much soul as they were capable of: only the music that came out, however honourably intended and technically proficient, proved to be mostly an academic exercise in a European idiom, irrelevant to the forces that were making America. For this reason, the massive scores have mouldered on the shelves of libraries, the dust being disturbed only very occasionally, when a research student produces a doctoral dissertation. Against all this earnest endeavour, only one nineteenth-century American composer maintains a modest creative spark; and we have seen that we remember Macdowell largely for his small piano pieces which, being a pseudo-celtic dream-music, are in part an escape from the American stresses. As dream-pieces, indeed, they may approximate to highly sensitive "entertainment music": which reminds us that it may not be an accident that the three nineteenth-century Americans whose music sounds as vital today as ever it did hardly claimed to be art-composers, but were content to be considered as popular entertainers. They were Stephen Foster, Louis-Moreau Gottschalk, and John Philip Sousa.

Foster was born in 1826, near Pittsburgh. Though the family was reasonably well-off, and most of them succeeded in business, Stephen had no settled career and no formal musical training. That he was brought up in Pittsburgh (and later in Cincinnati) is significant, for Pittsburgh was not New York or Boston, in touch with European culture; it was an urban industrial society—on the edge of a wilderness. This is literally true. As late as 1812 "savages" still "infested" the Alleghenies within two hundred miles of Pittsburgh, which was then a trading post. By the date of Foster's birth it was a town (which looks "dirty and smoky", as Stephen's sister Charlotte said); but though the Indians had gone, the wilderness remained. Here in Pittsburgh, Foster wrote, at first as an amateur, spare-time composer in such leisure as he had from work in office and printing press, quantities of parlour music that was neither better nor worse than the common denominator of taste permitted. His public was polyglot: English, Irish, German, Italian by ancestry, with a heavy leaning towards Puritan heritage.[1]

These urban people no longer sang folk songs, and if Foster ever heard any real folk music it would have been sung by Negroes working on the rivers. The genteel middle-class society, for whom Foster wrote, sang hymns and sentimental parlour songs of a type derived from the ballads of British composers such as Arne and Hook: and played salon pieces for piano in a degenerate rehash of the classical conventions of Europe. A new industrial town was too busy growing to admit to needs for artistic satisfaction. Nobody wanted more from art than a momentary respite from work: so those conventions that were handiest, and most familiar through usage, seemed the best.

But though Foster had no ambition other than to "give the public what it wanted", he knew what those wants were better than did the people themselves. This discovery he made in his "Ethiopian songs": which were based not on real negro spirituals or plantation songs, but

[1] "Come, Charlotte", said Mrs. Febiger, "before I ride, sing and play some of those favorite little airs of yours". Charlotte lifted her blue eyes and looked sweetly at Mrs. Febiger. She did not whine, nor look affected, nor did she undertake to excuse herself by saying she had a cold, or other such reprehensible devices, but walked modestly to the piano, and seating herself, sang "There's nothing true but Heaven" in a manner that touched the feelings and moved the hearts of all present. "It is, alas, the case", said Mrs. Woolley, "that we are continually deceived with the glitter of a delusive world. My dear little Charlotte, there is so much pathos in your song, do not leave the instrument until you have given us another." Charlotte immediately complied, then rose, and slightly curtsying, with a gentle Good Night, left the room." From Mrs. Elizabeth Foster's *Recollections*

on the songs of the Christy Minstrel shows. These were an exploitation of the Negro by white men with blackened faces—in an idiom closer to English ballad, march and hymn than to Negro music. The first black-faced minstrel was probably Daddy Rice who, around 1830, had won fame in the frontier settlements with his parody-imitations of an aged, rheumaticky Negro he had met in one of the river towns. The vogue spread, and reached a peak, interestingly enough, during the years of the Civil War. The conventionalized form of the Christy show, with its interlocutory figure and two stooges with tambourine and bones, crystallized the white myth of the wide-grinning, white-toothed, red-lipped nigger, lazy and good-for-nothing, yet innocently happy. Foster's genius lay in his revealing how the myth got it both ways, since the Negro, although happy, was also homeless, and therefore sad. The minstrel show took the savagery out of his merriment, making him a harmless figure of fun: while at the same time it related the Negro's homesickness, his sense of oppression, to the frustration and nostalgia inherent in every man, whatever the colour of his skin—and especially in man in a raw industrial society that knew but obscurely where it was going. Indeed the minstrel show as a whole was a presentation, as drama and entertainment, of the Great American Myth: which accounts for its prodigious appeal. It is, however, interesting that the show's positive evocation of the American Hero—who still appears as the figure of the Backwoodsman—should now be subservient to the American Innocent, as represented by the Comic Negro. Both the Hero and the Anti-Hero are treated facetiously, and the main dramatic items are burlesques of European classics. Significantly Washington Irving loved minstrel shows and had an almost extravagant affection for Foster's songs: which were all based on yearning for the Good Old Days: which mattered because they were true, and were true because they were innocent. But they were not innocent as real folk music is innocent, for they expressed modern man's *consciousness* of loss. This is why the songs are sentimental in no pejorative sense: and is also why the technique of the songs is at once simple and artificial. The ballad is an artefact—made in conventions derived from Europe: English ballad (especially Dibdin); French waltz; Italian opera; all of which had reached, in garbled form, the Pittsburgh parlour. In Foster's finest songs, however, the heartfelt simplicity transforms the artefact into something like folk art. We can see this in three different degrees, in three songs written at various periods of his life.

The first song on which we will comment was one of the last Foster wrote: money-grubbing publishers claimed it, along with several others, as positively *the* last. It is the closest to the American parlour, the furthest from Foster's mythical Ethiopia, of the songs to which we shall refer. Its technique is artificial in that it draws directly on clichés, if not conventions, from European art-music; and its text is a direct statement of the escape-motive. It invokes a "Beautiful Dreamer": presumably a young woman, whom Foster (or you, or I) can awake by song: who will then banish "sounds of the rude world" and disperse "all clouds of sorrow". Musically, it is a rudimentary version of the ballad-style of a composer such as Hook, with an infusion of French waltz in the rhythm and of Italian opera in the arpeggiated accompaniment and in the repetitions of the cadential phase. The tune, like the young woman, has an insidious memorability, perhaps because its symmetrical clauses, with falling arpeggio balanced by rising fifth, never defeat expectation. But there is something a little horrifying about the regularity of the tune's insistence; and this is related to the artificiality of the technique, especially the cadential modulation and the final repetition of the cadence phrase with sobbing grace-note:

EXAMPLE I

It is not that the feeling is fundamentally insincere—Foster wrote this song in New York, from a bitter awareness of what Broadway meant, as compared with the provincial Pittsburgh of his early days. It is rather that the feeling is knowingly indulged in: so that it sullies, at the same time as it reveals, the aspirations of the common heart.

One can see how a taint of "commercial" degeneration has crept into this song if one compares it with a dream-song of Foster's Pittsburgh period. Even in the words a difference is discernible: for whereas the words of "Beautiful Dreamer" are heavy with cliché, anticipating the moon-June convention of Tin Pan Alley, the words of "I dream of

Jeanie with the light brown hair" (1854) preserve a certain poetic freshness, along with a survival of eighteenth-century elegance:

> I dream of Jeanie with the light brown hair,
> Borne, like a vapor, on the summer air;
> I see her tripping where the bright streams play,
> Happy as the daisies that dance on her way.
> Many were the wild notes her merry voice would pour,
> Many were the blithe birds that warbled them o'er.
> Oh! I dream of Jeanie with the light brown hair,
> Floating, like a vapor, on the soft summer air.

Both the freshness and the elegance communicate themselves to the music. The lovely tune, with its gracefully balanced undulations, is haunting with the simplicity of an Irish or Scots folk-song, and even has a pentatonic flavour. Formally and tonally, of course, the song is artificial, with a modulation to the dominant to make the daisies dance on their way, a brief middle section for her merry voice and the blithe birds, and a little cadenza to take us back to the *da capo*, which ends with the tenderest cadential thirteenth on the word "summer":

EXAMPLE 2

Floating like a va - pour on the soft sum-mer air

But the simplicity of the art exactly matches the fragility of the dream; the song resembles an eighteenth-century British arrangement (and urbanization) of a celtic folk-tune, and is superior to the comparable pastoral songs of (say) Arne because the tune is so much more beautiful and memorable. Indeed, "Jeanie" is an art-song that has become a part of folk-culture, as no tune by Arne ever could; and this may be in part because the experience is particularized, as well as generalized. The Beautiful Dreamer of the New York song was, one suspects, a concoction of the fancy; Jeanie was a real girl, and Foster's wife, even though she seemed no more tangible than a vapour. "Jeanie" may well be so poignant *because* of the disparity between dream and reality.

Foster could see his Jeanie as lovely and merry only through a soft summer haze, since in fact their marriage was a failure.

The theme of lost innocence finds direct expression in the Ethiopian songs, including the most famous of them all, "The Old Folks at Home". Vestiges of eighteenth-century elegance have disappeared from this music; the harmony is almost consistently tonic, dominant and subdominant (chromatic passing notes and so on are later, non-Fosterian accretions), and the tune is restricted to five notes. Yet this song has become the apotheosis of the regressive instinct, known and sung all over the habitable world. It owes its obsessive quality to its very rudimentariness: the fourfold repeated phrases make their effect because they are *worth* repeating, for the leaping octave followed by a pentatonic minor third contains an age-old yearning, while the declining cadential phrase brings us safe to the security of Home:

EXAMPLE 3

The other internationally celebrated Ethiopian song, "My Old Kentucky Home", is hardly less primitive structurally, and melodically employs only six notes. It has nothing to do with genuine Negro music, not even the Westernized forms of the plantation song, and it is not true, never was true, that the sun always shone bright on the old Kentucky home, nor that the birds made music all the day. What is true is the singer's longing for release from weariness. It is this which has preserved the tune's potency throughout a hundred progressively wearier and less innocent years.

Foster's music is a quintessence of the Common Man's nostalgia, his yearning for innocence, his fear of experience. It is pertinent to note that, despite the fabulous appeal of his music, his life was an unsuccess story. If we think of him as one of the progenitors of the American pop-music industry, there is an allegorical appropriateness in the fact that he should have been congenitally mother-tied, a man "to whom

Home meant everything, and for whom home was impossible", as his brother Morrison put it. Morrison also tells us that Stephen's love for his mother "amounted to adoration . . . and there is not one reference to Mother in the homely words in which he clothed his ballads that did not come from the heart". Stephen had little general, as well as musical, education because he so frequently refused to leave home and attend school, where "there is too much confusion"; and it is clear from Mrs. Foster's *Recollections* that she encouraged her son to think of the White Cottage as an oasis in the hostile desert of the world:

> The sloping terraced grounds about the Cottage, dressed off with many a rose and dancing flower, laughed gaily on that sweet morning in the bright sunlight. I knew that a happy Home awaited me, with breakfast table laid, and husband kind, and infant footsteps pressing the green sod. . . . Is it that memory of long buried joyous hours comes o'er our spirits like a pleasing Dream, and drapes the loved ones in such Angelic Shapes as makes them seem indeed the favorites of a better world? When Fancy lends her wings to bend my memory back, it seems as if in some sweet dream my happy buoyant steps had been within Eden's walls.

Perhaps it was fortunate that this white-cottage Eden at Lawrenceville had to be sold when Stephen was still a small boy. But he never really escaped its obsessive memory: so that he lost his Jeanie, who might have helped him to grow up; succumbed to the Genteel Tradition; drank himself into ill-health; and died in a New York slum. His degeneration started, moreover, when he ceased to be an amateur song-writer and entered the commercial music racket. Then the Common Heart was overlaid with rhetoric; then other men began to reap material profit from his world-wide popularity.

That Foster was an urban American helped him to use the Negro's melancholy as a revelation of the white man's nostalgia. Another urban American, born three years later than Foster, in 1829, found in the Negro's music a more positive reminder of the qualities which urban man had lost. Louis-Moreau Gottschalk could do this because the environment in which he was nurtured was very different from Foster's Pittsburgh. As a boy he was brought up, in the brilliant and colourful world of New Orleans, by a Jewish-English father of German descent, and a French Creole mother who had aristocratic connections. New Orleans then had a Negro slave population of 465,000, with about 30,000 free blacks and the same number of whites. So the music of the Negro was a positive experience for Gottschalk as it could not be for Foster, who heard the Negroes singing in their industrial prison. One might say that Foster became aware of the white man's nostalgia through awareness of the black man's exile; Gottschalk, on the other hand, became conscious of the black man's vitality when he himself was exiled. The exile was self-induced, and very comfortable; through his mother's "connections" he was sent to Paris, to develop the talents which he had exhibited as a piano-prodigy. Even though the Principal refused him admission to the Conservatoire on the grounds that nothing could come out of America except steam-engines, Gottschalk soon achieved phenomenal success as a pianist, being praised by Chopin, Berlioz and Liszt. At the same time—still in his teens—he began to compose piano pieces based on reminiscences of the Creole and Negro music he had heard in New Orleans. This was originally intended as a serious artistic gesture; Gottschalk would create a New World complement to European nationalism, using the dances he had heard in childhood in the same way as Chopin had used Polish mazurkas, or Liszt used Hungarian czardas. In effect, however, Gottschalk produced something quite different, partly because the basic material was different, partly because of the way he treated it. Chopin's mazurkas are poetic commentaries, by a spiritually isolated artist, on folk material, and are in that sense romantically introverted. Gottschalk's dances are, in their exhibitionism, extroverted, re-creating in pianistic terms the communal vivacity of their prototypes. They are "people's music" in that there is a minimum intrusion of personal sentiment; and Gottschalk's genius lay in seeing how this "child-like" Negro vitality could reflect one aspect of his white America. Thus Gottschalk and Foster are complementary. The New Orleans man's life was as much a success story as Foster's was an unsuccess story; he was cosmopolitan, whereas Foster was provincial. Gottschalk's sex-life was as virtuosic as his piano playing (women fought to touch him, to tear tatters off his clothing, even to uproot locks of hair), whereas Foster's relationships with women were both tangled and sad. Gottschalk was technically adroit as composer, whereas Foster was amateurish; Gottschalk's best music is jauntily self-confident, whereas Foster's best music is nostalgic and insecure. They epitomize the two poles of entertainment music: physical dedication to the passing moment, and the retreat to day-dream. One is all action, of a rudimentary nature; the other substitutes reverie even for the possibility of action.

It is remarkable that Gottschalk seems to have realized intuitively the nature of his talent even when he was touring Europe as a young concert pianist, achieving a success that might well have encouraged delusions of artistic grandeur. His own account, in *Notes of a Pianist*, suggests that his tours rivalled Liszt's gladiatorial progress through Europe. When he reaches Latin America, he adds an additional New World touch of the fabulously absurd, for not even Liszt ever lived for some months on a rock projecting over the crater of an extinct volcano, rolling out his piano every evening (with appropriate caution, one presumes) in order to give a recital to the immense forests, waving savannahs, gibbering monkeys and howling jaguars. One cannot doubt that Gottschalk, unlike Thoreau, expected Nature to attend; and this "fabulous" self-salesmanship (even though he could hardly have expected any material reward from Nature animate or inanimate) points to the sense in which Gottschalk, although comparable with Liszt, was to become a Common Man's version of the travelling virtuoso. He had Liszt's exhibitionistic glamour, but not his more complex qualities, nor, of course, his awareness of a European heritage. This must have been why in 1853—when he was still only twenty-four —Gottschalk returned to the States and embarked on a prodigious round of piano-playing, performing to vast audiences in cities, shanty-towns and backwood settlements. He amassed an immense fortune, but gave most of his money away. What drove him onwards was apparently his American energy; even though he had been the inti-mate of Europe's cultural élite, himself preserved aristocratic preten-sions, and sometimes affected contempt for the crowd to whom he sold himself, he desired to make contact with as large and miscellaneous a public as possible. He wooed the Common Heart of America; and by this time his repertory included many pieces that were a pianistic complement to Foster's songs, being nostalgic and sentimental. These Dying Poets, Maiden's Blushes and Last Hopes achieved their end, for they became vastly popular. Gottschalk claimed that he improvised "The Last Hope" to ease the death-bed melancholy of a Cuban lady, and certainly had no objection to other young ladies soaking their handkerchiefs over it vicariously. Shorn of pianistic embellishments, the piece found its way into sundry hymnals and, in the days of the silent cinema, was still a favoured accompaniment to moments of religious elevation. This suggests that the feeling was synthetic in the first place; and explains why Gottschalk's sentimental numbers, with their chromatic arabesques and Lisztian fioriture, are now period pieces, whereas Foster's songs—which cannot hope to emulate Gottschalk's technical expertise—are still alive and kicking. Gottschalk's sentimental pieces seem quaint, even comic, and we play them, if at all, with an indulgent smile. Technical perfection is no substitute for the unforgettable tune which once heard, has to be borne with, even though we may come to think it mawkish or offensive.

In this connection a brief digression on Ethelbert Nevin is pertinent. Like Foster, Nevin was born in Pittsburgh (in 1862); like Gottschalk, he was musically educated in Europe. His songs include two of the supreme best-sellers of history—"Mighty lak a Rose" and "The Rosary", and his salon pieces for piano, including the ubiquitous *Narcissus*, were scarcely less popular. While he does not attain the inspired banality of Foster's revelation of the Common Heart, his expertly made music still has more of a kick than Gottschalk's sentimental numbers. The artifice of the technique—as compared with Foster's crudity—is related to the phoneyness of the sentiment; but that the best-sellers are still performed, even if provincially, suggests that the phoneyness is not the whole story. The question of sentimentality is complex. It has a positive aspect in "Mighty lak a Rose" for though the feeling is a bit "in excess of the object", the object (the baby) exists, and we recognize the feeling in the rising two-bar pentatonic phrase as true and touching. This being so, we do not mind being given a knowing little nudge by the harmonization of the high E with a dominant thirteenth. "The Rosary" is a different matter. Did it owe its prodigious success to the unconscious blasphemy of the words—which today we find ludicrous or shocking according to our religious proclivities? Or would the words have been powerless without the assistance of music so non-inventive in melody and harmony (a rising minor third, followed by a chromatic descent, repeated *ad nauseam*) as to be monstrous? Is the badness of this music itself a kind of inspiration —in that the average hack composer would not dare be as shameless? However this may be, it seems clear that Ethelbert Nevin, though he had less than Foster, had something that Gottschalk as sentimentalist had not. All the pieces of Gottschalk that still live have no connection with the sentimental aspects of popular music, but are related rather to popular music as an expression of physical immediacy. Deriving from recollections of Negro and Creole music heard at home, they were mostly written in his teens, when boyhood was a vivid memory.

One of the earliest is *La Bamboula* which, composed at the age of sixteen, is a pianistic arrangement of an authentic New Orleans dance. In Gottschalk's hands the cake-walk rhythm acquires a self-confident bounce that is reinforced by the bright, resonantly spaced piano texture, and by the glittering virtuosity of the variations in parallel sixths. Significantly, the Latin flavour of the music is modified by a Yankee swagger; the dancer wears his straw hat at a rakish angle, like the nigger in the minstrel show. The Yankeefying tendency is still more evident in *The Banjo* (1851), a "Fantaisie Grotesque" that introduces Foster's "Camptown Races" as coda. The piece begins as banjo-imitation of a most ingenious character. As the black-note F sharp major figuration grows increasingly rapid, the piece induces a sense of elevation and spring within its rhythmic momentum. This is even more prophetic of the "swing" of New Orleans jazz than the cake-walk of *La Bamboula*; and in this connection it is pertinent to note that the effect depends entirely on the rhythmic lift and the brilliant layout for the keyboard, the harmonic texture remaining throughout extremely simple:

EXAMPLE 4

and

Musically, the most interesting of Gottschalk's pieces are those which combine Negroid with Latin-American elements: primitive African rhythms meet Spanish tango and habanera, and French folk-tune and operetta. *La Bananier* is a charmingly elegant version of a French Creole tune with an African drone bass; *Pasquinade* has a French gavotte tune, with a striding ragtime bass and reiterated pianistic ornaments that anticipate the riffs of jazz; *Suis-moi* most seductively fuses habanera with cake-walk—a more refined version of a style later to be explored by Jelly Roll Morton. Perhaps the best piece of all is *Souvenir de Puerto Rico*, which is written in the much-favoured convention of the Patrol—a processional music that approaches from a distance, reaches a fortissimo, and then recedes into the distance. Most of Gottschalk's dance pieces are based on the variation principle, as jazz was to be later; here he employs variation in masterly accord with the programmatic convention. Starting with the barest indication of a march beat, the piano decoration cumulatively stimulates excitement. The march rhythm becomes mixed with the more voluptuous habanera; and in this piece even the harmony grows exciting as it indulges in "the full force of chromatic grapeshot and deadly octaves", to use Gottschalk's picturesque phrase:

EXAMPLE 5a

The climax, however, when the procession envelops us, is almost entirely a matter of rhythm—the 3 plus 3 plus 2 rumba metre that gives a forward lurch, and also a stasis, to the quaver pulse:

EXAMPLE 5b

This rhythmic spasm is very sexy yet feels also, in the context, slightly comic: so that it can combine with the exuberant colours of the piano-writing, the symmetry of the sequences, and the precise lucidity of the texture to preserve the music from any tinge of introspection. This extrovert quality is implicit too in the simplicity of the piece's structure; after the climax, the variations recur in reverse order, until the march beat fades into the night.

This piece—and a few other of Gottschalk's piano dances—is a near-perfect instance of the qualities essential to a good "light" music of a positive, rather than sentimental, type. In the first place, it is physical, connected with bodily (processional) movement, and therefore with the dance. Since the dance is a social act, a coming together of people, it is also communal rather than personal: a music of the Crowd which, inculcating bonhomie, makes us feel good in our social relationships. Personal experience has little to do with it: indeed, as we have seen, entertainment music may sometimes be a denial of the personal. This is why the tunes must be memorable without being too distinctive: why the harmonies may occasionally be piquant, but must always be subservient to physical movement. The problem—which Gottschalk solves so beautifully—lies in the achievement of a satisfactory balance between cliché (the public assumption) and creative invention. A piece that is too cliché-ridden may fortuitously hit the temper of the moment, but will not preserve its appeal. A piece that departs too far from convention, however, cannot be acceptable as entertainment, for it will disturb rather than comfort; and the function of entertainment is to confirm us in our prejudices. In *Souvenir de Puerto Rico* Gottschalk hits the balance exactly: the "chromatic grapeshot and deadly octaves" release from us the "oos" and "coos" occasioned by a pyrotechnic display, but we know that the fireworks are only a game, not an authentic conflagration. Though they may remind us, momently, of the vanity of human wishes, we know that our lives will go on, humdrum and comfortable as ever, when the fireworks are spent.

The relationship between Gottschalk's positive, incipiently jazzy, pieces and physical movement, brings us to the overtly functional aspects of music for moving to. In Europe had emerged the first school of composers to dedicate themselves to the production of "light" music as such. In origin the Viennese waltz was revolutionary, as compared with the aristocratic minuet; it was physical, a celebration of the sensual present; and it was addressed to a polyglot public—German, Italian, French, Spanish, Polish, Jewish, even Turkish—since eighteenth-century Vienna, like nineteenth-century America, was a melting-pot of the nations. It is not therefore surprising that the Johann Strauss band should have been rapturously received when it toured the United States: nor that the Americans should soon have evolved their own fresher, perkier, less traditionally ripe form of music for moving to. The Viennese waltz, newly democratic product of an old world, moved in a circle, combining the revolutionary dance stamped around the Bastille with the whirling of sexual play. The American march, newly democratic product of a new world, moves in a straight line, pressing forward with confident energy, but with comparatively little sexuality. As the new cities are shaped the vigour of the pioneer with his axe is subjected to military discipline. The codification of the march-form is even more rigid than that of the waltz; in both cases the code exists because the music is concerned with public co-operation, not private experience. The most effective march or waltz proves, however, what was implicit in the dances of Gottschalk. Conformity to convention is not, in itself, enough. One needs to be aware of a human being who is conforming: who must be individual enough to be recognized as human, but not so individual as to seem different from the rest of us.

So, just as the Viennese waltz had its undisputed master in Strauss (or perhaps one should say in the Strauss family), so the American march discovers its master in John Philip Sousa. Born in Washington, D.C., itself, in 1854, he was the son of a Spanish trombonist who played in the U.S. Marine band. Sousa has himself refuted the legend that his father's name was originally Antonio So, the letters U.S.A. being appended to his name as a tribute to his adopted country; but this remains one of the stories that ought to be true because in a sense it *is* true—truer than fact. The young Sousa did not, at first, manifest the patriotic fervour inherent in the mythical version of his name; that his boyhood ambition was to be a circus performer reflects, however, on the exhibitionism and braggadocio that was to distinguish his later career. At the age of thirteen he was steered away from the circus and into the marine band, by his father. Later he played in theatre orchestras—including that of Offenbach, when the Frenchman toured the States; returned to the marine band as leader at the age of twentyfive; and inaugurated his own band in 1892. This band became world-famous, far beyond the confines of the military framework in which it had originated. It did so because it epitomized the youthful enthusiasm and optimism of America, making the maximum appeal to body and nerves, the minimum to head—and maybe to heart also. Sousa himself said that his marches were "music for the feet instead of the head": that "a march should make a man with a wooden leg step out". He did not tell us how this electrifying effect could be achieved; but he knew that he achieved it, and that one of the better of his marches was worth all his operas, cantatas, and symphonic poems rolled together. He also knew that writing a good march is a difficult art. "A march speaks to a fundamental rhythm in the human organization and is answered. A march stimulates every centre of vitality, wakens the

imagination. . . . But a march must be good. It must be as free from
padding as a marble statue. Every line must be carved with unerring
skill. Once padded, it ceases to be a march. There is no form of composition wherein the harmonic structure must be more clear-cut. The
whole process is an exacting one. There must be a melody which
appeals to the musical and the unmusical alike. There must be no
confusion in counterpoints."

The basic convention—the public "mould"—for the march is
similar to the most rudimentary form of the Viennese waltz. After
four or sometimes eight bars of "dramatic" introduction, arresting the
public's attention with diminished seventh chords and occasional
chromatics, the verse-section of the march falls symmetrically into two
groups of sixteen bars. The first sixteen modulate to the dominant.
After the double bar, the second sixteen bars make only momentary
departures from the tonic, and are usually broader and more cantabile
in line, and slightly more "meaty" in harmony, with some chromatic
passing notes. The trio, like that of the waltz, is always passively in the
subdominant, always more lyrical, and usually quieter in rhythm. It
becomes, however, a chorus rather than an interlude; after its own
brief middle section, which sometimes opens in the relative minor and
always recaptures something of the rhythmic and even harmonic
strenuousness of the verse, the chorus trio is restated, still in the subdominant but very loud, fully scored. The most famous of all examples
—*The Stars and Stripes Forever*—is typical. The four-bar introduction
begins with an aggressive unison and a cocky syncopation in the second
bar, followed by a dramatically chromaticized cadence. We sit up, or
rather stand up, and take notice as the verse section proceeds in a
jerkily dactyllic rhythm over a swinging melodic bass. When in the
second sixteen bars the bass is transformed into a broad melody with
falling sixths and rising sevenths, the effect is like chest-expansion. The
bass—what we are based on—has become the tops, and the afflatus is
at once physical and moral, making us "feel good" in both senses of
the phrase:

EXAMPLE 6a

EXAMPLE 6b

The trio tune begins with a much narrower melodic range, centred around the third of the subdominant. Animated at first by the prancing bass and then by the fierce descending chromatics of the middle section it swings, however, into the familiar restatement, "molto grandioso".

The effect is psychologically, perhaps physiologically, interesting. The original, quiet statement of the trio tune would seem, like the trio of the waltz, to invoke domestic sentiment: to tell us that all the public well-being of the first section reflects on our own lives and on those of our family, friends and acquaintances. If one thinks of the march in military terms, the trio-chorus is What We are Fighting For, Hearth and Home; if the march is not military but belongs to fraternity, university or club, the trio takes us from a general awareness of Community to communion with Toms, Dicks and Harrys for whom we have a particular affection. Then, however, the chorus tune acquires, in its middle section, some of the aggressive punch of the verse section; and when it is restated, still in the subdominant but very grandly, we realize that its domestic security has been (democratically) identified with national glory. Hearth and Home *are* the Nation: which is why the march can end, fortissimo, and in the *sub*dominant, which might seem an odd thing for a progressive, optimistic piece to do. Even in the skittish $^6_8$ marches in horse-galloping two-step rhythm (*Washington Post, Liberty Bell, El Capitan*, to mention merely the more familiar), the lyricism of the trio tune rides triumphant through the mêlée of jigging movements. Usually the scoring helps to achieve this equation of the domestic with the national: the warm, homely chorus-tune turns into a blaze of brass, accompanied by screeching piccolos and clarinets, to which the drum-major twirls his baton in physical *joie de vivre*. Occasionally (as in *Power and Glory*, which has "Onward Christian, Soldiers" for its subdominant tune), the reprise of the trio theme is combined with the jauntier first theme, with shattering effect.

Sousa was writing marches in the eighteen-seventies, and some of them (consider the trio of *Our Flirtation*) are significantly Straussian in manner. He was still producing marches in the nineteen-twenties, and his eupeptic Americanism remained unadulterated. In between those years—and especially in his "middle period" around the turn of the century—he achieved a more vigorous inventiveness within his limited formula than any similarly restricted composer, with the possible exception of the younger Strauss: and his creativity would seem to have flourished in proportion to his subservience to function, for his rare attempts to depart from the conventional formula are not among his distinctive successes.[2] Though Sousa's death, and the end of the heyday of the American March, coincided with the Great Depression, his marches are still played, and will continue to be played, wherever a public occasion calls for communal rejoicing or even for mass hysteria. They are a necessary part of the experience of all common men (and of some uncommon ones), for they fulfil our most primitive instincts at the same time as they cage them in conformity. They are at once Revolutionary and Established!

If we consider these three composers—Foster, Gottschalk and Sousa —as a trio, we shall observe that their prophetic significance, in mutual interrelationship, is even greater than their intrinsic interest. Foster is all heart, Sousa is all body; neither of them demands much from the head. Foster is quintessentially regressive—to childhood and the womb; Sousa lives quintessentially in the present moment of physical activity. Foster's nostalgia is pessimistic, Sousa's buoyancy is optimistic: so they are prophetically the negative and positive poles of the vast industry of pop music that emerged as American civilization became mechanized. Gottschalk, the third member of the trio, stands between

---

[2] The exceptional cases may, however, be fascinating for extramusical reasons. One of Sousa's last marches, *New Mexico*, written in 1928 as a tribute to the Governor and people of that state, turns into a potted history of Mexico, with Indian drum effects, Spanish conquistadorial rhythms, arrival of the U.S. Cavalry, and a general reconciliation of the themes and the races at the end. Another late march, *Nobles of the Mystic Shrine* (1923) was written for the Shriners, a masonic lodge purporting to maintain the spirit of the medieval Crusaders. Sousa, who was himself a member of Almas Temple, suggests mystery and crusading orientalism by writing the verse section in the minor—a dashing and most unusual procedure— with sundry chromaticisms and clinking acciaccaturas. Harp, triangle and tambourine add Turkish colour, and a special part is written for Turkish Crescent, an arrangement of bells supported on a mace which was carried processionally, to accompany Very Important Persons. The mace had to be twirled by a highly skilled, as well as dignified, performer. Sousa saw a possible connection between this Oriental tradition and the drum-major's twirled baton. Characteristically, the Americans democratized the ritual instrument; they christened it "Jingling Johnnie"!

the two poles, embracing both the American vigour and also—if in corrupted form—the American nostalgia; and even the corruption is a part of his prophetic quality. He could do this because he was the only member of the trio who was directly in contact with Negro music: which was to become a new form of popular art. Though it started from the exiled Negro's sorrow and resilience, it became a universal—literally a world-wide—expression of the uprootedness of modern man. It is separate from the commercialized world of entertainment music which men such as Foster and Sousa inaugurated: yet it is never completely independent of that world, since that is the context within which it must exist. The relationship between jazz and commercial pop-music is thus a classic instance of love-hate. It may be that history will prove that a complete reconciliation of the folk integrity of jazz with commercial music's exploitation of the Common Dream can be achieved only when both approach the condition of Art. If this proves so, the figure of Louis-Moreau Gottschalk will loom larger than we or he suspected: for in the middle years of the nineteenth century he was a commercial entertainer who used Negro music like a "natural"; and was at the same time, within limits, a skilled, highly trained practitioner of his art.

II

Orgy and alienation: country blues, barrelhouse piano, and piano rag

The black man, forlorn in the cellar,
Wanders in some mid-kingdom, dark, that lies
Between his tambourine, stuck on the wall,
And, in Africa, a carcase quick with flies.

HART CRANE

Don't forget the crablike
hands, slithering
among the keys.
Eyes shut, the downstream
play of sound lifts away from
the present, drifts you
off your feet: too easily let off.

So look: that almost painful
movement restores the pull, incites
the head with the heart: a tension, as of
actors at rehearsal, who move
this way, that way, on a bare stage, testing
their diagonals, in common clothes.

DENISE LEVERTOV

In discussing the genesis of American popular music in the nineteenth century we observed that both its positive and its negative poles, as represented by Sousa and Foster respectively, were an evasion of "reality", whether through oversimplification or through escape. Jazz, which was ultimately to affect popular music all over the world, flowed parallel to the streams of Foster and Sousa, yet differed from them in that it flowed on the hardest rockbed of reality. It began as the music of a minority, a dispossessed race. This minority, having nothing more to lose, could accept its alienation and its isolation for what they were, with a desperate fortitude denied to the members of an ostensibly prosperous society. Yet in so doing this minority could imbue its awareness of dispossession with a universal significance, making its melancholy serve as symbol of the alienation of modern, urban man. D. H. Lawrence said that humanity today is "like a great uprooted tree"; and James Joyce made the hero of his modern Odyssey a Jew. The American Negro was literally uprooted from his home; the American Jew was a polyglot whose traditions had become so confused as to be inapprehensible. So, in the early days of jazz, the American Negro stood for the reality which the commercial world of the American Jew denied. Both asserted the vitality of Low Life as against the vested interests of "culture"; this may be why they had to seek, in Tin Pan Alley, a partial rapprochement—as we shall see when we consider the career of George Gershwin.

Having primitive and rural origins, the music of the American Negro was simultaneously a reminder of the physical energy inherent in an agrarian society: and also a revolt against the spiritual, as well as physical, prostitution that an urban community entails. In any big American city we may still find evidence of the qualities that have enabled the Negro to preserve, even in an industrial environment, the immediacy of folk-art. We may hear—city-recorded, quite recently— the work-song of a shoe-shine boy (1)[1]: in which the chanted ululation has functional purpose in that it helps him to shine better, while at the same time it expresses, through the melismatic intensifications and pitch-distortions of an age-old pentatonic formula, the loneliness of alienation. The work-rhythm goes back to the most primitively functional magic of African music; and the intensification of the vocal line by distortion may also derive from the traditional relationship between meaning and pitch-inflection in some of the African languages. At the same time both melody and rhythm are given a raw edge, a touch of physical and nervous laceration, by the modern Negro's awareness of deracination. In this cry there is a fierce undercurrent of pain; other vocal manifestations of urban life reflect physical pleasure unalloyed: for instance, this record of a Negro boy turning himself into an instrument, accompanying his yelled pentatonic incantation by slapping his thighs and thumping the resonator which is his chest. (2) There could hardly be a more basic manifestation of physical well-being; often the work-song and the play-song are combined—as in the record of the man who sings while battering on beer cans and a chair (3).

[1] In the chapters on jazz the bracketed numbers refer to the discography: wherein may be found the numbers of the records discussed, with details of personnel and dates.

Both in their "positive" virility and in their "negative" melancholy, these survivals of folk-reality are in direct descent from the music the African Negroes made when they were first transported to America as slaves. Then, indeed, they had little *except* music, for the visual and dramatic arts were banned by the landowners as distracting. Music was admitted in some (not all) areas only because it abetted labour: so most American Negro music was in origin work-song, with an occasional pleasure-song as a necessary but momentary respite from toil. Prison songs that have been recorded in comparatively recent times suggest that labour-music has changed little since the days of slavery, and indicate further that their characteristics were deeply embedded in the racial past. The stone-breaking song "I . . . be so glad" (4) is built out of very brief pentatonic phrases in rigid metrical patterns that are repeated in apparently endless incantation. The ritualistic hypnosis numbs pain and promotes physical habit; in so doing it induces obliviousness of time. A sugar-cutting song (5) has a similar incantatory technique, though the phrases are more lyrically extended, perhaps because cutting sugar is a less rhythmic and slightly less depressing activity than breaking stones. A remarkable afterwork song (6) shows an antiphonal style, with the leader chanting unaccompanied pentatonics, to which the group responds in triadic homophony that involves, however, no sense of harmonic progression. Both the antiphony and the incremental repetitions look backwards to a remote African ancestry, forwards to the vocal-instrumental duologue of the blues and to the riffs of instrumental jazz.

Transplanted to their new environment, the Negroes rapidly absorbed the Bible stories and Wesleyan hymns of Christianity; and did so the more readily because their earthly lot was wretched. The landowners encouraged them to look for a second chance, because hard labour in this life would seem easier to accept if it were rewarded with pie in the sky, by and by; on this basis the slave-owners even found it possible to give slavery moral justification, on the grounds that it was a means of converting the infidel! But although the Negroes gladly embraced Christianity, they did not so much take over the music of European Christendom as re-create their own music in the light of their Christian experience. Just as they preserved voodoo-worship while reconciling its symbolism with Christian mythology, so they transformed, in New Orleans, the techniques of the work-song into religious orgy. In a "shout" the pentatonic ululation, the hypnotically repeated riff-phrase, carry both chanters and listeners outside Time, as they do in the labour-songs: only here the chant becomes a positive rhythmic ecstasy, rather than a negative numbing of pain. (7) The most widespread, and the richest, type of Christianized Negro music was, however, that which achieved a union of indigenous roots with both the spirit and the technique of European hymnody. At first, "spirituals" were not, and were not intended to be, a harmonic music, *Trouble so hard,* for instance (8), is basically monodic as well as pentatonic, and such harmony as occurs is a heterophonic and accidental consequence of inflections in the single line, whereby the song's harsh realism is strengthened. But though harmony is not "natural" to a primitive people, the Negroes could respond spontaneously to its sensuousness when they heard it, especially in the shape-note hymns that spread rapidly over the continent, among the unlettered whites. Thus in a spiritual like *The new buryin' ground* (9) the triadic harmony comes from European hymns: but is employed with no sense of progression or development, so that it induces a feeling simultaneously sensual and ritualistic. This is closer in spirit to some early Renaissance music (in which composers were hypnotized by the sensuous euphony of parallel $\frac{6}{3}$ chords) than to anything in the music of eighteenth- or nineteenth-century Europe, or the more "cultivated" type of white American hymn. The spiritual may be a song of yearning and is usually a song of protest and oppression; but it is never merely a song of nostalgia or escape. The European harmony, even if chromatic, is given a sharp, harsh edge because the pitch-relationships are modified by the fortuitous intensifications of vocal monody: while the hymn's rhythmic complacency receives an injection of savage vigour from the thrust of work-movement and, maybe, from memories of the rhythmic displacements of primitive African dance. The music thus has a certain incantatory wildness that may momently remind us of the music of medieval Europe, and an earthiness that may recall the early Renaissance. It never reminds us of the politeness of the eighteenth century or the sanctimoniousness of the nineteenth; nor is chromatic nostalgia of the type associated with Delius's evocations of Negro life relevant to the genuine spiritual, though there is a link between the Negro's sorrow and Delius's sense of isolation. This is one reason why Delian chromatics became, much later, part of the harmonic dialect of jazz and of Tin Pan Alley; it was not a question of "influence", but of intuitive affinity.

However vigorously the Negroes responded to Christianity, they were separated from their own gods; and found the heart of their music not only in worship, but also in the however painful reality of their everyday lives. We can see this in the secular story-songs which the Negroes adapted from European ballads. Leadbelly's version of *John Henry* (10), for instance, translated into terms of Negro life and assimilated to a work-song, is a hero-worshipping Romance like the song of Roland or le Cid: but is vigorously non-sentimental and non-religious as compared with its European prototype; the more metrical, labour-dominated rhythm gives to the pentatonic tune a grim relent-lessness. This is true even of songs derived directly from white sources—like the Kentucky mountain music—which contain a dramatic situation: the traditional impersonality of folk-art—the concern with statement, not expatiation—is reinforced by the rhythmic hypnosis. This a-religious impersonality became the more marked when the slaves were emancipated. For although free, the Negroes were un-believably poor and underprivileged; in many ways their lot was harder than in the days of slavery. Whereas as slaves they had worked communally, they now tended to work alone, each man for himself, or in very small groups. Their work-songs returned to the most primi-tive "holler", part sung, part cried; and as they hollered to themselves in the empty fields the deepest, most primitive roots of their racial heritage seemed stretched in an ageless pain. In the astonishing *Wild Ox Moan* (11) the trance-like repetition of the brief, broken, pentatonic phrase induces an immense loneliness. The melismatic distortions of pitch sound more Eastern than European, transplanting into American English the pitch-inflections of the ancient African language. So evoca-tive a memory of so remote an antiquity makes the present moment's lonely dedication to toil seem the more forlorn.

The hollers were sung unaccompanied, of course, and were ad-dressed not to an audience but to the singer himself and to the job in hand. The work-songs and play-songs might be unaccompanied, or might be percussively supported by any banging or scraping instru-ments (pickaxes, washboards, knives, cans) that were being used in the act of work. The only authentic musical instruments that found their way into Negro music in the days of slavery were the "quills" or pipes, and the banjo, which seems to have been imported from Africa. Naturally enough, however, the Negroes picked up such European instruments as came—in however tattered and battered a condition—to hand, and were soon using violins along with the percussive instruments which they im-provised *ad hoc*. Most crucial of all was their discovery of the guitar: for while this instrument had affinities with their traditional banjo, it was musically much more rewarding. It could play pitch-distortions similar to those found in primitive monodic music, emulating with poignancy the melismata of the Negro speaking and singing voice: at the same time it could offer the sensual sonority of triadic harmony. The singer and his guitar could indulge in antiphonal dialogue comparable with that between the leader and the group in primitive African music. The difference was that the group was no longer present or, at least, need not be present: for through his guitar the deracinated Negro talked, alone, to himself—whoever might, fortuitously, be listening.

Though the blues derived directly from the field-hollers and in-directly from ballads, spirituals, and gospel shouts, they needed the guitar for their classic formulation. The twelve-bar structure of the blues—four bars of tonic moving to the seventh chord, two bars of subdominant, two of tonic, two of dominant seventh and two more of tonic—was a lowest common denominator of "form" within which improvisation could take place. The rudimentary sequence of chords was derived from the European hymn: (as T-Bone Walker said, "The blues comes a lot from the Church. . . . The first time I ever heard a boogie woogie piano was the first time I went to church. . . . That boogie-woogie was a kind of blues, I guess.") But there was no clear distinction between the convention of the Church and that of the saloon, so the blues-sequence provided the context within which the Negro, willy-nilly, had to live both musically and socially. The dialogue between voice and instrument thus complemented a deeper antiphony between the Negro's own experience and the (to him) strange world in which he found himself. The rigidity of the form was a part of his act of acceptance: a part, therefore, of the reality from which, without sentimental evasion or even religious hope, he started. This is why, though the blues are intensely personal in so far as each man sings, alone, of his own sorrow, they are also—even more than most folk-art—impersonal in so far as each man's sorrow is a common lot. Though the blues singer may protest against destiny, he is not usually angry, and seldom looks to heaven for relief. He sings to get the blues off his mind; the mere statement becomes therapeutic, an emotional liberation. "Bad time is upon me, everywhere the panic is on, I feel disgusted, all the good times done gone." But although it is he personally who feels disgusted, he immediately goes on to a general statement: "Everybody is cryin' they can't get a break. Tell me what's the matter. Everythin' seems to ache." So tragic passion is tempered by ironic detachment. When the blues singer advises us not to notice him because he's "just a poor boy in trouble tryin' to drive my blues away" by song we recognize that the detachment is part of the blues' honesty. Its truth is at rock-bottom: at the furthest possible remove from Stephen Foster's dream of the Old Kentucky Home.

In the country blues the rigid formal structure—which came from Europe and the town—is gradually imposed on folk sources that embrace the Negro's alienation, his search for love, his reliance on animal sensation, whether as substitute or as fulfilment. We can see this in *Skin-Game Blues* (12), as sung by Peg-Leg Howell. The beautiful tune preserves much of the pentatonic freshness and lyricism of the Appalachian folk-song from which it is derived; and that tune in turn descends directly from an Irish or Scottish original. In relationship to this tune, however, the effect of the guitar figuration, in the rudimentary harmonic sequence of the blues, is somewhat odd. It does not exactly cloud the vernal lyricism with a weight of sorrow; but it does suggest that, though the spirit wants to sing, it is nagged by the everyday round, by the wearisome burden of keeping alive. It is a gambling song that expresses not the exhilaration of gambling, but the realization that life itself is a gamble. This curiously numb quality is especially evident if one compares the guitar-accompanied *Skin-Game Blues* with an unaccompanied performance of the original Appalachian melody. In *Waking Blues* (13) the same oppressed and depressed feeling has become much more formidable and disturbing. It is as though the monotonous reiteration of the guitar, with chittering telescoped dissonances low in its register, is the reality that goes on and on, unalleviated: against which the voice can do no more than speak, rather than sing, broken, disjointed phrases, separated by silences.

In *Court-Street Blues* (14), however, we become aware of the Negro's resilience. While the primitive vocal line has lost the folk-like lyricism of *Skin-Game Blues*, it is undeniably a *song*, and the stove-pipe accompaniment indicates the singer's readiness to make music out of anything he finds handy, even an industrial implement; his acceptance may be comic at the same time as it contains an awareness of pain. In Bukka White's *Strange Place Blues* (15) lyricism returns in a different and potentially more significant form. The singer is standing by his mother's grave, and the melancholy he sings of is no longer merely a racial memory. We can see here how the blues singer creates, out of his passion, while he sings. The words fill up only two bars of the first four-bar period, leaving room for improvised dialogue between voice and guitar; and while the words are repeated to the conventional vamping bass the singer can be thinking up the second phrase. Personal feeling is responsible, too, for the sudden distortions of the voice in falsetto and in the "blue" notes whereby the third and seventh, and sometimes the sixths, are slightly flattened through subconscious recollection of folk-monody. The guitar may or may not emulate these distortions of pitch; since it is a harmony instrument, there is always a chance that its sharpened thirds may conflict in false relation with the voice's melodically flattened intervals. There is nothing specifically African about the so-called blues scale, for its fundamentally pentatonic modality is common to folk music all over the world. The characteristic flavour of jazz comes largely from a subterranean conflict between this age-old and instinctive approach to melody and the rudimentary harmonic and tonal structure which was inherited from Europe's and America's recent past; and this conflict is almost a musical synonym for the conflict between two worlds, old and new, black and white. Both worlds are accorded their value: though the harmonic sequence is basic, one cannot say that the blue notes are "out of tune", since they may merely be veering towards a Just Intonation that will not square with tempered harmony. So this ambiguity between vocal and instrumental style represents, musically, the Negro's attempt to come to terms with his new environment; and it is a two-way process. In *Skin-Game Blues*, we saw, the instrumental rhythm and harmony tend to negate the lyricism of the melody. In *Strange Place Blues*, on the other hand, the melodic distortions of pitch, which cannot be notated, arise from the singer's immediate awareness of suffering and also from the (for the dispossessed Negro) all-important dominance of the mother-image: while the rhythmic energy and harmonic solidity of the guitar become a powerful physical energy rather than a nervous freezing of the marrow. The reiteration of routine is now the clicking of the washboard, an economic and comfortably domestic instrument, associated with Mother. So the Negro learns to live with his melancholy, and although both the vocal technique and the force of the rhythm spring from his experience here and now, they serve too to carry him outside himself. In thus being a folk-song of isolation rather than of community *Strange Place Blues* approaches, more than any of the country blues on which we have commented, to the spirit of urban jazz.

In some country blues the jazz element finds expression in the instrumental commentary rather than in the vocal part itself. Lewis Black's version of *Gravel Camp Blues* (16), for instance, is vocally hardly distinct from a worksong or holler of despair; but the despair finds release in the emotionally expressive blue notes of the guitar, which speaks more passionately, more subjectively, than the voice itself. As voice, indeed, the singer is an anonymous member of his race; as guitar player he is a particular individual at a specific (gravel-pitted) time and place. In *Lonesome Blues* (17) a solo melody instrument (violin) dialogues with the voice while both are supported by guitar. This time the melismata and the blue intensifications of the fiddle both accentuate the singer's sorrow, and also effect the sorrow's release: for the fiddle is abandoned in its twiddling fioriture, almost gay despite the lonesomeness, so that in imitating the inflections of the human voice it frees them from a merely personal distress. Rigid though the blues form may be, it has no sense of beginning, middle or end. The blues are always with us; so, fortunately, is the possibility of creative arabesque. In this sense the blues are non-European, without the post-Renaissance time-sense. Here the music does not end, it merely tails off.

The folk-fiddle was a fairly popular melody instrument among the early country blues singers, and the fiddler in *Lonesome Blues* sounds remarkably like an early New Orleans clarinetist, who also imitated the inflections of the human voice. As the country blues became urbanized, instrumental techniques grew more varied and more complex, while the vocal elements absorbed a wider range of song-types. Blind Willie Johnson, for instance, singing *Nobody's fault but mine* (18), transforms the gospel shout directly into the blues, and his vocal production in "false bass" (a curious croaking from the back of the throat) emulates the "dirty" tone of the jazz trombone. Papa Charlie Jackson, on the other hand, singing *Airy Man Blues* (19) to his banjo, not guitar, links the blues with the vaudeville style of minstrel music, even with the songs of Stephen Foster. Leroy Carr—a country singer who went to work in Chicago, and favoured the piano as accompanying instrument, usually with the addition of guitar— tended to sophisticate the country blues, both in his lyrics and in his comparatively sweet and mild ballad style. In *Midnight Hour* (20), for instance, the music's poignancy depends on the slight disparity between the voice's lyricism and the full sweetness of the piano's harmony on the one hand, and on the other hand the wry, pinched, scrawny sound of Scrapper Blackwell's obbligato guitar. Carr's own guitar style—in, for instance, *Alabama Woman* (21)—tends to be richly plangent, with frequent *arpeggio* figures. A similar cross between traditional blues style and vaudeville or ragtime is evident in Lonnie Johnson's lyrical version of *Careless Love* (22); a more vigorous, perhaps more bouncily attractive, version of the compromise is offered when Washboard Sam sings *I been treated wrong* (23) to Memphis Slim's "corporeal", yet nervous, piano.

In the greatest of the male blues singers' performances there is usually little infiltration of vaudeville lyricism or pop music formality, though there is always an extraordinary development in guitar virtuosity to complement the poetic intensity of the words. Blind Lemon Jefferson, singing *Match Box Blues* ("got so many matches, got so far to go"), discovers a range of guitar sonorities, sometimes tenderly whimpering, more often hard and chippy, which is as variously emotive as his song-speech (24). Sleepy John Estes, on the other hand, in *Special Agent* (25), counteracts the speech-like pliancy and expressivity of his vocal line with a driving guitar rhythm hardly less potent than that of piano boogie: and generates from the contrast what one might call a *positive* hysteria. There is a similar flavour in Bukka White's version of *Fixin' to die* (26) and in Tommy MacClennan's *I'm a Guitar King* (27), but here the "shouted" vocal lines have the extrovert exuberance, which the violent contrasts of the "crying" guitar part tend to belie. In Blind Willie McTell's *Statesboro Blues* (28) this incipient sophistication begins to suggest the women blues singers of the cities, for he uses a nasal, earthily feminine vocal tone, over a guitar part of extreme rhythmic independence and of almost orchestral resonance, making great play with open strings.

Gradually, and inevitably, the introverted nervous tension within the blues gained ascendency over the extrovert qualities. In Charlie Pickett's *Down the Highway* (29), for instance, the rapid, obsessive, minor-keyed ostinato of the guitar reminds us, in its passionate remorselessness, of Spanish *flamenco*. The traditional fatalism of the blues changes, by way of the instrumental complexity, from passive suffering to something like desperation; and the music has lost the "positive" qualities we commented on in Sleepy John Este's *Special Agent*. In the work of Robert Johnson—a young man who was addicted to wine and women no less than to song, and who was murdered at the age of 21— we can hear how a personal, not merely racial, sense of persecution and alienation can give the blues a neurotic frenzy that has its counterpart in big-city life. *If I had possession on Judgement Day* (30) is in origin a gospel shout; but the wails and howls of the voice around the basically pentatonic phrases, reinforced by the high hammering and hard clanking noises of the guitar, transform the music into a personal desperation, awakening echoes in the hearts of all imprisoned victims of the city. In *Come on in my Kitchen* (31) Johnson treats ballad style in the

same way; while in *Stones in my passway* (32) or *Me and the Devil* (33)
he makes—by means of a wild intensification of the folk shout, howl,
shriek and falsetto yell—a savagely grotesque comment on the traditional irony of the blues. The chunky note-clusters of the guitar, its
extravagantly plangent vibrato, complement the varied vocal techniques; and this is still more evident in Johnson's tragic blues, which are
explicitly concerned with obsession and possession. In *At the Cross Roads*
(34) ("Ain't nobody seems to know me, everybody pass me by"), or in
the extraordinary *Hellhound on my trail* (35) ("Blues falling down like
hail this morning, I can't keep no money, hellhound on my trail") we
have reached the ultimate, and scarifying, disintegration of the country
blues. The howls and falsetto yells are now not only savage and grotesque,
they are also broken, lost, centreless. The almost lunatic emotional
excitement is reinforced by the harsh dissonances of the guitar, its
piercing vibrato scraped with knife-blade or bottle-neck on reiterated
single-notes; voice and instrument no longer comfort one another in
dialogue, but stimulate one another to further frenzy. On the words
"gotta keep moving" the blues-form is literally disrupted, the harmony displaced, the modulations weirdly awry. Sometimes Johnson
has no need of the conventional harmonic sequences, but makes do
with a quavering drone, as in the most primitive folk style; sometimes
he relinquishes song altogether and mutters to himself. The expression
of lonesomeness—the singer speaking with and through his guitar—
could be carried no further. This may be why the classic form of the
city blues, as developed by the women singers, had to involve participation between the singer and someone outside herself, whether it
were an instrumental soloist or a band.

Before this development could take place, however, there had to be
a growth within the techniques of instrumental jazz itself. This begins
to happen in the Mid-West logging and turpentine camps, where the
workers played instrumental blues for guitar or, more commonly, two
guitars, one playing the rhythm-harmony, the other the tune and
embroideries thereon. Since these pieces stressed the rhythmic excitement rather than the vocal melancholy of the blues, they were sometimes known as "Fast Western". Though a harsh, rough sonority could
be extracted from two guitars, the plangency of the instruments was
not naturally suited to this rawly masculine music: so the Fast Western
blues players seized avidly on the broken-down upright pianos that
came their way in the shanty-town bars and brothels. Most of the
players were camp-men, not professional musicians; even after barrel-

house piano music moved into the cities, the players were not always fully professional, but often taxi-drivers, ball-park or lavatory attendants or other public servants, who performed in bars and brothels in their spare time. Their instruments were essentially percussive; they had to make as much noise as possible if they were to be heard over the bar's babel. So the music played on barrelhouse pianos naturally represented the triumph of the guitar's percussion over the vocal lyricism of the country blues. The pianist's left hand becomes kinetic rhythm, creating, with complete denial of pianistic sophistication, a thick chugging of low-spaced triads in crotchets, then in quavers, then in the thrusting dotted rhythm of boogie-woogie. Against the remorseless bass, played without variation of dynamics, is the treble line, usually widely spaced, and often in complex cross-rhythms, pulling against the rhythmic-harmonic drive that apportions two chords to the bar, one on the first beat, the other on—or sometimes just before—the third. Fundamentally, barrelhouse piano is a two-voiced music for the player's left and right hand. The rhythmic momentum is everything, though the right hand uses percussive note-clusters to make the noise louder and wilder, and introduces crushed notes, chromatic slides, rapid repeated notes and tremolandi in an attempt to emulate, however crudely and raucously, the expressive devices of the more emotionally sensitive guitar. Pitch distortion was certainly part of the effect of the piano blues, but was an accidental, rather than deliberately expressive, effect: the tumble-down instruments were grievously out of tune, and the jangle was approved of, since it enhanced the clamour.

Not surprisingly, considering where it was played, barrelhouse piano is an extremely sexy music in which the incessant beat and thrust of the boogie rhythm become synonymous with male potency. However confused and confusing its etymology may be, there is no doubt that one of the meanings of the phrase boogie-woogie, as of the word jazz itself, is sexual intercourse; and what happens in the music is both descriptive and aphrodisiac. Thus the obsessively repeated rhythmic figurations of the "riff" phrase adapt a primitive orgiastic technique to the bar-parlour: while both the repetitions and the perpetual cross-rhythms of the right hand brace the body and the nerves against the forward thrust. The deeper implications of the act of coition come in, too, because in the relationship between the two voices or rather hands there is both a duality of tension, and also a desperate desire for unity which would, of its nature, destroy the forward momentum, make Time stop. From this point of view the significance of the *break* is interesting. Technically, it is simply a rest for the pianist's hard-stomping left hand; but it becomes, in the explosion of its cross-rhythms, literally a break in Time—a kind of seizure within the music's momentum. In this sense its effect is like an orgasm: though it is never finally resolutory. The piano blues is a communal act in that it is meant to be performed in public places; but the orgasm into which the listeners, along with the pianist, are "sent" remains as private, if elemental, as it would be when enacted in the room upstairs.

The twelve-bar blues form, though still present as a basic convention, has little formal significance in piano blues: what matters is the continuous drive that induces excitement and at the same time carries us beyond the self. One of the most primitive, and fascinating, of the early barrelhouse players was a character with the romantic-heroic name of Romeo Nelson. When he plays *Head Rag Hop* (36) his energy surges into the physical behaviour of his left hand, which generates the thrusting rhythm of boogie-woogie—tum-ti-tum-ti. It is interesting to recall that this rhythm is strictly comparable with the "unequal note" convention in classical baroque music, especially that of Louis XIV's France; and in the seventeenth and early eighteenth century the rhythm's physical energy was a celebration of the glory of the visible and tactile world. Boogie-woogie is a sensual celebration, too: but its creators, far from being lords of the earth, had nothing to celebrate but their own animal vigour. So the difference between Romeo Nelson's boogie and the dotted rhythm in Lully or Purcell lies in the fact that with the Europeans the rhythm's bounce is marshalled by the will into clearly defined harmonic and tonal periods, producing Order and Civilization, with a beginning, middle and end: whereas Romeo Nelson's energy exists apart from the will, or even the consciousness, and has no sequence or consequence. The right hand's arabesques, indeed, are not only widely separated from the boogie bass, they are also prevailingly pentatonic—a primitivism habitual in the vocal country blues, but rare in the later instrumental versions. The insistent thrust of the rhythm, the endless oscillation of pentatonic figures, the lack of recognizable "theme", make Nelson's barrelhouse style a raw, shanty-town form of ancient African ritual-music, rather than "art" in the post-Renaissance sense. It is irrelevant to complain that it goes on too long. Time is only a European notion. This music is not meant to be listened to as an end in itself; it is a background to action.

A more sophisticated form of barrelhouse piano can be heard in Montana Taylor's *Indiana Avenue Stomp* (37). The physical energy of the stomping bass has here a thick, viscid texture comparable with the guitar-bass of *Strange Place Blues*, and this time the widely separated right-hand tune does not merely—like Romeo Nelson's pentatonic doodlings—ride mindless and will-less over the boogie gallop; it acquires more melodic definition, and therefore a more positive identity, which is to some degree *opposed* to the bass's momentum. The twelve-bar blues structure is more evident: as is the fact that the essence of piano-blues style lies in tension between the remorseless potency of the bass-beat and the tune's attempt—by way of cross-rhythms, chromatic glissandi like guitar portamenti, high quivery tremolandi and guitar-jangling note-clusters—at "personal" expression. The dynamism of the bass both sustains and threatens the tune's lament or ecstasy. It is what keeps us going, and also what may obliterate us; and this may be literally true, for the more vehemently we live in our bodies (which are about all we have), the sooner we are worn out and die. In *Indiana Avenue Stomp*, certainly, the breaks in the line get more jittery, the hands' separation in the very high and very low registers of the keyboard more precarious: until the music thins out in chromatically descending thirds. This drooping melancholy seems an odd end to so energetic a piece. It *has* an end, unlike Romeo Nelson's boogies, which might as well go on for ever; but it stops not by will or by choice, but through sheer inanition, because the clock runs down, as did the nerves and bodies of so many early jazzmen. There is an incipiently tragic quality in *Indiana Avenue Stomp*, which reaches fulfilment in the work of the greatest of the barrelhouse pianists, Jimmy Yancey. Significantly, Yancey is the only early blues-pianist to play in comparatively slow tempi: the only one who—in a piece like the deeply poetic *At the Window* (38)— manages to suggest, on the mechanical and equal-tempered piano, something of the expressive plangency of jazz voice, guitar, and clarinet. He could play chromatic slides with such subtle control of tone-colour that they sound like true vocal portamenti; he could even create the illusion, by infinitesimal delays in attack, that a blue note was minutely off-key—not merely a minor, instead of a major, third or seventh. In Yancey's slower pieces the emptiness of the texture —the distant separation of treble and bass—becomes a poignant image of urban loneliness. The raw vitality of lumber-camp music merges into the melancholy of the big city.

In Yancey—and in *Indiana Avenue Stomp*—kinetic bass and potentially melodic treble are on more or less equal terms; sometimes, however, the physical drive of motor rhythm destroys any attempt at line and, living for itself in the present moment, becomes a kind of hysteria. This often happens in the train pieces, of which the most celebrated, and also the most impressive, is Meade Lux Lewis's *Honky Tonk Train Blues* (39). The Negro's obsession with the railroad has become a twentieth-century myth. The railway train—powerful at the head, snake-like in elongation—is probably a phallic image; and the railway also opened up and ravished the American wilderness. Although it represented an endless series of departures, there was always the hope that one might arrive somewhere wonderful at the end. The Negro himself worked on the railroad, and rode on it legitimately or as hobo; in any case he was a traveller moved on by economic necessity, living in the mere fact of motion because he had little else to live for. In *Honky Tonk Train Blues* the thrust of the chunky left-hand triads generates an immense momentum, which is enhanced by the right hand's fantastically complex (though of course intuitive) cross-rhythms. The interlocked energy of the rhythms is vigorously sexual; but again the orgasm is incomplete. We cannot conceive of motion except in relation to passion, feeling, growth; here, we are "sent" by the rhythm into a state of trance because we experience it without reference to melody or even harmony—for the note-clusters are, for the most part, percussive dissonances. For this reason, the motion itself becomes a kind of immobility; and the piece ends, through inanition, in the same way as *Indiana Avenue Stomp*. The train chuffs to stillness, just as the pendulum of the stomp's clock surrenders motion. This is indicated in the conventional fade-out on the flat seventh. Barrelhouse blues hardly ever end in tonic resolution, and Jimmy Yancey, whatever key he was playing in, tended to doodle out on the flat seventh of E flat. He was still travelling, never really at journey's end. We can observe something similar in Speckled Red's remarkable *Wilkins Street Stomp* (40), which combines the hysteria of movement-as-an-end-in-itself with the opposition between blues tune and boogie rhythm.

At the same time as the urban folk art of barrelhouse piano was evolving in bars and brothels, the Negro tried consciously to create a notated form of piano music that would be his own contribution to "art". This was piano rag: which is distinct from barrelhouse music in that it has no reference either to the blues or to improvisation. It was closely associated with the aggressively cheerful banjo music played in the minstrel shows—such as James Scott's *Ragtime Oriole* (41), which is a military two-step; and this in turn was related to the Cake-Walk, which had originally been a grotesquely prancing dance wherein the

Negro slaves competed—in parody-imitation of their white masters—
for a prize of cake. In every sense ragtime would thus seem to represent
the Negro's desire to get his own back. It is a composed music, like the
white man's Art; it flourished, during the first decade of the century,
in comparatively northern towns where music publishing was practic-
able; Scott Joplin, the leading writer of rags, was quite well read in
classical music and had ambitions to create large-scale works. (He
wrote a rag opera, *Treemonisha*, which was produced, though it was
unsuccessful.) Formally, rag derived—like banjo music—not from the
blues but from those more sophisticated white sources that had found a
home, along with slavery, in the Southern states. French quadrilles and
military two-steps that (as we saw in our account of Sousa) were closely
related to them merged to create rags in sixteen-bar strains—never in
the (elastic) twelve-bar strains of the blues. Usually there were four
themes: the first march-like, in two-step rhythm; the second lighter,
often upwards-soaring; the third darker and more cantabile, like the trio
of a march, usually in the subdominant but occasionally in the dominant;
and the fourth a blaze of triumph, returning to the tonic and to the mood
of the first strain. James Scott's *Frogs Legs* (42) is a classic example of the
norm, except that there is a repetition of the first strain after the soaring
counter-theme, and the trio tune is in the dominant, not subdominant.
Like all rags *Frogs Legs* is in $\frac{2}{4}$ and is of absolute metrical regularity, with
syncopations that enhance the jauntiness, but do not imply tension,
because the harmonic and formal structure is so simple and so clearly
defined.

Yet while rag is a composed music, an emulation of white techniques
that seems to belie the instinctual character of American Negro music,
it is also in an odd way a parody music—like the Cake-walk from
which it had descended. And we cannot be sure whether it parodies
the white man's image of the Negro or the Negro himself; we can only
feel that there is a certain pathos in the Negro's obsession with "white"
rondo form as an attempt to tame, even to "civilize", the rhythmic
hysteria of barrelhouse stomp, especially as exemplified in the train
pieces. The essence of the rag is its unremittent rhythmic *pattern* which,
though habitually syncopated, is never violent. The melancholy, the
frenzy, the ecstasy of the blues are all banished. Instead of lament or
orgy, we have a dead-pan manner that shuts out personal sensation.
The music is hard, bright, obstinately eupeptic and incorrigibly cheerful; in its machine-made way it is even elegant, like the Negro dandy
wearing his straw boater at a raffish angle. In so far as the inane grin

and the prancing vivacity attempt to shut out the painful actuality of the Negro's experience, there is an affinity between piano rag and the positively ebulliently entertainment music we referred to in the previous chapter: rag is the Negro's attempt at the buoyant optimism of the Sousa march and the brilliant elegance of the Gottschalk dance, and the mass feeling is depersonalized because personal feeling may be too much to bear. In this sense, rags are an *alternative* to the blues; and their use of the discipline of military music becomes equated with the disciplined non-humanity of a machine. This is literally true: for many rags were transferred to the pianola roll and, even if not played by a machine, should be played *like* a machine, with meticulous precision. Perhaps it is better to be a merry machine, the music says, than to be human but blue: so the queer, sad poetry of the best rags comes from the flimsiness of the gay mask they wear. Although this poetry may be inherent in the situation rather than in the music itself, the later rags of the master of the convention, Scott Joplin, unobtrusively readmit those elements of tension which the rag had tried to deny. *Euphonic Sounds* (43), for instance, written in 1909, has some oddly elliptical modulations in its second strain, wandering from tonic B flat to B minor, to E flat, and then from G minor to D flat major, changing to the relative B flat minor, and so back to tonic major; in the first strain it also indulges in syncopations in which the beat is merely implied. In the later *Magnetic Rag* (44) such elements of relative complexity are structural as well as incidental, for Joplin modifies the third and fourth strains so that they acquire some of the features of a sonata development. Joplin thus confesses to an element of duality, even of dubiety, in his attempt to relinquish the blues' tension. Related to this, perhaps, is the fact that his rags are often quite difficult to play; one cannot merely take them in one's stride—unless one's stride happens to be exceptionally large and agile.

The significance of piano rag in the history of jazz may be vicarious rather than intrinsic: it suggested to the more talented barrelhouse pianists possibilities of formal organization that need not conflict with their instinctive utterance. The presence of creative invention was, of course, obligatory, for formal control is meaningless unless there is something to *be* controlled. When Cow Cow Davenport plays *Atlanta Rag* (45) we feel that the discipline of rag-forms restricts the invention which he could exhibit as a boogie-woogie player. When, however, a player of the calibre of James P. Johnson performs *Riffs* (46) we hear how the spontaneity of barrelhouse style may be intensified, rather than weakened, by the influence of the rag's lucidity. In particular, the powerful "striding bass" characteristic of Johnson comes from the more sophisticated rag-technique, yet enhances the rugged virility of the barrelhouse chugging triads. A further stage is represented by many piano pieces of the first great master of jazz, Jelly Roll Morton. He also employs the stride bass, over which he manages to reconcile the rag's conscious if rudimentary artistry with both the improvisatory vigour of barrelhouse piano, and also with the passion of the blues. His *Kansas City Stomps* (47) is a superb example of the half-way house between barrel-house and rag. The sixteen-bar theme comes, by way of rag, from church hymn and military music, and the structure—with a "tuning up" section introducing an E flat theme stated twice, followed by a counter-subject also in the tonic, a trio theme in the subdominant rounded off by a varied restatement—derives simultaneously from rag and from the Sousa-type march. The complexity of the counter-rhythms, on the other hand, is an authentic barrelhouse style: while the tense displacements of accent and the recurrent false relations in the melody betray the flavour of the blues. In another version of this piece Jelly Roll employs the European convention of the rag-rondo in the evolutionary manner of jazz variation. The first theme A is followed by an improvised variation A¹; then the counter-subject B is followed by its variation B¹. Theme A then reappears in another variation A¹¹. Theme C, the trio section, is also succeeded by a variation; after which, as coda, theme A returns in a third variation A¹¹¹. This is a formal structure of the most satisfying solidity; the immediacy of jazz improvisation can be preserved because the structural symmetries are not static but evolutionary.

Morton's *King Porter Stomp* (48)—one of his most celebrated pieces—shows another variant of the formula. There is a four-bar introduction, then eight plus eight bars in A flat, with hints of B flat minor. This verse-section is characterized by four chugging barrelhouse beats a bar, with off-beat syncopations in the right hand. After the double bar, there is another section of eight plus eight bars, now in the relative, F minor; here the off-beat syncopations have become the basis of the melodic line, more sinewy and flexible than in the first section. The rising scale passage here generated turns into an octave passage marked "Interlude". This carries us into the trio, which is in the subdominant D flat, with a B flat minorish tinge, so that we feel that this more patently tuneful section is an evolution both from the F minor paragraph, and also from the incidental modulation in the verse's first few bars. The Trio leads into the Stomp, which does not return to the original A flat, but falls still flatter, from D flat to G flat. Yet it is truly a consummation of the previous music; and generates tremendous excitement from cross-accents between the right hand's chords (mostly 3 plus 3 plus 2 quavers) and the regular stomp of the bass, which tends chromatically to *rise*. The climax comes in a reiterated riff of blue notes, alternating between E natural (really F flat) and E flat: the music stops on the dominant seventh. Part of the effect of this piece depends on the way it grows more exciting as the tonality subsides flatwards. The same thing happens, we have seen, in Sousa marches, and Jelly Roll was a literate musician, brought up on classical pop music, both operatic and military. The authentically creative nature of his talent lies, however, in the fact that everything he borrows from "formal" sources is reborn. Perhaps one could say that in this case he makes the flatwards subsistence which, in the Sousa march had enshrined Hearth and Home, a wonderfully pertinent musical image for the coloured man's capacity for acceptance—and then for exuberant resilience. To describe his music as "bouncy" is both technically and emotionally accurate.

Work-songs and play-songs, spirituals and shouts, hollers and country blues were nation wide, coming to birth wherever the Negro needed to express his longing, his weariness, or his joy in the passing moment. Barrelhouse piano began in the Mid-West; piano rag, being a relatively sophisticated music that called for publishers and mechanized instruments, was centred in the cities. But Jelly Roll Morton—in whom all these elements and some others coalesced to create an art—was a New Orleans man; and it was in New Orleans—if not, as he liked to suggest, specifically with Jelly Roll himself—that jazz achieved its classic formulation. To the genesis of the New Orleans jazz band we must turn in the next chapter.

III

Heterophony and improvisation: the New Orleans jazz band and King Oliver; Bessie Smith and the urban blues

In the land of plenty, have
nothing to do with it
take the way of
the lowest,
including
your legs, go
contrary, go

sing.

CHARLES OLSEN

a little sunlight and less
moonlight ourselves against the worms

hate laugh shimmy

E. E. CUMMINGS

Nineteenth-century New Orleans—as we saw when discussing Louis Gottschalk—had been a vivid, cosmopolitan city, a melting-pot of the nations and races. The coloured people, more vigorously represented there than anywhere, were relatively prosperous; there had even been a Creole aristocracy—mostly the free descendants of mulattoes who had been the favoured mistresses of white men—to which Gottschalk's mother belonged. It was natural enough, therefore, that the Negro's music should flourish in this city, and that the richest flowering should occur with the final abolition of slavery. But if jazz was in one sense a music of rejoicing, of liberated ebullience, it was at the same time, even in New Orleans, still a music of protest: a democratic insistence on the vitality of the underprivileged, at a time when the priviledged were no longer having things all their own way. Jazz became dominant only when the pseudo-artistocratic "Creoles of colour" declined: and was essentially a music of low life, centred in the red-light district of Storyville. The escape or dream motive was alien to jazz, except in so far as its permutations of Christian mythology were such a motive. If they were, the Negro knew that his dreams would not be fulfilled in this life, and was content to base his art on the celebration of a real world, and real people. Canal Street and Perdido Street were round the corner; the characters referred to in the songs could be met with at any time, on the streets.

There were two positive elements in New Orleans jazz, in addition to those referred to in the previous chapter; both were consequent on the city's cosmopolitan flavour—a well-stirred mixture of French, German, Italian and Spanish settlers with a sprinkling of Anglo-Saxons, a vast Negro population, and a considerable body of Carib-beans, not to mention the variously shaded half- and quarter-breeds that resulted from interracial sexual relationships. The French, Spanish, and Caribbean infiltrations brought to New Orleans music a sensuality that was relatively easy and passive: without the frenzy of African rhythm, the tension of the blues, or the harshness of barrelhouse piano. A patois song (*c'été n'aut can-can*) rehashed by Kid Ory (1) indicates how the sun-baked Latin-American rhythm permeated French street song, and was even combined with reminiscences of the French theatre and Italian opera, which were immensely popular with the more well-to-do New Orleans public. In much of the music of Jelly Roll Morton, king of early New Orleans jazz, there is a direct merging of "cultivated" French and Italian theatre music with Latin American rhythm. He was especially fond of playing his ragtime version of the Miserere from *Il Trovatore* (2) in which passionate Italianism lends itself readily to transmutation into habañera and rumba rhythms. Morton tells us that as early as 1902 he had put "the Spanish tinge" into his *New Orleans Joys* (3) and goes on to say that "if you can't manage to put tinges of Spanish in your tunes, you will never be able to get the right seasoning for jazz". There may be something in the view that jazz's preoccupation with syncopation was deeply influenced by the dotted rhythm swing of the tango, and the delayed effect of the rumba's cross-accents; certainly Jelly Roll himself, in a splendid piece such as *Spanish Swat* (4) fuses Spanish tango and habañera with the military two-step of ragtime in a manner that is both positive and stimulating. This piano music is not less vigorous, but considerably richer and warmer, than the aggressive music of the Mid-West, for the piano texture preserves the scrunchiness and density of barrelhouse style, while the rhythm is relatively relaxed.

The other positive element in New Orleans music was military music itself. All over the South decrepit military instruments survived among the vestiges of the Civil War. The Negroes appropriated the instruments to their own use; and while their street bands imitated the Europeanized military music they had heard, they ragged it rhythmically and treated the tunes in improvisatory folk-heterophony, not having the skill or the learning to do otherwise. A superb record, made comparatively recently, but by old men, enables us to hear the *Gettysberg March* (5) played in this style. Here the individual embellishments of the line—whereby different players perform slightly different versions of the same tune—are far more important than the conventional march-harmony, in so far as it survives at all: so the disciplined, European-American march is remade in Negroid terms. The consequences of this in New Orleans music are again most richly revealed by Jelly Roll Morton, this time in a band piece—a version of the funeral music *Oh, Didn't he ramble*! (6). On the way to the funeral the band blows quasi-European hymnody to a slow military beat. On the way back, however, as they proceed to the junketing, the military march becomes a quick rag, the hymn becomes a blues, and Latin-American dance-song brings in hints of French and Italian opera, with maybe a whiff of Europeanized plantation music, in the manner of Stephen Foster, also. This melting-pot of a piece gives us an idea of the variety of music that shook New Orleans during the first two decades of the century. Parade bands in the streets were so numerous that they were apt to bump into one another, engendering rivalry sometimes friendly, sometimes highly inimicable. Party-bands in parks or squares might be playing Negro rags or Latin American tangos or French quadrilles or German waltzes. Every nationality had its feast days, and at Mardi Gras the celebrations were universal. There was music for every occasion—picnics, conventions, prize fights, race meetings, birthdays, weddings and—above all—funerals. And that all this multifariousness did not affect merely the surface of life is revealed in Jelly Roll's famous description of New Orleans funeral music:

> Of course, the dead man would always be laid out in the front and he'd be by himself most of the time and couldn't hear nothing we would be saying at all. He was dead, and there was no reason for him to be with us living people . . . We would stand up and begin

Nearer my God to Thee

very slow and with beautiful harmony, thinking about that ham—

Nearer to Thee

plenty of whiskey in the flask and all kinds of crazy ideas in the harmony
. . . We'd be sad, too, terribly sad . . .

In New Orleans very seldom they would bury them in the mud. They
would always bury um in a vault. So they would leave the graveyard . . .
the band would get ready to strike up. They'd have a second line behind
um, maybe a couple of blocks long with baseball bats, axe handles,
knives, and all forms of ammunition to combat some of the foe when
they came to the dividing lines. Then the band would get started and
you could hear the drums rolling a deep, slow rhythm. A few bars of
that and then the snare drummer would make a hot roll on his drums
and the boys in the band would just tear loose, while the second line
swung down the street, singing

> Didn't he ramble?
> He rambled.
> He rambled till the butcher cut him down.

In this and in many similar passages we can detect a strange medley of
primitive superstition, facile sophistication, naïve ebullience and canny
irony; and Jelly Roll's paradoxical personality is, indeed, an epitome of
the tangled skein of impulses that went to make jazz. Born in 1896, he
grew up in and around the brothels and bars of New Orleans. There
was a dark undercurrent in him that linked him to a remote African
past, and his conviction that he was the victim of a voodoo curse
grew on him in the later years of comparative misfortune. Yet at
the same time he was a light mulatto, proud of the fact that "all my
folks came from France", and this produced in him an odd dubiety, for
he felt that the "black" element both compromised his respectability
and was also evidence of his artistic truth. Tension between the harsh,
earthy vigour of black Negro music and the easy, almost elegant
relaxation of Creole music and of French, Italian and Spanish song and
dance generated his most characteristic creations; and this is true of
New Orleans jazz as a whole. Dr Bechet—Sidney Bechet's brother—
has pointed out that Creoles learned to play jazz only when they
associated with Negroes, since one could play hot only if one had lived
hard: "These hot people, they play like they're *killing* themselves, you
understand?"

So the classic style of New Orleans jazz, as it was formulated
during the first decade of the century, combined an easy spontaneity
with an uneasy strain. The easiness was a part of the Negro's empirical

inventiveness; Jelly Roll tells us that many characteristic jazz effects were discovered accidentally, as the Negro was larking around, doing an animal imitation or, for a joke, hitting the drum with a fly-swatter. Similarly he would supplement authentic "horns" with any *ad hoc* instrument he could improvise; and although we have no contemporary recordings of this music of extrovert gaiety, something comparable survives as late as the twenties, in the jug-bands of Memphis. In *Ripley's Blues* (7) Gus Cannon blows into a jug, in dialogue with Noah Lewis's harmonica, over a simple rocking bass on guitar; in *Harmonica Stomp* (8) harmonica and voice exchange a simple, almost infantile tune, interspersed with exuberant falsetto hoots and stimulating cross-rhythms on washboard and guitar. The *ad hoc* nature of the music is its charm; it goes on "regardless", until abruptly it stops on an unresolved dominant seventh. Similar music was made at Chicago rent-party sessions, and reappeared in the skiffle craze of the 1950s.

Even in the earliest New Orleans bands, however, the horn playing must have brought in something of the typical jazz "dirt" and anguish, if we can judge from Jelly Roll Morton's music and his comments on it. Neither Jelly Roll nor Louis Armstrong were by nature self-effacing personalities, yet they spoke in reverential terms of the legendary (because unrecorded) Buddy Bolden and Buddy Petit; and since we are told that "Bolden was the blowingest man who ever lived since Gabriel . . . he went crazy because he really blew his brains out through his horn", we can assume that their playing was not merely a matter of animal high spirits. A remote idea of what these bands sounded like may perhaps be obtained from the music of George Lewis, an instinctive jazzman of the old type, who never learned to read music: for in the forties he recorded with his New Orleans Stompers a number of early classics, using the old instrumentation, and the old style as he remembered it. The cornet—or later the trumpet—takes the lead and plays the tune, while the clarinet either doubles the cornet or "noodles" around it, playing heterophonic embellishments, usually at the octave. The trombone is the tenor part, accenting the beat and occasionally playing a very simple counterpoint to the melody. The tuba (or later the string bass) plays the bass line, and banjo (or later guitar) acts as harmonic fill-in. Still later the piano, which naturally did not figure in the early itinerant bands, was used simultaneously as harmony and rhythm instrument. In the first bands, however, the basis of the rhythm was the big military drum, with two beats a bar derived from the military two-step. Only when the rhythms grew more complicated and syncopated was there a change from two- to four- beat rhythm, wherein bass drum alternated with snare drum or a wood block, such as was common in minstrel shows.

The Stomper's version of *Just a closer walk with Thee* (9) derives directly from European hymn and march, for the melody is a hymn tune, which is treated in march rhythm. This rhythm becomes positive and ebullient, deprived of its restrictive discipline; the physical assault of the dotted rhythm, continuing unremittently, encourages forgetfulness of self, and so binds us in mutuality. In being together, as we beat the earth, we find a kind of freedom; tranced by the unrelenting metre and by the lowest common denominator of the harmony, we begin to grow individually alive even as we seem to lose our identities. The basis of the style is heterophony; the harmony does not matter, for in solidarity we all try to play the same tune, creating music for dancing to, and thereby identifying the group with ourselves. At the same time, the more worked up we become, the more prone are we to introduce embellishments into our part; and these embellishments become the heart of the music, creating fortuitous clashes similar to, if more raucous than, those that occurred in the heterophonic music of Europe's Middle Ages. This, indeed, is the medieval stage of jazz history, distinct from, even opposed to, later Western tradition. Since then jazz has grown—but not necessarily towards a conception of music comparable with that of Europe's Renaissance.

The creative embellishments which the players introduce into their collective heterophony may sometimes be disturbing and are often comic. In *Just a closer walk with Thee,* for instance, the repeated-note dithers suggest a tipsy abandon that is both a release from propriety and an ironic deflation. This tendency is more developed in the military-founded *Milenberg Joys* (10), for here there is a greater differentiation between the melodic parts and the rhythm-harmony section. Jittery repeated notes, riffs, "speaking" glissandi and portamenti adapted from the blues, convey a kind of naïve wit, if the term is not contradictory. A deeper note is sounded in *Two Ten* (8), which is a band version not of the hymn or military march, but of the blues itself. The traditional dialogue between voice and guitar becomes a conversation between tuba and trombone, which wailingly imitate the rough, "dirty" inflections of the speaking voice. The tone is not dirty because it is unpleasant, much less false: but rather because it is the true voice of a human creature, life as it is—raw because the Negro has no cocoon of pretence to wrap it in.

The classic form of the New Orleans band crystallizes, however, in the ensemble of Joe "King" Oliver, who, though born in the "District" in 1885, seems to have grown up in a slightly less seedy and shady environment than Jelly Roll Morton. He worked as a butler; but was playing in bands as early as 1894. In 1911 he made a big tour with the Original Creole Orchestra. His own group—consisting of himself as cornet-leader, Johnny Dodds as the most warmly expressive of New Orleans clarinetists, Honoré Dutrey as trombone, Bill Johnson as bass, Baby Dodds as drummer and Lil Hardin as pianist—was not finally established until 1920, two years after Oliver left New Orleans. The title of "King Oliver's Creole Jazz Band", adopted in Chicago in 1923, did not mean that the band played Creole music, only that their roots were in New Orleans. Like Jelly Roll Morton, Oliver sought for a compromise between Creole relaxation and Negro earthiness: so that when his band plays the celebrated *Mabel's Dream* (11) they start from a Creole-like sweetness of sonority, but make jazz in that they follow Louis Nelson's advice to "shove in cryin whenever you get the chance". They play with the heart and sinews as well as with the lungs: with the result that a blandly cheerful military strut is transformed, through the improvisatory chorus variations, into a blues. After an introductory strain, the second strain establishes the mood of the pop song on which the improvisations are based. The third strain invokes the hymn, with a close-textured, organ-like instrumentation, through which Oliver's silvery cornet, and then Dodd's clarinet, float and soar, growing increasingly ecstatic. Though the individual players are liberated by the mutuality, however, they do not aim to be soloists. This is still ensemble playing, more heterophonic than polyphonic. It differs from the very first bands, or from George Lewis's imitations of them, in that social solidarity now seems to imply a more harmonic style, based on four, not two, fastish beats to the bar. The harmony does not depart from the common denominator of the traditional blues progression, tonic, subdominant, tonic, dominant, tonic; but the chord progressions may be enriched by subsidiary sevenths, ninths, and even elevenths, so that more of Europe's "consciousness" is involved in the being together.

Perhaps one could define this technique as "heterophonic homophony": in playing the blues in this style the band seeks to render a music of solitariness socially amenable. Oliver tends to play the blues somewhat quickly, in a homogeneous sonority; in *Dippermouth Blues*, (12), for instance, the military rhythm remains unbroken through the improvisatory variations, though the separate parts are very blue. The jauntiness of Oliver's music reminds us of the rags: only it no longer disguises undercurrents of passion and sorrow. *Canal Street Blues* (13) or *Working Man Blues* (14) are both traditional twelve-bar blues, incorporating march and hymn in fastish tempo. While the music is still a co-operative act, the solos—especially those of Dodds—become increasingly important, and tension within the homophony literally sunders the ensemble—into "breaks". The interrelation between the solidarity of march and hymn and the solitariness of the blues is more subtly evident in *Chimes Blues* (15). The tune itself is a twelve-bar blues, but the improvisatory choruses create an A B C D C structure that comes straight from march music, with strain D serving as trio. After a two-bar introduction in which the youthful Louis Armstrong joins Oliver in duo, there are two bars of full ensemble music. Strains A, B and C have the same harmonic base, and each is repeated with improvised variation. Chorus 1 is for ensemble, chorus 2 for ensemble with clarinet solo, chorus 3 and 4 are for ensemble-homophony, with clarinet occasionally spilling into heterophonic arabesques. In choruses 5 and 6 the piano's chimes enter; they are the only passage that sounds dated, but are justified because they are decorated with a beautiful filigree on Oliver's muted cornet. This is answered, in choruses 7 and 8, by Armstrong's comparatively angular and frenetic solo. A more extended repetition of chorus 3 serves as coda; the equilibrium here achieved between the close homophony of the ensemble and Dodds's winging clarinet solo is truly consummatory.

It is interesting to compare the sound of King Oliver's Jazz Band with that of the Original Dixieland Jazz Band, which was its white complement. Though this band was the first recorded jazz ensemble, and antedates Oliver's band by some years, Jelly Roll Morton characteristically insists that it was only a white imitation of the band of Freddie Keppard, "'who had the best ear, the best tone, and the most marvellous execution I ever heard". Nick La Rocca's father had come from Italy to New Orleans in 1876; Nick's first job was as arc-light attendant at the Old French Opera, where he heard music that fascinated him almost as much as his supreme musical passion—the band of Sousa. From about 1905 he played cornet, usually in combination with violin, guitar, and bass, at dances and parties. By 1912 he had joined Jack Laine's Reliance Band, in which military instruments had superseded strings. From 1916 he led his own bands, playing music which absorbed ragtime and other aspects of Negro music into his reminiscences of Sousa's military one-steps and two-steps, and of the ensemble numbers of French operettas. *Livery Stable Blues* (16) (which made him famous) had a chord structure borrowed from Stephen Adam's *The Holy City*, with one chord changed and the last two bars omitted; the piece's notoriety depended largely on its animal imitations. *Tiger Rag* (17) borrows phrases from a French quadrille, from "London Bridge is falling down", and from the National Emblem March, while the riffs of the second chorus began as a comic imitation of the alto part of a German band. La Rocca claimed the piece as an original composition, though Jelly Roll Morton maintained that he wrote it. Certainly Morton demonstrates, most effectively, how he "put the tiger in" to the bits he picked up from other sources; and it is precisely the absence of the tiger-spirit that differentiates La Rocca's music from that of Jelly Roll, or from King Oliver's band. The wildness of the blues, the tension of the heterophony, have vanished, leaving only a eupeptic jauntiness. Oliver makes something positive, even gay, out of a painful reality; the Dixieland Band, purging away both the passion and the irony, leaves us with the inane grin of the black-faced minstrel. The brassy, reedy sonority of the Negro band—which can be simultaneously hard as nails and warmly sensitive—becomes a footling tootle; the perpetual jigging of the dotted rhythm becomes a jerking of puppets. All that comes over as genuine is an element of pathos beneath the merriment. If there was pathos in the vivacity of the Negro rags, it is sadder still to find white men, with or without blackened faces, wearing the same mask. The pathos is for the most part extra-musical.

Though King Oliver's Jazz Band was an ensemble, a miracle of intuitive co-ordination, the improvising soloist began increasingly to dominate it. The development of the soloistic approach is beautifully illustrated in the work of a group (including Dodds and Ory) which recorded under the name of the New Orleans Wanderers. If Oliver's Creole Jazz Band created heterophonic homophony, the New Orleans Wanderers approach a true polyphony; and although in *Papa Dip* (18), for instance, the "togetherness" of the driving rhythm is the main impetus behind the music, the collective security becomes the basis of personal fulfilment. Because we are all, as players, carried along by the thrill of the beat, we can blow our horns in uninhibited passion and in individual exuberance. In *Perdido Street Blues* (19) (in itself a most impressive minor-keyed melody) we experience the blue passion of the solo lines *against* the metrical patterns of the ensemble's harmony: which though still regular, are now broken, the segments separated by disturbing silences, within which the jets of melody shoot. One might almost say that the *break* is here the heart of the piece. Although a band-blues, its melancholy is solitary, like that of the vocal blues itself. Indeed, there is, in this classic phase of jazz, a complementary development both in band music and in vocal jazz. Within the band emerge the great improvising virtuoso soloists, such as Louis Armstrong and Sidney Bechet: while as the country blues singer moved into the towns he joined with the bands, becoming an obbligato singer strictly comparable with the obbligato trumpet or clarinet. The instrumentalist would emulate, imitate, underline, maybe ironically comment on the voice: which would, in its turn, learn subtleties of expressive inflection from the instrument. This we can observe in a wonderful record of *Death Sting Me Blues* (20) in which Sara Martin, a cabaret singer rather than a blues singer proper, is accompanied by a pick-up group featuring Oliver and Clarence Williams. The words themselves, a tragic statement of unrequited love, are poetry, combining rock-bottom truth with the surprise of revelation; and the "speaking" inflections of the voice have a similar immediacy, an awareness of a particular human situation, in a specific time and place. Oliver's superb cornet obbligato, however, answering the voice with sighs, sobs, and occasionally chuckles, renders the intensity of personal experience universal; we realize, from the range of his wordless lament, that this girl's experience might be our own, in a sense is so, since everyone is to some degree and in some manner betrayed. The ringing sonority of the (old-fashioned) tuba's isolated bass notes reinforces this effect, giving a solemn, almost liturgical flavour that carries the music beyond suspicion of personal indulgence.

These two marvellous pieces—*Perdido Street Blues* and *Death Sting Me Blues*—take us to the heart of jazz. In the first phase of the New Orleans band—that exemplified by George Lewis's Stompers—we have collective heterophony: a basically one-voiced music over a two-beat metrical bass, with only the most rudimentary harmony, if any. In the second stage we have the heterophonic homophony of King Oliver, which establishes the four-beat harmonic basis for collective improvisation; the harmonic solidarity, however simply derived from hymn, march and blues, is a developing stage in human togetherness, since more is involved in it than mutuality achieved merely through an orgiastic time-pulse. In the third stage—that represented by *Perdido Street Blues* and *Death Sting Me Blues*—the soloist emerges from the ensemble's homophony and from the percussion's metre. The individualized, improvised solo lines create a tension with the underlying beat (the progression of Time) and with the rudimentary harmony (which would tie us together, earth-bound). So as individuals we play or sing with an improvisatory freedom that attempts to override the earth-pull of metre and harmony. Syncopation itself is an expression of this desire: as are, more subtly, the misplaced accents, delays, anticipations, tonal distortions and intensification of pitch that are the jazz player's immediate response to reality. So the orgiastic submission to Time leads to liberation from it, and the *break* is only a consequence of what we are always trying to achieve. The difference between the break in barrelhouse piano and that in classic horn-playing jazz is that in the latter the break, being melodic, becomes a positive in its own right. It literally "breaks" both the metre and the harmonic solidity in lyrical cadenza, so that when we play or sing breaks we transcend both Time and human solidarity. Through our sense of community, we discover our personal identity; we are "sent" outside ourselves and our world, and play our breaks to God rather than to our fellow men. There is a valid relationship between the jazz break, in its melodic aspect, and the trope of plainsong. It is not merely the liturgical sound of the tuba that gives *Death Sting Me Blues* some of the qualities of a religious affirmation, even though—in its statement of a painful actuality—it asks for no metaphysical consolation.

This tension between the collective harmonic rhythm and the individual rhythms of the solo lines is what later came to be described as "swing". It is present in all good jazz of any period and derives, inevitably, from the music's corporeal nature. The rhythm of the human body and senses, precisely because it is human, will always be slightly different from, although related to, the metrical beat of Time; and Spengler may have been more than merely ingenious in identifying the post-Christian obsession with Time, as metrically exemplified in European music, with the Decline of the West. Of course, swing is present to some degree in all true music that involves any kind of motor rhythm: its presence or absence certainly helps to distinguish the good from the bad performance of Bach. It would seem legitimate to suggest, however, that jazz swing seemed so important to so many people in our vast industrialized world because it reminded us of an "organically" instinctual life from which (as Harry Partch and Edgar Varèse have told us) we have been too long separated. Perhaps it was not an accident that the simultaneously re-creative and nostalgic implications of jazz began to be explored when the blues singers moved into the towns and linked up with the bands: for no solo line could be more intimately expressive than that of the human voice—not even that of a clarinet or trumpet, which could extend, and even intensify, the voice's range.

Country-blues singers had been mainly, though not exclusively, male, and their art had grown from the ritual of work. Those men who raised blues-singing to professional status tended to be social outcasts, whether through temperamental malaise like Robert Johnson, or through physical affliction (usually blindness), like Blind Lemon Jefferson. They had no home, but wandered from city to city, seeking a livelihood from song. The city-dwellers who found in the blues a reflection of their own sorrows and desires were, however, for the most part female. This was because the band-trained, town-dwelling male Negro had learned to speak through his "horn": but also because the deep resonance of the female Negro voice came to represent the mother-image which seemed so significant to the rootless inhabitants of big cities. The first of the great women blues singers was known, indeed, at quite an early age, as "Ma" Rainey. When she sings *Titanic Man Blues* (21) we can hear how her metrically simple, rhythmically complex style does nothing to lull us into security, yet reminds us, in its raucous intensity, of our birthright. She is Mother Earth, and not the less so because the earth has grown dark and dirty. We have no choice but to accept it, and to make of it what we can.

The expressive devices of the blues singer are, of course, a performing technique which is incapable of notation. As appendix to Alan Lomax's classic book on Jelly Roll Morton, however, are printed a few literal transcriptions of Jelly Roll's performances; by examining one of these we can obtain some insight into the nature of the idiom. The *2.19 Blues* (22) was written and sung by Mamie Desdumes in the sporting house where both she and Jelly Roll worked.[1] In his version he alters the words in order to metamorphose the singer into a man, but the piece is a representative, if somewhat primitive, woman's blues. Jelly Roll plays a traditional four-bar introduction, the effect of which depends on the strong beats that are *not* present. Then he launches into the twelve-bar blues on the piano, very simply, with the conventional harmonies; the slightly nervous feeling is created by the displaced accents and by the blue notes which are appoggiaturas and also false relations, since the G sharps also sound like A flats. The verbal accents change in the traditional repetition of the first line of the song, stressing "my" in the first statement, "babe" in the second. The voice sticks to its pentatonic falling thirds when she sings of the hope that the train may some day

[1] See Appendix II

bring her lover back; and the hope seems the more forlorn because the voice's implied harmony remains tonic, while the piano is playing the dominant seventh cadence (this might not happen, of course, in the next performance). In the next verse the voice starts off-chord as well as off-beat; the flat sevenths make her "soakin' feet" the heavier. Against the dominant seventh cadence the voice whines pentatonic thirds, which are both the depressed monotony and also the despair of her begging; the contrast between sharp and flat third is here especially touching. The greater poignancy of the last verse comes from the fact that the "give a dollar" phrase for the first time involves a real, if momentary, modulation to the subdominant: and also from the hypnotic extension of the quaver triplets into crochets, which (with the help of the blue sevenths) both makes the dollar lousy and also contains the man's hunger, and the woman's hunger for the man's love. In the piano postlude the figuration is more fragmentary and the beats are usually implicit rather than explicit; the neurotic quality is perhaps emphasized by the cessation of movement on the drooping subdominant modulation.

2.19 Blues is an early New Orleans blues that Mamie Desdumes was singing in the first decade of the century. The hey-day of the city blues occurred, however, when the red-light district of New Orleans was cleaned up, and the Negro musicians migrated north. Oliver himself, we have seen, went to Chicago, and it was there the girl blues singers flourished—if the term is appropriate—in the twenties. There could have been no tougher and dustier environment: so it is not surprising that when Mary Johnson, in *Key to the Mountain* (23) talks with a trombone it is difficult to decide whether woman or instrument has the more lacerating vibrato. The warmth of Jelly Roll's New Orleans jazz has gone: as it has when Chippie Hill, who was what her name implies, sings-shouts *Charleston Blues* (24) to a hard-driving accompaniment, imitating with her searing voice the arpeggiated thrusts of the trumpet's obbligato. The background to Bessie Smith, who raised the urban blues to tragic intensity, is no less squalid. She was born at Chattanooga, eight miles north of the Tennessee-Georgia state boundary, in 1898. The population then numbered about 30,000, of which 13,000 were Negroes; this inevitably meant that large numbers of coloured people were unemployed, and lived in conditions of appalling indigence. Bessie Smith's family was no exception; and her talent was inseparable from the savage humiliations she suffered, in the same way as her improvisatory technique was inseparable from her illiteracy (she sometimes remembered things wrong, and the mistakes were a manifestation of genius). As a child she worked in travelling tent-shows and circuses, so she was a professional music-hall artist who preserved some of the qualities of a folk-singer. Though she made and squandered a fortune, she neither sought for nor received anything but dusty answers from men, gin, and drugs; and she died in 1937 because, having been injured in a car accident, she was refused admission to a white hospital. No wonder she sang: "You can't trust nobody, might as well be alone", "There ain't no place for a poor old girl to go"; no wonder she believed: "You reap just what you sow." Yet her malaise, her bitterness, sprang from what life did to her; her blues can become an epitome of urban man's frustration not merely because they are true, but also because they accept this truth with a tragic unsentimentality and a proud dignity to which most of the crippled inhabitants of big cities cannot aspire. She was not called "the Empress of the blues" merely because of her impressive physical proportions. There is a grandeur in her art, whereby her solitariness becomes Everyman's.

In the country blues words and tune were made up by some, often anonymous artist; with repeated performance by him and others words were changed, verses added, nuances of expression in the dialogue of voice and guitar modified. In the instrumental band-blues the tunes are again traditional, but since there are no, or at least only implicit, words, the possibilities for improvisation (by several performers instead of one) are more complex. The classic sung form of the town blues, as exemplified by Bessie Smith, combines the intimacy of the country blues with the relative complexity of the band-blues: for the singer is no longer accompanied by herself, but by the band's rhythmic-harmonic fundament of piano and bass, while the melodic line is shared between the vocalist and the band's soloist. The instrumentalist will sometimes take over from the singer for a complete verse, offering his wordless commentary on the human stories the vocalist tells. He is thus simultaneously one with the singer, and apart from her; the solitariness of the blues has become, paradoxically, a communal experience. How the urban blues evolved from the country blues is revealed in, for instance, Bessie Smith's singing of *Careless Love* (25). This modally lyrical blues derives from an Old Kentucky mountain song which, in its turn, came from an English Elizabethan source. Fletcher Henderson's piano, in conjunction with Charlie Green's trombome, makes a solid, harmonium-like sonority, sounding like a magnified rural accordion. Louis Armstrong's trumpet, on the other hand, though of folk-like spontaneity, introduces an element of urban intensity, for its spurting rhythms are ragged rather than easy, while its fioriture spill dissonantly over the simple harmonic base. Bessie Smith's vocal line is subtly intermediary; she sounds relaxed, timeless as a country singer, yet her unobtrusive rhythmic-harmonic ellipses make the relaxation weary—and therefore, perhaps, not relaxed at all. She may be careless, but is certainly not carefree; the apparent easiness is only a respite from pain. Indeed, being careless is not so far from being reckless; and in the famous *Reckless Blues* (26) she sings, with Armstrong's trumpet, unambiguously in his mood of urban tension. The juxtaposition of these two pieces demonstrates most movingly how the age-old, passive melancholy of the country blues acquired, in entering the city, a quality of nervous laceration. *Reckless Blues* projects—in its angular interlocking of the voice's intimacy with the trumpet's aggressive bravura—a hysteria latent within us all, and it can do so because its urban agitation contacts so long a tradition of passive suffering. That the keyboard instrument, played by Fred Longshaw, is in this case a harmonium—rural, domestic and pious—emphasizes the nervosity of the two solo voices.

Thrilling though this blues is, Bessie Smith's greatest achievements were not in partnership with Armstrong, probably because his personality was no less powerful than hers, so that it was difficult for them to achieve a personal-communal identity. Joe Smith—whose short life was as tormented as Bessie's and who died in a mental hospital—was her perfect partner: for we feel that his cornet obbligati are the spontaneous overflow of her vocal phrases. She sings, he comments; and although the commentary may introduce inflections that are his own, they seem to be inherent in the vocal phrases, waiting to be revealed. What his cornet adds is what Bessie's voice had implied, yet because it is added by someone else, it becomes our contribution, too; it is as though Joe Smith stands for us, identifying Bessie's experience with ours, and this effect is strictly comparable with the relationship between vocal line and instrumental obbligato in a Bach aria—if so sublime a comparison be permitted. A beautiful example of this is *Young Woman's Blues* (27), in which the dialogue of voice and cornet transforms social protest into an impersonal tragic lament, rooted in particular and personal experience:

> I'm a young woman, and I ain't done running round,
> Some people call me a hobo, some people call me a bum,
> Nobody knows my name, nobody knows what I've done.

I'm as good as any woman in your town:
I ain't no high yellar, I'm a deep yellar brown.
I ain't going to marry, ain't going to settle down,
I'm going to drink good moonshine, and run these browns down.
See that long, lonesome road? Don't you know it's got to end,
And I'm a good woman, and I can get plenty men.

The words' "low-down" medley of the outsider-mood with a pride that manages to be at once pathetic and formidable creates a tune that, in Bessie Smith's interpretation, is as powerfully dramatic as it is lyrical; and the singer's autobiographical fervour has inspired Joe Smith to perhaps his most masterly obbligato. The sudden modulation that *creates*, musically, the licence of the "running around" demonstrates the advantage of working within a rigidly limited convention: on the rare occasion when the performers depart from it the effect is overwhelming.

Such tragic-ironic blues are among the supreme achievements of jazz, and although they may not often have so directly autobiographical a connotation as *Young Woman's Blues* they always spring from, and owe their "universality" to, topical and local circumstance. In *Poor Man's Blues*, (28) for instance, the extraordinary gurgling of clarinet and saxophone at the opening combines with the misplaced accents and pitch distortions in the vocal line to give authenticity to words that, in themselves, are a slightly phoney, self-pitying piece of social criticism. That the music is at once savage and grotesquely comic removes the mawkishness and reveals the terror—bitterly, yet without anger. Complementary to this is a late recording like *Black Mountain Blues* (29), which is almost a parody of the narrative country blues. Bessie adopts the folk-raconteur's dead-pan manner, modified by a highly sophisticated innuendo in her vocal inflections, while Ed Allen's cornet catches and refracts these ironic overtones. Yet the effect is not in the least "smart"; the rural mode is not deflated, but rather re-created in an urbanly worldly-wise spirit that makes the blues seem at once as old as the hills and as new as today. Somewhat similar are certain narrative blues that celebrate topical events—such as the Mississippi flood number, *Backwater Blues* (30), to which James P. Johnson's piano contributes so vividly illustrative, yet tragically impersonal, a commentary. Bessie even managed to instil some genuine feeling into an offensively sentimental pop song called *Muddy Water* (31), based on this awe-ful theme; and this points to the fact that for a "natural" genius taste and artistry are synonymous with integrity. We do not know whether Bessie liked

the words of *Muddy Water;* we do know that she discovered pathos
and terror in the human predicament that lay behind them, and that
she lavished great care on expressing these qualities with all the conviction and precision of which she was capable. She was a folk-singer
in the immediacy of her response, a professional showman in her
ability to project her experience, to use her art to achieve the most
powerfully communicative effect. This applies to her rare comic
numbers, too. If in *Muddy Water* she brings the reality of the blues to
the evasive sentimentality of a pop number, in *Alexander's Ragtime
Band* (32) she uses rhythmic contractions and expansions combined with
pitch distortions to bring an almost febrile quality to a vacuous Tin
Pan Alley manifestation of nigger minstrel mirth. The tipsy gaiety
seems genuinely ecstatic, because we are aware of the tension that is
being released. Still more impressive is her version of *Nobody Knows
you when you're Down and Out* (33), a pop number she had picked up
from a Negro entertainer, Jimmy Fox, with whom she had worked.
Taking the song up towards the end of her career, at a time when its
autobiographical implications were all too clear, she turned it not so
much into a song of social protest as into a *cri de coeur*, a passionate
testament to her lonesomeness and still more to her feeling of baffle-
ment at the unpredictability of fortune and the frailty of human
loyalties. Her elongation of the syllable *no* in the opening phrase
suggests indignation, even anger, and at the same time a pathos destitute of self-pity; while the extraordinary discoloration of the tone
when she sings the words "fall so low" seems to drain off the blood,
almost to stop the pulse. Life is shut off, in a neutral limbo, and even
song breaks down, so that Bessie hums to herself. But the humming
is not an end; she sings again, with a wild, proud fortitude: which is
reinforced by Ed Allen's huskily strident cornet and by the solemn
resonance of Cyrus St Clair's tuba bass.

The flowering of instrumental jazz—notably in the various ensembles of Louis Armstrong—developed from the merging of the
traditions of the New Orleans band with those of the urban blues. In
New Orleans the blues was a low-life music which existed alongside the "Africanized" version of European military music, mixed
with the liquid and relaxed French Creole style, and the Spanish tinge of
Latin American music, to which Jelly Roll Morton had referred. The
hardness of the city blues was necessary before the "crystallizing"
phase of classical jazz could occur; this is why the synthesis was closely
associated with the river-boats that, plying up river from the Mississippi

Gulf, provided jobs for so many New Orleans jazzmen. Once they arrived north—at St Louis or St Paul, whence they moved on to Chicago —they were reluctant to return, for, as Zutty Singleton said: "Chicago! That was the place to be. Your friends would go there and after a while they would write back and say what a swell place it was—good jobs, lot more money than down south, and all that. Then as soon as you could you'd go there, too. Nobody thought at all about New York in those days." Singleton was invited to Chicago by Louis Armstrong, who had in turn been invited there by King Oliver in 1922; the Dodds brothers, Honoré Dutrey and other famous Oliver men had been there since 1920, Sidney Bechet had gone in 1918, and Jelly Roll Morton as early as 1908. When New Orleans jazz became finally established in Chicago, the blue element became equated with the nervous stresses of urban life, as it was in Bessie Smith's blues. We can see how jazz achieved a synthesis of "primitive" vitality with "modern" tension: can see, too, why it owes its mythological character to the fact that it is the most direct manifestation possible of what we have called—in the introductory chapter to Part I—the American innocence and the American violence. This is why Louis Armstrong is a symbol as well as a musician. To the traditional ensemble as employed by Oliver he adds an instrumental equivalent to the solo virtuosity of Bessie Smith. He thus brings to fruition the true jazz polyphony—as compared with Oliver's heterophonic homophony. The New Orleans "wanderers" have reached Chicago: where jazz has become the folk-song of the asphalt jungle.

IV

*From heterophony to polyphony: from
polyphony to the antiphony of the big
band: improvisation and
composition in the work of Louis
Armstrong, Jelly Roll Morton and
Count Basie*

> You have conquered the yearning, she said
> The numbers have entered your feet
> turn   turn   turn
> When you're real gone, boy, sweet boy . . .
>
> the human greenness
> tough as grass that survives cruelest seasons
>
> ROBERT DUNCAN

Louis Armstrong's triumphant part in the flowering of jazz is related
to the fact that, although born in New Orleans, in the year of the New
Century, he achieved artistic realization not in his native city but in
Chicago: to which urban metropolis he had followed his idol King
Oliver. From the first of his autobiographical volumes, *Satchmo: my
Life in New Orleans*, we can obtain a vivid impression of the background of violence against which his childhood was lived. He witnessed
razor-fights of the most hair-raising ferocity, between whores, pimps
and petty thugs; was himself repeatedly involved in brawls with a
succession of "stepfathers"; and was diurnally aware of the imminence
of death:

> Arthur Brown was one of my playmates at school. . . . He was going
> with a girl who had a little brother who was very cute. Too cute, I would
> say, since he was always playing with a pistol or a knife. We did not pay
> much attention to the kid, but one day when he was cleaning his gun he
> pointed it at Arthur and said "I am going to shoot." Sure enough, he
> pulled the trigger; the gun was loaded and Arthur Brown fell to the

ground with a bullet in his head. It was a terrible shock. We all felt so bad that even the boys cried. When Arthur was buried we all chipped in and hired a brass band to play at his funeral.

Thus Louis and his friends used music as a release from violence, just as his grandparents, who were slaves, must have done; and they could do this because their awareness of violence was inseparable from their vitality—their joy in living, even in conditions that would seem to us insupportable. At the time when the young Louis, a fairly innocent victim of Fortune's malignancy, was undergoing a period of "corrective detention" in a Waif's Home he can write like this:

> The Waif's Home was an old building which had apparently formerly been used for another purpose. It was located in the country opposite a great big dairy farm where hundreds of cows, bulls, calves and a few horses were standing. Some were eating, and some were prancing around like they wanted to tell somebody, anybody, how good they felt. The average square would automatically say those animals were all loco, to be running like that, but for me they wanted to express themselves as very happy, gay and contented.

That, surely, expresses Louis Armstrong's "religion", however much he learned from singing in church as a kid; and the attitude did not change after he became materially successful:

> I never deprived myself of things I thought absolutely necessary, and there are lots of things I never cared for, such as a flock of suits for example . . . what good does that do? The moths eat them up before you can get full use of them. . . . I have always believed in giving a hand to the underdog whenever I could, and as a rule I could. I will continue to do so as long as I live, and I expect to live a long, long time. Way past the hundred mark.

The remark about the underdog is touchingly illustrated by Armstrong's care for his cousin's child, Clarence, who was mentally retarded as the result of a fall. "Since Clarence has always been a nervous sort of fellow and was never able to work and earn his own living, I set up a routine for him in which he'd be happy for the rest of his days. I managed to teach him the necessary things in life, such as being courteous, having respect for other people, and last but not least, having good common sense." In Louis Armstrong's music there is violence in plenty and quite a lot of suffering; there is also happiness—and courtesy, respect and common sense.

As a boy, Louis "stood in" for Joe Oliver, "the King of all musicians, the finest trumpeter who ever played in New Orleans". When, in the

early twenties, he followed Oliver to Chicago, he formed his own Hot
Five, a recording group which started from, but gradually modified,
Oliver's collective improvisation. In basic New Orleans style, we saw,
the cornet had taken the melodic lead, with the clarinet adding heterophonic embellishments, while the trombone provided a tenor counterpoint over the bass, which was originally a military tuba, later a
plucked bass fiddle. The rhythm section marked the beat with insistent
regularity, at first merely on military drum and snares, later with the
harmonic support of banjo, or guitar, or piano, in that chronological
sequence. Usually the improvisation was collective, there being little
opportunity for extended breaks by soloists. This "heterophonic
homophony" was a necessary stage in jazz history, for only when
harmonic solidarity was so clearly defined that it could exert its
influence unconsciously could a true jazz polyphony be explored.
Armstrong's melodic lines often grow out of harmonic sequences, for
both trumpet and clarinet lend themselves naturally to arpeggiated
figures; but the more independent and lyrically sustained his melodic
improvisations become, the more they ride over the harmonic basis of
blues or hymn. The passion and power of the music are a direct consequence of this: as is the establishment of "three-section" jazz form in
which the numbers begin with an ensemble dominated by the cornet-
leader, while the second section is a series of solo or duet choruses in
improvising virtuosity, which sweep us into a final ensemble of collective improvisation. This third section is the more exciting because it
occurs as climax to the soloists' creative adventures. The substitution of
guitar for banjo adds plangency to the harmonic texture, as does the
more independent role given to the piano.

At the same time the drums develop far from their quasi-mili-
tary function: while still marking the beat, they are now counterpointed—with subtlety, if not with African complexity—against
the line's spring. We can see here the beginning of a characteristic
of jazz rhythm that complements the duality between primitive
melody and relatively sophisticated harmony on which we have commented: for while the metrical basis is modern and military, the rhythm
increasingly seeks for the flexibility of primitive music. In this sense the
primitivism is part of man's attempt to rediscover his "corporeal"
humanity; and Baby Dodds, greatest of the New Orleans drummers
who sometimes worked with Armstrong, has explained how the subtleties of his drumming style grew out of his respect for the individual
manners—the human identities—of the improvising soloists. "I feel them

all out. I work with all of them because they all belong to me. I feel I'm the key man in that band. In drumming you have got to pay attention to each, everyone. You must *hear* that person distinctly, and hear what he wants. You got to give it to him. . . . You must study a guy's human nature, study about what he will take, or see about what he will go for. All that's in a drum, and that's why all guys are not drummers that's drumming. . . . Now I know it sounds very funny to hear me say spirit. But *drumming is spirit*. You got to have that in your body, in your soul. . . . And it can't be an evil spirit. . . . If you're evil, you're going to drum evil, and if you drum evil, you're going to put evil in somebody else's mind. What kind of band have you got? Nothing but an evil-spirit band. And God help a bad-spirit band. They're subject to do anything. They're liable to step on each other's instrument. Anything. Might put limburger cheese in a man's piano. Anything. . . . So you've got to keep a spirit up. And it's a drummer's job because he's playing nothing. . . . His place is to help the other fellow, not make him play himself to death. . . . Without a drummer that knows how to *help*, there's no band."

Some such human contact, such "good spirit", comes over in two fascinating recordings of the Hot Five that let us into the inside of a jam session. For while Armstrong expressed pleasure in working with men who could read music, it is clear from the recording of *Heebie-Jeebies* (1) that familiarity with notation is subservient to the heat of the moment. Human contact is the music's inspiration; and because human beings are fallible, the musical climax here results in an improvised mistake! We may compare with this the manner in which the nineteenth-century American Primitives produced some of their most interesting music when their harmony was academically incorrect. *Skid-dat-de-dat* (2) also demonstrates the genesis of Armstrong's jazz, in that it consists of mutual imitation between the singing-speaking "scat" voice and the instruments. From such mutuality Armstrong derived his melodic style: which combines the stepwise flexibility of the talking voice with the instrumental arpeggio, which spreads the basic chords of jazz into line.

The maturing of Armstrong's style occurs in his association with the Dodds brothers, with Kid Ory, with Johnny St Cyr and other players worthy to stand up with him. The Hot Seven group, formed in 1927, recorded in *Willie the Weeper* (3) one of the first fully fledged examples of jazz polyphony; while *Wild Man Blues* (4) a joint creation of Armstrong and Jelly Roll Morton, indicates how inventive composition stimulates improvisational invention. Here Armstrong's trumpet becomes a voice that is more than a voice, intimate and personal in its "dirty" tone, yet grand and epic in its sweep. Dodd's chalumeau register clarinet has a similar immediacy, with a rhythmic ambiguity that hints at mysteries beneath the surface. The piece reaches a tremendous climax when at last the two solo voices meet in duologue in the final chorus, creating the wildest heterophonic dissonance that is yet, inevitably, The End, if only because one can conceive of no more riotous abandon. This is not just a "jungle" piece; it reveals, with almost tragic majesty, the wildness within the heart of the Negro—and of us all. *Potato Head Blues* (5) combines the improvisation of *Willie the Weeper* with the powerful soloistic development of *Wild Man*. The climax occurs, however, when the polyphony stops and Armstrong plays a solo of a type known to jazzmen as a "stop-time chorus". The description is precise: Armstrong's wildly jetting arpeggios, alternating with "speaking" phrases, soar and bound over stopped chords from the other players, separated by silences. Again, liberation occurs when the beat is broken; time stops as we are "sent".

Armstrong's emotional range is remarkably wide. *Savoy Blues* (6), for instance, a tune by Kid Ory, preserves something of the innocence of Creole music, as contrasted with the tense abandon or excitement of *Wild Man* and *Potato Head*. This is partly due to the nature of the charming tune itself; but the treatment matches the tune's simplicity, being a very clear variation technique. It is true that the permutations do not always fit the basic harmony; the consequent dissonances sound, however, at once wistful and humorously relaxed rather than tense—as though the players could not bother to play the "right" notes because the tune made them feel so "easy" (so that, in context, the right notes would be wrong). *Struttin' with some barbecue* (7) is comic in a more sophisticated way. Its cheeriness sounds as though it is going to be that of the inaner type of pop number: but is in effect deflated by a cryptic restraint, epitomized in the "throw-away" coda. The Negro simplicity thus becomes a kind of wit: adult compared with the commercial world's synthetic merriment.

So, beginning with the New Orleans march and hymn, Armstrong increasingly found impetus from other sources—from the traditional blues, from pop songs, from fragments of tune made up *ad hoc* by members of the band. Though he remained an intuitive, improvisational artist, there is a gradual increase in compositional sophistication through the series of bands that he directed during the 'twenties. The second Hot Five, established in 1927, makes a sound quite different from the first Hot Five or the Hot Seven; and the difference centres around the fact that the piano is much more prominent both as solo and as harmony instrument. Armstrong's earlier groups tend to make the harsh, fierce sound of the heterophonic phase of New Orleans jazz—intensified by big-city grittiness. The Second Hot Five makes a sound that is softer, more sophisticated; both the melodic flexibility and the harmonic texture are at once more complex and more sensuous than those of the earlier Five. That Armstrong's pianist, the great Earl Hines, is a much more sophisticated artist than Lil Hardin is not the basic reason for this distinction: for Armstrong used the kind of pianist that this music needed. The famous West End Blues (8) is Armstrong's masterpiece in this manner. It opens with an unaccompanied trumpet solo introduction, sad, but grand and dignified: an apotheosis of the blues typical of Armstrong at his finest. After the first chorus, however, Armstrong does not play trumpet; instead, he scat-sings in duologue with clarinet. As his voice imitates the instrument, and the instrument imitates him, it is as though he is talking to himself in the quiet of the night; the music is, for Armstrong, relaxed, yet the intimate tenderness of the vocal-instrumental line makes it seem also frail and forlorn. When Hines plays a tremulously fanciful piano chorus, full of fluttering Debussian chromatics, we can sense the relationship between the music's in-drawn melancholy and the nostalgia typical of pop music. But that the nostalgia is distilled—at once rarefied and intensified by being related to the Negro's deeper yearning for Home—is indicated when Hines's piano-dream is pierced by Armstrong's immensely long, high trumpet note: which brings us back to reality with what might be a scream or might be a desperate affirmation—and is probably both. The dream is then brushed away in a brief, laconic coda that ought to be the end. Unfortunately Hines adds a few bars of dreamy doodling which, whether or not they bubbled up spontaneously, are detrimental to the composition, since they weaken its imaginative point. This indicates how improvisation—when it reaches a certain level of complexity and subtlety—is to some degree dependent on the normal criteria of composition.

This point is further illustrated by the Savoy Ballroom Five, which, founded in 1928, was the last combo Armstrong directed during his Chicago days. In Weather Bird, (9), for instance, we have not a band piece, but an Oliver number treated as a duet between Armstrong and Hines. We would expect this to produce the freest, most rhapsodic improvisation: whereas, in fact, the sequence of choruses is most artfully planned to lead towards a climax of disrupted repeated notes; after which there is a disturbingly abrupt coda. Similarly, *Beau Koo Jack* (10), a piece in fast-driving rhythm, with a searing, sizzling solo, develops its orgiastic excitement climacterically: and so may be related, like the mood-nocturne of *West End Blues*, to the semi-composed pieces of Duke Ellington. The most remarkable of the Savoy Ballroom Five recordings is, however, *Tight like this* (11), recorded as a farewell to Chicago, just before Armstrong left for New York. It begins as a slow, grave blues in the minor. There is a beautiful, very sophisticated piano chorus from Hines, wide-spaced and lonely; then a solemn, organ-like sonority as background for, and inspiration to, a wild trumpet solo. Ostinato rhythms grow rather Spanish and seductively energetic as the trumpet reaches a high, exultant coda: but the coda-climax proves to be a negation, for although Armstrong has increasingly dominated three successive chorus variations and has increasingly tried to establish identity *against* the ensemble, he ends in a rhythmic stasis, with repeated note phrases dislocated off-beat. That is why the music—whatever the title is supposed to mean—is in fact *tight*, like this: a tragic frustration, or (more accurately) a frustrated tragedy. It is clear that since the music makes some such effect it must have, despite its basis in evolutionary variation, some sense of beginning, middle and end. This is another way of saying that Armstrong has proceeded from the heterophony of primitive jazz to a true polyphony: for of its nature polyphony involves tension between melodic direction and the fundaments of harmony and metrical Time.

So although *Tight like this* is a passionate search for the oneness of being "sent", it is also, in the relationship between solo and ensemble, dualistic. In this sense it is closer to us than is earlier jazz, and more diverse aspects of experience are involved in it. It is still closer to us, perhaps, because its dualism results in frustration, not fulfilment: from which point of view we may not sacrilegiously contrast its tension between melodic texture and rhythmic-harmonic drive with that in the music of Bach. The vitality of Bach's music is inseparable from the fact that its independently polyphonic texture creates inner tension: which is, however, absolved in the flow of the lines, the continuity of the rhythm. In Armstrong's music the tension is, in principle, the same; yet it results not in absolution and affirmation, but in frustration. This is not merely because Bach was a very great composer and Armstrong is a little one; it is also because Bach was a man of faith in an age of faith, whereas Armstrong is a man sometimes of spontaneous gaiety, always of rock-bottom fortitude, in an age of unfaith. Thus his best music, like the blues itself, tends to be religious ritual without religious belief; and this may be why the tension in *Tight like this* could not be long sustained. The commonly held view that Armstrong left his genius, if not his talent, behind him when he left Chicago is not entirely fair, for it would be truer to say that in New York, in a world of commercial exploitation, he found fewer men of calibre to play with him. That something happened to his talent is revealed, however, by his version of *St Louis Blues* (12), among many possible examples: for while this begins as an impressively driving tango, the energy gradually dissipates, and with it the melodic impulse. The solo breaks become the opposite of a liberation: a reaching for the high notes, which come to exist in isolation from melody or rhythm. Such preoccupation with "effect", divorced from music, has obvious commercial possibilities, whether or not Armstrong himself exploited them.

Exploitation is not, of course, confined to jazz; it is merely more noticeable in a music that owes everything to its spontaneity and honesty. It seems unlikely that we have lost much significant Armstrong music *because* he went to New York, for he, like all true jazzmen, had said what he had essentially to say in his early twenties. Jazz is of its nature an art of youth and adolescence, and the jazzman's spontaneity is most "maturely" realized when he is least inhibited. He achieves artistic fulfilment, if at all, at an age when the "straight" composer is still trying to learn a technique that may or may not enable him to discover what he has to say. So the jazz artist seldom "develops"; he either dies young, disappears into private life, enters the world of pop music or—if he keeps to the jazz path—refines and renders subtler his art without radically changing it. The exceptional jazz artist who does develop—for instance Ellington—does so only by a partial *rapprochement* with techniques and attitudes that do not belong to jazz at all. As an example of the non-developing jazz soloist who neither sought nor achieved wide popularity we may mention Armstrong's contemporary, Sidney Bechet, a New Orleans man born in 1897. In his art there is the profound melancholy of the blues, and there is often exuberance in plenty. Tension and angularity are, however, less evident than in Armstrong's playing; far from being "tight, like this", Bechet's music is relatively supple and flexible. This fact is related to his Creole ancestry —his direct affinity with Latin American relaxation, with French and

Italian opera, with waltzes, quadrilles and "mazookas". He changed from clarinet to soprano saxophone—which was not part of the original military instrumentation of the New Orleans band—because its liquid, voluptuous sonority could impart greater richness to the flowing cantilena that makes him the supreme lyricist of jazz. So the flexibility of his line does not promote screwed-up cross-rhythms, as it does in Armstrong; it rather enhances the "speaking" poignancy of the melody. It is here that Bechet's distinctively Negroid character is evident; no jazz player uses more extravagant portamenti and a wider vibrato, and while this does not destroy the line's lyricism, it gives it an almost hysterical edge. In the marvellous *Out of the Gallion* (13) the blues line is always winging and singing; yet the song becomes a sob, protected from self-indulgence because it does not break into fragments but remains suspended, air-borne. In *Really the Blues* (14) we find a comparable technique used not merely in monologue, but also in duologue with Tommy Ladnier's trumpet—a most sensitive player who, preserving Armstrong's ferocity, could yet adapt his trumpet sonority to the sensual contours of Bechet's sax. Frequent passages in parallel thirds emphasize the voluptuousness. In fast tempi Bechet does not relinquish his lyricism, so that the frenzy he generates remains untortured. In *Down in Honky-Tonk Town* (15) he plays with Armstrong in furiously ebullient comedy. The heterophonic final chorus is as exciting as Armstrong, though less "tight"; even the fortuitous dissonances are relaxed—a cascade of laughter.

In some ways comparable with Bechet is the clarinetist Jimmy Noone, who lacks Bechet's sensual passion, but has in common with him a plangent limpidity of tone, most beautifully manifested in his 1928 and 1936 record sessions, especially in *Sweet Lorraine* and *Apex Blues*. In *Keystone Blues* (16) he shares melodic solos with Nat Dominique's trumpet. Though not virtuosic, Dominique's style has the almost folk-like expressivity of early New Orleans jazz, and it serves as an admirable foil to Noone's liquid tremolos, his precise and elegant phrasing that remains melancholy even when, as in *New Orleans Hop Scop Blues* (17), the tempo is fairly fast. The lyricism of clarinet, trumpet and trombone is, in both pieces, the more touching by contrast with the hard, brittle, almost flamenco-like quality of the guitar as played by Lonnie Johnson. We are reminded of those country-blues in which the guitar accompaniment pricks the dream of the voice's song. From this point of view it is interesting to compare Jimmy Noone with Johnny Dodds as a partner for Johnson. Dodds, as we have seen, is a plangently lyrical clarinetist, but he embraces within his lyricism far more of the harshness, the "dirt", of blue melancholy, so that in their version of *Gravier Street Blues* (18) Dodd's piercing blue notes and Johnson's clinking acciacaturas reinforce one another. Perhaps no one has revealed the blues' basic sorrow more deeply than Dodds who, in *Red Onion Blues* (19), *Weary Blues* and *Bucktown Stomp,* for instance, uses pitch distortions as extravagant as Bechet's, while preserving a sense of laconic understatement—probably because the distortions of pitch are related to the weary displacement of the rhythm, which is in "drag" style. *Because* the rhythm seems to be running down, *because* the riff chords are savagely reiterated, the solo line cries and wails, cannot get on centre. Yet the point is that the line is not broken, that the melody remains lyrical.

Far more glamorous in reputation than Noone or Dodds, or even Bechet, was another soloist of Armstrong's generation, Bix Beiderbecke, whose relatively "soft" style, as compared with Armstrong's toughness, is attributable not to Creole but to white ancestry. The basis of Beiderbecke's playing was in the regular beat, the perky dotted-note fillip, the comparatively sweet sonority of the Original Dixieland Jazz Band; and the pathos inherent in this style became the more marked because his tone was gentle—purely Teutonic, with few of the African "vocalized" inflections of the Negro cornetist—and because his phrasing was so delicate, even when playing at very fast tempi. The sensitivity and refinement are indubitable and appealed, as a white man's gesture to them, to the great Negro horn players, who all revered Beiderbecke. Maybe something came over from a live performance that cannot be trapped on a record—except possibly in the celebrated solo in *Singin' the Blues*. To us, at this date, however, Beiderbecke's playing survives as much for social-historical as for musical reasons. We see him a symbol of the Jazz Age of Scott Fitzgerald: the white dweller in the Big City who, in the days of depression, gangsterism and prohibition, desperately sought an outlet for his nervous distresses, but who died young, at the age of twenty-eight, of a mixture of alcoholism and pneumonia. Always playing the old-world cornet rather than the more aggressive trumpet, Beiderbecke sought the presumed innocence of Negro music, but avoided, no less than did the white Dixieland Band, the hard realism of Armstrong or the ecstatic melancholy of Bechet. Instead he discovered, within the deliberate inanity of Dixieland style, a frail charm and plaintive nostalgia. It is not an accident that Beiderbecke was a pianist as well as a cornetist, and that as piano-harmonist he acquired a measure of academic know-how. His favourite concert works were the early pieces of Debussy (*Clair de Lune* and *L'Après midi d'un Faune*) and of Stravinsky (*Firebird* and *Petrouchka*), and the dream-land salon pieces of Macdowell (*To a Water Lily*). In his own piano piece *In a Mist* (20) he doodles, rather feebly, with the sensuous chromatics of Debussy; and when he introduces such sequential modulations and oozy harmonies into band pieces like *I'm Coming, Virginia* (21) or *Way down yonder* (22) the effect is to emphasize the dreamy, unreal flavour of the music. The sweetness has a certain pierrot-like charm; but it has become escape-art in a way that looks forward to Tin Pan Alley.

This is not necessarily a liability, and there is something to be said for the view that historically Beiderbecke is the most interesting of the white musicians who worked in Chicago during the 'twenties, precisely because he—unlike Frank Teschemacher, Pee-Wee Russell or Muggsy Spanier—made little direct attempt to emulate the inflections of Negro melody. Those horn-players were powerfully responsive to authentic Negro style, and Gene Krupa was probably the only white player before Dave Tough to stand on equal footing with the greatest Negro drummers. Yet although white Chicago jazz mirrored the tension of black jazz, it could not also reflect its earthly vigour. As a consequence the mood of these players' white Chicago style tended to be one of uneasy frustration, and they remained an isolated group who founded no school or tradition. Beiderbecke, on the other hand, being one of the first to explore the type of harmony that might be applicable to jazz, looks in this sense to the future. If there was an implicit compromise with pop art, this, too, was a historical necessity: as we shall see when, in the next chapter, we discuss the achievement of Duke Ellington. Armstrong is certainly a much more creative musician than Beiderbecke; but qualities represented by them both went to make an Ellington—and perhaps we may add a Gershwin also .

The harmonic phase of jazz was inevitable for the apparently paradoxical reason that, with men such as Armstrong and Bechet, the soloist had become all-important. For the more complex and subtle the soloists' lines became, both tonally and rhythmically, the less susceptible were they to *collective* improvisation. Though the freeing of the soloist was essential, the band must still be a band—a concourse of people coming together. The sweeter, more homophonic style of Beiderbecke suggests how jazz could not advance further except through a growing concern with harmonic mutuality: which skill would not be feasible without a measure of Bix's technical sophistication. Technical sophistication need not imply the white, franco-teutonic flavour that Beiderbecke gave to jazz; but it did imply some relinquishment of jazz's improvisatory wildness. The arranger—the composer or semi-composer—was a necessary consequence of the growth of the soloist, for having been "freed", the soloist had to be controlled in the interests of the total ensemble.

The earliest—and still highly impressive—manifestation of this process in Negro jazz is to be found in the band pieces that Jelly Roll Morton recorded with his Red Hot Peppers. Most of these were originally piano pieces based—like those we have already discussed—on the notated conventions of rag. The piano pieces were, we saw, composed music of some sophistication; the band pieces are composed in the sense that the themes and formal proportions are predecided, but are re-composed in that each player makes anew the material during the performance. The concourse of voices seems to "work" largely through a telepathic process that is part of the composer-arranger's talent. In this, no less than in sheer musical ability, Jelly Roll is a true forerunner of Ellington: which may be why Ellington has adopted a highly critical, even condescending, attitude to Morton. Jelly Roll's bumptious braggadocio, not to mention his diamond-stopped tooth, deserved the Duke's witty riposte: "Sure, Jelly Roll Morton has talent—talent for talking about Jelly Roll Morton"; but the quality of Jelly Roll's music must be estimated on purely musical criteria, and on the evidence of the Red Hot Peppers records it would seem to be high. A piece such as *Smokehouse Blues* (23) stands half-way between the soloistic chorus-variations of Armstrong and the "controlled sequence" of Ellington; and the Armstrong-like tragic authenticity and passionate detachment are in no way weakened by the Ellington-like sense of proportion. This is still more evident in Morton's more explicitly composed pieces, such as *The Chant* (24), a reincarnation of a stock arrangement of Stitzel's number which crystallizes into art-form most of the intuitive ingredients of jazz. African vitality is basic to the orgiastic riffs, blues intimacy to the solo lines; yet both seem to be generated by the tremendous rhythmic-harmonic drive, which creates complexities far beyond the metrical beat (for instance, the "Spanish tinge" of Latin American rumba rhythm, or 8 divided into 3 plus 3 plus 2). The extension of the blues melodies, the cumulative excitement of the riffs, lead to the true polyphony of the final ensemble: which therefore becomes a climax to the music's harmonic direction. The concept of harmonic direction can occur only in a music that is at least part-composed, and must be attributed to the guiding force of the composer-performer's genius. This is a splendid piece of controlled music which yet preserves, even enhances, jazz spontaneity, for the control means that there is no doodling around, no merely hopeful fortuity.

We shall not meet with anything as exciting, and at the same time cohesive, as this until the mature work of Ellington; but the control of the soloists by the composer-arranger became generally accepted practice, and a necessary stage in the evolution of jazz. This explains the historical significance of the band of Fletcher Henderson, who was a college-trained Negro, not a "low-down" jazzman: for he was the first band-leader to insist that members of the group he established in 1923 should be technically proficient, able to read music, and willing to submit to the discipline of concerted effort. He habitually employed written arrangements, sometimes by himself, sometimes by Don Redman; but that this discipline did not necessarily destroy the spirit of jazz improvisation is indicated by the fact that all the great jazzmen of this classic phase of the art were eager to play in Henderson's band. During the group's heyday—the five-year period beginning in 1924, when the band settled at the Roseland Ballroom, New York, playing for a mainly white public—the personnel included Coleman Hawkins, Joe Smith, Louis Armstrong, Buster Bailey, Benny Morton and Jimmy Harrison, among others. Even the great Louis was expected to show respect for group discipline; and there is evidence in the (somewhat inadequate) surviving recordings that such control could stimulate, rather than restrict, improvisatory creation: consider, for instance, *Henderson Stomp* (25) in which the rhythmic energy and figurative gaiety seems to "spill over" the arrangement, especially in Tommy Ladnier's trumpet and Fats Waller's piano solos. There is a similar ebullience in such boogie-rhythmed pieces as *Snag it*, or in their several performances of *Sugar Foot Stomp*, a version of Louis Armstrong's version of Oliver's *Dippermouth Blues:* or in slightly more sombre vein in Henderson's odd version of Stitzel's *The Chant*, in which Fats Waller plays an organ continuo to Ladnier's bounding trumpet!

The acceptance of the arranger, and of a more stream-lined technical efficiency, was to lead, however, to the temporary decline of the jazz soloist. The big-band movement of the thirties was based upon an extension of Henderson's methods, and even in the earliest and merriest manifestations of this trend—such as McKinney's Cottonpickers' version of *Skeedle-um-bum* (26)—the vigour of the attack is apt to sound aggressive; we are bullied into a self-confidence that we cannot unequivocally share. The swing bands that evolved out of this kind of music—for instance the band of Bennie Moten, that of the Dorsey brothers, and ultimately that of Benny Goodman—tended to separate a technically drilled brass section from a reed section (including saxophones), driving them over the vigorously mechanistic rhythm of a large percussion section, and so creating a brazen, big-city version of the traditional antiphony of African ritual music and of the gospel hymn. Since little room is given for *melodic* extemporisation, sheer physical power comes to stand in lieu of creation. The force of the rhythm, the barking riffs of the massed trumpets, trombones and saxes, epitomize the city's energy; although the effect may be one of well-being it is also, significantly, belligerent.

This is precisely what is revealed when this "powerhouse" style attained its maturity of technical expertise. For the big band that Count Basie evolved during the thirties in Kansas City demonstrates how the aggressiveness of powerhouse was in part a denial of the abandon it professed to express. As arranger, Basie had learned from Fletcher Henderson the virtue of economy. Concentrating on the basic blues form whether in slowish or (more commonly) in rapid tempo, he pared down the complexities of Chicago polyphony in order to allow for the sharpest antiphony between the band's sectional groups. He claimed that he depended more on team work than on star soloists, though each section of his band included—at least during its heyday—solo players' of great distinction. Among the trumpets there was Buck Clayton, among the trombones Dickie Wells, who gave to the trombone line a cantabile flow and a subtlety of nuance far removed from the vigorous but rough tailgate style cultivated in the days of Kid Ory. Among the saxes there was Lester Young, who developed an intimately "speaking" yet reticent fluidity that leads away from the ripe, full-bodied tone of Coleman Hawkins towards the more tired, neutral colorations of modern jazz. Basie's rhythm section—with himself as pianist, trained in the classical barrelhouse-rag tradition of James P. Johnson, and with Walter Page on bass, Freddie Greene on guitar, and Jo Jones on drums—was probably the most brilliant percussion combination in jazz history, and Jones was one of the first to perfect the drumming technique that became the basis of the swing era. The use of the "high-hat" cymbal, operated by a foot pedal, allowed for much freer activity in the rest of the percussion kit, and the alternation with cymbal helped the players to achieve the infinitesimally slight, yet powerfully effective, "lean" on the off-beats. We see again that as percussion techniques grow more sophisticated they also in a sense become more primitive, for having left behind the European military two-step, they approximate to the polyrhythms of African and Caribbean music.

Subterranean conflict between the modern and the primitive finds, indeed, explicit formulation in Basie's antiphony. Though he starts from the orgiastic repetition of a striking riff, and makes the solos ride on the tremendous drive which the percussion lets loose, the solos now unambiguously *fight against* the ensembles. Thus in *Gone with What Wind* (27) Basie himself opens with a hard, dry piano solo that grows gradually more powerful and, encouraged by the percussion, stimulates the soloists. Then gradually the soloists are separated from the raucous blasts of the chordal brass, which blows in furious antiphony over a battering of percussion. The remarkable *Tickle Toe* (28) shows this effect more subtly: Basie's typically thin, wiry, boogie-rhythmed piano solo, sharp as glinting glass, is shattered by explosive shouts of brass chords in lashing rhythm; or Lester Young's tenor sax, expressive but pallidly "lost", tries to hold its own against the stream-lined precision of the brass interjections—a savagely mechanized version of the relationship between soli and tutti in the baroque concerto. In King Oliver's music the soloists' freedom grows out of the mutuality of the ensembles. In Armstrong and Bechet the soloists' ecstasy becomes more important than the mutuality, and tension between soloist and ensemble leads to the soloist's triumph—or at least to the recognition that he *ought* to triumph. In Basie's music the outcome of the dualism is more ambiguous. The communal rhythmic orgy liberates the soloist, and yet at the same time threatens his individuality: just as the big-city worker is simultaneously freed and enslaved by industrial power. Basie thus gives a different stress to the traditional dualism of jazz, which was to begin with at once an assertion of animal vitality and a protest against oppression. Armstrong and Bechet state the dualism, but forget it in the monism of their ecstasy. Basie, on the other hand, revels in the dualism; and because his semi-arranged, semi-improvised music is avowedly dualistic it is a later stage in jazz history, as is sonata in classical music.

What Basie's soloists are protesting against—or trying to hold their own against—is the hard, sharp, predatory vigour of an industrial society, which barks in the brass, crashes and snaps in the percussion.

Yet that vigour is a positive, too, and the hardness of Basie's music is its authenticity, for it accepts the consequences of a machine-made world. Sometimes, when Basie uses a Tin Pan Alley tune as a basis for composition, he treats the machine-made product of commerce in a style that anticipates the deflatory style of some modern jazz, especially Thelonious Monk. In his version of *Blue and Sentimental* (29), for instance, the horns' slow wobbles are highly expressive; yet they slightly guy the tune's sentimentality, just as Basie's spare, sharp piano solo comments wryly on its blueness. There may be a similar quality in *Evil Blues* (30), in so far as the (in this case original) tune, though innocuous enough, even jolly, in its first presentation, grows gradually nastier, dirtier, more sleazy, until the horrid stuttering and lecherous gibbering of the final chorus. The "evil" here isn't so much primeval as the knowing smirk of commercial art, which Basie puts in its proper place. But what Basie here does deliberately could easily happen through a fortuitous emotional dishonesty. Certainly there were insidious seductions working against the kind of honesty he achieved in his powerhouse manner; when the softness of Beiderbecke and the white bands entered the Powerhouse, it tended towards emotional prostitution, wherein a streamlined technique mirrored a streamlined feeling. Even big bands (such as that of Benny Goodman) that produced some distinguished music were victimized by this substitution of power-in-the-head-and-fists for power-in-the-heart-and-loins.

A revealing example is Artie Shaw's pretentiously titled *The Blues* (31). The first half of this long performance is, in a mild way, not unpleasing; in the second half, however, the riff triumphs over the music. The repetitions cease to be exciting, because there is no longer any tension—as there is in Morton and Basie—between the rhythmic patterns and the thrust of the melodic lines: or if any excitement survives, it is only of the orgiastic, extra-musical type exemplified in the corruption of Rock 'n' Roll. The excitement is a formula, mechanical not because it grows from honest acceptance of life in a machine-dominanted civilization, but because it accepts the tabloid feeling that machine techniques all too often imply. Shaw's solo, as compared with the riffs, demonstrates the other side of commercial exploitation. The solo does not grow out of the momentum, nor is it poised against it. On the contrary, the drive stops; there is a formula of repeated chords, over which the soloist muses to himself. Though it is most beautifully played, the solo is the antithesis of the true blues spirit as revealed in Morton's *Smokehouse Blues*. Its Beiderbecke-like frailty is emotionally indulgent, and when the wildness goes out of the blue portamenti they become wistfully nostalgic, even self-pitying, as Armstrong's *West End Blues*, nocturnal mood-piece though it may be, is not. Thus the "reality" of jazz begins to approximate to the escapism of pop music. Throughout the 'thirties and 'forties Duke Ellington was pre-eminent, if not unique, in preserving the authenticity of jazz while achieving, too, tenderness and sensitivity—the essential human values within the context of a hard, brutalized, industrialized world. His stature cannot be separated from the fact that he discovered how to make creative—not escapist—use of elements derived from pop music, in association with the heritage he received from jazz.

V

Jazz polyphony and jazz harmony: Duke Ellington as composer

> so lonely growing up among
> the imaginary automobiles
> and dead souls of Tarrytown
>
> to create
> out of his own imagination
> the beauty of his wild
> forebears—a mythology
> he cannot inherit. . . .
>
> the recognition—
> something so rare
> in his soul,
> met only in dreams
> —nostalgias
> of another life.
>
> ALLEN GINSBERG

The improvisatory "reality" of folk art and the conventionalized "artistry" of commercial music had to meet—we suggested at the end of the previous chapter—if jazz was to become the representative music of our industrial world: for just as man in the big city cannot turn his back on the world of commerce, so a dispossessed minority, if it is to create an art relevant to urban society as a whole, must to some degree absorb the values of that society. Duke Ellington has shown that this marriage, which seems unholy, can be consummated without sacrilege, dishonesty, or evasion; this is his historical importance, which complements that of Gershwin. Ellington, starting from jazz, came to terms with Tin Pan Alley; Gershwin, starting from Tin Pan Alley, attained the integrity of jazz.

Ellington's youthful career bears directly on his later achievement. Born in 1899 in Washington, D.C., he knew nothing of the squalor and violence with which Louis Armstrong or Bessie Smith had to contend. His family was reasonably well-to-do, and if the Ellingtons thought of themselves as alienated through colour, this served merely to deepen their domestic loyalties. So Edward Kennedy Ellington's childhood was comparatively happy; and he earned his soubriquet of "Duke" as a boy, because of the dignity and confidence of his bearing. Having exhibited talents as a musician, he moved, in his early twenties, not to Chicago, but to New York—where Armstrong went, according to some reports, to the dogs. But James P. Johnson, who was Ellington's idol, flourished in New York; and Ellington was to emulate not only his piano playing—which combined the improvisatory passion of jazz with the formalized art of ragtime—but also the shape of his career, which hovered between the worlds of jazz, of art, and of commerce. Ellington's first professional engagements, way back in his Washington days, had been as a ragtime party-pianist working with "legitimate" musicians, creating functional music geared to social dancing and theatre-shows rather than to the blues. The experience was useful to him when he began to discover his gifts as a jazz creator; even in his earliest recordings we can see that although his music has affinities with chamber-music improvisation as practised by Armstrong in the 'twenties, none the less Armstrong's intuitive tendency towards formal discipline—with a beginning, middle and end—is, in Ellington, more strongly marked. Indeed, it has been suggested that in Ellington's early compositions he contributed the "art", while the "folk" element of blue improvisation came from his collaboration with his first trumpet, Bubber Miley. The collaboration would not have worked if the "blue" passion had not been latent in Ellington, waiting to be sparked off; but it would seem valid to say that the famous *East St Louis Toodle-oo* (1), which made Ellington's reputation in 1926, was a joint creation of Miley as improvising folk-artist, and of Ellington as a composer with a Negroid inheritance. The poignantly simple tune is Miley's creation; so are the improvised "bubberings" which, in emulation of the human speaking voice, he achieves on his muted trumpet. Beneath the tune Ellington adds a richly atmospheric ostinato of moaning saxophones and tuba: a sound lushly enveloping, as compared with Armstrong's sharp acidity, and at the same time a quasi-theatrical convention, because the ostinato is supposed to represent an old man shuffling monotonously down a dusty road. There is a fairly sophisticated romanticism in the idea: the shuffling ostinato becomes man's everyday destiny, from which the improvised solos speak yearningly. In this piece the "romanticism" implies, perhaps, an element of self-consciousness which is reflected in the alternation of the tune and the ostinato in rondo style; Miley's thirty-two-bar tune and his exquisitely resolutory epilogue have greater musical substance than the sixteen measures of Nanton's trombone, the sixteen of Bigard's clarinet, the eighteen bars of brass and the ten somewhat corny ensemble bars. None the less, the rondo-like nature of the piece hints at possibilities for future development. Scope is still given for improvisation, but the improvisation has become part of the composition—more than it is in Armstrong, almost as much as in Jelly Roll Morton's band pieces. It is significant that the improvisations in later versions of Ellington's pieces change only slightly, even when they are performed by different players. The part is not written down because the manner of performance must seem spontaneous; when once established, however, the music that is appropriate to the context remains constant.

Like Jelly Roll, Ellington achieved this one-man control over improvisation through a telepathic faculty and through sheer force of character. Human sympathy and intelligence, working together, helped him to find the collaborators he needed, and to keep them with him. Bubber Miley, Arthur Whetsol and Cootie Williams on trumpets, Sam Nanton on trombone, Barney Bigard on clarinet, Harry Carney on baritone sax and Johnny Hodges on alto stayed with Ellington through periods which, in the mutable world of jazz, seem like eternity; and Ellington is a new type of composer in that he has written, not merely for given resources and a specific function, but for a particular group of human beings, each with his own distinctive characteristics. "Sometimes I shift parts right in the middle," Ellington has said; "you see, the man has to match the music, in feeling, in character. No point in knowing the music unless you know the boys as individuals." From this point of view one can see Ellington's preoccupation with new sounds—with the sonorous variety possible through the use of different types of mute—as an extension of jazz's traditional concern with melodic inflections as a kind of human speech; each man must reveal more of himself, through his own accent or dialect, and in so doing will make the richer contribution to the whole. The more respect the band shows for the identities of the individuals who comprise it, the better it will be—so long as the cohesive power of the composer-arranger operates effectively. This is why there must always be a two-way relationship between the composer and the players:

> the music is mostly written down, because it saves time. It's written
> down if it's only as a basis for change. There's no set system. Sometimes

I write it and the band and I collaborate on the arrangement. Sometimes Billy Strayhorn does the arrangement. When we're all working together a guy may have an idea and he plays it on his horn. Another guy may add to it and make something of it. Someone may play a riff and ask How do you like this? The trumpets may try something together and say Listen to this. There may be a difference of opinion as to what kind of mute to use. Someone may advocate extending a note, or cutting it off. The sax section may want to put an additional smear on it.

The give and take is essential: but so is the controlling talent that makes the ultimate decisions. It was Ellington who produced from the band a sound such as had not been heard before, and who made the new sound formally and artistically convincing. Again, his relationship to "commerce" helped. Because he was now working at the Cotton Club as a show-band, not merely as a functional band for dancing to, he had opportunities to experiment with composed music as atmospheric accompaniment to a floor-show.

The organization which Ellington imposed was melodic, formal and harmonic—in that order of importance. One puts the melodic element first because the tune was traditionally the starting-point for jazz improvisation, and Ellington was the first jazz musician since Morton habitually to write his own tunes. On the whole, they are very good tunes; and Ellington's pieces prove, no less than Jelly Roll Morton's, that a distinguished melody is the best impetus to every aspect of jazz creation. Moreover, the nature of Ellington's tunes betrays the first, and the most positive, of the many influences that Tin Pan Alley has had upon him. Though the manner of performance may be blue and folklike, the tunes themselves are much closer to Gershwin and Cole Porter: as we may hear in, for instance, *Black Beauty* (2), a most touching melody that attains, largely through an unobtrusive irregularity of phrase, a typically precarious equilibrium between innocence and sophistication. Ellington's slow tunes, such as *Solitude* (3), have their prototype in the "lonesome" numbers of Tin Pan Alley; though their effect depends largely on the closely chromatic harmonies and the "clinging" instrumental coloration of the simple, homophonic accompaniment, they would not be so haunting if the tunes were not in themselves distinctive. It is interesting that the period during which Ellington produced his richest crop of hit tunes coincides with the period in which Arthur Whetsol took over from Bubber Miley as trumpet lead. Miley was a folk blues player; Whetsol's sweeter tone and more cantabile phrasing suggest Bix Beiderbecke in their subtlety and sensitivity, and so by implication have affinities with the world of

Gershwin. Incidentally, the occasional asymmetry of phrase to which Ellington became increasingly prone is one of the reasons why un-organized collective improvisation would be difficult to achieve in this music.

The second element of control in Ellington's music is his more formal treatment of rhythm *in relation to melody*. For instance, *Rockin' in Rhythm* (4) depends mainly, as the title suggests, on the physical stimulation of a metrical pulse. But the riffs in it differ from those in most Chicago jazz in being melodic: closely related to the tune, which is similar in character to *Black Beauty*. There is also a simple architec-tural structure, with a clear recapitulation. In *Hot and Bothered* (5), a busily exhibitionist version of *Tiger Rag* (6), the orgiastic excitement again submits to architectural symmetry: which is why the excitement is different in effect from that generated by Armstrong. The tragic element latent in Armstrong has been replaced by a quality almost comic; and perhaps this was inevitable as the blues were "civilized". The primitive fears, terrors and desires below the surface of our lives must be admitted to, but at the same time "placed", even gently laughed at. If this in a sense approaches the comparatively safe world of pop music, it does so with genuinely creative wit and zest. *Jungle Jamboree* (7), like most of Ellington's jungle pieces, is another instance; the tiger's growl is a joke, and has to be, if we are to face him: whereas Jelly Roll's *Wild Man*, as played by Armstrong, is comic and frighten-ing at the same time. One can take such savagery in New Orleans or Chicago, but not in the Cotton Club at New York. There the blueness will be affiliated to the sweeter tones of the Kentucky mountain song in one direction, and to the lures of Tin Pan Alley in the other. If the tiger should growl, ferociously, he will be "met only in dreams—nostalgias of another life".

For the alternative to treating the Unknown as comic is to regard it as romantic. We have seen that there is a strain of romanticism latent in Ellington's very first successful composition, the *East St Louis Toodle-oo* of 1926; many of his finest pieces exploit deliberately this "mythology he cannot inherit", creating atmosphere mainly through the third "compositional" element in Ellington's work—his highly personal harmonic texture and scoring. Like Bix Beiderbecke, Elling-ton explored impressionistic harmony not so much because it was "modern" (by the twenties it was so no longer), but because he realized intuitively that it was the only harmony that might be relevant to blues-derived jazz, since it was at once sensuous and non-developing.

Static sevenths, ninths and elevenths could enrich the "moment of sensation"; but in so far as they would inevitably weaken the momentum of line and rhythm, they would encourage the impulse to dream—at the expense of jazz "reality". This is why Ellington's harmony is another feature that links him with the world of pop music; and it is probable that he at first inherited Debussian and Ravelian harmonies from Tin Pan Alley rather than from direct sources. Later on, his favourite concert pieces were similar to those of Bix Beiderbecke, though more substantial: he refers repeatedly to Ravel's *Daphnis et Chloe*, to Debussy's *La Mer*, and to Delius's *In a Summer Garden*. We can see why these works would appeal to him, harmonically and colouristically; and yet may still think that his direct debt to them is small. For instance, while the similarity between his harmonic texture and that of Delius may come from a shared nostalgia, there is no comparison between the way in which Delius and Ellington employ their chromatics. Though Delius's music moves in no particular direction, it is all movement; the only thing that matters, he said, is the sense of flow, and this is why he needed time and space in which to express himself. For Ellington, the mood and the moment are everything. His harmonic texture is very close, the chromatic lines wriggling around one another in restricted space: while his forms are short, simple, economical, non-flowing. His larger works are suites—sequences of short pieces: or, if they attempt more complex and extended forms, are usually unconvincing.

While Ellington's creation of mood and atmosphere through harmony and instrumentation links him with the world of pop music, it is also the element wherein his personal sensitivity is most manifest. He makes the dream not a cliché, a substitute for reality, but a most delicate and moving apprehension of urban man's nostalgia for "the beauty of his wild forebears": so that again he brings jazz and pop together in authentic awareness of the temper of city life. *The Mooche* (8), for instance, is certainly not an escapist piece. The fine tune is very blue in feeling, and its grandly passionate descending chromatics are reinforced by the mutes and plungers through which Miley and "Tricky Sam" Nanton (so called because of his tricky agility with the mutes) bubber and growl. The muted colours give the music a mysteriously sensuous effect that removes the tune from the blues' hard reality; yet although the colours are romantic, and therefore dreamy, the piece remains slightly sinister in effect, largely because of the screwed-up cross-rhythms of Lonnie Johnson's guitar. The wordless scat singing of Baby

Cox is also equivocal in effect, for it sounds gaily abandoned, yet also a bit looney, and therefore potentially dangerous. So the romanticism of this piece doesn't evade the dark undercurrents of feeling which we sense beneath the surface. It does, however modify our attitude to them, since the sophistication implies a degree of conscious awareness. The classical symmetry of form, with a clear recapitulation, disciplines the elements in the music that might be a threat—just as the wit, in the jungle pieces, tames the snarl of the tiger. *Misty Mornin'* (9), another piece from the late 'twenties, has a similar mood, expressed largely by way of harmonic and tonal subtlety. The old New Orleans scoring for trumpet, low clarinet and trombone is used to create an entirely different effect; instead of the traditional earthy, salty tang, Whetsol's muted trumpet wanders dreamily through a texture of chromatic inner parts that sometimes creates whole-tone or even bitonal progressions. The poetically introverted quality is emphasized later in the piece by the extremely close part-writing for saxophones, and especially by Ellington's fondness for the sonority of the baritone sax, which often has unresolved sevenths in the bass line. One might say that the brooding, oily tone of Harry Carney's baritone sax epitomized what Billy Strayhorn has termed "the Ellington sound", which is the aural realization of his nostalgia; perhaps it is not an accident that Harry Carney is the one member of the early band who is still with Ellington after thirty-odd years. *Misty Mornin'* indicates, too, how closely the Ellington sonority is associated with his favourite harmonic mannerisms; the typical modulation to the flat submediant (from B flat to G flat) occurs with an effect of passive luxuriance strictly comparable with its effect in Schubert. The piece's moodiness is quintessentially romantic (Ellington said that in this number Whetsol's muted trumpet used to make "great big ole tears run down people's faces"): though again the sensuous indulgence is disciplined by the lucid structure, which is not misty at all. In the same way the intertwining chromatic part-writing of the most celebrated of all the mood pieces—*Mood Indigo* (10)—is balanced by the delicate equilibrium of the tune; we are shut within our melancholy, and at the same time detached from it.

In *Creole Love Call* (11), another mood piece from the late 'twenties, Ellington makes unexpected but evocative use of the high coloratura soprano voice which "calls", for the most part pentatonically, against the ripe Ellington ensemble. The high register, the pentatonicism, and perhaps the irregular five-bar phrasing, give the wordless vocal line a pristine innocence, despite the sensuous sinuosity of its contours; the typical nostalgia is inherent in the contrast between this line and the somewhat voluptuous, at times even savage, bubbling and gibbering of the instrumental horns. The marvellous *Black and Tan Fantasy* (12), for which Ellington has justly shown especial partiality, inverts the *Creole Love Call*'s relationship between solo and ensemble. Here the dream is contained most in the atmospheric background, consisting of liquid "Creole" clarinet and sax and muted brass: while Miley's twelve-bar blues tune on the classic harmonic progression, and the sequence of solos by Miley, Nanton and Ellington speak, painfully, of the heart's truth. The piece is almost an elegy on the "lost world" that the Negro cannot inherit: which is why the famous quotation from the Chopin Funeral March seems, when it is used as coda, both appropriate and inevitable. In an early version of the piece this coda is played in a manner that is simultaneously comic and pathetic—as is so much authentic New Orleans funeral music. In a later, 1938, version the coda becomes loud, rather wild and tragic. It would seem that the *Black and Tan Fantasy* owes its potency to the fact that it re-creates so much of the spirit of the blues and of New Orleans jazz, while achieving the precise realization of art. Because of the compositional quality, Ellington's world can become ours—not merely a world which we may enter vicariously, if with delight.

In the first phase of his career—that one can speak of his "development" itself suggests that he is more of a composer than any previous jazz musician—Ellington has thus effected, more or less intuitively, a fusion of procedures derived from folk-blues with art-conventions suggested by popular music. The more developed element of composition is manifest—we have seen—in the more organized nature of the tunes, which are usually Ellington's, and often comparable with those of Gershwin or Cole Porter: in an approach to a more architectural form through the use of ostinato-like refrains, ostinati and rudimentary recapitulations: and in an increasing sophistication of harmony, derived from impressionism via pop music, this harmony being non-developing, and therefore evocative of mood rather than of drama. The growing subtlety in tone-colour combinations was perhaps more empirical: an investigation of the expressive possibilities of jazz-band sound derived, through experiment with responsive colleagues, from an uncannily sensitive ear. Occasionally, not often, the scoring betrays a hint of Hollywood sentiment.

In the second phase of his career Ellington begins to reconcile blues tradition not only with pop music, but with some of the conventions of classical art-music also. This may have been part of his growing sophistication; he heard more music as he became famous and fêted. But the process was probably instinctive, too: for, being a real composer, he could not avoid seeing that the more he had to say, the more "technique" he would need, since the only kind of technique that matters is that which is the servant of necessity. Listening to "serious" music may have helped: though like Gershwin—who was trained not in the jazz world but in Tin Pan Alley—Ellington would have learned what he had to learn from experience. He was almost entirely a self-taught musician, after some boyhood piano lessons with a lady whose name has variously, but with equally sublime improbability, been transcribed as Mrs. Klingscale, Klinkscale and Chinkscale. According to the academic textbooks Ellington's part-writing is incorrect; according to his ear (and ours) it is correct, for the rules of European harmony were not devised to produce the effects that Ellington had in mind. His genius is to be equated with his ear, which is the servant of his experience. Any music-maker of whom this is not true is not a composer.

Ellington's development from jazz towards "art" can be illustrated by a sequence of pieces from his "middle" period, the early 'forties. Bubber Miley, the original folk-blues player of the band, had left in 1929; Arthur Whetsol died in 1940. The new, bigger band was centred around Cootie Williams and Rex Stewart on trumpet and cornet, "Tricky Sam" Nanton and Juan Tizol on trombones, Barney Bigard on clarinet, Otto Hardwicke, Johnny Hodges, Ben Webster and Harry Carney on saxes. Fred Guy's guitar and Sonny Greer's percussion remained, with Ellington on piano, as the rhythm section: which was, however, renewed, re-created by the sprightly counterpointed string bass of Jimmy Blanton, a player of remarkable inventiveness, who died of tuberculosis at the age of twenty-one. The difference between the Ellington band of the 'forties and traditional jazz is clear enough even in *Portrait of Bert Williams* (13), which is a jazz variation number in traditional style. We may express the distinction by saying that the jazz solos are now subservient to the composed form, being designed to *fit in*, rather than conceived as points from which the music *takes off*. Related to this is the nature of the tune itself, which is long and of remarkably wide range. On such a tune the improvisations could hardly be expansive; if they were not, to a degree, controlled, their relationship to the tune would be inapprehensible. Connected with the nature of the tune and its variations is the relaxed quality of the rhythm. The concern for clarity and balance inevitably brought a modified conception of rhythm, for the light must be let in if the relationship of parts to whole is to be manifest. So the old notion of the regular earth-beat against which the melodies pull and prance is in part superseded; the melodic movement of Jimmy Blanton's brass inaugurates—no less than the rhythm section of the Basie band—a new phase in jazz, where-in rhythm is an integral part of polyphony.

Portrait of Bert Williams is a song-style piece, blues derived; similar characteristics may be noted in purely rhythmic pieces, such as *Main Stem* (14). The rhythmic excitement, in association with the lucid texture and structure, is no longer orgiastic in the directly physical way of Armstrong's, or even Basie's, comparable numbers. The riffs have melodic appeal and structural purpose; while the muted, masked sonorities have the effect of distancing the frenzy, almost as though the music were laughing at itself—like Ellington's comic-grotesque beasts of the jungle. There is a similar effect in the sheer virtuosity of the building up of Latin-American cross-rhythms in *The Flaming Sword* (15): or in the cumulative increase in excitement, generated by Ben Webster's vibrant tenor sax, in the splendid *Cotton Tail* (16): which explodes in rhythmic contradiction, only to be deflated by the comic coda. The celebrated *Ko-Ko* (17) owes its almost unique position in Ellington's work to the fact that it is a ferocious rhythm-piece in which there is no ironic deflation. The element of formal control, with a decisive recapitulation, prevents the music from going mad; but there is no compromise in the fury of the scarifying ostinato figure that generates yells from the whirling extensions of the solos, barks from the brass tutti, and an extraordinary minatory venom from the piano's solo. This is a tragic piece worthy of comparison with the best of Armstrong: and more completely realized in terms of art.

It is, however, inherent in the nature of Ellington's artistic success that he should not often allow himself to become so directly involved. *Blue Serge* (18), for instance, has a poignant minor tune (by the Duke's son, Mercer) and a sombre but sensuous tone colour. The passion is unequivocal, the more striking because of the dramatic contrast between the mellifluous sonority of the opening and the dark hues of Nanton's chorus. Yet the contrast is a conscious sophistication; and the sophistication is a means of not being too implicated in the wildness and strangeness. The chromatic piano chords that spice the passion have the same effect of detachment: so does the wistful coda with unresolved added sixths, which succeeds the weird explosion of the last chorus. In *Sepia Panorama* (19) this sense of detachment finds a more comprehensive form: for the piece is a mood-picture of Harlem, and a wide range of apparently contradictory emotions are, in the melodic phrases, the harmonies and riffs, yoked together not by violence, but by the composer's art. The variety of mood and atmosphere reflects the multifarious variety of the Harlem world; this is not, like early jazz, a red-hot participation between composing performers and audience, or rather dancers, but is almost, in the Wordsworthian sense, emotion recollected in tranquillity. The piece is not entirely successful—Ellington seldom is when he goes beyond one-mood reverie or the celebration of the passing moment; yet it often makes a virtue of its indeterminacy, as in the savage brass intrusion into the forlornly wandering piano solo, and in the modulatory surprise in the coda. This is not only Harlem music, but also, in a general sense, urban music, comparable with Copland's *Quiet City*. The isolation of Negro and Jew are complementary.

This miniature tone-poem provides a transition to Ellington's concert music—his suites and larger compositions. It is often said that an element of pretentiousness creeps into these, and it is true that they convince most when they are formally simplest. His first experiment in "extended form", the *Creole Rhapsody* (20) of 1931, merely strings together a number of casually connected episodes, and the second version of the same piece gives up even the pretence of connectedness, since the sections are now played in clearly distinct tempi. His later, more successful attempts to create more sustained movements—such as *Reminiscin' in Tempo* (21) and *Diminuendo and Crescendo in Blue* (22)—depend more directly on traditional jazz techniques, for both rely on the incrementary riff, and differ from improvised jazz only in the art with which the rise and fall of excitement is controlled. It is true that the occasional use of irregular (five or fourteen bar) phrases hints at more complex formal processes; yet when in later years Ellington explored these possibilities he usually preferred to do so within a "closed", classical structure, relinquishing the "rhapsody" in favour of the suite—a number of comparatively small, self-contained pieces. We may take, as representative of this mode, some movements from his recent Shakespearean suite, *Such Sweet Thunder* (23). Of course, one should not think of this as an attempt to emulate Shakespeare, or to create music collateral to Shakespeare's characters. It is quintessentially Ellington's music, prompted by *his* reaction to Shakespeare; and that he should have experienced Shakespeare, at the American Stratford, is another aspect of his growing sophistication. Yet on becoming increasingly aware of the wide world around him, Ellington does not lose his innocence; and there is something deeply touching in the fact that he should have been so moved by his belated experience of Shakespeare as to want to, need to, create this music. "Being sophisticated" might have meant response to so many things less real, less human.

Not surprisingly, there are two pieces about Othello—Shakespeare's coloured hero. *Such Sweet Thunder* is the marvel-narrating Othello who casts his spell over Desdemona. A somewhat swaggering ostinato figure on trombones gives intimation of his adventurous glamour, but Ray Nance's trumpet solo has a faintly pathetic wobble in its singing nobility, and this prepares us for the other Othello piece, *Sonnet in Search of a Moor*: a very sad little piece in which there is none of Othello's *nobilmente* heroics, but much of his lost, alienated loneliness. The tune significantly reminds us of Gershwin's Porgy: so that Othello becomes a pathetic hero, the Negro in the big city, perhaps even Ellington himself. If the aereated hissing of percussion and the vacillating clarinet filigree suggest the mystery of the unknown, this only makes the tune sound the frailer; and the delicately stalking bass, prompted by Othello's footsteps through the night, hints that it is indeed himself, not Desdemona, that he is "in search of". Here, interestingly, we find the most obvious influence of "art" music; we may suspect that Ellington had been listening to Stravinsky's *Petrouchka*, especially the Moorish episode. *Petrouchka* is a ballet about puppets. The forlorn quality of Ellington's Moor may come from the fact that he is seen as the Negro-Clown, buffeted by, rather than heroically in control of, circumstances. The irony in this piece is wistful; in the wittily titled *Sonnet to Hank Cinq*, which is closer to jazz in spirit, it is more ebullient. A prancing, shooting trombone tune, nosing over a boogie-rhythmed beat, trenchantly suggests Harry's brassy insouciance, which is perhaps a very modern quality: shorn of the patriotism he is a twentieth-century smart-alec. Falstaff interjects baritone bantering, and the satirical note carries the day. In the comic coda patriotism is reduced to March of Time heroics, with a telescoped version of the newsreel's habitual harmonic cliché.

The Star-Crossed Lovers calls on Paul Gonsalves's tenor and Johnny Hodges's alto sax to sing the loves of Romeo and Juliet, in lyrical dialogue. The tune is extremely beautiful, in the ballad tradition of Gershwin. Being a pop number, it has an adolescent quality that makes it appropriate to twentieth-century teenagers in the big city; yet its sustained lyrical breadth, its deeply sonorous scoring, its disturbing harmonic and tonal twists give it a sad, hymnic, even tragic quality that is completely without sentimentality. If it evokes the world of *West Side Story*, it does so with the love, tenderness, compassion, even awe, which that work lacks. The piano cascades hint at the dangers inherent in reconciliation with pop music, for although presumably intended to express the turbulence within a society in conflict, they provoke irrelevant associations with the cocktail lounge. But if this is a blemish, it is not sufficient to affect the deeply moving character of the music. The piece is a small masterpiece and—in its threefold fusing of jazz, pop, and art music—is of some historical, as well as intrinsic, significance.

Madness in Great Ones again concentrates on the twentieth-century aspects of its subject. As a portrait of Hamlet it may not go far, for he was more than a mixed-up kid. It is none the less relevant to us in being concerned with the mixed-up element in modern youth, and in deliberately exploiting sensation, disruption, surprise. The sudden breaks (in both the literal and the technical sense), the conflicting sonorities, the simultaneous sounding of opposites are almost Ives-like, whether or not the Duke has ever heard any of Ives's music. The saving grace of the piece is that it is, in a wild way, funny, and its mad exhibitionism is as typical of us as it is of Hamlet. While it makes a hero of the mixed-up kid, it paradoxically deflates him simultaneously. Cat Anderson's stratospheric trumpet coda prevents us from taking the mixed-upness *too* seriously, though it does not promote contempt for the screwy. In *Half the Fun* the joke is all in the title. The music of this languid Cleopatra is serious enough and so it should be, for her sensuality is eternal and neither custom nor commerce can stale it. Ostinato patterns and tingling percussion are used as background to Oriental melismata that turn into the expressive jazz solo of Johnny Hodges' alto sax: in some ways, as we shall see, jazz has more in common with the linear techniques of Eastern music than it has with the European conventions with which it started. If this piece seems a little too long we must remember, again, that Time is only a European notion; the monotony is part of the music's hypnotic sensuality.

The suite concludes with *Circle of Fourths*, a quick coda-piece which represents the artist's (Shakespeare's or Ellington's) control over his creations by rushing pell-mell through a modulating cycle of fourths, covering the complete chromatic range. It has both the excitement and the wonder of creation; and ends with a terrific solo break when the creator steps forward from the created to take his bow. Ellington does not pretend to be a Shakespeare, but he stands there in his own right: the music has justified the pride he feels in his ability as artist, and he has created music that can be discussed on the same terms as any other composed music. The question is often asked: Is it still jazz? for the essence of jazz was that it began as a freeing of the libido: was negatively a protest against persecution, positively a rediscovery of the earth-rooted vigour that urban man had lost. It was also a refinding of the forgotten relationship between flesh and spirit, in that the best jazz, through its physical excitement, led to a condition of ecstasy comparable with some aspects of religious or mystical experience. It would seem inescapable that jazz cannot preserve its pristine identity: it cannot be a physical-mystical *act* if it is also composition, for a composer is one who places things together, making order from chaos. So the only question worth asking is not: Is it jazz? but: Is it good music— which preserves some of the lost virtues that jazz represents? On this basis one might claim that some interpenetration of the virtues of jazz, of pop music, and of art music is not only desirable, but also necessary, if there is to be a future for any of them.

That Ellington, in his latest and "artiest" phase, has not lost contact with the roots of jazz is proved by the record he has recently made in collaboration with Louis Armstrong (24). In their sixties, the two almost-old grand men of jazz have at last come together to play numbers that cover well over thirty years of the Duke's creative life. What Armstrong does to Ellington is to reveal afresh the wildness and strangeness beneath the surface; the art is not destroyed, though there is no compromise with the taming effect that pop music conventions may have. The superb new version of *Black and Tan Fantasy* preserves the mysterious flavour of Ellington's piece, into which Armstrong's solo injects sudden bursts of fury or ecstasy that are an apotheosis of the New Orleans-Chicago spirit. The "Ellington sound" thus acquires a strange vehemence; and the funeral march quotation loses all suggestion of pathos or grotesquerie, and seems to epitomize the sorrow of the ages. The new version of *Mood Indigo* is similar in its deepened range. It was always a beautiful nocturne, one of the most disturbing examples of Ellington's close-moving chromatic harmony that creates an atmosphere curiously dense and tense, despite the tune's relaxed nostalgia. Armstrong's fiercely asymmetrical solo deepens the indigo in the mood, and inspires clarinet and scat voice to jerks and wails of a piercing plangency. Ellington's piano arabesques have a comparable incisiveness; and throughout the record his playing creates extreme tension, largely by way of rhythmic displacements in a very thin texture. If it is true that, during most of his career, "the Duke has played the piano, but his real instrument is his band", he here becomes a pianist in his own right. Inspired by Armstrong, he has learned something relevant to his piano style from Count Basie also, as we can see from *Lucky So and So*, in which the elegance, the polish, the thin texture are Basie-like, though the tremolo effects and false relations have an Ellington-like ripeness. Delayed accents give the music a remarkable inner energy. *Duke's Place* achieves something similar in quick tempo, for the incantatory riff becomes atmospheric rather than orgiastic, and the hollow echo effect at the end introduces a new dimension—revealing, as does the new version of *Cotton Tail*, the Ellington poetry within the Basie Powerhouse. Taking it all round, indeed, this record is a most impressive tribute to the vitality of the human spirit. The heart of the matter survives in those who have the strength to apprehend it. The lures of "New York" have not destroyed the truths that Armstrong, as a young man, had blown for: nor are those truths denied by Ellington's necessary affiliation with a commercialized world.

VI

*From art back to jazz. Modern
jazz and the composing improviser:
Thelonious Monk and Charlie Parker,
Ornette Coleman and John Coltrane*

> I have heard the sound of revelry
> by night
> I have wandered lonely
> as a crowd.
>
> LAWRENCE FERLINGHETTI

> If we could hear all the sounds existing we'd soon be mad.
>
> CHARLIE PARKER

Ellington has proved that the merging of jazz, as an urban folk music, into "art" and "commerce" was necessary if the music of an alienated minority was to become the voice of industrial society as a whole. Clearly, however, there were perils involved in such a process; indeed, a composer of modest genius—such as Ellington—was needed to carry it off, and the process could not happen by wilful effort, only by subconscious permeation. So, for one Ellington there were a hundred jazzmen in whose work both jazz and art were swallowed whole by commerce, in that the box-office value of an immediate physical impact upon the audience was their first consideration. The music was still to be an orgy: but a *conscious* orgy—which is a contradiction in terms. Stan Kenton's big band may be cited as representative; and the chromium-plated, flashy vitality of his music is synthetic in a far more sinister way than the sentimental aspects of Hollywood's escapism. Of course, it is not really vital at all, only a surface pretence, a phoney sexuality "in the head": for musically it is all cliché, non-creative. The excitement is extramusical, a matter of rhythmic hypnosis and of the brash rowdiness of the sonority, which lacerates the nerves. It is better done by the dentist's drill. Moreover, Kenton's band tried to get it both ways: the bogus primitivism was complemented by an equally bogus artistic sophistication—Heaven defend us from Art, if it has anything to do with Kenton's grisly-titled *Artistry in Boogie* (1), wherein the streamlined slickness of technique and feeling is prostitution: as early jazz, played for prostitutes and their clients, was not.

At the height of the swing era Ellington and Basie were, we have observed, supreme in using the big band to expressive purpose: though this is not to belittle their debt to the bands contemporary with and sequent to Fletcher Henderson's—in particular to Bennie Moten's (in which Basie played piano); Chick Webb's; the Dorsey brothers' white band and, above all, the big bands of Benny Goodman and of Jimmy Lunceford. In so far as these bands created fine music they did so because the players, although working on the fringes of the commercial world, still had the blues in their blood and bones, as was most evidently true of Ellington and Basie. Yet the more the big band became an agent of emotional exploitation, the more equivocal the position of the true jazzmen became. Originally their art had been functional, music for dancing to; and much of the historical significance of jazz lay in the fact that it was a "corporeal" and celebrative art, flourishing at a time when the post-Renaissance dichotomy between spirit and flesh seemed to have reached a point of ultimate attenuation. Lester Young, who was one of the most highly influential figures among the creators of the new jazz, once said that the only worthwhile audience was an audience of active participants. Yet the music of the big bands grew increasingly remote from the dance, being designed to pulverize a captive public. The orgiastic vitality of jazz seemed, by this synthetic exploitation, discredited: so either jazz moved increasingly into the category of art-music, as with Ellington, who to some degree ordered and tamed the jungle; or it gave up the attempt to compromise with pop art and became, once more, an improvisatory folk art, now dedicated, however, almost exclusively to protest and withdrawal. The positive exuberance of traditional jazz was transformed into the nervous twitch, the highly strung quiver.

Although jazz ought, of its nature, to be a music for dancers, it could not be such if it had become an art of private withdrawal rather than a communal celebration. So the advanced jazzmen began to emulate the advanced straight musicians of a slightly earlier generation: they deplored the philistinism of their public, and played for themselves and their initiates. This attitude was mixed up with social ostracism and racial discrimination, the old jazz being despised as "Jim Crow music";

and the advanced jazzmen began to adopt ritual forms of dress to distinguish themselves as an *élite*, and even literally played with their backs to their audience. They attempted to make an asset of alienation: drank and drugged and took up with Oriental religions (especially the more passive Zen-Buddhistic kinds) as an escape from their sense of not belonging. Of course, drug addiction is not a prerogative of the exponents of Modern Jazz; it was common among jazzmen of the 'twenties, being in part a response to economic depression, to racial discrimination, and to industrial overcrowding. But the jazzman of the 'twenties—especially if coloured—really was a victim of social circumstances; by smoking his reefers he hoped to give himself the same kind of lift as he got from playing jazz. The position of the new jazzmen was different; they took the much more dangerous heroin as evidence of their wilful isolation, and because it induced a passivity similar to that which they sought in their music. The deliberate threat to health and life was a death-wish; shot-marks on the arm were publicly exhibited, as stigmata. Thus they expressed their hostility to society: and also the self-depreciation inherent in their basically insecure, defensive, inferiority-ridden art. It was not an accident that Modern Jazz evolved during and in the wake of the Second World War, in which the Negro had been forced to fight to defend a freedom that seemed dubiously applicable to himself.

In traditional jazz, we have seen, the neurotic element had always been present, but it was balanced by the vitality of innocence. Now only the neurosis is left, or the vitality itself has become hysteria. A highly neurotic art, as symptom of a highly neurotic civilization, cannot, however, be unexpected and may be valuable. *Because* it does not grow from a harmonious relationship between the individual and society it may help us to understand how our, as well as the artist's, neuroses may be lived with, if not dealt with. For, despite the incidental affectations, the best Modern Jazz preserves the integrity of the great days of jazz history; the dedicated players would not compromise, even though Ellington had shown that compromise was possible. Rather than compromise, they were prepared to accept madness or death; and although this statement may sound melodramatic it is strictly true. As long as they could, they would create a chamber music—even a soloist's music—of protest and rejection, playing for themselves as Outsiders. They would accept the fact that the only vitality they could encompass was the nervous frenzy of a jungle turned to asphalt. Their music was their religion in that they put into it all the skeletonic truth they knew.

Having played it, they died of consumption, drink, drugs or mental breakdown.

Interestingly enough, one of the starting-points for Modern Jazz—perhaps *the* earliest distinctive manifestation—was within the big band itself. A young guitarist called Charlie Christian came, it seems, from nowhere, with no musical antecedents, played with Benny Goodman's band for a brief period, revolutionized the technique of jazz guitar playing, and died of consumption at the age of twenty-one. He recorded both with Goodman's big band and with his Sextet or Septet, which included, beside Goodman on clarinet, Count Basie on piano, Jo Jones on drums, and Cootie Williams on trumpet: and if we listen to Christian in the number which gave him his greatest opportunity, *Solo Flight* (2), we shall understand how Basie's piano style was a generative force behind not only the later Ellington, but still more behind the new jazzmen. With Basie himself the sharp, brittle style of playing, though wry and anti-sentimental, remains confident and vivacious; but we can see that this style could easily become not bouncy but quivery, brittle as broken glass. Charlie Christian explores this quality on his guitar, which he regards not (in the traditional style of Bud Scott) as a harmonic fill-in, nor in the plangent melodic-harmonic style of Eddie Lang, but primarily as a melody instrument, with its tone electrically reinforced where necessary. He emphasizes the pinging, whining sonority of guitar line, rather than the instrument's potential harmonic sensuality, and in this particular significantly reminds us of a late country-blues singer like Robert Johnson, or a classic guitarist like Lonnie Johnson. But the bite of the string has become still more nervous and tight; and the tremor of the solo line—often of fantastic rapidity for a plucked string instrument—contrasts disturbingly with the regularity of the beat, in a manner that Christian is said to have represented onomatopoeically by the expression "be-bop". There may be an incipiently schizophrenic quality in the contrast between the grotesque grimace of the physical movement and the agonized tightness of the feeling; wherever the expression came from, it aptly characterizes the phase of jazz that Christian, among others, inaugurated.

While the line is changing, so is the nature of the beat itself. Carrying on from Basie's and Ellington's liberation of the rhythm section, Kenny Clarke treats the percussion almost as melody instruments. The beat is no longer compulsive, but is brittle, like the line—aerated with a shimmer of cymbals rather than driven by the boom of the drum. No longer does the beat necessarily mark the pulse of Time; on the contrary it may, acquiring some of the qualities of Oriental percussion, become a synonym for eternity. This is another reason—in addition to the music's relationship to early jazz—why harmony is comparatively unimportant in this music. Such harmony as there is is not so much chordal as implicit in Christian's tortuous lines. Despite the Oriental tendency of the percussion, this tortuousness allows for no relaxation, not even in a slowish piece like *Blues in B* (3), the bizarre key of which is probably a gesture of defiance. It is a particularly tricky key for the B-flat-centred melody instruments of traditional jazz.

Charlie Christian, working within the context of the big band world, was a precursor rather than a founder of the religion of Modern Jazz: which discovered its "high priest" in the appropriately named Thelonious Monk, its disciples among the jazzmen who met and played with him at Minton's. Monk, a truly creative if not virtuoso pianist composer, has established himself as one of the seminal forces in jazz-history; and since his piano style—and implicitly his compositional style—tends to be percussive in attack, we may directly associate his achievement with the liberation of the percussion initiated by Kenny Clarke. In his piano solo *Work* (4) Monk plays with two men—Art Blakey on drums and Percy Heath on bass—who developed further Clarke's rhythmic innovations. Blakey creates an almost incessant shimmer with the stick on the top cymbal, while exploring cross rhythms and double-time on bass drum and side drum, often with authentically African complexity. He also favours the hard, sharp tone of the cymbal with rivets: a complex use of tom-toms of different pitches: a subtle percussion rubato against the melodic lines: terrific solo-engulfing crescendi: and fierce stick-shots and rim-shots on both snare-drum and cymbal. He has aimed to make the percussion player not merely an equal partner in the band's concourse, but even to make him the band's leader. Here his somewhat aggressive but imaginative style meets its match in Monk's piano playing, which can hold its own with any percussion in precision and resilience. Again, the affinity of Monk's hard, sharp piano sonority with Basie's is obvious enough; but it is Basie gone "mixed up"—strictly so, indeed, for Monk plays in a linear style in which the parts are apt to bump into one another and the harmonies do not always make sense, being per-cussive note-clusters designed to sharpen the accents. Though the sound is sometimes similar to Ives's piano writing in its deliberate lack of grammar, it is never unselfconscious, as were the early boogie players. Perhaps one could say that it is what happens to the boogie player after he has been blessed, or cursed, with "the pain of consciousness". The music is like early jazz, and unlike Ellington, in having no development, in merely going on until suddenly it stops; it is deeply rooted in the blues and in the clean piano style of a classic jazz pianist like James P. Johnson. Yet at the same time, if this is "functional" music, like old-fashioned boogie, it is also agile and nervous, and the broken, bopping lines seem the more fragmentary because of the aerated percussion and the quasi-melodic bass. One finds similar characteristics in Monk's quartet pieces. *Five Spot Blues* (5) uses all the traditional formulae of barrelhouse piano: the boogie rhythm, the teetering blue thirds, the rocking tremolos, the sharply chittering repeated chords in the treble. While these features do not lose their earthy vigour, however, they acquire a wiry resilience; and this is still more evident in a more extended piece, such as the magnificent *Bolivar Blues* (6). Monk's boogie-style opening inspires Charles Rouse's tenor sax to a Parker-like tensity in melodic arabesque; and his own single-line piano extensions bound across the beat in sextuplet and quintuplet variation, the pinging, isolated notes being occasionally reinforced by percussive minor seconds. The nervosity that complements the earthiness increases with each blues-evolution, until Monk splinters the blues-bass with upward-spurting fioriture, mostly in minor seconds and major sevenths. Each upward spurt ends, as it were, hanging in mid-air. Even when Monk starts from the compulsive energy of Latin American rhythm, as in *Bye-ya* (7), the texture turns into this nervous re-creation of barrelhouse tradition. The sharp but sonorous spacing of the telescoped dissonances in the treble here reminds us of the machine-noises in Copland's later piano works.

If there is a neurotic element in Monk's jazz, we can see how the dry, chittering texture combines with the traditional virility to enable the composer-performer to get outside his neurosis, perhaps even to laugh at it. This is why in Monk's music an ironic, even wryly satirical flavour often complements the nervous agility. This is naturally evident when he adapts pop numbers. Sometimes, as in his version of *Body and Soul* (8), the high, chittering line, the sudden breaks, the occasional missing beat, the gruff percussive bass sonorities, are more disturbing than comic in effect. At other times, as in his version of the Jerome Kern tune *The way you look tonight* (9), the effect is both comic and acidulated at the same time—especially in contrast with Ellington's more positive treatment of the pop number. The fragmentation of tune and rhythm by Monk's chippy piano and Sonny Rollins's piercing sax extract a perverse gaiety from the destruction of the tune's sentimentality: she must look pretty shocking, not shockingly pretty. Something rather similar happens in one of Monk's quartet numbers, *Nutty* (10). The nutty tune is, indeed, almost infantile; and the piano's rhythmic contradictions give it a horrid lurch. The post-Parkerian saxophonic whirls of the brilliant John Coltrane are comic but screwy; Monk's piano chorus barely controls the screwiness by way of its hard, sharp clarity, though the acute dissonance of the note-clusters hurts. The element of pain beneath the comedy indicates how Monk's anti-sentimentality does not necessarily impose an embargo on tenderness. He can create, in a piece such as *Ruby my dear* (11), a most beautiful bluesy version of Coleman Hawkins's tune, with the nostalgia of a pop number: and can make it the more touching because of the detached, apparently uninvolved texture of his piano playing. Coltrane's saxophone here complements this, for his tone and phrasing combine something of Coleman Hawkins's traditional ripeness with Lester Young's neutral but expressive reticence. Monk's most famous piece—*'Round Midnight* (12)—effects a synthesis between his nervous heat and his relaxed coolness. It is a nocturnal mood-piece, like many of Ellington's; something of Ellington's warmth remains in the haunting tune, but the sinister stalking bass and the gaunt harmonic texture introduce a late-night queasiness. The night has gone murky; and the murk swallows "revelry by night" into lonesomeness.

Perhaps Monks's most remarkable music is contained in his solo piano performances that dispense even with bass and percussion. Certainly the highly personal character of this fantasy of lonesomeness, *'Round Midnight*, finds deeper expression when he plays it by and to himself alone. The beat is present only by implication; that we sense it is a tribute to Monk's art, for the pulse is so slow that the music seems about to reach immobility. Yet the marvellously spaced, sonorously scrunchy "added note" chords, the metallic, percussive acciaciaturas, the very high and very low tremolos, the self-communing chromaticism of the inner parts, are all tense, and the nervosity is reinforced by the sharp tone that Monk's piano technique extracts from the instrument: he plays with stiff—splayed out, not rounded—fingers. The solo piano version of *'Round Midnight* "lets in the silence" much more than does the ensemble version; the tension is increased because we are aware of the emptiness that surrounds it. There is a feeling of screwed-up expectancy; the music might, we suspect, break down at any moment, or it might explode into heaven or hell knows what. In fact, it does neither; it simply goes on until it stops. It owes its considerable emotional impact partly to the frustration it generates, partly to the fact that this frustration is accepted with "a kind of furious calm". This effect becomes still odder when Monk improvises on a standard pop number such as *I'm getting sentimental over you* (13) or Irving Berlin's *All alone* (14). The immensely slow pulse and the rhythmic hiatuses are not here ironic in effect, any more than are the sudden Tatum-like spurts of fioriture. The music moves like a bird with a broken wing; the pathos is that of the maimed creature, quite distinct from the self-induced sentiment of the pop originals.

In *I should care* (15) Monk carries this separation of the nervous agility of the component elements from the slowness of the pulse to almost pathological lengths, pressing down each note as though its disturbance of the silence is an agony: the denial of the beat seems a little frightening, because perverse. Yet if we put this piece beside the long, extremely beautiful slow blues *Functional* (16) we can see how the modern and the traditional elements in Monk's music are complementary. Here the pulse, slow though it is, is still present, along with the traditional boogie rhythm, the glinting tremolos, the reiterated chords, the percussive blue notes, false relations and note-clusters. All these elements seem, however, separated in space and time, surrounded by silence; and the passion and the silence are in perfect equilibrium. We can note here a characteristic that, in jazz terms, complements an effect we have observed in Copland's music; and we can also see that the simultaneous tension and relaxation in Monk's work may be related to the two main strands in Modern Jazz, epitomized in the playing of two great improvising instrumentalists, Charlie Parker and Miles Davis. In this chapter we shall be concerned with the tension, reserving the relaxation—and its implications in reference to jazz composition—for the chapter that follows.

Though for a time Charlie Parker and Miles Davis played together, and though they continued to admire one another's work, they were not temperamentally disposed to do their best in consort. The first phase of Modern Jazz was, indeed, not so much a revival of the chamber ensemble in place of the big band as a recrudescence of the soloist. As we have seen in considering Monk's solo piano playing, Man-alone tries to break the remorseless beat of Time, the clatter and bustle of a material world; and although this lonely assertiveness may sometimes be comic in effect—as in the relatively extrovert art of Dizzy Gillespie, whose virtuosity takes the breath away, inducing the nervous giggle—it finds its creative justification in Monk and in the tragic art of Charlie Parker. We may see the trumpeter Gillespie and the saxophonist Parker as complementary figures in the mythology of Modern Jazz. Gillespie was the Clown whose protest against a world that rejects him can be both a show-off and a show-down. His ability to ex-hibit, not in-hibit, his passion through the fantastic pyrotechnics of his trumpet playing at once fulfils his animal vitality and becomes a slightly desperate assertion of superiority over us, who are left to gasp; it is not an accident that Gillespie is one of the few Modern Jazzmen whose domestic and social life is fairly "normal". Parker, on the other hand, was the Tragic Fool whose protest against the society that rejected him was a pathologically extravagant assertion of his own individuality against the Rest. To assert his livingness he would eat, drink, sleep, fornicate, drug, experience more than twenty ordinary mortals, and would be prepared to take the consequences. Gillespie could find freedom in a dizzy game; Parker could find freedom only in death. His life was a *passionate* act of self-destruction: while his music was, in a different sense, an attempt at the destruction of the Self which, as man, he flaunted before the conventionalized stereotypes of the world.

Listen to him in *Slam-Slam Blues* (17), in which Slam Stewart's melodic bass, accompanied by vocal croaks, hums and grunts, serves to establish an atmosphere of self-communing: into which Parker injects a solo line that is broken, wild, wandering, giving to saxophone tone a savagery it had never known previously, yet changing momently to a murmuring tenderness. Always he speaks to himself, without audience. The fantastic virtuosity of his roulades is an outlet for suppressed passion, tense, breathless, yet—like Monk's music, only more so—therapeutic: a release of suffering, a tragic complement to Gillespie's comedy. Parker is the supreme master of the nervous 'forties, as Armstrong had been the master of the roaring 'twenties. In principle he is an old-style improvising soloist, but the difference between his music and that of any earlier soloist lies in his concern with shifting accents within small note-values that, in earlier jazz, would have been regarded as decorative passage-work. The "expressivity" of his music moves at a phenomenally rapid pace, as compared with traditional jazz; and in this particular he has affinities with the development in European art-music that was (contemporaneously) associated with Boulez, Stockhausen and Nono. In both cases the extreme rapidity of the expressive figuration involves a slowing down of the basic rhythmic-harmonic pulse: a veering towards an Oriental passivity, which alone can sustain so highly wrought a tension. In the very complexity of its energy, the flexibility of Parker's line, with its "numerical" rhythms and cross-accents and hiatuses, "breaks the Time barrier".

Parker's roots in tradition are, however, almost always evident, and he once said that the new, young jazzmen who were so eager to imitate him would never get anywhere if they neglected their birth-right, the blues. In *Parker's Mood* (18) we can see how his re-creation makes the blue passion nervously exacerbated; the pitch-distorted cries are broken, the wriggles agonized as well as ecstatic, the tone usually hard, the movement serpentine, full of self-contradictions yet never incoherent. The blue spirit survives in that the pain is also a release: we experience Parker's roulades against the background of John Lewis's still, dead-pan piano, and the comparatively gentle hiss of percussion. *Yardbird Suite* (19) shows a similar quality, now incorporated into the solo line itself. The chord-changes somewhere at the back of this number are those of a pop song, "I want to be happy!" Something of its slightly inane innocence comes over in almost Ellington-like style, but the ferocity of Parker's lashing arabesques contrasts weirdly with the wistfulness. The "recognition of other modes of experience that are possible" is certainly evident, though the effect is too strange to be described as witty. Parker's improvisations on pop numbers are, indeed, seldom ironic in effect, as Monk's may be. In *Hot House* (20), for instance, he improvises with fantastic rhythmic complexity and ambiguity on Cole Porter's "What is this thing called love?" The variations, being on the chord changes, do not reflect ironically on the tune, which is scarcely recognizable; they are, however, a most disturbing comment on the question that is the tune's title. Parker's destruction of the tune, when he works with pop music standards, usually means that he can adhere, whatever the basic material, to the spirit and technique of the blues, while finding stimulation in the slightly less rudimentary chord sequences which the pop numbers offer him.

Though blues-derived, most of Parker's numbers are very fast: not with the orgiastic fulfilment of Armstrong, but with a furious despera-tion wherein the art—the balance and contrast of the ever-mutable phrases—just prevents the fury from becoming hysteria. A marvellous example is *Bird gets the Worm* (21) wherein Parker's reedy, anguished tone is highlighted in contrast with Miles Davis's muted trumpet, which mutes the anger as well as the sonority. The tension is increased by the "throw-away" manner; and again the piece has a minimum of harmony and no beginning, middle and end. Again, in *Chasing the Bird* (22) we have a fascinating revival of jazz heterophony in that instead of a unison opening there is a strange, non-harmonic canon between Parker and Davis, broken and distraught, like a twentieth-century version of a medieval hocquet or hiccup. Dissonant heterophony reaches a climax in *Koko* (23), and is dependent on the polyrhythms inherent in the wild virtuosity of Parker's lines. The intuitive and implied harmonic complexities spring from the shifting accents of the eighth notes, which are taken, very fast, as the unit. When, towards the end of *Koko*, Parker and Davis play in parallel thirds the effect, within the dissonant-linear texture, is oddly pathetic. The thirds—which ever since the Renaissance have been associated with man's awareness of his humanity—sound little and lost amid the asphalt jungle's frenzy. There's a similar effect in *Moose the Mooche* (24), where the screwy distortion of the line explodes finally in a disruption of tonality. In *Chichi* (25) we can appreciate how Parker's conception of line and rhythm —wherein the quick-flickering phrases make their own logic as they ride over the beat and the implied harmony—directly affected Percy Heath's handling of the bass's pizzicato, and even Max Roach's quiveringly nervous, if high-powered, mastery of percussion. As Roach has said: "Bird was really responsible, not just because his style called for a particular style of drumming, but because he set the tempos so fast it was impossible to play on a straight, Cozy Cole, four style. So we had to work out variations." No doubt it took a musician of Roach's sensitivity to respond thus creatively; it is interesting that Roach recognized that the fury of Parker's line was also a desperate assertion of love: "He had a *secret* love life. He would get that loving sound that would come out of his horn. Everything else is incidental to one thing, and that is that Bird contributed more and received less than anybody."

Even when Parker played ensemble music it tended to be unisonal in principle, like the very earliest jazz. It could hardly have been otherwise, since his lines were so complex that the human ear and nervous system could not keep pace with more than one at a time. Even the most experienced jazzmen, indeed, found Parker's musical ideas difficult to "get", and Ross Russell tells us that at the notorious "*Relaxin' at Carmarillo*" session, just before Bird's nervous breakdown, the highly competent jazzmen were completely incapable of cottoning on to a thematic idea that Parker had scribbled on a bit of paper. This being so, it is not surprising that some of his most remarkable solos are in fact monodic, over an Oriental drone; *A Night in Tunisia* (26) (to which the eastern title was added as an afterthought) is a marvellous example, and it is interesting that Parker's playing here inspires Gillespie to remarkable imaginative—not merely stratospheric—heights. Yet while Parker was essentially a jazz improviser, his improvisation, being so complex, involved more "compositional" elements than did that of Louis Armstrong. He made careful sketches of melodic ideas prompted by given chord changes, and in playing from that basis made use not only of his inventiveness, but also of his phenomenally quick and retentive musical memory. In this connection the remarks of Earl "Fatha" Hines, in whose band Charlie played for a time, are worth noting:

> Charlie used to take his alto in the theatre between shows—and have an exercise book—that's all he did—sit down; between he and Dizzie, they ran over those exercises in these books they're studying up. One day they'd have the trumpet book and another day they'd have the alto book, they'd change around. And I think that where Charlie got his particular style from was the different inversions and phrases in those exercises he had. They'd insert these passages that they would play in tunes that would come up. Whenever a chord would strike them, with the memories both of them had, why they'd just strike up one of these passages from one of these exercises and insert them in one of these tunes. And I think that was the reason for them to create the style that they got. . . .
>
> And then all the musicians wanted to find out how fast they could get over that horn, listening to Charles. But you see, many of them made so many mistakes because they didn't realize this was *music* he was playing. They thought it was just out of his mind, so whatever they did was all the same as Charlie. . . . But Charlie knew what he was playing, and when he made those flatted fifths and what have you, it was written in those exercises, and Charlie was playing what he actually remembered from those exercises.

It is interesting, moreover, that Parker, aware that his improvisation involved intuitive composition, resented that fact that he had to make his living in cabaret and dance hall. He desperately wanted his art to be appreciated by people who were more capable of understanding some of its qualities than were the people with whom he habitually consorted. Edgard Varèse tells touchingly of how Parker "stopped by my place a number of times. He was like a child, with the shrewdness of a child. He'd come in and exclaim, 'Take me as you would a baby, and teach me music. I only write in one voice. I want to have structure. I want to write orchestral scores. I'll give you any amount you wish. I make a lot of money. I'll be your servant. I'm a good cook." I left for Europe and told him to call me up after Easter when I would be back. Charlie died before Easter. He spoke of being tired of the environment his work relegated him to, 'I'm so steeped in this and can't get out,' he said." Structure of an orthodox kind would have been useless to Bird, but his instinct was right in seeing that there was more composition in the improvisations he made on the fragments of tunes he jotted down in cabs, on his way to a recording session, than in the tunes themselves; and that he should have realized that Varèse, among "art" composers, might have something to teach him about the kind of structure that *would* be relevant testifies to his genius. His tragic division between two worlds was, as it were, a projection of his schizophrenia—of what the Bellevue Hospital report described clinically as "high average intelligence, a hostile, evasive personality with manifestations of primitive and sexual fantasies associated with hostility, and gross evidence of paranoid thinking and suicidal tendencies". Always a lone wolf, in every sense, he created an artefact out of his neurosis; yet the heart of his frustration was that the Beat Generation he sang for could but haltingly understand what he had to say. His music gave him the release from isolation that alcohol, sex and heroin could not lastingly offer; and perhaps the drugs triumphed because the beauty of the music was too scarifying to be finally accepted. "Everyone" tried to play like Charlie, who with Armstrong is perhaps the only jazz instrumentalist to whom the word genius seems appropriate. No one succeeded, because few could approach his technique, and those who could lacked his Blake-like quality of "terrifying honesty". It was easy enough to agree with him when he said "music is your own experience . . . if you don't live it, it won't come out of your horn"; it was more difficult to follow him when, admitting the full implications of this remark, he went on to add that there can be "no boundary line to art". The final tragic irony of Parker's parable-like career came at the funeral service. The Rev. David Licorish, orating over the corpse, said that Parker had been put into the world "to make people happy [!] and that if he were alive today he would say to his colleagues that it was time to be up and doing, because life is not an empty dream". The organist played Sir Arthur Sullivan's *The Lost Chord*, and the Rev. Licorish read "those old words about the search for the chord that sounded like the Last Amen".

Charlie Parker never found any lost chord. He accepted the traditional chord sequences; and his melodic honesty pierced through the pretences we have tried to live by in our machine-dominated world, annihilating with his rage the Rev. Licorish and his kind, absolving them with his love. "Sure," he once said, "civilization is a damned good thing; why doesn't somebody try it?" For all his influence on others his art is as forbiddingly lonely as that of Varèse, whom he admired more than any modern musician. Yet although no instrumentalist has achieved Bird's tragic intensity, there are fine players among those who, in various ways, have tried to copy him. We have met with Sonny Rollins in duo with Monk; on tenor, not alto, sax he has a technique hardly inferior to Parker's and, especially when he plays with Max Roach, can achieve a Parker-like febrility. In *Ee-ah* (27) he plays a fast blues built on a reiterated three-note figure. His tone is harsh, searing and blasting like microtonal motor-horns whipping in roulades that are consistently violent. The obsessive neurosis is authentic enough, although it is without the lyrical passion that Parker manages to distil from frenzy. This is why some of Rollins's best numbers tend towards irony—as we have seen in his slightly cruel treatment of *The way you look tonight*. This kind of effect is not, however, restricted to his adaptations of pop numbers. In *B Swift* (28) he transforms Parkerian frenzy-arabesques into a comic hysteria, aided by some particularly ecstatic "melodic" drumming by Max Roach. Occasionally, as in *Blue 7* (29), Rollins achieves a Parker-like intensity by way of true melodic variation, rather than improvisation on chord changes. This impressive piece explores, with evolutionary consistency, the melodic permutations of only two basic intervals, the tritone and the major third (which would sometimes be more accurately notated as a diminished fourth).

The pianist Bud Powell—like Parker, a highly disorganized and anguished character—has tried to discover a complement to Parker's line on the keyboard instrument: a difficult, if not impossible task, since equal temperament cannot lend itself to Parkerian subtleties. He did, however, create a new, excitingly tense sound in exploiting wildly cascading, brittle right-hand figurations against a fiercely stamping bass: as we can see in *Wee* (30), wherein his virtuosity is counterpointed against Gillespie's dizzy trumpet. That this tornado hides passional depths is suggested by *Meandering* (31), one of his infrequent slow numbers: a blues that is relaxed, as the title implies, yet at the same time harmonically acid. Lennie Tristano, a conservatory trained musician, has attempted something like a fusion of Parker's line with Monk's piano texture. His music is most interesting when closest to the blues, as in *Requiem* (32), after the slightly pretentious Debussian introduction: least convincing when it imposes Parker-like complexities of filigree on a sentimental tune such as "These foolish things." Here, perhaps, academic know-how gets in the way of creation; there is a separation between the impetus and the "treatment", as there never is with Parker. Cecil Taylor—another academically trained Negro musician who says he derives from Ellington, Monk, Bud Powell and Parker—has taken the bold step of creating a polyphonic texture in which all the lines attempt a Parker-like complexity. *Nona's Blues* (33) for instance, is basically a twelve-bar blues on the usual chord sequence. The tempo is furious, the drive dynamic, as the solo parts create heterophony that seeks only the minimum of harmonic congruity. The effect is wild and primitive, the sonority of the melody instruments being distinctly Asiatic in feeling, over the African voodoo rhythm. Sometimes the saxophone skirls and the piano's percussive note-clusters boil over in a crazy sizzling: the effect is comparable both with David Tudor's playing of graph pieces and with Charlie Mingus's *Lock 'em Up* (34)—a jazz stunt piece that reproduces the chaotic howls of the asylum. While the sonority that Taylor creates is startling, its violence defeats its own ends. *Mixed* (35), for instance, is a mixed-up love song that begins with slow, soupy piano chords, only for the pop number style to be destroyed by wildly contrary moods and vehement note-clusters; *Pots* (36) is a piece of primitive voodooism that grows gradually screwier, off beat, off chord, off key over the remorseless drumming, until it reaches complete disintegration. We can see that it combines primitive frenzy with the tortured modern mind; but unlike Parker's music—and like the Mingus piece—it is a gimmick rather than an experience. Forty years after *The Rite of Spring* it comes too late.

Cecil Taylor's music falls between the stools of improvisation and composition. If it were improvised, it would need a genius of Parker's calibre on each instrument, and would then be too much for the human ear and nerves to assimilate; as composition, however, it is defeated by its *wilful* primitivism. Perhaps it is significant that the first musician who has carried further some of the implications of Parker's line and rhythm should be entirely self-taught and musically unlettered (though he has recently taken lessons with Gunther Schuller). Certainly it is not an accident that Ornette Coleman has achieved this stylistic development by paring harmonic texture to a minimum: by discarding the piano as harmony instrument and exploring, more radically than Sonny Rollins, melodic variation on line, not on chord sequence. "I know exactly what I'm doing," he has said:

I'm beginning where Charlie Parker stopped. My melodic approach is based on phrasing, and my phrasing is an extension of how I hear the intervals and pitch of the tune I play. There is no end to pitch. You can play flat in tune and sharp in tune. It's a question of vibration. My phrasing is spontaneous, not a style. A style happens when your phrasing hardens. Jazz is the only music in which the same note can be played night after night but differently each time. It's the hidden things, the subconscious that lies in the body and lets you know: you feel this, you play this.

So Coleman scores for himself on alto sax, with Donald Cherry as a somewhat subservient but responsive, bird-like cornet, Charlie Haden on bass both plucked and bowed, and Billy Higgins on drums. The percussion player seems to have an instinctive understanding of the principles of Asiatic—as well as primitive African—drumming, and his complex, timeless pattern-making is the eternity against which the cries of Coleman's sax become apprehensible. This melodic line comes as close to surrealism as jazz has approached. In a quick number such as *Eventually* (37) or *Free* (38) the sax chuckles, gibbers, wails, howls, gurgles—like a bird, an animal, a baby, a man or woman in fear or distress or sudden joy. The variety of tone colour that Coleman achieves —whereby his horn becomes the multifarious voices of Nature—is remarkable; and the emptiness of the texture, the breaks in the line and the sudden silences, make Nature's creatures (including Coleman and us) seem at once passionate and forlorn, against the immensity of time and space. This becomes still more disturbing in slow numbers such as *Lonely Woman* (39). Here, against the eternal background of the "Oriental" percussion, sax and cornet begin chanting together a wild, reiterated phrase. The parts are usually dissonantly heterophonic, like very early New Orleans funeral music, but intermittently they come together to create concordant thirds: the effect is a weird extension of the famous thirds at the end of Charlie Parker's *Koko*. The sax line grows more madly contorted as the piece goes on, but with an odd, almost desperate irony the thirds return. In a still slower number, *Peace* (40), we can see how Coleman's primitivism, unlike Taylor's, derives from traditional jazz experience. The spirit is that of the blues, though the beat is broken (there are prolonged silences), the line fragmented, the harmony disguised or non-existent. The string bass plays—in wailing pizzicato glissandi and then in sepulchral bowed tones—an extraordinary unaccompanied solo, like the everlasting hum of the turning earth; and against this solo and the empty air that the drums open up, the solo line—chirruping like a bird, howling like an animal, sobbing like a woman, chanting like an angel—nurtures the pulse of life as best it may. The "peace", it would seem, is to be found only in the silence.

There are similar effects in *Ramblin'* (41), another blues-derived number with a mysteriously solitary bass solo, and in *Face of the Brass* (42), in which Haden's instrument, both plucked and bowed, sounds like a country-blues singer's guitar reverberating in a vast, empty cavern. Indeed, the music frequently reminds us of the primitive roots of the blues in the field hollers, as well as of the more neurotic development of blues singing by Robert Johnson. If we listen to Coleman's music after *Wild Ox Moan*, or Robert Johnson's *Hellhound on my Trail*, it is as though the age-old, instinctive cry of loneliness is not changed, merely deepened, by our awareness of "civilization" and the big city. We are reminded of Charlie Parker's words; it would certainly seem that civilization has not been "tried", or if tried has been ineffectual. It is pertinent to note that Coleman was born in Texas and has worked mostly on the West Coast, especially in Los Angeles. He himself has likened his improvisational composing processes (in which all the basic tunes are his own) to the painting of Jackson Pollock; and there is a clear affinity between his music and the vocal pieces (such as "She is asleep") of another West Coast musician, John Cage. We have related the silence in Monk's music to that in the music of Copland; similarly Coleman's silence may be related to the more radical conception of Cage. In *Free Jazz* (43) Coleman has worked with his own group plus Scott LaFaro on bass, Ed Blackwell on drums, Freddie Hubbard on trumpet and Eric Dolphy on bass clarinet, in an attempt to achieve complete improvisational spontaneity, without "theme", chordal bass or rhythmic structure. The resultant heterophonic, polyrhythmic hubbub may be directly compared with Cage's *Concert*, though the existence of the jazz beat renders the noise frantic rather than relaxed. The extreme (Parker-derived) rapidity of the melismata also relates the music to *avant-garde* developments in straight music—for instance, Boulez and Stockhausen and the Carter of the Double Concerto. All these manifestations tend to sound, to Western ears, excessively long, and the thirty-six minutes of Coleman's freedom seem interminable, despite the exciting aural incidents in which they abound. There would seem to be a basic conflict between the "corporeality" of jazz's nature and so complete a liberation from the shackles of time and mortality. Listening to this cataclysmic protest against Time one understands, at least, why Cage and Feldman have been necessary.

Perhaps only one young player, John Coltrane, has explored the most "far out" regions investigated by Coleman with complete spontaneity and emotional conviction. He started comparatively mildly, as a collaborator with Monk and Miles Davis; but in his recent work, such as *Out of this World* (44), he plays with post-Parker- and post-Coleman-like fury against piano, bass and percussion which generate tremendous orgiastic frenzy through the regular repetition of rhythmic patterns and chord sequences that are in themselves highly complex. The repetitions counteract the complexity, demolishing the temporal sense: and inspire Coltrane to melismatic arabesques which are, if anything, even more fantastically convoluted than those of Coleman. In effect, they are also more primitive, recalling not only field hollers and Asiatic music, but African ritual music itself. Coltrane's sax tone is consistently hard and harsh, without the varied coloration of Parker or Coleman, and this quality intensifies the "ritualistic" savagery of the music. When the remarkable pianist McCoy Tyner takes over, he comes as close as he can, on an equal-tempered piano, to Coltrane's abandon. Again, his chord changes, beneath the spilling and spurting fioriture, are often quite abstruse, but are rendered hypnotic through repetition. The reiteration of pattern makes us wait, breath-less, in mingled hope and dread, for the re-emergence of Coltrane's saxophonic yell. When finally it comes it provides the improvisation with a true coda, for the asymmetrical rhythms and pitch distortions go crazy until the music ends in the only way it could end—with an explosion. The pretence of control is finally abandoned; though its having been implicit during the piece explains why Coltrane's music has such authentic potency. The effect is not noticeably different even on the rare occasions when Coltrane plays in slower tempo, as in *Soul Eyes* (45). Even here the strident, unrelenting tone of the opening solo prepares us for the near-chaos that is to ensue.

Coltrane and Coleman would seem to represent the ultimate in the rediscovery of the wildness within the heart, which has only been exacerbated by the asphalt jungle. It is difficult to see how they can go much further in this direction; obviously their frenzy and loneliness, which further intensify the frenzy and loneliness of Parker, could not hope to come to terms with the world in the same way as Armstrong's exuberance and protest had led to Ellington. Several attempts were made to accommodate post-Parkerian wildness to the simpler, more animated rhythms of traditional jazz—for instance by Gigi Gryce, a trained Negro musician who was a pupil of Hovhaness in the States, and of Honegger in Europe. The compromise could not succeed, for the hectic line of post-Parkerian improvisation could not submit to an affirmative rhythm without destroying its nature; maybe the manner of Gryce and similar groups was christened "funky" not only because it was traditionally earthy, but also because it funked Parker's "terrifying honesty". If Parker, or Coleman, or Coltrane could not be accommodated to classical jazz, still less could they seek a compromise with pop music and the assumptions of a commercialized world. Some element of composition had none the less to be achieved, if the pressure was to be withstood. To some extent this is observable in the work of the bass player and composer, Charlie Mingus: for while he has, as a traditional jazzman, stated that "jazz by its very definition cannot be held down to written parts", he has made, as a trained musician, a deliberate attempt both to extend and to organize improvisatory variation. Thus whereas *Profile of Jackie* (46) reveals—despite the complex, quasi-Oriental percussion—how deeply Mingus's music is centred in the traditional blues, *Love Chant* (47) makes an interesting, if not altogether successful, move towards "extended form". It is based on a standard set of chord changes and rhythmic patterns or riffs, but these changes and patterns are enormously slowed down, so that there is room for stretches of purely linear variation. The "changes" are first heard in very slow, sustained notes: which the soloists "divide" into smaller note-values on a principle analogous to the seventeenth-century technique of divisions on a ground. Periodically the slow, sustained notes return in rondo fashion; but the divisions get progressively wilder and more heterophonic. If the design is Western, the slowness of the pulse and of the linear evolution is Eastern; and the two worlds do not quite come to terms.

More successful is *Pithecanthropus Erectus* (48), which uses evolutionary jazz-variation to describe the cycle of human life. The beautiful sustained sonority of the opening evokes, incantatorily, the void from which life springs; the soloists utter primitive heterophonic howls and screeches—the chatter of the jungle's monkeys, the scream of her parrots. The lines become more modally formed as they evolve, until man reaches his (relative) maturity in the urban blues. His "erect" state does not last long, however; the blues disintegrates into the music of the *asphalt* jungle, which is perhaps savager and more chaotic than the original verdant one. The monkey's gibber and the parrot's screech return, with more frenetic desperation. The piece ends with a recapitulation of the sustained tones of the void; and the cycle presumably starts

again. Though this music is highly effective, it is a little too simple to
be true. The Parkerian frenzy cannot be as easily placed as that; and it
would seem that Mingus can present it in these terms only because he is
an extremely fine comic, rather than tragic, artist. We noted this in the
literalism of his piece about the madhouse (*Lock 'em Up*); another
example is *A Foggy Day* (49), which exploits with comic realism the
noises of big-city life, without attempting to transmute them (as does
Varèse) into art.

So Mingus's music does not really suggest an alternative development to that of Parker, Coleman and Coltrane; it merely exists at a
less intense (though enlivening and entertaining), level. An alternative tradition had, however, evolved with men who had originally
played with Parker, and notably with Miles Davis, whose "cool"
jazz was music for a minority in which the players could still be
against the world, while belonging to one another. Parker, despite
the throw-away technique which gave to his playing "a kind of furious
calm", had been anything but cool, and Davis, playing with him, in
awe of his genius, had sometimes ineffectually tried to emulate his
fervour. Perhaps only Parker's early death enabled Davis to come into
his own: to create a more integrated—arranged or composed—
chamber-music texture which is relaxed, yet at the same time preserves
jazz's fundamental tension. His "cool" music never approaches the
excitement of the startling heterophonic canon that, in *Chasin' the Bird*,
he played with Parker; but the control does discipline something, the
nervosity of line and rhythm spring against the lucidity of the proportions, the mellowness of the sonority. Davis does not run away from
the latent hysteria, however uninvolved in it he may be, or seem to be.
To his work, and the composing tradition that springs from it, we must
turn in the next chapter.

VII

From jazz back to art. Modern jazz and the improvising composer: Miles Davis and Gil Evans; Gerry Mulligan and John Lewis

He grew up by the sea
on a hot island
inhabited by negroes—mostly.

There he built himself
a boat and a separate room
close to the water
for a piano on which he practised. . . .

Thence he was driven
out of Paradise.

WILLIAM CARLOS WILLIAMS

Vistas
of delight waking suddenly
before a cheated world.

WILLIAM CARLOS WILLIAMS

The cult of the Cool must of its nature involve order, control, and therefore composition, of a more "externalized" form than was manifest in Parker's subtly organized but intuitive heat. This is evident, when once Miles Davis has freed himself from Parker, even in Davis's most directly improvisational playing. We are told that his record *Kind of Blue* (1) consists entirely of first takes, with a minimum of preparation; it sounds like extremely ordered composition, partly because the basic material—both melodic phrases and chord changes—is so simple. In *So What* (2) there is a cool, Debussian prelude, with many parallel triads, followed by a long riff built on the verbal inflection of the shoulder-shrugging title phrase. This builds up expectation: which is fulfilled when the trumpet solo takes over, for although this is muted and "throw-away" in style, it gradually reveals an inner tension which the riff does not have. In a sense, that is, the solo contradicts the title; and that is true also of John Coltrane's nasally insinuating sax solo. *Blue in Green* (3) has a bass line with a lovely melodic curve and a quietly seductive ostinato thythm. Davis's muted trumpet plays the blue tune with the gentlest sighs and most intimately repeated speaking notes, so that we realize that he is a later, wearier, but no less lyrical successor to the nostalgia of a Johnny Dodds or a Sidney Bechet. Beneath and around the melody, Bill Evans's soft piano chords grow increasingly scrunchy and bitter-sweet; and as the piano's false relations dissolve away in the long-winding modalism of the trumpet line the music creates a big-city mood, while seeming at the same time immeasurably old. The sorrow within it, digging deep, frequently reminds us of the melancholy of Spanish flamenco. In *Blue in Green*—and still more in *All Blues* (4), in *Flamenco Sketches* (5), and in the later series of pieces directly inspired by Miles's visit to Spain—the fervent yet quiet modal arabesques and the pitch distortions link the sorrow of twentieth-century urban man to the centuries-old sorrow of a civilization grown hoary. The New World admits to its emotional exhaustion; and the flamenco flavour gives to the nostalgia an epic quality that releases it from mawkishness. In *Blue in Green*, beautiful though it is, the warmly enveloping piano chords imbue the trumpet's wandering melody with a brooding, somewhat enervating, introversion. In the later *Solea* (from *Sketches of Spain*) (6) the solitary desolation is no longer self-regarding. It has the tragic quality of flamenco music itself, transplanted to the urban metropolis; and the solo trumpet is here accompanied mainly by ostinato riffs, by drone chords, and by non-harmonic percussion. This development towards "objectivity" is significant, though *Blue in Green* remains the more representatively jazzy, and perhaps for us the more poignant, piece.

It is interesting to note what happens when Davis plays numbers derived directly from the "tense" strand of Modern Jazz. He makes Monk's *'Round Midnight* (7) much more seductive than Monk's own versions: partly because of Philly Joe Jones's insidious ostinato on percussion, partly because of his own flamenco-blue style, and partly because of the tone of John Coltrane's sax, which at this date had something of the ripeness of Coleman Hawkins, and something of the refined expressivity of Lester Young, but little of Parker's nervosity. When he plays Parker's own number *Ah Leu Cha* (8) Davis keeps it very quick, but remains unfrenzied. It becomes almost gay, like a fiddle-dance or square dance taking place in the Big City; and the complex counter-rhythms and glissando whines are always lyrical, wistful rather than hectic. In his early days, when he played with Parker and Gillespie, Davis was reproved for not being as dizzy as Dizzy. Now we can see that his talents tended from the start in a different direction: which is not less impressive, though it is, in every sense, more composed.

For whereas Parker's genius was expressed almost exclusively through creative improvisation as a soloist, Davis's work has always involved close co-operation with composing "arrangers" who had the talent to give him the material that would stimulate his improvisatory faculties. Both Davis himself and the arranger John Carisi are professionally trained musicians, and the interrelationship between the jazzboy and the Juilliard man may be inaugurating a new phase in musical history. In *Israel* (9), for instance, Carisi cunningly produces a composed-arranged blues with an archaic-modal flavour that is obviously suited to Davis's style of improvisation. The harmonic texture is dissonant and slightly dislocated, like Parker's melodic improvisation: quintuplet rhythms push against the beat, and the vagaries of tonality undermine the grave Dorian tune. Yet the fact that the melody is consistently modal (so that the blue notes are no longer exceptional, and are therefore more relaxed) gives the piece a solemn, even liturgical flavour, similar to that which we have commented on in Davis's free improvisation. Even the virtuosity is comparatively "easy", more reminiscent of Lester Young than of Parker's intensity; this makes the polytonal explosion at the end more, not less, impressive. It is a venomous threat to the music's hymnic character, and in retrospect we become aware that there has been a hint of threat throughout: which is what gives the music its power to disturb. None the less, the point lies in the fact that the players remain quiet, cool, even while the threat is manifest through them. Certainly the beautifully fresh yet mellow sonority is part of the ambiguity; "dirty" jazz tone has gone, and the brass voices are almost vibrato-less.

Move (10) is another piece with a chorale-like trombone melody, modal in contour. Virtuoso solos—with Parker-like displaced accents, though comparatively relaxed—whirl against the melody in a moto perpetuo. Against the *move* of the solos, John Lewis's piano chords are almost moveless: still and trance-like. Though Davis's solos here are more like Parker, being quivery and broken, their tone is gentle; and one finds a parallel relaxation in the piece's structure. Being arranged and harmonized music, these pieces have as much in common with

Ellington as with Parker: but compared with those of Ellington the arrangements of John Lewis and Gil Evans—who has become Davis's principal associate—are far less "classical" and symmetrical. In *Boplicity* (11), for instance, Lewis breaks away from the sixteen-bar tyranny, elides the introductory theme with the first chorus, and inserts additional bridge passages in polyphony. As a result the complicated solo paraphrases do not need to fight against the beat and the structural simplicity of the tune. For all their complexity, they may attain a quality of emotion recollected in tranquillity. This becomes explicit in Evans's *Moondreams* (12), a mood piece that has drifted further from jazz than any of Ellington's atmospheric numbers. The bird noises are fascinating, the sonority magical, and the brief nightmare episode just saves the music from a relaxation so extreme that it would be flabby.

Gil Evans, who has brought Davis's intuitions to artistic realization, is a man of an older generation than Davis; and although so expertly professional, is paradoxically a self-taught musician whose training has been largely empirical. As a boy he listened to the noises of the world around him, including motor-cars; as a young man he listened to recordings of the great jazzmen; as a professional orchestrator, working for show-business and radio, he used his acute ears to experiment in sound-creation. So the relationship between Miles Davis and Gil Evans inverts the habitual interdependence: the jazzman has some conservatory training, while the expert arranger is the empiricist. Evans has modestly stated that the kind of sonority we associate with him was not in fact his invention, but that of Claude Thornhill, with whom he worked in California. Even then, he has said:

> Claude had a unique way with a dance band. He'd use the trombones for instance, with the woodwinds in a way that would give them a horn sound. . . . I think he was the first among the pop or jazz bands to evolve that sound. Someone once said, by the way, that Claude was the only man who could play the piano without vibrato. Claude was the first leader to use French horns as a functioning part of a dance band. That distant, haunting, no-vibrato sound came to be blended with the reed and brass sections in various combinations. . . . A characteristic voicing for the Thornhill band was what often happened in ballads. There was a French horn lead, one or sometimes two French horns playing in unison or a duet depending on the character of the melody. The clarinet doubled the melody, also playing the lead. Below were two altos, a tenor and a baritone, or two altos and two tenors. The bottom was normally a double on the melody by baritone or tenor. The reed section sometimes went very low with the saxes being forced to play in a subtone and very soft. In essence, at first, the sound of the band was

almost a reduction to an inactivity of music, to a stillness. Everything—
melody, harmony, rhythm—was moving at minimum speed. . . .
Everything was lowered to create a sound, and nothing was to be used
to distract from that sound. The sound hung like a cloud. But once this
stationary effect, this sound, was created, it was ready to have other
things added to it. The sound itself can only hold interest for a certain
length of time. Then you have to make certain changes within that
sound; you have to make personal use of harmonies, rather than work
with traditional ones; there has to be more movement in the melody;
more dynamics, more syncopation; speeding up of the rhythms. For me,
I had to make those changes. . . . I would say that the sound was made
ready to be used by other forces in music. I did not create the sound;
Claude did. I did more or less match up with the sound the different
movements by people like Lester, Charlie and Dizzy in which I was
interested. It was their rhythmic and harmonic revolutions that had influenced me. I liked both aspects and put them together. . . . Those
elements were around, looking for each other.

So what Evans inherited from Thornhill was the sound of the band
that "calmed down the overall mood, but made everyone feel very
relaxed"; what he added was movement, which is life itself. It is
interesting that this most sensitive musician should have been self-
trained in the world of pop music: still more interesting that he should
have collaborated with one of the loneliest exponents of a Modern Jazz
that has consciously withdrawn from the commercial world: and most
interesting of all that Evans and Davis should have achieved their
finest work together by reaching out to pop music—not in order to
satirize it, but in order to embrace and to re-create it. Admittedly,
Gershwin's *Porgy and Bess* is pop music of unusual kind and quality;
yet it was the intuition of exceptional talent that enabled Evans
and Davis to realize that what they had to say and what Gershwin
had to say were intimately related. Their *Porgy and Bess* pieces (13)
stand, with the best of the later Ellington, as the most distinguished
music that has as yet been created through the historically significant
merging of the traditions of jazz, pop, and art music.

Though the pieces are art of a considerable degree of sophistication,
they do not destroy the popular appeal of Gershwin's tunes; at the
same time they uncover jazz roots of which Gershwin was probably unconscious. Thus "Gone, Gone, Gone" is a deeply moving instrumental
re-creation of the antiphonal lament of a Negro burial; Davis's pentatonic, pitch-distorted solo trumpet becomes the preacher's cry against
the dark, massed sonority of the communal voices, in which the interweaving of saxes and French horns creates an almost neurasthenically

oppressive effect. The unrelated triads of Gershwin's accompaniment prove harmonically and colouristically stimulating to Evans, melodically stimulating to Davis. In "Gone" the same disruptive harmonic motive lets loose a quick fantasy for solo percussion, relating the Negroid element directly to urban sophistication. Gershwin's marvellous cries for fisherman, strawberry woman and devil-crab man are transformed into a lovely blue lullaby, poetic in sonority, sleepy in rhythm, yet with Davis's muted line rhythmically taut within the quietude. The "Buzzard" song—musically the most complex number in Gershwin's score—lends itself to a pungent sonority, rapid rhythmic figurations, screwed-up appoggiaturas and wild chromatic skirls. The great lyrical numbers create a mood-fantasy out of a tune. Davis says that for some numbers Evans gave him not a chord-sequence but a "scale" to improvise on, meaning, one presumes, a series, row, or raga—a linear rather than a harmonic formula. Such linear improvisation goes to explain the complex harmonic texture which the music creates; and it could be risked, in so large and closely integrated an ensemble, only with performers of a considerable degree of sophistication. It called for an improviser of Davis's kind and quality to explore, through Gil Evan's arrangement, the tender frailty inherent in both the "Summer-time" tune—and in the mother-child relationship. Between them, solo line and harmonic colour create a music that is at once innocent and tense with apprehension. There is a similar quality in the muted colours and broken lyrical extensions of the love song, "Bess, you is my woman now"; while the version of the final elegy "Bess, Oh where's my Bess", superbly re-creates, in the questioning, delayed rhythm of the solo and the subdued, hushed scoring, the nostalgia of the search for the Eternal Beloved. The beat continues, ever so gently, like a heart that is almost stopping, against the wandering polyrhythms of the solo; the infinitely soft, indrawn, crunching sonority sounds as though Porgy is communing with himself, and we overhear because he, being Everyman, is ourselves. The version of Sportin' Life's "There's a boat that's leavin'" is the only number that sticks fairly close to the original tune, in the manner of the traditional jazz improvisation. This is appropriate, for Sportin' Life is not concerned with poetic undercurrents and overtones. The true jazz feeling of the improvisation reveals, however, that he is not entirely corrupted by "New York"; and this, as we shall see, is part of the point of Gershwin's opera.

The Evans-Davis *Porgy and Bess* achieves an emotionally powerful balance between jazz and art; perhaps it is pertinent to note that Davis is coloured, Evans a white man. Later developments of "cool" jazz have tended to emphasize art at the expense of jazz, to the detriment of both; and one of the most representative developments is that of Gerry Mulligan, a white saxophonist who at one time played with Miles Davis, but who split off to form his own all-white group, operating mainly on the West Coast. In most of his early work, especially that with largish bands, Mulligan was obviously—perhaps too obviously—indebted to Ellington, and an Ellingtonian mellowness survives in the more personal sonority of the Gerry Mulligan Quartet, which originally consisted of Chet Baker on trumpet, Chico Hamilton on drums, Bob Whitlock on bass, with Mulligan as baritone sax and arranger. Their music is in every sense easier than that of Davis or Monk—let alone Parker. It deliberately seeks a chamber-music style by scoring for melody instruments and percussion, without piano or any other harmonic fill-in. Though this linear scoring would seem to be a return to the old New Orleans tradition, if not to a neo-primitivism such as is favoured by Ornette Coleman, the effect is completely different since in the New Orleans bands the polyphony was both incidental and accidental, whereas in the Gerry Mulligan Quartet it is a conscious technique, related to the "composed" aspects of the harmony and form. Parker's or Armstrong's interior vitality has gone; there remains, in the better numbers, a precarious equilibrium between the fresh melodic and harmonic invention and the clarity of the form, which often includes academic counterpoint. A lovely example is *Darn that Dream* (14), a highly composed treatment (by Evans) of a pop number. The sonority is soft and mellow, with a prevalence of thirds: less disturbing than Gil Evans's typical sound. The tune is basically simple, not tortuous, like Parker's or Monk's treatment of pop numbers; and the form has an almost passacaglia-like rigidity, with a little three-note scale ostinato that keeps returning as counterpoint, both ways up. Towards the end it also appears in diminution, creating climax and resolution, so that in this sense the piece is closer to Ellington than to Parker, or even Davis.

Mulligan's characteristic note is a gentle wistfulness in place of Parker's frenzy or Davis's more searing melancholy; we may relate him to the white tradition inaugurated by Bix Beiderbecke. In faster tempi his music becomes more soloistic, for the obvious reason that harmonic polyphony of the type used in *Darn that Dream* could not be employed at fast speeds without a damaging simplification of the lines, or without accidental heterophony that would not fit into Mulligan's euphonious style. *Goldrush* (15) is a fast piece that can be compared with Parker, who was clearly the model for some of the solos. Yet the virtuosity has now become easy in its flexibility; there is plenty of pep but little inner passion. We are reminded that Mulligan greatly admires the music of Red Nichols and his Five Pennies, who were never less than six and sometimes as many as ten and who made a series of records, starting in 1926 . This all-white group included Jimmy Dorsey, Eddie Lang, Miff Mole, Benny Goodman, Pee Wee Russell, and sometimes Glenn Miller both as trombonist and arranger. Red Nichols's music (16) is harmonically euphonious, rhythmically simple, melodically tuneful, Bix-like, but without his nostalgic sweetness. Mulligan's faster numbers are a slightly more sophisticated re-creation of this music; and it is interesting to note that Nichols was a professional musician, son of a university music teacher, and himself teutonically trained, as was Beiderbecke. It is also relevant to note that the Five Pennies were centred on New York: and included players who later entered the world of pop music.

While Mulligan's best pieces are distinguished in a small way, and have a genuine relationship to traditional jazz, they also hint at a danger inherent in the cultivation of the Cool. It may, as with Davis, be a means of dealing with the darker fevers and passions that lurk beneath the surface of our lives; but it *may* be merely a turning away from uncomfortable reality with a shrug of the shoulders—in which case the players' contemptuous attitude to their audience is latent in the music itself. Technical skill, intellectual contrivance will not in themselves save one from madhouse or sanitorium: nor is relaxation in itself a virtue. There must be something to be controlled by the technique, some element of tension from which to be relaxed. The Modern Jazz Quartet, a Negro ensemble which is even cooler than Mulligan's Quartet, does not escape this danger, though all the players —especially John Lewis himself on piano and Milt Jackson on vibraphone—are able and sensitive musicians, as we can see from their sundry co-operations with Miles Davis. In their Quartet performances, however, the coolness of the music seems almost an affectation, since there is so little melodic, rhythmic or harmonic energy to be cooled. The "corporeality" of jazz can hardly survive in the improbable medium of vibraphone, piano, bass and percussion. If the sonority is supposed to be like that of Balinese music—which may be suggested by the trance-like, ritualistic manner in which the Quartet performs— one is forced to admit that there is an unbridgeable gulf between the two. The ritual of Balinese music is a positive religious act between performers and worshippers; how can there be a parallel to this in our world, and in a concert-hall wherein the performers deliberately avoid any sense of participation?

Moreover, the quality of the ritual, if it existed, could not be separated from the quality of the music: which, when once we have recovered from the impact of the novel sonority, is not always high. The Modern Jazz Quartet version of a pop number such as Judy Garland's *Over the rainbow* (17) may be interestingly contrasted with Ellington's version of a pop song (which re-creates it positively), or with Monk's version (which tends to destroy it). The John Lewis arrangement of *Over the rainbow* does neither; it expresses, with some delicacy, precisely the emotion of adolescent wonder that is inherent in the tune itself. It is more veiled and "poetic" in exploiting the commercial world's dreamland of Debussian and Ravelian chromatics; but it is closer to Disneyland than to Ravel. It may be indicative of the lack of robustness in Lewis's talent that his music improves when it departs further from pop music. His jazz fugues, which are supposed to be influenced by Bach, have charm and a certain desiccated energy, though they are not fugues and are not jazz. Jazz polyphony implies tension between line and beat, Bachian polyphony involves tension between line and harmony (which includes beat, too). Lewis's *Versailles* (18) has neither quality, and falls somewhere between Bach and Bali. As Bachian fugue, it lacks harmonic progression, and therefore a sense of growth from beginning to middle to end; as Balinese ritual music it lacks variety of texture, significance of gesture, and, of course, magical or religious conviction. We do not feel transported; we merely feel that it goes on too long.

The title of this piece is interesting, for it suggests that Lewis's partiality for the eighteenth century parallels his sympathy with Debussy and particularly Ravel; he sees the eighteenth century as a fairy-tale, a dream-world over the rainbow, an escape from Parker's asphalt jungle. This is borne out by the suite *Fontessa* (19), which is about the *Comedia dell'Arte*. Again the Ravel Pierrot-figure cries for the moon; and the suite begins with what might almost be a quotation from Ravel's *Pavane pour une Infante Défunte*—significantly an elegiac piece. Though this is hardly jazz, it is light music of charm, marred by a lack of Ravelian economy. Consider what happens in the improvisatory solo episodes, including Lewis's own. This is no longer Ravel's "green Paradise of childish loves", let alone the magic ritual of Balinese music; we are plumb in the middle of the Palm Court or cocktail lounge. Ravel's dream, if ideal not real, is true; Lewis's has become a cinematic wish-fulfilment.

That his talent is genuine is none the less proved by his film music itself which, perhaps because it has a function, is on a higher level than his concert music. Being related to story and character, it is less prone to expatiate: so that whereas his weaker music is "cinematic" in inverted commas, his best work is cinematic in that it refers directly to a human situation, dramatically depicted. A lovely example is the heroine's song from *One never Knows* (20), which in mood is related to Lewis's version of the Judy Garland song. Here the lyricism, though childishly simple, as befits the young girl, is given an inner fervency by a blue element in the line, and a suppressed Latin American thrust within the rhythm. These New World elements come to terms with the Old World wherein the drama takes place, so that the piece becomes a blue Neapolitan boat-song! At the same time it is an impressionist art-piece, too, with a beautifully evocative use of bell noises against the frail melody. In its subdued way, it is a subtle piece of characterization, conveying the girl's tenderness, loneliness, sadness. It is interesting that the piece was first performed in concert form along with works by Debussy and Satie. It is at home in that company, though it could learn something from the Frenchmen about economy, for it is, as usual, unnecessarily long.

This merging of the new and the old world occurs also in *Cortège*, based on the old man's theme. The tune is modal rather than blue:· related to Europe's past, elegiacally sad, like the modal tunes of Ravel. Its simple sobriety is preserved in the passacaglia-like gait, for it is a processional piece, however muted. As the procession moves on, however, the variations grow more jazzy and more Negroid; and Lewis has said that he could not keep reminiscences of New Orleans funeral music out of this Venetian ceremonial, however submerged they must be in the context of the past. Again, a sophisticated compositional element is imposed on jazz improvisation, and the cortège returns in a da capo, re-entering the stillness. The formal devices are as simple as Lewis's counterpoint; and he was justified in pointing out that in his music—perhaps in all jazz-derived music—they *ought* to be simple. The sonority in this piece is beautiful and unexpectedly varied. Milt Jackson's virtuosic sensitivity on vibraphone adds guitar-like overtones that are delicately integrated with the percussion.

The Golden Striker, which is the hero's theme, has a comparatively energetic tune and a Latin-American rhythm that is in part veiled by the "Balinese" overtone resonances. *The Rose Truc*, the "other man's" theme, is a quick blues with a brilliant bass part, creating a—for Lewis —strangely strenuous, whispered passion. In *Three Windows* there is more composition, for it combines the themes of hero, other man and old man, each of which has a fugal exposition. A coda rounds off the piece with the three themes simultaneously, over a Latin-American ostinato. The academic counterpoint comes off here, partly because it is simple and does not get in the way of the swing: partly because it has a dramatic purpose. This comparatively arty number is, indeed, more successful than *Venice*, a night-club tune not otherwise related to the action. The attempt to inject blue blood into the Italianized pop song goes soft at the centre, like "Over the rainbow". It is not more sensitive than the real thing, only feebler: and longer.

Outside his film music, Lewis's best work is probably the brassy music, *Three Little Feelings* (21), that he wrote for Gunther Schuller. The tender and intimate mood is the same as that of the music he writes for the tinkling sonority of his Quartet; but the music gains in pungency from the brassiness, the more so because Miles Davis is among the soloists. The first movement, or "feeling", is a skeletonic minor-keyed blues, with Davis playing on flugelhorn a broken, pathetic solo over simple harmony and a wandering fugato that creates a grave, rich sonority. In the second movement, which is in the major but is still more wistful, harmonic progression virtually stops as Davis, forlorn and lost, sings over two undulating chords on trombones and baritone sax. The deep texture and bluely nostalgic tune return in a "da capo", the enveloping sonority being characteristically "regressive". The third feeling opens with a romantic horn-call. The piece returns to the minor and to the mood of the first piece, though it is grimmer, with a stalking bass. It ends with the horn-call on four horns in unison. Perhaps it is invoking the past; it certainly is not a call to battle.

This work of romantic *simplesse* is truly touching: and shows that Lewis can write good music when he keeps within his limitations. If insubstantial compared with the work of the Miles Davis-Gil Evans collaboration, it has authenticity as well as charm. The compromise of the jazzman with Art is not always, or indeed often, so imaginatively justified: as we may see from the work of the Chico Hamilton Quartet which cultivated a muted sonority similar to that favoured by Lewis. Here melody instruments—flute, clarinet, alto and tenor sax, cello and guitar—create a chamber-music texture; and again the music invokes a Ravelian dream-world, but with greater insistence on the child-like aspects of the fairy-tale, so that the ostinato-like phrases frequently suggest Poulenc and Satie, as well as Ravel. *Sleep* (22) employs naïve, incantatory phrases on flute and cello, with an occasional Oriental twiddle, to concoct a rarefied, unraucous, unjazzy soporific. Abrupt contrasts of mood add to the wide-eyed effect, but the surrealism is paradoxically self-conscious. *Chrissie* (23) has a flute in fugato, over nursery rhythm ostinati with a Latin-American tinge. The little-girl cheekiness is similar to Poulenc; it is odd indeed that jazz, which began by reminding us of the jungle and of the rock-bottom realities of our urban lives, should ultimately arrive not at the child's spontaneity, but at this arch pretence of childishness: which is also a deliberate denial of reality.

Of course, there are better examples of this artily conscious cult of the naïve: we may mention the *Seven Pieces* (24) which Jimmy Giuffre, a musically educated white jazz composer, wrote for himself on clarinet or sax, with J. Hall on guitar and Red Mitchell on bass. In *Happy Man, Princess,* or *The Story,* simple, child-like noodling tunes, prevailingly pentatonic, are played in a wistfully neutral tone by Giuffre, while guitar and bass add nagging cross-rhythms in a rather bleak and empty texture. A certain fool-like pathos comes across, which sometimes reminds us of the "lonesome" moments in Copland's rustic works: so that the music has a more valid relationship to the world in which it was made than has the little-girl music of Hamilton. Coplandesque art here exists alongside hints of country blues guitar-playing, of flamenco, and of "timeless" Oriental percussion. In his more recent group, in which Paul Bley's piano comes in for the guitar, this mode reaches out to the more radically primitive hollering of Ornette Coleman. A slow number like *Cry-want* (25) begins with wanly pentatonic folk-monody, using the bass like a cavernous guitar; while the quick numbers in *Thesis* (26) explore a Coleman-like heterophony, both rhythmically and harmonically unlicensed. Finally, in pieces such as *Ornothoids, Propulsion* and *Yggdrasil* on the disc called *Free Fall* (27), Giuffre takes the ultimate step and dispenses with "beat" altogether, for these pieces are entirely improvised monodies without even the accompaniment of percussion. Both the complex numerical rhythms and the pitch distortions (achieved by split reeds and overblowing) have affinities with Asiatic techniques; and although there is a hint of self-consciousness in this paradoxically intellectualized surrealism, we can relate the music to certain central developments in American music—to the nocturnal bird and animal noises of Varèse and Partch, to the sound if not the philosophy of electronic music, and to both the sound and philosophy of the music of John Cage. As a result, Giuffre's music, if it hasn't the passionate authenticity of the "advanced" music of Coleman and Coltrane, at least seems relevant: whereas the intellectualism of Chico Hamilton's music is of its nature evasory. If Stan Kenton's music, flourishing at the end of the big swing era, corrupted the positive ingredient of entertainment music (physical immediacy), Hamilton's "masterpiece", *Gone Lover* (28), equally corrupts its negative ingredient (escape). Beginning with a quotation from Ravel, which we may or may not be expected to recognize as such, it relapses into a doodling that is as pretentious as it is emasculate. The mood is remarkably close to that of the pop music it affects to despise; nothing could be further from Ravel's heart-rending dream of beauty and transience. Kenton explodes jazz in mechanized vulgarity; in *Gone Lover* art peters out in inanition.

That the fusion of jazz and "art" is doomed as soon as it becomes self-conscious is suggested, too, by the career of Dave Brubeck, an academically trained white musician whose creation none the less springs from Tin Pan Alley. His (published) *Weep No More* (29) piano improvisation has the mood and feel of "These foolish things"—without the memorable tune. The cheapened Delian chromatics and the piano texture are much the same as those cultivated thirty years ago by Reginald Forsythe, and are not so far away from the once ubiquitous Billy Mayerl! *Two Part Contention* (30) illustrates the urge towards higher things. It is supposed to be a jazzed two-part invention, but, like Lewis's emulations of Bach, lacks the essential tension between linear movement and implicit harmony. When the harmony develops it is, again, cornily old-fashioned: which matters in this context, because the harmony is meant to be important. There is no composition in the piece, only continuation; climax is generated by the repetition of Brubeck's notorious "punch" chords. In this hypnotic repetition without temporality, the music is like a rudimentary version of Indian music, with line and rhythm rendered crude, and with unnecessary harmonic excrescences. The piece seems vastly too long because it does not, like real Indian music, escape temporality through ecstasy.

In some of the pieces from *Impressions of Eurasia* (31)—a title which telescopes Europe and Asia—Brubeck makes this Oriental affiliation explicit. *Nomad* has a tala rhythmic pattern, 3 plus 3 plus 4; but line and rhythm are puerile compared with the real thing, and jazz virtues are not present as substitute. Again the climax comes mechanically, through reiterated punch chords. There is no composition, as in Ellington or Davis-Evans: but no ecstasy, as in classical Indian improvisation, either. *The Golden Horn*, the Turkish piece, begins more promisingly. The modal incantation and the rhythmic pattern belong equally to jazz and to Turkish music, and the sharp, twanging noise suggested by Turkish instruments is fascinating. Then, however, Tin Pan Alley harmony cheapens both the Negroid and the Turkish elements. Ellington can make similar harmony sound fresh because it is inseparable from every other aspect—melody, rhythm, colour—of his personal idiom. The creative mind can be a maker, whether his materials be gathered from jazz, from pop music or from art; the uncreative mind will rely on the gimmick, the effectiveness of which is exhausted with its novelty.

Calcutta Blues, indeed, is an insult both to the Negro who made the blues, and to the ancient civilization of India. The square phrases make nonsense of the implied affinity with classical Indian music; the passages which use the piano as a folk percussion instrument are probably borrowed from Hovhaness. Again the piece seems interminable, since although without time-sense it never levitates. The "European" pieces in *Eurasia* are equally Hollywooden. The best of them, *Brandenburg Gate*, is more vigorous than Lewis's Bachian evocations, ending with a sturdy chorus of burgomasters; no more than Lewis, however, does it attain the Bachian equilibrium between linear independence, rhythmic continuity, and harmonic tension. The British piece—*Marble Arch*—is supposed to be funny, with parodies of the music-hall and perhaps of British jazz. The humour is jejune, in a manner related to Brubeck's improvisations on well-known tunes, such as *These foolish things* (32). These are not composition, but decomposition. The theme is taken to pieces, and Brubeck investigates the permutations and distortions to which it may be submitted. However clever these permutations and distortions may be incidentally (and the cleverness has been exaggerated), they are doodling rather than creation. The Brubeck-Bernstein collaboration—*Dialogues for Jazz Combo and Symphony Orchestra* (33)—is similar in effect. The jazz improvisation is by Brubeck and the orchestral composition by his brother Howard, conducted by Bernstein. The basic composition is undistinguished, the treatment more so: the effect is Hollywoodish, not so much because of the corny harmony as because of the emotional bulldozing.

Academy-trained jazz musicians, especially composers, are sprouting like mushrooms, and not many of them are as talented as Gil Evans, who was not trained at all except by using his ears, or as John Lewis, who wisely limited his range. Charles Bell's Contemporary Jazz Quartet of piano, guitar, bass and drums is directly modelled on Lewis's ensemble, and the white leader, a pupil of Nicolai Lopatnikoff, is clearly a fine musician. His music—influenced by white-note Stravinsky, by Prokoviev, perhaps by Bartók and in lighter moments by Poulenc—is formally lucid, fascinating in sonority, and of greater rhythmic energy than Lewis's work, probably because he has so remarkably talented a drummer in Allen Blairman. His simplest pieces, like *Last Sermon* (34), tend, following Lewis's precedent, to be more effective than his complex ones, such as *Counterpoint Study 2* (35), which suffers from the same disabilities as Lewis's fugal numbers. There is something a little clinical about Bell's music; and though he is a better-equipped musician than Lewis he is further from the spirit of the blues. His music includes little improvisation. Among other jazz composers, John Carisi, a pupil of Stefan Wolpe, has made somewhat self-conscious advances towards the East. *Moon Taj* (36) indulges in chromatic, near atonal melismata around an almost static harmony; but the piece—like the quicker *Angkor Wat* (37)—is more interesting as sonority than as composition.

More creatively vigorous than the academically trained jazz composers who stem from the manner of the Modern Jazz Quartet is George Russell, a highly sophisticated musician who has become guide and mentor to "advanced" developments. As a white man he has tried to do what Cecil Taylor attempted as a coloured man: and has, perhaps, failed for a reason that complements Taylor's failure. In Taylor's case, the compositional elements that were supposed to discipline the primitivism did not convince, and this made the primitivism itself seem suspect. In Russell's case we can have no doubt that his response to modern "art" music is genuine, and he uses a Bartók-like percussive dissonance, Stravinskian ostinati, even Schoenbergian variation techniques more adeptly than any jazzman. What seems more dubious is the occasional explosion of jazz licence which he feels he ought to encourage in his piano playing—the sudden, ungrammatical bangings up and down the keyboard, the glissandi swooping through the top registers or whooshing down to the bottom. Curiously enough, the most spontaneous features sound the most "thought up". This is probably why his most successful pieces are not those which are surrealistically "furthest out", nor those which are most consciously organized according to theory—he has evolved a "Lydian concept of tonal organization" which is a jazz complement to Harry Partch's justly intoned monody. Rather he creates his most exciting and forward-looking music when he is closest to tradition, and so does not need to think about the fact that jazz's desire to follow Nature is liable to conflict with the artifices that civilization has imposed. Playing his version of a Miles Davis standard, or a twelve-bar blues like *Sandhu* (38), composed by the young trumpeter Clifford Brown, he can reconcile the arty complexities of his piano style with the note-clusters, tremolos and rhythmic hiatuses of barrelhouse style, and can inspire the trumpet, trombone and sax of Don Ellis, Dave Baker and Don Young to Park-erian exuberance, if not to the Coleman-like immediacy of the field holler, or to Coltrane's neo-African violence.

But by far the most interesting attempts to combine jazz techniques with the sophisticated art-techniques of twentieth century music have been made, understandably enough, by Gunther Schuller: a fully trained "straight" composer who, as we have seen, has worked professionally in the jazz world. In his Variants on Monk's classic number *Criss-cross* (39) he scores for jazz players of the calibre of Ornette Coleman, Eric Dolphy, Bill Evans and Scott LaFaro, playing antiphonally with a string quartet, while a solo flute hovers between the world of art and that of jazz. The string and flute texture and sonority have affinities with the music of Webern and his imitators; and their "stillness" generates tension and energy from the improvising jazz soloists, so that the juxtaposition of styles is more than a technical device. The worlds of feeling overlap; and a true release is effected in the exciting cadenza for Dolphy's bass clarinet and Scott LaFaro's string bass, and in the lovely flute arabesques of the last variant. What Schuller has achieved here cannot of its nature, however, be done often: for the more conscious one becomes of an emotional interdependence between the two worlds, the less likely is that interdependence to "work". The piece called *Abstraction* (40), for instance, attempts to relate an impro-vising Ornette Coleman to a fully integrated serial composition, and it fails because, although both jazz and serialism are principles of variation, they are none the less radically opposed. Jazz is permutatory, serialism pre-ordained; we cannot feel, in this piece, that the one has anything to give to the other, whereas the point of *Criss-Cross* is evident in its title—the music's fusion of spirituality and corporeality is inseparable from its fusion of the genres.

This may indicate that jazz-as-composition is most likely to succeed if it remains relatively unpretentious, as in the pieces of John Lewis performed by the same players, such as the *Variants on Django*, a memorial to the jazz guitarist which has a particularly haunting tune (41). Despite the fascination of Schuller's work, it seems doubtful if the future of jazz can lie in the more intellectualized aspects of composition, any more than in the frenzy of the far-out boys—if only because such music, if we are to believe in it, calls for composers and players of something approaching genius. It seems more likely that the future lies in a synthesis of Parker's improvised heat and Davis's relatively composed coolness: with the understanding that—as we have seen—Bird was a composing improviser, and Miles an improvising composer. We can see this happening in both directions. Davis himself, for instance, playing *Milestones* (42) begins with a riff of short detached chords, marking off the miles against a gentle, regular beat. When the muted trumpet emerges from the beat of Time, however, the soft, suave tone veils tremendous passion: which gradually breaks through until the line whirls with almost Parker-like agitation. The effect of the piece depends on the contrast between the passion the line generates and the immensely ancient, modal quietude of its first statement. The continuity of riff and beat seem impervious to the soloist's speaking intensity: so the piece seems, although fairly fast, extremely sad, like most of Davis's music.

Something similar happened when Bill Evans, the white pianist who played so exquisitely with Davis in *Kind of Blue*, began to record on his own, accompanied by Scott LaFaro's bass and Paul Motian's percussion. He has made his own solo version of Davis's *Blue in Green* (43), and in this and in some moving versions of pop songs such as *When I fall in love* (44) or the Rodgers and Hart tune *Spring is here* (45) preserves the Miles-like sonority of his earlier playing. Both pulse and harmonic movement are immensely slow, the middle register chords scrunchily sensuous, the spacing warm, the texture enveloping; yet through and over this introverted quiet the melodic lines float and soar high in the treble, insinuate in the tenor range, and occasionally reverberate in the bass. Evans's ability to make melodic lines "speak" on the piano is of extraordinary subtlety; and always the sensuousness leads not to passivity but to growth. The dance-lilt flows into spring-like song; the inexhaustibly inventive cross-rhythms and counter melodies are never rebarbative, always supple and in that sense songful. Even when Evans plays quick numbers, such as *Autumn Leaves* (46) and *Witchcraft* (47), the rhythmic zest provokes song; and this may be why his piano encourages bass and drums to polyrhythmic dialogue both with himself and with one another. He can even play a Disney tune—*Some day my prince will come* (48)— preserving, as Lewis would do, its frail, adolescent simplicity, yet giving it, too, a most unDisney-like flow, floating cross-rhythms in waltz time against the boogie movement, dissolving melody into Tatum-like fioriture that remains always plastic and expressive.

Here, then, as in Miles Davis's later work, the passivity of Cool Jazz finds a more positive, a more creative extension. The Parker-Davis synthesis functions from the other direction in the playing and composing of a remarkable young trumpeter Clifford Brown, who was killed, at a very early age, in a car crash. Playing with Max Roach on drums, Ritchie Powell (Bud's brother) on piano, Harold Land on alto and George Borrow on bass, he achieves in *What am I here for?* (49) a Parkerian rage: and in *Jor-du* (50) a gravely swinging, sonorous modal tune that is Davis-like in its disciplined passion. His emotional range was much wider than that of most jazzmen; if *Jordu, Daahoud* (51) and *Dalilah* (52) (the last named not an original but a re-creation of the old tune by Victor Young) have a dark, even tragic quality related to Davis's flamenco manner, *Joy Spring* (53), with its bugle-call breaks, is high comedy, an emotional release. *Parisian Thoroughfare* (by Bud Powell) (54) is also an extrovert, illustrative piece based on the motor horns, traffic noises and chiming bells of Paris: which becomes a vivid, yet lucid, image of the introvert's mixed-up state. Finest of all is *The Blues Walk* (55), a fast blues, angry but ordered, neither haphazard nor gimmicky. This is one of the rare examples of true jazz polyphony— a hammer and tongs conflict between Brown's trumpet and Roach's drums, with Ritchie Powell playing piano in his brother's style, and with hardly less sizzling power.

In this splendid piece, and in the hauntingly melancholic *Jordu*, Brown plays in a style that is a cross between Parker's nervosity and Gillespie's virtuosity on the one hand, and Davis's speaking intimacy on the other. The heroic jazz trumpet comes into its own again, after Miles Davis's muted nervosity, or Don Ellis's attempt—in such African-rhythmed pieces as *Ostinato* (56)—to give to the trumpet a strangled jitteriness comparable with that of Charlie Parker's sax. This renaissance of the trumpet is continued by a very young player Booker Little who, in *Moods in Free Time* (57), borrows something from the veiled melancholy of Miles Davis's flamenco style, from Jewish cantillation, and from Asiatic melismatic techniques, while at the same time reminding us of the hard, bright, relatively extroverted sonority of Louis Armstrong.

The case of John Coltrane, indeed, suggests that even his "advanced" sax playing may convince precisely because he started from, and has never relinquished, a basis in traditional jazz: as we can see when, at the height of his progressive phase, he plays ballads and blues. In a tune such as *You don't know what love is* (58) both Coltrane and Tyner preserve the ballad's conventional nostalgia, with wailing refrain-phrase on sax and added note arpeggios on piano; and that Coltrane's biting tone and Tyner's sharp texture are anti-sentimental deepens rather than dissipates the nostalgia. Coltrane's variation technique is here a kind of *creative* dissection. He doesn't make the phrases of the tune unrecognizable nor does he ironically distort them as Monk sometimes does; but he reveals unexpected implications in dividing the phrases into shorter note-values, usually in irregular patterns and with distonations of pitch: so that the nostalgia changes from a dream of what might have been to a recognition of the disturbing possibilities of what *is*. Perhaps it is significant that this goes along with a destruction of the temporal sense; memory and desire dissolve into an ecstatic present, and this happens in the beautiful coda to this piece no less than in the numbers (such as *All or nothing*) (59) in which Coltrane deliberately indulges in what he calls "the arabian style", with bagpipe-like melismata over a complicated rhythmic ostinato or tala.

Jazz, pop, and composition are here creatively unified. When Coltrane plays the blues we reach at once the most mature and the most instinctive form of this meeting between traditional jazz and the compositional tendencies of the *avant garde*. *Blues to Elvin* and *Mr Syms* (60), for instance, are built on the traditional blues progression, on boogie rhythm, and on brief melodic formulae derived directly from old-style country blues. The broken rhythms, the wailing melismata, the nagging repetitions and sudden hiatuses of the sax line are both nervous and Oriental; and McCoy Tyner's fine piano solos have learned something from Bud Powell while harking back to the barrelhouse by way of Monk and Basie. There is no sharp distinction between these relatively traditional blues and a number such as *Mr Knight,* in which Coltrane's pentatonic ululations are more obviously Asiatic or flamenco-like, and in which the cross-rhythmed ostinati of piano (in empty fifths) and of percussion are intermittently Latin-American and primitively African. Even the most advanced of these blues preserve a creative relationship to tradition. *Mr Day*, for instance, doesn't exist passively in its Asiatic ecstasy, but depends on a classical jazz antithesis between the orgiastic repetition of the tala pattern and the desire of the solo lines—both sax and piano—to break free. This tendency is still evident in *Blues to You* and *Blues to Bechet*, pieces wherein the harmony instrument (piano) is abandoned: for although the melodic line can be all the freer for the lack of harmony, we none the less experience the noodling elaborations of phrase against the insistency of a beat. *Blues to Bechet*, in which Coltrane revives the soprano sax, is an authentic tribute to the classic master of that instrument, even though Coltrane's tight, pinched sonority is so different from Bechet's liquid voluptuousness. Indeed, the point of the piece lies in the manner in which the innocent, New Orleans bugle-phrase gradually ties itself into knots: which are not untied when the piece slides out on the traditional unresolved seventh.

This music proves again that the basic necessity for a jazzman, as for any kind of musician, is creativity; he must be a maker, not a dissector or an illustrator. Much modern jazz is not creation but gimmick-worship, and this is inevitable in a gimmick-ridden world. Brubeck, for instance, belongs to a commercial society because he exploits non-creatively things that have, or had, creative validity—such as the affiliation of jazz with the East. But the non-creative have always outnumbered the creative and always will; all that matters is that the non-creative techniques of a mechanized society should not stifle creativity altogether. Modern Jazz has produced one supremely gifted improvising musician in Charlie Parker, and two remarkably disturbing players in Ornette Coleman and John Coltrane; it has produced some impressive semi-composed music from Thelonious Monk, Miles Davis, Gil Evans and Charlie Mingus; and some sensitive if light-weight work from Gerry Mulligan and John Lewis. That is enough to indicate that jazz is still alive: that it may yet lead to a future wherein distinctions between art music and pop music—between art and commerce itself—will have become meaningless.

VIII

From jazz to pop: the decline of the big bands: pianists, cabaret singers and the "musical"

> not that mu-sick (the trick
> of corporations, newspapers, slick magazines, movie houses
> the ships, even the wharves, absentee-owned
>
> they whine to my people, these entertainers, sellers
>
> they play upon their bigotries (upon their fears
>   no moving thing moves
> without that song I'd void my ears of, the musicracket
> of all ownership . . .
>
> you sing, you
> who also
>
> wants.
>
>   CHARLES OLSEN

In the last chapter, and in the chapter on Ellington, we have observed the process whereby jazz turns into "art". We have also noticed the degree to which this process involves compromise with pop music; and we have further seen that the world of pop music may all too readily take over both art and jazz. Nor was capitulation to commerce a new phenomenon. It had happened in the 'twenties, the hey-day of classical jazz: for the Man in the Street gained his knowledge of jazz from the symphonic perversions of Paul Whiteman which, in attempting to make jazz respectable, deprived it of all validity. The soaring strings souped up the texture, the chromatic sequences inflated the feeling, the bulging brass elephantized the sonority, until the result was an exact musical equivalent for the "substitute living" of the worst aspects of Hollywood. The big bands of the 'thirties—as we saw in our account of Basie—had no truck with this manufactured feeling, for they excitingly expressed a reaction to a hard, machine-dominated world. That this world *was* machine-dominated, however, was a fact difficult to withstand: there was a remorseless tendency for the precision and non-humanity of the machine to supersede such human values as tried to survive. We commented on a pretentious example of this in the band of Stan Kenton: pretentious because the anti-feeling which the band's sensationalism represents claimed to be Art. More normally, the big band directed itself towards a mass audience, to whom it appealed at the most rudimentary level of physical assault. Even Benny Goodman, in his small groups a most sensitive as well as virtuoso performer, sometimes descended to this level in his big band work. More representative is the band of Glen Miller which, if less blatantly bogus than that of Kenton, is no less a well-oiled machine. The notorious *In the Mood* (1) is based on the traditional country-guitar vamp—and on nothing else. There is no melody, no rhythmic interest, and only the most rudimentary harmonic progression; such effect as it has on an audience (and it seems to have had considerable effect) depends entirely on repetition and on sudden changes of dynamics: substitute excitement as a part of substitute living. Of course, many of Miller's pieces have greater musical interest than this: *Tuxedo Junction* (2), for instance, makes some stimulating train noises and a version of Jelly Roll Morton's *King Porter Stomp* (3) benefits from the fact that a real piece of music is pulverized within the Miller machine. But all this music relies on the riff for its own sake; Basie's tension between the riff and the melodic-harmonic identity of the solos has gone—and with it the human truth of the music.

The approach of jazz to commerce was, none the less, not all loss. It was essential, we have seen, for Ellington's fulfilment; we might even say that a man of Benny Goodman's high abilities as administrator and impresario was necessary if true jazz was to become economically self-subsistent, not only with a Negro public, but in modern society as a whole. We should not forget that it was largely through Goodman that black and white performers were accepted on equal terms, even (ultimately) in the South. Goodman's flirtings with "straight" music—in particular with Mozart and Bartók—were also significant because, unlike Paul Whiteman's symphonic pretensions they were based on genuine ability and interest. Maybe Goodman played Mozart, and Mozart lost; Mozart would none the less have recognized validity and sensitivity in Goodman's phrasing, however extraneous it might seem to eighteenth-century Vienna, while Bartók must have been delighted with Goodman's spontaneous revelation of the affinity between jazz phrasing and the swing of Hungarian rhythm. The barriers were really broken down since a jazzman, born in Chicago, reared in the jazz world, had proved that he wanted to play Mozart and Bartók, not as a gimmick, but because he enjoyed their music. The divisions between jazz and art and pop had always been shadowy. During the 'thirties and 'forties they became still more dubiously defined; and it became evident that the dubiety might be a virtue.

While the most impressive instance of this is undoubtedly the later development of the Ellington band, it is more widely apparent in the solo performers, mostly pianists and singers, who now flourished not in bawdy houses and tent-shows, but in fashionable night-clubs, for the delectation of a white public. We may consider first the pianists, beginning with James P. Johnson, who, as we have seen, was trained in the old barrelhouse and ragtime tradition, but came to New York, not Chicago. Here, in the metropolitan centre, he influenced true jazzmen, as we have observed in our discussion of Ellington and Monk; at the same time he worked in cabaret and in Tin Pan Alley, writing musical comedy and even abortive works with grandiose symphonic pretensions. We do not remember him for his symphonic works, nor even for his theatrical pieces: though his creative modification of traditional jazz piano was certainly affected by the fact that he wrote music affiliated to both pop song and art. In his playing, indeed, there is a history of jazz in microcosm. In numbers such as *The Mule Walk* (4) or *Carolina Shout* (5) he looks back beyond jazz to the country dance fiddle-tunes and banjo music of the mid-nineteenth century, emulating the banjo's click with his bright acciacciaturas, yet jazzing the tunes slightly through his cross-rhythmed tenor parts. In *Worried and Lonesome Blues* (6) he starts from the chugging accompaniment of barrelhouse style, poising against it, however, a spry, almost elegant right-hand figure built on repeated notes. In *Hungry Blues* (7) he plays with the irresistible swing of classical jazz, developing in his opening statement a chanting lyricism that stimulates both the singer, Anna Robinson, and the trumpeter, Red Allen, to vibrantly blue performances in traditional style. In *If Dreams come True* (8) he manages to blend something of the simple gaiety of country dance tunes with the passionate exuberance of jazz; he thus creates the vital bounce of his characteristic "stride bass", against which the melodic line dances in sprightly rhythmic ellipses. At the same time the resonant spacing of the left hand's tenths, and the precision of the right hand's figurations tend away from authentic jazz towards the "positive", physically immediate aspects of pop music.

In *Lonesome Reverie* (9), on the other hand, Johnson starts from the "negative" or escapist properties of Tin Pan Alley—consider the parallel sevenths and inner chromatics of the opening—but gives them so sharp and clean a refurbishing through the lucidity of his spacing and the precision of his trills and tremolos that they, too, become positive and zestful, related to the swing of barrelhouse rhythm. Most beautifully characteristic of all is a piece like *Blueberry Rhyme* (10): the charming tune of which has the gay simplicity of a country dance, though the potent slow swing with which Johnson plays it is true jazz. The cleanness of the texture—the ripely spaced tenths, the noodling tenor part, the poetically delicate fioriture, the almost airy boogie chords in the left-hand figure—is highly art-ful, however, and we can understand why this music appealed strongly to such sophisticated players as Art Tatum and Thelonious Monk. A still more direct relationship between Johnson and these later pianists is evident in his playing of *Riffs*, to which we briefly referred in the chapter on barrelhouse piano. The sophistication of this music lies in its deliberate exploitation of the *contrast between* the rhythmic energy of the stride bass and the hard, clattering treble. This piece is less "happy" than Johnson's habitual manner, for the fioriture spurt through the rhythm, which becomes subject to odd hesitancies. It is as though the drive in itself is not enough; the melodies and figurations are not content to ride on it, but threaten to destroy it. This pianistic version of a band-music effect which we have observed in Armstrong and Basie will be developed by later pianists: but not by Fats Waller, whose style is related mainly to the positively vigorous and elegant aspects of Johnson's work.

Fats considered himself a disciple of Johnson, and recordings which he made in the 'twenties with Ted Lewis's (commercial) band show him as a traditional jazzman who could perform expertly in ensemble with such players as Muggsy Spanier and Benny Goodman. Their versions of *Dallas Blues* (11) and *Royal Garden Blues* (11) are particularly impressive, and prove that Waller's prancing and airy right-hand technique was wedded to a stride bass of remarkable potency. When he turned to solo playing he often returned to old-style stomp and barrel-house style, as we can see in *The Minor Drag* (12), usually extracting a somewhat ribald comedy, or even farce, from the traditional cross-rhythms. Although trained in authentic jazz traditions, Fats was always of a genial disposition, so that jazz tension was somewhat less meaning-ful to him than jazz exuberance. This is why he could spontaneously develop his jazz in the direction of pop music, preserving the driving rhythm of the bass and the vigour of the riffs, while his right-hand technique, full of twittering thirds in tremolando and dancing dotted arabesques, became increasingly delicate—as we can see from *Twelfth Street Rag* (13) or the famous *Truckin'* (14), in which the music's energy is wittily released by the repeated-note bass. Connected with the sprightly elegance of his pianism is his gift for the memorable tune: as he once said, "You got to have melody. Jimmy Johnson taught me that." So in becoming a popular entertainer he was not denying his nature. *Ain't Misbehavin'* (15) is an admirable tune, and played with Waller's typical bounce and elegance, sounds at its arabesque-decorated climax happy, even abandoned, but never wild. In both the words and tunes of all Fats's most characteristic songs it is no longer tension that complements the exuberance, but rather a clownish pathos. His singing of *I'm gonna sit right down and write myself a letter* (16) or of *Blue turnin' gray over you* (17) achieves gaiety out of the act of self-depreciation, and though Fats's vivacity may be one stage further from "reality" than Bessie Smith's intensity, it is no less honest. Perhaps the gaiety is a release from a basic unease; certainly it says something for the quality of Fats's merriment that he can make something both delightful and touching out of a tune as inane as *Tea for Two*. The tune hums to itself in the tenor register; the treble-twiddles comment on it and ride over it, with slightly ironic comedy, while the swinging bass gives its self-rotating imbecility an unexpected vitality. Even Waller's comedy turns—such as the wryly regretful anti-love song *Your feet's too big* (18)—are part of his jazz-like physical well-being; nor is jazz entirely banished from his more elaborate "piano arrangements" like that of his *Honeysuckle Rose* (19), which begins with sweetly elegant chromatic sequences in the sentimental manner of Gottschalk's or even Ethelbert Nevin's parlour pieces, but then hots up the charm with boogie rhythms, and ends by laughing at itself, crossing rag rhythms with a polite waltz.

Waller veers from jazz towards the "positive" aspects of pop music; Earl Hines, born a year later, in 1905, embraces both the positive and the negative (or escapist) aspects of pop music, and some features of art music, too. He thus started as a true jazzman, like Louis Armstrong, with whom he worked, as we saw, during the 'twenties: but became in later years a figure more comparable with Ellington, effecting a true and moving synthesis of worlds, as well as of techniques. *Caution Blues*, sometimes known as "Blues in thirds" (20), is a fine example. The hesitancy, which was perhaps fortuitous in James Johnson's *Riffs*, here becomes the essence of the tune and of its harmonization. The richly spaced tenths of the bass are a warm, sensual fulfilment: against which

Hines's famous "trumpet style" right hand—derived from an attempt to rival Armstrong—clatters in sharp octaves and arpeggios, springs and prances in pianistic abandon, while emulating brass vibrato. Emotionally, the effect is equivocal, and at bottom melancholy—as the more extrovert Johnson and Waller are not. Moreover, the hesitancy we referred to in Hines's treatment of the melody extends into an alternation between a hard, sharp directness and passages of dreamy pianistic impressionism. Hines does not turn round and laugh at these doodlings, as Waller does on the rare occasions when he is tempted to indulge in them. Hines rather exploits the dichotomy between the solo pianist-composer's sensory, "private" life and what had once been, in the barrelhouse, his social function. Perhaps it is also—since he often plays for a white audience in a cabaret show —the old dichotomy between primitive black and modern white, both states being within as well as without the player-composer's mind. This could be why the music tends to sound sad, as compared with Johnson and Waller.

While in Hines's earlier work this equivocation produces some moving music, it contains dangers which, in his later work, he cannot entirely resist. In *Diane* (21), for instance, the slow, moony introduction that comes from Chopin and Debussy via Hollywood has no necessary relationship to the swinging dance that follows it; and the fioriture and mandoline effects become emptily decorative. In *These Foolish Things* (22) the artifice tends to destroy the virtues of Tin Pan Alley—the fetching tune—as well as the virtues of jazz. There are, however, successes in this manner, notably *Rosetta* (23), in which the sonority is a fascinating and ingenious equivalent to the sound of the Ellington band. Again it is a very sad piece, with a romantically dwindling texture at the end. Perhaps Teddy Wilson—a Hines disciple—is the only pianist to develop this harmonic and textural sophistication without losing the rhythmic drive of traditional barrelhouse style, as we can see from his brilliant version of *Between the Devil and the Deep Blue Sea* (24).

The climax to the sophistication of jazz piano comes with the phenomenal figure of Art Tatum, an almost blind virtuoso who is the Big City's complement to the blind guitar-playing singers of the country blues. He was born in Toledo in 1910, and the origins of his art in traditional barrelhouse style are revealed when he plays the fast blues. In an extraordinary version of *Mr. Freddie Blues* (25), for instance, the James Johnson-like stride-bass, the strident chord clusters, the tremolos and riffs in complex cross rhythms are employed with an untraditional richness of harmony which is extraneous to barrelhouse style, and made possible only by Tatum's prodigious technique. This technique is not normally, however, lavished on the crudity of barrel-house music; Tatum, who worked always as soloist in night clubs or as radio pianist, was no less than Ellington a show-business man rather than a "functional" jazz musician who played for dancing. In *Sophisti-cated Lady* (26) he takes over an Ellington tune and treats it with a har-monic and figurative resource related to Ellington's, though it is derived, not from the interweaving of band-voices, but from the movement of his hands on the keyboard. The figuration is brilliant, hard, strident, with a furious exhibitionism that conflicts oddly with the sensual complexity of the harmonic texture. The rhythm, however, has tremendous bounce, preserving jazz vitality.

Often, especially in his later work, Tatum's experimental proclivities get the better of his musical instinct. The harmonic doodling, even if interesting in itself, destroys continuity; the fioriture, though in them-selves breath-taking, counteract rather than intensify the momentum, and lose their shock-value through excessive repetition. *Willow Weep for Me* (27) is an odd example: in which the extreme complexity of the rhythm does not get over because it does not "carry" the harmonic and modulatory excursions of the piano arabesques. We do not here feel that the conflict between the lines' direction and the complexities of the rhythm is the imaginative point of the composition: we merely feel that Tatum's obsession with rhythmic peculiarities gets in the way of the piece's evolution. There is a danger inherent in being a one-man band, as the virtuoso jazz-pianist hoped to be. His clever hands may carry the composer where his integrity would not want to go. What happens in *Willow Weep* could hardly happen in an Ellington piece, for Ellington must be aware of the band's identity as well as of his own. He cannot play himself tipsy.

The limitations of Tatum's achievement do not alter the fact that he made an historically significant impact on jazz, art music and pop music. All later jazz pianists are indebted to him, even one who, like Erroll Garner, is a "natural", entirely self-taught, academically illiter-ate. It is thus not surprising that some elements in his style should go back to the most primitive barrelhouse; he revives, with renewed *élan*, the chugging eight-chord-to-the-bar bass; but this bass releases right-hand figurations which, unlike old-style barrelhouse, have lyrical grace and vivacity as well as rhythmic excitement. The result—in, for instance, his own number *Play, Piano, play* (28)—has a fresh gaiety with little hint of Hines's dreamful melancholy. This is true even when he plays slowish, sentimental numbers such as *Body and Soul* (29) or *I cover the Waterfront* (30): for he usually introduces the tune with a stomping passage of great rhythmic energy, and the energy does not entirely evaporate when the tune takes over, supported by a slowly swinging lilt. Instead, the rhythmic vigour climbs deviously into the right hand's repeated chord figures, which spread upwards, quiveringly, from the chugging bass. This often (as in *I'm in the Mood for Love*) (31) creates a curious stuttering effect in the enunciation of the melody: so that although the boogie bass is lively and aerated, and the bounce frisks into merry fioriture in the right hand, there is yet a slightly nervous feeling beneath the happiness. This may suggest that at heart Garner is a very romantic player, despite his pep. Certainly on the rare occasions when he relapses into a dreamy mood, as in *Laura* (32), he indulges in Tatum-like modulations and arabesques, but substitutes a relaxed tenderness for Tatum's ripe assertiveness.

The relaxed piano mood, as contrasted with barrelhouse virility, has been further explored by Red Garland, who at one time played with Miles Davis. Though less inventive, his playing is related to that of Bill Evans, another associate of Davis. His left hand swings quietly, while the right hand alternates frail, halting fioriture with scrunchy added note chords, sometimes almost explosive in effect, high in the treble. The effect, at once wistful and slightly acid, comes across well in nostalgic ballads like Hoagy Carmichael's *The Nearness of You* (33), in which the chord progression is so slow that it almost stops: or Jerome Kern's *Long Ago and Far Away* (34), in which sudden Tatum-like spurts make the music more butterfly-frail, not more brilliant: or Ellington's *I Got It Bad and That Ain't Good* (35), in which repeated notes in cross-rhythm suggest a lost lonesomeness. In a sense, Red Garland complements Erroll Garner, for whereas Garner reveals a poetic romanticism beneath the gay gesture, Garland starts with the nostalgic dream but grows increasingly impatient with it. Most of his numbers end with a sudden, rather fierce, barrelhouse-like tremolo, banishing the self-indulgent brooding. If both players have become victims of their mannerisms, they at least had a manner—some creative originality— out of which the mannerisms could crystallize. A younger cabaret pianist, Oscar Peterson, seems in comparison, despite a brilliant technical equipment, parasitic, borrowing his sensuous complexity from Tatum and his vigorous immediacy from Garner.

In all the later pianists we have discussed the harmonic sophistications of the instrument tend to work against the "reality" of the blues. Certainly with only one performer—a singer—has the true flavour of the blues been carried into the world of the pop song; and there is little chance, at this date, of another Billie Holiday. Her life, as revealed in her most disturbing autobiography *Lady Sings the Blues*, had a background of squalor—of childhood rape, prostitution, drink and drugs— no less appalling than the career of Bessie Smith, despite the fact that in her days of affluence she lived, not in a Negro slum, but in the relative luxury of Tin Pan Alley. Throughout it all she preserved something of Bessie Smith's rock-bottom courage and dignity: which she managed to express through the often trite words of the pop numbers she sang. She was a blue singer but not a blues singer; it is encouraging that her revelation of reality beneath apparent sham met with a wide popular response.

In her autobiography Billie tells us that as a child she decided she would always try to speak the truth, or what she believed to be the truth, even though she knew that the world would kick her for it, and kick the harder because she was coloured. This desire for honesty had direct musical consequences, for although she was a pop singer she modelled herself on no preconceived cliché, and acknowledged a debt only to the two great improvising "realists" of jazz:

> Unless it was the records of Bessie Smith and Louis Armstrong I heard as a kid, I don't know of anybody who actually influenced my singing, then or now. I always wanted Bessie's big sound and Pop's feeling. Young kids always ask me what my style derived from and how it evolved and all that. What can I tell them? If you find a tune and it's got something to do with you, you don't have to evolve anything. You just feel it, and when you sing it other people feel something too. With me it's got nothing to do with working or arranging or rehearsing. Give me a song I can feel and it's never work. There are a few songs I feel so much I can't stand to sing them, but that's something else again.

Pop songs were the mythology of her urban world. Through this mythology Billie Holiday revealed "the heart of the matter" which Bessie Smith had discovered in the blues. Her success is indicated by the fact that the greatest jazz instrumentalists of her day were eager to play for her, as Louis Armstrong had played for Bessie.

The bases of her art may be studied in an early performance of *Eeenie meenie minie mo* (36), in which, as in many of her recordings, Teddy Wilson plays piano. Roy Eldridge—a fine trumpeter who provides a bridge between classical style and Dizzy Gillespie—plays an exciting, agitated solo while Wilson's spare piano-texture sounds cool and uninvolved. Billie Holiday's singing manages to fuse Eldridge's heat and Wilson's coolness simultaneously, for her speech-inflection is laconic, almost dead-pan, while her cross-phrasing generates a suppressed passion. It is not merely a matter of cross-rhythms; the basic tempo of the vocal line is at times different from the instrumental tempo. The effect, if stimulating, is slightly self-conscious; and self-consciousness is the last quality one would think of in connection with her later work. In this, the art that hides art is equally effective whether she sings pop numbers expressing the positive or the negative pole of entertainment music. Among the "positive" pieces—those concerned with physical immediacy, happiness in the present moment—we may mention *One, two, button my shoe* (37). A girl brought up as Billie had been brought up, who had received so many dusty answers from life, could hardly be expected to sing in pristine joyousness. Her tone remains neutral, almost off-hand, yet at the same time the subtlest delayed accents impart a sense of wide-eyed wonder, almost of adolescent innocence, to the sleazy atmosphere. This wondering quality is enhanced by Bunny Berigan's obbligato, for he plays his cornet with a tenderness strikingly reminiscent of Bix Beiderbecke. He, too—a white man playing the old-fashioned instrument—becomes the Little Boy Lost in a big city. *Nice work if you can get it* (38) is a still better example of Billie's singing in this mode, probably because both words and tune—by the Gershwins—are in themselves distinguished, delicately balanced between illusion and disillusion.

Some such equilibrium is precisely what Billie Holiday manages to instil into songs related to the "negative" pole of entertainment—the escape into dream. Whereas the words of the positive songs are often quite witty, the words of the negative songs are, almost consistently, bathetic. Yet Billie reveals the agony that may be behind inarticulate cliché: consider how, in *I've got a date with a dream,* (39) she sings the word "dream" in a disembodied, ghostly tone, ending in a glissando sigh: which indicates that she knows, in her heart, what the dream is really worth. The effect is beautifully complemented by Dickie Wells' reticently singing trombone. It is difficult to be sentimental, without also being unintentionally comic, on the traditional jazz trombone; in his most moving performance Wells preserves his instrument's dignity while giving it a songfulness, and also a subtlety of nuance and inflection, that matches Billie's voice. Indeed, he achieves on the trombone some of the traditional qualities of the jazz clarinet or sax, but with a lyrical gravity, even majesty, that befits his instrument.

It is, of course, not an accident that Billie Holiday's favourite obbligato instrument was the tenor sax: nor that Lester Young's playing of it should have complemented her vocal production as precisely as Joe Smith's trumpet complemented that of Bessie Smith. We have seen that Young, born not so far from New Orleans in 1909, became one of the creators of Modern Jazz; and it was Billie Holiday who christened him Pres, because she thought he was as great as Franklin D. Roosevelt. Like Billie, he was a lone wolf, speaking through his horn of the need for love, with a self-defensive laconicism. His plastic phrasing, and pallid, apparently dispassionate tone (often achieving, through "false fingering", subtly fluctuating densities on a single note), echo Billie's neutral style, and—no less than her singing— hide beneath their discretion an intense yearning. Nobody sings—and nobody plays—the word "hunger" and the word "love" as Billie and Lester play-sing them, and the confusion of terminology is appropriate, since Young's sax is a speaking voice and Billie's voice, however intimately associated with the meaning of words, sings like a horn. A lovely example is *Back in your own backyard* (40), a song about the Stephen Foster dream-home, where one is ever "safe from the wolf's black jaw, and the dull ass's hoof". The tender fluctuations in Billie's cool tone, her tremulous little mordents, expose the dream's pathos, as does the interwoven line of Young's wistfully wandering solo and the fragile fioriture of Wilson's piano: yet all three performers give to the frailty an unexpected strength, since their lines, however fine-spun, have the resilience of steel. *If dreams come true* (41) is another song about the "common dream" in which Billie sings not only with Lester Young and Teddy Wilson, but also with two other Basie-men, Buck Clayton and Jo Jones. Here the truth within the dream consists in the simplicity of the tune (she wants to believe), subtly modified by the lingering, lagging phrasing (she cannot believe). In *I'll never be the same* (42) there is a similar effect, for her continuously shifting verbal stresses (consider her singing of the words "there's such an ache in my heart") are echoed, rather than answered, by Young's sax: which suggests simultaneously an impersonal regret (as apposite to you and to me as to Billie), and a gentle, sad mockery. Occasionally an ironic note is explicit, as in *A Fine Romance* (43): note Billie's rhythmic contraction in singing the words "mashed potatoes", and Bunny Berigan's sweetly cheeky cornet obbligato.

But Billie Holiday's finest performances are those in which irony is no more than latent in the understatement of passion. They include all the songs that she "couldn't stand to sing" because the words or tunes or both had so personal a significance for her. This may have been for extramusical reasons, as in the extraordinary lynching song *Strange Fruit* (44), to which Billie's variety of coloration and paradoxically breathless sostenuto give a mysteriously venomous anguish; in the clinching phrases "for the sun to rot", "for the wind to suck", she may attack notes as much as a tone flat, dead and vibrato-less, whining up until they end absolutely on centre in a way that freezes the marrow, and burns with the fierceness of ice. Sometimes no personal reference was necessary to spark off this intensity in Billie: if the tune was good enough, and the words elemental enough, she could become every woman's representative. Her singing of the title phrase in *When a woman loves a man* (45) is a striking example. All the serious Gershwin love-songs, such as *The man I love* (46) or *Porgy* (47), inspired her, not surprisingly, to the best of which she was capable. Here she is as close to Bessie Smith, if more seedily sophisticated, as she is remote from any other pop singer, even the most technically expert. Contrast with Billie Holiday singing Gershwin, Ella Fitzgerald singing tunes from Rodgers and Hart musicals. In *Manhattan* (1925) (48) both words and tune are sprightly and amusing, in *Thou Swell* (1927) (49) the dream of Young Love is stated, verbally and musically, without excessive sentimentality and with some charm. Ella Fitzgerald sings these songs straight, with none of the harsh, "dirty" tone and little of the displaced rhythm of the blues, but with considerable variety of tone-colour and inflection, ranging from a tender, limpid high to a deep, sexy low register. In *My Romance* (50) (1935) the extreme simplicity of the tune, with its endlessly repeated upward rising scale of three notes, attains pathos in Ella's mordents for the "soft guitar", and even hints at the flexibility of jazz improvisation in the final chorus, while in *I wish I were in love again* (51) (1928) an almost identical phrase is made to express, by the singer's false accents, a make-believe gaiety. The words in these Rodgers and Hart numbers have a modest wit, the tunes are catchy and memorable if only because they are so simple and include so much repetition; and the performances are brilliantly professional, enjoyable, and sometimes genuinely touching. Yet they are never more than touching: for we know that while *I wish I were in love again* tells us, a little facetiously, something that is true about the state of being in love, it is true only if you cut out the element in love that is bound sooner or later—however happy you imagine yourself to be—to hurt.

The mixture of charm and facetiousness here involves a combination of extreme naïvety with sophistication, which two qualities are neatly epitomized in two of the most successful pop song composers of the twentieth century—Irving Berlin and Cole Porter.

Irving Berlin—born in Russia, as Izzy Baline, in 1888—is a twentieth-century equivalent to Stephen Foster; and it says something for the "common heart of humanity" that such a figure should survive two World Wars and a Depression. Taken to New York as a baby, he grew up the hard way in the Bowery and lower East Side. He had no musical training, except such as he picked up as a singing waiter in the Bowery saloons; even when he discovered that he had a gift for writing songs—both words and tunes—he was content to pick out the melodies with one finger on the piano, leaving them to be written down and harmonized by some professional. A legend has it that, after he had become rich and famous, Berlin had manufactured a pianistic contrivance that would provide the stock harmonies and modulations—derived from the Massenet-Grieg vocabulary of fifty years ago, and fitted into the thirty-two-bar tune (one four-bar or two two-bar phrases stated twice, two four-bar or four two-bar phrases of "contrast", rounded off by a repetition of the first eight bars, whether in "common" or in "three-quarter" tempo)—at the touch of a lever. The story is probably apocryphal, yet has a kind of rough truth. It was fair enough that Berlin, the folk artist of a commercial world, should allow a machine to do the donkey-work for him while he—a Little Man and a Common Man—created what he had in him to create: the lyrics and tunes that went straight to the hearts of the millions who were like him, except that they lacked his talent.

Certainly it is interesting, even comforting, to note that the lyrics and tunes of Berlin that have survived best seem—as one looks back at them over the years—to be those that most people liked most. Their range of feeling and of technique is as limited as that of the songs of Stephen Foster; and they have the same two basic themes—a simple, adolescent pleasure in the present moment, and an equally adolescent self-pity and nostalgia. *Alexander's Ragtime Band* (52), which we have met in Bessie Smith's unconventionally jazzy version, belongs to the first type and contains, in fact, virtually no jazz influence: only a catchy, reiterated tune-phrase that is a white equivalent to the brisk inanity of Negro ragtime. More interesting are songs like *Top hat, white tie and tails* (53) or *Cheek to cheek* (54), which Ella Fitzgerald sings with an exquisite dippy rapture. If we are young, we recognize the experience as our own—unless we are very hard-boiled and sophisticated. If we merely have once been young, we like being reminded of what young love felt like; and we cannot escape the tunes because, within their restricted vocal range and their simple stepwise movement, they more or less sing themselves. Yet they have their (purely instinctive) subtleties, too: consider how the repeated phrase in *Cheek to Cheek* is gradually extended upwards until it reaches its highest point on the words "hardly speak"; and it is interesting that most of the big successes contain such subtleties, whereas the numbers that have been forgotten do not. This is perhaps more evident in the tearful, self-pitying songs, which are based on the same formula of narrow-ranged, stepwise-moving melody as the simple pleasure songs, except that the phrases tend to fall instead of rise. *Let's face the music and dance* (55) advises us to "put aside the tear-drops" while there is still "music, and moonlight, and romance"; almost exactly the same repeated notes, lullingly regular rhythm, and symmetrical disposition of phrases (with a more rapid build-up of the repetitions to form the climax) occur in *How deep is the ocean?* (56) or *How about me?* (57) Such self-pitying songs may not help us to grow up; but they do insidiously correspond with feelings we have all had in adolescence, and we cannot deny the precision of their art, however instinctual it may be. Though these songs do not deny that love will hurt, as the "facetious" numbers of Rodgers and Hart tend to, they seek a vicarious pleasure from the hurt itself. So they, too, create an illusion that we can live on the surface of our emotions. Sincere, and true, and touching though they may be, their truth—compared with that expressed by Billie Holiday or by Gershwin or still more by the two of them together—is partial.

The world of musical comedy never gets beyond, or wants to get beyond, this illusion: which is why it is most convincing when, grown sophisticated, it makes an ironic point of its illusory nature. This brings us to Cole Porter, who is Berlin's complement and polar opposite. Whereas Berlin is the poor Jew who won fame and fortune, triumphing not through education or even skill, but through his knowledge of the common heart, Porter is the American playboy (the son of an immensely rich industrialist), who, having the knack, can write songs for fun, travelling to Europe for as much or as little training as he needs or desires. The cynical title of Porter's *Anything goes* is typical: so is the fact that, although it hits off the mood of the moment (the 'thirties), it does so with insouciant irresponsibility—without a trace of the bitterness typical of the social-political popular art of the time. The book—

improbably but sometimes comically based on a novel of P. G. Wodehouse—guys the Establishment, the English milord and all representatives of authority. Its ostensible hero is the American Outcast, or gangster. At the same time its heroine is a slightly blowsy English Rose (called Hope!) who has to express moral disapproval of the gangster, while the gangster himself turns out to be a most inefficient Public Enemy, no more than thirteenth on the list, and therefore a figure of fun, shorn of the horror and savagery which, in actuality, he represents. There is no "positive" value except for the rudimentary simplicity of the boy-girl relationship as expressed in the song *All through the Night* (58). In this the tune is merely a descending chromatic scale that, prompting dreamy, unconventionally vacillating modulations, induces a state of trance, which makes the love seem almost too innocent to be true. The limitation of vocal range and the *chromatic* scalewise movement seem to cast a slightly parodistic reflection on the *diatonic* love-songs of Irving Berlin. They also are in a sense too innocent to be true: only we believe in them while they last, whereas Porter's chromatics tell us, regretfully, that we know we are kidding ourselves.

The real vitality of *Anything goes* lies not here, but in a quality entirely alien to Berlin: in its debunking smartness, its desire to get a rise out of authority, to prick the bubbles of humbug—especially religious humbug. One of the most effective numbers, *Blow, Gabriel, blow* (59), is an anti-gospel song, a spiritual to end all spirituals. The destruction of pretence seems in itself to create rhythmic vivacity; and although the original source of the energy—the triplet cross-rhythm in the "blowing" phrase—is simple, the melodic and rhythmic momentum, once generated, carries us helpless and happy into the most unexpected adventures. Consider the D flat modulation, with swinging triplets, that arouses the fire and brimstone, and the comic "purgation" of the return, via B flat minor, to the E flat tonic: wherein both the excitement and the wit effect an emotional release. The well-known song *You're the top* (60) and the title-number *Anything goes* (61) work in rather the same way. The extravagant hyperboles of Porter's own lyrics deflate pretension by guying the poetic, and by equating a Shakespeare sonnet, the Mona Lisa and Mickey Mouse. The persistent syncopation of the clipped melodic phrase does this musically: yet at the same time it induces a positive zest as the phrase rises to high D and stays there while the music modulates rapidly through G minor and B flat and so back to the E flat tonic. The return to the da capo is so neat that we want to laugh; and in laughing we feel—even if with a self-depreciatory shrug—that we are indeed the tops, merely because we are not duped and have no illusions. In *Anything goes* the catchy C major tune is jerked wantonly into E major and A minor in the middle section, yet the point lies in the fact that we accept this licence as funny. Since "anything goes" we may not know where we stand, but at least we can laugh at ourselves—in the same way as the stanza gives the old-world Puritans a "shock" by yanking them up from C to the flat supertonic.

Though this kind of knowing *bonhomie* is, as a positive experience, distinctly limited, it has a queasy honesty such as we do not find in Rodgers and Hart, or even in the simple sentiment of Irving Berlin; and this may be why the sophisticated Cole Porter was able at times to approach, within the conventions of the pop number, a level of passion such as we find nowhere else outside Gershwin's music. There is a hint of this in *I get a kick out of you* (62), where the extension of the crotchet-moving phrase into minim triplets creates an effect both of cumulative obsession and of frustrated energy. *Night and day* (63), from one of the early Fred Astaire and Ginger Rogers musicals, is a more developed example; and it is worth enquiring what makes this song better not merely than the easy reiterations of the average commercial number, but better, too, than a fetching nostalgic number such as Jack Strachey's *These foolish things* (64). We recognize that this latter song has its limited kind of truth; we've all felt like that and have, up to a point, enjoyed the feeling. It is a harmless, or fairly harmless, self-indulgence which is directly related to the habituation of the repeated clauses: only the harmonic climax of the ninth chord that underlines the tune's climax reminds us of *you*—not ourselves, but the girl we're supposed to be thinking of and regretting the loss of. We feel sad, blue in the conventionalized sense, while the gently insistent boogie rhythm renders the sadness delicious. Cole Porter's *Night and day*, beginning with an onomatopoeic beat of the tom-tom and tick of the clock, leaves us for a while in doubt. But if we think the one-note repetitions might be comic, the restless modulations soon suggest otherwise: until the repeated notes grow into the refrain melody, the point of which is the desire of the undulating tune to break away from the repetitions. The ambiguity of the harmony (which begins somewhere between E flat minor and major), the persistent dissonant suspensions, and the descending chromatic sequences are balanced by the forward-thrusting triplets that carry the tune on; indeed, the song grows from a tension between the melody's yearning for lyrical continuity and the harmony's desire to relapse into the enveloping sequence. And the repeated notes, which might have been frustratingly obsessive, paradoxically become the source of the tune's power. They are not present merely to make the tune easily memorable; they serve an expressive purpose, since his obsession is also the urgency of his passion. The G flat modulation, and the oscillating syncopation on the "yearning-burning-inside-of-me" phrase, act the sense; and the melodic thrusting forward is complemented by the increasing animation of the Latin-American rhythm, which makes his heart beat in fevered irregularity. Such unembarrassed sensuality is rare in pop music; and since a real harmonic and tonal progression follows the growing urgency of melody and rhythm, there can be a true harmonic-tonal climax, succeeded by a consummation when the "night and day" phrase is recapitulated, moving to the higher octave no longer with yearning, but with triumph. Only the final return to the tonic, necessitated by the conventional cadence phrase, seems bathetic, letting down the passion as though even Porter is reluctant to admit that love has a power to disturb, irreconcilable with the conventions of Entertainment. At least the song proves that Porter knew that passion existed, even if it were better avoided; and it would be just to say of his more characteristic witty numbers that he seldom wrote a song in which wit stood as a substitute for, rather than an ironic commentary on, feeling.

The later history of the musical has witnessed sundry attempts to counteract its escapism with some kind of moral validity. Theatrically, the best of all latter-day musicals is probably Frank Loesser's *Guys and Dolls,* (65), based on the Damon Runyan stories. In its debunking wit, this is close to Cole Porter, and in particular to *Anything Goes*, for it, too, has as unhero the gangster-outcast, and makes an almost mythologic point of its moral dubiety. While the book is brilliant, however, the music is inferior to Porter's, and hardly succeeds in reconciling Broadway sophistication with old-time corniness. Perhaps only Kurt Weill, had he been born an American, could have caught the right note, though Marc Blitzstein might have approached it. The debunking musical is, however, grossly outnumbered by the semi-serious type, like the Rodgers and Hammerstein *South Pacific* (66), which introduces the fashionable themes of miscegenation and the mixed-up psyche. The miscegenation theme is, of course, treated wistfully, but with unshakeably simple-minded propriety; the mixed-up psyche is comfortably tidied up. It comes back to the amount of "felt life" in specific words and music, and there is more reality in Cole Porter's *Night and day*, let alone one of the love-songs of Gershwin, than in the whole of *South Pacific*, where the dramatic theme is belied by the synthetic sentiment of the harmonic clichés and the rhetoric of the inflated scoring. The pretence of real emotion might better have been avoided: as on the whole it is in the charming *Oklahoma* (67), which is a modern musical in dealing with ordinary folk in a comparatively realistic setting, but is old-fashioned in being satisfied with the superfices. The one composer of genius who, in the early part of his short career, devoted himself consistently to the musical certainly had no desire to plumb depths. George Gershwin was content with the frivolous literary theme as well as with the restricted musical diet of Tin Pan Alley; yet the songs that he wrote within the Alley's conventions revivify cliché in a manner comparable with Cole Porter's *Night and day*, only far more consistently.

The man I love (68), for instance, can stake a claim to being the most moving pop song of our time and, given Gershwin's genius, can do so because both lyric and music treat the stock theme of the Adolescent Dream with compassionate irony and ironic compassion. In his brother Ira, George Gershwin found the ideal collaborator: for he had the ability to write lyrics that resembled the stereotypes sufficiently to be acceptable to a popular audience, while at the same time giving to the formula the slight twist that can transform it into an unexpectedly fresh and adult experience. Thus the lyric of *The man I love* begins with the moon-June cliché and the vision of Prince Charming; simultaneously it admits that the dream, though true to the cravings of the youthful heart, is not likely to be true in fact. The girl laughs at herself ("the he for me") without destroying the reality of her tenderness. The music enacts this beautifully: four repeated E flats establish the intimacy of the speaking voice in youthful innocence, while the rising scale in dotted rhythm makes the flutter of hope in her heart. But the wistful mockery of the "he for me" phrase is reflected in the sophistication of the harmony—the augmented triad that leans towards the "he", the dominant ninth that gives a warm, slightly humorous self-indulgence to the word "me":

EXAMPLE I

Perhaps because of this touch of irony the restatement of the initial phrase is not merely a restatement. The repeated notes are harmonized with more austere G minor triads instead of the E flat concords, and the rising scale modulates sharpwards, so that the stanza can end with a kind of affirmation: we can believe that "to *me* it's clear that he'll appear", and the belief makes the dream more than a self-delusion.

The refrain, however, loses the innocence and becomes all yearning. The tune grows from the merging of the repeated notes into the dotted rhythm lilt of the rising scale, which leans upwards to the flat seventh while the harmony oscillates between the major and minor third; and the vision of the Man I Love as Hero, "big and strong", acquires pathos through being harmonized in *descending* sequences, drooping on to repeated Gs in minims (twice as slow as the original repeated notes) on the words "make him stay":

EXAMPLE 2

The effect is the more wistful because the last G is harmonized not with the expected E flat tonic, but with a delaying G minor. The conventional repetition of these eight bars of refrain unconventionally intensifies both the yearning and the pathos. The asymmetry of the phrase that rises to the blue flat seventh (the D flat occurs first on the third beat, then on the second) evokes the mixture of wonder and apprehension in the girl's meeting with her mythical lover: the more so because the hopefully lifting third is counteracted each time by "crying" descending chromatics in the instrumental parts. At the end of this repeat the long notes (in minims again) enact the speechlessness, and re-create the innocence, of the girl with her dream man.

The middle section moves to C minor and to more urgent harmonic movement, with two harmonies to a bar. Sighing, but acute, appoggiaturas and chromatic inner parts lift her out of her dream of longing, as she identifies her man's coming with a particular day and moment, Monday, Tuesday, or whenever: so that when we return to the original phrase we hear it afresh, as we hear the recapitulation of a sonata! The drooping sequences are still sad, but there is now a quiet confidence in the long, low repeated E flats. The girl has grown in the course of the piece, and we have grown with her: we have come to recognize that if one believes enough, dreams can come true. She will not find her fairy prince, but she will certainly find a young man she mistakes for one. The music tells us that the fact that she will be mistaken does not matter all that much; the joy of love can survive the fallibility of human nature, and the girl knows that, even before the love has happened to her.

There are many Gershwin musical comedy numbers which are almost as good as *The man I love*. In this field he was an adult and unexpectedly deep composer: whereas his first attempts consciously to expand his range and write "serious" music proved, in varying degrees, unfortunate. His association with the Paul Whiteman phase of symphonic jazz produced *Rhapsody in Blue* (69), the Piano Concerto in F (70), and a few smaller orchestral pieces. The tunes were so good that the symphonic apparatus could not sink these works—indeed, they are still afloat in the concert hall, long after the knowledgeable had predicted they would be sunk, encrusted with barnacles. It remains true, however, that the tunes in these works are complete in themselves, like Gershwin's musical comedy numbers, and are thus improved neither by the attempts at "development" nor by the Lisztian tinsel with which they are flimsily tied together. Here the world of art and the world of commerce cannot amalgamate; and in this case we certainly cannot say that art represents truth and commerce falsehood.

On one occasion, however, at the end of his "fabulous" life, Gershwin managed to start from the conventions of Tin Pan Alley, in which he had been nurtured, and to achieve a convincing fulfilment in the world of art. The two sides of his nature—the man of commerce who, with the help of remarkable talents, had made millions, and the man of art who wished to leave a legacy to America's future—became one. That they did so in a work for the theatre was not an accident, for Gershwin's professional training on Broadway meant that he felt and thought spontaneously in theatrical terms, whereas to create in terms of the concert hall went against the grain. But there is a deeper reason for the success of *Porgy and Bess*: which is that the theme of the opera is Gershwin's own life, his experience and ours—a modern myth. Indeed, to recognize DuBose Heyward's novel, when he came across it, as *his* was a part of Gershwin's genius: which a composer of talent might have passed by. Having recognized it, his greatest, his most emotionally involved numbers grew out of it. Because they were so involved with his own experience, they became inextricably involved with one another; as a result Gershwin raised the conventions of the musical to operatic stature.

IX

From pop to art: opera, the musical and George Gershwin's "Porgy and Bess"

> nothing
> inspires us but the love we want upon the frozen face of earth
>
> and utter disparagement turns into praise as generations read
> the message of our hearts in adolescent closets who once shot
> at us in doorways
>
> or kept us from living freely because they were too young
> then to know what they would ultimately need from a
> barren and heart-sore life
>
> the beauty of America, neither cool jazz nor devoured
> Egyptian heroes, lies in lives in the darkness I inhabit in the
> midst of sterile millions
>
> the only truth is face to face, the poem whose words become
> your mouth and dying in black and white we fight for what
> we love, not are.
>
> FRANK O'HARA

DuBose Heyward's novel *Porgy* is a parable about alienation, oppression, and the inviolability of a radical innocence of spirit, even in a corrupt world. George Gershwin was not, like Porgy, a Negro, nor, in the material benefits of life, was he in any way deprived. He was, however, a poor boy who made good: an American Jew who knew all about spiritual isolation and, in Tin Pan Alley, had opportunity enough to learn about corruption. He was not, like Porgy, a physical cripple. He was, however, an emotional cripple, being victimized, like so many of his generation, by nervous maladjustments and the usual escapes from them. So, in his opera, he sang with honesty and with unexpected strength of the spiritual malaise that is inherent in the twentieth-century pop song itself. His instinct for the nostalgia at the heart of the common man's experience rivals that of Stephen Foster: what makes him so much richer a composer is that his art intuitively recognizes the nostalgia as such. His opera is about the impact of the world of commerce on those who once led, would like to have led, may still lead, the "good life", based on a close relationship between man and nature.

This theme is stated explicitly in the verses that stand as prelude to the novel:

> Porgy, Maria and Bess,
> Robbins, and Peter and Crown,
> Life was a three-stringed harp
> Brought from the woods to town.
>
> Marvellous tunes you rang
> From passion, and death, and birth,
> You who had laughed and wept
> On the warm, brown lap of the earth.
>
> Now in your untried hands
> An instrument, terrible, new,
> Is thrust by a master who frowns,
> Demanding strange songs of you.
>
> God of the White and Black,
> Grant us great hearts on the way
> That we may understand
> Until you have learned to play.

The theme applies, obviously, to urban, industrialized man whatever the colour of his skin: the plight of the Negro merely gives one peculiarly pointed manifestation, because the contrast between his innocence and urban sophistication is acute. Gershwin sees the parable in terms of his own experience: which is why it is of no consequence that the book offers a synthetic picture of Negro life. Broadway is indeed a long way from the "warm, brown lap of the earth", and the strange song it sings may inculcate evasion rather than understanding. None the less, even on Broadway, Gershwin sounds the three-stringed lyre of passion and birth and death with unequivocal power. He accepts his world as it is, never loading the scales: we should honour him for his "great heart".

The opera opens in Catfish Row (Charleston), a Negro slum-tenement which had once (the point is not fortuitous) been a colonial-style palace occupied by "governors and the ambassadors of kings". The orchestral prelude evokes a Negro Eden: a state of happiness in the present moment, incarnated in rapid pentatonic figuration, non-developing ostinati, and a minimum of harmony, founded on oscillating pentatonic fourths. Only the persistent cross-accents suggest a jazzy agitation beneath the "pre-conscious" happiness: though the fourths of the ostinati gradually acquire higher chromatic discords until the curtain rises on Jazzbo Brown playing boogie piano on stage. While the chorus sing primitive pentatonic Da-doo-das, Jazzbo introduces the tawdry sophistications of Tin Pan Alley chromatics; the two worlds of the folk community and of New York are already juxtaposed.

This evocation of background merges into a musical-dramatic statement of the contrasting poles of experience. Clara, nursing her baby, sings the "Summer-Time" lullaby. The mother-child relationship is the basic human positive; but, being human, the song involves much more than the pre-conscious happiness of the prelude. Thus the words are a dream of Eden, when it is always summer-time, when "livin' is easy, fish are jumpin', an' the cotton is high: [when] daddy's *rich* an' ma is *good-lookin'*. But, though the line is still basically pentatonic, it is now not merely a gay doodling, but a pliantly expressive melody, the innocence of which is modified by the melancholy of the blue notes, the ellipses of the rhythms, and the nostalgia of the chromatic harmony, which is darkly sweet and sensuously yearning:

EXAMPLE I

Though within the convention of the pop number, the lullaby, like many of Gershwin's tunes, has the authentic spirit of the blues: which may be why true jazzmen have always admired him and have so frequently used his tunes as a basis for improvisation or (in the case of the beautiful Miles Davis-Gil Evans suite) re-composition. Moreover, the blue melancholy points to the deeper roots of this most haunting number: for the sadness is an admission that the Eden-dream will not square with the facts of experience. The baby *will* cry, and must one day "spread its wings". The desire for security ("Nothin' can harm you With Daddy an' Mammy standin' by") is in all of us: yet we have to pass beyond attachment to the mother, let alone regression to the womb. This equivocation is marvellously suggested by the static rocking chords combined with the ambiguous tonality, which oscillates between a Dorian B minor and a diatonic D major with whole tone implications. This tonal fluidity is the more expressive since it follows the nearly static E major innocence of the prelude.[1]

The lyricism of the mother-child relationship is abruptly swept aside by the violence of the crap-game. The significantly named Sportin' Life, a Negro who represents the new world of Commerce and New York, makes the appropriate verbal comment when, invoking the dice, he says, "It may be in the summer time an' may be in the fall, But yo' got to *leave* yo' *baby* an' yo' *home* an' all." All the simple human positives that are inherent in the Lullaby have to be sacrificed in a world of exploitation. If one cannot have a stable relationship to family and community, one has to accept the fact that life is a gamble; and most of the characters, "good" or "bad", are gamblers whose fecklessness is a consequence of their awareness that they do not belong. The only people who disapprove of the gambling are the religious fanatics, like Serena; and in the conversation between her and her husband Robbins we are implicitly told that worship of the Lawd can be as much an escape as the worship of chance or of the body. Jake's crap-game song, which excuses his gaming as a relief from toil, evokes more sympathy from the onlookers and us than Serena's liturgical incantation. Its rapid changes of metre and instable mediant modulations follow the heart's waywardness—as compared with his wife's rigidity.

Soon the two modes—the humanity of the mother-child relationship and the fecklessness of gambling—are counterpointed against one another, as Clara sings the Lullaby while the crap-game continues. It looks as though the fecklessness is destroying the humanity: for Clara's man Jake complains that she cannot get the baby to sleep, but he'll soon "fix it". So the Lullaby's ostinato turns quick and agitated in $\frac{3}{8}$;

[1] It is interesting that E major seems to be traditionally associated with Eden. It is the key of the "O past, O happy life" epilogue to Delius's *Sea-Drift*; was habitually Schubert's Eden key; has often this association in Beethoven, Mozart and Handel (consider Semele's dream of bliss). Can the association have arisen because, in the early days of diatonic homophony, E was the sharpest, most "upward-tending" key in reasonably common use?

and leads into a jazzy number in boogie rhythm, somewhat aggressively shouting that "A woman is a sometime thing". The key, G
minor, is the dark complement to the opera's key of simple happiness,
G major; and there seems to be a hint of frenzy in the rhythmic drive,
and in the chorus's broken ejaculations of the refrain to falling minor
thirds. Yet if the song is anti-woman and anti-mother ("Yo' mammy
is the first to name yo', and she'll tie yo' to her apron string, Then
she'll shame yo' and she'll blame yo', till yo' woman comes to claim
yo'"), we see in retrospect that it is a positive statement also. The
child's relationship to mother is not enough. We have to grow up;
and, as we shall see, the opera is about the difficulty of doing so in a
world dominated by Sportin' Life and commercial exploitation.

With the baby, Jake's cynicism is no more effective than its mother's
tenderness. It continues to wail; and the men laughingly remark that
Jake is better at crap-shooting than he is at nursing. A new world of
feeling is introduced by the appearance of Peter, the old honey-man,
crooning his pentatonic honey-call in G major, over a drone ostinato
and a soft, bee-like buzzing in flowing semiquavers, with Lydian sharp
fourths and flat sevenths:

EXAMPLE 2

The honey-man seems to come from a distant past: from a pristine
world where man and nature lived in harmony. Significantly, he
heralds, with a return to the initial pentatonic Eden music, the approach
of Porgy, in his goat cart. The opening paragraph of the novel runs:

> Porgy lived in a Golden Age. Not the Golden Age of a remote and
> legendary past; nor yet the chimerical era cherished by every man past
> middle life, that never existed except in the heart of youth; but an age
> when men, not yet old, were boys in an ancient, beautiful city that time
> had forgotten before it destroyed.

A little later we find:

> No one knew Porgy's age. . . . A woman who had married twenty
> years before remembered him because he had been seated on the church

steps, and had given her a turn before she went in. Once a child saw Porgy, and said suddenly, "What is he waiting for?" That expressed him better than anything else. He was waiting, waiting with the concentrated intensity of a burning-glass.

All this may be latent in his musical theme, which we now hear in the original E major:

EXAMPLE 3

The falling fifths have a primal, noble simplicity, but the blue minor thirds, approached by the "crushed" notes, are crippled, while the accompanying parallel triads begin in diatonic stability but grow chromatically disturbed, "waiting" for fulfilment. In parlando recitative the men tease Porgy about being soft on Crown's Bess, whom Maria (representative of the old communal values) and the religious Serena both dismiss as unfit for "Gawd-fearin" ladies to "'sociate with". Porgy denies any acquaintance with or interest in Bess; and introduces the theme of alienation when, in noble pentatonic arioso, he sings "When Gawd make cripple, he mean him to be lonely. Night time, day time, he got to trabble that lonesome road": a remark that applies to the Jewish or Gentile emotional cripple no less than to Porgy. Thus the opera's central theme is related to Gershwin himself—and to us.

With a violent hubbub and offstage shouts which "frighten children that run past the gate yelling", Crown enters, with Bess, to a ferocious syncopated rhythm that is associated with him throughout the opera:

EXAMPLE 4

Later on we shall realize that Bess's two lovers, Crown and Porgy, are not to be thought of as villain and hero; perhaps they are not so much opposed as complementary, separated parts of a human whole that ought to be indivisible. Porgy is pre-lapsarian man, innocent and good, but broken and unfulfilled. Crown is fallen man, yet a Lucifer figure, impressive in his pride, brute strength, and self-reliance. Both are immensely strong physically, though Porgy's strength is crippled because he is unaware of it. Both are operatically bass-baritones, and the same Negro singer was suggested to Gershwin as being suitable for the role of either Porgy or Crown. Both, in the crap-game, invoke fortune or the dice, Crown with a snarled curse, Porgy with a quasi-liturgical incantation to his "little stars". The simplicity of this sounds the more moving, and also the more vulnerable, because the crap-game is mostly spoken rather than sung, against a metrically aggressive background dominanted by minor seconds and by the sharp sonority of the xylophone. The "Woman is a sometime thing" tune is cynically intertwined in the gaming music.

The scene culminates in a fight, prompted by the drunken Crown, to music combining the metallic clatter of the crap-game music with Crown's sadistic syncopation. After a wild "ensemble of perplexity", Crown murders Robbins with a cotton-hook: which may also be, in Freudian terms, the fury of his uncontrolled sexual appetite. Everyone rushes off before the arrival of the police. Crown, with Bess's encouragement and financial help, goes to hide on Kittiwah Island, and Bess is left to fend for herself. She is alone with Sportin' Life, who, in plying Crown with rot-gut whisky and dope, has been indirectly responsible for letting loose chaos. He croons to Bess, in sleazy blue notes and chromatics, "I'se the only frien' yo' got left"; and she accepts a touch of happy dust to steady her nerves and shaking limbs. That Sportin' Life, a very light-coloured Negro, peddles dope is inseparable from his relationship to commerce, prostitution, and "New York"; he offers forgetfulness in exactly the same way as Tin Pan Alley. And although or because he is the snake in the grass, he has the serpent's insidious attractiveness, for Eve in Eden, for Bess, for Gershwin, and for us, too. Anyway, he is a fact, like Tin Pan Alley; he is what life is like, since the Fall, and it does not help to pretend he is not there. Bess, though she cannot resist the happy dust, resists his invitation to accompany him to New York, and it seems that, with Crown gone, she has no one to turn to. Maria—the old, pre-New York-conscious world—rejects her as a liquor-guzzling slut and she is left quite alone. It is then that crippled Porgy invites her into his hut; and the scene ends with a swelling theme growing from pentatonic simplicity, a lyrical extension of Porgy's arioso of loneliness:

EXAMPLE 5

We shall hear this again, in a very different context.

This incipient love-theme in F major remains, in its sequential thirds, more primitive, less adult, than the later song of love fulfilled. It is at this point that we begin to identify ourselves with Porgy, as Gershwin did: for we all tend to think of ourselves as good, if broken. There may be an Oedipan undercurrent, too, in so far as Bess is, for Porgy, not only passion and experience, but also the Eternal Beloved: Maria, in the novel, refers to her as Porgy's "she-Gawd". She is the balm for loneliness, and so not only lover but also the mother who will give the babe rest. From this point of view Crown is the father-figure, dreadful in his potency: against whom Porgy has to assert himself to conquer the infantile fear of impotence. Crown repeatedly taunts Porgy because he is crippled: "ain't there no whole ones left?" Something of this may be present in the postlude to the scene, for the wailing inner chromatics (also derived from the loneliness arioso) imbue the simple, pentatonic tune with an oddly febrile quality.

After the violent action of this scene, the second scene of Act I is static. It begins with a lament for the dead Robbins, in which solo voices declaim in pentatonic ululations, based on observation of genuine gospel "shouts". The chorus intone the word "gone" in a descending whole-tone progression, harmonized with unrelated diatonic concords:

EXAMPLE 6

Each triad sounds like a thudding of earth-clods, while the chords' lack of harmonic relationship suggests disintegration, the opening of an abyss. Though the harmony may have no affinity with real Negro music, it is equally remote from Tin Pan Alley. The key, G minor, seems in the opera to be a key of tragic reality, as it is in more reputable composers such as Mozart and Handel; but the tragedy is epic and communal rather than personal. Porgy and Bess come in to make their contribution to Robbins's "saucer-burial". Serena refuses the money until she learns that it comes from Porgy, not Crown; then we see that their action stands for life against the dirge. Everybody sings a spiritual, "Fill up de saucer till it overflow", in which descending chromatics wail against life, while the "overflow" phrase, growing gradually stronger, goes up diatonically.

The frenzied chanting is broken by the appearance of a white detective, investigating the murder. Like all the sequences in which white men appear, the interview with the detective is more spoken than sung. The upshot is that old Peter, the honey-man, is taken away to prison as a witness, pending the arrest of Crown. That Peter, representative of the pristine innocence of the old world, should be the scapegoat is not fortuitous, as Porgy points out in musing arioso; perhaps it is also not fortuitous that while Porgy admits to the unpredictability and injustice of life, chromatic weaving in the orchestra hints remotely at his adult song of love fulfilled. The arioso also leads into Serena's song of loss, "My man's gone now", wherein the tragic note is sounded for the first time in the opera. The pentatonically simple tune is modified by the fierceness of the false relations created by blue thirds; while the energy of the Creole rhythm is undermined by rapid, often semitonic modulations, and by the chromatic refrain in which the chorus participates. So, from the apprehension of loss comes an affirmation of the will to go on living. In the context, we probably associate the dead Robbins with the imprisoned Peter; and the loss of innocence is our loss: just as Crown's crime is ours because we are all fallen creatures and not many of us—as we shall see—are as courageous as Crown. The immediate effect of Serena's song is to induce compassion in the Negro undertaker, who agrees to save Robbins from the students' hospital even though the saucer has not produced sufficient money. Everybody joins in singing a spiritual of gratitude, in which rhythmic and harmonic ostinati become a train-piece. The Negro— and modern man in general—is heading for the Promised Land because he has no earthly home. The delirious pace of the choo-choo suggests that the promise is a long way off.

As an epic figure Porgy belongs, like Peter, to the Golden Age. Unlike Peter, however, he has to learn to deal with the world as it is; and both in Catfish Row and in New York the gold is tarnished. The second act of the opera concerns Porgy's attempt to grow from child to man; and although it begins in the morning, in a relaxed manner, we for the first time become conscious of the unconscious, which is the sea. Negro fishermen are repairing nets and singing a rowing song that begins pentatonically in G major but finds its way to the "reality" of G minor for the refrain, "It takes a long pull to get there". It does indeed, even though the verses pretend to be easy about the vast sea and the unknown mysteries: "if I meet Mister Hurricane and Hurricane tell me no, I'll take ole Mister Hurricane by the pants and I'll throw him in the jail-house do'." But, of course, we know that although you can lock up innocent Peter in a jail, you cannot do that to a hurricane; and in the refrain everyone seems to admit that in going over the unknown sea they are committing themselves to a pilgrimage that may or may not lead to that Promised Land.

Against this awareness of the eternal sea we are shown the simple human solidarity of the island picnic at which, care-free, we seek together happiness and a refuge from the unknowable. Porgy's banjo-song, "I got plenty o' nuttin'", is a personal complement to this. Growing from his invocation to the dice, it is a pre-purgatorial expression of the happiness of not having, once more basically pentatonic, in G major, over a rudimentary oompah accompaniment. He sings against the world of commercial exploitation and material possession.

> I got plenty o' nuttin',
> An' nuttin's plenty fo' me.
> I got no car, got no mule,
> I got no misery.
> De folks wid plenty o' plenty
> Got a lock on dey door,
> 'Fraid somebody's a-goin to rob 'em
> While dey's out a-makin' more.
> *What for?*

There is no cynicism but a melancholy irony in the fact that the hero of the playboy who made millions should croon these words; Porgy is to learn, as Gershwin himself learned, that "misery" is not as easily evaded as that. Perhaps he suspects this, in his heart, while he sings: for the G major tonality and the childish rhythm are disturbed by tentative, groping modulations to E and C sharp, which are abruptly, even shamefacedly, yanked back to G, as though he dare not follow the waywardness of his heart.

Pointedly, this happy song is succeeded by two (parlando) incidents which attempt, superficially and inconclusively, to banish evil. First,

Maria as spokesman of the old world gives a dressing-down to Sportin'
Life, while the orchestra plays his serpentine tritonal triplets. She says
someone has to carve him up and "set these niggers free", and it might
as well be herself. But although she threatens to offer his remains to the
buzzards and rattlesnakes, it is he, musically, who survives: for the
devilish tritones and triplets ultimately turn into his anti-creed song
"It ain't necessarily so". The comedy in Maria's berating of Sportin'
Life turns out to be double-edged; and the same may be true of the
next episode, wherein the Negro lawyer Frazier attempts to sell Bess a
divorce from Crown. There is a "complication", because Bess has
never been married; but while the parlando dialogue and the chorus's
interjections are very funny, we sense an element of uneasiness, too,
for the episode brings the theme of commercial exploitation into
Porgy's own experience. He pays up, though Bess tries to persuade
him not to; his "childish" credulity is part of his tragedy. In personal
terms Porgy's credulity parallels Jake's simplicity in taking his boat out
to the Blackfish Banks at the time of the September storms. Jake's
answer to his wife's fear is that if he doesn't make *money* he won't be
able to give their son a college education. The two worlds are in
conflict.

The Frazier incident is concluded by the appearance of the white
man Archdale, who cautions Frazier about his divorce racket, but lets
him off "this time". Archdale informs Porgy that he has stood bail for
Peter; there are general cries of gratitude. Immediately after the white
man's apparently disinterested action, however, a buzzard ironically
appears in the sky, and the cries of joy turn into yells of superstitious
horror. Porgy's "Buzzard" song is the turning-point of the opera, for
it forces him to face up to reality and suffering. The anguished appoggiaturas, the strained, gawky leaps and flapping-winged chromatics are
darker in character than any music we have heard previously, since the
anguish is now that of personal experience—of growing up—and is
not, like the dirges, a communal lamentation. The appearance of the
buzzard marks Porgy's realization of the significance of his love; and
although conflict is manifest in the rondo structure, the song turns into
a victory for love-life over death. "Ain' nobody *dead* dis mornin'",
says Porgy; "livin's jus' begun. *Two is strong* where *one* is feeble".
Man and woman, together, may share grief as they share laughter;
because there are "two folks livin' in dis shelter" there "ain' no such
thing as loneliness". Here the pop-music cliché of the eleventh chord
is given fresh meaning by its association with melodic climax:

EXAMPLE 7

So the buzzard keeps on flying; and the chromaticized A minor tonality ends in a resonant A major triad with added sixth.

Immediately afterwards Sportin' Life, whom Maria had called a buzzard as well as a rattlesnake, tempts Bess with his happy dust. The slithery chromatics and sequences of his song, "Picnics is alright for these small town niggers", reject the old world's solidarity in favour of "the big money" and New York: a use of pop music cliché for satirical effect which is also, once more, insidiously attractive. Bess contemptuously spurns his advances and Porgy overpowers him with the strength of his hand: "Gawd, what a grip for a piece of a man!" Sportin' Life, cursed by Porgy as rat, louse and buzzard, sneaks off: but not before he has reminded Bess, in a craftily chromatic recitative ending on a high A, that though her men may come and go, "ole Sportin' Life an' de happy dus' here all along".

Since both the buzzard and Sportin' Life are temporarily routed, the public merriment of the picnic can proceed; and Porgy can grow into his great song of adult love, "Bess, you is my woman now". This marvellous piece insists first on an awareness of personal identity ("you is, you is"), then on their togetherness ("two instead of one"). They belong to one another, if to nothing else; and this is contained in the sweep of the line. The strain that has gone to create this twoness is also present—in the leaps of sixth and seventh and ninth, in the blue notes and crushed notes that are a cry of pain, in the mediant modulations that seem to urge the music upwards:

EXAMPLE 8

The urgency is stilled in the falling fifths and rising fourths of the "mornin' time and evenin' time" refrain, which is a fulfilled metamorphosis of Porgy's "night time, day time" arioso of loneliness in Act I. The first ensemble number in the opera occurs when they sing the "I is, you is" chorus in duo, a third higher in D major. Bess vows to be Porgy's woman for ever, while he sings, to wistfully declining chromatics, "O my Bessie, we's happy now".

The extraordinary emotional weight which this song bears is achieved within a convention still recognizably that of the popular ballad, though Tin Pan Alley would have frowned on the wide vocal range, the difficult leaps, the unconventional modulations. The dramatic placing of the song is also masterly: for immediately after this liberation of personal feeling, the crowd surges in on its way to the picnic, singing a pentatonic song of simple gaiety, related to Porgy's banjo song, and in the same G major tonality. The community cannot follow Porgy through his purgatorial experience towards adulthood; and although Bess has just said she will stay with Porgy for ever, she submits to public opinion, and Porgy abets her, when Maria says she'll spoil the fun if she doesn't attend the picnic. This is the second turning-point in the tragedy. The duo has told us that the personal love-relationship is, in a shifting world, all-important: to relinquish it in favour of a simple, communal sociality is fatal. This must be why Bess's good-byes in rising thirds and sixths have a poignancy far in excess of their ostensible relation to the situation. When she has gone Porgy returns to his naïve banjo-song, but in E flat, flat submediant to the original G. Trivial though the incident may seem, it has acquired a quality which we may not extravagantly term tragic irony.

This is underlined by the picnic music that opens scene 2. There is something frightening, as well as exuberant, about the pounding tom-toms, the pentatonic ha-da-das, and the barbarous 3 plus 2 ostinato: for it is a denial of the complexity of the love relationship, as expressed in the duet. The words explicitly refer to a preconscious state: "like the moon, I ain't got no shame"—no awareness of guilt—"so I can do what I like". Then Sportin' Life, in his anti-creed song "It ain't necessarily so", betrays the link between this unthinking and ultimately unfeeling animality and the modern corruption. Having no shame, doing what I like, though potentially a virtue, may become a vice: the "easy livin'" of urban sophistication. Yet Sportin' Life's vice remains attractive. Gershwin's direction that he should sing "happily, with humour" is not ironic, and in a sense what he says is true: life *is* like this and, for most of us who cannot live through the Porgy-Bess experience, it *ain't* necessarily so. The verbal wit of Sportin' Life's inverted gospel-sermon takes the mickey out of "religious" innocence, which we have seen to be inadequate; and his serpentine triplets and devilish tritones become blandly humorous now they have grown into so captivating a tune:

EXAMPLE 9

It ain't ne-ces-sar-il - y so

The savage wa-dos that return as a ritornello seem in the context ludicrous; and it is appropriate that their key should be E flat, that of Bess's good-byes, of Porgy's last version of the banjo-song—and of the stock Tin Pan Alley ballad: as compared with Sportin' Life's honestly dishonest G minor.

Certainly when Serena answers Sportin' Life with quasi-liturgical incantation, accompanied by the savage drum-beats of the picnic music, we see that her response is no answer at all. The Tin Pan Alley sevenths and ninths of Sportin' Life's song, cumulatively reinforcing the swing of the tune, have in the context more real vitality than this primitive pentatonicism; and one reason why the opera is so moving and so relevant to us is that it admits that there is no answer to Sportin' Life's anti-creed except the struggle towards personal fulfilment and togetherness that Porgy and Bess seek. The religious certainties of the old world of Maria and Serena have gone, destroyed by Sportin' Life's New World of commerce; wishful thinking will not bring them back. So it is at the picnic, on the island, after the junketings, that Bess re-meets Crown, man fallen but devastating in courage and potency. The interview, mainly spoken against his cruel, jagged rhythm, is superb theatre. She tries to speak on behalf of Porgy, who needs her; but her frenzied song "What you want wid Bess?" is, in its thrusting triplet syncopations, as much sexy as desperate. Enharmonic modulations from the initial B major become wild as Crown joins her in the opera's second ensemble number, and the contact with his hands—about which Bess sings a weird wailing ululation—is too much for her. Fearfully, delightedly, she yields to him, to the violence which is in all of us, and perhaps has to be admitted to. Crown's triumph is a rau-cously scored version of the Bess-Crown duo, violently syncopated, yet unmistakably related—in its falling fifths and energetic sixths (which are Porgy's thirds inverted)—to Porgy's theme. This relationship makes its effect, though we do not as yet realize how Porgy and Crown are complementary, if not in a sense identical.

After this tremendous climax, the third scene of Act II returns to Catfish Row at dawn. Quietude is expressed by way of chiming bells built from superimposed fourths—the static chord of the first act's prelude; but sliding chromatic sequences suggest unease beneath the calm. The gently rocking sea of the $\frac{12}{8}$ larghetto is pierced by sighing false relations; and fishermen set out to the rowing song, reminding us that they will "anchor in de Promise' Lan' ". The deceptive tranquillity is broken by cries from Bess, offstage in Porgy's room. After being three days away with Crown, she has returned delirious, in a fever; she screams of hands and rattlesnakes on Kittiwah Island, her yells being accompanied by oscillating tritones. At the height of Bess's sickness, Peter returns from prison. He sings an exquisitely simple G major arietta of acceptance ("White folks put me in, an' de white folks take me out, an' I ain' know yet what I done"), which gives a hymnic resolution to Porgy's falling fifths:

EXAMPLE 10

Perhaps it even suggests a fusion of the black spiritual with the white hymn. Certainly its freshness is no longer a mere return to primal innocence, for it pours balm on Bess's Lydian agitations: induces Porgy to croon to her a lullaby, related to Peter's tune but with blue ambiguities, since he is suffering in this world, not a vision from afar: and leads Serena to pray for her, with declamatory encouragement from Porgy and Peter. With the release of Peter, the religious sanctions of the old world become momentarily operative again: so Serena's pentatonic incantation summons, ritualistically, the street-criers: honey-man, strawberry-woman, and even devil-crab man. The effect of these calls, wondrously re-created from folk sources, is literally magical. Time stops—there is no harmonic movement, only a drone with added sixth; and this return to Eden, complete with crab (apples) that are sold for money ("I's talkin' about yo' pocket book") recovers Bess from madness. While the clock chimes its fourths she comes out to greet Porgy on the step. The love-song sounds distantly, while he whispers "Thank Gawd".

Outside Time, this lovely passage looks forward to a day when spiritual innocence and the material world of buying and selling will be compatible. It is a vision, not a fact: as is indicated in the pathos of the dialogue that follows. Bess says she has been lonesome in there by herself; and they whisper in haltingly tender arioso of Porgy's intuitive knowledge that she has been with Crown, of her fear of Crown's inescapability, of their need for one another, while thinly scored fragments of the love-song sound frailly forlorn. But the adult love-song cannot re-establish itself. Bessie's aria "I want to stay here, but I ain't worthy" regresses to the embryonic love-theme that had concluded Act I scene 1, in the same key of F. The broken arch of the melody, rising through pentatonic thirds, pausing at the top, and then falling, conveys the vacillation within her feelings: the wave that cannot reach the shore. The orchestra's false relations add to the ambiguity. Only in the middle section, when she sings of Crown's return, of how he'll handle her and hold her and it'll be "like dying", does the movement press forward, reinforced by chromatically rising ninths. Porgy promises to protect her: so they sing the "I wants to stay here" song da capo, in duo, and faster. Bess's broken waves, stretching from a low B flat to a high A, sound more desperate, if less forlorn, than when she sang alone.

Out of the strange pathos and ultimate desperation of this scene comes the hurricane, expressed musically through sliding chromatics related to the buzzard skirls, through Sportin' Life's tritones, and through Crown's syncopation. The outburst of elemental fury abruptly concludes the scene; and in the next scene the Negroes are huddled in Serena's room, praying in multifarious pentatonic yells, over a G minor drone, while the storm howls outside. Among those appealing to God to spare his *children*, Sportin' Life remains himself, and by no means unsympathetically cynical: "We had storms befo'. I ain't so sure this is Judgment Day." While Porgy and Bess converse in a corner, he confident of her, she thinking of Crown on Kittiwah Island, the Negroes break into a spiritual, "Oh, de Lawd shake de Heavens": while Clara, singing the "Summer-time" lullaby to her baby, counterpoises the security of the womb against the chaos that has been loosed within the mind and without. At the height of the storm there is a

terrifying banging at the door. The Negroes scream that it must be
Death, and lurch into a hysterical chanting of "O dere's somebody
knockin' at de do'". When, as magnificently theatrical climax, the
door is scrunched in, the visitor proves to be not Death but Crown,
come through the storm to claim his Bess. Against his violent rhythm
he taunts Bess and Porgy: "You ain' done much for yo'self while I
been gone . . . does yo' call dat a *man?*" As Bess screeches that he
should keep his *hands* off her, he comes sublimely, Lucifer-like, into his
own. Shouting a fierce chant, mostly on high Cs, he defies Porgy, the
crowd, and God: "If Gawd want to kill me, He had plenty of chance
between here an' Kittiwah Island. . . There ain' nothin' He likes
better den a scrap wid a *man*; Gawd an' me is *frien.*" Horrified by
this blasphemy, the crowd roar a spiritual about the sky tumbling.
But Crown shouts them down: "Don' you hear God a'mighty laughin'
at yo? . . . Gawd laugh, *an' Crown laugh back.*" His rhythm takes
over, and he swings into a triumph song about his sexual attractiveness—a crude barrelhouse tune about the red-headed woman who,
though she may make a choo-choo (to the Promised Land?) jump
its tracks, will never make a goddam fool of Crown. Everybody
yells "Lawd save us, don't listen to that Crown". But they do listen;
and Crown's supreme moment is still to come. Clara, at the window,
suddenly screams, for she has seen her husband's boat wrecked.
Handing the baby to Bess, she rushes out into the hurricane. Bess
says someone must go to help her. After further jibes at Porgy—
"Yeah, where is a man?"—Crown, fallen man as hero, goes unafraid
to the rescue. As the door opens, contrary motion chromatics act the
storm's putting out of the lights. The scene ends, in every sense, in
darkness, the Negroes returning to their pentatonic incantations over a
G minor drone, to a dolorous thudding of timpani. While the crowd
pray to be released into the "golden meadows", Crown stands alone,
breasting the storm.

But Crown fails, no less than Porgy. Though he survives, for a time,
he does not save Clara and Jake; and Act III opens with the chorus
trying to re-establish the tribal innocence, singing to dead Clara and
Jake: follow Jesus, and be *safe*. The hypnotic falling fourths of the
chant, the lack of harmonic movement, the D flat tonality with flat
sevenths, induce a state of trance—at the furthest possible pole from
Crown's music. And again Sportin' Life's cynicism stands, in a sense,
for life: "I ain't see no sense in makin' such a fuss over a man when
he's *dead*". When Maria reprimands him he gloats over his power over

Bess who, in having two men, has none: for the light and the dark forces will destroy one another, if they have not already done so. It may be at this point that we realize intuitively that Porgy and Crown are, or ought to be, one man. Porgy's simple nobility and Crown's dark passion and courage should be complementary, since both are necessary for growing up. What prevents their working in harmony is the no-values of commerce, prostitution, and Sportin' Life, whereby the savagery becomes callous, the innocence itself savage. Porgy and Crown are both gamblers, and both lose. What they lose is Bess, as mother, lover, and Eternal Beloved.

So the nemesis that follows is the unfolding of what has already happened: which is suggested musically by the fact that the second murder takes place to a modified recapitulation of the music for the first act murder. Bess is singing the "Summer-time" lullaby to Clara's baby which is now vicariously hers, while Crown approaches stealthily through the night to a dry, sinister repetition of the crap-game music. Attempting to enter Bess's window, he is stabbed and then strangled by Porgy's strong *hands*. The son-against-father motive becomes explicit here. Porgy has to acquire Crown's sexual violence to assert his rights over Bess, so the scene ends with his hysterical guffaws of triumph ("yo got a *man* now"), accompanied by *Crown's* rhythm, and rounded off by a raucous permutation of his falling fifth tune which emphasizes its relationship to Crown's theme. He becomes Crown, instead of being fused with, reconciled to, him. That is the tragedy, the disharmony for which Sportin' Life is responsible.

The second scene opens with a necessary relaxation of tension. The pentatonic figures suggest the bustle of everyday life—now centred on F sharp minor, rather than in an E major Eden. The enquiries of the white detective and coroner are counterpointed against the Negro innocence; but this time the situation is inverted, because the innocence is really craft. The comedy of the trio of women who "aint seen nothin'" relates back to the Frazier episode of Act I; the difference is that whereas in the first act Porgy faced up to the buzzard, defeated Sportin' Life, and sang his chant of adult love, this time his credulity undoes him. Asked to go and identify Crown's body, he trembles with superstitious dread: which Sportin' Life exploits by insinuating that Crown's wounds will bleed as soon as his murderer looks on them. At this point Sportin' Life parodies Porgy's pentatonics. When Porgy has been carried off, encouraged by Bess who says that he can keep his eyes tight shut, needn't see what he doesn't want to see, Sportin' Life teases

her, too. He convinces her that Porgy's guilt is already known or will
be known, and that he'll be lucky if he's locked up for life, rather than
executed. Whereas he exploits Porgy's innocence, he exploits Bess's
weariness. He knows that life has taught her that things usually go
wrong, and he offers her the way out: the happy dust that will scare
away those lonesome blues. She may not have a man, nor a baby, but
she will have the Good Time and the release from fear.

So he croons to her his marvellously seductive song "There's a boat
dat's leavin' soo-hoon for New York, Come wid me", with its serpentine chromatic bass. Yet although he invites her to a world with no
roots, in a music that starts from the tawdriest clichés of Tin Pan
Alley, the song has a remarkably positive jauntiness also. The upward
thrust of the tune, the Lombard syncopations, the blue flat seventh on
the word "Come" fascinate; while the intrusive rumba rhythms and
the increasingly chromatic harmonization of the rising arpeggio create
a cumulative energy that becomes irresistible. When he sings, prancing
up through a B flat arpeggio to a high G flat (a pungent twelfth superimposed on a dominant ninth chord):

EXAMPLE II

and then up to B flat to clinch the assertion that "Dat's where we
belong", we have to admit that he is right, if one can talk of belonging
in so rootless a world. Perhaps it is not an accident that the key, B flat,
is that of Porgy's love-song; and that the middle section in which he
tempts Bess with silks and satins is in the "real" key of G minor.
However morally dubious, that dream at least could come true. Porgy
is destroyed because part of him cannot grow up and accept Crown.
Crown is destroyed because his passion cannot rediscover Porgy's
innocence. Bess, losing them both when she needed them both, is left
with the eternal serpent. Though she rejects his invitation with fury,
while the orchestra screeches devil-tritones, Sportin' Life leaves the
happy dust on the door step as he slinks out, and the orchestra plays a

triumphant version of his New York song, a tone higher. By implication the opera says that we—and Bess—have no choice but to accept Sportin' Life and "New York". Having done so, it is up to us to find new life, rather than death: to make the happy dust dream come true, or to substitute a better dream for it.

Certainly the last scene is in part a rejection of the old life. It opens with a ballet of Negro work and play which includes a children's Eden-song in E major, mainly in primitive, pre-pentatonic falling fourths, identical with those of the trance-song over the dead Clara and Jake. "Yes, you boun' to go to Heaven . . . If yo' good to yo' mammy an' yo' pappy", the words interestingly tell us. Into this apparent Paradise Porgy returns, released after a period of imprisonment for contempt of court, since he refused to look at Crown's body: the half of himself that he had slain. The music recapitulates the original prelude music, and the *first* version of Porgy's tune. Returned to his pre-purgatorial state, he is full of pride at having defied the white men, and is laden with presents which he ritualistically distributes. He is a god offering largesse, the biggest presents being reserved for Bess. He returns, with unconscious irony, to his G major banjo-song; but fragments of the love-theme wander through mediant modulations as he gradually realizes that something is wrong. It is Maria who tells him, with some self-satisfaction, that Bess has gone, with Sportin' Life and the happy dust, to New York, leaving the baby with Serena. There is a hint of G minor as his theme sounds in its original form and in augmented inversion as bass; but Porgy brushes aside Maria's denunciatory morality as the music sweeps back to E major. He sings his great final aria, "Oh Bess, oh, where's my Bess", wherein the love-song is transmuted into a triple-rhythmed song of yearning for the Eternal Beloved, and for the state of togetherness as opposed to lonesomeness. The upward octave leap and the strained chromaticism are balanced by the painful dissonance of the blue flat third:

EXAMPLE 12

This intense longing for Eden, that now comes *from* the pain of consciousness, is strikingly similar to the "O past, O happy life" epilogue to Delius's *Sea-Drift*, which is in the same key.

After Porgy has sung his aria alone, Maria and Serena join in, singing quite different music, trying to convince him that Bess was worthless, that she deserved nothing better than Sportin' Life. The modulations in this almost Mozartian ensemble grow increasingly unstable as he appeals to them "won't somebody tell me where's my Bess?", but return to E major when he stops addressing the women and asks God to give him the strength and show him the way. Flat sevenths on the words "where? tell me the truth", fight up to the sharp seventh, and then to resolution on to the tonic. The appeal to God is not now an escape but a plea for fortitude. Perhaps, now Crown is dead, he can grow up, reconciling Crown's virtues with his own; perhaps there is point in the fact that he sets out, in his goat-cart, for New York, though it be at the ends of the earth or even "in a heavenly land". Of course, there is no hint, in the final spiritual "O Lawd! I'm on my way", with its rising arpeggio theme and its potent rumba lilt, of a conventional happy ending. He will not find Bess or New York; and she is more likely to succumb to the happy dust than to discover new life in a new world. But he makes a symbolic gesture in going, even in a goat-cart, crippled as he is, towards New York and Bess; and there is a sense in which the Promised Land *is* New York, where the new life can grow only when he and Bess can meet, accepting the city as home, and Sportin' Life as no longer buzzard or serpent. The opera thus states explicitly the theme which we have seen to be latent in the history of American civilization; and it had specific personal implications for Gershwin himself in so far as he hoped that the element within him that was Porgy might one day come to terms with the element that was Sportin' Life. Certainly the cathartic effect of the opera depends on its achievement of "restitution", in psychological terms. Porgy's credulous nobility, Crown's ruthless courage, Bess's divided passion are all human characteristics, alike in their strength and limitation. Porgy and Crown are forgiven for their murders, Bess for her defection; even Sportin' Life, who is the cause of their non-fulfilment, is forgiven for being what he has to be. The act of forgiveness is Gershwin's forgiveness of himself: and of us, in so far as he "stands for" a lost, alienated race.

The end of the opera is, in this respect, significantly different from the novel, which leaves Porgy crippled in every sense, "an old man

. . . alone in an irony of morning sunlight". So negative a conclusion would not have been theatrically effective; but that Gershwin can bring off his more positive end is a tribute not merely to his theatrical instinct, but also to the much deeper human implications his opera raises. The sentiment is never sentimental, because the opera never takes sides, and can afford not to do so because it springs so deeply from Gershwin's experience. What would have happened had he not died so soon after *Porgy* was completed? Was this intuitive self-knowledge the beginning of his career as an artist? Or had he, in making his testament—which stood for an epoch—said all he had to say?

We shall never know the answer, but the opera remains, and its impact increases, rather than diminishes, with the passage of years. This is the ultimate test: which discounts the fact that the music is not good all the time. There are occasions when pop music clichés are not used creatively—as they are in the Sportin' Life passages—but merely fill in the gaps: chromatic sequences in some of the atmospheric interludes sounded Hollywoodish, and the fights and hurricane music have little substance. Even this, however, may be part of Gershwin's theatrical instinct, for early Verdi and Donizetti have proved that it may be an asset for a theatre composer to be able to produce inferior music where necessary. At times, theatrical elements have to take over from musical: what matters is that the moments of feeling should all be musically true. In this, Gershwin never lets us down. The tunes are probably the best that even he ever wrote, and are more memorable than those of any twentieth-century opera: a quality by no means to be sniffed at in a theatrical work. The harmonies are re-created where re-creation is necessary, and not least in the Sportin' Life passages, which directly evoke Tin Pan Alley. The orchestral textures, if often plummy, are varied and often imaginative. The relationship of parts to whole is, as we have seen, a genuine musical-dramatic integration; and the degree to which this is due to design or to the kind of accident that happens to genius is unimportant. There are greater twentieth-century operas: but not one which offers more of the qualities that opera used to have in its heyday, and must have again if it is to survive. Gershwin's *Porgy*, like the operas of Mozart or Verdi, is at once a social act, an entertainment, and a human experience with unexpectedly disturbing implications. Historically it is a work of immense, if as yet only potential, significance. Its historical significance could not, however, exist if it were not the achieved work of art it demonstrably is.

X

From art to pop: Marc Blitzstein's "Regina" and Leonard Bernstein's "West Side Story"; the rebirth of wonder

I am waiting for my case to come up
and I am waiting
for a rebirth of wonder
and I am waiting for someone
to really discover America . . .
amd I am waiting
for the Age of Anxiety
to drop dead . . .
and I am waiting
for a reconstructed *Mayflower*
to reach America
with its picture story and TV rights
sold in advance to the natives
and I am waiting
for the lost music to sound again
in the Lost Continent
in a new rebirth of wonder.

LAWRENCE FERLINGHETTI

Genius does not often flourish in the environment of Tin Pan Alley; but it is not common anywhere, and we have noted that Gershwin was in no way frustrated by the commercialized conventions within which he had to work. When Ravel said that he had nothing to teach Gershwin, he probably meant what he said. He did not mean—as Gershwin's disciples gleefully maintained—that the Master had been endowed direct from heaven with a complete technical equipment; nor did he mean—as the academically respectable liked to think—that the commercial song-plugger was congenitally incapable of learning his craft. He meant that Gershwin's technique was precisely adequate to what he had in him to do. In this connection a comparison with Menotti is pertinent.

Gian-Carlo Menotti has grown up twenty years later than Ger-

shwin, when the techniques of commercial music have been sophisticated by years of application to the cinema and, more recently, to TV.
Being highly intelligent, and technically well equipped both as
musician and as man of the theatre, he has adapted cinematic techniques
to solve one of the basic problems of opera in a democratic society. Of
its nature, opera is a highly stylized art that flourishes best in a society
dominated by complex and "artificial" conventions of behaviour and
feeling. Menotti, taking his cue from Hollywood and from Puccini,
has created an operatic stylization that seems almost as natural—and
therefore acceptable to a popular democratic audience—as realistic
drama. In no discreditable sense, he has also learned how to exploit
themes that go home to his public. *The Consul* is a genuinely frightening vision of the dehumanized world of bureaucracy, with the added
advantage that it can, if need be, be imbued with political significance—
on either side. *The Medium* exploits both our pseudo-scientific desire to
debunk the irrational and our vague yearning for supernatural excitement, if not satisfaction. *The Telephone* makes amusing and theatrically
ingenious use of a modern gimmick. Yet Menotti, who seems to have
liberated commercial cliché in making it emotionally more malleable,
is much more a product of industrialized inhumanity than Gershwin:
because although his musical and dramatic technique is more complex
and sophisticated, the music itself is neither good nor bad, but so
cinematically parasitic as to be without identity. Though the pieces
live, if at all, because they are "good theatre", they are theatrical in
both the positive sense (given the premises, the dramatic argument is
logical and gripping) and also in the negative sense (the premises are
contrived). The music, almost consistently, is part of the contrivance.
It "effectively" brings Puccini up to date, while depriving him of the
lyrical panache and harmonic punch that justified his theatricality. In
this sense Menotti is the perfect television composer, using a naturalistic
medium to create an illusion of reality. A Gershwin tune exists in its
own right. Menotti's parlando lyricism has no existence apart from his
theatrical illusion.

Obviously theatre music ought first and foremost to come off in the
theatre. Good theatre music has, however, always been able to stand
musically on its own feet, and the words that Marc Blitzstein wrote
thirty or more years ago are still relevant: "I have heard that a theatre
song, being plugged, need only be pluggable, while a concert song can
take its time, make its points more musically; in other words, don't be
too good a composer and you may write a successful theatre song. It

doesn't make sense to me. The good theatre songs of the past seem to have lasted, the poor concert songs seem to have died; and Time and Tarnish go their own sweet way, plucking off the cheaper products without regard to category." It would seem that from a theatrical composer we need both Menotti's stage sense and also Gershwin's instinctive musicianship. From Blitzstein himself we certainly get both; and whereas Gershwin was nurtured in Tin Pan Alley and became an artist almost by accident, Blitzstein—another American composer whose name has allegorical overtones—was born in Philadelphia in 1905, in relatively affluent circumstances, and as a young man did the cultural tour of Europe, studying both at the Boulangerie and with Schoenberg. His early works, almost all disowned by the composer, were "abstract" to the point of vehemence: fiercely protestant, dissonant, and percussive, as the work of a young American was prone to be. He turned to the theatre from inner conviction. It was useless, he felt, percussively to batter in a void. If, as an anti-traditionalist, one is going to hit out, it is as well to hit something. His musical development parallels a growing social conscience: though he gave up non-theatrical music for fundamentally aesthetic, not political, reasons.

In *The Cradle Will Rock*—his first opera, or "play in music", as he called it—Blitzstein took over the framework of the commercial musical, with spoken dialogue, set numbers, and various kinds of compromise between music and drama. To this he added—as Menotti was to do later—many techniques suggested by the cinema. Music in the theatre may be background, providing atmosphere or underlining dramatic significance, often ironically. It may be foreground, directly furthering the action through the participation of the characters in song, march or dance. Speech may pass into song; words underpinned by music may pass into action while the music carries on; silence may be used when action or phrase needs sudden or startling relief. None of these techniques was in itself new; no one before Blitzstein, however, had used them so consistently, so coherently, and to such imaginative purpose. This remains true even though Blitzstein is the first to admit his debt to Kurt Weill, of whose *Threepenny Opera* he has made a most successful American translation and adaptation. His own works, from *The Cradle Will Rock* onwards, have justified his confidence in himself as a theatre composer. As he has said, "Music in the theatre is a powerful, an almost immorally potent weapon. It will do things you would never dream of; it will be fantastically perfect for one scene; it can louse up another scene to an extent that is unbelievable. There is only one rule I know: follow your theatre instinct. You discover you have got it very much in the same way as you first discovered you were a composer. You may be wrong on both counts; but your inner conviction is all you have got."

All Blitzstein's libretti have been written by himself, in a style which invests the inflections of American speech with the pungency and pith of art. The remarkably varied musical and dramatic treatment to which these texts lend themselves is illustrated by the Drugstore Scene from *The Cradle*. It opens with spoken dialogue. The druggist is chatting in witless contentment to his son Steve, while the orchestra plays an amiable little tune in $\frac{6}{8}$:

EXAMPLE I

The lilt of this tune manages to suggest both a catlike pleasure in the warm sun and the complacency of the small property-owner: while at the same time the hovering tonality imbues the Common Man's unimaginative silliness with a certain pathos. The tune and its harmonization tell us that he is genuinely happy, incorrigibly stupid—and pitifully vulnerable. Steve blows away his pipe-dream by jerking him back to reality: what about the mortgage, he asks, in an agitato rhythmic figuration, oscillating ambiguously between the triads of F minor and E major. This prepares the way for the appearance of the hired thug, agent of the villianous capitalist, Mister Mister, who wants to use the pull of the mortgage to involve the druggist in the frame-up of an innocent young Pole. These sinister goings-on unfold ironically, but significantly, against the bland, blind complacency of the song tune; the final machinations are entirely unaccompanied. Then Gus and his wife Sadie, the victims of the frame-up, enter to sing a love-song, in slow waltz time, about the baby Sadie is expecting. The lyricism of this is in striking contrast to the squalor of the spoken dialogue that has preceded it, so that its musical and dramatic effect is in part dependent on its context.

At the same time it is in its own right music of considerable beauty, deep in its simplicity. We may quote it complete:

EXAMPLE 2

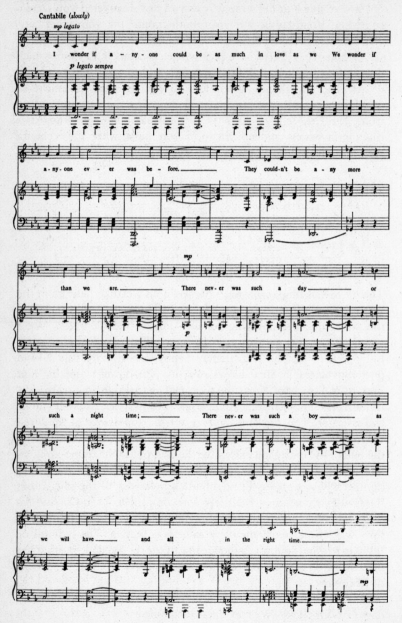

EXAMPLE 2 *(continued)*

Its form, superficially considered, is that of the commercial ballad, beginning with two eight-bar clauses each of which describes a slowly rising arch; the second arch rises a fifth higher than the first. These are answered by a four-bar phrase which, while forming a similar, smaller arch, is pathetically broken in rhythm. Then there is a middle section in which all the phrases have this fragmentary tenderness; and an instrumental da capo of the first section, under spoken dialogue. The effect of this gently caressing melody is inseparable from its subtle harmonization. It opens in tonal ambiguity—in something that might be F minor with sharp sixth and flat seventh. At the top of the second (climacteric) arch the sharp sixth becomes a dissonant bass to the harmony. The brief phrases of the middle section pass through almost continuous enharmonic modulation: which proceeds back from D minor, by way of linearly related triads of C minor and E minor, to the veiled tonality of the opening. The slow, arching growth of the tune, with its warmly tranquil harmony, makes us feel not merely Gus's tenderness, but also the growth of the child within the womb: while at the same time the ambiguity of the initial tonality, the softly piercing dissonance on the high E flat, and the broken rhythm and shifting modulations of the middle section imbue the music with a questioning wistfulness, a sense of mystery and wonder. The song is instinct with both the beauty and the frailty of life: love itself is so intangible, the child that is love's creation will be so tiny, so unprotected. So not only musically but also psychologically the Gus and Sadie song balances the fundamentally unfeeling, as well as unthinking, lyricism of the druggist's tune at the beginning of the scene. Both Gus and Sadie and the druggist are happy: and also frail. The Gus and Sadie love-song moves us so much more deeply because so much more is at stake. In the dramatic context this is emphasized by the fact that Gus and Sadie will shortly walk out into the bomb-plot—as we know, but they do not. The effect of the song in itself, however, has nothing to do with this dramatic irony. It moves us because its equivocation between life-creating love and the threat of mutability is inherent in life. If the musical, like the political, conventions of *The Cradle* now seem slightly dated ("thirty-ish"), this song certainly demonstrates one of the qualities that distinguishes Art from Entertainment or from Propaganda; it is a "moment of truth", and its truth is impervious to Time.

We have analysed this little song in perhaps extravagant detail because there is no better example of Blitzstein's ability to achieve, within his self-imposed limitations, a range and depth of experience comparable with that of much more complex "art" music. In *The Cradle Will Rock* most of the song numbers are closer than this to popular convention. Sometimes, as in *Honolulu*, they guy their prototypes by reducing their clichés *ad absurdum*; sometimes, as in *Croon-Spoon*, they parody the real thing only by their ironic text and by their level of musical accomplishment. The serious or ironically tragic songs usually keep to the ternary convention, though the diatonic tunes have an alertness and flexibility that often prompts enharmonic modulations. In the title-song, *The Cradle Will Rock*, the tonality suggests the uprooting, revolutionary tempest by hovering between a Phrygian E flat minor and E major with chromatic alterations: ending with fortissimo triads of B, A, D and A flat, harmonizing a line rising from D sharp up the scale of E major. *Joe Worker* is tonally less adventurous, but still more powerful. The passionate indignation of the words spills over into music which uses the rigidity of the convention to tighten the force.

The Cradle Will Rock is a satirical piece with tragic undertones; Blitzstein's second "play in music", *No for an Answer*, is a tragedy with satirical implications. It tells a grim story of a group of New York waiters victimized by Big Business. Apart from the superb torch song and *Penny Candy*, there are fewer set numbers than in *The Cradle*: or rather the song-tune tends to merge into a wonderfully sensitive treatment of speech inflection—a kind of "American recitative" in which Blitzstein reveals the roots of some features of jazz in American dialect. In a piece such as the character-sketch of Mike this vocal line provides a link between musically accompanied speech and song: the transitions are so subtle that "real life" dialogue dissolves into music in a way that makes Menotti's parlando line seem relatively crude in range and expressiveness. As in the earlier play in music, tenderness and strength are here allied. The Joe and Francie love scenes—especially the exquisite, vocalized D flat nocturne—develop the manner of the Gus and Sadie episodes with still greater poignancy; and compassion now embraces many of the "unsympathetic" characters also. The character-sketch of Mike referred to above makes us feel both with and for the young tough guy; and the chromatic arioso of the rich boy Paul ("the sky is black and blackening"), followed by his slow waltz harmonized in rich but tremulously fluctuating sevenths, involves us in the disintegration of his world. We weep for him, as he asks us to, and for his blundering good intentions: the song is at once satirical and beyond the range of parody. The strength of the fierce songs of the *Joe Worker* type is also developed, in the second opera, on an altogether grander scale, especially in the choruses. The final oration over the dead Joe is a fine example. The vocal line is stark in its diatonicism, yet rhythmically resilient; again the movement of the parts creates an alert expectancy from enharmonic modulation, and it is this element of precariousness that relates Blitzstein's power to his sensitivity. Even when his use of patterned figurations in ostinato rhythms attains a steely monumentality there is no emotional bullying, for the lines preserve their nervous vitality.

Blitzstein's equilibrium between power and compassion seems, at first glance, to be somewhat disturbed in his third opera, *Regina*. The book of this he adapted, with characteristic tact, from Lillian Hellman's play *The Little Foxes*; it suffers from the play's grimly negative nature. Blitzstein's previous works had dealt with corruption and a decaying world; but in them the positive forces of love and courage were at least an equal match for the negative forces. In *Regina* the central character is a villainess-heroine; and the action centres around the money-grubbing intrigues of the Hubbard family. Admittedly, the opera concludes with the escape of Zan, Regina's daughter, from the corruption of the Deep South, which represents decaying capitalism in general. But she exists in the opera mainly as a foil to her mother: though she is "realized" musically with considerable insight, Blitzstein hardly allows himself time to establish her character in relation to Regina. The only other people for whom sympathy is invited are Horace, bullied by his fearsome wife, and in the last stages of physical decay: and Aunt Birdie, who is a secret drunkard. While Blitzstein makes us feel for these sad creatures, this sympathy is hardly an adequate substitute for the relationship between Gus and Sadie, or between Joe and Francie, in the earlier works.

Yet in total effect *Regina* marks, as we shall see, a further creative development in Blitzstein's work. The Southern setting makes it possible for him to use the Negro element as a choric commentary: Negro life and music become an ideal representation of the fundamentals of the Good Life, as opposed to the savage lunacy of Regina's obsession with Things. We may recall Porgy's banjo-song "I got plenty o' nuttin' "; but as in Gershwin's opera the jazz element in *Regina* is double-edged, since if it connects on the one side with primitive simplicity, on the other side it is linked with commercial exploitation. The nastiest characters in *Regina* have a bastardized musical idiom hovering between jazz and the nineteenth-century salon. The manner in which, at the opening of the second act, a Negro jazz band and a white drawing-room trio are counterpointed on stage is brilliant theatre: and provides evidence as to the way in which the good dramatic composer has sometimes to write music that seems trivial— without being so, in relation to the work as a whole.

This scene is, indeed, the turning-point of the opera. Up to this moment Blitzstein has presented Regina as a fully "rounded" character —a Verdian heavy mezzo with a range from G below middle C to C in alt; and has shown us how her corrupt passion is related to the degeneracy of the society she lives in. She has sold everything for power, setting brother against brother and son against father. Now, to complete her latest and shadiest deal, she has brought her sick husband home from the sanatorium, exploiting his natural affection for his daughter to this end. He is in her power because he is weak and ill; the others are in her power because the deal, in which they are involved, is dependent on Horace's money. Zan is to be married to Leo to keep the money in the family. At this point the tension explodes in music that is also dramatic action.

The piano on stage, playing ("in the style of Louis Moreau Gottschalk") prettified arpeggios in the fancy key of B major, is the tawdrily elegant facade behind which lurks the fury. This breaks out, first, in the chorus of merrymakers who attend the party, given by the Hubbards to clinch the deal. The chorus is in E flat (which has become the stock key of Tin Pan Alley) and the tune is both brutal and banal, its pulsing rhythm crude. Yet tune and rhythm have a vigour comparable with early Verdi: which fact tells us that though the Hubbards may be exploiters ("Young and old among the lot of us, There's none they haven't double-crossed. They foot the bill So swill Right hearty"), none the less their power cannot be gainsaid. "What's become of

dignity and true gentility?" indeed; "We've just sighed, And pocketed
our pride, And sold it down the river." The chorus ends in a drunken
frenzy: "Eat, gobble, guzzle, swill, perish, rot, For what? FOR
HUBBARD."

After this party-chorus, spoken dialogue against a tenuous orchestral background tells us that Horace intends to change his will, and that
Leo plans to steal the bonds on which the deal depends, since Horace
refuses to hand them over. Like Gershwin in *Porgy*, Blitzstein effects
subtle transitions between speech and song, music disappearing as
commercial self-interest comes uppermost. It is at this point that the
Negro intervenes as a positive. Addie, the old Negro servant who
comes from, and still represents, the old world, beckons Miss Birdie
away from the party and tries to persuade her not to tipple. Birdie's
secret drinking indicates what happens to weak, decent, sensitive
people who have to live in the Hubbard's world. So Addie, in an
A flat blues—*sub*dominant to the Hubbards' raucous E flat—invokes
the night, which can relieve care, "rubbing out memories". "If you
were like the night," she sings, "you'd be blue like you ain't never been
before; if you knows the woes that's making folks so blue-tonight,
you'd let your own alone, and they'd just go out like the night." This
most poignant song, with its arpeggio-based melody and yearning flat
sevenths, its low, indrawn tessitura, its quietly rocking rhythm, makes
the Negro alto voice both the consciousness of the dark that envelops
us, and the solace of an eternal Mother Earth:

EXAMPLE 3

And it is placed immediately before Regina's waltz-song which, expressing her obsession with Things, becomes the opera's climax. Furious with Horace for not conniving in her plot, she flirts with John Bagtry, an old beau. The surging rhythm of her waltz, with many duple groupings across the triple beat, suggests her driving vitality, while the repeated breaks in the upward-thrusting phrases and the continual modulations give the music a frantic—both restless and directionless—quality:

EXAMPLE 4

In being monstrously contemptuous of Bagtry she dismisses the old world of "comeliness and grace" and invokes "a new century"—the action takes place in 1900—as she screams an increasingly hysterical chant of possession. "I'm no simpering saint with wings To whom vacuous virtue clings, I don't mind handling money, handfuls of money, money means THINGS, and the things I can do with things." Yet her obsession gives no real satisfaction: as is indicated by the irresolute cadential phrases, shifting uneasily between B flat, F and E flat. In spoken interludes against her song Leo returns, having stolen the bonds, and Ben informs Marshall, the big-time capitalist, that the deal is settled: so we are not surprised when Regina's waltz—it is really a soliloquy in which she talks to herself, not Bagtry—explodes into an appalling gallop. The World or Society is swept into her possessed hysteria, and the chorus's sweaty "whews" reinforce the horror of Regina's yells of hatred as she whirls tauntingly past her husband in the dance. She is left alone with her unaccompanied curtain phrase, complete with high C: "I'll be waiting"—for you to die.

This magnificent theatrical stroke depends for its full effect on its context: for the next and last act opens with the opera's most extended statement of positives. Although these positive values are not incarnated in characters as convincingly as they are in the earlier plays in music, this "Rain" quartet, sung by all the "good" characters—the adolescent Zan, the maimed Horace and Birdie, and the choric figure of Addie—is musically Blitzstein's most mature affirmation, and the most beautiful and original music he has thus far created. The orchestral fabric, with its rarefied texture of open seconds, sevenths, and ninths, is Coplandesque; but when the voices sing "Make a quiet day, let's keep it steady and low", the music acquires a touching freshness unlike any other composer. Blitzstein has not Gershwin's melodic genius: perhaps his greater sophistication precludes such haunting memorability. On the other hand, the typical note of the "Rain" quartet—keeping it low and steady—is something we do not find in Gershwin's more passionately Jewish sense of alienation. In Blitzstein's music the Jewish flavour is part of the polyglot texture of metropolitan life; there is a delicate balance between an ironically tight-lipped understatement (consider the comedy of Addie's bellow) and a deep seriousness when the patter-song of the rain evolves into Horace's aria of growth: "Consider the friendly rain that"—unlike the predatory Hubbards—"*serves* the earth, then moves on again":

EXAMPLE 5

When the aria turns into an ensemble, with Zan's high soprano soaring on top, the simplicity of the rising-scale lyricism, with the intermittently unexpected diatonic harmony, creates a compassionate detachment that Gershwin, with his commercial background, could not have. For Gershwin involvement was everything; he wrote real music because he was Porgy—and Crown, and Sportin' Life, and even Bess. His melodic and harmonic potency could discover the heart's tenderness through the machine-made sentimentality that Tin Pan Alley wrapped around it. Blitzstein's spare texture and unassuming lyricism do not lacerate or pierce, for they reveal common humanity's heart as clear, clean, and vulnerable—as is Sadie's unborn baby in *The Cradle Will Rock*.

This freshness and vulnerability, the sense of something *waiting to be born*, is Blitzstein's characteristic note; and it is the opposite pole to the Hubbards' assertiveness which, superficially, is part of the American "go". The fact that Blitzstein's positives are, as it were, latent beneath the surface—that his music is "waiting for a rebirth" of the lost music in the lost continent—may mean that his instinct was right when he did not allow his positives to be fulfilled in terms of character. They have, none the less, their manifestations in human development, the first of which occurs immediately after the "Rain" quartet. Birdie sings an aria that, beginning in fuddled nostalgia, looks back to the Old Days, to the family estates in Lionnet, to What Might Have Been. In a sonorous D flat major, with drooping thirds and fifths and wistful flat sevenths, she invites herself to "remember Lionnet", the lawn down to the river, the lovely parties, the music: a vision which, in its luminous scoring and open texture, is the more precariously moving by contrast with the squalid present:

EXAMPLE 6

But the nostalgia is a starting-point for growth. The old-fashioned European coloratura—just beginning in the last measure of the above quotation—expresses the pathos both of her tipsiness and of her yearning for music and "culture". It looks back to her music-lesson aria in Act I: but becomes increasingly distraught as she gradually admits to herself that the dream was a dream; that Oscar married her for her money, not for love; that she knows in her heart that her own son is a brute; that she knows that everyone knows what her "headaches" mean. The verbal acrobatics, become hysteria, have also become a kind of truth: so she can go off with Zan, salvaging a little of the human potentiality that was in her vision of Lionnet. As the music returns to D flat, after the wild modulations of the arioso, we know that her dream, though it turned into nightmare, was not entirely false.

Zan's own song "What will it do for me?" shows a comparable psychological subtlety. This time it has no relation to "Europe" and to art-music. It looks like a corny commercial number because it is Zan's music, and therefore adolescent; at the same time it shows an awareness of the realities of adolescent feeling which the commercial number usually belies. Thus the first rising phrase beautifully suggests the girl's search for an answer to Young Love's dream: while the unexpected modulation to the *minor* of the dominant, and the different harmonization of the E flat each time it appears, intimate that she is half eager, and half afraid, to find what she seeks:

EXAMPLE 7

It is significant, too, that this song is not just a "number"; its relationship to the central theme of the opera is crucial. Thus its tune is closely allied to Horace's song about the friendly rain; and in the finale Zan's going away—her personal rebellion against her mother—is identified with the rain-growth theme and with the "new life" of the spiritual "Certainly, Lord". So the opera ends with an affirmation: even though its fulfilment, either in personal or in social terms, cannot be yet. The spiritual is the answer to Ben's cynical song, accepting willy-nilly Regina's mercenary terms: "The century is turning, opening up so big, so grand, And hundreds of Hubbards, just like us, will own this land". At the end, however, it is Regina who has her tremor of fear; and it is her daughter who asks, "What's the matter, mother? Are you afraid? Is a new day coming?"

Regina is a fully-fledged opera, which has grown out of the conventions of popular music. It deals directly with the impact of commercial interests upon human society, not in sociological terms, but in terms of individual human experience; and Blitzstein's great achievement is that he has imbued techniques borrowed from the commercial world with the power to hit back—to stand for, rather than against, the human spirit. His embryonic awareness of emerging life, in his "low and steady" mood, is the real America, beneath the push and go, the America that is still waiting to be born: so it is significant that Blitzstein usually identifies this mood with youth. Unless one counts the experimental *Reuben Reuben*, which was theatrically unsuccessful, Blitzstein has not yet attempted to enter the "young" field of the musical proper. Another highly intelligent and sophisticated composer of the "art" world, Leonard Bernstein, has however used this medium: for in *West Side Story* he has tried not merely to use popular conventions for his own purposes, but to create a musical, specifically about youth, which can take its place against commercial competition on Broadway.

At some levels, he has been brilliantly successful. *West Side Story* is a musical, popularly accepted as such, and easily the most distinguished, both musically and dramatically, that has yet appeared. For this, much of the credit must go to Jerome Robbins, the talented choreographer whose idea *West Side Story* originally was. This is not, like the conventional musical comedy, escape art. It has a serious theme related to our time, being a modern version of the Romeo and Juliet story, set in the slums of New York. There are two rival gangs of young people, the Jets and the Sharks, teenage New Yorkers and invading Puerto Ricans; and the war between them brings in most of the urgent contemporary problems, racial, sexual, political, social and economic. One of the New York boys falls in love with a Puerto Rican girl, but in the frenzy of gang-war is forced into a murder; the murdered man is the girl's brother. After a visionary episode in which we are told that in a better, if far distant, world love might prove stronger than hate, the boy is shot in reprisal.

Since the theme turns on the conflict between young love and the destructive force of social and economic pressures, the piece has much in common with Blitzstein's plays in music, and a less direct relationship to Gershwin's *Porgy*. The main difference is that Blitzstein's pieces, being plays in music, attempt and achieve the greatest degree of realism that is reconcilable with a sung drama, whereas *West Side Story*, being a musical, mixes drama with ballet. It is extremely forceful and original ballet; yet the mere fact that it is ballet, deprives it of some degree of reality. This technical distinction has its counterpart in the musical-dramatic treatment of the subject.

Thus the negative elements—the destructiveness of the gang life—are splendidly realized in balletic terms, both in the music of the Jets or New Yorkers and in that of the Sharks or Puerto Ricans. The texture, like that of much Modern Jazz, is bare and hard in the Jets' music, with many parallel fourths and fifths, and a minimum of harmony apart from percussive minor seconds. The tunes are fragmentary, dominated by tritones, the rhythms nervously jittery. In the *Jet Songs* hypnosis is generated by a $\frac{3}{4}$ rhythm against a $\frac{6}{8}$ beat. The persistent dislocation of the accents is both physical (this is how they walk) and emotional; and the tendency to bitonality—or rather to two-part writing in which one part is unresolved appoggiatura to the other—suggests their disconnectedness:

EXAMPLE 8

The words of the *Jet Song* tell us that though the boys do not belong to Society, they belong to one another, and so can exhibit a couldn't-care-less defiance of the world. This is vividly expressed in "Cool", based on the twittering tritones; the coolness is the heartlessness of the manner, not in the least "low and steady", but savage behind the tight lips. The Puerto Rican gang-music, being Latin American in origin, has more animal vitality and harmonic punch than that of the jerky New Yorkers, though it, too, has become jittery and dehydrated. *The*

Chacha is brittle, twitchy, disoriented, "light and dry". *America* is
an ironic deflation, juxtaposing Puerto Rico as dream-island and as
island of disease and poverty, with Manhattan as paradise of the
automobile and washing-machine—and of the sell-out to commerce.
The rhythmic subtleties of Latin American music have here become
parodistic, jangled, mixed-up: like the modulations, which are as
flickering and directionless as Blitzstein's gallop.

These negative, destructive numbers could hardly be better done;
but the link between them and the "positives" does not convince, as it
does in Blitzstein's work. Tony's first song, "Somethin' Comin',"
promises well, for the cross-rhythms and dislocations over the fourth-
founded ostinato convey expectancy, if not Blitzstein's tender awareness of something waiting to be born. What comes of the expectancy
does not ring true however: as we can see by considering Zan's song
from *Regina* alongside Tony's adolescent love-song, "Maria". This
begins with incantatory pentatonics in B major; we cannot quite
swallow their innocence, as we can that of the comparable passages in
Gershwin's *Porgy*. The tune itself, in E flat, incorporates the Jets'
tritones, but resolves them melodically:

EXAMPLE 9

Though the tune is memorable enough, it hardly avoids the pop
number's synthetic sentiment. Listening to Zan's song, we say: Yes,
this sounds like a corny pop number, and of course that is how an

adolescent girl, in our world, would express herself; yet the expression remains true, and we found the evidence for this in the incidental subtleties that Blitzstein unobtrusively introduces into popular cliché. In "Maria", cliché takes over. One even wonders whether in the "say it soft and it's almost like prayin'" passage Bernstein may not have his tongue in his cheek, for however much Tony is victim of a commercialized world, he would not feel like this if he were really in love: nor would he reach for his high B flat in the adagio coda.

The famous love-song "Tonight" has greater authenticity. The melodic contours, with their obsessive repeated Fs, are rudimentary compared with Porgy's great love-song. This is probably appropriate, however, to these urban adolescents; and the free modulations, especially to mediants and to keys a tone or semitone apart, suggest the restless unease beneath their being together. Though less subtle than Blitzstein, less hauntingly memorable than Gershwin, the song does just what it should do in the context. In the Marriage Scene and the G flat duo "Make of our hands one hand", however, Bernstein once more glamorizes simple sentiment. The ritualistic repeated notes, the falling pentatonic fourths and thirds, complete with churchy moonbeams through the skylight, are a Hollywood corruption of Blitzstein's parallel love-scenes between Gus and Sadie, Joe and Francie. The tenderness is given an aura, almost a halo; and what Blitzstein calls—in the beautiful little aria from *Reuben Reuben*—"the moment of truth" is thereby obscured.

The "Tonight" ensemble that concludes the first act counterpoints the love-song against the gang's fury; epitomizing the dramatic theme, it makes a fine curtain. After the interval, Maria's "I feel pretty" is the most genuine positive statement in the piece. The words are smart but true: "I feel dizzy, I feel sunny, I feel fizzy and funny and fine, And so pretty Miss America can just resign". This, unlike the Marriage Scene, is how she would think and feel; and the lilting buoyancy of the Puerto Rican waltz, simply diatonic, matches the words:

EXAMPLE 10

The rapid modulations here suggest a happy freedom, while reminding us of young love's precariousness and—in this violent world—of its instability. The dream sequence ballet that occurs after the murder—the dream of life and love fulfilled—destroys this emotional delicacy by too great explicitness. "*Somewhere* there's a place for us, Peace and quiet for us, Open air waits for us, Somewhere; we'll find a new way of living; we'll find a new way of forgiving." The rising seventh and falling triad of the tune—tentatively entering in canon in the orchestra —beautifully suggest both longing and resignation; but the symphonic and balletic development seems otiose. In Blitzstein the longing for the "rebirth of wonder" remains latent in the music; here the pretentiousness of the development destroys the theme's truth. One must admit, of course, that Blitzstein nowhere attempts so direct a compromise with musical comedy convention.

Blitzstein, in "purifying the dialect of the tribe", creates works which are related to musical comedy but could not be mistaken for it; Bernstein, in writing a musical comedy, cannot entirely avoid capitulation to commercial values. This is why *West Side Story* is most effective when it claims least. The most dramatic number in the score is "A boy like that", a duo between Anita, full of fury at Tony the murderer, and Maria, who still cannot help loving him and believing that love is better than hate. Though this number is heavily indebted to Kurt Weill, it achieves, in its nervously oscillating duple-triple rhythm, its savage ostinato and upward-jagging chromatics, a raw passion most effectively counterpointed against Maria's lyrical confession of love. This is a truly dramatic—operatic rather than balletic—duo-ensemble wherein the stabbing repeated phrases that express hate are gradually transformed into stepwise song as the power of love grows stronger. The clinging, possessive cantilena broadens to soaring sevenths when Maria triumphs, and the two girls sing together "I have a love". This is probably the only moment, however, when *West Side Story* raises the musical to the musical-dramatic entity which is opera. For the rest, the moments that come off best are the ballets of violence, which are all dance and mime: and the music-hall turns, such as the brilliant *Officer Krupke*, which in both words and music parodies the serious theme of delinquency. This is a vaudeville patter-song in which the wrong notes, flickering modulations (through every key of the chromatic scale) and unexpected disruptions of rhythm are as wildly funny as the words. But the number is a set-piece; if one extracts it from the context it loses little, and this may indicate that Bernstein's con-

tribution towards a musical of greater maturity and deeper awareness
is less impressive than, superficially, it seems. It comes back to the fact
that his talents flourish best in the expression of negative, rather than
positive, experience. The derogatory, debunking numbers are all, we
have seen, first-class; the positive manifestations of love and compassion
all tend to be phoney or, if they are not false, to be deficient in character—like the funeral music for the tragic conclusion which, though
theatrically effective and even beautiful, is parasitic on Copland no
less than "A boy like that" is parasitic on Weill. One could say something similar of Bernstein's prize-winning score to Elia Kazan's film
On the Waterfront. The score is extremely eclectic, borrowing widely
from Copland and Stravinsky, from Schoenberg's thematic serialism,
from Mahlerian orchestration, from Puccinian harmony, from folk-
song and from jazz. For the most part the eclecticism is brilliantly
justified: the professional craftsman uses what comes to hand for a
functional purpose, underlining the visual images, and helping to
intensify dramatic coherence by structural and thematic relationships
of considerable complexity. The score demonstrates how Schoenbergian "developing variation" and Stravinskian ostinati lend themselves
readily to cinematic use, and the sharp, thin textures and acid sonorities
that Bernstein favours are apposite to the film's grimness, and miles
removed from the orchestral soup that Hollywood usually pours over
even the toughest subject. None the less it is significant that the score's
only failures occur in the music accompanying the love-passages:
wherein the string texture and Wagnerian sforzandi may suddenly and
bathetically recall the glycerine tears of Hollywood. In this particular—
and it is essential—Copland's film scores, though less professionally
developed and integrated than Bernstein's, and apparently of more
limited emotional range, are the truer. Love may not often be fulfilled
in Copland's dramatic music—his finest film score is significantly that
to *The Heiress*, which is a cinematic version of Henry James's novel
about the frustration of love; but the feeling is never forced and remains, in its frustration, both tender and resilient. In comparison the
sheer efficiency of Bernstein's film music would seem to indicate that
in the modern world there may be a price to be paid for competence: a
point we commented on, indeed, in discussing recent developments in
"concert" music.[1]

Certainly Bernstein himself seems to have paid it in his failure to
fulfil his remarkable talents. He has obviously enjoyed and deserved his

[1] See Appendix III.

phenomenal success as conductor, as pianist, as TV personality as well as composer; but he has produced no sequel to *West Side Story* apart from a revised version of the earlier *Candide* which, though often incidentally clever and amusing, lacks the imaginative core and the centrality of *West Side Story*. The dissipation of Bernstein's creativity seems, indeed, almost a moral tale which has more than personal significance. We cannot merely say that he has not "had time" to create, for no true artist ever put anything before creation. If he has found more satisfaction in the various roles he has decided to play so brilliantly, that is at least in part a comment on the society that has produced him. A failure in creativity, we have seen, is also a failure in love; and this is why American civilization—as the music of Blitzstein and Gershwin has told us—is still "waiting" for the Promised Land.

From this point of view the mid-century development of pop music has some documentary interest. Rock 'n Roll is the music of the new generation, of the young people Blitzstein and Bernstein have written of and potentially for. Yet this "young" music has found its impetus in the earliest, most primitive forms of the country blues: that music of a dispossessed people which grew up painfully, in remote rural areas of the new world, and was gradually translated into the urban folk-music of jazz. The old tradition is still active, as we can see from the work of a travelling blues singer such as John Lee Hooker. His style is extremely primitive; melodically he sings in consistent pentatonicism and sometimes employs no more than three tones (tonic, fourth and fifth), chanting and shouting rather than singing, over a guitar twanged and banged with fateful remorselessness and with a minimum of harmony. If we compare his singing of "I can't believe"—in which song is frozen and stifled in the horror of his woman's betrayal—with a classical blues singer such as Lightnin' Hopkins singing *Worried Blues*, we can appreciate both the power and the limitation of his archaism. Hopkins's vocal lines and solo-line guitar preludes and antiphonies are still pentatonic, but are much more lyrically extended than Hooker's; and they are complemented by a chordal guitar part, based on the traditional blues progression, that lends itself to great variety of harmonic coloration. So in his music the dichotomy, typical of classic jazz, between primitive (black) line and sophisticated (white) harmony is clearly evident. It is not, however, the true jazz of Hopkins's blues, but the primitivism of Hooker's that is behind Rock 'n Roll; and the work of singers such as Brownie McGhee and Sonny Terry indicates how the transition was effected.

Their vocal style and wonderfully nuanced harmonica playing are directly within country-music tradition; their guitar harmony is much simpler, less subtly related to the words than Hopkins's, yet of some structural purpose as compared with Hooker's mainly percussive bangings and scrapings. Positively, the harmony becomes allied with the straightforward rhythmic lilt; and it was these cruder—not necessarily more primitive—aspects of the country blues that could be and were exploited by Madison Avenue: the more so because teen-agers in an affluent society are no longer commercially negligible. Despite the exploitation, it remains significant that young people have wanted, needed, to go back to the *beginnings* of a new world's music, associating themselves with the sense of oppression, of revolutionary protest, and of animal vigour that had gone to create that primitive art. There is thus a difference between Rock 'n Roll's commercial mechanization of the country blues and the big band's mechanization of classical jazz during the pre-Second World War years. Rock 'n Roll is at least active, not passive, a music for celebrants. The phrase itself is, of course, unambiguously sexual, though there is little pleasure left in a sexuality that has been mechanized. So the fundamentally human togetherness of sex is paradoxically dehumanized in a *communal* ritual of separateness. The dancers, frozen faced, jerk alone, without a partner; the lonesome band together *because* each one is individually alone. They would be freed of "consciousness", celebrating in their physical ritual nothing beyond the mere fact of being, after a fashion, alive rather than dead. In a post-atom bomb world this may be something worth making a song-and-dance about; if it is a kind of hysteria, a substitute for the faculties of love and wonder, we can hardly blame the average teenager for it when a man as highly endowed as Bernstein has failed in this particular.

We should also refer, in this context, to the development of the work of William Russo, who has made a consistent attempt to recon-cile the worlds of jazz, of art music and of pop music. Bernstein started as a "straight" composer, and embraced jazz and pop; Russo started as a jazzman in Stan Kenton's smaller band of the 1950s; was impressed by the dubious "artistry" of Kenton's arranger Pete Rugolo, who had orthodox musical training; and embarked himself on collaborations between jazz convention and improvisation and some of the techniques of modern art music. The results, as exemplified in the Violin Con-certo he wrote for Yehudi Menuhin, are not notably happier than any other conscious attempts at collaboration, such as the Brubeck-

Bernstein effort referred to above, or the British association between Matyas Seiber (a composer of much greater distinction than Bernstein or Russo) and Johnny Dankworth. This being so, it is interesting that in the most recent phase of his work Russo seems to be seeking not greater sophistication (as does Gunther Schuller) but a lowest common denominator of the worlds of art, jazz and pop. His opera *John Hooton*, which translates the Othello story to modern America, as *West Side Story* had transplanted Romeo and Juliet, attempts a spareness reminiscent of Kurt Weill, but achieves no more than a self-conscious approximation to the manner of the country blues, from which Rock 'n Roll derived. The convention, not surprisingly, cannot support the violent tragedy and passion of the Shakespearian Othello, and the effect of the art-singers is to weaken, not to deepen, the impact of the pop-singers with whom they co-operate. The *inarticulateness* of the music and the characters is the point; it admits to its, and our, inadequacy to deal with the realities of the human predicament, which is today much as it has always been, except that man's ability to control or disrupt Nature is so wildly at odds with his ability to understand himself. Russo is not, compared with Weill, a good composer, so his operatic myth doesn't strike home as it might. Yet his music does consciously and too deliberately what the teenager's music does intuitively: it protests against the world that is exploiting both it and the audience, and it intimates that it might be possible to *begin again*. In this sense "Third Stream" jazz manifests an affinity not only with Blitzstein and Bernstein but also—equally and simultaneously—with the teenagers' pop music and with the *ab ovo*-ism of the American *avant-garde*. This is encouraging rather than discouraging: for in so far as music may begin again there is always a chance that love and wonder might once more prove stronger than the juke box, since while there is life there is hope.

So if ever the lost music sounds again in the lost continent—which means virtually the whole of the "civilized" world—we shall remember how Gershwin and Blitzstein had sung directly of the need for a rebirth of love and wonder. We shall also recall how closely allied their song is to such apparently diverse manifestations of love and wonder as the music of Ives, Ruggles, Carter, Copland, Riegger, Sessions, Varèse and Cage, of Louis Armstrong and Bessie Smith, of Duke Ellington, Charlie Parker, Thelonious Monk and Miles Davis. We shall know at last that there is no differentiation between the genres. The only valid distinction is between those who stand for life and those who are against it; and this distinction is as old as the history of civilization or, indeed, of man himself. All true American sound-creators could say with Thoreau: "I long for wildness, a nature which I cannot put my foot through, woods where the woodthrush for ever sings, where the hours are early-morning ones, and there is dew on the grass, and the day is for ever unproved, where I might have a fertile unknown for a soil about me . . . A New Hampshire everlasting and unfallen."

Americans are the last "first" people; they, and we, await the consummation.

EPILOGUE

In the form of two poems by Louis Simpson

A siren sang, and Europe turned away
From the high castle and the shepherd's crook.
Three caravels went sailing to Cathay
On the strange ocean, and the captains shook
Their banners out across the Mexique Bay.

And in our early days we did the same.
Remembering our fathers in their wreck
We crossed the sea from Palos where they came
And saw, enormous to the little deck,
A shore in silence waiting for a name.

The treasures of Cathay were never found.
In this America, this wilderness
Where the axe echoes with a lonely sound,
The generations labor to possess
And grave by grave we civilize the ground.

From *Orpheus in America*

This is the New England—rocks and brush
Where none may live but only tigers, parrots,
And mute imagining—
America, a desert with a name.

America begins antiquity.
Confronted with pure space, my Arcady
Has turned to stone . . .

Let music then begin. And let the air
Be passing sweet,
Music that scarcely wakes
The serpent in her trance
And leads the lion out into the dance.
And let the trees be moved.
And may the forest dance.

Then shall intelligence and grace
Join hands and sing: Goodbye to Arcady!
Another world is here, a greener Thrace!
Here are your meadows, Love, as wide as heaven,
Green spirits, leaves
And winds, your ministers,
In this America, this other, happy place.

Appendix I

Mr John Kirkpatrick has gathered together some MS. jottings—made by Ives on scraps of paper, without thought of publication—that indicate how logical and consistent—according to his lights—Ives's compositional processes and methods of notation were. Far from being a (fitfully) inspired barbarian, he knew what he was doing, even when *not* knowing, with the conscious mind, was the heart of the matter. Thus he replies to a "rather overrated, celebrated piano player's" criticism of the opening of the Alcott's movement from the "Concord" Sonata as follows:

> He said somepin' like this. "In the 3rd movement on the front page the chord of A♭ E♭ & C is played in the L H but the signature is A♭—now the signature of E♭ would do just as well for A♭ & E♭ & c— & the R H part is in sig. B♭ tho' running sometime way out." "This man" he said "doesn't understand tonality—the A♭ signature is wrong & so is the R H". That is a typical get off lily-eared softy. That first page is one of the simplest & most obvious things in the whole book—when Rollo says that the E♭ would be better than the A♭ he says the subdominant chord is exactly the same as the tonic in its relation to the nice scale. Almost any conductor of the Philharmonic or Boston Symphony could see even that. The L H is in A♭—in that key, no other key—keeps in that key—is that key—it intends, does (meant to do) that, could(nt?) do anything else & will always put the players L H mind in that nice key of A♭ & nothing else (for old man Alcott likes to talk in A♭ & Sam Staples likes to have his say over the fence in B♭) & the nice soprano sings in B♭—no, Rollo the subdominant & tonic are not the same chords.

Speaking of the apparently irrational notation of some of his polyglot chords Ives says:

> they seem (to the nice class room) to be a nice sign that they are part of the dominant seventh— & must act obediently—but the "ear" sometimes doesn't feel that exactly that way—so we must be fair and change that sign. Suppose 2 curves, an up & down, start on E♭ & D♭— & are held down hard thro' the arpeggio & back, and we don't land in A♭ major—that sign isn't fair—Rollo—it paints us the wrong way. So the sign-maker makes it C♯ & E♭ and the music via ((the)) ear takes its own way up the mountain better & feels better about it. For instance, just as an illustration or instance ((that)) wrong signs may mean right or at least away from a misleading tendency—see pg 61 Thoreau—2nd brace chord beginning of 6th ♩ beat. This is R H $\begin{pmatrix} B♭ \\ F♭ \\ G♯ \end{pmatrix}$ L H $\begin{pmatrix} E♭ \\ F♯ \\ C♯ \end{pmatrix}$—if the R.H.

G♯ had been put on A♭, the eye would probably to most have suggested a resolution to a nice E♭ maj. tonic chord even in spite of the C♯ in L.H. with F♯ & E over ((it)) which may seem to lean towards a B♯ gate—but it doesn't get there, Rollo!—This is just one technical explanation of why certain notes have been written as they have (in the Sonata & other music) no more technical notes & explanations today, Rollo etc.— —

Then to my way of hearing & thinking a ♯ is a kind of underlying sign of, or senses or reflects or encourages an upward movement—tonal & more perhaps spiritual—at a thing, somewhat more of courage & aspiration towards than the ♭ carries or seems to. The ♭ is more relaxing, sub((?)) looking for rest & submission—((They are)) often used as symbols as such—when not needed as signs of tonality in the usual way.

On "form" in the "Concord" Sonata, and implicitly in his other works, he writes:

For the most part the Sonata was decided and sensed to a great extent by the ear & mind (to say nothing of the left side of the breast) before much went down on paper. It has seemed to me for a long while back that too much went down on paper too soon—the pen & eye are inclined by habit & custom to make the music somewhat more static than it should be—that is, more in the customary conventions than the ear & mind would agree to, or like enough to use—(if they had more chance to hear & think about new fields, substances & visions in music which they are not used to, as the pen & eye help the ear & mind keep too easily & steadily to their nice old customs & habits.) Maybe that may be some of the reason of some musicians who have written me & made some remark & criticism—say, that the music wasn't quite as awful as it looked—and a few musicians who took enough trouble & time to try to be fair enough to get into it in some way at least and went at it seriously said that it sounded (after some study & familiarity by "ears") better, more logical than it looked—on that nice paper—& more musically understandable.   One even said quite "eloquent"—tho' I didn't mean it to be especially.

And when the Nice Old Ladies say "no design", "formless"—"all music should have design & form". "Yes, Sarah, but not your design & form—no siree!" In this sonata they are spitting about, there is design—somewhat more than should be it seemed to me & the "form" is obvious but it isn't drabbed on every mile stone on the way "up" or "to" or "on"—it takes care of itself so to speak and isn't yanked back every 32 measures by those nice apron strings hanging on the class-room scroll. A natural procedure in a piece of music, be it a song or a week's symphony, may have something in common—I won't say analogous—to a walk up a mountain—its foot—its summit, then the valley. The climber looks, turns & looks down or up:—he sees the valley but not at exactly the same angle he saw it at the last look, & the summit is changing with every step— & the sky—even if he stands on the same rock at the top & looks at "Heaven & Earth" he is not in just the same key he started in or in the same moment of existence. That a symphony, sonata or jig, that all nice music should end where it started on the doh key, is no more a natural law than that all men should die in the same town & street number in which they were born. The "academics" "$50, please" fall back over the nice "waste basket" & say "natural laws"—that's an easy excuse—anything their ears & that above their ears wherever that is hasn't heard for 33 years or before, don't like, don't understand etc. etc. etc. '/. '/. '/. they scold & say "not a, or against, natural law."—in other words anything that is not easy to play, hear & sell.

The more one studies & listens and tries to find out all he can in various ways technically, mathematically, acoustically & aurally he begins to feel & more than that, actually know & sense that the world of tonal vibrations, in its relation to the physiological structure of the human ear has unthought-of because untried possibilities—for man to know & grow by—greater and more transcendental than what has too easily & thoughtlessly been called—a natural law! Just a few months study of what can be found in the tables of acoustics—vibrations of overtones, beats, etc. as found in Helmholtz et al. & it will be realized that nature's laws are greater than (?) So, Sarah, let the music move as the mountain does & it will be a bigger thing than Mus. Dock".

Appendix II

N.B. *Morton's unique ad lib. vocal interpretation has been preserved intentionally in this version, even though at times it may seem at variance with the piano score.*

Mamie's Blues
(219 Blues)
Words and Melody by
MAMIE DESDUME

Transcribed and Edited by
J. Lawrence Cook

Arranged by
FERDINAND J. MORTON
(Jelly Roll)

Appendix III

A note on Musical Comedy, Cinema and TV

Musical comedy—a Plain Man's popular art—had its origins in the impact of democracy on opera, which had been initially an aristocratic art—an imitation of human action which, *because* it was sung not spoken, could readily become a ritual of humanism, expressing the belief that man might attain godlike potentialities. Italian *opera buffa*, German *Singspiel*, French *opéra comique* and English ballad opera all parodied this idea by inversion, seeking the Hero and Heroine among the poor or, more commonly, the middle class; all of them tended towards naturalism in abandoning the musical stylizations proper to opera in favour of a spoken play into which musical numbers could be interspersed. Yet while the idea was that the spoken play would be more real, more like everyday life, more common if not more commonplace, because it was spoken, in fact the combination of the spoken play with music worked in the contrary direction. Full opera came to seem, and indeed to be, more "real" than the hybrid play-opera (with a very few exceptions, such as *Fidelio* and *Carmen*) because, having established its own conventions, it remained true to them. The stylization of people conversing in song may make people larger than life, but we accept that if we can imaginatively enter their world. In the Heroic Age people entered the mythological world of opera because to them it seemed true, or at least potentially true, of their society's experience. Even when opera was no longer a socially sanctioned mythology, it was still possible to find in Verdi's operas themes concerning human relationships which had wide social implications; and it was still possible to enter Wagner's operatic universe, because his plumbing of the ego's depths involved themes that were important enough, and "universal" enough, to take operatic exaggeration.

Comic opera, however, after Mozart and (more equivocally) Rossini, tended—as we saw in discussing Rossini and Offenbach—to become an escape art; and whereas in these two composers the music explored a reality which the play denied, by the time we reach Gilbert and Sullivan and the Edwardian musical comedy the function of the music itself has become an attempt to blanket reality, to forestall threat. In true opera song intensifies drama; in musical comedy the intrusion of song into spoken dialogue inevitably suggests illusion, encouraging us to believe that the happenings cannot be true, and so can be taken as a game. The nature of the music, moreover, does everything possible to foster this illusion—as we saw in our comments on Irving Berlin, Rodgers and Hart, and even Cole Porter, in so far as his cynicism is an inversion of Berlin's sentimentality. All attempts to evolve an emotionally more "mature" type of musical comedy are thus up against an equivocation inherent in the form's nature. Menotti, we saw, created an operatic technique which is "popular" and reconcilable with the conventions of naturalistic drama, but only by a journalistic prostitution of truth which is a more streamlined, cinematically effective version of the methods of *verismo* opera. We accept the illusion while it lasts, yet even while we experience the opera never quite forget—as we do when we watch Mozart's or Verdi's or Wagner's operas—that it is an illusion. This is why *The Consul* is not, as it pretends, a blow for the Free World: we are never less free than when knowingly having our withers wrung. In Bernstein's *West Side Story* the music, as we saw, brilliantly reinforces a drama which is deeply serious in its implications; yet the reinforcement works only in a negative direction, and the positive songs, nearly if not quite always, deflate the theme's sincerity. The dream-sequence—prophecy of a Better Life— is unconvincing because it is a balletic wish-fulfilment in a naturalistic context. We cannot accept it as a social ritual as we can accept the ballets in heroic opera: so it seems no more than a fairy-tale which can have no credible relation to the human situation that the piece is about. Perhaps only Gershwin and Blitzstein have solved the problem of the "democratic" musical; and Gershwin, in solving it in *Porgy and Bess*, reverts to full-scale opera with a minimum of spoken dialogue, and that almost all musically accompanied: while Blitzstein either adopts the same course (in *Regina*) or employs Brechtian combinations of music and speech which, however effective, are not as yet popular at all.

The same problems crop up, more acutely, in filmed musicals. Film, being visual, is a spatial before it is a temporal art. Its technique of "cutting" tells against temporal continuity, and in the silent cinema the function of music had been mainly to suggest a continuity which the succession of visual images did not intrinsically possess. This function still survives in the sound film, though there is now a more complex integration with the audible noises of the drama. It is significant, however, that so much of the most musically distinguished film music has been written to accompany movies that do not move, or move very slowly—as we observed in commenting on the film music of Copland and Thomson. When we come to films wherein the music is not merely an accompaniment to the drama but an important part of the total experience, we are more than ever conscious of the temporal difficulties involved in the film's naturalism. The succession of "moments" visualized, the technique of the close-up, invites intimacy with the characters and destroys the sense of the proscenium arch. With it goes the sense of distance, the norm of unreality without which musical comedy can hardly exist. Thus the filmed version of *West Side Story* magnificently exploits its cinematic possibilities in using movement in space and visual grouping; yet as a total work of art the film may be less convincing than the stage version, because in the film we are more conscious of the disparity between the naturalistic and the poetic levels. Similarly the film version of *Porgy and Bess* may superficially appear more "real" than the stage version because the rape is ferocious and the murders bloody and because we become acquainted with Porgy and Bess and Sportin' Life in the super-close quarters of the close-up. This reality, however, disrupts the more significant reality created by Gershwin's music and the choric movement. You cannot have it every way; and we need the distance of the proscenium arch if the elements are to appear to exist on the same level.

This is why there has as yet been no successful filmed version of any kind of opera; still less has there been any operatic success in the field of television, for

TV's limited range obviates against adequate use even of the virtues proper to cinema. Maybe some solution will have to be found if there is to be a real future for either the opera or the musical; thus far, certainly, no successful music-dramas have been written specially for television. Naturalistic pieces dealing with Modern Life (usually facetiously) get snagged on the problems of convention and stylization discussed above; while the allegorical or historical pieces tend to become pretentious or Hollywooden—or both. Interestingly enough, the better composers, despite the obvious material temptations, seem to have avoided the genre, or if, like Stravinsky, they have attempted it, to have failed. Even if *The Flood* contains music which is good Stravinsky (and this is debatable), it is certainly a failure as TV drama and as entertainment, and has been an embarrassment all round.

Appendix IV

RECOMMENDED BOOKS

This is not a comprehensive bibliography, but an acknowledgment to a number of books which the author has found helpful while working on this study. Creative literary works are not here included: for these see Index of Literary Quotations.

GENERAL

Van Wyck Brooks, *Makers and Finders:* a history of the writer in America 1800–1915; five volumes (Dutton; English edition J. M. Dent)
Lewis Mumford, *The Golden Day* (Boni and Liveright)
Henry Bamford Parkes, *The American Experience* (Vintage Books)
Alan Pryce Jones (editor), *The American Imagination* (Cassell)
Gertrude Stein, *Lectures in America* (Beacon Press)
William Carlos Williams, *In the American Grain* (New Directions)

PART I

J. Murray Barbour, *The Church Music of William Billings* (Michigan State University Press)
William Billings (edited by Hans Nathan), *The Continental Harmony* (John Harvard Library)
John Cage, *Silence* (Weslyn University Press)
John Cage and Kathleen Hoover, *Virgil Thomson, his Life and Music* (Thomas Yoseloff)
Gilbert Chase, *America's Music* (McGraw Hill)
Aaron Copland, *Copland on Music* (Doubleday)
Henry Cowell, *American Composers on American Music* (Oxford University Press)
Henry and Sidney Cowell, *Charles Ives and his Music* (Oxford University Press)
Charles Ives, *Essays before a Sonata* (Oxford University Press)
Harry Partch, *Genesis of a Music* (University of Wisconsin Press)
Virgil Thomson, *The State of Music* (Vintage Books)

PART II

Louis Armstrong, *Satchmo* (Prentice Hall)
Elizabeth Foster, *Recollections* (University of Pittsburgh Press)
Louis Moreau Gottschalk, *Autobiography* (out of print; in process of being re-edited by Jeanne Behrend)

Nat Hentoff, *The Jazz Life* (Apollo Books) (Peter Davies)
Billie Holiday, *Lady sings the Blues* (Barrie Books)
Alan Lomax, *Mr Jelly Roll* (Universal Library)
Francis Newton, *The Jazz Scene* (MacGibbon and Kee)
Paul Oliver, *Blues fell this morning* (Cassell)
George Reisner (editor), *Bird, the Legend of Charlie Parker* (Citadel Press)
Kenneth Rexroth, *Bird in the Bush* (New Directions)
Nat Shapiro and Nat Hentoff (editors), *Here me talkin' to ya* (Penguin Books)
  (Reinhart & Co. Inc.)
Marshall Stearns, *The Story of Jazz* (Mentor Books)

DISCOGRAPHY

In addition to gramophone companies' catalogues, the *Schwann* and *Gramophone* cumulative catalogues and the monthly publication *New Records*, the following have been consulted:

CLOUGH AND CUMING	*World's Encyclopaedia of Recorded Music and Supplements* (Sidgwick & Jackson Ltd.)
CAREY AND MCCARTHY	*Jazz Directory*, Vol. I–VI (Vol. I op, Vols. II–VI pub. Cassell & Co. Ltd)
FOX, GAMMOND *et al*	*Jazz on Record* (Grey Arrow Books)
DELAUNEY	*Hot Discography* (2nd ed. 1938)
	New Hot Discography (1946)
HARRIS AND RUST	*Recorded Jazz—a critical guide* (Pelican Books)
JEPSEN	*Jazz Records* 1942–1962 (Vols. 5 and 6—all pub. Nordisk Tidsskrift Forlag A/S, Denmark)
RUST	*Jazz Records* 1897–1931 (privately printed)

American Record Guide	*Music Quarterly*
Down Beat	*Notes*
Gramophone	*Record Review*
Jazz Journal	*Records and Recordings*
Jazz Monthly	
Jazz Hot	

Appendix V

Discography

INTRODUCTION

This discography does not claim to be exhaustive. No attempt has been made to list every reputed issue of each work referred to in the text since such a task could have no practical value in the present context which is to bring to the notice of the reader those recordings which are most likely to be accessible to him. Bearing in mind that the book is addressed as much to British readers as to American and that the work of American composers is extremely poorly represented in British catalogues, first choice in the selection of examples is of those recordings which have appeared in British catalogues even though they may subsequently have been withdrawn. In the case of recordings which have appeared only in the United States of America those issued by the major companies have been given precedence over those issued by private companies. This should not be construed as implying that the versions chosen are necessarily superior to those not included, merely that the former are likely to be more easily obtained. A list of addresses of all companies whose records are cited is appended. Though as much care as possible has been taken to ensure the accuracy of these details no guarantee can of course be given either that the records are available or that the companies represented are necessarily still in being.

The discography is arranged in two sections corresponding to the two parts of the book. A third list is appended primarily for the benefit of British readers, of recordings of the works, other than those which appear in Part One, of all American composers which have been released in Great Britain irrespective of whether the composers are discussed in the text or not. In these cases, however, no details other than the composer's name, title of the work and the catalogue numbers are given.

Part One, which deals with the works of American composers, is arranged under the composer's name and, as far as possible, in the order in which the works are discussed. Items are listed as follows: composer's name: title and date of composition (if known): soloist(s) (if any): orchestra: conductor. The record catalogue numbers follow, American issue mono and stereo [indicated (s)] then British issues in the same order. (Note: mono and stereo are divided by a colon; American and British issues by a semi–colon).

Part Two covers popular, light classical and jazz music. Those items, such as Foster's songs and Sousa's marches, which have been the subject of intensive recording could not, for obvious reasons, be listed in great detail, consequently only representative modern recordings have been included. Listing of these items and of the stage works discussed in the last chapters of the book is done in exactly the same manner as Part One. Jazz has been treated somewhat differently for the following reasons.

By its nature Jazz has no definitive performance; each performance has its own intrinsic interest. There is therefore no value in listing items under composer's names. The author and I have decided to number these items in the text for easier reference, beginning from 1 in each chapter, and to list them under these numbers. Further, because the variety of treatment of each item is in itself of interest, even when recorded by the same performers, an attempt has been made to include as many alternative versions as are likely to be readily available. Though the standard method of identifying jazz performance on record is by reference to the Matrix or serial number allocated by the recording engineer to each "take" it has not been thought necessary to include these here except in the rare cases where alternative "takes" of the same performance have been released.

The listing of Jazz items follows the same basic pattern as other entries with the following modifications: the personnel is given in full where possible and the date and place of recording is added. Though such instances have been kept to a minimum some items referred to have not been reissued on long-playing records. In these cases it is the 78 rpm version which has had to be listed though, in most cases, suitable alternatives on long-playing records have been included. The 78 rpm will no longer be generally available though they may be obtainable through the many dealers on both sides of the Atlantic who deal in historical jazz recordings. In these cases it is the latest known issue which is quoted as that most likely to be available to the curious reader.

Except as already stated only long-playing records have been included, though a number of historical recordings have been listed in Part One where it is considered likely that they may be found in special libraries or public collections. All records are 12-inch except where otherwise described, and in general are drawn only from American and British catalogues though where items of special interest are included in catalogues likely to be accessible to the general reader, they have been included.

In conclusion I should like to express my gratitude for all the assistance and advice freely given by my many friends in libraries and in the trade, especially to Mrs. Wilshire of the United States Information Service Library at the U.S. Embassy in London, and to Mr. Morris Hunting and his staff at The Diskery, 82a Hurst Street, Birmingham, for bringing to my attention much special information which I should otherwise have certainly overlooked. Errors and omissions are, of course, my responsibility. I have tried to ensure the accuracy of what is contained here and would appreciate any major errors or omissions being brought to my notice. Finally, special thanks are due to my wife, Irene, for her enduring patience under what have often been trying circumstances.

KENNETH W. DOMMETT

Birmingham
1964

ABBREVIATIONS

GENERAL

(acc)	accompanied by
(del)	deleted (i.e. withdrawn from catalogue and no longer generally available)
(E)	British release
(F)	French release
(G)	German release
(l.ed)	limited edition (i.e. under 100 copies pressed)
(m)	monophonic (single channel) recording
(p.ed)	private edition (i.e. normally only obtainable direct from manufacturer)
(s)	stereophonic (twin channel) recording
(US)	American release

INSTRUMENTAL

(alt)	contralto, alto saxophone
(alt.hn)	alto horn
(bar)	baritone, baritone saxophone
(bar.hn)	baritone horn
(bass)	bass, contra- or double-bass
(b.clt)	bass clarinet
(b.d)	bass drum
(b.sax)	bass saxophone
(bjo)	banjo
(bon)	bongos
(bsn)	bassoon
(c.a)	cor anglais
(cel)	celeste
(clt)	clarinet
(cnt)	cornet
(con.d).	conga drums
(d)	drums
(el.g)	electric guitar
(fl)	flute
(fr.hn)	french horn
(g)	guitar
(hca)	harmonica
(hpd)	harpsichord
(mar)	maraccas
(mba)	marimba
(mel)	mellophone
(narr)	narrator
(ob)	oboe
(org)	organ
(perc)	percussion
(pno)	piano
(prep)	prepared
(reeds)	orchestral section comprising clarinets and saxophones
(sax)	saxophone
(sop)	soprano, soprano saxophone
(s.d)	snare drum
(s.pipe)	stove-pipe
(s.w)	swanee whistle
(tbn)	trombone
(ten)	tenor, tenor saxophone
(tpt)	trumpet
(tu)	tuba, brass bass
(vcl)	violoncello
(vib)	vibra-phone, -harp
(vla)	viola
(vln)	violin
(voc)	vocal
(v.tbn)	valve trombone
(wbd)	washboard
(xyl)	xylophone

PART ONE

CHAPTER I

Various	The Bay Psalm Book (1640) (excerpts)
	Margaret Dodd Singers; Gordon Myers (Precentor)
	NRI 2007 (10″) (del): ARS 32 (del)
	Music of the Pilgrims: excerpts from the Ainsworth Psalter
	New England Conservatory Alumni Chorus
	HSL 2068 (del)
The American Primitives	The American Harmony: Hymns and fuguing tunes
	Maryland University Chapel Choir—Fague Springmann
	Wash. 418: S418 (s)
William BILLINGS (1746–1800)	Easter Anthem (in anthology 'Easter')
	Robert Shaw Chorale
	Vic. LM-1201
William BILLINGS	*I am the Rose of Sharon*
Jacob FRENCH Daniel READ	*The death of General Washington*
	Sherburne
	The Abbey Singers
	Dec. 10073: 710073(s); Bruns(E) AXA 4518: SXA 4518 (s)
John ANTES and others	Arias, Anthems and Chorales of the American Moravians,
	Vol. 1
	Moravian Festival Chorus and Orchestra—Thor Johnson
	Col. ML-5427: SM-6102 (s)
Johann Friedrich PETER and others	Arias, Anthems and Chorales of the American Moravians,
	Vol. 2
	Moravian Festival Chorus and Orchestra—Thor Johnson
	Col. ML-5688: MS-6288 (s)
Johann Friedrich PETER (1746–1813)	6 Quintets for strings
	Moravian Quintet
	NRI 2013-5 (10″) (del)
John ANTES (1740–1711)	3 Trios for strings (2 vln, vcl)
	Moravian Trio
	NRI 2016 (del)
Various	Patriotic music in Early America
	NRI 2011 (10″) (del)
Alexander REINAGLE (1756–1809)	Sonata in E for piano
	A. Loesser
	NRI 2006 (10″) (del)
Horatio PARKER (1863–1919)	*Hora Novissima,* Op. 30 (1893)
	G. Hopf, E. Wein, E. Kent, W. Berry—
	American Record Society Chorus and Orchestra—
	Strickland
	ARS 335

Horatio PARKER (1863–1919)— *contd.*	*Mona,* Op. 71 (1912): Interlude Hamburg Philharmonic Orchestra—Korn Allo. 3150 (del)
George CHADWICK (1854–1931)	Symphonic Sketches, Suite for orchestra (1907) Eastman-Rochester Symphony—Hanson Mer. 50104: 90019 (s) *Tam O'Shanter,* Symphonic ballad (1914–15) American Recording Society Orchestra—Schönherr ARS 29
Arthur FOOTE (1853–1937)	*Night Piece* for flute and strings (1917) J. Baker (fl); S. Shulman, B. Robbins (vln); H. Coletta (vla); B. Greenhouse (vcl) Dec. DL-4013 (10″) (del); Bruns(E) AXL 2015 (10″) M. Sharp (fl)—Cleveland Sinfonietta— Lane (orchestral version) Epic LC-3574: BC-1116 (s) Suite in E for strings (1910) Eastman-Rochester Symphony—Hanson Mer. 50074
Edward MACDOWELL (1861–1908)	Concerto No. 2 in d for piano, Op. 23 (1890) Cliburn—Chicago Symphony Orch.—Hendl Vic. LM-2507; LSC-2507; RCA(E) RB 16244; SB 2113 (s) Rivkin—Vienna State Opera Orch.—Dixon West. 18367; Nixa (E) WLP 5190 (del) Mitchell—American Arts Orch.—Strickland Van. 1011 *Woodland Sketches,* Op. 51 *Sea Pieces,* Op. 55 *Fireside Tales,* Op. 61 *New England Idylls,* Op. 62 John Kirkpatrick (pno) Col. ML-54572 (del) *Woodland Sketches,* Op. 51 Marjorie Mitchell (pno) Van. 1011 *Woodland Sketches,* Op. 51 Vivian Rivkin (pno) West. 18201 *Woodland Sketches,* Op. 51 (excerpts) 1. To a wild rose 6. To a water lily Leonard Pennario (pno) Cap. P-8541: SP-8541 (s) (US & E) Songs: There are no modern recordings of MacDowell's songs. A number are to be found on deleted 78 rpm records, notably by Schumann-Heink and Nelson Eddy
Henry F. GILBERT (1868–1928)	*Dance in Place Congo,* ballet (1918) Janssen Symphony of Los Angeles—Janssen Art. 100 (del)

Douglas   Symphony in A (1946)
MOORE   American Recording Society Orchestra—Dixon
(1893–)   ARS 5
                   Japan Philharmonic Orchestra—Strickland
                   CRI 133
                 The Ballad of Baby Doe (1956)
                   B. Sills, F. Bible, W. Cassel—New York City Chorus
                     and Orchestra—Buckley
                   MGM 3-GC-1: S3-GC-1 (s)

Quincy   String quartet No. 8 (1950)
PORTER   Stanley Quartet
(1897–)   CRI 118

Howard   Symphony No. 2 *Romantic*, Op. 30 (1930)
HANSON   Eastman-Rochester Symphony—Hanson
(1896–)   Col. ML-4638
                 Symphony No. 4 *Requiem*, Op. 34 (1943)
                   American Recording Society Orchestra—Dixon
                   ARS 6
                   Eastman-Rochester Symphony—Hanson
                   Mer. 50077
                 Symphony No. 5 *Sinfonia Sacra* (1954)
                   Eastman-Rochester Symphony and Chorus—Hanson
                   Mer. 50087
                 Cherubic Hymn, Op. 37 (1949)
                   See above

Walter   Symphony No. 6
PISTON   Boston Symphony Orchestra—Munch
1894–)   Vic. LPM-2083 (del); RCA(E) RB 16030

                         CHAPTER II

Charles IVES   *Two little flowers; The circus band; The side show;*
(1874–1954)   *In the cage* and other songs
                   E. McChesnay (ten); O. Herz (pno)
                   CHS C.7 (3 records) (78 rpm) (del)
                 Twenty-four songs
                   H. Boatwright (sop); J. Kirkpatrick (pno)
                   Over. 7
                 Eleven songs
                   J. Greissle (sop); J. Wolman (pno)
                   SPA 9
                 Eight songs
                   C. Curry (sop); L. Vosgerchian (pno)
                   Cam. 804: (1804 (s)
                 The Indians (1912)
                   Boston Chamber Ensemble—Farberman
                   Cam. 804: 1804 (s)
                 Three Places in New England (1903–14)
                   (i) *The Reddings at Boston Common;* (ii) *Putnam's Camp;*
                   (iii) *The Housatonic at Stockbridge*

Charles IVES
(1874–1954)—
contd.

Eastman-Rochester Symphony—Hanson
Mer. 50149: 90149(s); Mer(E) MMA 11010: AMS
16083(s) (del)

Central Park in the dark (1898–1907)
Polymusic Chamber Orchestra—Cherniavsky
Polym. PR 1001 (del)
Oslo Philharmonic Orchestra—Strickland
CRI 163

The Pond (1906)
Boston Chamber Ensemble—Farberman
Cam. 804: 1804(s)
Oslo Philharmonic Orchestra—Strickland
CRI 163

Hallowe'en (1911); *Over the pavements* (1913)
Polymusic Chamber Orchestra—Cherniavsky
Polym. PR 1001 (del)
Boston Chamber Ensemble—Farberman
Cam. 804: 1804(s)

Hallowe'en (1911)
Oslo Philharmonic Orchestra—Strickland
CRI 163

The Unanswered Question (1908)
Polymusic Chamber Orchestra—Cherniavsky
Polym. PR 1001 (del)
Zimbler Sinfonietta—Foss
Siena 100–2

Sonata No. 2 for piano *Concord Mass., 1840–1860* (1909–15),
John Kirkpatrick (pno)
Col. ML-4250 (del)
A. Kontarsky (pno); T. Plümacher (vla); W. Schweger (fl)
Time 58005: 8005(s)
G. Pappa-stavrou (pno); B. Lichter (fl)
CRI 150

Sonata No. 1 for piano (1902–10)
William Masselos (pno)
Col. ML-4490 (del)

String quartet No. 2 (1913)
Walden Quartet
Per. SPLP 501 (del)

Washington's Birthday from Symphony: Holidays (1913)
Tokyo Imperial Philharmonic Orchestra—Strickland
CRI 163

Decorations Day from Symphony: Holidays
Louisville Orchestra—Whitney
Lou. 621

Symphony No. 2 (1897–1902)
Vienna Orchestra—Adler
SPA 39

Symphony No. 2
New York Philharmonic Symphony Orchestra—
Bernstein
Col. KL-5489: SL-6155

Symphony No. 3 (1901–11)
   Baltimore Little Symphony—Stewart
   Van. 468
   Eastman-Rochester Symphony Orchestra—Hanson
   Mer. 50149:90149(s); Mer(E) MMA 11010: AMS 16083(s) (del)
Symphony No. 4
   No commercial recording of this work exists but a private
      recording of part of it is believed to be in the U.S.
   Embassy Library in London
Sonata No. 2 for violin and piano (1907–10)
   Rafael Druian (vln); John Simms (pno)
   Mer. 50097
Sonata No. 3 for violin and piano (1902–14)
   As above
Sonata No. 4 for violin and piano, *Children's Day at the
   Camp Meeting* (1916)
   As above
Tone Roads No. 1 (1911) and No. 3 (1915)
   Boston Chamber Ensemble—Farberman
   Cam. 804: 1804(s)
Psalm 67 (c. 1898)
   Hamline Singers—Holliday
   NRI 305 (10″) (del)
   Columbia University Teachers College Choir
   Music Lib. 7071
Harvest Home Chorales Nos. 1–3 (1898–1912)
   Shaw Chorale—Shaw
   Vic. LM-2676: LSC-2676
No. 3 only:
   Columbia University Teachers College Choir
   Music Lib. 7071

CHAPTER III

Carl RUGGLES
(1876–   )

Lilacs from *Men and Mountains* (1924)
   Juilliard String Orchestra—Prausnitz
   Col. ML-4986
Portals (1926 rev. 1952–3)
   As above
Evocations—four chants for piano (1937–43 rev. 1954)
   John Kirkpatrick (pno)
   As above
Organum (1949)
   Japan Philharmonic Symphony Orchestra—Watanabe
   CRI 127

Roy HARRIS
(1898–   )

Concerto for piano, clarinet and string quartet, Op. 2 (1930)
   Aeolian String Quartet and soloists
   Col. 68138–40D (78 rpm) (del)
Sonata for piano (1929)
   Johana Harris (pno)
   Vic. 12445–6 (78 rpm) (del)
Soliloquy and Dance (1941)
   William Primrose (vla); Johana Harris (pno)
   Vic. 11–9212–3 (78 rpm) (del)

Roy HARRIS   Trio for violin, cello and piano (1934)
(1898-)—   University of Oklahoma Trio
contd.   U. Okla. 1
        Quintet for piano and strings (1937)
          Johana Harris (pno); Coolidge Quartet
          Vic. 17750-3S (78 rpm) (del)
        Symphony No. 3 (1938)
          American Recording Society Orchestra—Hendl
          ARS 28
          Eastman-Rochester Symphony Orchestra—Hanson
          Mer. 50077; Mer(E), MMA 11097 (del)
          New York Philharmonic-Symphony Orchestra—Bernstein
          Col. ML-5703: MS-6306
        Symphony No. 7 (1951) with (†) Symphony No. 1 "1933"
          Philadelphia Symphony Orchestra—Ormandy
          (†) Boston Symphony Orchestra—Koussevitsky
          Col. ML-5095

William   Symphony No. 5 for string orchestra (1943)
SCHUMAN   Pittsburg Symphony Orchestra—Steinberg
(1910-)   Cap. S 8212; Cap(E) CTL 7039 (del)
        Judith, Choreographic poem (1950)
          Louisville Orchestra—Whitney
          Lou. 604, Mer. MG 10088 (del)
        Credendum (Article of Faith)
          Philadelphia Symphony Orchestra—Ormandy
          Col. ML-5185

Peter   String Quartet No. 2
MENNIN   Juilliard Quartet
(1923-)   Col. ML-4844
        Symphony No. 3 (1946)
          New York Philharmonic-Symphony Orchestra—
             Mitropoulos
          Col. ML-4902
        Symphony No. 5 (1950)
          Louisville Orchestra—Whitney
          Lou. 613
        Symphony No. 6 (1953)
          Louisville Orchestra—Whitney
          Lou. 545-3

Robert   Quartet for piano and strings (1948)
PALMER   John Kirkpatrick (pno); Walden Quartet
(1915-)   Col. ML-4842
        Memorial Music (1957)
          Orchestre Solistes of Paris—Husa
          Cor.U. N80P

CHAPTER IV

Aaron   Passacaglia (1922)
COPLAND   Webster Aitken (pno)
(1900-)   Lyr. 104

Two pieces for Strings (1928)
  MGM String Orchestra—Solomon
  MGM 3117 (del)
Piano Variations (1930)
  Webster Aitken (pno)
  Lyr. 104
  William Masselos (pno)
  Col. ML-5568: MS-6168(s)
  Frank Glazer (pno)
  Con-Disc 1217: 217(s); Saga XIP 7010(m)
  Of historical interest is an old recording by the composer
    on Col. 68320–1D (78 rpm) (del)
Concerto for piano and orchestra, "Jazz Concerto" (1926)
  L. Smit (pno)—Radio Rome Symphony Orchestra—Copland
  CHS 1238 (del)
    E. Wild (pno)—Symphony of the Air—Copland
  Van. VRS-1070: VSD-2094(s)
Statements for Orchestra (1933–35)
  London Symphony Orchestra—Copland
  Ever. 6015: 3015(s)
Billy the Kid, Ballet suite (1938)
  As last
  Ballet Theatre Orchestra—Levine
  Cap. P-8238 (del); Cap(E) CTL 7039 (del)
  New York Philharmonic-Symphony Orchestra—
    Bernstein
  Col. ML-5575: MS 6175; Phi(E) ABL 3357: SABL 192(s)
  London Symphony Orchestra—Dorati
  Mer. 50246: 90246(s); Mer(E) MMA 11172: AMS
    16122(s)
  Philadelphia Symphony Orchestra—Ormandy
  Col. ML-5157
  London Symphony Orchestra—Susskind
  WRC(E) T.92
Rodeo, Ballet suite (1942)
  Ballet Theatre Orchestra—Levine
  Cap. P-8196 (del); Cap(E) CCL 7516 (10″) (del)
  New York Philharmonic-Symphony Orchestra—Bernstein
  As for *Billy the Kid*
  Minneapolis Symphony Orchestra—Dorati
  Mer. 50172: 90172(s); Mer(E) MMA 11005: AMS 16021(s)
Appalachian Spring, Ballet suite (1944)
  Boston Symphony Orchestra—Copland
  Vic. LM-2401: LSC-2401(s); RCA(E) RB 16232:
    SB2104(s)
  New York Philharmonic-Symphony Orchestra—
    Bernstein
  Col. ML-5755: MS-6355; CBS(E) BRG 72074:
    SBRG 72074(s)
  London Symphony Orchestra—Dorati
  See *Billy the Kid*
  London Symphony Orchestra—Susskind
  Ever. 6002: 3002(s); WRC(E) T.92

Aaron
COPLAND
(1900–   )—
contd.

Appalachian Spring (complete)
  Philadelphia Symphony Orchestra—Ormandy
  Col. ML-5157
Our Town, Orchestral suite (1940)
  Utah Symphony Orchestra—Abravanel
  Van. 1088: 2115(s)
  Little Society Orchestra—Scherman
  Dec. DL 7527 (10″) (del); Bruns(E) AXL 2006 (10″) (del)
Quiet City, Incidental music for a play (1941)
  H. Glantz (tpt); A. Goltzer (c.a)—Concert Arts Orchestra
    —Golschmann
  Cap. P-8245; Cap(E) CTL 7056 (del)
  S. Mear (tpt); R. Swingley (c.a)—Eastman-Rochester
    Symphony Orchestra—Hanson
  Mer. 50076; Mer(E) MG 40003 (del)
  Utah Symphony Orchestra—Abravanel
  Van. 1088: 2115(s)
Music for Radio (*Saga of the Prairies*) (1937)
  MGM Orchestra—Winograd
  MGM 3367 (del)
Sonata for piano (1941)
  Webster Aitken (pno)
  Lyr. 104
  Leon Fleischer (pno)
  Epic LC-3862: BC1262(s)
  Harry Somer (pno)
  CRI 171
  Andor Foldes (pno)
  DGG(E) DGM 18279 (del)
Sonata for violin and piano (1943)
  J. Fuchs (vln); L. Smit (pno)
  Dec. 8503; Bruns(E) AXTL 1047 (del)
  C. Glenn (vln); H. Somer (pno)
  CRI 171
  (excerpt)
  Y. Menuhin (vln); M. Gazelle (pno)
  in 2-Vic. LM-6092; HMV (HMS) HLP 27
El Salon Mexico (1936)
  Utah Symphony Orchestra—Abravanel
  West 18840: 14063(s)
  Columbia Symphony Orchestra—Bernstein
  Col. CL-920; Phi(E) NBR 6019 (del)
  New York Philharmonic-Symphony Orchestra—Bernstein
  Col. ML-5755: MS-6355; CBS(E) BRG 72074: SBRG
    72074(s)
  also
  Col. ML-5841: MS-6441
  Minneapolis Symphony Orchestra—Dorati
  Mer. 50172: 90172(s); Mer(E) MMA 11005; AMS
    16021(s)
  National Symphony Orchestra—Mitchell
  West 18284; Nixa WLP 5286 (del)

> In the Beginning (1947)
>> San José College Choir
>> Music Lib. 7007
>
> Twelve Poems of Emily Dickinson (1950)
>> M. Lipton (sop); A. Copland (pno)
>> Col. ML-5106
>
> Quartet for piano and strings (1950)
>> New York Quartet
>> Col. ML-4421
>
> Piano Fantasy (1957)
>> William Masselos (pno)
>> Col. ML-5568: MS-6168(s)
>
> *The Tender Land*, Suite (1954)
>> Boston Symphony Orchestra—Copland
>> Vic. LM-2401: LSC-2401(s); RCA(E) RB16232;
>> SB2104(s)
>
> *The Second Hurricane*, Opera for schools (1937)
>> New York City High School of Music and Art Chorus—
>> New York Philharmonic-Symphony Orchestra—
>> Bernstein
>> Col. ML-5581: MS-6181(s)

CHAPTER V

Elliott
CARTER
(1908–   )

> Tarantella (Prelude to *Mostellaria*) (1936)
>> Harvard Glee Club
>> Car. 118
>
> Sonata for piano (1946)
>> Beveridge Webster (pno)
>> ARS 25
>> Charles Rosen (pno)
>> Epic LC-3850: BC-1250
>
> *The Minotaur*, Ballet suite (1946)
>> Eastman-Rochester Symphony Orchestra—Hanson
>> Mer. 50103; Mer(E) MRL 2515 (del)
>
> Sonata for cello and piano (1948)
>> B. Greenhouse (vcl); A. Markas (pno)
>> ARS 25
>
> String Quartet No. 1 (1951)
>> Walden Quartet
>> Col. ML-5104
>
> Variations for Orchestra (1955)
>> Louisville Orchestra—Whitney
>> Lou. 58-3
>
> String Quartet No. 2 (1960)
>> Juilliard Quartet
>> Vic. LM-2481: LSC 2481(s)
>
> Double Concerto for harpsichord, piano and two chamber
>> orchestras (1961)
>> R. Kirkpatrick (hpd); C. Rosen (pno)—Chamber
>> orchestras—Meier
>> Epic LC-3830: BC-1157(s)

Elliott
CARTER
(1908–   )—
contd.

Sonata for flute, oboe, cello and harpsichord (1952)
   A. Brieff (fl); J. Marx (ob); L. Bernsohn (vcl); R. Conant
   (hpd)
   Col. ML-5576; MS-6176(s)

CHAPTER VI

Wallingford
RIEGGER
(1885–1961)

Trio for piano, violin and cello, Op. 1 (1919–20)
   J. Covelli (pno); W. Kroll (vln); A. Kouguell (vcl)
   Col. ML-5589: MS-6189(s)
New Dance, Op. 18b (1934)
   Eastman-Rochester Symphony Orchestra—Hanson
   Mer. 50078
Symphony No. 3, Op. 42 (1946–7)
   Eastman-Rochester Symphony Orchestra—Hanson
   Col. ML-4902
Variations for Piano and Orchestra, Op. 54 (1952–3)
   B. Owen (pno)—Louisville Orchestra—Whitney
   Lou. 545–3

Roger
SESSIONS
(1896–   )

The Black Maskers, Incidental music (1923)
   Eastman-Rochester Symphony Orchestra—Hanson
   Mer. 50106: 90103(s); Mer(E) MMA 11145:
      AMS16093(s)
Symphony No. 2 (1937)
   New York Philharmonic-Symphony Orchestra—
      Mitropoulos
   Col. ML-4784 (del)
String Quartet No. 2 (1950)
   New Music Quartet
   Col. ML-5105
Idyll of Theocritus for Soprano and Orchestra (1954)
   A. Mossaman (sop)—Louisville Orchestra—Whitney
   Lou. 57–4

Andrew
IMBRIE
(1921–   )

String Quartet No. 1 in B flat (1944)
   Juilliard Quartet
   Col. ML-4844
String Quartet No. 2 (1953)
   California Quartet
String Quartet No. 3 (1957)
   Walden Quartet
   Cont. 6003: 7022(s)
Legend for Orchestra (1959)
   San Francisco Symphony Orchestra—Jorda
   CRI 152

Ben WEBER
(1916–   )

Symphony on Poems of William Blake, Op. 37 (1952)
   W. Galjour (bar)--Leopold Stokowski Orchestra
   CRI 120

Hugo
WEISGALL
(1912–   )

The Stronger (1952)
   A. Bishop (sop)—Columbia Chamber Orchestra—
      Antonini
   Col. ML-5106

Ross Lee
FINNEY
(1906–)
	Symphony No. 2
	  Louisville Orchestra—Whitney
	  Lou. 625
	String Quartet No. 6 in E (1950)
	  Stanley Quartet
	  CRI 116

Leon
KIRCHNER
(1919–)
	Concerto for violin, cello, ten wind instruments and percussion (1960)
	  T. Spivakovsky (vln); A. Parisot (vcl)—Chamber
	    Orchestra—Kirchner
	  Epic LC-3830: BC-1157(s)
	Concerto for Piano and Orchestra (1952–3)
	  L. Kirchner (pno)—New York Philharmonic-Symphony
	    Orchestra—Mitropoulos
	  Col. ML-5185

Irving FINE
(1914–62)
	Quartet (1952)
	  Juilliard Quartet
	  Col. ML-4843
	Fantasy Trio
	  Illinois University School of Music Trio
	  CRS 5 Vol. II (p.ed)

George
ROCHBURG
(1918–)
	Symphony No. 2 (1958)
	  New York Philharmonic-Symphony Orchestra—
	    Torkanowsky
	  Col. ML-5779: MS-6379

CHAPTER VII

Charles T.
GRIFFES
(1884–1920)
	Roman Sketches, Op. 7 (1917) (complete)
	  Lenore Engdahl (pno)
	  MGM 3225 (del)
	  Leonard Hambro (pno)
	  Lyr. 105
	The White Peacock Op. 7/1
	Clouds, Op. 7/4
	  Eastman-Rochester Symphony Orchestra—Hanson
	  Mer. 50085: Mer(E) MRL 2544 (del)
	Sonata for piano (1919)
	  Del Purves (pno)
	  Music Lib. 7021
	  Leonard Hambro (pno)
	  Lyr. 105
	  William Masselos (pno)
	  MGM 3556 (del)
	The Pleasure Dome of Kublai Khan (1920)
	  Eastman-Rochester Symphony Orchestra—Hanson
	  Mer. 50085; Mer(E) MRL 2544 (del)

Henry
COWELL
(1897–)
	Piano music
	  Henry Cowell (pno)
	  Folk. 3349
	  (*N.B.* All items cited in text are on this record)

| Henry COWELL (1897–)— *contd.* | Henry Cowell (pno) |
| | CRI 109 |

Set of Five for violin, piano and percussion
A. Ajemian (vln); M. Ajemian (pno); E. Bailey (perc)
MGM 3454 (del)
Toccanta for soprano, flute, cello and piano
H. Boatwright (sop) and ensemble
Col. ML-4986
Symphony No. 4, *Short Symphony*, (1946)
Eastman-Rochester Symphony Orchestra—Hanson
Mer. 50078; Mer(E) MMA 11136
Symphony No. 11, *Seven Rituals of Music* (1954)
Louisville Orchestra—Whitney
Lou. 545-2 *and* Col. ML-5039

Henry BRANT *Galaxy 2* (1954)
(1913–) *Signs and Alarms* (1953)
Col. ML-4956 Chamber Ensemble—Brant
Angels and Devils: Concerto for Flute (1932)
F. Wilkins (fl)—Flute Orchestra—Brant
CRI 106

Alan Concerto No. 1 for piano and orchestra, *Lousadzak* (1944)
HOVHANESS M. Ajemian (pno)—MGM String Orchestra—Surinach
(1911–) MGM 3674 (del)
Concerto No. 2 for violin and orchestra (1957)
A. Ajemian (vln)—MGM String Orchestra—Surinach
MGM 3674 (del)
Concerto No. 1 for Orchestra, *Averekal* (1951)
Eastman-Rochester Symphony Orchestra—Hanson
Mer. 50078; Mer(E) MRL 2556 (del)

Lou Mass for mixed chorus, trumpet, harp and strings
HARRISON R. Kutik (tpt)—New York Concert Choir and Orchestra,
(1917–) directed by Margaret Hillis
Epic LC-3307 (del)
Suite No. 2 for String Quartet (1948)
New Music Quartet
Suite for cello and harp (1949)
S. Barab (vcl); L. Lawrence (harp)
Col. ML-4491 (del)
Suite for Symphonic Strings (1936 rev. 1960)
Louisville Orchestra—Whitney
Lou. 621
Canticle No. 1 for percussion (1940)
Manhattan Percussion Ensemble
Time 58000: 8000(s)
Canticle No. 3 for percussion (1941).
American Percussion Society—Price
Uran. 106: 5106(s)

Daniel Concerto for celeste and harpsichord soli (1955)
PINKHAM E. Low (cel) and D. Pinkham (hps)
(1923–) CRI 109

Edgard
VARÈSE
(1885–)

Offrandes (1922)
 D. Precht (sop)—Columbia Symphony Orchestra—Craft
 Col. ML-5762: MS-6362(s); CBE(E) BRG 72106:
  SBRG 72106(s)
Ionisation (1931)
 Craft Ensemble
 Col. ML-5478: MS-6416; Phi(E) ABL 3392
 Juilliard Percussion Orchestra—Waldman
 EMS 401
 American Percussion Society—Price
 Uran, 106: 5106(s)
Density 21.5 for solo flute (1936)
 Unnamed soloist (Arthur Gleghorn?)
 Col. ML-5478: MS-6416; Phi(E) ABL 3392
 Rene LeRoy (fl)
 EMS 401
Intégrales (1926); *Octandre* (1924)
 Craft Ensemble
 Col. ML-5478: MS-6416; Phi(E) ABL 3392
 New York Wind Ensemble; Juilliard Percussion Orchestra—
  Waldman
 EMS 401
Arcana (1927); *Deserts* (1954)
 Columbia Symphony Orchestra—Craft
 Col. ML-5762: MS-6362; CBS(E) BRG 72106:
  SBRG 72106(s)
Poème électronique (1958)
 Direct composition on magnetic tape
 Col. ML-5478: MS-6416; Phi(E) ABL 3392

CHAPTER VIII

Harry
PARTCH
(1901–)

U.S. Highball (1956)
 T. Coleman—Instrumental Ensemble—McKenzie
 Gate 5 Issue B (p.ed)
EvenWild Horses (1953)
 A. Louw (voc)—Gate 5 Ensemble of Sausalito—Schwartz
 Gate 5. Issue C (p.ed)
Ring round the Moon
 L. Ludlow—Gate 5 Ensemble of Sausalito—Schwartz
 Gate 5. Issue C (p.ed)
Castor and Pollux from "Plectra and Percussion Dances"
 Gate 5 Ensemble of Sausalito—Schwart 2 (1953)
 Gate 5 Issue C (p.ed)
Poems by Li-Po (1931–33)
 W. Wendlandt, H. Partch (voc); H. Partch (prep. vla)
 Gate 5. Issue A (p.ed)
Bless this home (1961)
 H. Partch (voc, prep.vla); V. Prockelo (ob); D. Mitchell
  (kithara, harmonic cannon); J. Varhula (mazda marimba)
 Gate 5. Issue A (p.ed)
Cloud-chamber Music (1950)
 Instrumental Ensemble
 Gate 5. Issue A (p.ed)

Harry
PARTCH
(1901–)—
contd.

The Bewitched (excepts) (1956)
 F. Pierce (sop); W. Olson (narr)—Gate 5 Ensemble of
  Illinois University—Garvey
 Gate 5. Issue E (p.ed)

Revelation in the Courthouse Park (1960)
 Soloists—Gate 5 Ensemble of Illinois University—Garvey
 Gate 5. Issue F (p.ed)
Water! Water! An Intermission (1961)
 Soloists—Gate 5 Ensemble of Illinois University—Garvey
 Gate 5. Issue G (p.ed)
Windsong (excerpt from film soundtrack) (1958)
 Gate 5. Issue A (p.ed)

John CAGE
(1912–)

Amores for prepared piano and percussion (1943)
 Manhatten Percussion Ensemble
 Time 58000: 8000(s)
Aria (1958)
 Cathy Berberian (mezz)
 Time 58003: 8003(s)
String Quartet (1950)
 New Music Quartet
 Col. ML-4495 (del)
Sonatas and Interludes (1946–48)
 Maro Ajemian (pno)
 Dial 19 (del)
The Wonderful Widow of 18 Springs (1942)
 A. Carmen (alt); J. Cage (pno)
She is asleep (1943)
 (i) Quartet for twelve tom-toms
  Manhatten Percussion Ensemble
 (ii) Duo
  A. Carmen (alt); J. Cage (pno)
Music for Carillon (1954)
 David Tudor
Concert for piano and orchestra (1957–58)
 D. Tudor (pno)—Cunningham Orchestra—Cunningham
Construction in metal (1937)
 Manhatten Percussion Ensemble
Williams Mix (1952)
 Electronic tape
 All above items in 3-Avakian JC-1; JCS-1(s)
Fontana Mix (1958)
 Electronic tape
 Time 58003: 8003(s)

Earle BROWN
(1926–)

Music for violin, cello and piano (1952)
 M. Raimondi (vln); D. Soyer (vcl); D. Tudor (pno)
Music for cello and piano (1955)
 D. Soyer (vcl); D. Tudor (pno)
Hodograph No. 1 (1959)
 D. Hammond (fl); P. Kraus (bells, vib, mba); D. Tudor
  (pno, cel)
 Time 58007: 8007(s)

Morton
FELDMAN
(1926–)

Structures for String Quartet (1951)
  M. Raimondi (vln); J. Rabushka (vln); W. Trampler (vla);
    S. Barab (vcl)
Projection 4 for violin and piano (graph) (1951)
  M. Raimondi (vln); D. Tudor (pno)
Three Pieces for String Quartet (1954–56)
  See "Structures" above
Piece for four pianos
  M. Feldman, D. Tudor, R. Sherman, E. Hymovitz (pno)
    all above in Col. ML-5403: MS-6090(s) (del)
Durations (1960–61)
  M. Raimondi (vln); D. Hammond (alt.fl); D. Soyer (vcl);
    P. Kraus (vib); D. Tudor (pno); D. Butterfield (tu)
  Time 58007: 8007(s)

CHAPTER IX

Samuel
BARBER
(1910–)

Dover Beach, for Baritone and String Quartet, Op. 3 (1931)
  S. Barber (bar); Curtis Quartet
  Vic. 8998 (78 rpm) (del). Reissued on Vic. LCT-1158
  J. Langstaffe (bar); Hirsch Quartet
  HMV C.4201 (78 rpm) (del)
  P. King (bar); Hartt Quartet
  Cl.Ed 1011 (del)
Symphony in One movement, No. 1, Op. 9 (1936 rev. 1943)
  Eastman-Rochester Symphony Orchestra—Hanson
  Mer. 50087 and 50148; Mer(E) MMA 11097 (del)
  Japan Philharmonic Orchestra—Strickland
  CRI 137
Capricorn Concerto, Op. 21 (1944)
  J. Mariano (fl); R. Sprenkle (ob); S. Mear (tpt)—Eastman-
    Rochester Symphony Orchestra—Hanson
  Mer. 50224: 90224(s); Mer(E) MMA 11148: AMS 16096(s)
Adagio for Strings (from Quartet, Op. 11) (1936)
  NBC Symphony Orchestra—Toscanini
  Vic. 11-8287 (78 rpm) (del); HMV DB.6180 (78 rpm) (del)
  Eastman-Rochester Symphony Orchestra—Hanson
  See "Capricorn Concerto" above. Also Mer(E) xep 9000
  NB. There are other versions of this piece too numerous to
    list exhaustively.
Adagio: Quartet version
  Borodin Quartet
  MK-1563
  Stradivari Records Quartet
  Strad. 602
Sonata for piano, Op. 26 (1949)
  Vladimir Horowitz (pno)
  in 2-Vic. LD-7021; RCA(E) RB 6555
Songs to Poems by James Joyce, Op. 10
  P. King (bar); S. Quincey (pno)
  Cl. Ed 1011 (del)
Hermit Songs (1953)

Samuel   L Price (sop); S. Barber (pno)
BARBER   Col. ML-4988
(1910-)—   *Vanessa,* Opera in four Acts. Libretto G-C Menotti(1958)
contd.   E. Steber, N. Gedda, R. Elias, G. Tozzi, R. Resnik—
                       Metropolitan Opera Orchestra and Chorus—
                          Mitropoulos
                       3-Vic. LM-6138: LSC-6138(s)
                    Knoxville: Summer of 1915, for Soprano and Orchestra (1948)
                       E. Steber (sop)—Greater Trenton Orchestra
                       Harsanyi
                       Stand 420: 7420(s)
                       E. Steber (sop)—Dumbarton Oaks Chamber Orchestra—
                          Strickland
                       Col. ML-5843

Theodore   Epitaphs (1937–40)
CHANLER   P. Curtin (sop); F. Ryan Edwards (pno)
(1902–61)   Col. ML-5598: MS-6198(s)

Virgil   Variations on Sunday-school Tunes (1927, 1930)
THOMSON   Marilyn Mason (org)
(1896–)   Eso. 522
                    Capital, capitals, for four men and a piano (1927).
                       Text by G. Stein
                       J. Crawford, C. Turner (ten); J. James (bar); W. Smith
                          (bass); V. Thomson (pno)
                       Col. ML-4491 (del)
                    The Mother of us all, Orchestral suite
                       Janssen Symphony of Los Angeles—Janssen
                       Col. ML-4468
                    Four Saints in Three Acts, Opera. Libretto: G. Stein (abridged)
                          (1934)
                       B. Robinson-Wayne, I Matthews (sop); A. Hines (Mezz);
                          R. Greene (alt); C. Holland, D. Bethea (ten);
                          R. Robinson (bar); A. Dorsey (bass)—Chorus and
                          Orchestra—Thomson
                       Vic. LCT 1139 (del)
                    Five Songs from William Blake
                       M. Harrell (bar)—Philadelphia Symphony Orchestra—
                          Ormandy
                       Col. ML-4919 (del)
                    A Solemn Music (1949)
                       Eastman-Rochester Symphonic Wind Ensemble—Fennell
                       Mer. 50084: Mer(E) MRL 2535 (del)
                    The Plow that broke the Plains, Film music (1936)
                       Little Society Orchestra—Scherman
                       Dec.DL-5727 (10″) (del); Bruns(E) AXL2006 (10″) (del)
                       Symphony of the Air—Stokowski
                       Van. 1071: 2095(s)
                    The River, Film music (1942)
                       ARS Orchestra—Hendl
                       ARS 8
                       Symphony of the Air —Stokowski
                       Van. 1071: 2095(s)

Louisiana Story—Arcadian songs and dances (1948)
 Little Society Orchestra—Scherman
 Dec. 3207 and 9616; Bruns(E) AXTL 1022 (del)
 Cleveland Pops Orchestra
 Epic LC-3809: BC-1147
Three Pictures for Orchestra (1947, 48, 52)
 Philadelphia Symphony Orchestra—Thomson
 Col. ML-4919

Bernard
ROGERS
(1893–)

Leaves from *The Tale of Pinocchio* (1950)
 M. Mackown (narr)—Eastman-Rochester Symphony
  Orchestra—Hanson
 Mer. 50114; Mer(E) MMA 11064 (del)
Once upon a time, Five fairy tales (1934)
 Eastman-Rochester Symphony Orchestra—Hanson
 Mer. 50147: 90147(s); Mer(E) MMA 11158:
  AMS 16104 (s)
Variations on a Song by Mussorgsky (1960)
 Rochester Philharmonic Orchestra—Bloomfield
 CRI 153

CHAPTER X

Harold
SHAPERO
(1920–)

Sonata No. 1 for piano (1944)
 Frank Glazer (pno)
 Con-Disc 1217: 217(s); Saga XIP 7010
 Sylvia Marlowe (hpd)
 Dec. 10021: 710021(s)
Symphony for Classical Orchestra (1948)
 Columbia Symphony Orchestra—Bernstein
 Col. ML-4889

Alexei
HAIEFF
(1914–)

Concerto for Piano and Orchestra (1952)
 L. Smit (pno)—ARS Orchestra—Hendl
 ARS 9
 S. Bianco (pno)—Hamburg Philharmonic Orchestra—
  Walther
 MGM 3243 (del)
String Quartet (1951)
 Juilliard Quartet
 Col. ML-4988

Robert
MOEVS
(1920–)

Sonata for piano (1950)
 Joseph Bloch (pno)
 CRI 136

Milton
BABBITT
(1916–)

Du, Song cycle (1951)
 B. Beardslee (sop); R. Helps (pno)
 Son-Nova 1: S1(s)
Composition for twelve instruments (1948)
 Hartt Chamber Orchestra—Shapey
 As above
Composition for four instruments (1948)
 J. Wummer (fl); S. Drucker (clt); P. Marth (vln);
  D. McCall (vcl)
 CRI 138

Milton   Composition for viola and piano (1950)
BABBITT   W. Trampler (vla); A. Bauman (pno)
(1916–   )–*contd.*   CRI 138

Melvin   Divertimento for five winds (1956)
POWELL   Fairfield Wind Ensemble
(1923–   )   CRI 121
                          Divertimento for violin and harp (1955)
                            L. Sorkin (vln); M. Ross (harp)
                            CRI 121
                          Haiku Settings (1960)
                            Bethany Beardslee (sop); R. Helps (pno)
                            Son-Nova 1: S1(s)
                          Filigree Setting for string quartet (1959)
                            Claremont Quartet
                            Son-Nova 1: S1(s)
                          Electronic Setting (1961)
                            Electronic mixer
                            Son-Nova 1: S1(s)

Seymour   Serenade for five instruments (1955)
SHIFRIN   M. Kaplan (ob); C. Russo (clt); R. Cecil (fr.hr);
(1926–   )   Y. Lynch (vla); H. Wingreen (pno)
                            CRI 123: 123SD(s)

Gunther   Seven Studies on a theme of Paul Klee
SCHULLER   Minneapolis Symphony Orchestra—Dorati
(1925–   )   Mer. 50282: 90282; Mer(E) MMA 11151: AMS 16099(s)
                          Symphony for brass and percussion, Op. 16
                            Jazz and Classical Music Society Ensemble—Schuller
                            Col. CL-941 (del)
                          String Quartet (1957)
                            Walden Quartet
                            CRS 5. Vol. III (p.ed)

Lukas FOSS   String Quartet No. 1 (1947)
(1922–   )   The American Art Quartet
                            Col. ML-5476
                          The Song of Songs, for Soprano and Orchestra (1947)
                            J. Tourel (sop)—New York Philharmonic-Symphony
                                Orchestra—Bernstein
                            Col. ML-5451: MS-6123(s)
                          Psalms (1957)
                            Roger Wagner Chorale
                            CRI 123: 123-SD(s)
                          Concerto No. 2 for piano and orchestra
                            L. Foss (pno)—Los Angeles Festival Orchestra—Waxman
                            Dec. 9889 (del)
                          A Parable of Death
                            R. Robinson (ten); M. Hayes (narr)—Pomona Glee
                                Clubs—Foss
                            Educo 4002
                            F. Stevens (ten); V. Zorina (narr)—Louisville
                                Orchestra—Whitney
                            Col. ML-4859

    Time Cycle
      A. Addison (sop); L. Foss (pno); R. Dufallo (clt); H. Colf
        vcl); DeLancey (perc)—Columbia Symphony
        Orchestra—Bernstein
      Col. ML-5680: MS-6280(s)

Hall
OVERTON
(1920–)
	Sonata for viola and piano (1960)
	  W. Trampler (vla); L. Greene (pno)
	Sonata for cello and piano (1960)
	  C. McCracken (vcl); L. Greene (pno)
	EMS 403: S-403(s)

Billy Jim LAYTON (1924–)	String Quartet in two movements (1955–6) Claremont Quartet CRI 136

William
SYDEMAN
(1928–)
	Concerto da Camera (1958)
	  M. Polikoff (vln)—CRI Chamber Ensemble—Wolfe
	Seven movements for Septet (1958)
	  CRI Chamber Ensemble
	CRI 158

Charles WUORINEN (1938–)	Symphony No. 3 (1959) Japan Philharmonic Orchestra—Watanabe CRI 149

Yehudi
WYNER
(1929–)
	Concert Duo for violin and piano (1956)
	  H. Raimondi (vln); Y. Wyner (pno)
	  CRI 161
	Serenade for seven instruments (1958)
	  J. Baker (fl); R. Froelich (fr.hn); R. Nagel (tpt); K. Brown
	  (tbn); H. Zaratzian (vla); C. McCracken (vcl); Y. Wyner
	  (pno)—Torkanowsky
	  CRI 141

Ralph SHAPEY
(1921–)
	Evocation, for violin, piano and percussion (1959)
	  M. Raimondi (vln); Y. Wyner (pno); P. Price (perc)
	  CRI 141

Walter
MOURANT
(1910–)
	Valley of the Moon (1955); *Air and Scherzo* (1955);
	  Sleepy Hollow (1955)
	  Symphony Orchestra—Camarata
	  CRI 157

Gilbert
TRYTHALL
(1930–)
	Symphony No. 1 (1958)
	  Knoxville Symphony Orchestra—Van Vactor
	  CRI 155

PART TWO

CHAPTER I

Stephen
FOSTER
(1826–64)

Song collections
  Nelson Eddy (bar)
    Col. ML-4099
  Robert Shaw Chorale
    Vic. LM-2295: LSC-2295(s)
  Roger Wagner Chorale
    Cap. P-8267: DP-8267(s)
  Halloran Choir
    Con-Disc 1030: 30(s)
  Richard Crooks (ten)
    Cam. 124 (del)
  Bing Crosby
    Dec. 83; Bruns(E) LA8571 (10″) (del)
  Roger Wagner Chorale
    Cap(E) CTL 7073 (del)

Note: There are other collections on the American lists,
notably those on Avoca 2002; Kapp 1140: 3023(s) and
Request 8028, but the two cited above appear to be the only
collections to have appeared on British lists.
Individual songs, too numerous and too diverse in treatment
to list in detail, are to be found in various collections.
Recordings of Foster songs by the following singers may be
of special interest:

  Jussi Bjorling (ten)
    Vic. LM-1771; HMV ALP 1857
  John McCormack (ten)
    Ang. COLH 124; HMV COLH 124
    HMV 7er.5181 (del)
  Paul Robeson (bass)
    HMV DLP 1165 (10″)

Ethelbert
NEVIN

Mighty lak a rose, Ballad
  Geraldine Farrer (sop); Fritz Kreisler (vln)
    in 2 Vic. LM-6099; RCA(E) RB 6525
  Paul Robeson (bass)
    HMV DLP 1155 (10″), 7eg.8677
The Rosary, Ballad
  Paul Robeson (bass)
    HMV DLP 1155 (10″)
  Lauritz Melchoir (bass)
    MGM(E) *ep* 577 (del)
  John McCormack (ten)
    Cam. 635; Cam(E) CDN 1029
  Beniamino Gigli (ten)
    HMV 7er.5187
Narcissus, Op. 13 N9. 4

No straightforward performance of this once popular piano
piece appears to be available now, though it is of course
possible that one may be hidden away in the many miscellaneous piano recitals on record.

Louis-Moreau
GOTTSCHALK
(1829–69)
	Piano Music
	  Eugene List (pno)
	  Van. 485
	  Note: All items discussed in the text are on this record)
	Le Bananier, Op. 5
	  Frank Glazer (pno)
	  Con-Disc 1217: 217(s); Saga XIP 7010

John Philip
SOUSA
(1854–1932)
	March collections
	There are so many of these on the American lists that there
	is no point in listing them all. Readers should therefore make
	their own selection. Those shown below have been released
	in both countries:
	  Eastman-Symphonic Wind Ensemble—Fennell
	  Mer. 50264: 90264(s); Mer(E) MMA11134: AMS16081(s)
	  Mer. 50284: 90284(s); Mer(E) MMA11163: AMS16110(s)
	  Mer. 50291: 90291(s)
	  Band of the Grenadier Guards
	  Lon. 1229: 139(s); ACl ACL 1032: Dec(E) SKL 4062(s)

CHAPTER II

*(Note: Further coverage of titles or genre marked thus ★ will be
found in the Addenda at the end of each chapter.)*

  Percy RANDOLPH (voc)
1 *Shine*   New Orleans, 1957
  Folk. FA2461; Top(E) 12T 53

  Unidentified youth (voc, chest-slapping)
2 *Hambone*   New Orleans, 1957
  As above

  Unidentified street musician (chair, beer cans)
3 Untitled percussion solo   New Orleans, 1957
  As above

  ★Ed. LEWIS (voc) and Group
4 *I be so glad*   Parchman Miss. Summer, 1959
  Atl. 1346: S1346(s); Lon(E) LTZ-K15209: SAH-K6131(s)

  ★Ernest WILLIAMS (voc) and Group
5 *Ain't no more cane on this Brazos*   Sugarland, Tex. 1933
  Lib. Con AAFS L3

  ★Clyde HILL (voc) and Group
6 *Long hot summer days*   Brazoria, Tex. 1939

7 ★A selected list of Gospel Shouts and Songs will be found in the Addenda

  Vera HALL (voc)
8a *Trouble so hard*   Livingstone, Ala. 1937
  Lib. Con AAFS L3

8b *Trouble so hard*   Livingstone, Ala. Summer 1959
   Atl. 1346: S1346(s); Lon(E) LTZ-K15209: SAH-K6131(s)

Willie WILLIAMS (voc) and Group
9 *The New Burying Ground*   Richmond, Va. 1936
   Lib. Con AAFS L3

*Arthur BELL (voc)
10 *John Henry*   Gould, Ark. 1939
   Lib. Con AAFS L3

Vera HALL (voc)
11 *Wild Ox Moan*   Livingstone, Ala. Summer, 1959
   Atl. 1348: S1438(s); Lon(E) LTZ-K15211: SAH-K6133(s)

Peg-Leg HOWELL (voc, g)
12 *Skin Game Blues*   Atlanta, Ga. 9 Nov. 1927
   Not issued in U.S.; Phi(E) BBL 7369(m)

Otis HARRIS (voc, g)
13 *Waking Blues*   Dallas, Tex. 8 Dec. 1928
   As above

'STOVEPIPE No. 1' (Sam Jones) (voc, s-pipe); David CROCKETT (g)
14 *Court Street Blues*   Atlanta, Ga. Mar. 1927
   As above

Bukka WHITE (voc, g); unknown (wbd)
15 *Strange Place Blues*   Chicago, June 1940
   As above

Lewis BLACK (voc, g)
16 *Gravel Camp Blues*   Dallas, Tex. 10 Dec. 1927
   As above

Henry WILLIAMS (voc, g); Eddie ANTHONY (voc, vln)
17 *Lonesome Blues*   Atlanta, Ga 20 Apr. 1928
   As above

Blind Willie JOHNSON (voc, g)
18 *Nobody's fault but mine* (Gospel song) Dallas, Tex. 3 Dec. 1927
   Folk. FG3585; Fon(E) *tfe 17052*

'Papa' Charlie JACKSON (voc, bjo)
19 *Airy man Blues*   July 1924
   Folk. RF-202 (excerpt only); Her(E) 1011 (l.ed)

Leroy CARR (voc, pno); Francis 'Scrapper' BLACKWELL (g)
20 *Midnight Hour Blues*   Chicago 16 Mar. 1932
   Col. CL-1799; Fon(E) *tfe 17051*

Leroy CARR (voc, pno); Francis 'Scrapper' BLACKWELL (g)
21 *Alabama Woman Blues*   Chicago Oct. 1930
   Folk. RF-1

Lonnie JOHNSON (voc, g)
22 *Careless Love*   New York City 16 Nov 1928
   Folk. RF-1

'WASHBOARD SAM' (Robert Brown) (voc, wbd); 'MEMPHIS SLIM'
(Peter Chatman) (pno); 'Big Bill' BROONZY (g); Alfred ELKINS (bs)
23 *I been treated wrong*   Chicago 4 Nov. 1941
   As above

Blind Lemon JEFFERSON (voc, g)
24 *Matchbox Blues*   Chicago 14 Mar. 1927
     As above, Folk. FG3585

Sleepy John ESTES (voc, g); unknown (g)
25 *Special Agent*   New York City 27 Apr. 1938
     Folk. RF-1

Bukka WHITE (voc, g); unknown (wbd)
26 *Fixin' to die*   Chicago May? 1940
     As above

Tommy McCLENNAN (voc, g); unknown (bs)   no details
27 *I'm a guitar king*
     As above

Blind Willie McTELL (voc, g)   no details
28 *States boro Blues*
     As above

Charlie PICKETT (voc, g)   no details
29 *Down the Highway*
     Folk. RF-202

Robert JOHNSON (voc, g)
30 *If I had possession over Judgement Day*   San Antonio, Tex. 27 Nov. 1936
31 *Come on in my kitchen*   San Antonio, Tex. 23 Nov. 1936
32 *Stones in my passway*   Dallas, Tex. 19 June 1937
33 *Me and the Devil Blues*   Dallas, Tex. 20 June 1937
34 *Crossroads Blues*   San Antonio, Tex. 27 Nov. 1936
35 *Hellhound on my trail*   Dallas, Tex. 20 June 1937
     Col. CL-1654; Phi(E) BBL 7539 (include all above titles)

Romeo NELSON (pno, voc)
36 *Head Rag Hop*   Chicago 5 Sept. 1929
     Bruns 54014 (del); Crl(E) LVA 9069

Montana TAYLOR (pno)
37 *Indiana Avenue Stomp*   Chicago 23 Apr. 1929
     As above

Jimmy YANCEY (pno)
38 *At the window*   Chicago Dec. 1943
     Pax 6011 (del); Vog(E) *epv 1203*

Meade Lux LEWIS (pno)
39a *Honky Tonk Train Blues*   Chicago Dec. 1927
     Riv. Folk. FA 2801; Lon(E) AL3506 (10") (del), Phi(E) BBL 7511
39b *Honky Tonk Train Blues*   Chicago 21 Nov. 1935
     Dec. DL 5133 & 5249 (10"); Bruns. (E) LA8544 (del), Col(E) *seg 5728* (del)
39c *Honky Tonk Train Blues*   Chicago 7 Mar. 1937
     Vic.LRP-2321; Cam(E) CDN 118
39d *Honky Tonk Train Blues*   Hollywood 22 Apr. 1946
     Clef MGC506 (10") (del); Col(E) 33C 9021 (10") (del)

(*Note:* Further versions of *Honky Tonk Train Blues* were recorded by
Lewis for The Library of Congress in 1938 and in 1940 for Blue Note
(BN 15) but neither appears to have been reissued.)

'SPECKLED RED' (Rufus Perryman) (pno); unknown (voc)

40   Wilkins Street Stomp   Chicago 14 Oct. 1929
       Bruns. 54014 (del); Crl(E) LVA 9069

RAGTIME (performances transcribed from pianola rolls made between 1902 and 1912. The date following the title is the date of composition; the name following this that of the composer)

James SCOTT (pno), (recorded 1911)

41   *The Ragtime Oriole* (1911), (James Scott)
       Riv. 12-126; Lon(E) AL 3503 (10″) (del)

Unknown (pno) (recording date unknown)

42   *Frogs Legs Rag* (1906) (James Scott)
       Riv. RLP 1049 (10″) (del); Lon(E) AL 3542 (10″) (del)

Unknown (pno) (recording date unknown)

43   *Euphonic Sounds* (1909) (Scott Joplin)
       Riv. 12-110; Riv(E) RLP 12-11 (del)

Unknown (pno) (recording date unknown)

44   *Magnetic Rag* (1914) (Scott Joplin)
       Riv. RLP 1049 (10″) (del); Lon(E) AL 3542 (10″) (del)

Charlie 'Cow-Cow' DAVENPORT (pno)

45   *Atlanta Blues* (*Rag*)   Richmond, Ind. Mar. 1929
       Riv. RLP1034 (10″) (del); Lon(E) AL 3537 (10″) (del)

James P. JOHNSON (pno)

46a   *Riffs*   New York City 29 Jan. 1929
       Phi(E) BBL 7511

James P. JOHNSON (pno); Eddie DOUGHERTY (d)

46b   *Riffs*   New York City 28 June 1944
       Dec. DL-5190 (10″) (del); Bruns(E) LA 8548 (10″) (del)

Ferdinand 'Jelly Roll' MORTON (pno)

47a   *Kansas City Stomps*   Richmond, Ind. 18 July 1923
       Riv. 111; Riv(E) RLP12-111 (del)

47b   *Kansas City Stomps*   Washington, D.C. May–July 1938
       Riv. 9003, Riv. 132; Riv(E) RLP 12-132 (del)

JELLY ROLL MORTON and his RED HOT PEPPERS
    Ward Pinkett (tpt); Geechie Fields (tbn); Omer Simeon (clt); Jelly Roll Morton (pno); Lee Blair (bjo); Bill Benford (tu); Tommy Benford (d)

47c   *Kansas City Stomps*   New York City 11 June 1928
       Vic. LPM-1649; RCA(E) RD27113

Ferdinand 'Jelly Roll' MORTON (pno)

48a   *King Porter Stomp*   Richmond, Ind. 17 July 1923
       Riv. 111; Riv(E) RLP 12-111 (del)

48b   *King Porter Stomp*   Chicago 20 Apr. 1926
       4-Dec. DX-140, Dec. 8398; Bruns(E) LAT 8166

48c   *King Porter Stomp*   Washington, D.C. May–July 1938
       Riv. 9003, Riv. 9010, Riv. 132; Riv(E) RLP 12-132 (del)

48d   *King Porter Stomp*   New York City 14 Dec. 1939
       Comm. 30001; Vog(E) *epv 1126*

King OLIVER (cnt); Jelly Roll MORTON (pno)

48e   *King Porter Stomp*   Chicago Dec? 1924
       Riv. 130; Riv(E) RLP 12-130

ADDENDA

The undermentioned records are intended to amplify the examples
discussed in the text and listed in detail above. They are not intended to
be an exhaustive coverage of the field, and for reasons of space, the only
title given is that under which the album appeared.

4–6 WORK SONGS—Collections

Anthology of American Folk Music—6 records	6-Folk. FA2951–3
Music from the South—10 records	Folk. FA2650–9
Negro Music of Alabama—6 records	Folk. FE4417–8, 4471–4
Negro Worksongs and Calls	Lib. Con AAFS L8
Negro Prison Worksongs	Folk. FE4475
Negro Prison Songs (coll. Lomax)	Trad. 1020; Nixa (E) NJL 11
(British issue entitled—Murderers Home)	
Angola Prison Worksongs	Flk. Lyr 5; Coll(E) JGN 1006

7 GOSPEL SHOUTS and SONGS
See also items 1–3 above

Introduction to Gospel Song (ed. Charters)	Folk. RF-5
Angola Prison Spirituals	Flk. Lyr 6; 77 LA 12/13
Negro Church Music	Atl. 1351: S1351(s);
	Lon(E) LTZ-K15214: SAH-K6136(s)
Negro Spirituals	Vog(E) LAE 12043 (del)

Many recent collections of Gospel music are in a more sophisticated
style than the examples discussed in the text. Instances of this kind of
treatment will be found in the collections already quoted; others will be
found under the names of Alex Bradford, the Drinkard Singers, the
Fisk Jubilee Singers, the Staple Singers and the Clara Ward Singers.
Similarly the styles of the solo singers who have contributed to the genre
vary from the roughnesss of Blind Willie Johnson to the relative
smoothness of some of the modern singers. Johnson, one of the earliest
and most important Gospel Singers, is represented only by the records
cited at 18 in the main section above, though individual tracks are to be
found scattered throughout the various Folkways anthologies.
Here is a selection:

'Cat Iron'—Blues and Hymns	Folk. FA 2389
Blind Gary Davis—Harlem Street Singer	Blues. 1015; Fon(E)688. 303ZL
Mahalia Jackson—various titles	Col.; Phi(E)
Marie Knight—Songs of the Gospel	Mer. 20196
Rosetta Tharpe—Gospel Train	Dec. 8782; Bruns(E) LAT 8290
Ernestine Washington—Gospel	West. 6089
Negro Spirituals—Hall and Reed	Folk. FA 2038 (10")
Preachers and congregationss	Fon(E) *tfe 17265* (del)

10 JOHN HENRY
This Ballad has attracted the attention of a great variety of singers from
Paul Robeson down. The version quoted in the main section is that to
which the author specifically refers but as it is not easily obtainable a
few idiomatic and more readily accessible recordings are included.

'Leadbelly' (Huddie Ledbetter) (1942/3)

	Stin. SLP17; Mel(E) MLP511 (both 10")
'Leadbelly' (1948)—Last Session	2-Folk. FA2941; Mel(E) MLP 12–113
'Big Bill' Broonzy—Sings Folk Songs	Folk. FA2328

'Big Bill' Broonzy—Last Session III   Ver.3003; HMV CLP 1562
Furry Lewis—Blues   Folk. FS3823
'Guitar' Welch, Hogman Maxey, Robert Pete Williams (voc. trio) (in
    Angola Prison Work Songs)   Flk. Lyr 5; Coll(E) JGN 1006
Brownie McGhee and Sonny Terry
                            Folk. FA 2327 (10″); Top(E) 10T 59 (10″)

12-28 COUNTRY BLUES and URBAN BLUES
    This is an inexhaustable field of enquiry ranging from the early twenties
    to the current rhythm and blues movement. Unfortunately few good
    collections are available, especially of the great singers of the past. In
    addition to the two quoted in the main section, a third, entitled *Bad
    Luck Blues,* has been issued on Bruns(F) and Bruns(G) and contains
    examples by Kokomo Arnold, Sleepy John Estes, Lightnin' Hopkins
    and others. Coverage of the output of individual singers is also uneven,
    especially in Great Britain where the major companies seem very
    reluctant to reissue archival material.
Kings of the Blues—Vols. 2 and 3   RCA(E) *rcx 203, 204*
    (Include Sleepy John Estes, Sonny Boy Williamson, Furry Lewis, Jazz
    Gillum, Arthur Crudup etc.)
American Folk Blues Festival   Poly(E) LPHM46397; SLPHM237597(s)
    (Memphis Slim, T-Bone Walker, John Lee Hooker etc.)
Blues in the Mississippi Night   UnA. UA 4027; Nixa NLJ 8
Angola Prison Blues   Flk.Lyr 3; Coll(E) JGN 1003
Blues n' Trouble   Arhoo 1006
Blues Roll On   Atl. 1352: S1352(s); Lon(E) LTZ-K15215; SAH-K6137(s)
The Rural Blues (ed. Charters)   Folk. RF-202 (2 records)
    (Readers should note that this last collection is designed to illustrate a
    lengthy essay on the nature of the Rural Blues by the editor and that the
    majority of items in it are excerpts only)

INDIVIDUAL ARTISTS
Blind BLAKE (died c. 1932)
             JCl(E) JFL 2001 (10″), *jel 4,* Her(E) 1011 (l.ed.), Ris. LP18(10″)
'Big Bill' BROONZY (1893–1958)   many collections available
Big Boy CRUDUP   RCA(F) 130.284 (10″)
Ray CHARLES   many collections available
Sleepy John ESTES   Del. 603; Esq. 32–195
Sleepy John ESTES   RCA(F) 75.752 (*)
    (*) One track by Son BOND
Blind Boy FULLER (1903–40)   Phi(E) BBL 7512
Jazz GILLUM   RCA(F) 130.273 (10″); RCA(F) 130.257 (10″)
John Lee HOOKER   many collections available
Lightnin' HOPKINS   many collections available
Blind Lemon JEFFERSON (died c. 1930)
    Riv. 125, 136; Lon(E) AL 3508, 3546, 3564 (10″) (all del), JCl(E) *jel 8,*
    jel 13, Her(E) 1007 (l.ed)
Lonnie JOHNSON   Blues. 1007; Blues(E) 1007 (del) others on Blues. (US)
'LEADBELLY' (1888–1949)   many collections available
Furry LEWIS   Folk FS 3823, Blues. 1036, 1037
Big MACEO (Maceo Merryweather)   RCA(F) 130.246 (10″)
Tommy McCLENNAN (died ?)   RCA(F) 130.274 (10″)
Brownie McGHEE and Sonny TERRY   many collections available
Blind Willie McTELL (died ?)   Blues. 1040

MEMPHIS SLIM   many collections available
MUDDY WATERS (McKinley Morganfield)   Chess 1427, 1449
Big Joe WILLIAMS—*Blues on Highway 49*   Del. 604; Esq. 32-191, other
                                               examples available
WASHBOARD SAM (Robert Brown)   RCA(F) 130.256 (10″)
Sonny Boy WILLIAMSON (original)   RCA(F) 130.238 (10″)

The following companies are especially active in the recording of contemporary blues singers and in the reissue of historical material. All are American but may be obtainable through specialist dealers: Arhoolie, Bluesville, Checker, Chess, Delmar, Origin, Stinson, Tradition, Vee Jay, Collector (British)

CHAPTER III

KID ORY'S CREOLE JAZZ BAND
Mutt Carey (tpt); Kid Ory (tbn, voc); Omer Simeon (clt); Buster Wilson (pno); Bud Scott (g); Ed Garland (bs); Alton Redd (d)
1   *Creole Song*   Hollywood, 3 Aug. 1944
     GTJ. L12022; Vog(E) LAG 12104

Jelly Roll MORTON (pno)
2   *Miserere* (*Il Trovatore*: Verdi trans. Morton)
                                   Washington, D.C., May–July 1938
     Riv. 9001, Riv. 113; Riv(E) RLP12-113 (del)
3   *New Orleans Blues/Joys*   As last
4   *Spanish Swat*   As last
     Riv. 9004, Riv. 132; Riv(E) RLP12-132 (del)

KID RENA'S DELTA JAZZ BAND
Kid Rena (tpt); Jim Robinson (tbn); Louis 'Big Eye' Nelson (clt); Alphonse Picou (E flat clt); Willie Santiago (g); Albert Gleny (bs); Joe Rena (d)
5   *Gettysburg March*   New Orleans, 1940
     Riv. 119; Riv(E) RLP12-119

KID ORY'S CREOLE JAZZ BAND
Personnel as 1 above except Darnell Howard (clt) replaces Simeon.
6   *Oh, Didn't he ramble!*   Hollywood, Sept. 1945
     GTJ. L12022; Vog(E) LAG 12104

✶CANNON'S JUG STOMPERS
Gus Cannon (bjo, jug); Elijah 'Lige' Avery (g); Noah Lewis (hca)
7   *Ripley's Blues*   Memphis, Tenn. 9 May 1928
     RCA(E) *rcx 202*; no U.S. reissue known

Sonny TERRY (hca); Blind Boy FULLER (g); 'OH RED' (George Washington) (wbd)
8   *Harmonica Stomp*   no details c1939
     Folk. RF-202

GEORGE LEWIS'S NEW ORLEANS STOMPERS
Avery 'Kid' Howard (tpt); Jim Robinson (tbn); George Lewis (clt); Lawrence Marrero (bjo); Chester Zardis (bs); Edgar Mosley (d)
9   *Just a closer walk with Thee*   New Orleans, 16 Mar. 1943
10   *Milenburg Joys*   The same
     BN 1205-6; Vog(E) LAE 12005

KING OLIVER'S CREOLE JAZZ BAND

King Oliver, Louis Armstrong (cnt); Honore Dutrey (tbn); Johnny
Dodds (clt); Lillian Hardin (pno); Johnny St. Cyr (bjo); Charlie Jackson
(b. sax); Baby Dodds (d)

11a	*Mabel's Dream*	Chicago, c26 Oct. 1923

Epic LN-3208; Phi(E) 7181
As last except St. Cyr out

11b *Mabel's Dream*   Chicago, c24 Dec. 1923
Riv. 122; Riv(E) RLP12-122 (del)
As last except Bill Johnson (bjo, voc. break) added; Charlie Jackson out

12a *Dippermouth Blues*   Richmond, Ind. 6 Apr. 1923
Riv. 122; Riv(E) RLP12-122 (del)
As last except Bud Scott (bjo, voc. break) replaces Johnson

12b *Dippermouth Blues*   Chicago, 23 June 1923
Epic LN-3208; Phi(E) BBL 7181
Personnel as 12a above

13   *Canal Street Blues*   Richmond, Ind. 31 Mar. 1923
Riv. 122; Riv(E) RLP12-122 (del)
Personnel as 11a above

14   *Working Man Blues*   Chicago, c26 Oct. 1923
Epic LN-3208; Phi(E) BBL 7181
All details as 13 above

15   *Chimes Blues*

*ORIGINAL DIXIELAND JAZZ BAND

Nick LaRocca (cnt); Eddie Edward (tbn); Larry Shields (clt); Henry
Ragas (pno); Tony Sbarbaro (Spargo) (d)

16   *Livery Stable Blues*   New York City, late Feb. 1917
RCA(E) *rcx 1028*
As last

17a *Tiger Rag*   Camden, N.J., Mar. 1918
Vic. 'X' LX3007 (10″) (del); HMV DLP 1065 (10″) (del)
As last except J. Russel Robinson (pno) replaces Ragas

17b *Tiger Rag*   London, 19 May, 1919
No U.S. release; Par(E) PMC 1195
As ORIGINAL DIXIELAND FIVE: Personnel as last

17c *Tiger Rag*   New York City, 25 Sept. 1936
Vic. 25524 (78) (del); HMV B.8642 (78) (del)

NEW ORLEANS WANDERERS

George Mitchell (cnt); Kid Ory (tbn); Johnny Dodds (clt); Joe Clark
(alt-1); Lillian Armstrong (pno); Johnny St. Cyr (bjo)

18   *Papa Dip-1*   Chicago, 13 July 1926
19   *Perdido Street Blues*   The same
Epic 16004; Phi(E) BBL 7136

Sara MARTIN (voc) acc. CLARENCE WILLIAM'S ORCHESTRA

King Oliver (cnt); Charlie Green? (tbn); Arville Harris (clt); Clarence
Williams (pno); Cyrus St. Clair (tu)

20   *Death Sting Me Blues*   New York City, Nov. 1928
Riv. 121, 130; Riv(E) RLP12-121, 12-130 (both del)

*'Ma' RAINEY (voc) acc. HER GEORGIA JAZZ BAND

Joe Smith (cnt); Charlie Green (tbn); Buster Bailey (clt); Fletcher
Henderson (pno); Charlie Dixon (bjo); unknown (bs)

21 *Titanic Man Blues*   New York City *c.* 1924
    Riv. 113

Jelly Roll MORTON (pno, voc)
22 *2.19 Blues*   Washington, D.C. May–July 1938
    Riv. 9007, Riv. 140; Riv(E) RLP12–140 (del)

Mary JOHNSON (voc) acc. Ike RODGERS (tbn); unknown (pno) (Henry BROWN?)
23 *Key to the Mountain*   Chicago, 1929
    Riv. 121; Riv(E) RLP12–121 (del)

Bertha 'Chippie' HILL (voc) acc. BABY DODDS'S STOMPERS
Lee Collins (tpt); Freddy Shayne (pno); John Lindsay (bs); Baby Dodds (d)
24 *Charleston Blues*   Chicago, 5 Feb. 1946
    Riv. 121; Riv(E) RLP12–121 (del)

*Bessie SMITH (voc) acc. Louis ARMSTRONG (cnt); Fred LONGSHAW (pno –1, harmonium –2)
25 *Carless Love* –1   New York City, c26 May 1925
26 *Reckless Blues*–2   New York City, 24 Jan. 1925
    4-Col. CL-855; Phi(E) BBL 7019 (del)

Bessie SMITH (voc) acc. Joe SMITH (cnt); Buster BAILEY (clt); Fletcher HENDERSON (pno)
27 *Young Woman's Blues*   New York City, 26 Oct. 1926
    4-Col. CL-857; Phi(E) BBL 7042 (del)

Bessie SMITH (voc) acc. Joe WILLIAMS (tbn); Ernest ELLIOTT, Bob FULLER (clt, alt); Porter GRAINGER (pno)
28 *Poor Man's Blues*   New York City, 24 Aug. 1928
    4-Col. CL-856; Phi(E) BBL 7020 (del)

Bessie SMITH (voc) acc. Ed ALLEN (cnt); Clarence WILLIAMS (pno)
29 *Black Mountain Blues*   New York City, 22 July 1930
    4-Col. CL-856; Phi(E) BBL 7020 (del)

Bessie SMITH (voc) acc. James P. JOHNSON (pno)
30 *Backwater Blues*   New York City, 17 Feb. 1927
    4-Col. CL-858; Phi(E) BBL 7049 (del)

Bessie SMITH (voc) acc. HER BLUE BOYS
Joe Smith (cnt); Charlie Green (tbn); Buster Bailey (clt); Fletcher Henderson (pno); Charlie Dixon (bjo); Kaiser Marshall (d)
31 *Muddy Water*   New York City, 2 Mar. 1927
32 *Alexander's Ragtime Band*   The same
    4-Col. CL-857; Phi(E) BBL 7042 (del)

Bessie SMITH (voc) acc. Ed ALLEN (cnt); Clarence WILLIAMS (pno); Cyrus St. CLAIR (tu)
33 *Nobody knows you when you're down and out*
                                                New York City, 17 May 1929
    4-Col. CL-856; Phi(E) BBL 7020 (del)

ADDENDA

1 CREOLE SONG
   This is a version of a traditional Creole patois song *C'ete n'aut' Can-can.*
   Other versions are available though not necessarily under this title. One

idiomatic version is that by Jelly Roll Morton in the full documentary
set recorded for the Library of Congress in 1938 and available on
twelve long-playing records (Riv. 9001–12). These have not been issued
in Great Britain but may be obtained through specialist dealers and are
highly recommended.

6   OH, DIDN'T HE RAMBLE!
Like the previous item this W. C. Handy version of the traditional New
Orleans funeral procession has been frequently recorded by bands other
than that referred to in the text. The following are two good, idiomatic
performances, though only the second is at present available.
a. Jelly Roll Morton's New Orleans Jazzmen (1939)
    (inc. Sidney de Paris, Sidney Bechet, Albert Nicholas, Claude Jones)
    Bb.B-10429 (78); HMV B-9217 (78)
b. (entitled *New Orleans Function*)
    Louis Armstrong's All Stars (1950)
    (inc. Barney Bigard, Jack Teagarden, Earl Hines) Dec. 8329; AH.
    AH18

7   JUG BANDS
The RCA(E) *ep* record quoted contains three vocal items by Cannon's
Jug Stompers in addition to the purely instrumental item referred to in
the text. Two more examples of this exuberant music, one by Cannon's
group, the other by the Memphis Jug Band, are included in the Charters
collection on Folk. RF-1 entitled *The Country Blues,* to which reference
has already been made. A fine collection of rare items is to be found on
Origin OJL 44 (l.ed) entitled *Jugs 1927–33,* and odd examples are to be
found in the various anthologies as well as in the collection entitled
American Skiffle Band on Folk. FA2610

8   HARMONICA STOMP
A further version of this by Sonny Terry, though not with Fuller,
is available on Folk. FA2035 (10″); Top(E) 10T 30 (10″)

16/17 ORIGINAL DIXIELAND JAZZ BAND
The earliest recording by this band, and the first jazz record issued, is
available on Phi(E) *bbe 12489.* The fine series of Victor recordings is
no longer available in l.p. form but a selection of titles recorded in
London for Columbia are still available on Col(E) 33S1087. A further
selection is on Riv. 126–7, not issued in Great Britain. Two late items,
dating from 1922, are in *Jazz Sounds of the Twenties—Vol. 2,* Elec.
832480 Par(E) PMC 1171

21   'MA' RAINEY
This important singer is not well represented on record, nor are those
which are obtainable always pleasurable to listen to. The most representative collection of her work appeared in Great Britain on three 10″
Lon(E) records—AL 3502, 3538 and 3558. Some of the items were
reissued on 12″ Riv(E) RLP12–108 while others were to be found on
Riv(E) RLP12–121. Both these are no longer available. Items are to be
found in Folk. anthologies and American readers will find the following
still available: Riv. 108, 137 and Riv. 134

25ff BESSIE SMITH
Representation of Bessie Smith on British catalogues is now exceedingly
poor. The four-volume set referred to in the main section is still
available in America and, apparently, on the Continent. The only

British issue now available is of a collection of very fine early blues
(1923) on Phi(E) BBL 7513, though there is one important track—
Dyin' by the Hour—on Fon(E) TFL 1523 (not issued in U.S.)

FEMALE BLUES SINGERS—General
In addition to the collection referred to in the main section (i.e. Riv. 121;
Riv(E) RLP12–121) a magnificent collection is available on *Jazz Sounds
of the Twenties—Vol. 4* (Elec. 83250; Par(E) PMC. 1177) which includes
'Chippie' Hill, Sippie Wallace, Victoria Spivey and others. Further
important singers are to be found on the Fon(E) release referred to under
Bessie Smith above.

CHAPTER IV

LOUIS ARMSTRONG AND HIS HOT FIVE
Louis Armstrong (tpt, voc); Kid Ory (tbn); Johnny Dodds (clt); Lillian
Armstrong (pno); Johnny St. Cyr (bjo)

1   *Heebie Jeebies*   Chicago, 26 Feb. 1926
   Col. CL-851; Par(E) PMC 1140
   As last
2   *Skid-dat-de-dat*   Chicago, 16 Nov. 1926
   Col. CL-851; Par(E) PMC 1142

LOUIS ARMSTRONG AND HIS HOT SEVEN
Louis Armstrong (tpt); unknown (tbn) (probably John Thomas);
Johnny Dodds (clt); Lillian Armstrong (pno); Johnny St. Cyr (bjo);
Pete Briggs (tu); Warren 'Baby' Dodds (d)

3   *Willie the Weeper*   Chicago, 7 May 1927
4   *Wild Man Blues*   The same
5   *Potato Head Blues*   Chicago, 10 May 1927
   Col. CL-852, Par(E) PMC 1142
   As previous Hot Five plus Lonnie Johnson (g)
6   *Savoy Blues*   Chicago, 13 Dec. 1927
   Lonnie Johnson out
7   *Struttin' With Some Barbecue*   Chicago, 9 Dec. 1927
   *Col CL-851; Par(E) PMC 1146

LOUIS ARMSTRONG AND HIS HOT FIVE
Louis Armstrong (tpt, voc); Fred Robinson (tbn); Jimmy Strong (clt,
ten); Earl Hines (pno); Mancy Cara (bjo); Zutty Singleton (d)

8   *West End Blues*   Chicago, 28 June 1928

LOUIS ARMSTRONG (tpt); EARL HINES (pno)

9   *Weatherbird*   Chicago, 5 Dec. 1928

LOUIS ARMSTRONG AND HIS SAVOY BALLROOM FIVE
Personnel as 8 above plus Don Redman (alt, arr); Armstrong, Redman
talking in (1)

10   *Beau Koo Jack*   Chicago, 5 Dec. 1928
11   *Tight Like This* (1)   Chicago, 12 Dec. 1928
   *Col.CL-853; Par(E) PMC 1150

LOUIS ARMSTRONG AND HIS ORCHESTRA
Louis Armstrong (tpt, voc); Henry Allen, Otis Johnson (tpt); J. C.
Higginbotham (tbn); Albert Nicholas (clt, alt); Charlie Holmes (alt);

Teddy Hill (ten); Luis Russell (pno); Will Johnson (g); Pops Foster (bs);
Paul Barbarin (d)

12   *St Louis Blues*   New York City, 13 Dec. 1929
Vocalion 3008 (78) (del); Par(E) R.618 (78) (del)

MEZZROW-BECHET QUINTET
Milton 'Mezz' Mezzrow (clt); Sidney Bechet (sop); Fitz Weston (pno);
Pop Foster (bs); Kaiser Marshall (d)

13   *Out of the Gallion*   New York City, 29–30 Aug. 1945
CH(E) J.1257–8

TOMMY LADNIER AND HIS ORCHESTRA
Tommy Ladnier (tpt); Milton 'Mezz' Mezzrow (clt); Sidney Bechet
sop); Cliff Jackson (pno); Teddy Bunn (g); Elmer James (bs); Manzie
Johnson (d)

14a   *Really the Blues*   New York City, 28 Nov. 1938
Vic. 'X' LVA3027 (del); HMV DLP 1110 (10″) (del); FrHMV FCLP 103
14b   The same (alternative Matrix)
Bb. B10089 (78) (del); HMV B.9236 (78) (del)

MEZZROW-BECHET QUINTET
Milton 'Mezz' Mezzrow (clt); Sidney Bechet (sop); Sox Wilson (pno);
Wellman Braud (bs); Warren 'Baby' Dodds (d)

14c   *Really the Blues*—Pts I–II   New York City, 18 Sept. 1946
CH(E) J.1257–8

LOUIS ARMSTRONG AND HIS ORCHESTRA
Louis Armstrong (tpt); Claude Jones (tbn); Sidney Bechet (sop, clt); Luis
Russell (pno); Bernard Addison (g); Wellman Braud (bs); Zutty
Singleton (d)

15   *Down in Honky-Tonk Town*   New York City, 27 May 1940
Dec. DL-8283; Bruns(E) LAT 8146, *oe 9287*

★JIMMY NOONE AND HIS ORCHESTRA
Natty Dominique (tpt); Preston Jackson (tbn); Jimmy Noone (clt);
Richard M. Jones (pno); Lonnie Johnson (g); John Lindsay (bs); Tubby
Hall (d)

16   *Keystone Blues*   Chicago, 5 June 1940
17   *New Orleans Hop Scop Blues*   The same
Dec. DL-8283; Bruns(E) LAT 8146, *oe 9342*

★JOHNNY DODDS AND HIS ORCHESTRA
Personnel as last, except Johnny Dodds (clt) replaces Noone. Date and
record details as last

18   *Gravier Street Blues*
19   *Red Onion Blues*

LEON 'BIX' BEIDERBECKE (pno)

20   *In a Mist* (Bixology)   New York City, 9 Sept. 1927
3-Col. CL-844-6; Phi(E) BBL 7014 (del), *bbe 12368*

FRANK TRUMBAUER AND HIS ORCHESTRA
'Bix' Beiderbecke (cnt); Bill Rank (tbn); Don Murray (clt, bar); Frank
Trumbauer (C-mel. sax); Red Ingle (alt); Itzy Riskin (pno); Eddie
Lang (g); Chauncey Morehouse (d)

21   *I'm coming, Virginia*   New York City, 13 May 1927
22   *Way down yonder in New Orleans*(★)   The same
3-Col. CO-844-6; Phi(E) *bbe 12053* ((★) only), Col(E) *seg 7566* (del) (both)

*JELLY ROLL MORTON'S RED HOT PEPPERS
George Mitchell (cnt); Kid Ory (tbn); Omer Simeon (clt); Jelly Roll Morton (pno); Johnny St. Cyr (bjo); John Lindsay (bs); Andrew Hilaire (d)

23	*Smokehouse Blues*	Chicago, 15 Sept. 1926
24	*The Chant*	The same

Vic. LPM-1649; RCA(E) RD27113
See Addenda for references to the following:

25 FLETCHER HENDERSON AND HIS ORCHESTRA

26 McKINNEY'S COTTON PICKERS

COUNT BASIE AND HIS ORCHESTRA
Ed Lewis, Harry Edison, Buck Clayton, Al Killian (tpt); Dan Minor, Vic Dickenson, Dicky Wells (tbn); Earl Warren, Jack Washington, Lester Young, Buddy Tate (reeds); Count Basie (pno); Freddy Green (g); Walter Page (bs); Jo Jones (d)

27 *Gone with 'what' wind*　　　　New York City, 31 Mar. 1940
Epic LN-3169 (del); Phi(E) BBL 7141 (del)
As last

28 *Tickle Toe*　　　　New York City, 19 Mar. 1940
2-Epic SN-6031, Epic LN-3577; Phi(E) BBL 7141 (del), Fon(E) TFL 5065

COUNT BASIE AND HIS ORCHESTRA
Ed Lewis, Harry Edison, Buck Clayton (tpt); Dan Minor, Eddie Durham, Benny Morton (tbn); Earl Warren, Jack Washington, Hershal Evans, Lester Young (reeds); Count Basie (pno); Freddy Green (g); Walter Page (bs); Jo Jones (d)

29 *Blue and sentimental*　　　　New York City, 6 June 1938
Dec. 8049 (del); Bruns(E) LAT 8028

COUNT BASIE AND HIS ORCHESTRA
Ed Lewis, Harry Edison, Buck Clayton, Shad Collins (tpt); Dan Minor, Dicky Wells (tbn); Earl Warren, Jack Washington, Lester Young, Chu Berry (reeds); Count Basie (pno); Freddy Green (g); Walter Page (bs); Jo Jones (d); Jimmy Rushing (voc)

30 *Evil Blues*　　　　New York City, 2 Feb. 1939
Dec. 8049 (del); Bruns(E) LAT 8028

*ARTIE SHAW AND HIS NEW MUSIC
John Best, Malcolm Crain, Tom di Carlo (tpt); Harry Rogers, George Arus (tbn); Artie Shaw (clt); Les Robinson, Harry Freeman, Tony Pastor, Jules Rubin (sax); Les Burness (pno); Al Avola (g); Ben Ginsberg (bs); Cliff Leeman (d)

31 *The Blues* (Pts. I–II)　　　　New York City, 4 Aug. 1937
No LP re-issue. Bruns. 7947 (78) (del); Par(E) R.2790 (78) (del)

ADDENDA

LOUIS ARMSTRONG
The 64 titles recorded by Armstrong with the Hot Five and Hot Seven between 1925 and 1928 are available in Great Britain on the four Par. quoted, and are especially interesting as the recordings are presented for the first time on long-play in chronological order. The set does not, so

far, appear to have been issued in America, though a number of Armstrong's records of this period are available.

The post-1928 period of Armstrong is not well represented in British catalogues, though representative selections will be found on Phi(E) BBL 7218 (del) (1929–31) and RCA(E) RD27241 (1932–34). These are available in America as follows: Col. CL-854 and Vic. LPM-2322. In addition there was a good anthology on Fr. Odéon 33T OSX144 and several *eps.* of Armstrong with Luis Russell's Orchestra and that of Les Hite. Some of these are available in America on Elec. 83262.

JIMMY NOONE

Despite his great reputation, Jimmy Noone is poorly represented on record. The items quoted in the text are about all that remain, and are by no means representative. The following collections should be sought by anyone wishing to make a closer acquaintance with Noone at his best.

Jimmy Noone and his Apex Club Orchestra (1927) (inc. *Apex Blues & Sweet Lorraine*)	Bruns. BL58006 (10″) (del); Cor(E) LRA10026 (10″) (del)
Jimmy Noone's New Orleans Band (1936)	Par(E) *gep 8605* (del)

JOHNNY DODDS

Though Dodds is much better served by the recording companies than is his great contemporary, Noone, a good deal of his best work is still absent from the catalogues. Apart from Epic 16004; Phi(E) BBL 7136 listed under New Orleans Wanderers in Chapter III, which also contains the sides made under the name of the New Orleans Bootblacks and some as the Chicago Footwarmers, Dodds is featured in the King Oliver and early Armstrong recordings and in the interesting collection of Washboard Band recordings reissued on Act of Hearts AH55. Other interesting collections containing much of Dodds' very finest recordings are:

Johnny Dodd's Washboard Band (1928) and Trio (1929) (inc. *Weary Blues* and *Bucktown Stomp*)	Vic. 'X' LX3006 (10″) (del); HMV DLP 1073 (10″) (del), *eg8233* (del)
Johnny Dodds' Black Bottom Stompers and Beale Street Washboard Band	Cor(E) LRA 10025 (10″) (del)
See also	Riv. 104, 135; Riv(E) RLP 104 (del); Lon(E) AL3505, 3513, 3555, 3560 (all del)

BIX BEIDERBECKE—FRANK TRUMBAUER

Bix Beiderbecke made a number of recordings with small groups under his own name. Some of these are available in Great Britain, though the best general collection is undoubtedly the set available on U.S. Columbia, which has not been issued in its entirety in this country. In addition to these, which date from 1927–9, there are the earliest examples of his work with the Wolverines, and some examples of his last years with Goldkette and Whiteman.

The Bix Beiderbecke Story	3-Col. CL-844–6; Phi(E) *bbe12125, bbe 12368,* Fon(E) *tfe 17059–61, tfe 17252,* Col(E) 33S 1035 (10″)

Bix and the Wolverines (1924) Riv. 123; Riv(E) RLP 123 (del)
with Goldkette, Whiteman, etc. Vic. LPM-2323; RCA(E) RD27225

JELLY ROLL MORTON'S RED HOT PEPPERS

Virtually all the most important recordings Morton made for the Victor Company between 1926 and 1930 have been made available on long-play, though in some cases different masters have been used from those on 78 rpm reissues, many of which are still to be found. Some of these appeared on the l.p. versions issued by French RCA, though, as is the case with some of the British RCA, the dubbings are very poor.

Jelly Roll Morton's Red Hot Vic. 'X' LVA3028 (del); RCA(E)
Peppers and Trio RD-27184. Also HMV DLP1016,
 1044, 1071 (all del)

FLETCHER HENDERSON AND HIS ORCHESTRA

This important orchestra has for long been most inadequately represented on records. Recently there has been a marked improvement in this direction, and there is now enough available to enable the reader to make an assessment of the orchestra's work throughout the whole period of its long existence. The records cited in the text are to be found in the Col.(/) CBS collection.

A Study in Frustration—4 vols. Col. C4L–19, CL-1682/5; CBS(E)
(1923–1938) BPG 62001/4
Connie's Inn Orchestra AH.AH41
'Smack' (1934) AH.AH61

McKINNEY'S COTTON PICKERS

A good selection of the recordings of this important large orchestra featuring such artists as Joe Smith, Rex Stewart, Don Redman, Coleman Hawkins, Fats Waller and others, dating from 1929–31, has recently appeared on British RCA, having been available in France for some years. It does not appear to have been released in U.S.A. An example of their work does, however, appear in the excellent anthology of Big Band Jazz before 1935 on Folk. 2808 which includes the bands of Benny Moten, Charlie Johnson, Luis Russell and Ben Pollack.

McKinney's Cotton Pickers RCA(E) RD-7561
(16 items)

OTHER LARGE BANDS (1930–40)

Big Band Jazz of the late 'twenties and early 'thirties is at present under something of a cloud. Outside the historical anthologies which are apprently more popular in America than in Great Britain there is very little of importance to be found. Continental issues have more to offer though with the exception of the admirable series of reissues on French RCA for the average collector they are difficult to obtain. A selection of the more representative bands of this period is given below to enable the reader to fill in any gaps which may be felt in the text.

Henry Allen and his Orchestra RCA(F) 430.602
(1929) Vic. LVA 3033 (del); HMV *7eg8112*
 and *7eg 8136* (both del)

Count Basie and his Orchestra Bruns. 45012
(1936–40) Bruns(E) LA 8589 (10″) (del)
Lester Young Memorial 2-Epic SN-6031; Fon(E) TFL 5064-5
 (see also main entry above)

Bunny Berigan's Orchestra Cam. 550; Cam(E) CDN 159
(1937–40)

Bunny Bergian's Boys (1935–7)	Epic 16006; Col(E) 33 SX 1491
Cab Calloway and his Orchestra	Epi LN-3265 (del); Fon(E) *tfe 17216* (del)
Bob Crosby Orchestra (1937–40)	Dec. DL-8061; Bruns(E) LAT 8050 AH. AH29
Dorsey Brothers Orchestra (1934–5)	Dec. 8631; Bruns(E) LAT 8256
Tommy Dorsey and his Orchestra (1936–41)	2-Vic. LPM 1432–3, Vic. LPM-1229; RCA(E) RD27069, *rcx 1002, 1012, 1023*
(post 1941)	Cam. 650: S650(s); Cam(E) CDN 153
Lionel Hampton and his Orchestra (1937–40)	Cam. 402, 517; Cam(E) CDN 129, CDN 138
Spike Hughes and his All-American Orchestra (1933)	Lon(US) LL1387 (del); ACl ACL 1153
Andy Kirk's Clouds of Joy (1936–41)	Cor. 56019 (del); Col(E) *seg7607, seg 7646* (both del)
Jimmy Lunceford's Orchestra (1934–41)	Dec. 8050; Bruns(E) LAT 8027 (del) Col. CL-634 (del); Phi(E) BBL7037 (del)
The Missourians (1928–30)	RCA(F) 430.385
Benny Moten's Kansas City Orchestra (1926–28)	RCA(F) 130.282 (10″) Vic. LX3004 (del), LVA 3025 (del); HMV DLP 1057 (10″) (del)
Don Redman and his Orchestra (1931)	in Bruns(E) LA 8565 (10″) (del)
Luis Russell's Orchestra (1928–32)	Od(F) 33T XOC 145
Artie Shaw Orchestra (1938–41)	Good selection on Victor (US), Cam. 465, 584; Cam(E) CDN 127, 5107
Chick Webb's Orchestra (1937–9)	AH. AH32, 36
Anthologies:	
Encyclopedia of Jazz—Vol. 2	Dec. 8939; Bruns(E) LAT 8167
Five Feet of Swing	Dec. 8045; Bruns(E) LAT8037 (del)
Guide to Jazz	Vic. LPM-1393
New York Scene (1914–45)	Folk. RF-3
Dictionary of Jazz	RCA(E) RC 24002
Jazz Greats—Vol. 1	RCA(E) *rcx 1027*

CHAPTER V

DUKE ELLINGTON AND HIS ORCHESTRA

Bubber Miley, Louis Metcalf (tpt); Joe Nanton (tbn); Otto Hardwicke, Rudy Jackson (clt, alt); Harry Carney (clt, bar); Duke Ellington (pno); Fred Guy (bjo); Bass Edwards (tu); Sonny Greer (d)

1a *East St. Louis Toodle-oo*   New York City, 14 Mar. 1927
Bruns. 54007 (del); AH. AH 23
As last

1b *East St. Louis Toodle-oo*   New York City, 22 Mar. 1927
3-Col. C3L-27; CBS(E) BPG 62178, Phi(E) *bbe 12403*
Wellman Braud (bs) replaces Edwards

1c *East St Louis Toodle-oo*   New York City, 19 Dec. 1927
Vic. 'X' LVA 3037 (del); HMV DLP 1094 (10″) (del)
As last, plus Arthur Whetsel (tpt)

2a   *Black Beauty*   New York City, 21 Mar. 1928
      Vic. 'X' LVA 3037 (del); HMV DLP 1094 (10″) (del)

DUKE ELLINGTON (pno. solo)
2b   *Black Beauty*   New York City, 1 Oct. 1928
      Par(E) PMC 1184 (no US LP reissue)

DUKE ELLINGTON AND HIS ORCHESTRA
Freddy Jenkins, Cootie Williams, Arthur Whetsel (tpt); Joe Nanton,
Lawrence Brown (tbn); Juan Tizol (v-tbn); Barney Bigard (clt, ten);
Johnny Hodges (alt, sop); Otto Hardwicke (alt); Harry Carney (alt,
bar), Duke Ellington (pno); Fred Guy (g); Wellman Braud (bs); Sonny
Greer (d)
3   *Solitude*   New York City, 12 Sept. 1934
    3-Col. C3L-27; CBS(E) BPG 62179, Phi(E) *bbe 12404*

DUKE ELLINGTON AND HIS ORCHESTRA
Freddy Jenkins, Cootie Williams, Arthur Whetsel (tpt); Joe Nanton (tbn),
Juan Tizol (v-tbn); Barney Bigard (clt, ten); Johnny Hodges (alt, sop),
Harry Carney (alt, bar); Duke Ellington (pno); Fred Guy (bjo); Wellman
Braud (bs); Sonny Greer (d)
4a   *Rockin' in Rhythm*   New York City, 8 Nov. 1930
    3-Col.C3L-27; CBS(E) BPG 62178, Par(E) PMC 1184
    As last
4b   *Rockin' in Rhythm*   New York City, 14 Jan. 1931
    Bruns. 54007 (del); Cor(E) LRA 10027 (10″) (del)
    As last
4c   *Rockin' in Rhythm*   New York City, 16 Jan. 1931
    Cam. 328 (del); Cam(E) CDN 118

DUKE ELLINGTON AND HIS ORCHESTRA
Bubber Miley, Arthur Whetsel (tpt); Joe Nanton (tbn); Barney Bigard
(clt, ten); Johnny Hodges (alt, sop); Otto Hardwicke (alt, b.sax);
Harry Carney (alt, bar); Duke Ellington (pno); Fred Guy (bjo); Lonnie
Johnson (g); Wellman Braud (bs); Sonny Greer (d) Baby Cox (voc)
5   *Hot and Bothered*   New York City, 1 Oct. 1928
    3-Col. C3L-27; CBS(E) BPG 62178, Par(E) PMC 1154
    Arthur Whetsel, Bubber Miley, Freddy Jenkins (tpt); Joe Nanton (tbn);
    Barney Bigard (clt, ten); Johnny Hodges (alt, sop); Otto Hardwicke
    (alt, b.sax); Harry Carney (alt, bar); Duke Ellington (pno); Fred Guy
    (bjo); Wellman Braud (bs); Sonny Greer (d)
6   *Tiger Rag*   New York City, 8 Jan. 1929
    Br. 54007 (del); Cor(E) LRA 10028 (10″) (del)
    Arthur Whetsel, Freddy Jenkins, Cootie Williams (tpt); Joe Nanton (tbn);
    Barney Bigard (clt, ten); Johnny Hodges (alt, sop); Harry Carney (bar,
    alt); Duke Ellington (pno); Fred Guy (bjo); Wellman Braud (bs); Sonny
    Greer (d)
7a   *Jungle Jamboree*   New York City, 29 July 1929
    AH. AH47
    Arthur Whetsel (tpt); Joe Nanton (tbn); Barney Bigard (clt, ten); Duke
    Ellington (pno); Fred Guy (bjo); Wellman Braud (bs); Sonny Greer (d)
7b   *Jungle Jamboree*   New York City, 2 Aug. 1929
    Par(E) PMC 1154
    Arthur Whetsel, Bubber Miley (tpt); Joe Nanton (tbn); Barney Bigard
    (clt, ten); Johnny Hodges (alt, sop); Harry Carney (bar, alt); Duke

Ellington (pno); Fred Guy (bjo); Lonnie Johnson (g); Wellman Braud
(bs); Sonny Greer (d); Baby Cox (voc)
8a   *The Mooche*   New York City, 1 Oct. 1928
3-Col. C3L-27; CBS(E) BPG 62178, Par(E) PMC 1154
As last, except Johnson and Baby Cox out
8b   *The Mooche*   New York City, 17 Oct. 1928
Br. 54007 (del); Cor(E) LRA 10027 (10") (del)
As last, except Miley out. Hodges and Carney play clt.
8c   *The Mooche*   New York City, 30 Oct. 1928
Vic. 'X' LVA 3037 (del); HMV DLP 1094 (10") (del)

DUKE ELLINGTON AND HIS ORCHESTRA
Personnel as 5 above, except Freddy Jenkins (tpt) added. Baby Cox out
9   *Misty Mornin'*   New York City, 20 Nov. 1928
Par(E) PMC 1154

DUKE ELLINGTON AND HIS ORCHESTRA
Arthur Whetsel (tpt); Joe Nanton (tbn); Barney Bigard (clt); Duke
Ellington (pno); Fred Guy (bjo); Wellman Braud (bs); Sonny Greer (d)
10a *Mood Indigo (Dreamy Blues)*   New York City, 17 Oct. 1930
Br. 54007 (del); Cor(E) LRA 10027 (10") (del)
As last
10b *Mood Indigo*   New York City, 30 Oct. 1930
3-Col. C3L-27; CBS(E) BPG 62178, Phi(E) *bbe 12029* (del)
As last
10c *Mood Indigo*   New York City, 10 Dec. 1930
Vic. *epa 5054*; RCA(E) *rcx 1022*
Bubber Miley, Louis Metcalf (tpt); Joe Nanton (tbn); Rudy Jackson,
Otto Hardwicke (clt, alt); Harry Carney (bar, clt); Duke Ellington
(pno); Fred Guy (bjo); Wellman Braud (bs); Sonny Greer (d); Adelaide
Hall (voc)
11   *Creole Love Call*   Camden, N.J., 26 Oct. 1927
Vic. LPM-1364; RCA(E) RD 27134
Personnel as at 1a above
12a *Black and Tan Fantasy*   New York City, 7 Apr. 1927
Br. 54007 (del); Cor(E) LRA 10027 (10") (del), AH. AH23
As last, except Wellman Braud (bs) replaces Edwards
12b *Black and Tan Fantasie* (sic)   New York City, 6 Oct. 1927
Vic. 'X' LVA 3037 (del); HMV DLP 1094 (10") (del)
As last, except Jabbo Smith (tpt) replaces Miley
12c (i) *Black and Tan Fantasy* (Mat. 81776-A) New York City, 3 Nov. 1927
3-Col. C3L-27; CBS(E) BPG 62178
(ii) The same (Mat. 81776-C)
AH. AH23

DUKE ELLINGTON AND HIS ORCHESTRA
Wallace Jones, Cootie Williams (tpt); Rex Stewart (cnt); Joe Nanton,
Juan Tizol Lawrence Brown (tbn); Barney Bigard (clt); Johnny Hodges,
Otto Hardwicke (alt); Ben Webster (ten); Harry Carney (bar); Duke
Ellington (pno); Fred Guy (g); Jimmy Blanton (bs); Sonny Greer (d)
13   *Portrait of Bert Williams*   Chicago, 28 May 1940
Vic. LPM-1364; RCA(E) RD 27134
As last
Main Stem   Hollywood, 26 June 1940
The Flaming Sword   New York City, 17 Oct. 1940

16   *Cotton Tail*   Hollywood, 4 May 1940
      Vic. LPM-1364; RCA(E) RD 27134
      As last
17   *Ko-Ko*   Chicago, 6 Mar. 1940
      Vic. LPM-1715; RCA(E) RD 27133
      As last
18   *Blue Serge*   Hollywood, 15 Feb. 1941
19   *Sepia Panorama*   New York City, 24 July 1940
      Vic. LPM-1364; RCA(E) RD 27134

DUKE ELLINGTON AND HIS ORCHESTRA
Arthur Whetsel, Cootie Williams, Freddy Jenkins (tpt); Joe Nanton,
Juan Tizol (tbn); Barney Bigard (clt, ten); Johnny Hodges (alt, sop);
Harry Carney (bar, alt); Duke Ellington (pno); Fred Guy (bjo);
Wellman Braud (bs); Sonny Greer (d)

20a   *Creole Rhapsody*   New York City, 20 Jan. 1931
      Bruns. 54007 (del); Cor(E) LRA 10028 (10″) (del)
20b   *Creole Rhapsody* (extended version)   Camden, N.J., 11 June 1931
      Cam. 459 (del); Cam(E) CDN 119

DUKE ELLINGTON AND HIS ORCHESTRA
Arthur Whetsel, Cootie Williams (tpt); Rex Stewart (cnt); Joe Nanton,
Juan Tizol, Lawrence Brown (tbn); Barney Bigard (clt, ten); Johnny
Hodges (alt, sop); Otto Hardwicke (alt); Harry Carney (bar); Duke
Ellington (pno); Fred Guy (g); Hayes Alvis and Billy Taylor (bs);
Sonny Greer (d)

21   *Reminiscin' in Tempo*
      Col. CL-663; Phi(E) BBR 8086 (10″) (del) (*NB*. The Phi(E) contains only
      Parts I and II of the original recording: The American is complete)

DUKE ELLINGTON AND HIS ORCHESTRA
Personnel as last, except Hayes Alvis out

22   *Diminuendo and Crescendo in Blue*   New York City, 20 Sept. 1938
      3-Col. C3L-27; CBS(E) BPG 62180

DUKE ELLINGTON AND HIS ORCHESTRA
Willie Cook, Cat Anderson, Clark Terry, Ray Nance (tpt); Quentin
Jackson, Britt Woodman, John Sanders (tbn); Jimmy Hamilton (clt,
ten); Johnny Hodges, Russell Procope (alt); Paul Gonsalves (ten); Harry
Carney (bar); Duke Ellington (pno); Jimmy Woode (bs); Sam
Woodyard (d)

23   *Such Sweet Thunder*   New York City, Apr./May 1957
      Col. CL-1033: CS-8091(s) (del); Phi(E) BBL 7203

DUKE ELLINGTON with LOUIS ARMSTRONG'S ALL STARS
Louis Armstrong (tpt, voc); Trummy Young (tbn); Barney Bigard (clt);
Duke Ellington (pno); Mort Herbert (bs); Danny Barcelona (d)

24   *10 Ellington titles*   New York City, 3 Apr. 1961
      Rou. 52074: S52074(s); Col(E) 33SX 1400: SCX 3430(s)

ADDENDA

Early Ellingtonia has almost entirely disappeared from American lists
with the exception of the three-record set on Columbia, advertised as
Ellington Era—Vol. 1, a title which presupposes other volumes to follow.
British collectors are more fortunate. In addition to the collections

already referred to, the commendable Ace of Hearts have given us a further collection of extremely rare items covering the period 1926–30 to which reference should certainly be made.

The Duke in Harlem (1926–3)   AH.47

Many important items from the Thirties still await re-issue. It is to be hoped that the original version of *Creole Rhapsody* (20a above) will shortly reappear, and that the Victor–RCA(E) companies will release some of the material of this period available to them.

Of post-1950 Ellington a fairly wide selection is still available though of variable quality. Ellington's qualities as a solo performer have recently been spotlighted in a number of recordings with musicians whose styles would appear to be at variance with his own. One of these, the collaboration with Armstrong, has been listed. Of additional interest are the following:

Meets Coleman Hawkins	Imp. 26: S26(s); HMV CLP 1644: CSD1494
With John Coltrane	Imp. 30: S30(s); HMV CLP 1657
Money Jungle—with Mingus and Roach	UnA.14017: 15017(s); UnA(E) ULP 1039
Ellington plays Ellington	Cap(US) (E) T.477

CHAPTER VI

STAN KENTON AND HIS ORCHESTRA

Chic Alvarez, Johnny Anderson, Buddy Childers, Ken Hanna, Ray Whetzel (tpt); Harry Forbes, Milt Kabak, Bart Varsalona, Kai Winding (tbn); Al Anthony, Boots Mussulli, Bob Cooper, Vido Musso, Bob Gioga (reeds); Stan Kenton (pno); Bob Ahern (g); Eddie Safranski (bs); Shelly Manne (d)

1   *Artistry in Boogie*   Hollywood, 9 Aug. 1946
      Cap. WDX-569; Cap(E) LC6676 (10″) (del)

*BENNY GOODMAN AND HIS ORCHESTRA

Alec Fila, Irving Goodman, Jimmy Maxwell, Cootie Williams (tpt); Lou McGarity, Cutty Cutshall (tbn); Benny Goodman (clt); Gus Bivona, Skippy Martin, Bob Synder, George Auld, Toots Mondello (sax); Johnny Guarnieri (pno); Charlie Christian (el-g); Arthur Bernstein (bs); Dave Tough (d)

2   *Solo Flight*   New York City, 4 Mar. 1941
      Col. CL-652; Phi(E) BBL 7172 (del)

BENNY GOODMAN SEXTET

Benny Goodman (clt); Lionel Hampton (vib); Johnny Guarnieri (pno); Charlie Christian (el-g); Dave Tough (d)

3   *Blues in B*   New York City, 22 Mar. 1941
      As last

THELONIUS MONK TRIO

Thelonius Monk (pno); Percy Heath (bs); Art Blakey (d)

4   *Work*   Hackensack, N.J., 22 Sept. 1954
      Pres. PRLP-7169; Esq. 31–115

THELONIUS MONK QUARTET

Charlie Rouse (ten); Thelonius Monk (pno); John Ore (bs); Frankie Dunlop (d)

5	*Five Spot Blues*	New York City, 6 Nov. 1962
6a	*Bolivar Blues*	New York City, 31 Oct. 1962
7a	*Bye-ya*	New York City, 31 Oct. 1962

Col. CL-1965; CS-8765(s); CBS(E) BPG62135: SBPG62135(s)

THELONIUS MONK SEXTET
Ernie Henry (alt); Sonny Rollins (ten); Thelonius Monk (pno); Oscar
Pettiford (bs); Max Roach (d)

| 6b | *Ba-Lue Bolivar Ba-lues-are* | New York City, Dec. 1956 |

Riv. 226: 1174(s); Riv(E) RLP12-226 (del)

THELONIUS MONK TRIO
Thelonius Monk (pno); Gary Mapp (bs); Art Blakey (d)

| 7b | *Bye-ya* | New York City, 15 Oct. 1952 |

Pres. PRLP-7159; Esq. 32-119

THELONIUS MONK (pno. solo)

| 8 | *Body and Soul* | New York City, 1 Nov. 1962 |

Col. CL-1965: CS-8765(s); CBS(E) BPG62135: SBPG62135(s)

SONNY ROLLINS QUARTET
Sonny Rollins (ten); Thelonius Monk (pno); Tommy Potter (bs); Art
Taylor (d)

| 9 | *The way you look tonight* | Hackensack, N.J., 25 Oct. 1954 |

Pres. PRLP-7169; Esq. 32-115

THELONIUS MONK TRIO
Thelonius Monk (pno); Percy Heath (bs); Art Blakey (d)

| 10a | *Nutty* | Hackensack, N.J., 22 Sept. 1954 |

As last

THELONIUS MONK QUARTET
John Coltrane (ten); Thelonius Monk (pno); Wilbur Ware (bs); Shadow
Wilson (d)

| 10b | *Nutty* | New York City, 16 Apr. 1957 |

Jld. JLP 46: 946(s) (US and E)

THELONIUS MONK TRIO
Thelonius Monk (pno); Gene Ramey (bs); Art Blakey (d)

| 11a | *Ruby, My Dear* | New York City, 24 Oct. 1947 |

BN. BLP-1510

THELONIUS MONK SEPTET
Ray Copeland (tpt); Gigi Gryce (alt); Coleman Hawkins (ten); John
Coltrane (ten); Thelonius Monk (pno); Wilbur Ware (bs); Art
Blakey (d)

| 11b | *Ruby, My Dear* | New York City, 26 June 1957 |

Riv. 242: 1102(s); Riv(E) RLP-242

THELONIUS MONK QUARTET
John Coltrane (ten); Thelonius Monk (pno); Wilbur Ware (bs); Shadow
Wilson (d)

| 11c | *Ruby, My Dear* | New York City, 16 Apr. 1957 |

Jld. JLP 46: 946(s) (US & E)

THELONIUS MONK QUINTET
George Taitt (tpt); Sahib Shihab (alt); Thelonius Monk (pno); Robert
Paige (bs); Art Blakey (d)

| 12a | *'Round Midnight (Round about Midnight)* | New York City, 21 Nov. 1947 |

BN. BLP-1510

THELONIUS MONK (pno. solo)
12b   *'Round Midnight*   New York City, 12 Apr. 1957
       Riv. 235; Riv(E) RLP12-235

THELONIUS MONK QUARTET plus TWO
       Joe Gordon (tpt); Charlie Rouse, Harold Land (ten); Thelonius Monk
       (pno); John Ore (bs); Billie Higgins (d)
12c   *'Round Midnight*   San Francisco, 29 Apr. 1960
       Riv. 300: 1138(s); Riv(E) RLP-300 (del)

THELONIUS MONK QUARTET
       Gerry Mulligan (bar); Thelonius Monk (pno); Wilbur Ware (bs); Shadow
       Wilson (d)
12d   *'Round Midnight*   New York City, 13 Aug. 1957
       Riv. 247: 1106(s); Riv(E) RLP-247

THELONIUS MONK (pno. solo)
13   *I'm getting sentimental over you*   New York City, 12 Apr. 1957
14   *All alone*   The same
15   *I should care*   The same
16a   *Functional*   The same
       Riv. 235; Riv(E) RLP-235
16b   *Functional* (alternative master)   The same
       Jld. JLP 46: 946(s) (US & E)

RED NORVO'S SELECTED SEXTET
       Dizzy Gillespie (tpt); Charlie Parker (alt); Flip Phillips (ten); Teddy
       Wilson (pno); Red Norvo (vib); Slam Stewart (bs); Specs Powell (d)
17   *Slam Slam Blues*   New York City, 5 June 1945
       Parker 408, Bar. B-105; CH(E) BJ-1204

*CHARLIE PARKER'S ALL STARS
       Charlie Parker (alt); John Lewis (pno); Tommy Potter (bs); Max Roach (d)
18   *Parker's Mood*   New York City, Sept. 1948
       Savoy 12000, 12009; Rlm. RM-131

CHARLIE PARKER SEPTET
       Miles Davis (tpt); Charlie Parker (alt); Lucky Thompson (ten); Dodo
       Marmorosa (pno); Arvin Garrison (g); Victor Macmillan (bs); Roy
       Porter (d)
19   *Yardbird Suite*   Hollywood, 28 Mar. 1946
       Parker 407, Bar. B-105; CH(E) BJ-1204

DIZZY GILLESPIE'S ALL STAR QUINTET
       Dizzy Gillespie (tpt); Charlie Parker (alt); Curly Russell (bs); Al Haig
       (pno); Sid Catlett (d)
20a   *Hot House*   New York City, 11 May, 1945
       Savoy 12020; Emb(E) EMB-3344, WRC(E) R29 (del?)

QUINTET OF THE YEAR
       Dizzy Gillespie (tpt); 'Charlie Chan' (Charlie Parker) (alt); Bud Powell
       (pno); Charlie Mingus (bs); Max Roach (d)
20b   *Hot House*   Massey Hall, Toronto, Can. 15 May 1953
       Fan. 6003; Vog(E) LAE 12031, *epv 1104*

CHARLIE PARKER ALL STARS
       Red Rodney (tpt); Charlie Parker (alt); Al Haig (pno); Tommy Potter
       (bs); Max Roach (d)

20c   *Hot House*   New York City, 18 Feb. 1950
       Jazz-Wkshp. JW-500 (del?); Mel(E) 12–105, *dep 36*

CHARLIE PARKER ALL STARS
Miles Davis (tpt); Charlie Parker (alt); Duke Jordan (b); Tommy Potter
(bs); Max Roach (d)
21   *Bird gets the worm*   Detroit, Dec. 1947
       Savoy 12000, 12014; Rlm RM-123
       As last, except Bud Powell (pno) replaces Jordan
22   *Chasin' the Bird*   New York City, May 1947
       Savoy 12001, 12009, 12014; Rlm. RM-121

CHARLIE PARKER'S RE-BOPPERS
Dizzy Gillespie (tpt, pno); Charlie Parker (alt); Curley Russell (bs); Max
Roach (d)
23   *Ko-Ko*   New York City, 26 Nov. 1945
       Savoy 12014, 12079; Rlm. RM-120

CHARLIE PARKER SEPTET
Personnel, place, date as 19 above
24a   *Moose the Mooche*
       Parker 407, Bar. B-105; CH(E) BJ-1204

CHARLIE PARKER SEXTET
Charlie Parker (alt); probably Walter Bishop (pno); Barney Kessel (g);
Teddy Kotick (bs); Max Roach (d)
24b   *Moose the Mooche*   New York City, 1950–51
       Parker 401; Esq. 32–157

CHARLIE PARKER QUARTET
Charlie Parker (alt); Al Haig (pno); Percy Heath (bs); Max Roach (d)
25   *Chi-Chi*   New York City, 4 Aug. 1953
       Ver. 8005, (Mat. 1246–143)
       Ver. 8409; HMV CLP 1538 (Mat. 1246–6)

PARKER-GILLESPIE QUINTET
Dizzy Gillespie (tpt); Charlie Parker (alt); John Lewis (pno); Al McKibbon
(bs); Joe Harris (d)
26a   *A Night in Tunisia*   Carnegie Hall, N. York, 29 Sept. 1947
       Roost *2234* (del); Col(E) 33SX 1555

CHARLIE PARKER SEPTET
Miles Davis (tpt); Charlie Parker (alt); Lucky Thompson (ten); Dodo
Marmorosa (pno); Arvin Garrison (g); Victor Macmillan (bs); Roy Porter
(d)
26b   *A Night in Tunisia*   Hollywood, 28 Mar. 1946
       Parker 407, Bar. B-105; CH(E) BJ1204, Esq. *ep57*

QUINTET OF THE YEAR
Dizzy Gillespie (tpt); 'Charlie Chan' (Charlie Parker) (alt); Bud Powell
(pno); Charlie Mingus (bs); Max Roach (d)
26c   *A Night in Tunisia*   Massey Hall, Toronto, Can., 15 May 1953
       Fan. 6003; Vog(E) LAE 12031, *epv 1104*

SONNY ROLLINS QUARTET
Sonny Rollins (ten); Kenny Drew (pno); George Morrow (bs); Max
Roach (d)
27   *Ee-ah*   Hackensack, N.J., 7 Dec. 1956

28   *B. Swift*   The same
     Pres. PRLP-7207; Esq. 32–175
     Sonny Rollins (ten); Tommy Flanagan (pno); Doug Watkins (bs);
     Max Roach (d)
29   *Blue Seven*   New York City, 22 June 1956
     Pres. PRLP-7079; Esq. 32–045

     QUINTET OF THE YEAR
     Personnel as at 26c above. Place, date and record numbers the same.
30   *Wee*

     CHARLIE PARKER QUARTET
     Miles Davis, Dizzy Gillespie (tpt); Charlie Parker (alt); Argonne Thornton
     (pno); Curly Russell (bs); Max Roach (d)
31   **Meandering*   New York City, 26 Nov. 1945
     Savoy 12079; Rlm. RM-120

     LENNIE TRISTANO (pno)
32   *Requiem*   New York City, 1955
     Atl. 1224, 1334; Lon(E) LTZ-K15033 (del)

     CECIL TAYLOR QUARTET
     Steve Lacy (sop); Cecil Taylor (pno); Buell Neidlinger (bs); Dennis
     Charles (d)
33   *Nona's Blues*   Newport, R.I., 6 July 1957
     Ver. 8238; Col(E) 33CX10102 (del)

     CHARLIE MINGUS GROUP
     Lonnie Hillyer, Ted Curson (tpt); Charlie McPherson, Eric Dolphy (alt);
     Booker Erwin (ten); Paul Bley (pno); Charlie Mingus (bs); Danny Rich-
     mond (d)
34   *Lock 'em Up*   New York City, 11 Nov. 1960
     Candid CMJ 8021; 9021(s); (E) 8021 (del)

     CECIL TAYLOR SEPTET
     Ted Curson (tpt); Roswell Rudd (tbn); Jimmy Lyons (alt); Archie Shepp
     (ten); Cecil Taylor (pno, arr); Henry Grimes (bs); Jimmy Murray (d)
35   *Mixed*   New York City, 10 Oct. 1961
36   *Pots*   The same
     Imp. A-9: S-9(s)
     (*Note:* This record released under the name of Gil Evans)

     ORNETTE COLEMAN QUARTET
     Don Cherry (cnt); Ornette Coleman (alt); Charlie Haden (bs); Billy
     Higgins (d)
37   *Eventually*
     Atl. 1317: S-1317(s)

     ORNETTE COLEMAN QUARTET
     Don Cherry (cnt); Ornette Coleman (alt); Charlie Haden (bs); Billy
     Higgins (d)
38   *Free*   New York City, 1960
     Atl. 1327: S-1327(s); Lon(E) LTZ-K15199; SAH-K6099(s)

     ORNETTE COLEMAN
     Personnel, place, date and record numbers as 37 above
39   *Lonely Woman*
40   *Peace*

ORNETTE COLEMAN QUARTET
Personnel, place, date and record numbers as 38 above.
41   *Ramblin'*
42   *The face of the brass*

ORNETTE COLEMAN AND GROUP
Freddy Hubbard (tpt); Ornette Coleman, Eric Dolphy (alt); Charlie Haden (bs); Ed. Blackwell (d) and others
43   *Free Jazz*—a collective improvisation
    Atl. 1364: S–1364 (s)

JOHN COLTRANE QUARTET
John Coltrane (ten); McCoy Tyner (pno); Jimmy Garrison (bs); Elvin Jones (d)
44   *Out of this world*   New York City, 1962
45   *Soul Eyes*   The same
    Imp. 21: S–21(s); HMV CLP 1629: CSD 1483 (s)

CHARLIE MINGUS GROUP
Jackie McLean (att); J. R. Monterose (ten); Mel Waldron (pno); Charlie Mingus (bs); Willie Jones (d)
46   *Profile of Jackie*   New York City, 30 Jan. 1956
47   *Love Chant*
48   *Pithecanthropus erectus*
49   *A Foggy Day*
    Atl. 1237; Lon(E) LTZ-K15052 (del)

ADDENDA

1 *Artistry in Boogie*. In common with many of Kenton's most spectacular successes this title has been recorded more than once by later orchestras. It has not been considered necessary to chart these re-creations in any detail. Many examples of this kind of music are to be found under Kenton's name in both American and British lists.

2 BENNY GOODMAN AND HIS ORCHESTRA with various small groups
Strictly speaking this, the most famous and most successful of all swing orchestras, should have been included in the Addenda to Chapter V, but since it was being discussed here, even though only in the context of Charlie Christian, it was considered better to transfer a list of its records to this chapter.
Of the hundreds of records Goodman made in his hey-day a mere handful remain on the catalogues, though there are signs that a revival of interest in this period of Jazz history may not be long delayed so that re-issues may be expected. The most complete representation of the Goodman orchestra and of the small groups which Goodman created to play intimate, sophisticated yet swinging Jazz, are of public performances and radio broadcasts, though there are some studio recordings to be found, particularly the great five-volume set on Victor.
Carnegie Hall Jazz Concert (1938)
3-Col. CL-814/6, 2-Col. OSL-160; Phi(E) BBL 7441/2
Golden Age of Goodman (1935–8)
Vic. LPM-1099
Golden Age of Swing (1935–9)

5-Vic. LPT-6703; excerpts on RCA(E) *rcx 1009, 1019, 1026, 1033, 1036, 1059, 1064, 1065*
King of Swing
3-Col. CL-817/9, 2-Col. OSL-180
Swing, Swing, Swing (1935–8)
Cam. 624:S-624(s?); Cam(E) CDN-148
Treasure Chest (1937–8 broadcasts)
3-MGM 3E9; MGM(E) C805, 807, 810
Trio-Quartet-Quintet
Vic. LPM-1226
The earliest recording period of Goodman (1927–34) was represented on the following record now apparently deleted both in America and Great Britain, though almost certainly still to be had in France or Germany
B.G. 1927–34
Bruns. 54010; Cor(E) LVA 9011

CHARLIE PARKER
The recordings of Charlie Parker, especially those recorded for Ross Russell's *Dial* label, have appeared under so many different imprints that it is now a major task to unravel the various sessions. I do not pretend that the numbers attached to the examples quoted are the only ones available. I only hope they are the correct ones.

31   *Meandering*
The text refers to the pianist on this session as being Bud Powell though it is, I believe, now more or less generally accepted that it was Argonne Thornton, a pianist whose talents have received little publicity.

WOODY HERMAN
Although no reference to the bands led by Woody Herman appears in the text his style and presentation have undoubtedly exerted great influence on modern big-band Jazz. Like Kenton, Herman has retired from the recording scene from time to time to emerge with a newly-constituted band, or Herd, each having clearly defined characteristics which mark it from its predecessors. The first three Herds are certainly the most important and it is fortunate that three records covering the whole of Herman's career between 1945 and 1947 have recently made their appearance in Great Britain. Although it may be felt by some readers that Herman really belongs, like Goodman, in Chapter V, the dates of his most representative recordings, to say nothing of their style, make them clearly stable companions of Kenton's.
The Thundering Herds
3-Col. C3L-25; CBS(E) BPG62158/60
A single record collection covering 1945–7, 1953–4 may still be found and is an excellent introductory.
Col. CL-592 (del); Phi(E) BBL 7123 (del)
A more recent recrudescence.
The Fourth Herd (1959)
Jld. JLP-17: 917(s); Riv(E) JLP-17

CHAPTER VII

1   *Kind of Blue* (album title: details see 2–5 below)
MILES DAVIS SEXTET
Miles Davis (tpt); Cannonball Adderley (alt, except –1); John Coltrane (ten); Bill Evans (pno); Paul Chambers (bs); James Cobb (d)

2	*So What*	New York City, 2 Mar. 1959
3	*Blues in Green* –1	The same
4	*All Blues*	The same
5	*Flamenco Sketches*	The same

Col. CL-1355: CS-8163(s); CBS(E) BPG62066: SBPG62066(s)

MILES DAVIS (tpt) with GIL EVANS' ORCHESTRA

6	*Solea*	New York City, 11 Mar. 1960

Col. CL-1480: CS-8271; Fon(E) TFL 5100 (del): STFL 531(s) (del)

MILES DAVIS QUINTET

Miles Davis (tpt); 'Charlie Chan' (Charlie Parker) (ten); Walter Bishop (pno); Percy Heath (bs); Philly Joe Jones (d)

7a	*'Round Midnight*	New York City, 30 Jan. 1953

Pres. PRLP-7044; Esq. 32–030

Miles Davis (tpt); John Coltrane (ten); Red Garland (pno); Paul Chambers (bs); Philly Joe Jones (d)

7b	*'Round Midnight*	New York City, 1956

Pres. PRLP-7150; Esq. 32–100
Same personnel

7c	*'Round Midnight*	New York City, 1956

Col. CL-949: CS-8649(s); Phi(E) BBL 7140 (del), *bbe 12266*
Same personnel

8	*Ah-leu-cha*	New York City, 1956

Col. CL-949: CS-8649(s); Phi(E) BBL 7140 (del), *bbe 12351*

MILES DAVIS ORCHESTRA

Miles Davis (tpt); J. J. Johnson (tbn); Sanford Siegelstein (fr. hn); Lee Konitz (alt); Gerry Mulligan (bar); John Lewis (pno); Nelson Boyd (bs); Bill Barber (tu); Kenny Clarke (d)

9	*Israel*	New York City, 1949

As last, except Kai Winding (tbn); Junior Collins (fr. hn); Al Haig (pno); Joe Schulman (bs); and Max Roach (d) replace Johnson, Siegelstein, Lewis, Boyd and Clarke.

10	*Move*	New York City, 1948

Personnel and date as 9 above

11	*Boplicity*	

Miles Davis (tpt); J. J. Johnson (tbn); Lee Konitz (alt); Gerry Mulligan (bar); John Levy (pno); Al McKibbon (bs); Max Roach (d)

12	*Moondreams*	New York City, 9 Mar. 1950

All above Cap. T-1974; Cap(E) T-762

MILES DAVIS (tpt, flg-hn) with large orchestra directed by Gil Evans

13	*Porgy and Bess* (Gershwin arr. Evans)	New York City, 1958

Col. CL1274: CSL-1274(s); Fon(E) TFL5056: STFL 507(s)

GERRY MULLIGAN QUARTET

Chet Baker (tpt); Gerry Mulligan (bar); Carson Smith (bs); Larry Bunker (d)

14	*Darn that dream*	Hollywood, Apr. 1953

Pac. Jazz 8; Vog(E) LAE 12268 (del)

Bob Brookmeyer (v-tbn); Gerry Mulligan (bar); Red Mitchell (bs); Frank Isola (d)

15	*Gold Rush*	Paris, Summer, 1954

As last

16 RED NICHOLS AND HIS FIVE PENNIES
    (See Addenda at end of Chapter)

MODERN JAZZ QUARTET
John Lewis (pno); Milt Jackson (vib); Percy Heath (bs); Connie Kay (d)
17 *Over the rainbow*   New York City, 22 Jan. 1956
18 *Versailles*   The same
19 *Fontessa*   The same
    Atl. 1231: S-1231(s); Lon(E) LTZ-K 15022; SAH-K6031(s)
    Same personnel
20 *One never knows*   New York City, 23 Aug. 1957
    Atl. 1284: S-1284(s); Lon(E) LTZ-K15140: SAH-K6029(s)

BRASS ENSEMBLE OF THE JAZZ AND CLASSICAL MUSIC
SOCIETY cond. Gunther Schuller
21 *Three Little Feelings* (J. Lewis)
    2-Col. C2L-31: C2S-831(s)

CHICO HAMILTON QUINTET
Buddy Collette (fl, reeds); Jim Hall (g); Fred Katz (vcl); Carson Smith
(bs); Chico Hamilton (d)
22 *Sleep*   California, 1956
23 *Chrissie*   The same
    World 1216; Vog(E) LAE 12045 (del)

JIMMY GIUFFRE THREE
Jimmy Giuffre (clt, ten, bar); Jim Hall (g); Red Mitchell (bs)
24 *Seven Pieces*
    Ver. 8307: 68307(s)

JIMMY GIUFFRE THREE
Jimmy Giuffre (clt), Jim Hall (g); Ray Brown (bs)
25 *Cry Want*
    Ver. 8397: 68397 (s)
    Same personnel
26 *Thesis*
    Ver. 8402: 68402(s)
    As last
27 *Free Fall*
    Col. CL-1694: CS-8764(s)

CHICO HAMILTON QUINTET
Personnel, place, dates and record details as 22 above
28 *Gone Lover*

DAVE BRUBECK QUARTET
Paul Desmond (alt); Dave Brubeck (pno); Gene Wright (bs); Joe Morello
(d) Carmen McRae (voc)
29 *Weep no more*   New York City, Dec. 1960
    Col. CL-1609: CS-8409 (s); CBS(E) BPG62076: SBPG 62076 (s)

DAVE BRUBECK (pno. solo)
30 *Two Part Contention*   New York City, 18/19 Apr. 1956
    Col. CL-878; Phi(E) BBL 7147, *bbe 12291*

DAVE BRUBECK QUARTET
Paul Desmond (alt); Dave Brubeck (pno); Joe Benjamin (bs); Joe
Morello (d)

31   *Impressions of Eurasia*   New York City, 1958
     Col. CL-1251: CS-8058 (s); Fon(E) TFL 5051 (del): STFL 508 (del), 2
     items on Fon(E) *tfe 17199*
     As last, except Norman Bates (bs) in place of Benjamin

32   *These foolish things*   Los Angeles, 1 May 1957
     Col. CL-1034; Fon(E) TFL 5002

DAVE BRUBECK QUARTET with NEW YORK PHILHARMONIC-SYMPHONY ORCHESTRA cond. Leonard Bernstein

33   *Dialogues for Jazz Combo and Orchestra* (H. Brubeck)
     Col. CL-1466: CS-8257(s); CBS(E) BPG 62071: SBPG 62071(s)

CHARLES BELL CONTEMPORARY JAZZ QUARTET

Charles Bell (pno); Bill Smith (g); Frank Trafficante (bs); Allen
Blairman (d)

34   *The last sermon*   Pittsburgh? c. 1961
35   *Counterpoint Study No. 2*   The same
     Col. CL-1582: CS-8382(s) (del)

JOHNNY CARISI ORCHESTRA

Johnny Glasel, Joe Wilder (tpt); Urbie Green (tbn); Bob Brookmeyer
(v-tbn); Jimmy Buffington (fr. hn); Hervey Phillips (tu); Phil Woods
(alt); Gene Quill (alt, bar); Eddie Costa (vib, pno); Milt Hinton (bs);
Osie Johnson (d); Johnny Carisi (ldr, comp, arr)

36   *Moon Taj*   New York City, 10 June 1961
     As last, except Doc Severinsen (tpt) and Art Davis (bs) replace Wilder
     and Hinton

37   *Angkor Wat*   New York City, 14 Sept. 1961
     Imp. A-9: S-9(s)
     (*Note*. This record has been issued under the name of Gil Evans, though
     Evans does not appear to have any connexion with its contents.)

GEORGE RUSSELL SEXTET

Don Ellis (tpt); Dave Baker (tbn); Dave Young (ten); George Russell
(pno); Chuck Israels (bs); Joe Hunt (d)

38   *Sandhu*   New York City, 20 Sept. 1960
     Dec. 4183: 74183(s)

UNNAMED GROUPS

Robert de Domenica (fl); Eric Dolphy (fl, bs.clt, alt); Ornette Coleman
(alt); Bill Evans (pno); Eddie Costa (vib); Jim Hall (g); Scott la Faro,
George Duvivier (bs); Sticks Evans (d); Contemporary String Quartet—
Charles Libove, Roland Vamos, Harry Zaratzian, Joseph Tekula.

39   *Four variants on a theme of Theolonius Monk* (Criss Cross) (G. Schuller)
     Ornette Coleman (alt); Jim Hall (g); Scott la Faro (bs); Sticks Evans (d)
     with Contemporary String Quartet

40   *Abstraction* (G. Schuller)
     Personnel as 39, except Coleman out; Dolphy plays fl. only

41   *Three variants on a theme of John Lewis* (Django) (G. Schuller)
     Atl. 1365: S-1365(s)

BILL EVANS TRIO

Bill Evans (pno); Scott la Faro (bs); Paul Motian (d)

42   *Milestones*   New York City, 25 June 1961
     Riv. 399: Riv. 9399(s) (US & E)

Same personnel
43 *Blues in Green*   New York City, 1959
44 *When I fall in love*   The same
45 *Spring is here*   The same
46 *Autumn Leaves*   The same
47 *Witchcraft*   The same
48 *Some day my Prince will come*   The same
    Riv. 315: 1162 (s); Riv(E) RLP12–315 (del)

CLIFFORD BROWN–MAX ROACH QUINTET
Clifford Brown (tpt); Harold Land (ten); Richard Powell (p); George
Morrow (bs); Max Roach (d)
49 *What am I here for?*   Los Angeles, 25 Feb. 1955
    Mer. MG36036; EmA(E) EJL 1250 (del)
    Same personnel
50a *Jor-du*   Los Angeles, 3 Aug. 1954
    Mer. MG36036; EmA(E) EJL 1250, Mer(E) MMC 14041
50b *Jor-du*   Los Angeles, 30 Aug. 1954
    GNm, LP6, LP18 (both del); Vog(E) LAE 12036 (del)
    Same personnel
51 *Daahoud*   Los Angeles, 6 Aug. 1954
    Mer. MG36036; EmA(E) EJL 1250 (del)
    Same personnel
52 *Delilah*   Los Angeles, 2 Aug. 1954
    Mer. MG36036; EmA(E) EJL 1250 (del)
    Same personnel
53 *Joy spring*   Los Angeles, 6 Aug. 1954
54a *Parisian thorofare*   The same, 2 Aug. 1954
    Mer. MG36036; EmA(E) EJL 1250, Mer(E) MMC 14041
54b *Parisian thorofare*   Los Angeles, 30 Aug. 1954
    GNm. LP6, LP18 (both del); Vog(E) LAE 12036 (del)
    Same personnel
55 *The blues walk*   Los Angeles, 24 Feb. 1955
    Mer. MG36036; EmA(E) EJL 1250 (del)

DON ELLIS
Don Ellis (tpt); Paul Bley (pno); Gary Peacock (bs); Nick Martinis (d)
56 *Ostinato*
    Pac. Jazz PJ55   c. 1962

BOOKER LITTLE
Booker Little (tpt); Julian Priester (tbn); Eric Dolphy (fl, bs.clt, alt), Don
Friedman (pno); *Art Davis or Ron Cartes (bs); Max Roach (perc)*
57 *Moods in free time*   New York City, Mar./Apr. 1961
    Candid 8027: 9027(s)

JOHN COLTRANE QUARTET
John Coltrane (ten); McCoy Tyner (pno); Jimmy Garrison (bs); Elvin
Jones (d)
58 *You don't know what love is*   New York City, 13 Nov. 1962
59 *All or nothing at all*   The same
    Imp. 32: S–32 (s); HMV CLP 1647: CSD 1496 (s)
    Same personnel
60 *Coltrane plays the blues*   New York City, 24 Oct. 1960
    Blues to Elvin; Mr Syms; Mr Knight; Mr Day; Blues to You; Blues to Bechet
    Atl. 1382: S–1382 (s); Lon(E) HA-K8017: SH-K8017(s)

RED NICHOLS AND HIS FIVE PENNIES

This group, rarely confined to its eponymous number, enjoyed one of the most successful recording careers in Jazz history. Between 1926 and 1933 these groups, assembled for recordings only, numbered among their members some of the most illustrious names in white Jazz, some of whom, Benny Goodman, Jack Teagarden, Eddie Lang, Joe Venuti, Glenn Miller, the Dorsey brothers, Miff Mole, Bud Freeman for example, are to be heard in the records listed below.

1926–30
Bruns. 54008 d(el); Bruns(E) LAT 8307 (del)
Red Nichols Story (1926–33)
Bruns. 54047
1926–31
AH. AH63 (contains some titles from first item)
Thesaurus of Classic Jazz—Vol. 3 (Red Nichols and the Charleston Chasers)
Col. CL-1523, 4-Col. C4L-18; Phi(E) BBL 7433
(*Note*. This last collection, though not strictly the Five Pennies, is an admirable anthology of white jazz of the 'New York' style. The other volumes in the set are devoted to Miff Mole, Nichols with the Arkansas Travellers, and with a number of miscellaneous allied groups including the Venuti-Lang orchestra.)

CHAPTER VIII

GLENN MILLER AND HIS ORCHESTRA

1	*In the mood*	New York City, 1939
2	*Tuxedo Junction*	The same, 5 Feb. 1940
3	*King Porter Stomp*	The same, 27 Sept. 1938

Vic. LPM-1192; RCA RD-27068

JAMES P. JOHNSON (pno. solo)

4	*Mule walk stomp*	New York City, 14 June 1939
	As last	
5	*Carolina Shout*	New York City, 18 Oct. 1921
	As last	
6	*Worried and lonesome blues*	New York City, 28 June 1923

Col. CL-1780; CBS(E) BPG 62090

JAMES P. JOHNSON AND HIS ORCHESTRA

Henry Allen (tpt); J. C. Higginbotham (tbn); Eugene Sedric (ten); James P. Johnson (pno); Eugene Fields (g); Pops Foster (bs); Sidney Catlett (d); Anna Robinson (voc)

7	*Hungry Blues*	New York City, 15 June 1939
	As last	

JAMES P. JOHNSON (pno solo)

8	*If dreams come true*	New York City, 14 June 1939
9	*Lonesome reverie*	The same
10	*Blueberry Rhyme*	The same
	As last	

TED LEWIS AND HIS ORCHESTRA

Fats Waller (pno, voc) and large orchestra featuring Muggsy Spanier (cnt), Benny Goodman (clt) and George Brunis (tbn) directed by Ted Lewis.

11a   *Dallas Blues*   New York City, 6 Mar. 1931
11b   *Royal Garden Blues*   The same
      Col.6127 (del); Phi(E) *bbe 12106* (del)

FATS WALLER AND HIS BUDDIES
      Charlie Gaines (tpt); Charlie Irvis (tbn); Arville Harris (clt); Fats Waller
      (pno); Eddie Condon (bjo)
12   *The minor drag*   New York City, 1 Mar. 1929
      Vic. LPM-1246; RCA(E) *rcx 1010*

FATS WALLER AND HIS RHYTHM
      Herman Autrey (tpt); Rudy Powell (clt, alt); Fats Waller (pno); James
      Smith (g); Charlie Turner (bs); Arnold Boden (d)
13   *12th Street Rag*   New York City, 1938
14   *Truckin'*
      No LP reissues of these known.
      (13) Vic. 25087 (78) ⎫
      (14) Vic. 25116 (78) ⎬ HMV BD 262 (78) (all del)
                            ⎭

FATS WALLER (pno solo)
15a   *Ain't misbehaving*   Camden, N.J., 2 Aug. 1929
      Vic. LPM-1246; HMV DLP 1008 (10″) (del)
      As last
15b   *Ain't misbehaving*   New York City, 11 Mar. 1935
      RCA(E) RD-7553

FATS WALLER AND HIS RHYTHM
      Benny Carter (tpt); Alton Moore (tbn); Gene Porter (clt, ten); Fats
      Waller (pno, voc); Irving Ashby (g); Slam Stewart (bs); Zutty
      Singleton (d)
15c   *Ain't misbehaving*   Hollywood, 23 Jan. 1943
      Cam. 473; Cam(E) CDN-131
      Herman Autrey (tpt); Rudy Powell (clt); Fats Waller (pno, voc); Al
      Casey (g); Charlie Turner (bs); Harry Dial (d)
16   *I'm gonna sit right down*   New York City, 8 May 1935
      Vic. LPM-1246, *epa 5140*; RCA(E) *rcx 1053*
      Personnel as last, except Eugene Sedric (clt, ten) and Slick Jones (d)
      replace Powell and Dial
17a   *Blue turning gray over you*   New York City, 9 June 1937
      Vic. LPT-14 (10″) (del); HMV DLP1017 (10″) (del), *7eg 8148* (del)

FATS WALLER (pno. solo)
17b   *Blue turning gray over you*   New York City, 11 Mar. 1935
      RCA(E) RD-7553

FATS WALLER AND HIS RHYTHM
      John Hamilton (tpt); Gene Sedric (clt, ten); Fats Waller (pno, voc); John
      Smith (g); Cedric Wallace (bs); Slick Jones (d)
18   *Your feet's too big*   New York City, 3 Nov. 1939
      Vic. LPM-1246; RCA(E) *rcx 1053*

FATS WALLER AND HIS RHYTHM
      Personnel as last
19a   *Honeysuckle Rose*   New York City, 2 Aug. 1939
      RCA(E) RD-7552

FATS WALLER (pno. solo)
19b   *Honeysuckle Rose*   New York City, 11 Mar. 1935
      RCA(E) RD-7552

FATS WALLER AND HIS RHYTHM
Bill Coleman (tpt); Gene Sedric (clt); Fats Waller (pno, voc); Al Casey (g); Billy Taylor (bs); Harry Dial (d)

19c   *Honeysuckle Rose*   New York City, 7 Nov. 1934
Vic. *epa 5005*; RCA(E) *rcx 1010*

EARL HINES (pno. solo)
20   *Caution Blues*   Chicago, 9 Dec. 1928
Fan. 3238; Phi(E) BBL 7185 (del)

EARL HINES TRIO
Earl Hines (pno); Al McKibbon (bs); J. C. Heard (d)

21   *Diane*   New York City, 17 July 1950
22   *These foolish things*   The same
23   *Rosetta*   The same
Fan. 3238; Phi(E) BBL 7185 (del)

TEDDY WILSON (pno. solo)
24   *Between the Devil and the deep blue sea*   New York City, 2 Nov. 1937
Phi(E) BBL 7511

ART TATUM (pno. solo)
25   *Mr Freddy Blues*   Hollywood, *c.* 1956
20-Fox 3033 : S-3033(s); Emb. EMB 3326
26   *Sophisticated lady*   New York City, 21 Mar. 1933
Epic 3295 (del); Phi(E) BBL 7511, Fon(E) *tfe 17235*
27a   *Willow, weep for me*   New York City, Sept. 1949
Har. HL-7006; Phi(E) BBL 7511
27b   *Willow, weep for me*   Hollywood, *c.* 1956
20-Fox 3033 : S-3033(s); Emb. EMB 3326

ERROLL GARNER (pno. solo)
28a   *Play, piano, play*   Hollywood, 10 June 1947
Roost 2213 Vog(E) LAE 12209 (del), Col(E) 33SX 1557

ERROLL GARNER TRIO
Erroll Garner (pno); John Simmons (bs); Shadow Wilson (d)

28b   *Play, piano, play* (f)   New York City, 11 Jan. 1961
29a   *Body and Soul*
30a   *I cover the waterfront*
31a   *I'm in the mood for love*
32a   *Laura*
Col. CL-6173; Phi(E) BBL 7192 (del) (f) *bbe 12345* (del)

ERROLL GARNER (pno. solo)
29b   *Body and Soul*
30b   *I cover the waterfront*
Savoy 12002; Lon(E) LTZ-C 15125 (del)
31b   *I'm in the mood for love*
32b   *Laura*
Savoy 12003; Lon(E) LTZ-C 15126 (del)

RED GARLAND TRIO
Red Garland (pno); Larry Ridley (bs); Frank Grant (d)

33   *The nearness of you*

34   *Long ago and far away*
        Jld. JLP 62 : 962(s)

RED GARLAND QUINTET
Donald Byrd (tpt); John Coltrane (ten); Red Garland (pno); George
Joyner (bs); Art Taylor (d)

35   *I got it bad*   Hackensack, N.J., 15 Nov. 1957
        Pres. 7181; Esq. 32–136

*TEDDY WILSON AND HIS ORCHESTRA
Roy Eldridge (tpt); Benny Morton (tbn); Chu Berry (ten); Teddy
Wilson (pno); Dave Barbour (g); John Kirby (bs); Cozy Cole (d);
Billie Holiday (voc)

36   *Eeny meeny miney mo*   New York City, 25 Oct. 1935
        Phi(E) BBL 7510

BILLIE HOLIDAY AND HER ORCHESTRA
Bunny Berigan (tpt); Irving Fazola (clt); Clyde Hart (pno); Dick
McDonough (g); Arthur Bernstein (bs); Cozy Cole (d); Billie Holiday
(voc)

37   *One, two, button your shoe*   New York City, 29 Sept. 1936
        Fon(E) TFL 5106

TEDDY WILSON AND HIS ORCHESTRA
Buck Clayton (tpt); Prince Robinson (clt); Vido Musso (ten); Teddy
Wilson (pno); Allan Reuss (g); Walter Page (bs); Cozy Cole (d); Billie
Holiday (voc)

38   *Nice work if you can get it*   New York City, 1 Nov. 1937
        Fon(E) TFL 5106

BILLIE HOLIDAY AND HER ORCHESTRA
Buck Clayton (tpt); Dicky Wells (tbn); Lester Young (clt); Queenie
Johnson (pno); Freddy Green (g); Walter Page (bs); Jo Jones (d); Billie
Holiday (voc)

39   *I've got a date with a dream*   New York City, 15 Sept. 1938
        Phi(E) BBL 7510
        As last, except Benny Morton (tbn) and Teddy Wilson (pno) replace
        Wells and Johnson. Lester Young reverts to (ten).

40   *Back in your own back-yard*   New York City, 12 Jan. 1938
        3-Col. C3L-21; CBS(E) BPG62038, Phi(E) BBL 7510
        As last (as Teddy Wilson and his Orchestra)

41   *If dreams come true*   New York City, 6 Jan. 1938
        3-Col. C3L-21; CBS(E) BPG62038, Fon(E) TFL 5106

TEDDY WILSON AND HIS ORCHESTRA
Buck Clayton (tpt); Buster Bailey (clt); Lester Young (ten); Teddy
Wilson (pno); Freddy Green (g); Walter Page (bs); Jo Jones (d); Billie
Holiday (voc)

42   *I'll never be the same*   New York City, 1 June 1937
        3-Col. C3L-21; CBS(E) BPG62037, Fon(E) TFL 5106

BILLIE HOLIDAY AND HER ORCHESTRA
Bunny Berigan (tpt); Irving Fazola (clt); Clyde Hart (pno); Dick
McDonough (g); Arthur Bernstein (bs); Cozy Cole (d); Billie Holiday
(voc)

43   *A fine romance*   New York City, 29 Sept. 1936
        3-Col. C3L21; CBS(E) BPG62037, Phi(E) BBL 7510

Frank Newton (tpt); Tab Smith, Kenneth Hollon, Stanley Payne (sax);
Sonny White (pno); Jimmy McLin (g); John Williams (bs); Eddie
Dougherty (d); Billie Holiday (voc)

44   *Strange fruit*   New York City, 29 Mar. 1939
Comm. 30008; State. 10007
As 40 above: all details the same

45   *When a woman loves a man*
Buck Clayton, Harry Edison (tpt); Earl Warren (alt); Lester Young
(ten); Jack Washington (bar); Joe Sullivan (pno); Freddy Green (g);
Walter Page (bs); Jo Jones (d); Billie Holiday (voc)

46   *The man I love*   New York City, 15 Dec. 1939
3-Col. C3L-21; CBS(E) BPG62039

BILLIE HOLLIDAY

Billie Holiday (voc) acc. Bobby Tucker (pno); Mundell Lowe (g);
John Levy (bs); Denzil Best (d)

47   *I wants to stay here* (Porgy)   New York City, 10 Dec. 1948
Dec. 8702; AH. AH57

*ELLA FITZGERALD (voc) with various accompaniments

48   *Manhattan* (Rodgers and Hart)
49   *Thou Swell* (Rodgers and Hart)
50   *My romance* (Rodgers and Hart)
51   *I wish I were in love again* (Rodgers and Hart)
Ver. 4002-2, Ver. 4022: 64022(s); HMV CLP 1116
52   *Alexander's Ragtime Band* (Irving Berlin)
53   *Top hat* (Irving Berlin)
54   *Cheek to cheek* (Irving Berlin)
55   *Let's face the music and dance* (Irving Berlin)
56   *How deep is the ocean?* (Irving Berlin)
57   *How about me* (Irving Berlin)
2-Ver. 4019-2, Ver. 4030: 64019-2(s), 64030(s); HMV CLP 1183
58   *All through the night* (Cole Porter)
60   *You're the top* (Cole Porter)
61   *Anything goes* (Cole Porter)
62   *I get a kick out of you* (Cole Porter)
63   *Night and day* (Cole Porter)
2-Ver. 4001-2; HMV CLP 1083-4
See Addenda for following:
59   *Blow, Gabriel, blow* (Porter)
64   *These foolish things* (Strachey)

FRANK LOESSER
65*   *Guys and Dolls* (selection)
Members of original New York cast
Dec. 9023: 79023(s); Bruns(E) LAT 8022

RICHARD RODGERS AND OSCAR HAMMERSTEIN
66   *South Pacific*
Members of original New York cast
Col. OL-4180: OS-4200(s); Phi(E) BBL 7157
67   *Oklahoma*
Members of original New York cast
Dec. 9017: 79017(s); Bruns(E) LAT 8001

GEORGE GERSHWIN (1898–1937)
68   *The man I love*
       Ella Fitzgerald (voc) with acc.
       5-Ver. 4029–5, 4025: 64029–5, 64025(s); HMV CLP1339: CSD1293(s)
69   *Rhapsody in Blue* (Orchestral version) (1924)
       L. Bernstein (pno)—Columbia Symphony Orchestra—Bernstein
       Col. ML-5413: MS-6091(s); CBS(E) BRG 7280: SBRG72080(s)
       L. Pennario (pno)—Whiteman Orchestra
       Cap. T-1678: DT-1678(s); Enc. ENC 123
       J. Katchen (pno)—Mantovani Orchestra
       Lon. 1262: Dec(E) LXT 5069
       E. List (pno)—Eastman-Rochester Symphony Orchestra—Hanson
       Mer. 50138: 90002(s); Mer(E) MMA 11046: AMS 16026(s)
       Rhapsody in Blue (piano version)
       George Gershwin (piano roll)
       20-Fox 3013; Emb. EMB 3315
       Vic. LPM-2058
       (both American companies advertise stereo versions of these releases)
70   *Concerto in F* (1925)
       Coupled with *Rhapsody in Blue* above, see Katchen
       List

ADDENDA

20   *Caution Blues*. A further version of this piece exists under the title *Blues
     in Thirds* played by Sidney Bechet, Earl Hines and Baby Dodds. This
     was recorded in 1940 and is one of the great jazz performances. It is
     now no longer available in U.S.A. or Great Britain apparently but is
     available on French RCA. It was originally issued on Vic. LPT-22;
     HMV DLP 1042.

TEDDY WILSON AND HIS ORCHESTRA
     Although listed above under the name of Teddy Wilson, all the records
     quoted are to be found listed in catalogues under the name of Billie
     Holiday. The bands under both Wilson's and Holiday's names were
     studio groups assembled merely for recording sessions.

ELLA FITZGERALD
48ff   The problems involved in listing anything like a representative collection
       of these titles were too manifold for the result to justify the labour
       involved. It was considered sufficient under the circumstances to list
       only the collections of songs by the composers concerned made by
       Ella Fitzgerald. Though these will not, naturally, satisfy every reader,
       they are in general felt to be faithful performances and are very well
       sung.

     Blow, Gabriel, blow
       Miss Fitzgerald does not appear to have included this in her collection of
       Cole Porter songs, possibly because it really requires a chorus. There are
       a number of performances but they are too varied in style to justify
       selecting any one as really representative, though readers may be in-
       terested to know that recordings exist by singers as widely separated in
       idiom as Ethel Merman and Caesar Siepi.

These foolish things
In general the same remarks apply to this most popular song. Readers should seek out a performance by a singer whose style is known to satisfy them.

65–67 SHOWS
For the sake of conciseness only the original theatrical cast recordings have been listed here. In most cases, especially *South Pacific*, film sound track versions exist which are as well, if not better known than the stage versions. These are still available in both countries.

69 *Rhapsody in Blue*
This work has been subjected to as much variety of treatment as any show tune and the number of performances on record make selection difficult. Those chosen appear in both countries and are all by pianists of merit who have featured the work in the concert hall.

CHAPTER IX

George
GERSHWIN
(1898–1937)

Porgy and Bess, Opera in 3 Acts (1935)
C. Williams, I. Matthews, J. McMechan, L. Winters, A. Long, W. Coleman—Chorus and Orchestra—L. Engel
3-Col. OSL-162; Phi(E) NBL 5016–18 (del), excerpts— Phi(E) GBL 5517

CHAPTER X

Gian-Carlo
MENOTTI
(1911   )

The Consul, Opera in 3 Acts (1950)
P. Neway, C. MacNeil, M. Powers and others—Orchestra L.Engel
2-Dec. DX-101; Bruns(E) LAT 8012–3 (del)
The Medium, Opera in 1 Act (1946)
M. Powers, E. Keller, B. Dame, C. Mastice, F. Rogier— Orchestra—Balaban
2-Col. OSL-154; Phi(E) ABL 3387
The Telephone (1947)
As last
2-Col. OSL-154; not issued in UK

Marc
BLITZSTEIN
(1905–64)

The Cradle will rock, Opera (1937)
Original cast—Blitzstein
Musicraft Set 18 (78 rpm) (del)
No for an answer
Original cast—Blitzstein
Theme 103 (del)
Regina, Opera (1949)
New York City Opera Company—Krachmalnick
3-Col. O3L-260; O3S-202(s)

Leonard
BERNSTEIN
(1918–   )

West Side Story, Musical
Original New York cast
Col. OL-5230: OS-2001; Phi(E) BBL7272: SBBL 504(s)
Film soundtrack
Col. OC-5670: OS-2070(2); CBS(E) BPG 62058; SBPG 62058(s)
On the Waterfront, Film music (1955)
N.Y. Philharmonic-Symphony Orchestra—Bernstein
Col. ML-5651: MS-6251(s)

Leonard   *Candide,* Musical
BERNSTEIN   M. Adrian, R. Rounseville and original New York cast—
(1918–   )—   Orchestra cond. S. Krachmalnick
contd.   Col. OL-5180: OS-2350; Phi(E) BBL 7305

William RUSSO   The items referred to in the text are not recorded. The
(1928–   )   following are indicative of the composer's style:
                   Fugue for Jazz Orchestra
                       Gld. Cr. 1002: S-1002(s)
                   Stereophony
                       FM. 302: D302(s)
                   Seven Deadly Sins
                       Rou. 52063: S-52063(s)
                   Russo in London
                       Col(E) 33SX1508: SCX 3478(s)

Matyas SEIBER—   *Improvisations* (1960)
Johnny   Johnny Dankworth Orchestra—London Philharmonic
DANKWORTH   Orchestra—Rignold
                       Rou. 52059: S-52059(s); Saga XIP 7006

SUPPLEMENT

This supplement, which has been prepared for the benefit of British readers,
lists all major works by American composers not discussed in the text which
have been issued on long-playing records in Great Britain. Where a version was
available at the closure of this discography (31 December 1963) no deleted
versions have been listed. Because a work is no longer available in Great
Britain it should not, of course, be assumed that it is likewise unobtainable in
America.

(i) Available on British catalogues on 31 December 1963

Samuel BARBER
   Essay for Orchestra, No. 1, Op. 12 (1937)
   Eastman-Rochester Sym. Orch.—Hanson   Mer. *xep 9000*
   Medea—Ballet, Op. 23
   Eastman-Rochester Sym. Orch.—Hanson   Mer. MMA11148: AMS16096(s)
   Souvenirs—Ballet, Op. 28 (1952)
   Philharmonia Orch.—Kurtz   HMV BLP 1080, hbt413 (tape)
   Summer Music (1956)
   N.Y. Woodwind Quintet   Saga XIP 7009

Robert BENNETT (1894–   )
   Song Sonata
   Jascha Heifetz (vln)   RCA RB16243
   Symphonic Songs
   Eastman-Rochester Wind Ens.—Fennell   Mer. MMA11152: AMS16100(s)

William BERGSMA (1921–   )
   Gold and the Senor Commandante—Ballet
      (1941)
   Eastman-Rochester Sym. Orch.—Hanson   Mer. MMA11167: AMS16117(s)

Aaron COPLAND
   Danzon Cubano (1942)

Minneapolis Sym. Orch.—Dorati   Mer. MMA11005 : AMS16021(s)
Symphony No. 3 (1946)
London Symphony Orch.—Copland   WRC CM34 : SCM34(s)

Norman DELLO JOIO (1913–)
   Sonata No. 3 (1947)
   Frank Glazer (pno)   Saga XIP 7010

Alvin ETLER (1915–)
   Quintet for winds (1955)
   N.Y. Woodwind Quintet   Saga XIP 7009

Paul FETLER (1920–)
   Contrasts for Orchestra
   Minneapolis Sym. Orch.—Dorati   Mer. MMA11151 : AMS16099(s)

George GERSHWIN
   An American in Paris (1931)
   Various recordings available
   Cuban Overture (1934)
   Minneapolis Sym. Orch.—Dorati   Mer. MMA11185 : AMS16135(s)
   Eastman-Rochester Sym. Orch.—Hanson   Mer. *xep 9074*
   Hollywood Bowl Sym. Orch.—Newman   Cap. P8581 : SP8581(s)
   I got rhythm—Variations
   Hollywood Bowl Sym. Orch.—Newman   Cap. P8581 : SP8581(s)
   Three Preludes (1936)
   Sergei Fiorentino (pno)   Saga XID 5130
   Frank Glazer (pno)   Saga XIP 7010
   Rhapsody No. 2 (1931)
   Pennario—Hollywood Bowl Sym. Orch.—   As above
     Newman

Morton GOULD (1913–)
   Fall River Legend (1948)
   Spirituals for string choir and orchestra
     (1941)
   Eastman-Rochester Sym. Orch.—Hanson   Mer. MMA11133 : AMS16080(s)
   Latin-American Symphonette (1940)
   Hollywood Bowl Sym. Orch.—Slatkin   Cap. P8474 : SP8474(s)
   West Point (Symphony for Band) (1952)
   Eastman-Rochester Wind Ens.—Fennell   Mer. MMA11152 : AMS16100(s)

Charles GRIFFES
   Poem for flute and string orchestra (1918)
   J. Baker (fl)—Orch.—Saidenberg   Bruns. AXL 2015 (10″)

Ferde GROFE (1892–)
   Grand Canyon Suite (1931)
   Mississippi Suite
   Hollywood Bowl Sym. Orch.—Slatkin   Cap. P8347 : SP8347(s)

Walter HARTLEY (1921–)
   Concerto for 23 wind instruments
   Eastman-Rochester Wind Ens.—Fennell   Mer. MMA11131 : AMS16078(s)

Victor HERBERT (1869–1924)
   Concerto No. 2 in E for Cello and
     Orchestra, Op. 30

C. Mignelli—Eastman-Rochester Sym. Mer. MMA11173: AMS16123(s)
 Orch.—Hanson
Natoma—Opera (1911): Aria
John MacCormack Cam. CDN 1023

Alan HOVHANESS
 Six Greek folksongs
 J. Sebastian (hca), R. Josi (pno) DGG SLPM136024(s)

Kent KENNAN (1913–)
 Three pieces for Orchestra (1936)
 Eastman-Rochester Sym. Orch.—Hanson Mer. MMA11158: AMS16104(s)

Gian-Carlo MENOTTI
 Amahl and the Night Visitors
 Soloists, Orchestra—Schippers HMV ALP 1196

Douglas MOORE
 The Pageant of P. T. Barnum
 Eastman-Rochester Sym. Orch.—Hanson Mer. MMA11179: AMS16129(s)

Walter PISTON
 The Incredible Flutist (1938)
 As last
 Symphony No. 3 (1947)
 Eastman-Rochester Sym. Orch.—Hanson Mer. MMA11136

Vincent PERSICHETTI (1915–)
 Symphony No. 6 (for Band)
 Eastman-Rochester Wind Ens.—Fennell Mer. MMA11131: AMS16078(s)

Wayne PETERSON (1927–)
 Free variations for Orchestra
 Minneapolis Sym. Orch.—Dorati Mer. MMA11177: AMS16127(s)

Wallingford RIEGGER
 Concerto for piano and woodwind
  quintet (1953)
 F. Glazer (pno)—N.Y. Woodwind Saga XIP 7009
  Quintet

Deems TAYLOR (1885–)
 Song for lovers, Op. 13/2
 K. Flagstad (sop) HMV ALP 1309

Clifton WILLIAMS (1923–)
 Fanfare and Allegro (1956)
 Eastman-Rochester Wind Ens.—Fennell Mer. MMA11152: AMS16100

Julian WORK (1910–)
 Autumn Walk
 As last
   (ii) The following, previously available, have now been deleted

George ANTHEIL (1900–)
 Capital of the World—Ballet (1953)
 Ballet Theatre Orch.—Levine Cap. CTL7081

Seymour BARAB
 Child's Garden of Roses
 Russell Oberlin Ens. Cpt. CPT 939

Samuel BARBER
  Concerto for Cello and Orchestra, Op. 22
  Nelsova—New S.O. America—Barber   Dec. LX 3048 (10″)
  Excursions, Op. 20
  Andor Foldes (pno)   DGG DGM18279
  School for Scandal, Ov. Op. 5
  Eastman-Rochester Sym. Orch.—Hanson   Mer. *xep 9014*, MG 40002
  Symphony No. 2, Op. 19
  New S.O. America—Barber   Dec. LX 3050

Wayne BARLOW (1912–)
  Winter's Past—Rhapsody for oboe and
    orchestra (1938)
  Sprenkle—Eastman-Rochester S.O.—   Mer. MG 40003
    Hanson

Sidney BECHET (1897–1956)
  La nuit est une sorciere—Ballet
  Bechet—Orchestra—Bazire   Lon. Int. WV91050

Leonard BERNSTEIN
  Facsimile—Ballet (1946)
  Ballet Theatre Orch.—Levine   Cap. P8320
  Fancy Free—Ballet (1944)
  Ballet Theatre Orch.—Levine   Cap. P8196
  Symphony No. 2 (*Age of Anxiety*) for Piano
    and Orchestra (1949)
  Foss—N.Y. Philharmonic Sym. Orch.—   Phi.
    Bernstein

John Alden CARPENTER (1876–1951)
  Adventures in a perambulator (1915)
  Eastman-Rochester Sym. Orch.—Hanson   Mer. MMA11043 : AMS16015(s)

Abram CHASINS (1903–)
  Three Chinese pictures
  Sura Cherkassy (pno)   HMV ALP1527

Aaron COPLAND
  Four Piano Blues
  Aaron Copland (pno)   Dec. LX 3042 (10″)
  The Red Pony—Film music (1948)
  Little Orchestra Society   Bruns. AXTL 1022

Paul CRESTON (1906–)
  Two Choric Dances (1938)
  Con. Arts Orch.—Golschmann   Cap. CTL 7056
  Quartet, Op. 8
  Hollywood Quartet   Cap. CTL 7063
  Sonata for saxophone and piano
  M. Mule (sax), S. Robin (pno)   Dec. LXT 5221
  Symphony No. 2, Op. 35
  Symphony No. 3, Op. 38
  Washington Nat. Sym. Orch.—Mitchell   Nixa WLP 5272

David DIAMOND (1915–)
  Rounds for string orchestra
  Con. Arts Orch.—Golschmann   Cap. CTL 7056

Don GILLIS (1912–)
  The Alamo
  Symphony No. 5½
  New Sym. Orch. America—Gillis   Dec. LM4510 (10″)
  The man who invented music
  Portrait of a Frontier town
  New Sym. Orch. America—Gillis   Dec. LK4014 (10″)

Morton GOULD
  Interplay for piano and orchestra
  Hague Philharmonic—Otterloo   Phi. NBR 6029
  Piano pieces
  Cor de Groot (pno)   Phi. *nbe 11016*

Howard HANSON
  Chorale and Alleluia (1953)
  Eastman-Rochester Wind Ens.—Fennell   Mer. MRL 2535
  Fantasy variations on a theme of youth
  Eastman-Rochester Sym. Orch.—Hanson   Mer. MMA11064
  March Carillon
  Eastman-Rochester Wind Ens.—Fennell   Mer. MRL 2512
  Merry Mount Suite (1934)
  Eastman-Rochester Sym. Orch.—Hanson   Mer. MMA11008: AMS16007(s)
  Pastorale for oboe, strings and harp (†)
  Serenade for flute, strings and harp
  Eastman-Rochester Sym. Orch.—Hanson   Mer. MG 40003, (†) *xep 9014*

Wells HIVELY (1902–)
  Three hymns
  Eastman-Rochester Sym. Orch.—Hanson   Mer. MRL 2551

Hunter JOHNSON (1906–)
  Letter to the World—Ballet
  Concert Hall Sym. Orch.—Hull   Nixa CLP 1151

Norman KAY
  Miniature quartet for wind instruments
  London Baroque Quartet   Pye-Nixa CCL30120

Charles LOEFFLER (1861–1935)
  La Bonne Chanson
  Memories of my childhood
  Eastman-Rochester Sym. Orch.—Hanson   Mer. MRL 2544
  Pagan Poem (after Vergil), Op. 14
  Paris Philharmonic Orch.—Rosenthal   Cap. CTL 7033

Robert McBRIDE (1911–)
  Mexican Rhapsody (1934)
  Eastman-Rochester Sym. Orch.—Hanson   Mer. MMA11012

Harl McDONALD (1899–)
  Suite from childhood
  Con. Arts Orch.—Slatkin   Cap. CTL 7057

Edward McDOWELL
  Concerto No. 1 in a for piano and orchestra
  Rivkin—Vienna Opera Orch.—Dixon   Nixa WLP 5190

Peter MENNIN
Canzona for wind instruments
Eastman-Rochester Wind Ens.—Fennell   Mer. MRL 2535

Gian-Carlo MENOTTI
Amelia al Ballo (1937)
Soloists, Orchestra of La Scala, Milan   Col. 33CX1166
The unicorn, the gorgon and the manticore—
    Ballet
N.Y. Ballet Co. Orch.—Schippers   Col. 33CX1543

Douglas MOORE
The Devil and Daniel Webster—Folk opera
Soloists, Chorus and Orch.—Aliberti   West OPW11032: WST14050(s)

Burrill PHILLIPS (1907–)
Selections from McGuffey's Readers (1934)
Eastman-Rochester Sym. Orch.—Hanson   Mer. MMA11043: AMS16015(s)

Walter PISTON
Sonata for flute and piano
P. Rampal (fl); Veyton-Lacroix (pno)   Fel. RL89007
Tunbridge Fair
Eastman-Rochester Wind Ens.   Mer. MMA11009

Quincy PORTER
Poem and Dance (1932)
Eastman-Rochester Sym. Orch.—Hanson   Mer. MRL 2551

Owen REED (1910–)
La fiesta Mexicana
Eastman-Rochester Sym. Orch.—Hanson   Mer. MRL 2535

Wallingford RIEGGER
New Dance
Eastman-Rochester Sym. Orch.—Hanson   Mer. MRL 2556

Bernard ROGERS
Soliloquy for flute and orchestra (1925)
Eastman-Rochester Sym. Orch.—Hanson   Mer. MG 40003
Three Japanese dances (1928)
Eastman-Rochester Wind Ens.—Fennell   Mer. MMA 11034

Ned ROREM (1923–)
Piano sonata No. 2
Julius Katchen (pno)   Dec. LXT 2812

Miklos ROZSA (1970–)
Concerto for violin and orchestra (1956)
Heifetz Dallas Sym. Orch.—Hendl   RCA RB16009
Sonata for piano (1948)
Leonard Pennario (pno)   Cap. P8376

William SCHUMAN
George Washington Bridge—an impres-
    sion (1950)
Eastman-Rochester Wind Ens.—Fennell   Mer. MMA11009
Undertow—Ballet (1945)
Ballet Theatre Orch.—Levine   Cap. CTL 7040

Howard SWANSON (1909–   )
  Night music
  Orchestra—Mitropoulos   Bruns. AXTL 1054

Deems TAYLOR
  Through the Looking Glass, Op. 12
  Eastman-Rochester Sym. Orch.—Hanson   Mer. MG 40008

Virgil THOMSON
  Ten Etudes for piano
  Max Shapiro (pno)   Bruns. AXL 2009 (10″)

Harold TRIGGS (1900–   )
  Bright Land
  Eastman-Rochester Sym. Orch.—Hanson   Mer. MMA11064

List of Record makes and abbreviations

N.B. Country of origin of records issued internationally is indicated in the discography by suffix letter in brackets. (e.g. Col(E) = British Columbia).

ACe	Ace of Clubs (British)	Cor	Coral
AH	Ace of Hearts (British)	Cpt	Counterpoint (American)
Allo	Allegro (American)		
Arhoo	Arhoolie (American)	CRI	Composer's Recordings Inc. (American)
ARS	American Recording Society	CRS	Custom Recording Society (American)
Art	Artist (American)		
Atl	Atlantic (American)	Dec	Decca
Bar	Baronet (American)	Del	Delmar (American)
Bb	Bluebird (American)	Dial	Dial (American)
Blues	Bluesville (American)	DGG	Deutsche Grammophon Gesellschaft
BN	Blue Note (American)		
Bruns	Brunswick	Educo	Educo (American)
Cam	Camden	Elec	Electrola (American)
Candid	Candid (American)	EmA	EmArcy (American)
Cap	Capitol	Emb	Ember (British)
Car	Carillon (American)	EMS	Elaine Music Shop (American)
CBS	CBS (British)		
Chess	Chess (American)	Enc	Encore (British)
CH(E)	Concert Hall (British)	Epic	Epic (American)
CHS	Concert Hall Society (American)	Eso	Esoteric (American)
		Esq	Esquire (British)
Cl.Ed	Classic Editions (American)	Ever	Everest (American)
		Fan	Fantasy (American)
Clef	Clef	Fel	Felsted (British)
Col	Columbia	Folk.	Folkways (American)
Coll	Collector (British)	Flk.Lyr	Folk Lyric (American)
Comm	Commodore (American)	FM	FM (American)
Con-Disc	Concert Disc (American)	Fon	Fontana
Cont	Contemporary (American)	Gate 5	Gate 5 (American)
		Gld.Cr	Golden Crest (American)
Cor.U	Cornell University (American)	GNm	Gene Norman (American)

GTJ	Good Time Jazz (American)	Polym	Polymusic (American)
		Pres	Prestige (American)
Har	Harmony (American)	RCA	RCA (British)
Her	Heritage (British)	Ris	Ristic (British)
HMV	His Master's Voice	Riv	Riverside (American)
HMV(HMS)	His Master's Voice (History of Music in Sound)	Rlm	Realm (British)
		Roost	Roost (American)
		Rou	Roulette (American)
HSL	Haydn Society	Saga	Saga (British)
Imp	Impulse (American)	Savoy	Savoy (American)
Jazz Wkshp	Jazz Workshop (American)	77	77 (British)
		Siena	Siena (American)
Jcl	Jazz Collector (British)	Son-Nova	Son-Nava (American)
Jld	Jazzland (American)	SPA	Society of Participating Artists (American)
Lib.Con	Library of Congress (American)	Stand	Stand (American)
Lon	London (American)	Stin	Stinson (American)
Lon.Int	London International (British)	Story	Storyville (Danish, British)
Lou	Louisville University (American)	Strad	Stradivarius (American)
		Theme	Theme (American)
Lyr	Lyrichord (American)	Time	Time (American)
Mel	Melodisc (British)	Top	Topic (British)
Mer	Mercury	Trad	Tradition (American)
MGM	Metro–Goldwyn–Mayer	20-Fox	Twentieth Century Fox (American)
MK	MK (USSR)		
Musicraft	Musicraft (American)	UnA	United Artists (American)
Music Lib	Music Library (American)	U.Okla	University of Oklahoma (American)
Nixa	Nixa (British)		
NRI	New Recordings Inc. (American)	Uran	Urania (American)
		Van	Vanguard (American)
Od(F)	Odeon (French)	Ver	Verve (American)
Over	Overton (American)	Vic	RCA-Victor (American)
Pac.Jazz	Pacific Jazz (American)	Vog	Vogue
Par	Parlophone (British)	Wash	Washington (American)
Parker	Parker (American)	West	Westminster (American)
Per	Period (American)	World	World (American)
Phi	Philips (British)	WRC	World Record Club (British)
Poly	Polydor (British, German)		

DISCOGRAPHY SUPPLEMENT, 1975

John CAGE
 Music for Keyboard (1935-48)
 Kirstein (prepared piano, toy piano)   Col. M2S-819
 String Quartet in 4 Parts (1950)
 Concord Quartet (plus string quartet works by Brown,
  Crumb, Druckman, Feldman, Hiller, Kirchner, Wolff and
  Wolpe)   Vox SVBX-5306
 3 Dances for 2 Amplified Prepared Pianos (1944-5)
 Thomas, Grierson   Angel S-36059

Elliott CARTER
    Concerto for Orchestra
    Bernstein, N.Y. Philharmonic   Col. M-30112
    Double Concerto for Harpsichord, Piano and *2 Chamber
        Orchestras*
    Jacobs, Rosen, Prausnitz, English Chamber Orchestra (plus
        Carter's *Variations for Orchestra*)   Col. MS-7191
    String Quartet No. 1 and 2
    Composers Quartet   Nonesuch 71249
    String Quartet No. 3
    Julliard String Quartet (plus Carter's *String Quartet No. 2*)   Col. M-32738

George CRUMB
    Ancient Voices for Children
    DeGaetani, Dash, Weisberg Ensemble   Nonesuch 71255
    Black Angels for Electric String Quartet
    New York Quartet   CRI S-283
    Echoes of Time and the River
    Mester, Louisville Symphony   Louisville S-711
    Eleven Echoes of Autumn, 1965
    Aeolian Quartet   CRI S-233

Charles IVES
    Browning Overture (1911)
    Various recordings available
    From the Steeples and the Mountains, Chromatimelodtune
    American Brass Quintet   Nonesuch 71222
    Schuller, Orchestra (plus *Hallowe'en, Sets*)   Col. MS-7318
    General William Booth Enters Into Heaven
    Smith Singers, Ithaca Coll. Chorus, Texas Boys Chorus
        (plus *Psalms 24, 67, 90, 100, 150*, and other works)   Col. MS-6921
    Hallowe'en, The Pond
    Schuller, Orchestra   Col. MS-7318
    Music for Theatre Orchestra
    Sinclair, Yale Theatre Orchestra   Col. M-32969
    Piano Music (complete)
    Mandel   Desto 6458/61
    Psalms 14, 25; 54, 135
    Smith, Columbia Symphony and Chamber Ensemble,
        Smith Singers, Texas Boys Chorus   Col. MS-7321
    Sonata No. 1 for Piano
    Masselos   Odyssey 32160059
    Sonata No. 2, "Concord, Mass., 1840-1860"
    Various recordings available
    Sonatas 1-4 for Violin and Piano
    Zukofsky, Kalish   Nonesuch 73025
    String Quartets 1 and 2
    Various recordings available
    Symphony: Holidays (complete)
    Various recordings available
    Symphony No. 4
    Serebrier, London Philharmonic, Alldis Chorus   Col. MS-6775
    Three Places in New England
    Tilson Thomas, Boston Symphony   DG 2530048

Unanswered Question
Various recordings available
The Music of Charles Ives
5 record set including: *The Fourth of July, Hymn, Variations on "America," In Flanders Field, The Celestial Country, Majority (or The Masses), They Are There!, Lincoln, the Great Commoner, 25 Songs,* and recordings of Ives at the piano performing transcriptions of and improvisations on the *"Concord" Sonata.* Performers include: Bernstein, Schuller, Stokowski, Zukofsky, Gregg Smith Singers, Helen Boatwright, John Kirkpatrick, and Charles Ives.   Col. M4-32504

Harry PARTCH
  And On the Seventh Day Petals Fell in Petaluma
  Partch, Gate 5 Ensemble   CRI S-213
  The Bewitched
  Garvey, University of Illinois Musical Ensemble   CRI SD-304
  Daphne of the Dunes, Barstow, Plectra & Percussion Dances: Castor & Pollux
  Danlee Mitchell, Ensemble   Col. MS-7207
  Delusion of the Fury
  Mitchell, Ensemble   Col. M2-30576
  Windsong, Bewitched: Scene 10 and Epilogus, *Plectra & Percussion Dances: Castor & Pollux, Cloud Chamber Music, Wayward: Letter*
  Partch; Pierce, Garvey Illinois University Gate 5 Ensemble   CRI 193

Carl RUGGLES
  Angels
  Foss, Buffalo Philharmonic   Turnabout 34398
  Men and Mountains
  Foss, Buffalo Philharmonic   Turnabout 34398
  Sun-Treader
  Tilson Thomas, Boston Symphony   DG 2530048

ACKNOWLEDGMENTS

MUSICAL

Grateful acknowledgment is made to the following publishers who have given permission for the reproduction of copyright works listed below. Without their co-operation the value of the book would have been greatly diminished.

Associated Music Publishers, Inc., New York: Elliott Carter. String Quartet No. 1 (1951) (copyright © 1955, 1956 by Associated Music Publishers, Inc.); String Quartet No. 2 (1959) (copyright © 1961 by Associated Music Publishers, Inc.); and Cello Sonata.

——: Roy Harris. Trio for violin, cello and piano.

——: Charles Ives. Sonata No. 2 for piano ("Concord").

——: Wallingford Riegger. Dichotomy, Op. 12.

Boosey & Hawkes, Inc., New York: Theodore Chanler. Eight Epitaphs.

——: Aaron Copland. Billy the Kid; Piano Variations; Quiet City; Twelve Poems of Emily Dickinson; Sonata for Piano; Two Pieces for string quartet.

——: Virgil Thomson. Sonata da Chiesa (copyright 1945 by Virgil Thomson; reprinted by permission of Boosey & Hawkes, Inc., sole agents).

R. J. Carew, Tempo-Music Publishing Co., 818 Quintana Place, N.W., Washington 11, D.C.: Jelly Roll Morton. Mamie's Blues (219 Blues) (arranged by Jelly Roll Morton, transcribed and edited by J. Lawrence Cook; copyright 1939, 1940, 1948 by Tempo-Music Publishing Co.; international copyright secured; all rights reserved; USED BY PERMISSION).

Chappell & Co., Inc., New York: George Gershwin. Porgy and Bess (copyright 1935 by Gershwin Publishing Corporation, New York, N.Y.; copyrights renewed).

——: Marc Blitzstein. The Cradle Will Rock (copyright © 1938 by Marc Blitzstein; Chappell & Co., Inc., owner of publication and allied rights); and Regina (copyright © 1949, 1953, 1954 by Marc Blitzstein; Chappell & Co., Inc., owner of publication and allied rights).

Franco Colombo, Inc., New York: Virgil Thomson. Five Songs from William Blake (copyright 1953 by G. Ricordi & Co., New York; by courtesy of Franco Colombo, Inc., New York).

——: Edgard Varèse. Density 21.5 (copyright 1946 by Edgard Varèse; copyright assigned 1956 to G. Ricordi & Co., New York; by arrangement with Franco Colombo, Inc., New York); Integrales (copyright 1926 by Edgard Varèse; copyright assigned 1956 to G. Ricordi & Co., New York; by courtesy of Franco Colombo, Inc., New York); and Octandre (copyright 1924 by Edgard Varèse; copyright assigned 1956 to G. Ricordi & Co., New York; by courtesy of Franco Colombo, Inc., New York).

Curwen Edition, J. Curwen & Sons, Ltd., London: Carl Ruggles. Angels.

Carl Fischer, Inc., New York: Lukas Foss. Three Psalms for Chorus and Two Pianos and A Parable of Death.

The H. W. Gray Company, Inc., New York: Virgil Thomson. *Missa pro defunctis* (copyright 1960 by The H. W. Gray Company, Inc.; used by permission).

Hinrichsen Edition, Ltd., London: John Cage. *Concert* for piano and orchestra; *Music for Carillon; Music of Changes; She Is Asleep;* Sonatas and Interludes.
———: Morton Feldman. *Last Pieces* for piano.
———: Lou Harrison. *Suite for Symphonic Strings.*

Edward B. Marks Music Corporation, New York: Roger Sessions. String Quartet No. 2.

Merion Music, Inc., Bryn Mawr, Pa.: Charles Ives. *Tom Sails Away; Two Little Flowers.*

Mercury Music Corporation, New York: Elliott Carter. Sonata for Piano.
———: Charles Ives. *Harvest Home Chorales.*
———: Virgil Thomson. *Four Saints in Three Acts.*

G. Ricordi & Co.: *see* Franco Colombo.

G. Schirmer, Inc., New York: Samuel Barber. Adagio for strings; *Hermit Songs;* and *Knoxville: Summer of 1915.*
———: Leonard Bernstein. *West Side Story* (copyright, 1957, 1959 by Leonard Bernstein and Stephen Sondheim).
———: Charles Griffes. Sonata for piano.
———: Roy Harris. Symphony No. 3.
———: Charles Ives. Sonata No. 2 for violin and piano.
———: William Schuman. *Judith.*
———: Roger Sessions. Symphony No. 2.
———: Virgil Thomson. *Louisiana Story* (copyright 1949 by G. Schirmer, Inc.; used by permission).

Southern Music Publishing Co., Inc., New York: Charles Ives. Sonata No. 1 for piano (copyright 1954 by Peer International Corporation; used by permission).

LITERARY

Grateful acknowledgment is made to the following publishers for permission to quote extracts from literary works.

City Lights Books, San Francisco: Allen Ginsberg. "Wild Orphan," from *Howl & Other Poems.*

Corinth Books, Inc., New York: Charles Olson. *The Maximus Poems* (copyright © by Charles Olson; a Jargon Book published in association with Corinth Books, Inc.).

The Dial Press, Inc., New York: James Baldwin. *Nobody Knows My Name.*

Doubleday & Company, Inc., New York: DuBose Heyward. *Porgy* (copyright 1925 by Doubleday & Company, Inc.).
———: Billie Holiday. *Lady Sings the Blues* (copyright © 1956 by Eleanora Fagan and William F. Dufty).

Grove Press, Inc.: Robert Duncan. "The Dance," from *The Opening of the Field* (copyright © 1960 by Robert Duncan).

Harcourt, Brace & World, Inc., New York: E. E. Cummings. *Poems 1923–1954*.

Holt, Rinehart and Winston, Inc., New York: "Birches," from *Complete Poems of Robert Frost* (copyright 1916, 1921 by Holt, Rinehart and Winston, Inc.; copyright renewed 1944 by Robert Frost; reprinted by permission of Holt, Rinehart and Winston, Inc.).

Houghton Mifflin Company, Boston: Willa Cather. *My Antonia.*

Alfred A. Knopf, Inc., New York: Wallace Stevens. "L'Esthetique du Mal," from *The Collected Poems of Wallace Stevens.*

Liveright Publishing Corporation, New York: Hart Crane. "The Bridge" and "White Buildings," from *The Collected Poems of Hart Crane* (copyright © renewed 1961 by Liveright Publishing Corporation).

New Directions, New York: Lawrence Ferlinghetti. *A Coney Island of the Mind* (copyright 1955, © 1958 by Lawrence Ferlinghetti).

———: Denise Levertov. *With Eyes at the Back of Our Heads* (copyright © 1958, 1959 by Denise Levertov Goodman).

———: William Carlos Williams. *The Collected Earlier Poems of William Carlos Williams* (copyright 1938, 1951 by William Carlos Williams).

W. W. Norton & Company, Inc., New York: Charles Ives. *Essays before a Sonata and Other Writings* (edited by Howard Boatwright; copyright © 1961, 1962 by W. W. Norton & Company, Inc.).

Prentice-Hall, Inc., Englewood Cliffs, N.J.: Louis Armstrong. *Satchmo: My Life in New Orleans.*

Random House, Inc., New York: William Faulkner. "Delta Autumn," from *Go Down, Moses*

———: Robinson Jeffers. "Wind-struck Music," from *The Selected Poetry of Robinson Jeffers.*

———: Gertrude Stein. *The Autobiography of Alice B. Toklas* (copyright 1933 and renewed 1960 by Alice B. Toklas).

Wesleyan University Press, Middletown, Conn.: John Cage. *Silence.*

———: Louis Simpson. "To the Western World" and "Orpheus in America," from *A Dream of Governors* (copyright 1957 by Louis Simpson).

Acknowledgment is also made to Mrs. H. T. Ives and John Kirkpatrick for permission to reprint the "Jottings" of Charles Ives, and to Frank O'Hara for extracts from his poem. Harcourt, Brace & World, Inc., publish Charles Olson's *Call Me Ishmael.*

INDEX OF MUSIC EXAMPLES

INDEX OF LITERARY QUOTATIONS

This index includes quotations from poetry and prose writings; and also verbal statements about their art by musicians.

GENERAL INDEX

Abstraction (Schuller), 366
Adagio for strings (Barber), 196
Adam, Stephen, 289
Aeolian Harp, The (Cowell), 150
Agee, James, 202, 203
Ah-Leu-Cha, 352
Ain't Misbehavin', 375
Airy Man Blues, 270
Alabama Woman, 270
Alcott, Bronson, 48, 53, 54
Alcott, Louisa, 48, 53, 54
Alexander's Ragtime Band, 297, 383
All alone (Monk), 338
All Blues, 352
Allen (Ed.), 296, 297
Allen (Red), 373
Allison, R. 6
All or nothing, 369
All through the Night, 385
Amahl and the Night Visitors (Menotti), 203
Amanda (Morgan), 9–10
American Dances (Gilbert), 30
American march, 256–61
American Hero, The, 19
America's Music (Chase), xiii
Amérique (Varèse), 157
Amores (Cage), 178
Anderson, Cat, 328
Andover (Holyoke), 11
Angels (Ruggles), 67
Angels and Devils (Brant), 153
Angker Wat, 365
Antes, John, 18
Antheil, George, 159n, 182n, 209n
Antigone (Orff), 173
Antiphony no. 1 (Brant), 152
Anything Goes, 374–5, 387
Apex Blues, 307
Apollon Musagètes (Stravinsky), 155
Appalachian Spring (Copland), 89–90, 98, 99
Après-midi d'un Faune, L' (Debussy), 309

Arcana (Varèse), 164
Arevekal (Hovhaness), 154
Armstrong, Louis, xiv, 285, 288, 290, 294–5, 297, 298, 299–306, 307, 308, 309, 310, 311, 313, 316, 317, 318, 320, 325, 329, 333, 339, 340, 342, 343, 348, 357, 369, 374, 375, 376, 379
Arne, Thomas, 19, 245, 248
Arnold, Matthew, 195
Artistry in Boogie, 332
As it fell upon a day (Copland), 83
Astaire, Fred, 386
Atlanta Rag, 278
At the Cross Roads, 272
At the Window, 275
Auden, W. H., 228
Autobiography of Alice B. Toklas, 208n
Autumn Leaves, 367

Babbitt, Milton, 223–4
Bacchae (Euripides), 174
Bach, J. S., 17, 25, 64, 128, 131, 305, 359
Back in your own back yard, 381
Backwater Blues, 296
Bailey, Buster, 311
Baker, Chet, 357
Baker, Dave, 366
Baline, Izzy (Irving Berlin), 383
Ballad of Baby Doe, The (Moore), 32
Ballads and story-songs, 366
Ballet méchanique (Antheil), 159n, 182n
Bananier, La (Gottschalk), 254
Bamboula, La (Gottschalk), 253, 254
Banjo, The (Gottschalk), 254
Banshee, The (Cowell), 150
Barber, Samuel, 195–203, 220
Barber of Seville, The, 240–1
Barnefield, Richard, 83
Barrère, George, 160
barrelhouse piano, 272–6
Bartók, Bela, 60, 84, 105, 113, 114, 115, 138, 150, 231, 365, 372